Investment Analysis and Management

Second Edition

Investment Analysis and Management

Stanley S. C. Huang
Rider College

Maury R. Randall
Rider College

Allyn and Bacon, Inc.
Boston London Sydney Toronto

Copyright © 1987, 1981 by Allyn and Bacon, Inc.
A Division of Simon & Schuster
7 Wells Avenue
Newton, Massachusetts 02159

Library of Congress Cataloging-in-Publication Data

Huang, Stanley S. C.
   Investment analysis and management

   Bibliography: p.
   Includes index.
   1. Investment analysis.   2. Portfolio management.
3. Investments. I. Randall, Maury R. II. Title.
HG4529.H8   1987   332.6   87-986
ISBN 0-205-10501-7

Production coordinator: Helyn Pultz
Editorial-production service: Nancy Benjamin
Cover administrator: Linda K. Dickinson
Cover designer: Susan Slovinsky

Printed in the United States of America

10 9 8 7 6 5 4 3 2 1 91 90 89 88 87

Contents

Preface   xiii

7153430

PART I   INTRODUCTION   1

1   Introduction to the Investment Process   3

Real Investment and Financial Investment   3
Investment Planning   3
Security Analysis and Portfolio Management   5
Investment and Taxes   7
Investment versus Speculation   7
Ingredients in a Successful Investment Strategy   8
The Economic Function of the Investment Process   9
Summary   10
Questions and Problems   10
References   11

2   Types of Financial Assets   12

Bonds   12
Money Market Instruments   14
Common Stocks   15
Convertible Bonds, Preferred Stocks, and Convertible Preferred
    Stocks   16
Options   17
Warrants   17
Futures Contracts   17
Investment Companies   17
Money Market Funds and Accounts   18
The Rate of Return   18
Components of Risk   19
Measuring Risk   21
Historical Performance   22
Summary   24
Questions and Problems   25
References   25

3   Securities Markets   27

Primary Markets and Investment Banking   27
Secondary Markets: Exchanges, Dealers, and Brokers   28
Regulation of Securities Markets and Investor Protection   46
Summary   49
Questions and Problems   50
References   52

4   Sources of Investment Information   53

Newspapers   54
Financial Magazines   54
Investment Advisory Services   55
Reports Issued by Corporations   58
Publications of Brokerage Firms   60
U.S. Government Publications   61
Trade Publications   62
Computer-Based Data Files   62
Indexes of Securities Prices   63
Market Movements and Differences in Market Indexes   73
Questions and Problems   77
References   78

PART II   MACROECONOMIC ANALYSIS AND THE ANALYSIS OF FIXED INCOME SECURITIES   79

5   Business Conditions Analysis, Corporate Profits, and Stock Prices   81

Security Prices and the Economy   81
Methods of Forecasting   82
Changes in Real GNP, Corporate Profits, and Stock Prices   96
Summary   102
Questions and Problems   104
References   105

6   Interest Rate Forecasting and Analysis   107

Importance of Interest Rate Forecasts   107
Structure of Interest Rates   107
The Federal Reserve and Interest Rates   109
Inflation and Interest Rates   112
Methods of Forecasting Interest Rates   113
Summary   121

Questions and Problems   121
References   122

7   Interest-Bearing Assets: Markets and Characteristics   123

Instruments of the Money Market   123
Features of Bonds   130
Summary   145
Questions and Problems   145
References   146

8   Valuation and Yields of Bonds   148

Bond Value Determination   148
Yield to Maturity   150
Maturity, Coupon, and Price Fluctuation of Bonds   155
Duration   157
Level of Yield Effect   161
Immunization of Investments in Bonds   162
Yield Curve Analysis: The Term Structure of Interest Rates   164
Yield Spreads   169
Bond Strategies   173
Summary   175
Questions and Problems   175
Appendix: The Time Value of Money   177
Future Values with Compound Interest   177
Present Value of a Single Payment   177
Present Value of an Annuity   182
Estimation of Yields for Zero-Coupon Bonds   183
References   185

PART III   ANALYSIS OF VARIABLE INCOME SECURITIES — COMMON STOCKS   187

9   Industry Analysis   189

Importance of Industry Analysis   189
Classification of the Economy into Industries   189
Stages of Industry Development   191
Evaluation of the Industry Life-Cycle Theory   193
Structure and Operational Characteristics   194
Input-Output Analysis   197
Researching an Industry   199
Summary   207
Questions and Problems   207
References   208

10   Financial Statement Analysis   210

Financial Statements   210
Basic Accounting Concepts   212
Deficiencies of Financial Statements   213
Manipulating Income by Management   218
Quality of Earnings   219
Analysis of Dow Chemical Statements   221
Summary   236
Questions and Problems   236
References   237

11   Growth Analysis   239

Importance of Growth of Earnings per Share   239
Determinants of Earnings per Share   241
Three Approaches to Estimating Growth Potential of EPS   244
Summary   259
Questions and Problems   260
References   262

12   Analysis and Measurement of Uncertainty of Return of Common Stocks   263

How to Deal with Uncertainty   264
Subjective Probability — the Markowitz Approach   267
Risk of Investment Measured by Standard Deviation   270
Calculating Risk and Return of Portfolios Using the Markowitz
    Approach   273
Our Views on How Best to Deal with Problems of Uncertainty   274
Value Line System of Measuring Risks of a Stock   287
Summary   289
Questions and Problems   290
References   292

13   Valuation of Common Stock   294

Expected Dividend Valuation   294
The Price-Earnings Ratio   302
Valuation of Stocks on the Basis of Cash Flow   309
Price/Sales per Share Ratio (P/S)   310
Graham's Intrinsic Value Approach to Common Stocks   311
Valuation of the General Market   314
Summary   322
Questions and Problems   323
**Appendix: Derivation of the Valuation Formula (Equation 13.3) with
    Constant Growth Rate of Dividend   325**
References   325

PART IV   ANALYSIS OF PREFERRED STOCK, CONVERTIBLE SECURITIES, OPTIONS, AND FINANCIAL FUTURES   329

14   The Hybrids: Preferred Stock, Convertible Preferred, and Convertible Bonds   331

Preferred Stock   332
Convertible Preferred Stock   334
Convertible Bonds   337
Performance of Convertible Securities   342
Questions and Problems   344
References   344

15   Options and Warrants   346

Options   346
The Options Markets   346
Call Options   348
Put Options   352
Combinations of Options   355
Hedging Strategies   356
Optimum Option Strategy with Different Expectations   360
Options on Market Indexes   362
Factors Affecting Option Premiums   363
Determining the Value of Options   364
The Role of Options in an Investment Program   370
Warrants   371
Summary   373
Questions and Problems   375
References   376

16   Financial and Other Futures   378

History of Futures Markets in the United States   378
Listings of Futures Prices   379
Participants in Futures Trading   382
Margin and Variation in Equity   385
Purchase of Precious Metals versus Precious Metals Futures
      Contracts   386
Types of Orders   388
Differences Between Options and Futures   389
Hedging with Futures   389
Programmed Trading   393
Futures Options   395
Spread Strategies   396
Rules that Experienced Traders Observe   398
Summary   399

Questions and Problems   400
Appendix A: Volume and Open Interest   403
Appendix B: Price Forecasting   403
Fundamental Approach   403
Technical Approach   404
References   406

PART V   SHORT-TERM TRADING IN SECURITIES   409

17   Technical Analysis   411

Technical Analysis versus Security Analysis   411
The Dow Theory   411
Other Technical Theories and Indicators   414
Technical Analysis of Individual Stocks   430
The Random-Walk Theory and Technical Analysis   438
Summary   440
Questions and Problems   441
References   441
**Appendix: Number of Stocks Reaching New Annual Highs and Lows
     Compared to the DJIA, April–August, 1979**   443

PART VI   MODERN PORTFOLIO THEORY   445

18   Efficient Portfolios   447

Return and Risk of a Security   447
Expected Return of a Portfolio   449
Expected Risk of a Portfolio   450
Efficient Portfolios   455
Attitudes of Investors Toward Risk and Return   456
Optimum Portfolio for a Given Investor   457
Difficulties in Applying Markowitz's Portfolio Theory   459
Correlation of Return of Securities to Returns on Market Index   459
Modified Efficient Frontier with Possibilities of Lending and
     Borrowing   463
Summary   475
Questions and Problems   477
**Appendix A: Calculation of Alpha, Beta, and Residual Variance: The
     Palmer Company**   480
**Appendix B: Calculation of Standard Deviation of Annual Return σ_i,
     Covariance σ_{ij}, and Coefficient of Correlation P_{ij} Between Returns
     of Two Companies**   481
References   482

19   The Efficient Market Hypothesis and the Capital Market Theory   484

Three Forms of the Efficient Market Hypothesis   484
Empirical Evidence for the Efficient Market Hypothesis   485
Empirical Evidence Against the Efficient Market Hypothesis   491
Evaluation of the Efficient Market Hypothesis   495
Capital Market Theory   497
Arbitrage Pricing Theory   508
Summary   509
Questions and Problems   509
References   510

20   Evaluation of Portfolio Performance   512

Rate of Return   513
Measurement of Risk   516
Risk-Adjusted Return   517
Evaluation of Investment Performance of Mutual Funds   522
Summary   525
Questions and Problems   526
References   527

21   Investment Decision Making by Individuals   528

Personal and Family Financial Planning   528
Factors Determining Appropriate Investment Policy   529
The Passive Investor Desiring Minimum Risk Exposure   530
The Passive Investor Assuming Moderate Risk   531
The Active Investor Assuming Moderate Risk   531
The Active Investor Assuming High Risk   532
The Speculative Investor   533
Reviewing the Experience of Equity and Bond Investment in the Last
      Thirty-Five Years   533
Questions and Problems   536
References   536

PART VII   ALTERNATIVE INVESTMENTS, INTERNATIONAL INVESTING, AND USE OF THE PERSONAL COMPUTER   539

22   Investing in Mutual Funds   541

The Advantages of Investing in Mutual Funds   542
Selecting No-Load Mutual Funds   543
Studies on Performance of Mutual Funds   548
Sources of Information on Mutual Funds   548
Summary   555

Questions and Problems   555
References   556

23 Home Ownership as an Investment and Real Estate Investment Trusts   557

Home Ownership versus Renting   557
Real Estate Investment Trusts   565
Summary   566
Questions and Problems   566
References   567

24 Other Investment Opportunities: Foreign Investments and Precious Metals   568

International Investing   568
Precious Metals   575
Summary   579
Questions and Problems   579
References   580

25 The Investor and the Personal Computer   581

How Computers Can Help Investors   581
Computer Software   582
Sources of Information   585
Summary   586

Glossary   589
Index   599

Preface

Investment Analysis and Management is designed for both one-semester and two-semester courses on investments. The book is written for students at the junior and senior level as well as those who are taking an introductory investments course in an MBA program. The book contains a balanced mix of theoretical concepts, institutional material, and real-world applications. Topics are presented in a logical and clear manner, and many examples are provided throughout the book to illustrate investment concepts and strategies. This second edition is a thoroughly updated and revised version of the first, and it contains five new chapters.

ORGANIZATION OF TOPICS

The twenty-five chapters which comprise this book are grouped into seven parts:

Part I contains introductory material, with Chapter 1 providing a discussion on the needs, constraints, and tradeoffs that investors should consider in formulating their objectives. In Chapter 2 we present an overview and brief discussion of the many types of financial assets that investors may purchase. Chapter 3 relates how securities markets function, and it includes some quantitative analysis of margin accounts and short sales. Chapter 4 reviews many sources of investment information.

Part II deals with analyses of business conditions, interest rates, and interest-bearing assets. In Chapter 5 we discuss the relationship between security prices and economic conditions. Special emphasis is placed on methods of economic forecasting, determinants of corporate profits, and the impact of profits on stock prices. Chapter 6 is devoted to interest rate forecasting and analysis. In Chapter 7 characteristics of interest-bearing assets and their markets are examined, while Chapter 8 is devoted to the valuation and theoretical analysis of those securities.

Part III is concerned with the subject of common stock analysis and valuation. Chapter 9 describes the importance of industry factors in stock selection. Chapter 10 describes how information from published financial statements is used to evaluate companies. Factors underlying earnings per share growth are examined in Chapter 11 and risk analysis is presented in Chapter 12. Chapters 9 through 12 provide the background for Chapter 13, which focuses on the actual techniques used in valuation of common stock.

Part IV examines convertible securities, warrants, options, and futures. Chapter 14 discusses preferred stock and convertible bonds. In Chapter 15 stock options are thoroughly examined and warrants are analyzed. Financial and other types of futures are described in Chapter 16. In the chapters on options and futures, special emphasis is placed on the various types of hedging strategies employed to reduce investor risk.

Part V deals with the subject of short-term trading. Chapter 17 provides a thorough examination of technical analysis. Although this topic is controversial, it does merit attention because a number of individual investors and portfolio managers do take into account the findings of the technicians.

In Part VI we discuss modern portfolio theory. In Chapters 18 and 19 we examine the subjects of efficient markets, the Capital Asset Pricing Model, and Arbitrage Pricing Theory. In Chapter 20 methods of evaluating portfolio performance are described, and in Chapter 21 portfolio selection for individual investors is discussed.

In Part VII we take up the topics of home ownership as an investment, mutual funds, international investing, and investor use of the personal computer. Chapter 22 provides an in-depth study of investing in mutual funds. Chapter 23 describes how one can analyze whether it is better to buy a house or rent an appartment. In Chapter 24 we describe international investing and issues related to investment in precious metals. Chapter 25, which concludes the book, examines how the personal computer can be used as an investment tool.

ACKNOWLEDGMENTS

The authors thank all who have provided assistance to them in writing this book. The comments and suggestions of the reviewers of the book were sincerely appreciated. In particular, the comments of John Dunkelberg, Wake Forest University; and C. R. Sprecher, New Mexico State University, were most helpful. We also wish to express gratitude to our wives, Aileen and Mirim. Their support, encouragement, and understanding were extremely important in enabling us to complete this project.

S. S. C. H.
M. R. R.

Investment Analysis and Management

Introduction

1

Introduction to the Investment Process

The subject of investments embodies the study of many types of assets and how they may be held or used for the financial benefit of investors. In purchasing such assets, investors commit funds at one point in time with the expectation of future returns. These expected returns should be sufficient to compensate the investor for the time the funds are committed and for the risks associated with the particular investment. In this book we analyze the many choices available to investors, how to estimate returns and assess risk, and how investment plans may be formulated.

REAL INVESTMENT AND FINANCIAL INVESTMENT

Real investment refers to the purchase of tangible assets such as land, houses, precious metals, buildings, and equipment. *Financial investment*, on the other hand, refers to the purchase of "paper" assets, which are collectively called securities. Among these assets are bonds, common stocks, preferred stocks, convertible securities, mutual funds, and short-term money market instruments. While the major emphasis of this book is on financial investments, tangible assets and home ownership as an investment are also analyzed.

INVESTMENT PLANNING

Investment planning begins with the establishment of objectives by the investor, based on personal financial needs, preferences, and constraints. A strategy can then be formulated and a portfolio (or group) of assets can be selected. The first step, then, is to examine some of the elements that determine investment objectives. Investors should ask themselves several questions:

- How much money do I need to live on now?
- How much do I need for the fundamental security of life, property, and casualty insurance?

The answers to these questions tell the individual how much income remains that can be used for investing.

- How much in assets do I have available for investment purposes?

Certain types of investments require a substantial amount of cash, such as $100,000 certificates of deposit (CDs) from commercial banks. The more funds one has to invest, the greater the number of options. Nevertheless, even individuals of relatively modest means still have many investment opportunities.

- What are my liquidity requirements?

Liquidity refers to the ability to convert an asset into cash rapidly and with no loss in value of principal. Examples of liquid assets include money market instruments and accounts and a number of types of savings accounts. Individuals require liquid assets in order to pay for anticipated expenditures in the very near future. A down payment for a new car, a vacation, or other major expenses would be financed with such assets. Liquid assets are also needed for unanticipated events, such as emergencies or special purchase opportunities. If one is planning to purchase stocks, real assets, or make some other investment soon, an appropriate level of liquid assets should be available.

- What is my current tax status and how do I expect it to change in the future?

Investors are concerned with after-tax rates of return in deciding which assets to purchase. Those who are in a high tax bracket may prefer securities whose income is exempt from federal taxation even if other securities pay a higher interest rate before taxes. Many investors open Individual Retirement Accounts (IRAs) or establish other tax deferred investment plans. In an IRA account the investor, if qualified, gets tax deductions for contributions, and taxes are not assessed until the future when withdrawals are made. Each individual must decide whether the net benefits of a tax-advantaged investment outweigh the net benefits from alternative investment strategies.

- What is the purpose of my investment?

The answer to this question involves determining how much income is needed, and when. For example, retirees generally require a safe, steady income from their investments. They tend to hold a high proportion of their assets in Treasury securities or other safe income-producing investments. Younger people who are working are more inclined to invest in stocks that pay little or no dividends but offer the prospect of substantial capital gains.

• What is my tolerance for risk?

Investment opportunities differ in risk and expected return. The notion of investment risk involves the uncertainty of future outcomes, and investors must decide how much such risk they can live with. Investment risk is measured by the volatility or unpredictability of returns. For example, consider three different types of investments: common stocks, corporate bonds, and Treasury bills. In the sixty-year period from 1926 through 1985, common stocks were the most volatile. Bond returns historically have been less so, and Treasury bills have fluctuated the least of the three. Over that same period, the average annual return from common stocks was approximately 12 percent, more than double that of the two alternatives. Thus, in making decisions, investors must recognize that there is a trade-off between expected return and risk.

Even though there is no guarantee that the future will repeat the past, an investor's knowledge of the historical record is important in planning an investment timetable, and in attempting to determine one's tolerance of risk. In the end, only the investor can answer the question of how much risk is acceptable. Some people are perfectly comfortable taking the higher risk of investing in the stock market; others who do so can't sleep at night.

SECURITY ANALYSIS AND PORTFOLIO MANAGEMENT

Once investment objectives are established, one selects investments using security analysis and portfolio management. *Security analysis* deals with analysis of past performance and evaluation of future prospects of individual securities. *Portfolio management* involves the analysis of potential portfolios in order to find the set of securities that best meets the objectives of an individual investor or group of investors. Specifically, portfolio managers have to answer these questions: How well-diversified should the portfolio be? That is, how many different issues should be included, and what should the mix be of securities having different return patterns over time? What portfolios are efficient? By "efficient" we mean those that will maximize return at a given level of risk, and at the same time will provide a given level of return at a minimum level of risk. Finally, which efficient portfolio is optimal in light of the objectives specified for the investor?

The process of investment management is summarized in Figure 1–1. Using information about the investor, goals are established. With information obtained through security analysis, portfolio management is performed, and a strategy is devised to best meet the needs of the investor. Portfolio management is an ongoing, dynamic process. An individual's objectives will likely change in response to fluctuating economic conditions, such as changes in interest rates, and the related developments in financial markets. In addition, an individual's financial position changes through life, typically

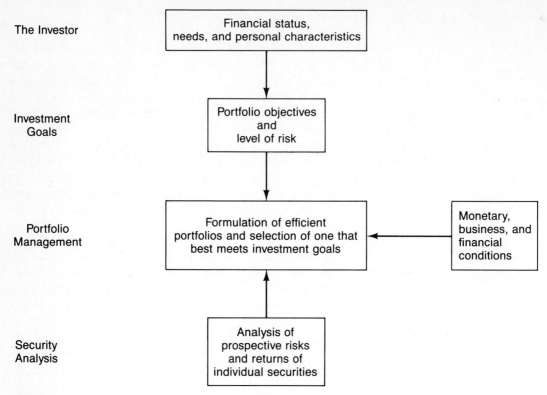

The Investor

Investment
Goals

Portfolio
Management

Security
Analysis

Financial status,
needs, and personal characteristics

Portfolio objectives
and
level of risk

Formulation of efficient
portfolios and selection of one that
best meets investment goals

Monetary,
business, and
financial
conditions

Analysis of
prospective risks
and returns of
individual securities

FIGURE 1–1   The Process of Investment Management

because of increased employment earnings, but in some cases as a result of extraordinary events such as inheritance or a sudden windfall.

Investment Advice and Costs

Among the considerations that help one determine an investment portfolio is the cost of information. Some individuals manage their own portfolio because they have the knowledge and time to study individual securities and the latest developments in financial markets. Others do not have this option. Clearly, if one relies on others for advice, the advisor must be both honest and competent. For example, registered stockbrokers can provide the investor with very helpful information. Yet one should be aware that there have been cases where brokers have churned accounts, encouraging investors to buy and sell primarily to generate commissions. Similarly, a number of those who have advertised themselves as financial planners were actually salespeople trying to sell specific financial products such as insurance policies or certain mutual funds. As in any such situation, the buyer must be careful.

INVESTMENT AND TAXES

In the fall of 1986 a major overhaul of the federal tax system was enacted into law. The basic effect of the law was to reduce tax rates and eliminate or reduce many itemized deductions. As stated earlier, taxes are an important consideration in developing an investment strategy. However, because the tax system is very complicated, we will review at this point only some of the basic provisions that apply to 1987 and beyond.

Taxable income is essentially calculated as wages, salaries, and other income less various deductions. The federal tax system had been quite progressive prior to 1987 with fourteen tax brackets. Under the 1986 law, new tax rates were scheduled to be phased in during 1987 with five tax brackets applicable in that year. For 1988 and beyond two tax brackets, 15 percent and 28 percent, would exist.[1]

The 1986 tax reform law also established new rules for long-term capital gains. Capital gains occur when an investor sells stocks or real assets at a profit, and these gains are considered long-term if the holding period is more than six months. If the holding period is six months or less, the gains are considered to be short-term. Prior to 1987, 60 percent of long-term capital gains were excluded from taxable income while 100 percent of short-term gains were included as taxable income. Starting in 1987 all long-term gains and short-term gains would be subject to taxation; for 1988 and beyond, the new 15 percent and 28 percent tax brackets would be applicable to long-term and short-term capital gains.

Various deductions are available to investors who itemize (as opposed to those who take a standard deduction). Individuals who borrow to purchase an investment can deduct interest expenses subject to certain ceilings and other limitations on the deductions. Similarly, expenses associated with investments such as costs of investment publications, storage fees, and management fees are deductible subject to certain exclusions and restrictions.

INVESTMENT VERSUS SPECULATION

As mentioned above, the purchase and ownership of securities involve different risk-return trade-offs. These are important in distinguishing between investment and speculation. Here we will contrast the behavior of an investor and a speculator.

[1] It is possible that an investor's overall marginal income tax rate will be higher than 28 percent in 1988 and beyond. For example, this could occur because of the added effect of state and local income taxes, and because of a scheduled federal surtax which would be applicable in certain income ranges.

Investor	Speculator
1. Interested in the long-term holding of securities, usually for at least one year.	1. Usually interested in short-term holdings. The holding period for a security may be a few days, weeks, or months.
2. Willing to assume moderate risk and generally buys securities issued by established companies.	2. Willing to assume high risks, often buying volatile issues (that is, with wide price fluctuation) or lower-grade securities.
3. Interested in current return in the form of interest income or dividends as well as the possibilities of capital appreciation.	3. Primarily interested in rapid price appreciation. Current income in the form of interest or dividends and long-term growth prospects are given low priority.
4. Expects a moderate rate of return in exchange for assuming a moderate amount of risk.	4. Expects a high rate of return in exchange for the high risk assumed.
5. The decision to buy is made after careful analysis of the past performance and future prospects of the issuing company and its industry. The analysis may be performed by the investor or by someone he trusts.	5. The desire to buy is usually based on intuition, rumors, charts, or market analysis, which concerns itself with the analysis of the stock market itself.
6. Uses own money rather than borrowed funds to buy securities.	6. Usually borrows money from brokerage firms to buy stock.

Some securities buyers are outright investors or speculators, while most others fall somewhere in between. It is worth noting that the same security could be purchased by both a speculator (who believes its price will rise quickly) and an investor (who believes in its long-term growth potential).

INGREDIENTS IN A SUCCESSFUL INVESTMENT STRATEGY

Success in any business is not easy, and the same may be said of investment management. Successful investing requires four ingredients:

1. A sound knowledge of investment fundamentals.
2. Self-knowledge.
3. Possession of good investment habits.
4. Good sense in judging investment values.

Knowledge of financial markets includes having an understanding of financial statements, economics, security analysis, investment strategies, and the functioning of security markets. Self-knowledge means knowing one's temperament and ability to assume risk. Good investment habits refer to setting appropriate objectives and formulation of an investment program to achieve those objectives. In following through to attain objectives, one should: make decisions after careful analysis; stick to an investment program as long as it is correct for oneself; and recognize that there are dangers in following fads.

The last of the four ingredients is to have good sense in judging investment values. Judgment, as a skillful application of knowledge and experience, is related to good common sense. By learning from both successes and failures, good judgment often follows.

Common Errors of Individual Investors

Although some errors are inevitable in the process of investment management, a number can be avoided. The following suggestions may help investors avoid some common mistakes:

1. Maintain proper diversification of a portfolio. Some portfolios are overdiversified, containing so many issues that the investor cannot follow closely the developments in those companies. Other portfolios are overconcentrated in too few types of securities.
2. Be sure the type and quality of the securities are consistent with stated investment goals. Too frequently, those who require safety are assuming excessive risk.
3. Monitor the performance of investments and keep the investment plan up-to-date. Needs may change and the investor may have to alter the strategy. Changing conditions in the economy, tax environment, or new opportunities may require new investment decisions.

THE ECONOMIC FUNCTION OF THE INVESTMENT PROCESS

When the investment management process is working well, it does more than just earn profits for the individuals involved. Participants play an important role in evaluating the performance and outlook of different firms, and in efficiently allocating capital resources within the economy. Companies that require funds to build plant and equipment issue equity and debt in financial markets. Security analysts study these companies and evaluate the securities they have issued or plan to issue. The limited quantity of funds available for investment in the economy annually tends to flow to well-managed companies regarded as being the most profitable and offering the highest returns in the future, given the perceived level of risk. Companies that are inefficient or uncompetitive and have poor prospects for profitability will have great difficulty obtaining funds and will be under pressure to curtail their activities. In short, with the help of investors, the most efficient and profitable firms that are meeting the growing needs of the marketplace are able to acquire funds and expand their operations.

SUMMARY

Investment management begins with the establishment of investor objectives based on personal financial needs, preferences, and constraints. Consideration must be given to liquidity requirements, taxes, risk-return trade-offs, needs for income, and total funds available for investing. Selection of securities involves the performance of security analysis and portfolio management. Security analysis consists of analyzing past performance and the evaluation of future prospects of individual securities. Portfolio management is concerned with the analysis of potential portfolios in an effort to find the set of securities that best meets the objectives of an individual investor or group of investors.

Investors and speculators have different objectives and follow different strategies. Investors have a longer-term perspective and assume moderate risks in order to obtain moderate returns. Speculators generally have a short-term perspective and assume high risks in the quest for high returns.

QUESTIONS AND PROBLEMS

1. What considerations enter into the formulation of investor objectives?
2. Contrast security analysis with portfolio management.
3. Why is portfolio management an ongoing process?
4. What are the risks and benefits of using investment advisers?
5. What types of investments provide tax advantages?
6. Are any important changes in tax laws currently being considered by Congress that would affect investors?
7. What is the difference between investment and speculation?
8. What are some of the common errors of individual investors?
9. What do individual investors require to be successful in their investments?
10. How does the investment process contribute to economic efficiency?

REFERENCES

D'Ambrosio, Charles S. *A Guide to Successful Investing*. Englewood Cliffs, N.J.: Prentice-Hall, 1970, Chapters 1–4.

Ellis, Charles D. "The Loser's Game," *Financial Analysts Journal*, July/August 1975.

Fielitz, Bruce, and Muller, Frederick. "The Asset Allocation Decision," *Financial Analysts Journal*, July/August 1983.

Financial Analysts Research Foundation. *The Economic Framework for Investors*. University of Virginia, 1975.

Fischer, Donald E., and Jordan, Ronald J. *Security Analysis and Portfolio Management*, 2nd ed. Englewood Cliffs, N.J.: Prentice-Hall, 1979, Chapters 1–2.

Graham, Benjamin. *The Intelligent Investor*, 4th ed. New York: Harper & Row, 1972.

Graham, Benjamin. "The Future of Common Stocks," *Financial Analysts Journal*, September/October 1974.

Lease, R., Lewellen, W., and Schlarbaum, G. "The Individual Investor: Attributes and Attitudes," *Journal of Finance*, May 1974.

Lorie, J. H., Dodd, M. P., and Kimpton, M. *The Stock Market: Theories and Evidence*. Homewood, Ill.: Irwin, 1985.

Maginn, John, and Tuttle, Donald, eds. *Managing Investment Portfolios*. Boston: Warren, Gorham & Lamont, Inc., 1983.

Malkiel, Burton G. *A Random Walk Down Wall Street*. New York: W. W. Norton, 1981.

Mayo, Herbert. *Basic Investments*. Hinsdale, Ill.: The Dryden Press, 1980.

Nicholson, S. F., Smith, M., and Willis, R. B. "Investment Perspectives — 150 Years," *Financial Analysts Journal*, November/December 1979.

Smith, Milton. *Money Today More Tomorrow*. Cambridge, Mass.: Winthrop Publishers, 1981.

2

Types of Financial Assets

In this chapter we review the basic characteristics of the different types of financial assets, or securities, commonly available. We first examine different debt securities and then describe several types of equity securities. In later chapters we will return to the subject of these securities and analyze them in greater detail. We conclude the chapter by returning to the fundamental concepts of risk and return and how to measure them.

BONDS

There are three major groups of bonds available in the market, categorized by the issuer: corporate bonds, state and local government bonds (also known as municipals), and U.S. government bonds. Bonds are *debt instruments* — they represent money loaned to the issuer by the investor. Essentially, all bonds are long-term promissory notes and usually mature ten to thirty years after issuance. Most of them have *coupons*, which means they promise to pay a fixed amount of interest periodically (usually semiannually), and the *par* or *face value* on the day of maturity. The interest payment, expressed as a percentage of par value, is called the *coupon rate*. Some bonds, called *zero-coupon bonds*, pay no annual interest. These securities sell for less than par, but at maturity they pay the par value. For example, an investor may pay $200 for a zero-coupon bond that matures in fifteen years at $1,000. The difference ($1,000 − $200 = $800) represents the investor's interest during the fifteen-year period.

Corporate Bonds

There are many types of corporate bonds. One of the most common is a *debenture*. A debenture is unsecured, meaning that no specific asset serves as collateral. Debentures are backed only by the general credit of the issuing corporation. *Mortgage bonds* have a mortgage, meaning that designated real property, such as land, buildings, or equipment, serves as security to guarantee repayment.

Each set of bonds has an *indenture*, which is a contract between the issuing company and the bondholders. The bond indenture includes a number of protective clauses or covenants. These clauses specify provisions, such as limits on indebtedness of the corporation, restriction on dividends, call provisions, and maintenance of a minimum current ratio. Trustees, usually commercial banks, are appointed to look after the interests of bondholders.

' The *call provisions* in the indenture give the issuing corporation the right to call in a bond for redemption before the date of maturity. Call provisions generally state that the company will pay an amount over and above the par value of the bond. This additional sum is known as the *call premium*.

Since a bond is a debt, the corporation is obligated to fulfill its promises on interest and principal. If the corporation fails to do so, bondholders can bring suit and force the corporation to declare bankruptcy. Because of these characteristics, bonds in general are a safer investment than common stocks, and bond prices usually fluctuate much less than prices of common stocks. People who buy bonds are generally interested in a fixed, dependable current income rather than the prospect of capital appreciation.

Treasury Securities

The U.S. government issues a variety of debt securities known as *Treasuries*. They have the highest credit rating of all securities because they are backed by the full faith and taxing powers of the U.S. government. Because so many of these bonds are outstanding, and large numbers are traded daily, they are more liquid than other securities of equal maturity. The income from Treasury securities, while subject to federal tax, is exempt from state and local taxes.

Treasury securities vary in length of maturity. *Treasury bills (T-bills)* are short-term, with initial maturities ranging from ninety-one days up to one year. They are sold weekly and have a minimum denomination of $10,000. Investors can buy previously issued T-bills through brokerage firms. New issues are sold by the U.S. Treasury at a discount from face value, and are similar to zero coupon bonds in this regard. *Treasury notes* have maturities of ten years or less, and *Treasury bonds* have maturities of ten years to thirty years. Both notes and bonds have coupons and pay interest on a semiannual basis.

Federal Agency Securities

Short-term and long-term securities are issued by agencies that have various affiliations with the federal government. These agencies include the Federal National Mortgage Association (FNMA or "Fannie Mae"), Federal Home Loan Banks, Federal Farm Credit Banks, and the Government National

Mortgage Association (GNMA or "Ginnie Mae"). While all are regarded as safe investments, only GNMA securities have the full guarantee of the U.S. government.

State and Local Government Bonds

State and local governments—including counties, school districts, townships, and other special agencies—issue large numbers of long-term debt securities to finance a variety of projects, such as schools, highways, bridges, tunnels, sewers, and water, electric, and gas facilities. State and local government bonds, commonly referred to as *muncipal securities*, are generally of two categories: general obligation bonds and revenue bonds. *General obligation bonds* are backed by the full faith and credit of the state or local government that issued them. *Revenue bonds*, on the other hand, are secured by a specific source of income. For example, when revenue bonds are issued to finance the construction of a bridge, the bridge's toll income may be pledged to pay interest and principal on the bond. It should also be noted that, like the federal government and a number of corporations, some state and local governments issue short-term securities.

Most municipal bonds are issued in serial form. That is, the total amount of an issue is usually divided into several portions, with each portion carrying different maturities and yields. The advantage of the serial bond is that the debtor can plan the repayment of the total debt in installments to suit its estimated requirements.

In most cases the interest income from securities issued by state and local governments is exempt from federal income tax. Under the 1986 tax reform law, all municipal bonds issued prior to 1986 have the federal tax exemption. Municipal bonds issued in 1986 and beyond which are used for essential government activities will continue to be federally tax-exempt. However, under the 1986 law, new bonds used to finance what is considered to be nonessential government activities would not be federally tax-exempt. In short, the investor should check on the tax status of a municipal bond before purchasing it.

MONEY MARKET INSTRUMENTS

The following securities have maturities of one year or less when they are issued, categorizing them as *money market instruments:*

1. *Treasury bills* are issued on a discount basis (below par value) and mature at par. Most mature three or six months after issuance, and the longest maturity is one year.

2. *Commercial paper* consists of unsecured promissory notes issued by large and well-known business concerns. Maturities range from four to six months.
3. *Negotiable certificates of deposit* are issued by commercial banks. They are transferable, and their yields generally increase with maturity.
4. *Bankers' acceptances* are drafts that originate in the financing of foreign trade, and are accepted or guaranteed by a commercial bank for payment at a specific time. Their maturity is usually four to six months.
5. *Eurodollars* are interest-bearing deposits held in banks located outside the United States. The banks may be foreign subsidiaries of American banks or they may be foreign-owned banks. The participating institutions are located primarily in Europe and Asia.
6. *Repurchase agreements* represent the sale of securities to an investor with an agreement to repurchase them at a later date. On the repurchase date the investor receives the principal plus some interest.
7. *Short-term tax-exempt securities* are like municipal bonds except that they mature within one year.

COMMON STOCKS

Common stocks are probably the securities that most often come to mind when people think of investments. Common stocks are equity securities, that is, they represent ownership of a corporation. The rights of holders of common stock are established by the laws of the state in which the firm is chartered and by the terms of the charter granted by that state. Usually, common-stock holders as a group enjoy the following rights:

1. To amend the charter
2. To adopt and amend bylaws
3. To select the directors of the corporation
4. To authorize the sale of fixed assets
5. To enter into mergers
6. To change the amount of authorized common stock
7. To issue preferred stock, bonds, and other securities

Common-stock holders have legal control over the corporation through voting privileges. As a practical matter, however, the principal officers in many corporations are also the most influential members of the board of directors and usually secure approval of their policies and decisions, including selection of their own successors in management. Nevertheless, if the common-stock holders as a group are dissatisfied with the performance of the current management of the corporation, they can vote their shares to change the management in a *proxy battle*.

The common-stock holder bears the ultimate risk and reward of the corporation. If the corporation fails to earn an adequate return on its assets, its stock price will most likely fall. If the corporation is forced into liquidation, the common-stock holder will usually get nothing because corporate assets, when sold, most often do not bring in sufficient funds to cover the claims of creditors. On the other hand, if the corporation is prosperous, the common-stock holder will enjoy rising dividends and, more importantly, substantial capital gains as the stock price rises.

CONVERTIBLE BONDS, PREFERRED STOCKS, AND CONVERTIBLE PREFERRED STOCKS

Convertible bonds are like other bonds, with the added feature that the owner may convert them into a certain number of shares of common stock. If a corporation becomes prosperous, as the price of the common stock rises, the convertible bond may be worth more as stock than as a bond, and the owner may receive some capital gains as a result. However, the investor pays a price for this advantage. The convertible bond is usually issued at a lower interest rate than is a straight bond. The investor must decide whether the advantage of having a conversion feature is worth the loss in interest income.

Preferred stock is a fixed-income security because the dividend is of a fixed amount. Preferred stock has priority over common stock in the distribution of dividends and in the allocation of assets in the event of liquidation. Preferred stock usually has a par value; this value is a meaningful quantity. It establishes the amount due to the preferred stockholders in the event of liquidation. Dividends on preferred stock are usually cumulative. Dividends omitted in one year have to be made up in the following years before dividends on common stock can be paid. An advantage of owning preferred stock is a reasonably steady income. In addition, in the event of liquidation, preferred-stock holders will have preference over common-stock holders in the distribution of assets. Many corporations, such as insurance companies, hold preferred stocks as investments because federal tax law provides that 80 percent of dividends received by corporate investors are tax-exempt. This feature, however, does not apply to individual investors.

Convertible preferred stocks are similar to convertible bonds in that preferred stock may be converted into a certain number of shares of common stock. If the corporation prospers, the owner may benefit from the rising price of common stock. However, as with ownership of convertible bonds, this advantage is obtained at a price. Convertible preferred stock is usually issued at a lower dividend rate than is straight preferred stock. The investor has to decide whether the advantage obtained is worth the price paid.

OPTIONS

Options are not securities, but rather the right to buy or sell securities. The right to buy a stated number of securities at a specified price (the *striking price*) is referred to as a *call option*. The right to sell a stated number of securities at a specified price is called a *put option*. If you buy a call, you are betting the price of a certain security will rise; if you buy a put, you are betting its price will fall. The *options markets* offer standardized expiration dates (of less than one year) and exercise prices. These markets have made the purchase and sale of options as simple as the purchase and sale of securities. The actual selling (or writing) and buying of options is done by investors and speculators. Options are listed on various exchanges, such as the Chicago Board Options Exchange and the American Stock Exchange.

WARRANTS

Warrants are similar to call options, for they allow the holder to purchase a certain number of shares of stock at a stated price within a specified time period. However, warrants differ from calls in several ways. First of all, they are issued by the firm itself. They give the holder more time to purchase the shares; when they are issued they are usually valid for at least three years, compared to less than a year for a newly issued call. When warrants are issued they are usually attached to a new set of bonds or preferred stock sold by the corporation.

FUTURES CONTRACTS

Futures contracts allow individuals to place bets regarding the future prices of various items. Contracts exist on commodities, foreign currency, interest rates, indexes of stock prices, and even the rate of inflation. Denominations are high in these contracts, and the risks can be great. There are methods, however, in which futures contracts can be used to reduce risk for financial institutions, business enterprises, and for some investors. These methods are called *hedging strategies* (see Chapter 16).

INVESTMENT COMPANIES

Investment companies are firms that pool shareholders' money to invest in a diversified portfolio of securities. An investor who buys shares in an investment company is, in effect, a partial owner of the company, and thus is also a partial owner of the company's portfolio. Investment companies are regulated by the Securities and Exchange Commission.

There are two types of investment companies. *Closed-ended investment companies* are like business corporations in that the amount of common equity, or capitalization, is fixed (closed), and the firm's shares are traded on the organized stock exchanges. The *open-ended investment company*, commonly called a *mutual fund*, does not have a limit on its common equity. It sells and redeems its shares without limit directly to the public at the net asset value (the total market value of the portfolio less liabilities, divided by the number of shares outstanding). The net asset value is computed daily.

There are more than 1500 mutual funds in existence, and each one has specific investment objectives. Some funds seek growth by investing in common stocks of companies the management believes offer large capital gains. Other funds seek income and invest in securities that have attractive interest rates and dividend yields. There are funds that specialize in specific securities, like bonds, foreign securities, GNMA securities, or high-tech stocks. The basic idea is the same: Individual investors secure the skills of professional fund managers, who use the pooled money to purchase a diversified portfolio designed to achieve specified investment objectives.

Some investment companies are *load companies*, that is, a portion of an investor's equity is deducted as a sales commission for the sales representative. *No-load companies*, which sell their shares directly to the public over the telephone and through the mail, charge no commission. All funds do have management fees, which are deducted when their net asset value is computed.

MONEY MARKET FUNDS AND ACCOUNTS

Money market funds are mutual funds that invest in the various money market instruments. Denominations of these instruments range from $10,000 for Treasury bills to over $200,000 for certain types of Eurodollar certificates. Money market fund managers pool deposits of small and large savers, use the funds to buy money market instruments, and then pay money market rates less a component allocated for the expenses of the fund. Initial deposits may be as low as $1,000, and the funds are usually set up like no-load mutual funds.

An alternative to money market funds are *money market accounts* at commercial banks and savings institutions. They accrue interest at rates similar to those of the funds.

THE RATE OF RETURN

Investing in the numerous instruments described in this chapter involves accepting the risk that the actual return might be less than expected. *Risk* involves the idea of uncertainty about future returns. The terms "risk" and "uncertainty" are often used interchangeably in investment analysis. What causes future returns to be unpredictable, that is, to vary? In other words, what causes risk? Before answering that question, we need to clarify what we mean by the term "return." The *return* on an investment is the actual dollar amount of the increase in wealth the investment provides. In order to compare alternative investments, however, we use the *rate of return*, which is the rate of increase in wealth, expressed as a percent. The rate of return for a given period includes both the cash flow from an investment (either dividends on stock or interest on bonds), plus the change in the value of the investment. The following equation is used in the computation of the rate of return:

$$r = \frac{(V_E - V_B) + CF}{V_B} \tag{2.1}$$

where:

r = Rate of return
V_E = Value of investment at end of period
V_B = Value of investment at beginning of period
CF = Annual cash flow (dividends or interest paid)

For example, if you buy a portfolio of stocks for $10,000 at the beginning of the year, receive $400 in dividends, and sell the portfolio for $11,000 at the end of the year, your rate of return for the year is $[(11,000 - 10,000) + 400]/10,000 = .14$.

COMPONENTS OF RISK

Systematic Risk

Systematic risk is the term given to forces of an economic, political, and sociological nature that are beyond the control of an individual firm, and affect all securities. Three components of systematic risk are inflation risk, interest-rate risk, and market risk.

    Inflation risk, or purchasing-power risk, has to do with the effect that generally rising (or falling) prices in the economy have on an investment. Suppose you purchase a security that gives you a 10 percent rate of return. If the expected rate of inflation is 6 percent, you anticipate a real rate of return of $10\% - 6\% = 4\%$. In other words, 6 percent of the total 10 percent return on the security keeps you just even with inflation; the real benefit to you is the 4 percent you get over the rate of inflation. Now suppose that your expectations turn out to be incorrect and the rate of inflation is actually 8 percent. You emerge with a 10% − 8% = 2% real rate of return. Given that the future inflation rate cannot be accurately predicted, some inflation risk is incurred in making investment decisions.

The holders of fixed-income securities (and other investments) are exposed not only to risks from changes in price levels but also to changes in interest rates, termed *interest-rate risk*. As rates move up, the prices of existing fixed-income securities move down, and vice versa. This reflects the fact that investors are unwilling to buy a bond (or other fixed-income security) at par when its fixed coupon interest rate is lower than the prevailing interest rate on bonds of comparable grade. For example, suppose the prevailing interest rate is 10 percent, and you pay $1,000 for a newly issued 10-percent security that promises a fixed payment of $1,100 ($1,000 principal plus $100 interest) at the end of one year from the date of issue. Assume prevailing interest rates for comparable investments rise to 12 percent in the next month. Now newly issued one-year securities that cost $1,000 have a fixed payment of $1,120 at the end of one year. Because your security promises only $1,100 you cannot sell it for $1,000, and you will have to accept less if you want to sell it immediately. When interest rates drop, the reverse occurs.

Interest rates also affect stock prices. When rates rise, some investors will be tempted to sell shares in order to obtain the new higher yields on fixed-income securities. Rising rates may also be a sign that adverse economic conditions will soon develop, and this may also affect stock prices.

Market risk is discussed primarily in the context of common stocks when price fluctuations of individual stocks are associated with movements in the market as a whole. The causes of the fluctuation vary, but economic, political, or other news or rumors can affect investors' expectations and cause substantial increases or decreases in prices throughout securities markets.

Unsystematic Risk

Unsystematic risk is the term applied to those factors peculiar to a particular firm or industry, and are to some extent controllable. For example, many factors that cause business risk (see below) and decisions on financing the firm, which relate to financial risk, also underly unsystematic risk.

Business Risk and Financial Risk

Business risk refers to the unpredictability in a firm's profits due to variations in revenues and operating expenses. It is caused by factors that are both internal and external to the firm. Internal factors include management decisions, labor relations, and the development of new products. Some important external factors are domestic and foreign competition, and general economic conditions. *Financial risk* is risk attributable to the use of borrowed funds (debt). Business risk and financial risk cause fluctuations in returns (stock prices and dividends) and also movement in bond prices via changes in the safety ratings of a firm's fixed-income securities.

MEASURING RISK

In Chapter 1 we saw that risk can be measured in terms of the volatility or unpredictability of returns. We compared the highly volatile nature of stock returns over the years with the less volatile returns of bonds and Treasury bills. How can we measure the risk of future returns?

Standard Deviation

A measure widely used in security valuation and portfolio theory is the *standard deviation*, which measures the degree of uncertainty because it gauges the probability of returns far from the expected return. If widely varying returns are probable, then the standard deviation will be high. If there is little difference among the possible returns, then the standard deviation will be low. A standard deviation of zero indicates that an investor is certain that the actual return will be the same as the expected return. In other words, the investment is risk-free. The larger the standard deviation, the riskier the investment. It is generally believed that people are risk-averse, that is, they will avoid risky investments unless they are compensated with a relatively high expected rate of return.

Beta

Security prices are affected to some extent by the overall state of the economy, and most stocks tend to fluctuate together. An important finding of modern portfolio theory is that investors can reduce their risk by selecting a diversified portfolio of stocks. For, a portion of the riskiness of a security depends on how movements in its rate of return are correlated with returns on other securities in the portfolio. A stock that performs poorly when the other stocks in a portfolio also perform poorly makes for a risky portfolio because it has no diversification potential. A portfolio of two oil company stocks is less diversified, and tends to be riskier than a portfolio of one oil company stock and one automobile stock. A decline in world oil prices might cause both oil stocks to decline in value, but it would have a positive effect on the auto company stock.

A measure called *beta* (β) may be used by investors to gauge how a security's rate of return is related to the returns on other securities in a well-diversified portfolio. Beta is a measure of market risk and relates the variation in the value of a security to the variation in an index of market performance. One such index, the Standard and Poor's Index of 500 stocks

(S&P 500) is frequently used to measure stock market performance and to calculate betas.

The point of reference with respect to beta is the number 1. A stock with a beta of 1.0 fluctuates to the same extent as the market, as measured by the index. In other words, it is about as risky as the overall market. A stock with a beta greater than 1.0 tends to have a greater fluctuation than the market, while a stock with a beta less than 1.0 tends to have less fluctuation. Stocks with betas larger than 1.0 are riskier than the overall market, while those with betas less than 1.0 are not as risky. If a stock has a beta of 2.0, and the market's overall return increases 2 percent, the stock should increase 4 percent (2% × 2.0). On the other hand, if a stock has a beta of 0.5 and the market decreases 2 percent, the stock should decrease only 1 percent. Thus a portfolio of high beta stocks is a risky portfolio, and a portfolio of low beta stocks is a safer, more conservative portfolio.[1]

Financial Ratios

Another aspect of risk lies in the credit-worthiness of a firm and the default risk of its fixed-income securities. To estimate this risk a number of financial ratios are employed. Useful ratios include the current ratio, debt to total assets, times interest earned, fixed-charges coverage, and various profitability ratios (see Chapter 10). These ratios also have a bearing on the riskiness of a company's stock, for as the risk associated with the firm and its debt increases, so too will the risk of its equity.

HISTORICAL PERFORMANCE

See Table 2–1 for the annual rates of return on several types of securities from 1950 to 1984. The return on common stocks is based on the S&P 500. The return for each year includes the dividends on the stock plus changes in price, as specified in Equation 2.1. Similarly, bond returns are based on the cost of a portfolio of bonds at the beginning of the year, the value of the portfolio at year-end, and the interest received. The composition of the securities in both the government and corporate bond portfolios changed over time. In the case of Treasury bills, the average rate on new bills issued during the year was taken as an approximation of an annual return because Treasury bills are short-term securities that fluctuate relatively little in price, and investors who purchase new issues often hold them to maturity.

The rate of inflation in this table is that measured by the Consumer Price Index. By deducting the rate of inflation from the return on a security,

---

[1]There are problems in making use of beta numbers, and these are discussed in Chapter 19. Also note that other factors exclusive of the market, such as industry competition, the acceptance of the company's product line, and management competence, will have a great effect on a firm's stock price movements.

TABLE 2–1   Annual Rates of Return on Stocks, Bonds, and Treasury Bills

Year	Common Stocks	Corporate Bonds	Government Bonds	Treasury Bills	Rate of Inflation
1950	31.71	2.12	.06	1.20	5.79
1951	24.02	−2.69	−3.94	1.49	5.87
1952	18.37	3.52	1.16	1.66	.88
1953	−.99	3.41	3.63	1.82	.62
1954	52.62	5.39	7.19	.86	−.50
1955	31.56	.48	−1.30	1.57	.37
1956	6.56	−6.81	−5.59	2.46	2.86
1957	−10.78	8.71	7.45	3.14	3.02
1958	43.36	−2.22	− 6.10	1.54	1.76
1959	11.95	−.97	−2.26	2.95	1.50
1960	.47	9.07	13.78	2.66	1.48
1961	26.89	4.82	.97	2.13	.67
1962	−8.73	7.95	6.89	2.73	1.22
1963	22.80	2.19	1.21	3.12	1.65
1964	16.48	4.77	3.51	3.54	1.19
1965	12.45	−.46	.71	3.93	1.92
1966	−10.06	.20	3.65	4.76	3.35
1967	23.98	−4.95	−9.19	4.21	3.04
1968	11.06	2.57	−.26	5.21	4.72
1969	−8.50	−8.09	−5.08	6.58	6.11
1970	4.01	18.37	12.10	6.53	5.49
1971	14.31	11.01	13.23	4.39	3.36
1972	18.98	7.26	5.68	3.84	3.41
1973	−14.66	1.14	−1.11	6.93	8.80
1974	−26.47	−3.06	4.35	8.00	12.20
1975	37.20	14.64	9.19	5.80	7.01
1976	23.84	18.65	16.75	5.08	4.81
1977	−7.18	1.71	−.67	5.12	6.77
1978	6.56	−.07	−1.16	7.18	9.03
1979	18.44	−4.18	−1.22	10.38	13.31
1980	32.42	−2.62	−3.95	11.24	12.40
1981	−4.91	−.96	1.85	14.71	8.94
1982	21.41	43.76	40.37	10.53	3.87
1983	22.30	6.70	2.00	8.60	3.90
1984	6.20	16.20	14.60	9.60	4.00

Averages and Variation over Major Intervals*

		Common Stocks	Corporate Bonds	Government Bonds	Treasury Bills	Rate of Inflation
1950–69	Average	14.8	1.5	.8	2.9	2.4
	High	52.6	9.1	13.8	6.6	6.1
	Low	−10.8	−8.1	−9.2	.9	−.5
1970–84	Average	10.2	8.6	7.5	7.9	7.2
	High	37.2	43.8	40.4	14.7	13.3
	Low	−26.5	−4.2	−4.0	3.8	3.4
Total Period:						
1950–84	Average	12.8	4.5	3.7	5.0	4.4
	High	52.6	43.8	40.4	14.7	13.3
	Low	−26.5	−8.1	−9.2	.9	−.5

* Averages, highs, and lows rounded to 1/10 of 1 percent.

Sources: 1950–1982: Roger G. Ibbotson and Rex A. Sinquefield, *Stocks, Bonds, Bills and Inflation, 1926–1982.* (Charlottesville, Vir.: Financial Analysis Research Foundation, 1983). 1983–1984: Estimated by authors.

one can compute the gain or loss in terms of purchasing power. Thus, someone who held Treasury bills in 1980 received a negative real return because an inflation rate of 12.4 percent offset an 11.24 percent annual return. A holder of T-bills in 1982 who received 10.53 percent did much better because inflation was only 3.87 percent.

As we might expect, the stock market produced the highest average annual return, 12.8 percent, over the entire 1950–84 period. Stocks also had the greatest variation in rates of return, ranging from +52.62 percent in 1954 and −26.47 percent in 1974. The next best performers were Treasury bills (5 percent), followed by corporate bonds (4.5 percent), and long-term government bonds (3.7 percent). The worst performance of bonds occurred during the period 1950–69, when both corporates (1.5 percent) and governments (0.8 percent) produced average returns less than the rate of inflation (2.4 percent). For the 1970–84 period, bonds had an average positive real return, but while corporate bonds (8.6 percent) had a higher return than Treasury bills (7.9 percent), long-term government bonds (7.5 percent) actually had a lower return than Treasury bills.

Why did bonds have such low real returns, and why did they perform poorly relative to Treasury bills, which have much less risk as measured by variation in return? The answer lies in the difference between actual and expected returns. During much of the 1950–84 period, inflation was increasing, as were interest rates. Most investors did not anticipate the severity of the inflation and the extent to which interest rates would rise. As noted earlier, rising interest rates cause bond prices to drop.

What all this means is that the following occurred: The market had expected bonds to perform better than Treasury bills and to provide generally positive real returns. In fact, bond yields, based on interest payments and excluding the price changes due to interest rate variations, generally exceeded Treasury bill rates. However, due to unanticipated inflation and rising interest rates, bond prices dropped. Actual returns for bondholders were less-than-expected returns, which were also below the average Treasury bill rate during that period. Thus, while there is normally a trade-off between expected return and risk, one may find that over an extended period of time there is not an obvious trade-off between actual return and risk among investments.

SUMMARY

There are a large number of investment alternatives available. Interest-bearing securities include bonds, notes, and various types of money market instruments. Equity investments include common and preferred stocks. In addition, there are hybrid investments, such as convertible bonds, that have characteristics of both debt and equity instruments.

This chapter also briefly described other types of investment media. Investment companies pool shareholders' money to purchase diversified portfolios of securities. Options represent the right to buy or sell securities under specified terms. Futures contracts allow investors to buy or sell certain commodities or financial instruments for future delivery. Finally, concepts of risk and return were discussed and common measures of risk used by investment analysts were introduced. In particular, standard deviation and beta are two measures of variation that one frequently encounters.

QUESTIONS AND PROBLEMS

1. What is the difference between
   a. Bonds with coupons and zero coupon bonds?
   b. Debentures and mortgage bonds?
   c. Treasury bonds and Treasury notes?
2. What is meant by a bond indenture? What provisions does it usually contain?
3. a. Which securities are known as tax-exempts?
   b. What is the difference between general obligation bonds and revenue bonds?
4. Which securities are known as money market instruments? Who issues them, and for what purpose?
5. Compare and contrast common stock and preferred stock.
6. Why are corporate investors usually more interested than individual investors in purchasing preferred stocks?
7. From the standpoint of investors, are convertible bonds better than straight bonds?
8. Explain the difference between load mutual funds and no-load mutual funds.
9. a. Are options securities?
   b. Explain call options and put options.
10. a. Discuss systematic risk and the factors that contribute to it.
    b. What is unsystematic risk?
11. Discuss the measures of risk used in investment analysis.
12. a. Does higher risk guarantee higher return?
    b. How are risk and return related?
13. "A U.S. government bond is risk-free, because it is backed by the full faith and credit of the United States." Comment on this statement.

REFERENCES

Cohen, J., Zinbarg, E., and Zeikel, A. *Investment Analysis and Portfolio Management*. Homewood, Ill.: Irwin, 1982, Chapter 1.

Cook, T., and Summers, B., eds., *Instruments of the Money Market*. Federal Reserve Bank of Richmond, 1981.

Darst, David M. *The Complete Bond Book*. New York: McGraw-Hill, 1975, Chapters 6–10.

Fabozzi, F., and Pollack, I., eds., *The Handbook of Fixed Income Securities*. Homewood, Ill.: Dow Jones–Irwin, 1983.

Fisher, Lawrence, and Lorie, James H. *A Half Century of Returns on Stocks and Bonds*. Chicago: The University of Chicago Graduate School of Business, 1977.

Ibbotson, R., and Sinquefield, R. *Stocks, Bonds, Bills, and Inflation, 1926–1982*, Charlottesville, Vir.: Financial Analysts Research Foundation, 1983.

Sharpe, W. F. *Investments*. Englewood Cliffs, N.J.: Prentice-Hall, 1981.

Sharpe, W. F., and Cooper, G. M. "Risk-Return Classes of New York Stock Exchange Common Stocks," *Financial Analysts Journal*, March–April 1972.

Sumutka, Alan, and Randall, Maury. "Some Tax Advantaged Investments — Part I," *CPA Journal*, February 1984.

Valentine, Jerome L., and Mennis, Edmund A. *Quantitative Techniques For Financial Analysis*, rev. ed. Homewood, Ill.: Richard D. Irwin, Inc., 1980.

3

Securities Markets

We can examine securities transactions from several perspectives—from the points of view of dealers, brokers, investment bankers, and other participants in securities markets. In this chapter we will also examine characteristics of the markets and some important investment strategies.

PRIMARY MARKETS AND INVESTMENT BANKING

The markets that deal with newly issued securities are called *primary markets*. These markets perform an important economic function. Savings of individuals are channeled to companies that use the funds to purchase new capital (for example, plant and equipment). In return, new securities are issued to savers, either directly or indirectly through financial intermediaries (such as financial institutions or mutual funds).

In primary markets, organizations called *investment bankers* specialize in the marketing of new securities. Investment bankers perform two functions: advising and underwriting. The investment banker acts as an advisor to corporations that plan to issue new securities, and in this capacity counsels the issuer on the types of debt and equity securities that can be sold. In the case of bonds, required interest rates, possible maturities, and other terms of the issue would be considered. When equity is to be sold, the impact of new shares on the current stock price would be examined. In the planning process the investment banker and the corporation also consider the proper time to issue securities in light of existing supply and demand conditions.

When investment bankers act as *underwriters*, they guarantee a specific price for the securities to be sold. This is done in an agreement with the corporation that states that they will buy the entire issue at a stated price per security and will deliver the proceeds to the issuer before a certain date. In such cases, investment bankers intend to resell the securities to the general public at a higher price and take the difference as their profits. However, security markets change quickly, and sometimes it is impossible to sell the entire issue without substantially lowering its price. An investment banker could end up either taking losses or buying some of the securities with its own capital.

Generally, investment bankers are only willing to underwrite issues from large and well-known firms. When small and less-known companies wish to sell securities, investment bankers may be willing to market the issue only on a "best efforts" basis. In these cases investment bankers are not underwriting, but merely pledging to do their best to sell the security. They receive a commission on securities sold, and the unsold securities are returned to the issuer.

SECONDARY MARKETS: EXCHANGES, DEALERS, AND BROKERS

Existing securities, which have been sold to the public in primary markets, are also traded in secondary markets. These markets have an important economic function in the capital allocation process by providing liquidity for new issue buyers. Investors would be reluctant to purchase newly issued securities from corporations and governments unless there were secondary markets in existence to sell those securities for cash at a convenient time prior to maturity.

Secondary markets consist of two principal components: organized exchanges and the over-the-counter (OTC) market. On exchanges, such as the New York Stock Exchange, securities are bought and sold in a central location. When one investor sells, the securities are sold on the exchange floor by a broker to another investor. The proceeds go to the seller, not to the company that issued the security. On the over-the-counter market, trading is performed over the telephone by securities dealers who buy from and sell to investors.

National and Regional Exchanges

In the United States there are two national stock exchanges: The New York Stock Exchange (NYSE) and the American Stock Exchange, (AMEX), both of which are located in New York City. They are national in that companies listed or traded on the exchanges are relatively large and are headquartered in many different locations around the United States. Of these two exchanges, the NYSE has more corporations listed, and the firms are also larger. Regional exchanges list companies that, generally, are smaller and more locally oriented than those in the national exchanges. Included among the regional exchanges are the Boston, Cincinnati, Midwest (Chicago), Pacific (San Francisco and Los Angeles), and Philadelphia-Baltimore-Washington stock exchanges.

The relative importance of these exchanges is shown in Table 3–1, in which we see, by shares and by values, the volume transacted on the NYSE, AMEX, and all other exchanges. In terms of 1984 share volume, the NYSE represents about 82.6 percent, the AMEX 5.2 percent, and all others combined 12.2 percent. In terms of value, the NYSE represents an even higher percentage, 85.7 percent.

TABLE 3–1

Shares sold on registered exchanges

	Number of shares (millions)			Percent of total		
	NYSE	ASE	Other exchanges	NYSE	ASE	Other exchanges
1935	513.6	84.7	63.6	77.6%	12.8%	9.6%
1940	282.7	47.9	41.4	76.0	12.9	11.1
1945	496.0	152.4	96.1	66.6	20.5	12.9
1950	655.3	114.9	86.9	76.5	13.4	10.1
1955	820.5	243.9	148.0	67.7	20.1	12.2
1960	958.3	300.6	129.6	69.0	21.6	9.3
1965	1,809.4	582.2	195.3	69.9	22.5	7.5
1970	3,213.1	878.5	444.1	70.8	19.4	9.8
1971	4,265.3	1,049.3	601.1	72.1	17.7	10.2
1972	4,496.2	1,103.2	699.8	71.4	17.5	11.1
1973	4,336.6	740.4	653.2	75.7	12.9	11.4
1974	3,821.9	475.3	541.9	79.0	9.8	11.2
1975	5,056.5	540.9	637.6	81.1	8.7	10.2
1976	5,649.2	637.0	749.5	80.3	9.1	10.7
1977	5,613.3	651.9	758.2	79.9	9.3	10.8
1978	7,618.0	992.2	872.6	80.3	10.5	9.2
1979	8,675.3	1,161.3	1,026.2	79.9	10.7	9.4
1980	12,389.9	1,658.8	1,437.0	80.0	10.7	9.3
1981	12,843.1	1,472.3	1,594.9	80.7	9.3	10.0
1982	18,210.8	1,582.6	2,662.1	81.1	7.0	11.9
1983	24,253.5	2,209.4	3,683.8	80.5	7.3	12.2
1984	25,150.2	1,584.0	3,722.3	82.6	5.2	12.2

Market value of shares sold on registered exchanges

	Market value (millions)			Percent of total		
	NYSE	ASE	Other exchanges	NYSE	ASE	Other exchanges
1935	$ 13,335	$ 1,205	$ 736	87.3%	7.9%	4.8%
1940	7,166	643	595	85.3	7.7	7.0
1945	13,462	1,728	1,036	83.0	10.6	6.4
1950	18,725	1,481	1,571	86.0	6.8	7.2
1955	32,745	2,593	2,530	86.5	6.8	6.7
1960	37,960	4,176	3,083	83.9	9.2	6.8
1965	73,200	8,612	7,402	82.0	9.7	8.3
1970	103,063	14,266	13,579	78.7	10.9	10.4
1971	147,098	17,664	20,169	79.5	9.6	10.9
1972	159,700	20,453	23,873	78.3	10.0	11.7
1973	146,451	10,430	21,156	82.3	5.9	11.9
1974	99,178	5,048	14,023	83.9	4.3	11.9
1975	133,819	5,678	17,595	85.2	3.6	11.2
1976	164,545	7,468	22,956	84.4	3.8	11.8
1977	157,250	8,532	21,421	84.0	4.6	11.4
1978	210,426	15,204	23,625	84.4	6.1	9.5
1979	251,098	20,596	28,279	83.7	6.9	9.4
1980	397,670	34,696	43,485	83.6	7.3	9.1
1981	415,913	26,385	48,390	84.8	5.4	9.9
1982	514,263	20,731	69,054	85.1	3.4	11.4
1983	815,113	31,501	110,505	85.2	3.3	11.5
1984	815,655	21,349	115,143	85.7	2.2	12.1

Source: NYSE Fact Book, 1985.

The New York Stock Exchange

Since the New York Stock Exchange is the dominant institution among the exchanges and because its organizational pattern is followed by the other exchanges, it merits our particular attention. The NYSE is an association of members organized for the purpose of facilitating the buying and selling of securities. The NYSE, now a corporation, provides the physical facilities for its members to trade in securities. Its membership has been fixed at 1366 members since 1953. Members of the NYSE are usually said to have a "seat" on the exchange, which can be bought and sold, although each transfer must be approved by the NYSE board of directors. The board of directors is made up of representatives of the security industry, listed companies, and the investing public. Ten directors are chosen from the membership, and ten are chosen from outside the industry. The chairman of the exchange is selected by the board of directors, which brings the total membership of the board to twenty-one.

Only members of the NYSE can buy and sell securities on its trading floor. The trading floor, about the size of a football field, has fourteen U-shaped counters known as trading posts. Listed securities of the NYSE are assigned to each of these posts for trading.

FUNCTIONS OF MEMBERS   In accordance with the functions performed, members of the NYSE can be classified into commission brokers, floor brokers, floor traders, odd-lot dealers, and specialists.

Commission brokers. A member of the NYSE may be a general partner or holder of voting stock in one of the brokerage concerns which, by virtue of exchange membership, is known as a member firm or member corporation. About half the members of the NYSE are partners or officers in member organizations doing business with the general public. These members execute customer orders to buy and/or sell on the exchange, and their firms receive commissions on these transactions. Many firms have more than one member.

Floor brokers. These members assist the commission brokers in the execution of their orders. In compensation for their services, they share a part of the commission earned by commission brokers. Floor brokers generally are "independents" who are not employees of a commission broker's firm.

Registered traders. These members trade for their own accounts. They do not act for the public or for other members.

Odd-lot dealers. These members serve investors who purchase or sell a few shares at a time rather than the conventional one hundred-share units known as a *round lot*. The odd-lot member acts as a dealer, not a broker. He buys from or sells to other members doing a public business.

Specialists.[1] About one-fourth of all members of the NYSE are called specialists because they specialize in "making a market" for one or more

---

[1]Much of the material in this section is drawn from a NYSE publication, *The Specialist — Key Man in the Exchange Market*, March 1973.

stocks. They perform two principal functions. First, they execute limit orders that other members of the exchange leave with them. These limit orders are left with a specialist when the current market price differs from the price of the order. For example, a commission broker may receive an order when the shares are selling at $60 to wait to buy at $58. By executing these orders on behalf of other exchange members when the market price finally reaches the price stated on the orders, the specialist makes it possible for these members to transact other business elsewhere on the exchange floor. In handling these orders, the specialist acts as a broker or agent.

The second, more complex role of specialists is that of dealer or principal for their own accounts. As dealers, specialists are expected, as far as is practical, to maintain continuously fair and orderly markets in the stocks assigned to them. When there is a temporary disparity, for example, between supply and demand, they usually buy or sell for their own account to narrow price changes between transactions and to give depth to the market. By doing this, they keep price continuity more orderly than it would otherwise be; they contribute to the liquidity of the market; and they make it possible for investors' orders to be executed at better prices when temporary disparities occur.

To maintain the market, specialists may purchase stock at a higher price than anyone else is willing to pay. For example, assume that a stock has just sold at 55. The highest price anyone is willing to pay is $54\frac{1}{4}$ (the best bid), and the lowest price at which anyone is willing to sell is $55\frac{1}{4}$ (the best offer). The specialist, acting as a dealer for his or her own account, may now decide to bid $54\frac{3}{4}$ for one hundred shares, making the quotation $54\frac{3}{4}$–$55\frac{1}{4}$, which narrows the spread between the bid and offer prices to $\frac{1}{2}$ point. Now, if a prospective seller wishes to sell one hundred shares at the price of the best bid, the specialist will purchase the stock at $54\frac{3}{4}$. By doing this, the specialist not only provides the seller with a better price but also maintains better price continuity, for the change from the last sale is only $\frac{1}{4}$ of a point.

In other cases specialists may sell stock from their own account to maintain a market. Assume that with the last sale in a stock at $62\frac{1}{4}$, the best bid is 62 and the best offer 63. The specialist offers shares at $62\frac{1}{2}$ from his own account, changing the quotation to 62–$62\frac{1}{2}$. A buyer enters the market and buys the stock from the specialist. Thus the buyer purchases the stock $\frac{1}{2}$ point cheaper than would have been the case without the specialist's offer. Again, better price continuity and depth have been maintained.

In their efforts to maintain an orderly market, sometimes specialists make both the best bid and best offer for a stock in their own account. Many times when specialists do not have sufficient stock in their inventory, they will *sell short* to maintain a market. In doing this, they must observe all the rules and regulations governing short selling.

Specialists record all limit orders in their books under each price category in the sequence in which they are received. For each of their orders, specialists show the number of shares and from whom it was received. They represent those orders in the market, and when they are successful in executing those orders on their books, they send reports to the members for whom they have acted according to the sequence of listing under each price category.

Because specialists stand at the center of the marketplace at the NYSE, they are closely regulated and supervised. Specialists are prohibited by exchange rules from buying for their account at a given price while they hold an order to buy at that price for someone else. Specialists must not buy stock at any price for their own account while holding an order to buy that stock "at the market" (the best available price). The same holds true with respect to specialists selling for their own account while holding a sell order for someone else. They cannot compete at the same price, for their own account, with orders they hold as a broker's broker.

Specialists are required to submit to the exchange, about eight times a year, details of their dealings for unannounced one–week periods selected at random by the exchange. Actions taken by specialists, price movements in stocks which they cover, and spreads in quotations are examined carefully by the exchange to determine their effectiveness in maintaining fair and orderly markets.[2]

The main source of the specialists' income is the floor brokerage commissions they earn by acting as an agent in executing the orders left with them by other members. The floor brokerage commission is paid to the specialist out of the commission that the commission broker receives from his customer. There is no extra charge to the investor when the specialist's services are used. On the other hand, specialists in their capacity as dealers buy and sell securities for their own account. The specialist's success in making a profit, as in the case with all other dealers, is largely determined by his or her own judgment and astuteness as well as by general market conditions. Specialists do have one intangible advantage over others. For the stocks in which they trade, they keep limit orders in their books, and, therefore, they know more than others about the supply and demand schedule for these stocks.

LISTING REQUIREMENTS   To have its stock listed (traded) on the New York Stock Exchange, a company is expected to meet certain qualifications and to be willing to keep the investing public informed on the progress of its affairs. The company must be a going concern, or be the successor to a going concern. In determining eligibility for listing, particular attention is given to such qualifications as the degree of national interest in the company, its relative position and stability in the industry, and whether it is engaged in an expanding industry with prospects of at least maintaining its relative position.

---

[2]There are limits to the intervention of the specialist. If new information suddenly becomes available, the price of the stock could change sharply with no intervention by the specialist until the appropriate new price is reached.

Other factors relating to listing involve minimum levels of assets, market value of shares, number of shares, and number of shareholders. Of the organized exchanges, the NYSE has the highest standards of requirements for listing.

TYPES OF ORDERS   Investors can use several different methods to instruct their brokers to buy and/or sell securities.

Market order. The most common order used on the exchange, the market order directs the broker to buy or sell securities immediately at the best price presently obtainable. The "best price" is the lowest price for a buy order and the highest price for a sell order. The obvious advantage of a market order is its rapid execution, especially when the market is changing quickly. The disadvantage is that the investor does not know the exact execution price until later notified by the broker.

Limit order. A limit order instructs the broker to execute the order within certain price limits set by the customer, no higher than the limit price in a buy order and no lower than the limit price in a sell order. The disadvantage of the limit order is that the order may never be executed and the investor may have missed the market by only a small fraction.

Stop order. The use of the stop order is an attempt by the investor to limit a loss or protect part of a profit. It has advantages as well as limitations and should be used with care. Defined in the simplest terms, a stop order is an instruction to the broker to buy or sell a given stock at or close to a certain price. The stop order becomes a market order as soon as the price of the stock reaches, or sells through, the price specified by the investor in the stop order.

For example, assume you buy a given stock at $35 in anticipation of a higher price, and you want to limit your loss if the market turns against you. You can place with your broker a stop order to sell at, say, $32. This order will be transmitted by your broker to the floor representative of the firm. The floor representative, in turn, will deliver the order to the specialist in that stock. The stop order becomes a market order if and when the price declines to $32 or less and the specialist will get the best price possible for you.

There are also some limitations in the use of the stop order. First, if the stop order is placed with a specified price too close to current market price, the investor may be in danger of being closed out by a minor fluctuation in the price of the stock, even though later developments may prove that the original decision was correct. Second, in active, rapidly changing markets, an accumulation of stop orders that have been converted into market orders could result in the execution of these orders at a large variation from the stop order price.

Time limit of orders. The time limit of orders is specified by the investor. Most orders are day orders, that is, they expire at the close of the day if they are not executed by that time. Market orders usually belong in this category. On limit orders and stop orders, the investor can specify the time limit: a day, a week, a month, or for an indefinite period until the order is canceled.

Odd-lot orders. An order for the purchase or sale of less than the unit of trading (usually 100 shares) is an odd-lot order. As in the case of a round-lot order (100 shares or a multiple of 100), the investor can specify a time limit for the order. Because the odd-lot order goes through odd-lot dealers, a fee known as an *odd-lot differential* is paid for their service. The charge is $\frac{1}{8}$ of a point per share for a stock selling below $55, and $\frac{1}{4}$ of a point for a stock selling for $55 or more. The per-share charge is added to the actual purchase price of a stock. In the case of a sell order, the per-share charge is subtracted from the actual selling price per share.

Sell-short order. A short sale means that a seller sells a given stock without owning it. He or she borrows the stock from the broker, who in turn borrows the stock from other customers (usually margin account customers) or other brokerage firms. The short-seller expects the stock to decline in price and, therefore, the stock can be repurchased later at a lower price and returned to the broker. The danger lies in that the price of the stock may rise rather than fall. Theoretically, the potential loss can be unlimited. To prevent the possibility that the short-seller may arbitrarily drive down the price of a stock through successive short sales, the Securities and Exchange Commission (SEC) has ruled that a short sale must be designated when the order is placed and may not be executed at a price below the last preceding regular sale. This is known as an *up-tick,* that is, a short sale must be made at a price higher than the last regular trade, or at the price of the regular trade only when the price was higher than the previous transaction. The short-seller is also obligated to make good to the lender of stock any dividends declared on the stock during the time when the short sale is in effect.

ORDER EXECUTION   The operation of the NYSE can perhaps be best understood by describing what happens when an order is placed. Suppose an investor in Baltimore decides to buy stock in General Motors. A call is made to a broker or registered account executive in a local brokerage firm to find out the price of GM. Using a computer terminal the broker obtains the latest price and reports to the investor that the price for GM is $50 bid and 50\frac{1}{4}$ asked. The investor instructs the broker to buy one hundred shares of GM at the market. The broker then writes out an order and has it transmitted to the NYSE through the Designated Order Turnaround System (DOT). Super-DOT is an electronic order-routing system through which member firms transmit market and limit orders in NYSE-listed securities directly to the post where the securities are traded or to the member firm's booth. After the order has been executed, a report of execution is returned directly to the member firm office over the same electronic circuit that brought the order to the trading floor.

If the investor's order is not 100 shares, but an odd-lot, say of forty shares, then the member partner on the floor gives the order to the odd-lot dealer in GM stock. The odd-lot dealer will fill the order at a price based on the next round lot transaction in GM stock plus an odd-lot fee of $\frac{1}{8}$ or $\frac{1}{4}$ of a point per share, depending on whether the price of the stock is below or above $55.

After the transaction is completed, the investor has five business days to pay for the securities purchased. For example, an investor who buys a security on Tuesday can pay for it by the following Tuesday. The certificate can be sent to the investor in about a month, or it can be sent to the brokerage firm for safekeeping.

MARGIN TRADING   Securities may be purchased entirely with the funds of the buyer or may be bought on *margin* — with some investor funds plus some funds borrowed from the brokerage firm. The percentage of funds that can be borrowed is determined by the Federal Reserve Board. A margin requirement set by the Federal Reserve at 60 percent means that the investor must provide at least 60 percent of the required funds (the investor's equity) and borrow as much as the remaining 40 percent from the brokerage firm. In this case, the securities purchased will be kept by the brokerage firm as collateral for the loan to the customer. The margin requirement set by the Federal Reserve Board is called the *initial margin* and applies only on the day of purchase.

In addition to federal regulations of credit, the NYSE itself has certain credit requirements. No one may open a margin account with a member firm without depositing at least $2,000 or its equivalent in securities. The exchange also sets requirements for the maintenance of margin, as distinguished from the initial margin requirements of the Federal Reserve Board. Generally speaking, a customer's equity (market value of securities less borrowed funds) may at no time be less than 25 percent of the market value of securities on deposit with the broker. Most member firms actually require a higher maintenance margin, usually 30 percent. If the equity of an investor falls below the required maintenance margin of the brokerage firm, the firm will send out a request — known as a *margin call* — for an additional deposit of funds. If the investor fails to deposit new funds or the equivalent in new securities, the brokerage firm will sell the securities in order to protect itself against possible losses. Therefore investors who have margin accounts must know the value of their equity margin. The formula for calculating the equity margin is as follows:

$$EM = \frac{E}{MV} \tag{3.1}$$

where:

EM = Equity margin

E = Investor's equity

MV = Market value of securities subject to margin

The investor's equity (E) is equal to the market value of assets less the market value of any liabilities in the account, including broker loans. *MV*, the market value of securities, includes both the value of securities purchased and the value of securities sold short. We will analyze short sales in a later chapter, but for now we will consider a simple example in which shares have been bought. Assume an investor buys 200 shares of stock R at $50 per share, with a total cost of $10,000. At that time the margin requirement set by the Federal Reserve is 50 percent, and the investor will borrow the maximum amount permitted. This means that $5,000 is borrowed from the brokerage firm, and the investor puts up $5,000 of personal funds, which constitute investor equity. The initial position is:

	Assets (A)	Liabilities and Equity (L + E)
	$10,000 Stock R (200 shares)	$5,000 Broker Loan $5,000 Equity

$$EM = \frac{5,000}{10,000} = .50$$

Now let us consider the new value of equity margin if the price of stock R falls to $40. The account has changed to the following:

	A	L + E
	$8,000 Stock R (200 shares)	$5,000 Broker Loan $3,000 Equity

$$EM = \frac{3,000}{8,000} = .375$$

The value of the 200 shares drops to $8,000, but there is no change in the liability to the broker. Therefore, equity declines to $3,000 and the new equity margin falls to 37.5 percent.

How could one compute the price of the stock at which a margin call would occur if the minimum maintenance margin is 30 percent. First note that with *BL* equaling the broker loan,

$$E = MV - BL \tag{3.2}$$

Next, note that the margin call will occur when EM = 30 percent.

$$EM = \frac{E}{MV} = .30$$

Substituting for E,

$$\frac{MV - BL}{MV} = .30$$

Since BL = \$5,000,

$$\frac{MV - 5,000}{MV} = .30$$

Multiplying each side of the equation by MV,

$$MV - 5,000 = .30\ MV$$
$$.70\ MV = 5,000$$
$$MV = 7,142.86$$

$$\text{Price of stock R} = \frac{7,142.86}{200} = \$35.71$$

Let us carry our analysis one step further and assume the price of the stock suddenly falls below \$35.71 to \$30. What would be the amount of the margin call or, in other words, what is the amount of additional equity required to restore the 30 percent maintenance margin?

Market Value of Stock R: \$6,000
Equity: \$6,000 − \$5,000 = \$1,000
Required Equity: .30 × \$6,000 = \$1,800
Margin Call: \$800

Borrowing to purchase shares, such as in margin trading, is an example of a *levered investment strategy*. The advantage of using borrowed funds is that the investor's potential return is higher. The disadvantages are that risk, as measured by the variation in the rate of return, is greater, and potential investment losses are also greater. Let us consider cases that illustrate these points. Assume an investor has \$1,000 that will be used to purchase stock in Firm Y, currently priced at \$10 per share. The investor will either buy 100 shares or will borrow $1,000 from the broker and purchase 200 shares. The initial balance sheets are shown below:

No Margin		Margin	
A	L + E	A	L + E
$1,000 Stock Y (100 shares)	$1,000 Equity	$2,000 Stock Y (200 shares)	$1,000 Broker Loan $1,000 Equity

Assume the interest rate on the loan is 1 percent per month, and the investor holds the shares three months. We will calculate the rate of return on the investor's equity under three different outcomes. For simplicity, commissions and taxes are not included, and no dividends are paid on the stock. Under these conditions we can calculate the return on equity during the three months as

$$r_e = \frac{\Delta E - INT}{E_0} \tag{3.3}$$

where:

r_e = rate of return on equity during holding period

ΔE = change in value of equity

E_0 = initial value of investor equity

INT = interest paid to broker

The rate of return is the capital gain or loss less interest paid to the broker, divided by the initial investment. Also note that r_e is the return for the holding period, in our example three months, and it has not been annualized.[3]

Outcome 1: No Change in Price

Given that there is no price change, $\Delta E = 0$, and in the no-margin case, $INT = 0$. Hence, the return on equity equals zero. However, in the case of $1,000 borrowed, there is an interest expense of $.03 \times \$1,000 = \$30$, and

$$r_e = \frac{0 - 30}{1000} = -.03$$

---

[3] If there were a quarterly dividend it would be added to the numerator of Equation 3.3.

Outcome 2: Price Drops to $8.50

No Margin		Margin	
A	L + E	A	L + E
$850 Stock Y	$850 Equity	$1,700 Stock Y	$1,000 Broker Loan
			$700 Equity

$$\Delta E = 850 - 1,000 = -150 \qquad \Delta E = 1,700 - 2,000 = -300$$

$$r_e = \frac{-150}{1,000} = -.15 \qquad r_e = \frac{-300 - 30}{1,000} = -.33$$

The return in the no-margin case is merely the percentage drop in price. In the margin case, the dollar drop in equity is twice as great because twice as many shares are held. With the added interest expense the loss is 33 percent.

Outcome 3: Price Rises to $11.50

No Margin		Margin	
A	L + E	A	L + E
$1,150 Stock Y	$1,1150 Equity	$2,300 Stock Y	$1,200 Broker Loan
			$1,000 Equity

$$r_e = \frac{150}{1,000} = .15 \qquad r_e = \frac{300 - 30}{1,000} = .27$$

Here the return on equity is higher in the margin case. The investor borrowed $1,000 and paid 3 percent, or $30, but earned 15 percent, or $150, on that $1,000. The net gain of $120 added to the $150 earned on the $1,000 of the investor's funds provides a total dollar profit of $270 or 27 percent.

In summary, we see that potential gains and potential losses are greater in margin trading. In comparing outcomes 2 and 3 we also see that the margin account has a larger variation in rate of return as prices fluctuate. Thus the use of margin to purchase stock is appropriate only for investors who have strong confidence in their selection of stocks and who are willing to assume the higher degree of risk.

Short Sales and Margin Accounts

If an investor or speculator anticipates a drop in share prices, a short sale may be implemented. Assume stock Z is selling at $50 per share, and you expect its price to fall to $40. If you sell 100 shares of margin account stock Z short, the borrowed shares are sold for $5,000. If you are correct and the price does drop to $40, you can repurchase the shares for $4,000 and realize a $1,000 profit. If you are wrong and the price rises to more than $50, you have a loss. Let us examine the account of an investor who engages in a short sale. For the moment, assume the account was initially empty.

Initial Position after Short Sale

A	L + E
$5,000 Cash	$5,000 Stock Z (liability of 100 shares)

When the $5,000 of stock Z is sold there is a cash balance of $5,000 from selling the shares, and there is liability of $5,000 to the lender of the shares. Note that the short sale generates no equity and, therefore, none of the cash can be withdrawn. In fact, the broker will require some additional cash or securities in the account so that there will be a specified minimum level of equity. To see why this requirement exists, consider the impact of an increase in the price of stock Z on the previously shown balance sheet. If the price of Z rises to $52 we have

A	L + E
$5,000 Cash	$5,200 Stock Z ($200) Equity

The liability of the borrowed shares would increase to $5,200. Given $5,000 in cash assets, equity would drop to −$200. Since brokers require a positive amount of equity, implicit in the minimum maintenance margin, the margin requirements are applicable to short sale transactions.

Before we compute the equity margin for a short sale, we will define two terms: long position and short position. A *long position* simply represents shares that have been purchased for price appreciation and where the investor gains if the price rises. A *short position* is just a short sale. In Equation 3.1 we defined equity margin as the ratio of the investor's equity to the sum of long positions plus short positions. If the initial required margin is 50 percent, and if 100 shares of stock Z are sold short at $50 per share, the investor must have equity equal to 50 percent of the value of the short position. Thus the investor must deposit $2,500 in cash or securities, and when this is done, as shown in the table below, $EM = \$2,500/\$5,000 = .50$.

A	L + E
$5,000 Cash proceeds from sale of Stock Z $2,500 Additional cash or securities	$5,000 Stock Z (short position) $2,500 Equity

Let us now consider an investor who is holding some stocks long and some stocks short, and calculate the equity margin.

A	L + E
$6,000 Stock Y $5,500 Cash	$5,000 Stock Z $2,100 Broker loan $4,400 Equity

$$EM = \frac{4,400}{11,000} = .40$$

We again use Equation 3.1. The value of equity, $4,400, is in the numerator, and the sum of the market values of all long and short positions, in this case $6,000 (Stock Y) + $5,000 (Stock Z) = $11,000, is in the denominator.

Over-the-Counter Market (OTC)

The over-the-counter market (OTC) does not have a central physical marketplace as the organized exchanges do; rather, it is a market composed of thousands of security dealers throughout the country and linked by telephone and computer. It is a *negotiated market* as distinguished from the organized exchange, which is an *auction market*.

SCOPE OF THE MARKET   The OTC market encompasses all securities not traded on organized exchanges. Bond trading is more important than stock trading on the OTC market; currently, most of the bonds of the U.S., state, and local governments, and of private corporations are traded there. For trading common stocks, the organized exchanges, especially the NYSE, are more important. However, common stocks of many financial institutions, such as banks, insurance companies, and open-end investment companies, are traded in the OTC market. Common stocks of thousands of small companies are also traded there.

BROKER-DEALERS   Firms making up the OTC market are investment bankers, brokers, and dealers. The dealers, however, constitute the backbone of this market. There are thousands of dealers; some are wholesalers, some are retailers, and some are both. A wholesale dealer buys and sells for his own account. These dealers make markets by standing ready to buy or sell securities. They maintain an inventory position in many securities in which they are actively engaged as principals.

THE NASDAQ SYSTEM   The National Association of Securities Dealers Automated Quotation system, (NASDAQ), is an electronic system that collects, stores, and displays up-to-the-second quotations from a nationwide network of OTC dealers making a market in stocks. Securities salespeople can get current bid and ask prices on OTC securities from a terminal electronically connected to NASDAQ. They can then contact the dealer offering the best prices and negotiate a trade for their customers.

REGULATION   Brokers and dealers who conduct an over-the-counter securities business are required by the Securities Exchange Act of 1934 to register with the Securities and Exchange Commission (SEC), which regulates their activities. In addition, dealers in the OTC market are members of the National Association of Securities Dealers (NASD). This organization establishes and enforces fair rules of business conduct for its members and promotes ethical trade practices. Any violation of its rules can result in suspension or expulsion from the association.

Brokers and Dealers

The function of a broker is to bring buyers and sellers together. In performing this function the broker receives a commission that depends on the value of the transaction. Unlike a broker, a dealer takes ownership of the item being transferred. A firm that is a dealer of a certain security will either buy or sell that security. The price the dealer pays is called the "bid" price, and the price at which the dealer sells is called the "asked" price. At any given time, the asked price is higher than the bid price, for the dealer's income is based on the difference between those two prices. In this respect, a securities dealer is like other dealers, such as those who buy and sell foreign currency, coins, or consumer products. However, securities markets are quite "efficient," that is, the spread between bid and asked prices is relatively small compared to spreads in coin and consumer goods markets.

When an investor sells stocks or bonds on the over-the-counter market, both brokers and dealers are involved. The task of the seller's broker is to transfer the securities to the dealer offering the highest bid. An investor who wants to purchase those securities also uses a broker, who finds the dealer with the lowest ask price. The investor who buys and later sells on the over-the-counter market pays commissions to buy and sell, and also incurs the cost of the spread between bid and ask.

SELECTION OF A BROKER   In selecting a broker, individuals may choose either a discount or a full-service broker. *Full-service brokers* provide the investor with research reports and other information and advice relating to specific securities. *Discount brokers,* on the other hand, do not provide research or advice on stocks or bonds that may interest the investor. In exchange for the assistance they provide, full-service brokers charge higher commissions. The extent of savings in commission fees one realizes by going to a discount broker varies depending on which firm is selected and on the number and value of shares traded.

There are several points to consider in whether to choose a full-service or a discount broker (assuming both are equally convenient and fully insure your account). If you have your own sources of information, and you are not interested in advice from a broker, buying from a discount broker offers advantages. If, however, you have poor access to research, or time is very limited, the benefits of a good full-service broker might well be worth the extra cost.

Share Ownership: Individuals and Institutions

Shares are owned by the public in a variety of ways. Some investors own corporate stock while others hold shares in mutual funds. We see in Table 3–2 that in mid 1983 over forty-two million people owned stock or held shares in stock mutual funds. This represents an increase of almost 150 percent since 1962. Moreover, if one were to include those who are participants in pension plans that purchase stock, an even larger number of people have a financial interest in the stock market. There has also been a substantial increase in the number of investors who directly own shares listed on the NYSE. Their number grew by almost 140 percent since 1962, to over twenty-six million.

Although there has been rapid growth in the number of individuals who directly own stock listed on the NYSE, the growth of institutional activity has been even more rapid. In Table 3–3 we see the types of institutions that presently hold shares. In 1980, insurance companies, investment companies (mainly mutual funds), pension funds, nonprofit institutions, and foreign institutions were the largest holders. The most rapid growth from 1960 to 1980 was in the pension group. Holdings of corporate and other private funds plus state and local pension funds totaled $219 billion in 1980, an increase of 1,400 percent since 1960! Based on market value, institutional investors controlled 35.4 percent of NYSE-listed stock in 1980, over double their 1960 share of the market.

In terms of trading securities, institutions are even more important than as holders of securities. See Table 3–4 for the breakdown of daily volume attributable to institutions and individuals. In 1980, almost 65 percent of average daily volume was due to activities of institutions, over twice their 1960 market share. Reflecting the increase in importance of institutional trading, there has been a sharp increase in *block trading,* single trades involving 10,000 or more shares. In 1984, block trades accounted for nearly 50 percent of total volume, compared to only 3 percent in 1965.

TABLE 3–2   Highlights of Seven NYSE Shareowner Surveys

	1962	1965	1970	1975	1980	1981	1983
Number of individual shareowners (thousands)	17,010	20,120	30,850	25,270	30,200	32,260	42,360
Number owning shares listed on NYSE (thousands)	11,020	12,430	18,290	17,950	23,804	24,504A	26,029
Adult shareowner incidence in population	1 in 6	1 in 6	1 in 4	1 in 6	1 in 5	1 in 5	1 in 4
Median household income (prior year)	$8,600	$9,500	$13,500	$19,000	$27,750	$29,200	$33,200
Number of adult shareowners with household income:							
under $10,000 (thousands)	10,340	10,080	8,170	3,420	1,742	2,164	1,460
$10,000 & over (thousands)	5,920	8,410	20,130	19,970	25,715	26,912	36,261
$15,000 & over (thousands)	2,823	3,796	12,709	15,420	22,535	24,375	33,665
$25,000 & over (thousands)	780	1,073	4,114	6,642	15,605	17,547	25,086
$50,000 & over (thousands)	N/A	N/A	N/A	1,216	3,982	5,457	7,918
Number of adult female shareowners (thousands)	8,290	9,430	14,290	11,750	13,696	14,154	20,385
Number of adult male shareowners (thousands)	7,970	9,060	14,340	11,630	14,196	15,785	19,226
Median age	48	49	48	53	46	46	45

Note: Characteristics are for all individual shareowners, except where "adult" is designated.

N/A: Not available.

A: Adjusted.

Source: NYSE Fact Book, 1985.

There are several implications in the growing dominance of institutions. In one sense, it may contribute to market efficiency because institutions have more information than individual investors. Thus share prices may better reflect the intrinsic or true underlying value of stocks. However, in another respect, market efficiency might be hampered. With a smaller group of traders doing most of the buying and selling, there is a relative reduction in market liquidity, and perhaps share prices will show greater variation.

The Third Market

The term *third market* refers to over-the-counter trading in listed stocks, primarily those listed on the NYSE. It is a negotiated market rather than an auction market, and most of the activity is attributed to institutional

TABLE 3–3   Estimated Holdings of NYSE-listed Stock by Selected Institutional Investors (in billions)

Type of Institution	Year End					
	1955	1960	1965	1970	1975	1980
U.S. institutions:						
Insurance companies:						
Life	$2.2	$3.2	$6.3	$11.7	$21.6	$38.1
Non-life	4.2	6.0	10.1	12.2	11.6	26.9
Investment companies:						
Open-end	6.3	12.4	29.1	39.0	35.0	38.1
Closed-end	4.6	4.2	5.6	4.1	5.5	5.1
Noninsured pension funds:						
Corporate & other private	3.4	14.3	35.9	60.7	82.5	166.0
State & local government	0.1	0.3	1.4	9.6	24.4	53.0
Nonprofit institutions:						
Foundations	6.9	8.0	16.4	17.0	20.8	32.4
Educational endowments	2.3	2.9	5.9	6.6	7.7	12.1
Common trust funds	0.9	1.4	3.2	4.1	5.2	9.5
Mutual savings banks	0.2	0.2	0.5	1.4	2.4	1.5
Subtotal	$31.1	$52.9	$114.4	$166.4	$216.7	$382.7
Foreign institutions	N/A	N/A	N/A	N/A	25.1	57.5
Total	$31.1	$52.9	$114.4	$166.4	$241.8	$440.2
Market value of all NYSE-listed stock	$207.7	$307.0	$537.5	$636.4	$685.1	$1,242.8
Estimated % held by institutional investors	15.0%	17.2%	21.3%	26.1%	35.3%	35.4%

N/A: Not available.

Source: NYSE Fact Book, 1985.

investors. At the heart of this market is a small group of firms actively engaged as principals in buying and selling exchange-listed securities.

Toward a Central Market

With the advance of modern electronic technology, communication links among financial markets in the U.S. and abroad have greatly improved. Consequently, more and more markets will be linked electronically. A number of exchanges in the United States are exploring the possibilities of linking up with each other or with foreign exchanges. In the not-too-distant future, we may see a number of domestic markets and some important international exchanges tied together, and trading may occur twenty-four hours a day.

TABLE 3–4   Public Volume on NYSE* (in millions)

Period	Total	Daily Volume**		Percentage Distribution	
		Individuals	Institutions	Individuals	Institutions
Fourth Quarter 1980	71.4	25.0	46.4	35.1%	64.9%
First Quarter 1976	44.1	18.8	25.3	42.7	57.3
First Quarter 1974	23.2	9.5	13.7	41.1	58.9
First Half 1971	26.6	10.7	15.9	40.3	59.7
Second Quarter 1971	25.0	9.4	15.6	37.6	62.4
First Quarter 1971	28.3	12.1	16.2	42.6	57.4
Full Year 1969	18.0	7.9	10.1	44.1	55.9
Second Half 1969	18.0	7.8	10.2	43.5	56.5
First Half 1969	18.1	8.1	10.0	44.6	55.4
October 1966	10.7	6.1	4.6	57.0	43.0
March 1965	8.9	5.4	3.5	60.7	39.3
October 1963	9.4	6.5	2.9	69.1	30.9
September 1961	5.7	3.8	1.9	66.7	33.3
Spetember 1960	5.1	3.5	1.6	68.6	31.4
June 1959	5.1	3.6	1.5	70.6	29.4
September 1958	7.0	5.0	2.0	71.4	28.6
October 1957	3.8	2.7	1.1	71.1	28.9
March 1956	5.6	4.2	1.4	75.0	25.0
June 1955	5.3	4.0	1.3	75.5	24.5
December 1954	6.1	4.8	1.3	78.7	21.3
March 1954	3.3	2.3	1.0	69.7	30.3
March 1953	4.0	3.0	1.0	75.0	25.0
September 1952	2.6	1.8	0.8	69.2	30.8

* Excludes member trading.
** Shares bought and sold.
Source: NYSE Fact Book, 1985.

REGULATION OF SECURITIES MARKETS AND INVESTOR PROTECTION

The securities markets in the United States have been closely regulated by the SEC since 1934. Let us review the main features of those laws which were designed to regulate the securities markets and protect the interests of investors.

Securities Act of 1933

This "truth in securities" law has two basic objectives: to provide investors with material financial and other information concerning securities offered for public sale; and to prohibit misrepresentation, deceit, and other fraudulent acts and practices in the sale of securities generally.

Before the public offering of new securities, a registration statement must be filed with the SEC by the issuer, setting forth the required information. When the statement has become effective, the securities may be sold. The purpose of the registration is to provide disclosure of financial and other information on the basis of which investors may appraise the merits of the securities. Investors must be furnished with a prospectus containing the salient data set forth in the registration statement to enable them to evaluate the securities and make informed and discriminating investment decisions.

Securities Exchange Act of 1934

By this act, Congress extended the "disclosure" doctrine of investor protection to securities listed and registered for public trading on U.S. national securities exchanges. The enactment in August, 1964, of the Securities Acts Amendments applied the disclosure and reporting provisions to equity securities of hundreds of companies traded over the counter if their assets exceed $1 million and their shareholders number 500 or more.

Companies that seek to have their securities listed and registered for public trading on an exchange must file a registration application with the exchange and the SEC. A similar registration form must be filed by companies whose equity securities are traded over the counter if they meet the size test. The law prescribes penalties for filing false statements and reports with the SEC, as well as provision for recovery by investors who suffer losses in the purchase or sale of registered securities after relying on those statements.

The Securities Exchange Act also provides a system for regulating trading practices in both exchanges and the over-the-counter market. The system seeks to curb misrepresentations and deceit, market manipulations, and other fraudulent acts and practices, and to establish and maintain just and equitable principles of trade conducive to the maintenance of open, fair, and orderly markets.

The law also requires the registration with the SEC of "National Securities Exchanges" (those having a substantial securities trading volume), and brokers and dealers who conduct an over-the-counter securities business in interstate commerce. To obtain registration, exchanges must show that they are so organized as to be able to comply with the law and that they can maintain fair and orderly markets to protect the investor. Among other things, the exchanges must have rules for the expulsion, suspension, or other disciplining of members for conduct inconsistent with just and equitable principles of trade.

By an amendment of the law enacted in 1938, Congress also provided for the creation of a self-policing body among over-the-counter brokers and dealers. This organization must also have rules for the disciplining of members for their misconduct. The National Association of Securities Dealers was organized in 1939 under this law and is registered with the SEC under the provision of this law.

Trust Indenture Act of 1939

This act applies in general to bonds, debentures, notes, and similar debt securities offered for public sale that are issued pursuant to trust indentures under which more than $1 million of securities may be outstanding at any one time. Even though these securities may be registered under the Securities Act, they may not be offered for sale to the public unless the trust indenture conforms to specified statutory standards of this act designed to safeguard the rights and interests of the purchasers.

This act requires that the indenture trustee be free of conflicting interests that might interfere with the faithful exercise of its duties on behalf of the purchasers of the securities. It requires also that the trustee be a corporation with minimum combined capital and surplus and imposes high standards of conduct and responsibility on the trustee.

Investment Company Act of 1940

Under this act, the activities of companies engaged primarily in the business of investing, reinvesting, and trading in securities, and whose own securities are offered and sold to and held by the investing public, are subject to certain statutory prohibitions and to SEC regulation in accordance with prescribed standards deemed necessary to protect the interests of investors and the public.

In addition to a requirement that these companies register with the SEC, the law requires disclosure of their financial condition and investment policies to afford investors full and complete information about their activities, and it prohibits these companies from changing the nature of their business or investment policies without the approval of the stockholders.

Investment Advisors Act of 1940

This law establishes a pattern of regulation of investment advisors that is similar in many respects to Securities Exchange Act provisions governing the conduct of brokers and dealers. It requires, with certain exceptions, that persons or firms who engage for compensation in the business of advising others about their securities transactions to register with the SEC and conform their activities to statutory standards designed to protect the interests of investors.

The registration of investment advisors may be denied, suspended, or revoked by the SEC if, after notice and hearing, it finds that a statutory disqualification exists and that such action is in the public interest.

Securities Investor Protection Act of 1970

During the period from 1968 to 1970, the securities industry experienced many difficulties, and many brokerage firms were forced into liquidation. Through the activity of the NYSE trust fund, hundreds of thousands of customers were saved from major losses.

However, in any future large-scale emergency, the current system of voluntary protection through the NYSE trust fund will most likely prove to be inadequate for the protection of investors. Accordingly, Congress enacted the Securities Investor Protection Act of 1970, creating the Securities Investor Protection Corporation (SIPC). This agency provides insurance for customer accounts of all registered broker-dealers, with a maximum limit of $500,000 for each customer, of which $100,000 may be in cash.

SUMMARY

New securities are traded in the primary markets where investment bankers play an important role. Existing securities are traded in the secondary markets, which include organized exchanges and the over-the-counter market.

Among the organized exchanges, the New York Stock Exchange is the most important, accounting for about 80 percent of the volume traded on all exchanges. The NYSE has 1366 members, of which roughly half are commission brokers, doing business with the public for commissions. About one-fourth of the members of the NYSE serve as specialists who are charged with the responsibility of maintaining orderly markets in the stocks for which they serve as specialists. The remaining one-fourth of the membership of the NYSE are floor brokers, floor traders, and odd-lot dealers.

The specialists play an important role in maintaining an orderly market. When there is a wide gap between supply and demand of a given security, the specialist is obligated to step in to buy or sell the security in order to bridge the gap and maintain an orderly market.

The over-the-counter (OTC) market is a market composed of thousands of security dealers across the country and linked by telephone and computers. It is a negotiated market, as distinguished from the organized exchange, which is an auction market. The OTC market encompasses all securities not traded on organized exchanges. Most of the bonds issued by governments and corporations are traded in the OTC market, even though some corporate bonds are also traded on the NYSE. Common stocks of tens of thousands of small companies are also traded there.

The securities markets in the United States have been closely regulated since 1934. The governing legislative acts have been:

Securities Act of 1933
Securities Exchange Act of 1934

Trust Indenture Act of 1939
Investment Company Act of 1940
Investment Advisors Act of 1940
Securities Investor Protection Act of 1970

The Securities Amendments Act of 1975 called for creation of a more competitive securities trading system. Under the concept, markets across the country are to be linked by an electronic communications system and are to compete directly with one another in offering the best price for security purchases and sales. Some progress has been made toward the goal of establishing a fully competitive central market, but a full operation of this system is still in the future.

QUESTIONS AND PROBLEMS

1. What are the differences between the organized exchanges and the over-the-counter market?
2. What is meant by the term "investment banking"? What roles do investment bankers perform?
3. What is the role of the specialist? What is the source of his income?
4. Explain the function performed by each:
   a. Commission brokers
   b. Floor brokers
   c. Odd-lot dealers
5. What are the listing requirements on the NYSE?
6. Explain the different types of orders:
   a. Market order
   b. Limit order
   c. Stop order
7. Indicate the circumstances under which you would like to use a (1) market order, (2) limit order, and (3) stop order.
8. Explain the following:
   a. Selling short
   b. Initial margin
   c. Maintenance margin
   d. Margin call
9. Are there any disadvantages to using margin credit? If a securities buyer uses margin credit liberally, is he or she an investor, speculator, or both?
10. How do you calculate the equity margin of a customer? Under what circumstances would one receive a margin call from one's brokerage firm?

11. Where is the over-the-counter market situated? Is it a market where only common stocks of small companies are traded?
12. What does NASDAQ stand for? What functions does it perform?
13. Consider an investor whose account appears as follows:

A	L + E
$6,000 Stock Y	$5,000 Stock Z
$5,500 Cash	$2,100 Broker loan
	$4,400 Equity

Assume positions in Stock Y and Stock Z each consist of one hundred shares. Calculate equity margin if
a. The price of Stock Y rises by $10 but Stock Z is constant.
b. The price of Stock Z rises by $10 but Stock Y is constant.
c. Both stocks increase by $10.

14. Assume an investor has $4,000 to buy Stock R at $40 per share. Initial equity margin is 40 percent, and the broker charges interest at 12 percent per year. Calculate the rate of return on the investor's equity for a six-month holding period, assuming margin is used in the following two cases:
a. Price of R rises to $48.
b. Price of R falls to $32.

15. Mr. A has $12,000. He is very optimistic about the outlook of the stock market. He borrows $10,000 from his margin account and invests the total $22,000 in the following securities:

Security	Price per Share	Shares	Value
1	$40	100	$ 4,000
2	50	100	5,000
3	30	200	6,000
4	35	200	7,000
		Total:	$22,000

Unfortunately, the stock market declines substantially against his expectations. Now his securities are selling at these prices:

Security 1 $20 per share
        2   30 per share
        3   10 per share
        4   25 per share

The current maintenance margin of his brokerage firm is 30 percent.

a. What is the amount of Mr. A's equity and equity margin now?

b. Does he get a margin call from his brokerage firm? If so, for how much?

c. If he cannot put up more cash as required by his brokerage firm, what will happen? What is the extent of his loss?

d. What lesson can you draw from this example?

REFERENCES

Dougall, Herbert E., and Gaumnitz, Jack E. *Capital Markets and Institutions*, 4th ed. Englewood Cliffs, N.J.: Prentice-Hall, 1980.

Cohen, J., Zinbarg, E., and Zeikel, A. *Investment Analysis and Portfolio Management*. Homewood, Ill.: Irwin, 1982.

Garbade, Kenneth D. *Securities Markets*. New York: McGraw-Hill, 1982.

Goldberg, L., and White, L. *The Deregulation of the Banking and Securities Industries*. Lexington, Mass.: Lexington Books, 1979.

Kidwell, David S., and Peterson, Richard L. *Financial Institutions, Markets, and Money*, 2nd ed. Chicago: The Dryden Press, 1984.

Mendelson, M., and Peake, J. W. "Which Way to a National Market System?" *Financial Analysts Journal*, Sept.–Oct. 1979.

Mendelson, M., and Robbins, S. *Investment Analysis and Securities Markets*. New York: Basic Books, 1976, Chapters 1–3.

New York Stock Exchange. *1985 Fact Book*.

———. *The Specialist—Key Man in the Exchange Market*, 1973.

Peake, J. W. "The National Market System." *Financial Analysts Journal*, July–Aug. 1978.

Schaefer, J. M., and Warner, A. J. "Concentration Trends and Competition in the Securities Industry." *Financial Analysts Journal*, Nov.–Dec. 1977.

Securities and Exchange Commission. *The Work of Securities and Exchange Commission*, 1973.

———. *The Future Structure of the Securities Market*, 1972.

4

Sources of Investment Information

In this chapter we discuss sources of investment information and price indexes of securities. There are many sources of investment information: the trade press, national trade associations, newspapers, advisory financial services, bank letters, the issuing company, financial and business magazines, brokerage firms, and, finally, the largest single publisher of statistics and economic information, the United States government. The information investors seek falls into three categories:

1. *Information on general business conditions in the economy and in securities markets.*

   Investors would like to know the rate at which the economy is growing, the current rate of inflation, trends in interest rates, and general conditions in different sectors of the securities markets. This information will help them decide whether or not it is a good time to invest, and if so, what types of securities to buy.

2. *Information on different industries.*

   Even though the economy as a whole may be expanding at a certain time, different industries do not progress at the same rate. Some sectors may have internal problems, while others may be much more promising. The information on different industries can help investors decide in which ones to invest.

3. *Information on specific corporations.*

   Clearly, the corporations within any industry differ from one another. Some are strong in one or more areas, such as technology, organization, marketing, finance, or general production. Very few are strong in all. Sometimes the outstanding companies are recognized by too many investors and, as a result, they are overpriced in the marketplace. Information on specific corporations helps investors decide whether the company is strong and also whether the company's shares are overpriced or underpriced.

Let us now examine the major sources of investment information.

NEWSPAPERS

The best known newspaper that specializes in reporting business and financial news is the *Wall Street Journal*. Published five days a week by Dow Jones & Company and available nationally, the *Journal* provides full coverage of business and financial news on the economy and on various industries and corporations.

The *New York Times* is a general newspaper, but it has an extensive section on business and financial news. Many investors would rank it second only to the *Wall Street Journal*. It reports national business and financial news and developments in various industries and major corporations. It also provides data from various markets.

Investor's Daily is a newspaper designed specifically for investors. It includes many interesting features, such as:

- Rankings of firms according to growth in earnings per share.
- Relative price strength of securities.
- Different market indexes for sectors like consumer companies, high-tech firms, small, rapidly growing companies, cyclical stocks, defense stocks, and other groups as well.
- Graphs of up to ninety common stocks that hit new highs on the NYSE, AMEX, or over-the-counter market.

FINANCIAL MAGAZINES

Barron's is a national business and financial weekly published by Dow Jones & Company. The first half usually includes feature articles of investment interest, investment views on some selected stocks, as well as departments, such as "The Week in Bonds," "The Trader," and "Short Interest." The second half of the magazine carries the quotations of shares traded on NYSE, AMEX, and OTC markets in the previous week. At the back of the magazine is "*Barron's* Market Laboratory," which contains valuable statistical information on the economy and the securities markets.

Published twice a month, *Forbes* regularly contains articles on developments in industries and major corporations. Topics include views on current market conditions, selected stocks, and investment policies at the moment. The January issue is particularly interesting; *Forbes* ranks 1000 firms, classified by industry, in terms of profitability and growth, two measures of management performance.

The *Commercial and Financial Chronicle* appears twice a week, on Mondays and Thursdays. The Monday issue contains, for the most part, statistical information. The Thursday issue contains articles by analysts and texts or summaries of speeches by corporate executives.

Financial World is published biweekly. It includes articles on trends of the market, developments in selected industries, and analyses of selected corporations.

Business Week is a well-known, general business, weekly publication. In addition to business news, one may find articles on finance, markets and investments, and money and credit.

Fortune is a biweekly publication that carries in-depth articles on industries and individual corporations. The "Business-Roundup" section, which reports current developments on major sectors in the economy, offers its editors' interpretations and views on the direction and outlook of general business.

Money is a monthly magazine that contains articles about investment alternatives and strategies for the person with relatively small amounts to invest. It includes advice about taxes, family budgeting, and career planning. It also provides rankings of mutual funds and articles about specific stocks.

Financial Analysts Journal, published bimonthly, is a publication of the Society of Professional Analysts. The articles are written primarily by practicing analysts and cover different phases of investment analysis and management.

In addition to the major financial publications mentioned above, there are others of interest and use to serious investors: *Journal of Finance, Journal of Portfolio Management, Financial Executive, Journal of Financial & Quantitative Analysis, Finance, Investment Dealers Digest, Trusts & Estates, The Institutional Investor, The Media General Financial Weekly,* and *Wall Street Transcript.*

Two basic references to current periodicals and articles are *Business Periodicals Index* and *F&S Index of Corporations & Industries.* Both are excellent sources for locating interesting articles on economics, finance, investments, and specific companies and industries.

INVESTMENT ADVISORY SERVICES

A large amount of information comes from investment advisory services. Three firms are especially well-known in this area: Standard & Poor's (S&P), Moody's, and *Value Line.* In the sections below we describe the different publications they provide.

Standard & Poor's Corporation

Corporation Records. These are thick reference volumes, arranged in alphabetical order. They are kept up-to-date by daily bulletins.

Stock Reports. A loose-leaf service of two-page reports on thousands of companies. Each report gives the fundamental position, finances, earnings, recent developments, and prospects of the company.

Stock Guide. A pocket-size monthly publication that provides essential information on nearly 5000 common and preferred stocks. Information includes principal business, price range, earnings, dividends, financial position, and capitalization. It also provides S&P's rating of the stock plus an estimate of earnings per share for the current year. Two pages of this guide are shown in Figure 4–1.

The Outlook. A weekly publication designed mainly to help individual investors. It reviews market conditions in the previous week, expresses its views on investment policy, and recommends a selected list of securities.

Industry Surveys. These cover more than forty industries. For each industry, a "basic analysis" is prepared once a year plus periodic updates in "current analysis."

Analysts' Handbook. This provides for each major industry per-share data on sales, earnings, operating profit margin, net profit margin, return on book value, and price-earnings ratios. These figures can be readily compared with those of individual corporations in the industry or of other industries. This statistical information is extremely useful for comparative analysis.

Other Publications. The following S&P publications should also be of interest to investors: *Bond Guide; Earnings Forecaster; Poor's Register of Corporations, Directors, and Executives; Statistical Service; Municipal Bond Selector;* and *Opportunities in Convertible Bonds.*

Moody's Investors Service

Moody's Manuals are reference volumes classified under the following titles: Bank & Finance, Industrial, Municipal & Government, OTC Industrials, Public Utility, and Transportation. These volumes are kept up-to-date by weekly or semiweekly supplements. Each volume contains reports on thousands of corporations, giving a brief history of the company and its operations, products, officers, financial statements, financial ratios, and general market data on their securities.

Moody's Investor Fact Sheets. These sheets, similar to S&P's *Stock Reports,* provide information on the nature of the business, recent developments, and prospects for the firm. They also include basic financial statistics of the firm for the last seven years. They cover, in addition, current news items and recent financial statements.

Stock Survey. This weekly publication is similar to S&P's *Outlook.* It reviews current market conditions, sets forth views on investment policy, and recommends a selected list of securities.

Moody's Bond Record. This is a monthly publication that provides summary information on thousands of corporate and municipal issues. Information includes such data as call price, recent price, price ranges, and ratings.

Moody's Bond Survey. A weekly publication that reviews the bond market and outlook of general business. It also includes buy, sell, and hold recommendations.

90 **Fir-Flo** Standard & Poor's Corporation

¶S&P 500 •Options Index	Ticker Symbol	Name of Issue (Call Price of Pfd. Stocks)	Market	Com. Rank. & Pfd. Rating	Par Val.	Inst.Hold Cos	Inst.Hold Shs. (000)	Principal Business	Price Range 1971-83 High	1971-83 Low	1984 High	1984 Low	1985 High	1985 Low	Mar. Sales in 100s	March, 1985 Last Sale Or Bid High	Low	Last	%Div. Yield	P-E Ratio
1	FNS	First Natl St Bancorp	NY,M	↑A	6¼	53	1929	Multi-bank hldg: New Jersey	42⅜	15¾	46⅞	31¼	50⅜	45½	1653	49½	46⅞	48⅞	5.9	7
2	Pr B	Adj Rt[52]10.97%cmB Pfd([54]103)	[1]	NR	No	3	92		105¼	97	107⅜	90⅛	103¼	99	650	102½	101¼	99B	11.1	..
3	FOOD	First Nat'l Supermkts	OTC	B–	1¢	11	520	Supermkts: Ohio,N.E., N.Y.	23½	3¾	17¾	7¾	15¾	13¼	2042	15¾	14¾	15½B	0.1	d
4	FNFC	First Nationwide Fin'l[56]	OTC	NR	10¢	27	2217	Hldg co: savings & loan	34	16¾	22½	12½	16¼	13¾	1619	16¼	15¾	15¾B	...	10
5	FIRO	First Ohio Bancshares	OTC	A+	6¼	11	918	Bank hldg,Toledo,Ohio	34	6½	35½	30½	40	35½	210	40	38¼	38¾B	4.6	8
6	FOKL	First Okla Bancorp	OTC	B–	5	19	4867	Bank hldg:Oklahoma City	26½	5⅛	15⅛	8⅛	11⅜	8¾	2310	10¾	8¾	9B	...	d
¶7	FPA	First Pennsylvania	NY,B,C,M,P,Ph	C	1	40	3812	Bank hldg co: Philadelphia	52¾	2⅜	7½	4½	7⅞	5⅞	6531	7⅝	6½	7	...	d
8	Pr	$2.625Cv[57]Dep Pfd([58]27.3625[59])	[2]NY	B–	No	22	1934		26	24¾	28⅛	20¼	30¼	25¼	3316	29½	27½	28	9.4	..
9	FRRG	First Railroad & Bkg	OTC	B+	66⅔¢	20	930	Bk hldg,Georgia:R.E.,sv	27¾	5½	29	23½	37	26	7726	37	32½	33B	2.9	11
10	FSAW	First Svgs Assn Wis[61]	OTC	NR	1	8	214	East'n Wisconsin sv & loan	18¾	4¼	14	7¼	10	7½	1405	10	9¼	9¾B	...	d
11	FSCO	First Security	OTC	A	1¼	49	4653	Multiple bk hldg:interstate	27⅜	9 9/16	23	15	26	19⅛	5835	24⅞	23½	23⅞B	4.6	13
12	FTEN	First Tenn Nat'l	OTC	A+	2½	51	3557	Multiple bank hldg:Memphis	28	5¾	30⅞	21⅛	35⅝	29	4575	35⅝	32⅛	35⅜B	4.5	9
13	FUNC	First Union Corp	OTC	↑A	3⅓	99	7456	Bank hldg: 1st Un NB No Car	28⅛	4½	35	23⅛	39¾	34⅝	16558	39⅜	35⅞	37⅞B	3.0	9
14	FUR	First Union RE EqSBI	NY,M	NR	1	44	3903	Ohio real estate invest trust	24	3⅞	28¾	20	31⅞	25¾	2179	31⅞	30½	31⅛	6.2	15
15	FVB	First Virginia Banks	NY,M,Ph	↑A+	1	42	2244	Bank holding, Virginia	20	4	20	14¾	22⅜	19	4148	22⅜	20	21½	3.9	9
16	FWES	First Western Fin'l	OTC	B	1	7	60	Savings & loan in Nevada	9⅜	1	8⅜	5	7	5	3121	6⅜	5½	6⅛B	s3.3	5
17	FWB	First Wisconsin	NY,B,M	A	2½	35	2971	Multiple bank hldg:Milw	24⅜	5	24¾	16	28⅛	24¼	2261	27½	25⅛	26⅜	4.5	8
18	Pr A	$6.25 cm A Pfd([63]53.125)	NY	BBB–	1	1	20		52½	49½	52½	45⅞	52	49½	26	50¾	49½	50	12.5	..
19	FWO	First Wyoming Bancorp	AS	↓B+	No	16	820	Multi-bank holding co	18⅝	4⅞	13⅞	11	13½	11¼	679	13½	11¾	12½	6.4	10
20	FSTW	Firstar Corp[67]	OTC	A–	5	3	88	Multi-Bank hldg:Appleton,Wis	21⅜	6¼	24½	13½	25½	18½	66	20	18½	19B	...	d
21	FSTG	FIRSTGULF BANCORP[68]	OTC	A	4	...	....	Bank hldg: Mobile,Alabama	28½	8⅛	42½	23	48	42½	11	47	46	46B	2.4	14
22	FRST	FirsTier, Inc	OTC	A	5	25	736	Bank hldg:Omaha Nat'l Bk	41½	14	48	38½	48½	44	211	48½	46	47½B	4.6	7
23	FIS	Fischbach Corp	NY,B,M	A	1	27	1880	Electric/mech contractor	69½	14	55½	30¼	41	30¾	2833	41	36¾	37¼	2.7	36
24	FP	Fischer & Porter	AS,B	B–	1	12	1287	Process control instruments	17⅞	2¼	16½	11⅝	15	11⅞	525	14½	11⅞	12	s...	21
25	FHR	Fisher Foods[70]	NY,M	B–	No	21	2846	Supermarkets:Chicago & Ohio	22⅜	5⅝	12⅛	8¼	11⅛	10⅛	1428	11	10½	10½	0.5	d
26	FISNY	Fisons PLC ADR	OTC	NR	£1	1	800	Agrochemical:drugs: sci eq	13	2⅛	14⅜	9	15½	12¼	1884	15½	12⅜	15⅜B	1.4	18
27	FGE	Fitchburg Gas & Elec	AS,B	NR	10	4	92	Elec & nat'l gas, Mass	26¼	7¾	19⅞	8⅜	11⅞	7⅛	719	8⅞	8	8⅛	...	4
28	Pr	$4.00 cm Pfd([75]29:SF25)1/4 vtg	AS	BB–	1	...	....		32¼	25	28¾	22¾	27¾	23⅝	81	26	23⅝	24⅝	16.2	..
29	BDL	Flanigan's Enterprises	AS	C	10¢	3	23	Pkg liquor stores: cocktail lg	20½	2¼	12⅛	8⅛	10⅝	8½	489	9½	8½	9⅛	...	d
30	FLAR	Flare, Inc.	OTC	NR	1¢	4	489	Develop,market seismic data	5⅛	1¾	2⅝	¼	⅜	¼	1164	⅜	⅜	⅜B	...	d
31	FLT	Fleet Financial Gr	NY,B,M	A+	1	80	7036	Bank hldg:Ind'l Nat Bk R.I.	25⅜	4⅝	28⅞	20¼	34¼	28½	4844	33¾	31⅜	32	4.1	8
32	Pr	Adj Div[79]8.30% cm Pfd([80]51.50)	NY	NR	1	5	136		50	36¾	47½	42½	47	43½	435	46½	45½	46B	9.0	..
¶33•[3]	FLE	Fleetwood Enterpr	NY,B,M,P,Ph	B+	1	125	9776	Mobile homes: travel trailers	41⅞	1¾	30¾	14⅛	28¾	20⅛	30337	25⅞	20⅛	21	1.7	8
34	FLM	Fleming Cos	NY,M	A+	2½	105	7894	Whlse food to affil stores	31⅛	4¼	35⅜	22¼	39½	32	4014	39½	36	39¼	2.2	15
35	FLX	Flexi-Van[82]	NY,M	B	1¢	36	3129	Worldwide lessor of cargo	32⅛	6¼	30⅞	23¾	33¼	29	3883	33¼	30⅜	33⅛	2.4	15
36	Pr	$1.61 cm Pfd ([85]15.81)	NY	BB	1	4	198	containers,chassis & trailers	15	9¼	12⅝	10¼	13¼	12⅛	364	13¼	12¼	12⅜	13.0	..
37	FLXS	Flexsteel Indus	OTC	B+	1	13	795	Quality upholstered furniture	19¼	1	17⅝	10	16½	13¼	1475	14⅞	13⅝	14B	3.4	9
38	FSI	Flightsafety Int'l	NY,M	↑A–	10¢	83	5647	Aircraft & marine training	39⅛	⅝	35	19½	37⅞	30	4254	35¼	30	31½	0.8	17
39	FLP	Floating Point Sys	NY,M	B+	No	63	4211	Array processor computers	44⅞	4¼	36¾	12½	31¼	19¼	4447	29¾	24	27	...	15
40	FLOK	Flock Industries	OTC	B–	1¢	...	....	Mfr fabric,textile,material	40⅝	⅛	5½	2¾	3¾	3	30	3¾	3⅝	3⅝B	...	8
41	FIIF	Florafax Int'l	OTC	B–	10¢	4	2547	Flower-by-wire service	13½	⅜	8⅞	3¼	5⅜	3⅜	3495	4⅞	3⅜	3⅜B	...	d
42	FLBK	Florida Com'l Bks	OTC	A	1	1	15	Bank hldg, Florida	22⅛	2¼	27⅛	18⅞	29½	24¼	174	29½	28¾	29½B	s1.9	15
43	FCYP	Florida Cypress Gdns	OTC	B–	25¢	6	390	Tourist attraction:central Fla	12¾	1	4⅜	2⅞	4⅜	3⅜	265	4	3⅝	3¾B	5.3	37
44	FLA	Florida East Coast Indus	NY,M	B+	6¼	18	355	Hldg co:Fla RR,land hldgs	35⅞	3 9/16	36⅞	29¾	40	34¼	556	39¼	37½	39	†0.5	12
45	FLFE	Florida Fed'l S/L Assn[90]	OTC	NR	1¢	37	1070	Savings & loan,Florida	24¼	13	17¾	13⅛	19½	15¼	7432	18⅛	15¼	16⅞B	1.2	10
46	FGLFS	Florida Gulf Rlty Tr SBI	OTC	NR	10¢	8	378	Real estate investment trust	14¾	3⅜	18¼	13½	16⅝	15½	1259	16½	15¾	16¼B	...	..

Uniform Footnote Explanations—See Page 1. Other: [1]NY([10]). [2]Ph. [3]AS:Cycle 2. [51]Restated fr $7.27,'83. [52]⊙$6.36,'84. [53]Thru 3-31-85:min 6¼%,max 12 3/4%. [54]Fr 3-31-88 to 3-31-93,then $100. [55]$11.33 fr 4-1-85(rate 11.33%). [56]Apply for NYSE listing. [57]Restr to 11-15-85(com price equals150%Cv price). [58]To 11-14-85,scale to $25 in'93. [59]Dep for¼ shr of $10 1/2 Cv Pfd. [60]⊙$2.90,'84. [61]First Fin'l(Wis)plans acq. [62]△$0.66,'82. [63]⊙$1.83,'84. [64]Incl $0.447 cap gains. [65]Fr 6-15-88,scale to $50 in'93. [66]⊙$1.34,'83. [67]Marine Corp plans acquis,$28 or 1.167 shr. [68]Apprv mgr into AmSouth Bancorp,$47 or 2.1 shrs. [69]⊙$1.76,'84. [70]Plan spinoff warehouse division. [71]□$0.06,'80. [72]△$3.54,□$1.70,'81. [73]Approx. [74]100% nontaxable'84. [75]To 5-31-87,scale to $25 in'97. [76]△$0.01,□$0.04,'82. [77]□$0.27,'83. [78]⊙$3.63,'84. [79]Thru 5-31-85:min 6%,max 12%. [80]Fr 3-1-88 thru 2-28-93,then $50. [81]⊙$2.57,'84. [82]Plan mgr with Castle & Cooke,2.2 com &1.1Pfd. [83]□$2.85,'80. [84]⊙$2.13,'84. [85]To 4-30-85,scale to $15 in 2000. [86]⊙$0.27,'83. [87]□$0.47,△$0.06,'80. [88]□$0.05,'81. [89]△$0.37,'80. [90]Plan name chge to Florida Fin'l. [91]Mar 70.06% nontaxable'84.

Common and Preferred Stocks **Fir-Flo** 91

Splits ◆ Index	Cash Divs. Ea. Yr. Since	Dividends Latest Payment Per$	Date	Ex. Div.	Total $ So Far 1985	Ind. Rate	Paid 1984	Financial Position Mil-$ Cash& Equiv.	Curr. Assets	Curr. Liab.	Balance Sheet Date	Capitalization Lg Trm Debt Mil-$	Shs. 000 Pfd.	Com.	Earnings $ Per Shr. Years End	1980	1981	1982	1983	1984	Last 12 Mos.	Interim Earnings Period	$ Per Shr. 1983	1984	Index
1◆	1812	Q0.72	4-1-85	3-1	1.44	2.88	2.70	Book Value $36.02			12-31-83	p90.1	1918	p10652	Dc	▲4.85	■5.66	▲6.59	■[51]•5.49	P△[52]6.67	6.67				1
2	1983	2.743	4-1-85	3-1	5.723	[56]10.97	1.701	...	...	...		...	350	...	Dc	...	...	...	b1.14	...	...				2
3	1978	0.02	12-7-84	11-23	....	0.02	0.02	17.0	130.	125.	12-8-84	119.	...	2610	Mr	△1.91	□1.58	•2.68	△d3.73	...	d2.41	36 Wk Dec	d1.24	•△0.08	3
4	....	None Since Public			....	Nil	....	Book Value $21.44			9-30-84	2157	...	15053	Dc	1.82	0.84	△0.31	▲□2.14	P△1.52	1.52				4
5◆	1949	Q0.45	3-15-85	3-5	0.45	1.80	1.75	Book Value $32.30			12-31-84	...	...	2053	Dc	3.09	■3.75	4.05	■4.44	▲4.88	4.88				5
6	.....	0.16	10-1-83	9-9	....	Nil	....	Book Value $16.83			9-30-84	48.3	812	9819	Dc	■2.58	■2.53	■1.87	▲d4.50	Pd2.15	d2.15				6
7	.....	0.11	4-1-80	3-3	....	Nil	....	Book Value $8.28			12-31-84	165.	1867	17452	Dc	■d10.47	■▲d0.40	■d1.66	d1.10	△d0.13	d0.13				7
8	1984	Q0.65⅝	5-15-85	4-10	1.31¼	2.62½	2.50½	Cv into 3.225 com,$7.75				...	7459	...	Dc	...	...	...	...	b0.99	...				8
9	1866	Q0.24	2-15-85	1-30	0.24	0.96	0.88	Book Value $21.99			12-31-84	79.5	126	8861	Dc	1.50	■1.76	■▲3.96	■▲3.40	■[60]3.11	3.11				9
10	.....	None Since Public			....	Nil	....	Book Value $16.20			9-30-84	123.	...	1251	Dc	△□0.93	■d10.66	[62]△d9.70	d8.69	Pd5.54	d5.54				10
11	1935	Q0.27½	3-11-85	2-15	0.27½	1.10	1.10	Book Value $28.94			12-31-84	259.	31	12136	Dc	■3.18	■3.39	■4.42	■1.75	P[63]1.90	1.90				11
12	1895	Q0.40	4-1-85	3-11	0.80	1.60	1.40	Book Value $26.53			9-30-84	64.6	...	9253	Dc	▲2.60	■2.73	■2.90	▲3.31	P4.10	4.10				12
13◆	1914	Q0.28	3-15-85	2-8	0.28	1.12	0.976	Book Value $25.00			12-31-84	142.	...	19829	Dc	■2.59	▲■2.03	■2.87	■3.60	■4.33	4.33				13
14◆	1962	Q0.48	4-30-85	4-3	0.94	1.92	[64]1.64	Equity per shr $9.16			12-31-84	205.	...	12144	Dc	▲1.28	▲1.79	▲1.74	▲1.90	▲2.07	2.07				14
15	1960	Q0.21	4-15-85	3-25	0.42	0.84	0.78	Book Value $13.49			9-30-84	45.8	251	14313	Dc	■1.42	■1.60	■2.00	▲2.30	P2.44	2.44				15
16◆	1984	Q0.05	3-31-85	2-8	0.05	0.20	s0.147	Book Value Neg			9-30-84	87.8	154	4604	Dc	1.22	0.24	d0.80	□1.43	P△1.23	1.23				16
17◆	1940	Q0.30	2-15-85	1-29	0.30	1.20	1.17½	Book Value $34.22			12-31-84	57.2	500	8465	Dc	▲■2.23	3.32	■3.43	■3.78	▲3.40	3.40				17
18	1983	Q1.56¼	2-15-85	1-29	1.56¼	6.25	6.25	...	...	...		...	500	...	Dc	...	...	...	b1.11	b1.09	...				18
19◆	1970	Q0.20	4-26-85	3-25	0.40	0.80	0.80	Equity per shr $15.66			9-30-84	23.3	...	4004	Dc	■2.12	■2.22	■1.42	▲[66]1.51	P1.21	1.21				19
20◆	1965	0.30	12-10-84	11-26	....	Nil	1.20	Book Value $26.17			9-30-84	6.73	...	987	Dc	■2.38	■1.05	■1.54	■•2.98	Pd2.77	d2.77				20
21◆	1866	Q0.28	4-1-85	3-11	0.56	1.12	1.12	Book Value $25.71			12-31-83	p23.5	...	p2463	Dc	■3.41	3.47	■2.59	3.16	P3.22	3.22				21
22	1935	Q0.55	3-15-85	2-25	0.55	2.20	2.15	Book Value $47.53			9-30-84	15.0	...	2355	Dc	■5.05	■5.66	■6.08	6.52	P7.26	7.26				22
23	1962	Q0.25	3-1-85	2-11	0.25	1.00	2.23¾	17.7	333.	193.	12-31-84	25.5	...	3866	Sp	4.62	6.59	7.59	7.39	□[68]1.83	1.04	3 Mo Dec	□0.88	□0.09	23
24◆	.....	5% Stk	4-4-85	2-25	5% Stk	Stk	5% Stk	2.87	88.7	30.1	9-30-84	17.7	50	±3694	Dc	0.33	0.38	0.20	•0.09	P•▲0.56	0.56				24
25	1969	0.05	12-28-84	12-10	....	0.05	0.05	34.5	88.8	44.3	10-6-84	33.3	20	4995	Dc	□[71]1.11	△[72]□1.63	△d0.30	△•0.04	Pd1.12	d1.12				25
26	1968	[73]0.127	7-17-85	5-6	[73]0.217	0.22	0.23	148.	220.	72.2	j12-31-83	68.2	...	44792	Dc	□d0.32	□0.33	□0.63	□0.84	...	0.84				26
27	1859	0.35	11-15-84	10-29	....	Nil	[74]2.30	1.34	9.81	26.4	12-31-84	22.1	215	1316	Dc	2.78	3.72	1.86	2.43	2.02	2.02				27
28	1982	Q1.00	3-1-85	2-13	1.00	4.00	4.00	Red restr(16%)to 5-31-87				...	180	...	Dc	...	...	b1.58	b1.95	b2.18	...	SF 9,000 min Jun'88, $25			28
29	.....	0.10	7-5-76	6-21	....	Nil	....	1.73	7.92	6.93	12-29-84	16.8	...	922	Sp	▲0.53	▲■d0.88	0.01	d0.08	d0.43	d0.58	3 Mo Dec	0.44	0.29	29
30	.....	None Since Public			....	Nil	....	0.02	1.47	4.39	12-31-84	1.63	...	7049	Je	0.04	0.19	[76]△0.41	□[77]0.20	■d0.05	d0.30	6 Mo Dec	0.15	d0.10	30
31◆	1791	Q0.33	4-1-85	3-11	0.66	1.32	1.20	Book Value $20.95			9-30-84	★443.	1000	p15511	Dc	▲2.28	■2.65	■3.14	■3.45	P[78]3.89	3.89				31
32	1983	1.068	3-1-85	2-8	1.068	4.15	4.625	...	...	...		...	1000	...	Dc	...	...	...	b1.15	...	...				32
33◆	1965	Q0.09	5-8-85	3-29	0.18	0.36	0.33	108.	282.	118.	1-27-85	...	...	23285	Ap	▲d0.37	▲0.10	▲0.41	▲1.33	2.71	2.52	9 Mo Jan△	1.89	1.70	33
34◆	1927	Q0.22	3-8-85	2-13	0.22	0.88	0.84	79.6	516.	265.	10-6-84	151.	...	19820	Dc	1.60	□1.77	1.98	2.36	P[81]2.70	2.70				34
35	1975	Q0.20	1-31-85	1-9	0.20	0.80	0.80	2.74	71.9	61.6	9-30-84	276.	2500	7860	Dc	[83]□2.22	□▲d0.11	▲3.24	■d0.29	P[84]2.20	2.20				35
36	1979	Q0.40¼	1-31-85	1-9	0.40¼	1.61	1.61	...	...	...		...	2500	...	Dc	b1.34	b0.98	b1.38	b0.96	...	...				36
37◆	1938	Q0.12	4-8-85	3-21	0.24	0.48	0.46	6.68	44.7	9.48	9-30-84	7.01	...	4795	Je	0.74	•1.01	1.06	1.16	1.61	1.51	6 Mo Dec	0.71	0.61	37
38◆	1976	Q0.06	5-14-85	4-17	0.11	0.24	0.20	50.4	69.2	32.4	9-30-84	24.4	...	14799	Dc	0.95	▲1.31	1.46	1.52	P1.81	1.81				38
39◆	.....	None Since Public			....	Nil	....	31.8	96.9	36.9	1-31-85	3.09	...	8109	Oc	□0.58	0.81	1.32	1.47	1.77	1.79	3 Mo Jan△	0.37	0.39	39
40◆	.....	None Paid			....	Nil	....	0.05	13.4	10.8	9-30-84	2.21	...	1000	Dc	d0.75	d0.55	•0.14	•[86]0.49	.....	0.47	9 Mo Sep	•0.49	•0.47	40
41◆	.....	None Since Public			....	Nil	....	0.53	10.0	9.96	11-30-84	0.41	30	4328	Au	△[87]d0.40	•0.30	•0.34	•0.47	■d0.41	d0.52	6 Mo Feb△	0.03	d0.08	41
42◆	1965	Q0.14	3-29-85	3-14	0.14	0.56	s0.533	Book Value $14.21			9-30-84	15.4	...	3357	Dc	■1.30	▲1.84	▲1.56	■1.91	P2.00	2.00				42
43	1975	S0.10	1-18-85	12-24	0.10	0.20	0.20	2.19	4.32	1.52	10-31-84	3.11	...	2862	Oc	0.54	□[88]0.30	0.32	△0.27	0.10	0.10	3 Mo Jan△	d0.12	d0.12	43
44◆	1980	Q0.04	3-29-85	3-11	0.04	0.21	†0.16½	20.2	59.8	31.8	9-30-84	...	...	9271	Dc	△[89]1.70	1.27	1.36	△4.26	P3.13	3.13				44
45	1984	0.05	3-15-85	2-22	0.05	0.20	0.10	Book Value $25.37			6-30-84	p499.	...	9350	Je	...	...	...	...	•1.61	0.95	6 Mo Dec	0.71	△0.05	45
46◆	1973	0.20	7-16-84	6-26	....	Nil	[91]0.40	Equity per shr $5.45			4-30-84	p13.8	...	p3357	Ap	0.45	0.54	0.82	0.42	0.20	0.13	9 Mo Jan△	0.10	0.03	46

◆ **Stock Splits & Divs By Line Reference Index** [1]Adj to 5%,'81. [5]10%,'82:3-for-2,'83. [13]3-for-2,'84. [14]3-for-2,'81. [16]10%,'83:Adj to 5%,'84. [17]2-for-1,'83. [19]10%,'80,'81,'82. [20]10%,'83. [21]Adj to 5%,'80(ex'79). [24]Adj to 5%,'85. [31]2-for-1,'84. [33]2-for-1,'83. [34]2-for-1,'83. [37]6-for-5,'81:2-for-1,'83. [38]3-for-2,'80,'81:To split 3-for-2,hldrs Apr 23. [39]2-for-1,'81. [40]1-for-5 REVERSE,'82. [41]3-for-2,'83:5-for-4,'84. [42]3-for-2,'82,'83:Adj for 5%,'84. [44]4-for-1,'81. [46]2-for-1,'81.

FIGURE 4–1 Sample Listings from *Standard & Poor's Stock Guide*

Source: Standard & Poor's Stock Guide, April 1985.

Value Line Investment Survey

The *Value Line Investment Survey* covers more than 1700 stocks in over ninety industries. Each stock report is revised once every three months. The survey is divided into thirteen weekly editions; each week one of the thirteen editions is revised.

The weekly edition of the survey consists of three parts: Ratings and Reports, Summary of Advice and Index, and Selection and Opinion.

Ratings and Reports contains stock reports that provide financial statistics of companies for up to eighteen previous years. Information in the report includes the nature of the business, earnings, dividends, sales, profit margin, working capital, capital structure, and current developments. Other helpful features in the survey are:

- Estimates of sales, earnings, and dividends per share of the firm for the current year and for the next year.
- Estimates of the beta of the stock.
- Ranking of the stock in terms of safety and relative price performance in the next twelve months.
- Reporting of corporate insiders' actions — buying or selling.
- A rating of the company's financial strength, stock price stability, and earnings predictability.
- Organization of stock reports by industry, including a few pages on industry trends.

The *Value Line* report on General Electric is reproduced in Figure 4–2.

The *Summary of Advice and Index* provides a summary of important information on all 1700 stocks under review. In addition, it groups stocks by category: timely stocks, conservative stocks, high-yield stocks, high three-to-five-year potential appreciation stocks, stocks at discount from liquidating value, best-performing stocks, and worst-performing stocks. There is also a table of relevant information for buyers and sellers of options.

Selection and Opinion gives *Value Line*'s opinion of the market and the economy and analyzes stocks that are recommended in particular for income, safety, or appreciation. It also carries *Value Line*'s composite stock indexes and articles of interest.

REPORTS ISSUED BY CORPORATIONS

Reports by the corporation itself constitute one of the most important sources of investment information. Major corporations publish annual reports, quarterly reports, and also 10-K annual reports, which they file with the SEC.

Annual reports are detailed audited reports sent to shareholders. They usually contain more information than is found in manuals and stock reports

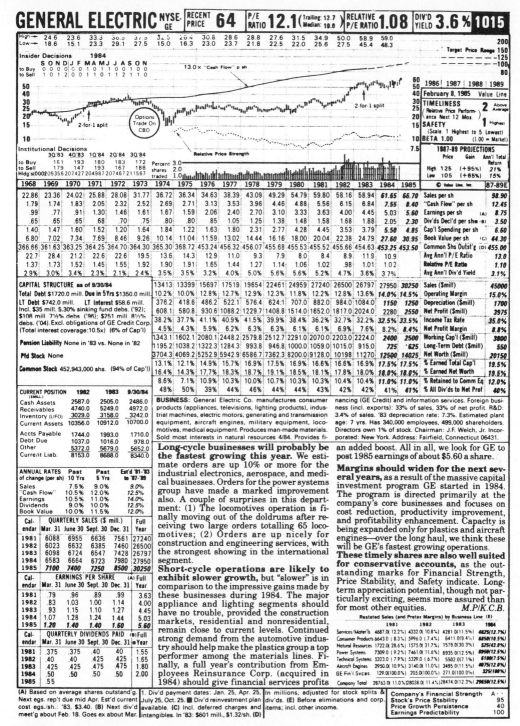

FIGURE 4–2   Value Line Report on General Electric

Source: Value Line Investment Survey, February 8, 1985. © Value Line, Inc. Reprinted by permission.

of investment advisory services. For example, reports of large firms may contain the following information:

- Operational highlights of sales and net income of the most recent two years, including a breakdown of net sales and operating income into major product lines.
- Operational results of various divisions and subsidiaries.
- Analysis of changes in earnings per share.
- Sales by product groups and geographical areas for the most recent five years.
- Analysis of changes in earnings per share.
- Research and development expenditures by product groups.
- Capital expenditures by line of products and geographical area.
- A summary of the significant alternative accounting principles selected for consolidation, depreciation and depletion, income taxes, inventory valuation, and pension plans.
- Consolidated income statements.
- Consolidated balance sheets.
- Statement of changes in consolidated financial position.
- Statement of consolidated shareholders' equity.
- Notes to financial statements concerning employee stock options, equity in affiliates and foreign subsidiaries, foreign exchanges, income taxes, inventory valuation, leases and contingent liabilities, legal proceedings, key employee bonuses, long-term debt, pension plans, research and development expenditures, and replacement cost data.
- Ten-year financial summary.

Interim reports are published quarterly, are not as detailed as annual reports, and they are not usually audited. However, they are important to investors because they do possess some information about prospects for the corporation in the near future.

10-K reports are annual reports by the corporation filed with the SEC. The SEC has a standard format for the 10-K report and requires a great deal more information from the corporation than what is generally available in the annual report sent to shareholders. Consequently most analysts believe that reading the 10-K report is a must in the analysis of a corporation. The 10-K report is available in SEC libraries and also at the NYSE if the stock is listed there. Many major corporations today are willing to send stockholders copies of their 10-K report on request.

PUBLICATIONS OF BROKERAGE FIRMS

The brokerage firm with which an investor deals constitutes another source of investment information. It may subscribe to a number of investment advisory services or, as many do, have its own research department staffed by analysts who are usually industry experts. They provide industry studies as well as analyses of individual corporations.

Brokerage firms usually have a few market letters reviewing current market conditions and suggesting different stocks for purchase or sale for different classes of investors. Major brokerage firms also provide services in the analysis of portfolios of individual customers. However, investors should be aware of the drawbacks in using the literature and advice from brokerage firms. Many have been known to be biased on buy recommendations.

U.S. GOVERNMENT PUBLICATIONS

Publications of the U.S. Government and its agencies represent the most important source of investment information on overall economic and financial conditions of the economy, including trends in various industries. Below we note some of the more important publications:

The *Survey of Current Business*, a monthly publication of the U.S. Department of Commerce, is one of the most useful sources for current business statistics.

The *Business Conditions Digest* is a monthly publication of the U.S. Department of Commerce. It contains many charts, showing GNP and its components; cyclical leading, coincidental and lagging indicators, and data on anticipations and intentions of business firms and consumers. It is very useful for understanding current trends in the economy and for forecasting the outlook of general business.

The *Federal Reserve Bulletin*, a monthly publication by the Federal Reserve System, contains articles and statistics on conditions in the money and capital markets.

The Monthly *Review* publications of individual Federal Reserve Banks, the twelve Federal Reserve Banks in New York, St. Louis, Boston, and so on, have monthly reviews that discuss the economy and financial markets. In addition a few, such as the Federal Reserve Bank of St. Louis, have separate publications showing recent data on money supply, interest rates, economic activity, and inflation.

The *Economic Report of the President and Annual Report of the Council of Economic Advisors* is published annually in February. It discusses economic and business conditions in the economy, and includes forecasts.

The *U.S. Industrial Outlook* is an annual publication by the U.S. Bureau of Domestic Commerce. It reports recent trends and a ten-year outlook for more than 200 industries.

The *Quarterly Financial Report for Manufacturing Corporations* is published by the SEC and the Federal Trade Commission. It reports corporate profits and contains income statements and balance sheets for all manufacturing corporations, classified by both industry and asset size.

TRADE PUBLICATIONS

There are many trade publications for each industry. Analysts who specialize in an industry need to review some of these trade publications regularly. The New York Society of Security Analysts has published a *Guide to Industry Publications for Securities Analysts,* which covers many industries.

COMPUTER-BASED DATA FILES

Major investment advisory services and other organizations store financial data concerning securities in computer files. Investors with access to a computer who are willing to subscribe may use these data bases. Computer data bases are very useful in performing research: For example, if an investor wants a list of stocks on the NYSE possessing certain characteristics, such as a given earnings growth rate, dividend yield, or price-earnings ratio, the computer can quickly retrieve them from a list of all NYSE securities. In the past, much time was spent by analysts to calculate such factors as financial ratios, growth rates, and measures of risk of securities; now the computer performs these tasks. Analysts and investors alike have more time today to evaluate the intangible factors and to form overall judgments about the security. Below are a few better-known data banks.

Dow Jones News Retrieval Service

This service provides subscribers with a great deal of information on thousands of companies. Among the items available are income statements on a quarterly and annual basis, balance sheets, and estimates of earnings per share obtained from about 1000 analysts who work in sixty brokerage houses. Through this service one may also obtain news stories that appeared in the *Wall Street Journal* or *Barron's* within the most recent ninety days.

Compustat

Investor's Management Services (IMS), a subsidiary of the Standard & Poor's Corporation, developed a major data compilation known as Compustat. Compustat is available on magnetic tape to subscribers either directly from IMS or indirectly through a number of time-sharing systems.

The Compustat tapes contain twenty years of annual data for approximately 3500 stocks. Quarterly data since 1962 are also available for about 2700 stocks. The tapes are updated regularly.

Value Line Data Base

Value Line's data file is known as *Value Line* Data Base. It contains comprehensive annual balance sheet and income statement information for

1700 industrial companies, finance companies, and savings and loan associations. The data base also includes such items as ratios, earnings estimates, beta, price ranges, trading volume, accounting methods, and growth rates.

CRSP Tapes

Monthly stock price data for corporations on the NYSE from as far back as 1926 are available on tapes. The data are adjusted for splits and stock dividends and have been compiled by the Center for Research in Security Prices (CRSP), located at the Graduate School of Business at the University of Chicago. Data on daily stock prices of NYSE companies is also available from as far back as the early 1960s.

INDEXES OF SECURITIES PRICES

Indexes of securities prices indicate the level and direction of securities prices, either of the general market or of a particular group of securities. Investors need this information to perceive trends in securities prices and to compare them with price changes of securities in their own portfolios.

Dow Jones Average

The Dow Jones Averages are probably the best known and most widely quoted indicators of stock market performance on the investment scene. The index includes four stock averages, six bond averages, and an average of yields on a group of bonds. The stock averages include indexes of thirty industrial common stocks, twenty transportation common stocks, and fifteen utility common stocks, as well as a composite average of all sixty-five issues.

Computing the Industrial Average[1]

The thirty stocks used to compute the Dow Jones Industrial Average were selected because of their total market value and broad public ownership. They are all high-quality securities of well-established firms, and fluctuations in their combined value generally reflect overall market activity.

But as companies split their stocks to keep prices within the reach of smaller investors, or when a merger, bankruptcy, or extreme lack of price activity causes a particular stock to be dropped from the index, as sometimes happens, the averages must be readjusted to reflect the change.

For example, if three stocks, A, B, and C, sell at $5, $15, and $10, respectively, the average price of all three is $10—their total value divided by 3. But suppose stock B is split, with three $5 shares exchanged for one $15 share. And suppose further that on the day the split occurs, the market goes

---

[1]Based on the pamphlet, *The Dow Jones Averages: A Non-Professional's Guide,* Educational Service Bureau, Dow Jones & Company, 1984.

up, with the $5 stock (A) closing at up one point at $6, the split stock (B) closing at up one point from $5 to $6, and the $10 stock (C) closing at up one point at $11. When we total the prices of stocks A, B, and C, we get a combined value of $23, which divided by 3 yields an average of only $7.67. This figure is less than the $10 average we determined before stock B was split, even though the value of each stock actually went up one point.

To compensate for this distortion, the divisor used to determine the average is changed according to an accepted formula:

$$\frac{\text{Former divisor}}{\text{Former total value}} = \frac{\text{New divisor}}{\text{New total value}}$$

Note that computation of the averages is a continuous process, carried on from day to day. Changes in the divisor are predicated on adjustments and readjustments made many times throughout the years that the averages have been calculated.

Looking again at our simplified example with three stocks, we see that the average price of stocks A, B, and C on a given day is $10. Remember that this is a simple mathematical average—the total of all three stock prices divided by 3—and is used solely for the sake of explanation. The divisor used to compute the Dow Jones average is never the number of stocks listed.

On the day stock B is split, the previous day's closing prices are totaled again, but this time the split stock is added in at its reduced price ($5 + $5 + $10 = $20). Then the $20 total is divided by the previous day's average ($\frac{\$20}{\$10}$), and the resulting figure—in this case, 2—becomes the divisor used to compute the current day's average.

Now the current day's closing prices are added ($6 + $6 + $11), and since each stock has closed at up one point, the current total is $23. When this figure is divided by 2, the new divisor, the current day's average is $11.50, which is an accurate reflection of the true stock value.

The divisor obtained by this method is used until another stock split or substitution occurs, and will yield an accurate average no matter how much the individual stocks in the listing rise or fall in price. (The divisor is not changed if the stock split causes a distortion in the average of less than five points.)

The Transportation Average includes twenty transportation common stocks, including railroads, airlines, freight forwarders, and mixed transportation companies. The Public Utility Average includes fifteen stocks. The method of computation for these averages—transportation, utility, and 65 composite—is the same as that described for the computation of the industrial average.

The 20-Bond Average represents the combined averages of ten public utility bonds and ten industrial bonds. It is determined by computing the simple mathematical average of closing prices in each group of bonds included, and then averaging these two figures to yield an overall average of all twenty bonds.

In Figure 4–3 we see the daily chart of the Dow Jones Industrial, Transportation, and Utilities averages as they appeared in the daily issue of the *Wall Street Journal*. The stocks used in computing the Dow Jones Averages are listed in Table 4–1.

TABLE 4–1   Stocks Used in Computing Dow Jones Stock Averages

Industrials

Allied Corp	IBM
Aluminum Co	Inter Harvester
Amer Brands	Inter Paper
Amer Can	Merck
Amer Express	Minnesota M&M
Amer Tel & Tel	Owens-Illinois
Bethlehem Steel	Procter & Gamb
Chevron	Sears Roebuck
DuPont	Texaco
Eastman Kodak	Union Carbide
Exxon	Union Carbide
General Electric	United Technologies
General Foods	US Steel
General Motors	Westinghouse El
Goodyear	Woolworth
Inco	

Transportation

AMR Corp	Overnite Transp
Amer President	Pan Am World Air
Burlington North	Santa Fe Indust
Canadian Pacific	Transway Int'l
Carolina Freight	Trans World
Consolid Freight	UAL Inc
CSX Corp	Union Pac Corp
Delta Air Lines	USAir Group
Eastern Air Lines	
Federal Express	
Norfolk Southern	
Northwest Air	

Utilities

Am Elec Power	Niag Mohawk P
Cleveland E ILL	Pacific Gas & El
Colum-Gas Sys	Panhandle Eastern
Comwlth Edison	Peoples Energy
Consol Edison	Phila Elec
Consol Nat Gas	Pub Serv E&G
Detroit Edison	Sou Cal Edison
Houston Indus	

Source: The Wall Street Journal, Education Edition, Dow Jones & Company, 1984/85.

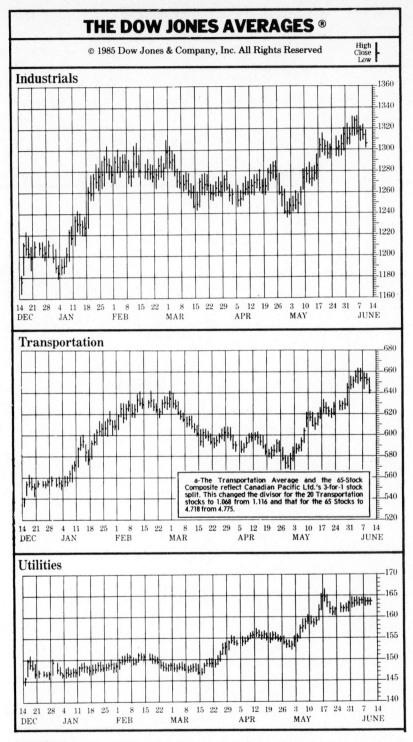

THE DOW JONES AVERAGES ®

© 1985 Dow Jones & Company, Inc. All Rights Reserved

High
Close
Low

Industrials

14 21 28 | 4 11 18 25 | 1 8 15 22 | 1 8 15 22 29 | 5 12 19 26 | 3 10 17 24 31 | 7 14
DEC | JAN | FEB | MAR | APR | MAY | JUNE

Transportation

a-The Transportation Average and the 65-Stock Composite reflect Canadian Pacific Ltd.'s 3-for-1 stock split. This changed the divisor for the 20 Transportation stocks to 1.068 from 1.116 and that for the 65 Stocks to 4.718 from 4.775.

14 21 28 | 4 11 18 25 | 1 8 15 22 | 1 8 15 22 29 | 5 12 19 26 | 3 10 17 24 31 | 7 14
DEC | JAN | FEB | MAR | APR | MAY | JUNE

Utilities

14 21 28 | 4 11 18 25 | 1 8 15 22 | 1 8 15 22 29 | 5 12 19 26 | 3 10 17 24 31 | 7 14
DEC | JAN | FEB | MAR | APR | MAY | JUNE

FIGURE 4–3

Source: Wall Street Journal, June 13, 1985. Reprinted by permission of *The Wall Street Journal,* © 1985, World rights reserved.

Standard & Poor's Price Indexes

Next to the Dow Jones Industrial Average, probably the most widely known index is that prepared by the Standard & Poor's Corporation. The S&P indexes include a composite index of 500 stocks, an industrial index based on 400 industrial common stocks, a transportation index of twenty stocks, a utility index of forty stocks, and a finance index of forty stocks.

The S&P index is a weighted index and related to a base period of 1941–43. The index is computed in this way: The current price of each stock in the index is multiplied by the number of shares outstanding. The market values of these stocks are then added together to arrive at an aggregate value of these stocks in the index. The aggregate value is then divided by the aggregate value of these stocks during the years 1941–43. The ratio thus derived is further divided by 10, and the result is the index at the current moment.

Because the index reflects the relative change in the total value of stocks outstanding, it is unaffected by stock splits and dividends, and therefore, no adjustments have to be made for them. See Figure 4–4 for the S&P indexes of industrials, utilities, transportations, financials, and their subgroups.

NYSE Common Stock Price Index

In 1966, the NYSE established its Common Stock Price Index to provide a comprehensive measure of the market trend of all stocks listed on the exchange. It is a weighted index. The method of computation is the same as that used for the S&P indexes. The price of each stock is weighted by the number of shares outstanding. The aggregate market value of all stocks on the NYSE is then expressed relative to the base period. The base index was 50 on December 31, 1965.

Changes in capitalization, new listings, and delistings are handled by adjusting the base period value. For example, if a new issue is listed, the base value is increased so that the addition of the current market value does not distort the index values.

In Figure 4–5 we see the growth rates in the NYSE common stock index for the period 1968–83. The data provides a broad picture of the stock market over recent years. First, the annual average growth rate of this index from 1969 to 1978 was about .4 percent. Second, from 1978 to 1984, the index increased 10.3 percent per year. These statistics reveal that one can either do well or do poorly over extended periods of time. It should be noted, however, that the table understates the investor's returns because dividends are not included.

See Figure 4–6 for a chart of the NYSE common stock index that appears each Sunday in the *New York Times*. There is weekly data for several averages: Dow Jones, Standard & Poor's, and the NYSE itself. In addition, it includes a bar graph showing the weekly trading volume for a two-year period.

FIGURE 4–4 S&P Indexes of the Securities Markets

	Apr. Month End	% Change from Prev. Month	Apr. Avg.	May 1	— 1985 Range — High	Low
500 Composite	179.83	− 0.5	180.62	178.37	183.43	163.68
400 Industrials	199.94	− 0.9	201.13	198.32	205.15	182.24
20 Transportation	148.11	− 4.3	152.12	147.43	162.54	141.56
40 Utilities	81.46	+ 1.4	81.25	80.94	82.30	74.70
40 Financial	21.25	+ 3.2	21.00	20.99	22.00	18.37
Capital Goods	180.13	− 0.9	182.94	178.19	193.57	171.26
Consumer Goods	173.51	+ 2.0	177.40	171.29	180.40	157.73
High Grade	135.84	0	136.22	134.11	138.29	124.90
Low Priced	521.32	− 2.2	531.73	515.50	537.97	466.69
Industrials						
Aerospace/Defense	273.81	− 3.8	277.37	271.07	301.74	250.55
Aluminum	126.21	− 6.8	133.47	124.75	157.60	124.75
Automobile	96.05	− 5.6	102.45	94.46	116.97	94.46
Excl. General Motors	41.64	− 2.7	44.02	41.09	48.65	41.09
Auto Parts — After Mkt.	23.18	− 4.7	24.32	23.15	26.88	23.15
Auto Parts — Orig. Equip.	28.08	− 4.9	28.67	27.88	31.25	27.88
Auto Trucks & Parts	56.67	−11.9	61.37	55.98	75.26	55.98
Beverages: Brewers	94.89	+ 4.2	93.67	93.19	94.70	84.27
Distillers	337.76	+ 2.0	336.30	330.54	347.90	304.48
Soft Drinks	205.64	+ 2.6	207.04	202.18	209.06	177.62
Building Materials	94.36	− 2.6	95.98	93.68	104.36	91.53
Chemicals	69.91	+ 4.3	68.95	68.91	70.71	63.14
**Chemicals (Diversified)	20.17	− 4.1	20.84	20.08	21.95	19.56
Coal	281.15	− 0.1	286.55	282.91	312.10	266.72
Communication — Equip/Mfrs.	33.29	− 5.2	34.54	32.96	41.59	32.94
Computer & Bus. Equip.	177.97	− 1.7	181.09	176.54	197.47	172.71
Excl. I.B.M.	262.71	− 5.2	273.25	261.30	319.01	261.30
Computer Services	40.33	− 3.7	42.22	40.44	44.98	37.55
Conglomerates	35.52	+ 0.3	35.26	35.61	35.73	30.22
Containers: Metal & Glass	84.88	+ 2.5	84.32	84.59	85.69	75.30
Paper	361.89	− 3.5	368.82	359.60	428.40	358.34
Copper	47.62	− 2.1	48.05	46.88	49.11	36.58
Cosmetics	50.86	+ 2.2	50.72	50.36	51.79	48.14
Drugs	314.01	− 1.6	317.80	310.82	321.35	283.64
Electrical Equipment	534.77	− 2.3	550.17	532.78	574.43	504.48
Electronic Major Cos.	195.25	− 0.1	197.70	192.17	211.66	181.14
Electronics — Instrumentation	59.18	− 6.0	62.70	58.81	70.80	58.81
Semiconductors/Components	41.46	− 8.3	44.48	40.69	51.44	40.69
Entertainment	341.83	+ 2.4	343.98	338.36	351.13	260.73
Fertilizers	17.04	− 8.0	18.16	16.97	18.48	16.97
Foods	169.67	− 2.1	169.93	166.81	172.34	152.89
Forest Products	20.39	+ 0.3	20.68	20.03	23.67	20.03
*Gaming Cos.	16.39	− 1.0	16.97	15.96	17.34	12.65
Gold Mining	126.47	− 7.8	134.14	125.28	136.65	107.53
Hardware & Tools	12.93	− 3.8	13.29	12.87	15.30	12.87

FIGURE 4–4, continued

	Apr. Month End	% Change from Prev. Month	Apr. Avg.	May 1	— 1985 Range — High	Low
Homebuilding	41.22	− 2.7	41.50	40.47	50.34	40.04
Hospital Management	61.75	− 8.3	63.96	60.99	67.57	53.92
Hospital Supplies	68.42	− 2.9	68.48	67.29	69.50	56.71
Hotel-Motel	127.04	+ 2.3	130.08	127.74	130.61	108.31
Household Furnish. & Appliances	269.82	− 5.9	278.44	269.35	301.33	269.35
Leisure Time	134.73	− 2.5	139.49	134.24	146.50	125.57
Machine Tools	147.75	− 3.8	151.50	146.90	178.15	142.18
Machinery; Agricultural	38.91	−10.6	40.57	38.19	46.65	38.19
Construction & Mat. Handling	241.17	− 1.6	244.48	238.19	257.55	230.96
Industry/Specialty	143.53	− 1.8	147.11	141.58	158.75	140.63
**Manufactured Housing	107.23	− 8.8	115.66	105.61	154.38	105.61
Metals — Miscellaneous	102.38	− 4.1	105.91	100.32	109.34	96.71
Offshore Drilling	111.10	+ 1.5	108.73	113.22	116.29	96.06
Oil Composite	368.64	+ 4.0	356.35	372.03	372.03	310.56
Crude Producers	704.41	− 0.3	703.02	700.49	809.94	658.29
Integrated: Domestic	446.73	+ 4.6	424.20	456.55	456.55	369.30
Int'l. Integrated	155.61	+ 3.7	152.65	155.29	155.45	132.60
Oil Well Equip. & Service	1216.60	+ 2.9	1193.45	1201.00	1296.47	1075.29
*Canadian Oil & Gas Exploration	23.21	+ 1.9	23.08	23.21	23.46	18.47
Paper	367.52	+ 2.0	367.30	363.96	376.84	353.24
Pollution Control	72.57	− 1.9	73.44	70.05	75.46	61.67
Publishing	948.59	− 0.3	955.79	936.74	976.88	826.87
Publishing (Newspapers)	80.47	− 1.1	80.09	79.48	81.59	68.02
Radio-TV Broadcasters	1633.19	+ 3.5	1604.61	1631.13	1646.39	1079.06
Restaurants	100.02	+ 1.3	99.48	97.90	101.15	82.91
Retail Stores Composite	168.07	+ 0.2	167.49	166.00	170.70	149.35
Department Stores	380.71	+ 1.5	375.28	377.15	386.07	323.06
Retail Stores (Drug)	66.56	− 7.7	69.22	66.42	74.58	63.35
Food Chains	117.60	− 1.6	119.17	116.12	120.33	105.07
Gen. Merchandise Chains	13.26	+ 0.7	13.14	13.08	14.01	12.28
Retail (Miscellaneous)	257.96	+ 3.7	255.22	252.87	263.15	200.85
Shoes	122.98	− 1.4	122.01	122.59	127.79	107.26
Soaps	227.63	− 3.5	228.93	226.61	237.65	225.80
Steel	35.40	− 4.9	35.92	35.20	41.38	35.20
Excl. U.S. Steel	29.61	− 8.5	30.59	29.22	37.69	29.22
Textiles: Apparel Mfrs.	81.50	+ 0.9	81.80	81.81	82.79	64.30
Textile Products	99.58	− 2.5	101.39	98.96	109.45	98.22
Tires and Rubber Goods	191.57	+ 0.6	194.67	191.62	198.46	175.86
Tobacco	200.55	− 8.6	216.76	195.35	219.99	186.14
Toys	24.10	+ 2.6	23.74	23.52	24.31	18.79
Utilities						
Electric Companies	44.78	+ 1.2	44.87	44.41	45.38	41.97
Natural Gas Distributors	131.95	− 2.0	134.70	132.41	136.96	124.88
Pipelines	299.52	− 3.2	299.54	307.84	307.84	240.25
Telephone (New)	124.84	+ 2.7	123.25	123.44	125.42	115.42

(continued)

FIGURE 4–4, continued

	Apr. Month End	% Change from Prev. Month	Apr. Avg.	May 1	— 1985 Range — High	Low
Transportation						
Air Freight	35.16	− 0.5	35.65	35.10	37.34	32.07
Airlines	162.58	− 8.6	171.94	161.98	178.64	161.98
Railroads	111.74	− 2.8	113.56	111.26	121.91	103.94
Truckers	158.05	− 7.0	167.02	158.73	196.51	158.73
Financial						
Banks — New York City	82.02	+ 2.5	83.55	81.30	86.20	70.87
Outside N.Y.C.	104.66	+ 5.4	101.61	103.67	105.86	94.87
Life Insurance	582.46	− 2.7	573.38	572.73	615.08	533.25
Multi-Line Insurance	33.84	+ 3.7	32.86	33.37	34.43	28.94
Property-Casualty Insurance	243.38	+ 8.7	230.30	238.50	241.35	194.22
Savings & Loan Holding Cos.	29.09	− 5.1	30.72	29.04	32.55	27.28
Personal Loans	145.75	− 2.9	147.66	144.34	149.20	134.71
*Brokerage Firms	50.49	− 5.7	52.63	49.90	60.27	43.34
*Real Estate Investment Trusts	4.27	− 2.4	4.30	4.27	4.38	3.94
*Investment Cos.	58.97	− 2.1	59.46	58.87	62.24	58.87
*Investment Cos. (Bond Funds)	8.79	+ 1.6	8.70	8.79	8.91	8.50

*Not included in composite indexes.
**Name Changes: Chemicals (Misc.) became Chemicals (Diversified) on 4/10/85. Mobile Homes became Manufactured Housing on 3/20/85.
†Figures for 500 Composite, Industrials, Transportation, Utilities, and Financial based on daily indexes. All others based on weekly indexes.
‡February figures revised. Brokerage Firms: 56.45; Real Estate: 4.32.
Source: The Outlook, May 8, 1985. © Standard & Poor's Corporation.

Value Line Averages[2]

Value Line has constructed its Stock Market Averages on the theory that it is important for the investor to see how the stocks of most companies are faring in the marketplace. Therefore, the *Value Line* Averages are broadly based (consisting of 1492 industrial stocks, 158 utility stocks, and fifteen rail stocks). Each stock in the *Value Line* Average is equally weighted. A stock with 2 million shares outstanding takes the same weight in the *Value Line* Average as a stock with 10 million shares outstanding.

Other well-known weighted averages, such as the New York Stock Exchange Composite Index and Standard & Poor's Averages, are more representative of the big companies than of the majority of companies. These averages are constructed by multiplying the price of each stock by the number of its shares outstanding.

[2]Arnold Bernhard. *Value Line Methods of Evaluating Common Stocks*, Arnold Bernhard, 1979, p. 64.

FIGURE 4–5 Compounded Growth Rates in NYSE Index*

	Initial Year															Index at Year-end
	'69	'70	'71	'72	'73	'74	'75	'76	'77	'78	'79	'80	'81	'82	'83	
'69																51.53
'70	−2.5															50.23
'71	4.6	12.3														56.43
'72	7.8	13.3	14.3													64.48
'73	0.1	1.0	−4.2	−19.6												51.82
'74	−6.9	−7.9	−13.8	−25.1	−30.3											36.13
'75	−1.3	−1.1	−4.1	−9.6	−4.1	31.9										47.64
'76	1.7	2.4	0.5	−2.7	3.8	26.6	21.5									57.88
'77	0.2	0.6	−1.2	−4.0	0.3	13.3	5.0	−9.3								52.50
'78	0.4	0.8	−0.7	−3.0	0.7	10.4	4.0	−3.8	2.1							53.62
'79	1.9	2.4	1.2	−0.6	3.0	11.4	6.8	2.3	8.6	15.5						61.95
'80	3.8	4.5	3.6	2.4	6.0	13.7	10.3	7.7	14.0	20.5	25.7					77.86
'81	2.7	3.2	2.3	1.1	4.0	10.2	6.9	4.2	7.9	9.9	7.1	−8.7				71.11
'82	3.5	4.1	3.3	2.3	5.1	10.6	7.9	5.8	9.1	10.9	9.4	2.0	14.0			81.03
'83	4.5	5.0	4.5	3.6	6.3	11.4	9.0	7.4	10.4	12.2	11.3	6.9	15.7	17.5		95.18
'84	4.3	4.8	4.2	3.4	5.8	10.3	8.1	6.6	9.1	10.3	9.2	5.5	10.7	9.1	1.3	96.38

*Index figures taken at year-end.
Source: NYSE Fact Book, 1985.

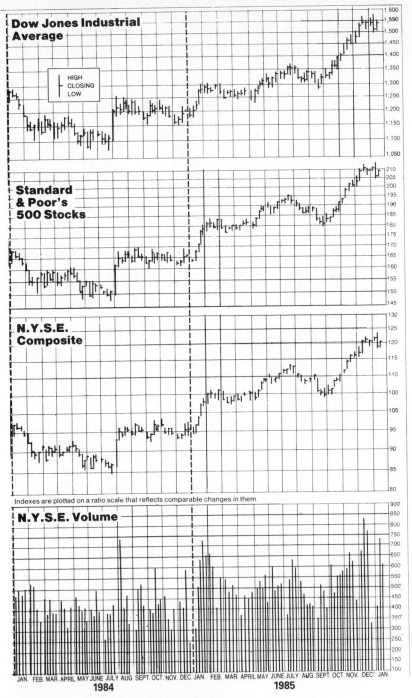

FIGURE 4–6   New York Stock Exchange

Source: The New York Times, January 17, 1986. Copyright © 1986 by the New York Times Company. Reprinted by permission.

When stock splits or dividends occur, the preceding day's price is adjusted accordingly, and the index of change computed thereafter. As stocks are added to the *Value Line Investment Survey,* the average is enlarged. Additions and deletions of stocks present no problem to the average because of its large base and method of construction.

In Figure 4–7 A and B we show the *Value Line* Composite index as well as the Dow Jones Industrial Average from 1966 to 1985. The relative strength line is an index of the ratios of the two indexes. While there is a correlation in the movement of the indexes, there are deviations, as we see in the relative strength line. Different indicators do not move exactly parallel to each other because they do not contain the same stocks, and the weights used are different.

MARKET MOVEMENTS AND DIFFERENCES IN MARKET INDEXES

Movements in market indexes may be used by investors to estimate the percentage change in the average price per share. If the Dow Jones Industrial Average moves from 1900 to 1919, the average price per share in the index increases by $\frac{19}{1900} = 1\%$. Indexes that are very broad in their coverage provide an estimate of overall market performance. Over extended periods of time, market indexes tend to move in the same direction, although the percentage changes differ. The differences are due not only to the different indexes containing different collections of companies but also to the different methods of calculating index numbers.

To illustrate this, assume the Dow Jones, S&P, and *Value Line* indexes all contain only three stocks with the following prices and shares outstanding:

Stock	Price ($t = 1$)	Shares Outstanding in Market	Price ($t = 2$)
A	$10	300	12
B	15	200	16.50
C	20	400	21

We initially assume that all three indexes are 100 at time $t = 1$. Let us now consider what each index will equal at time $t = 2$.

Dow Jones Method

First we take a simple average, Av, of the three prices at $t = 1$ and $t = 2$:

$$Av_1 = \left(\frac{10 + 15 + 20}{3}\right) = 15$$

$$Av_2 = \left(\frac{12 + 16.50 + 21}{3}\right) = 16.5$$

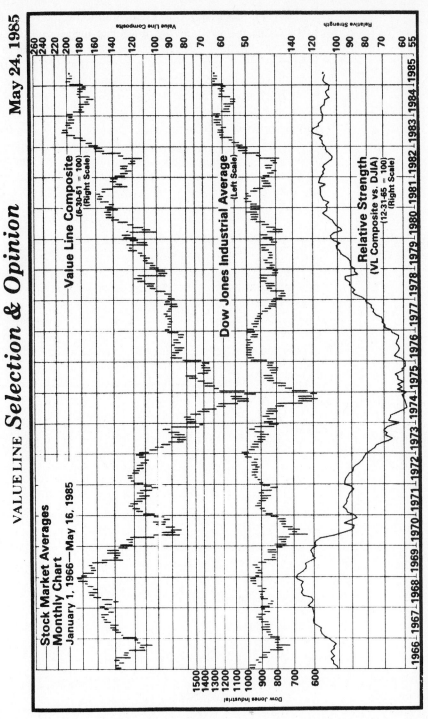

FIGURE 4–7A   *Value Line Selection & Opinion*

74

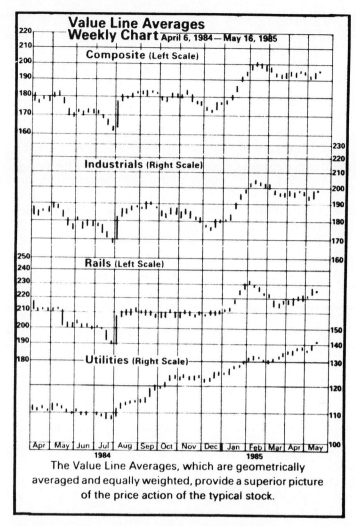

FIGURE 4–7B *Value Line* Selection & Opinion

Source: The Value Line Investment Survey, May 24, 1985. © Value
Line, Inc. Reprinted by permission. .

The index values are then calculated with 15 as a basis, for we assumed the value of each index was 100 at $t = 1$.

$$I_1 = \frac{15}{15} \times 100 = 100$$

$$I_2 = \frac{16.60}{15} = 110$$

Thus the index increased by 10 percent.

S&P Method

The S&P technique involves weighting prices by number of shares out-standing in the market. First we calculate the market value of those shares at $t = 1$ and $t = 2$, and then we divide by the total number of shares (900). In this way we obtain an average price per share during each period.

Stock	Market Value	
	$t = 1$	$t = 2$
A	$10 \times 300 = \$3000$	$12 \times 300 = 3600$
B	$15 \times 200 = 3000$	$16.5 \times 200 = 3300$
C	$20 \times 400 = 8000$	$21 \times 400 = 8400$
	$\$14,000$	$\$15,300$

$$Av_1 = \frac{\$14,000}{900} = \$15.56 \qquad Av_2 = \frac{\$15,300}{900} = \$17$$

Next, we calculate indexes with \$15.56 as a basis so that we have the assumed value of $I_1 = 100$.

$$I_1 = \left(\frac{15.56}{15}\right) \times 100 = 100$$

$$I_2 = \frac{17.00}{15.56} \times 100 = 109.3$$

Under the S&P method, the market rose less than under the Dow Jones technique. The difference is due to greater weight given to stock C, which has the highest market value of the three stocks but rose by only 5 percent (from 20 to 21). Stocks A and B both rose by higher percentages, and under the Dow Jones approach, the three stocks were weighted equally.

Value Line Method

Under the *Value Line* approach, we calculate an average growth factor from $t = 1$ to $t = 2$, and we define the index to be 100 at $t = 1$. Then we calculate growth factors for each stock in the index by taking the ratio of prices at $t = 2$ to $t = 1$.

Stocks	Growth Factors
A	$\dfrac{12}{10} = 1.2$
B	$\dfrac{16.5}{15} = 1.1$
C	$\dfrac{21}{20} = 1.05$

Note that the growth factor is merely 1 plus the growth rate in price. Since all stocks increased in price, the factors are all greater than 1. However, if some prices drop, the growth factors for those stocks will be less than 1.

We now calculate the geometric mean of the growth factors. When multiplied by 100 it will give us the market index at $t = 2$.

$$I_2 = \sqrt[3]{1.2 \times 1.1 \times 1.05} \times 100 = \sqrt[3]{1.386} \times 100$$

$$I_2 = 111.5$$

This market index has risen by 11.5 percent. It is higher than that found using the S&P method because stock C is weighted the same as stocks A and B; it differs also from the Dow Jones method in the calculation procedure.

QUESTIONS AND PROBLEMS

1. Where can one obtain information regarding the state of the general economy?
2. What are some of the sources of industry information?
3. What are some of the important publications by the Standard & Poor's Corporation that may be useful to investors?
4. Does the Dow Jones Industrial Average measure the overall stock market?
5. What are some of the well-known financial periodicals investors should consult?
6. How is the *Value Line* Average computed? What does it try to measure?
7. Where do you obtain information on a specific company?
8. Compare and contrast the information that appears in the *Federal Reserve Bulletin* and the *Survey of Current Business.*
9. Explain how the *S&P Stock Price Indexes* are constructed.
10. Indicate the types of information on a particular company that are available in the *Value Line Investment Survey.*

11. What are some of the advantages offered by computerized data files?
12. Name a few important publications of the U.S. government and its agencies that would be useful to investors.

REFERENCES

Bernhard, Arnold. *Value Line Methods of Evaluating Common Stocks.* Arnold Bernhard, 1979.

Bostian, David B., Jr. "The Impact of Institutions on the Market," *Financial Analysts Journal,* Nov.–Dec. 1973.

Butler, H. L., and Allen, J. D. "The Dow Jones Industrial Average Reexamined." *Financial Analysts Journal,* Nov.–Dec. 1979.

Dow Jones & Company, *The Dow Jones Averages: A Non-Professional's Guide,* Educational Service Bureau, 1984.

Good, Walter R. "Interpreting Analysts' Recommendations," *Financial Analysts Journal,* May–June 1975.

Latane, H. A., Tuttle, D. L., and Young, W. E. "Market Indexes and the Implications for Portfolio Management," *Financial Analysts Journal,* Sept.–Oct. 1971.

Logue, D. E., and Tuttle, D. L. "Brokerage House Investment Advice," *The Financial Review,* 1973.

Nevans, Ronald. "The Market Opinion Letters: How Good are They?" *Financial World,* July 16, 1975.

Reckers, Philip, and Stagliano, A. J. "How Good are Investor's Data Sources?" *Financial Executive,* April 1980.

Rogers, R. C., and Owens, J. E. "The Impact of *Value Line* Special Situation Recommendations on Stock Prices," *The Financial Review,* May 1984.

Smith, R. G. E. "Uncertainty, Information and Investment Decision," *Journal of Finance,* March 1971.

Macroeconomic Analysis and the Analysis of Fixed Income Securities

5

Business Conditions Analysis, Corporate Profits, and Stock Prices

SECURITY PRICES AND THE ECONOMY

Both fixed-income securities and common stocks are affected by economic factors. One element of the economic environment, interest rates, has a direct impact on bond prices and strongly influences stock prices. Other economic factors, such as expectations of sales and profits, play a major role in the stock market and also affect the risk in holding corporate bonds.

See Figure 5–1 for some relationships between fluctuations in the economy, corporate profits, and stock prices from 1959 to 1985. The shaded areas represent periods of recession. Associated with each recession was a decline in corporate profits and stock prices. Generally, the stock market starts to fall prior to the beginning of a recession and hits bottom prior to the end of the recession. This occurs because stock prices move in anticipation of future profits, and the market generally anticipates a recession or an economic expansion prior to its occurrence.

Firms vary in their sensitivity to general economic conditions. For example, automobile firms are more sensitive than electrical utilities. Some industries, such as residential construction, are strongly affected by movements in interest rates. Thus, the economy does not affect all firms in the same way at the same time. Several studies have examined the extent to which individual stock prices can be attributed to different factors.[1] Of total price movements, approximately 30 to 35 percent are due to market forces that affect all stocks; 15 to 20 percent are due to industry factors; events confined to the individual company account for 30 to 35 percent, and 15 to 20 percent are attributable to other factors.

---

[1]For example, see Richard A. Brealey, *An Introduction to Risk and Return from Common Stocks* (Cambridge, Mass.: MIT Press, 1969), pp. 59–61.

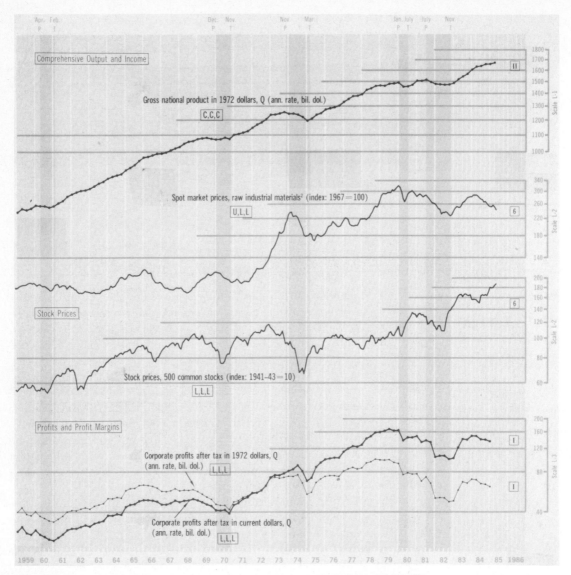

FIGURE 5–1   Economic Fluctuations, Stock Prices, and Corporate Profits
Source: U.S. Department of Commerce, *Business Conditions Digest,* June 1985.

METHODS OF FORECASTING

Because of the relationship between stock and bond prices and economic conditions, investors of all kinds, regardless of their objectives and practices, are all keenly interested in economic forecasts. Of course, most individual investors are unable to make their own forecast because they lack training and experience, and therefore must depend on the opinions of others — primarily economists employed by public and private institutions. Economists use a variety of concepts and techniques to forecast business. In the following sections we discuss six techniques used by professionals:

1. Economic indicators and diffusion indexes
2. Business and consumer surveys
3. National income and product accounts
4. Econometric models
5. Monetary measures
6. Futures markets

For the purpose of making a short-term economic forecast, a government publication, *Business Conditions Digest,* is particularly useful. It contains many charts and tables showing a large number of economic series. In the discussion that follows we will use a number of charts from that publication. Details on how data is presented in the *Digest* appear in Figure 5–2.

Short-Term Forecasting on the Basis of Economic Indicators

The National Bureau of Economic Research (NBER) is noted for its pioneering and comprehensive statistical studies of business cycles. In 1938 the NBER published its first list of business cycle indicators, as compiled by Wesley C. Mitchell, Arthur F. Burns, Geoffrey Moore, and Julius Shiskin. The list has been expanded several times with the most well-known series being the list of twelve leading indicators. The 1985 list is shown in Table 5–1 together with the median number of months by which the indicators have historically led the economy at peaks and troughs of business cycles.

See Figure 5–3 for the composite indexes of the twelve leading indicators, four coincident, and six lagging indicators during the period 1948 to 1985.

By closely watching the movements of the twelve leading indicators and their composite index, investors gain some perspective on what the economy will do in the next year or so. However, as shown in Figure 5–3, the composite index of the twelve leading indicators sometimes hesitates or pauses temporarily and may even decline for a month or two before resuming its upward movement. Investors should not jump to conclusions whenever the composite index of leading indicators turns downward. Rather, they should examine the individual leading indicators that have brought down the composite index. Some leading indicators portray basic economic processes, such as future production and, therefore, are more important than other leading indicators. Generally, if the composite index of leading indicators has

HOW TO READ CHARTS

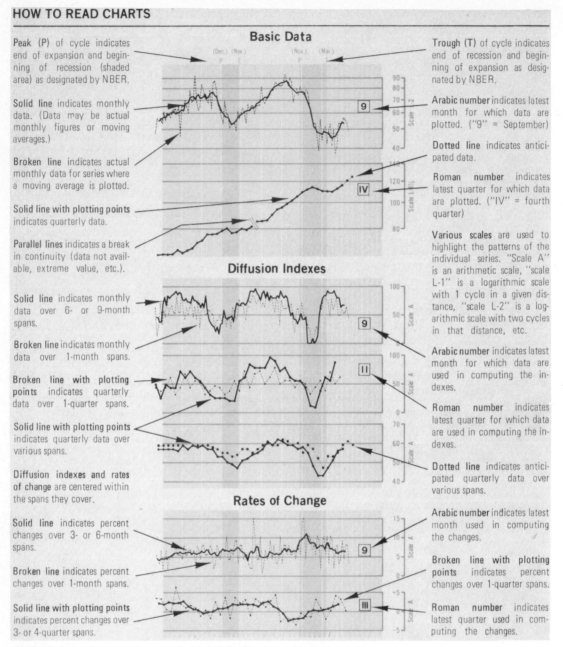

Peak (P) of cycle indicates end of expansion and beginning of recession (shaded area) as designated by NBER.

Solid line indicates monthly data. (Data may be actual monthly figures or moving averages.)

Broken line indicates actual monthly data for series where a moving average is plotted.

Solid line with plotting points indicates quarterly data.

Parallel lines indicates a break in continuity (data not available, extreme value, etc.).

Solid line indicates monthly data over 6- or 9-month spans.

Broken line indicates monthly data over 1-month spans.

Broken line with plotting points indicates quarterly data over 1-quarter spans.

Solid line with plotting points indicates quarterly data over various spans.

Diffusion indexes and rates of change are centered within the spans they cover.

Solid line indicates percent changes over 3- or 6-month spans.

Broken line indicates percent changes over 1-month spans.

Solid line with plotting points indicates percent changes over 3- or 4-quarter spans.

Basic Data

Diffusion Indexes

Rates of Change

Trough (T) of cycle indicates end of recession and beginning of expansion as designated by NBER.

Arabic number indicates latest month for which data are plotted. ("9" = September)

Dotted line indicates anticipated data.

Roman number indicates latest quarter for which data are plotted. ("IV" = fourth quarter)

Various scales are used to highlight the patterns of the individual series. "Scale A" is an arithmetic scale, "scale L-1" is a logarithmic scale with 1 cycle in a given distance, "scale L-2" is a logarithmic scale with two cycles in that distance, etc.

Arabic number indicates latest month for which data are used in computing the indexes.

Roman number indicates latest quarter for which data are used in computing the indexes.

Dotted line indicates anticipated quarterly data over various spans.

Arabic number indicates latest month used in computing the changes.

Broken line with plotting points indicates percent changes over 1-quarter spans.

Roman number indicates latest quarter used in computing the changes.

FIGURE 5–2   Explanation of Charts in *Business Conditions Digest*
Source: U.S. Department of Commerce, *Business Conditions Digest*.

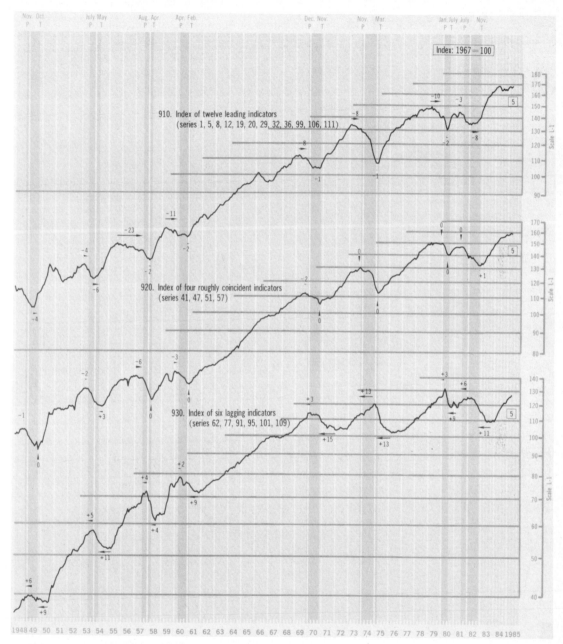

FIGURE 5–3 Composite Indexes of the Economy

Source: U.S. Department of Commerce, *Business Conditions Digest,* June 1985.

TABLE 5–1   Leading Indicators of Economic Activity, 1985

	Median Lead (in months)	
	Peak	Trough
1. Average weekly hours of production of nonsupervisory workers, manufacturing	11	1
2. Average weekly initial claims for unemployment insurance, state programs	12	0
3. Manufacturers' new orders in 1972 dollars, consumer goods and materials industries	11	1
4. Vendor performance, percent of companies receiving slower deliveries	6	4
5. Index of net business formation	13	1
6. Contracts and orders for plant and equipment in 1972 dollars	8	1
7. Index of new private housing units authorized by local building permits	13	2
8. Change in manufacturing and trade inventories on hand and on order in 1972 dollars, smoothed	11	1
9. Change in sensitive materials prices, smoothed	9.5	3.5
10. Index of stock prices, 500 common stock	9.5	4
11. Money supply (M2) in 1972 dollars	16	3
12. Change in business and consumer credit outstanding	11	2

Source: U.S. Department of Commerce, *Handbook of Cyclical Indicators: A Supplement to the Business Conditions Digest.* Washington, D.C.: U.S. Government Printing Office, 1984.

been rising and then changes direction with three consecutive monthly declines, there is reason to expect that a business slowdown or recession will soon occur. In addition, one should examine the coincidental indicators and their underlying strength. A relatively strong upward momentum can suggest that the pause or decline of the composite index of twelve leading indicators may more likely be just temporary. Sometimes some leading indicators point to a change, while others do not. To deal with that, a diffusion index can be constructed.

Short-Term Forecasting on the Basis of a Diffusion Index

The *diffusion index* is a statistical series indicating the percentage of items in a group that are rising at any given time. Thus, if the diffusion index of the twelve leading indicators is 67 percent, eight of the twelve indicators are higher in the measured period than in the previous period. The diffusion index, like rates of change, tends to change direction ahead of the aggregate. For example, we show a hypothetical case of the diffusion index of corporate profits of 1000 firms in the United States in Figure 5–4. The aggregate

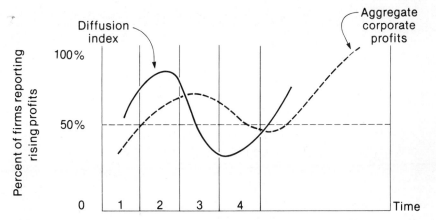

FIGURE 5–4   Diffusion Index of Corporate Profits of 1000 Firms: A Hypothetical Case

corporate profits of the 1000 firms measured by the vertical scale on the right shows fluctuations over a business cycle. The vertical scale on the left measures the diffusion index of corporate profits, that is, the percentage of firms reporting rising profits.

The diffusion index leads the aggregate. It can foretell what the aggregate will likely do in the near future. Of course, in an actual case, the diffusion index curve will not be as smooth as we have shown here. Nonetheless, it should not be difficult to recognize the direction in which the diffusion index is moving in an actual case.

As a tool in the forecasting of short-term business developments, the diffusion index can be either related to a group of NBER indicators or to a given economic process or significant factor, such as corporate profits, average workweek, or new orders for durable goods. The *Business Conditions Digest* regularly publishes a group of diffusion indexes, some of which appear in Figure 5–5. Looking over these diffusion indexes, note that before the economy emerged from the 1981–82 recession most of the diffusion indexes had already been increasing for several months to over a year. Diffusion indexes, therefore, if carefully watched and evaluated, can provide valid clues to the short-term business outlook.

Forecasting with Business and Consumer Surveys

Another source of information used by forecasters consists of surveys of plans made by companies and consumers.[2] Some of the major surveys usually available in a good library are:

[2]See Morris Cohen, "Surveys and Forecasting," in William Butler, Robert Kavesh, and Robert Platt, eds., *Methods and Techniques of Business Forecasting* (Englewood Cliffs, N.J.: Prentice-Hall, 1974), pp. 76–95.

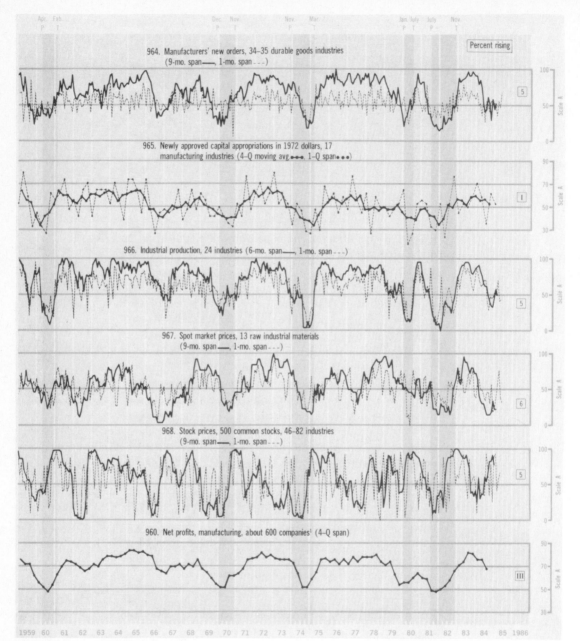

FIGURE 5–5   Diffusion Indexes

Source: U.S. Department of Commerce, *Business Conditions Digest,* June 1985.

1. *Plant and Equipment.* Department of Commerce-SEC and McGraw-Hill surveys of spending plans; Conference Board survey of capital appropriations, McGraw-Hill survey of new order expectations of nonelectrical machinery manufacturers.
2. *Consumer Surveys.* Census Bureau survey of buying plans; Conference Board survey of attitudes and buying plans; University of Michigan Survey Research Center consumer sentiment index.
3. *Sales and Inventories.* Department of Commerce survey of manufacturers' expected sales and inventories.
4. *Home Building. Fortune* survey of homebuilders.

Most business forecasters would readily agree that surveys are valuable. However, plans and intentions, whether by business firms or individuals, are subject to periodic revisions or sudden changes. Business and consumer plans for investments and purchases in the near future can be modified or, occasionally, completely abandoned or reversed. For example, oil companies suddenly and severely cut capital budgets in early 1986 in response to the rapid steep decline in world oil prices. Therefore, to be most useful, surveys must be periodically updated, preferably on a quarterly basis. While up-to-date information on spending plans by business firms and consumers are valuable, forecasters in general rarely make a forecast based solely on information from surveys.

Short-Term Forecasting on the Basis of National Income and Product Accounts

A widely used technique for short-term forecasting today employs the national income and product accounts. There are many advantages to this approach. The Gross National Product (GNP) represents the market value of all final goods and services currently produced by the nation during the year; or, alternately, the sum of expenditures by consumers, government, and business, and the net difference between exports and imports. Detailed figures for each component of the GNP for many years are available. Through regression analysis, valuable historical relationships can be found among the different components and subcomponents of the GNP. Additionally, the current data of each component or subcomponent of the GNP can be used as a starting point in the estimates for the next period. Under this approach, the forecaster can weigh diverse elements and make a final judgment as to the probable size and timing of a particular component of the GNP. Specifically, he will examine:

1. The factors that are currently affecting the type of expenditure under consideration.
2. The historical relationship between the type of expenditure under consideration and other economic series.

3. Probable future developments, such as governmental policies and institutional changes, which will likely affect the item under consideration.

In other words, this approach is flexible enough to allow the incorporation of results from other forecasting methods mentioned and, more importantly, the full exercise of the forecaster's judgment.

There are several steps in this forecasting process.

1. Listing the assumptions under which the economy is expected to operate in the forthcoming period. The assumptions usually relate to war or peace, major strikes, taxes, relationship between the government and the business community, and so forth.
2. Estimating individually the major components of the GNP and then adding them, yielding the forecast of the GNP. The major components are:
    a. Government expenditures on goods and services (excluding transfer payments):
        *   federal nondefense expenditures
        *   federal defense expenditures
        *   state and local government expenditures
    b. Gross private-domestic investment
        *   nonresidential structures
        *   producers' durable equipment
        *   residential structures
        *   changes in business inventories
    c. Personal consumption expenditures
        *   durable goods
        *   nondurable goods
        *   services
    d. Net export of goods and services

3. Estimating independently the GNP on the basis of assumptions relating to:

    *   civilian labor force
    *   length of workweek
    *   unemployment rate
    *   increase of productivity per man-hour
    *   increase in general price level

4. Reconciling the estimates from steps 2 and 3 to arrive at a final estimate of the GNP.

Among the components of the GNP, four areas are the most difficult to forecast. They represent postponable expenditures by business and consumers:

1. Capital spending on plant and equipment
2. Residential construction
3. Changes in business inventories
4. Consumer purchases of durable goods

Capital spending on plant and equipment depends on a variety of factors, including corporate cash flow (retained earnings plus depreciation allowance), rate of capacity utilization in manufacturing, profit margins, and increase in labor cost. It is difficult to find consistent relationships over time between capital spending and other factors, especially in the short term. Analysts, therefore, lean quite heavily on spending anticipations of business from surveys by McGraw-Hill, the Department of Commerce, the Securities and Exchange Commission, and the National Industrial Conference Board.

The forecasting of residential construction is complicated because the residential housing cycle differs significantly from the cycles of the general economy. On the demand side, residential construction depends primarily on the rate of family formation and on levels of disposable income. Availability and cost of credit, together with changes in regulations affecting government financing, on the other hand, dominate the supply side. The figures by F. W. Dodge on contract awards of residential construction and the results from some housing surveys are often referred to for indications.

The forecasting of changes in business inventory is often considered the least successful aspect of short-term business forecasting. Lack of current data on inventories and quick changes in inventory policy by business are cited by some leading business analysts as the most vexing problems in the area. In developing their projections, forecasters would have to examine a number of factors, including the prospective demand in major industries, the extent of price increases expected and their possible influence on inventory policies, the pattern of inventory/sales ratio in the past, and projections by business managers about their own stocks as revealed by surveys.

The fourth area listed above as difficult to forecast is purchases of consumer durable goods. In the past these purchases were found to be quite responsive to the rate of gain of personal income as well as to its absolute level. Automobiles, appliances, and furniture represent 90 percent of the total expenditure on durables. The forecasting of new car sales is by far the most important because of its relative size as well as its volatility.

Unfortunately, economic forecasting at the current stage of development is still no less an art than a science. A good forecaster needs to have a solid theoretical knowledge of business cycles as well as of methods and techniques in statistical analysis. Moreover, he or she should be endowed with the ability to exercise good judgments in making estimates and projections.[3]

Econometric Methods

Econometrics involves the application of mathematical and statistical analysis to the study of the economy. Because of the technical nature of the subject, we will provide only some basic information about how econometrics is used by forecasters.

Econometrics involves the construction of mathematical models that consist of one or more equations that are designed to explain relationships between economic variables. In specifying relationships, the analyst would use economic theory to determine which variables should be included in each equation. Suppose, for example, we want to forecast new car sales. We assume new car sales (S) are primarily a function of GNP, interest rates (i), and the average age of existing automobiles (A). We now write the following equation, which defines a relationship for each period t:

$$S_t = a_0 + a_1 \, GNP_t + a_2 i + a_3 A_t + u_t \tag{5.1}$$

In Equation 5.1 each a is a constant to be calculated, and u_t, called the *disturbance term*, contains all the other factors that affect S_t. The factors underlying u_t are assumed to be of minor importance in affecting S_t. Next, given that there are ample data on all of the variables of Equation 5.1 for a sufficient number of periods, we can estimate the a values with statistical methods such as least square regression analysis. Suppose that something like the following emerges.[4]

$$S = 2.7 + .02 \, GNP - 1.5i + .49A \tag{5.2}$$

To check whether the results are reasonable, we start with the signs of the coefficients. We would expect that sales would increase with higher GNP and a larger stock of older cars. In addition, as interest rates rise, we expect sales to decline due to higher financing costs. If the signs had turned out otherwise, we would have had to reconsider the equation we specified.

There are also a number of statistical measures that must be checked to determine if results are satisfactory. For example, an R^2 value is normally calculated by the computer program used in a study. The R^2 tells us the

[3]For more detailed discussions on how to make up a short-term forecast of the economy, consult the following: E. C. Bratt, *Business Cycles and Forecasting*, 5th ed. (Homewood, Ill.: R. D. Irwin, 1960), Chapters 17 and 18; and William Butler and Robert Kavesh, "Judgemental Forecasting the Gross National Product," *Methods and Techniques of Business Forecasting* (Englewood Cliffs, N.J.: Prentice-Hall, 1974), pp. 207–21.

[4]The size of the coefficients depends on the measures of variables used. For example, coefficients will differ if the GNP is measured in millions rather than billions of dollars.

amount of variation in S that is explained by our model. If $R^2 = .82$, it means we have explained 82 percent of the variation in S using GNP, i, and A.

While we have only looked at a single equation model, multiequation systems are often used, and some may contain well over 100 equations. Such complexity, however, does not imply accuracy. Accurate forecasts of inflation, for example, have been elusive, sometimes no better than uninformed guesses. GNP forecasts over the long run have been respectable, but not perfect. Among the problems that can occur are the following:

1. To use a model in forecasting, one may have to predict some or all of the explanatory variables for future time periods. If they cannot be accurately predicted, the forecast will not be reliable.[5]
2. Some important variables may be missing from the econometric model, which can lead to errors.
3. Relationships may change. The model's coefficients are estimated based on historical data, and what was true in the past may not be true in the future.
4. There are a number of technical mathematical and statistical problems that can invalidate a model.

In short, while econometric models can be useful, one must be cautious in relying upon them.

Monetary Measures as Forecasting Tools

Economists who stress the role of money supply in forecasting GNP are known as *monetarists*. Their analysis makes use of the *Quantity Equation of Exchange*:

$$\text{GNP} = MV = PQ \tag{5.3}$$

where:

M = a measure of money supply
V = income velocity of the money supply measure
P = price level index
Q = index of real GNP

Equation 5.3 is true by definition, for income velocity is defined as GNP/M. P and Q are also defined so that their product will equal GNP.

Under the monetarist view, movements in velocity are relatively stable or predictable, and changes in the money supply represent the main factor

---

[5] To the extent that lagged variables are used, fewer predictions of explanatory variables may be necessary.

influencing GNP. Monetarists recognize that there are lags between changes in monetary policy and changes in the economy. In addition, if monetary growth increases, total spending will be reflected in a mix of rising output and price increases. The lower the rate of unemployment, the greater will be the impact on prices, and the smaller the effect on output.

While the monetarist approach is most concerned with the relationship between money supply and GNP, it has also been used in forecasting stock prices and interest rates. Other variables besides money supply are used as explanatory variables, but the money supply receives particular emphasis.[6]

Futures Markets

One of the easiest and least expensive ways of obtaining financial forecasts is to look up the "Futures Prices" section in the *Wall Street Journal*. Futures markets are discussed in detail in Chapter 16, but a few listings are shown here in Figure 5–6.

Note the right-side settle columns for the Treasury bill and Bank CDs listings. On the date the listing appeared, the market expected that the three-month Treasury bill rates would be 7.38 percent in September 1985, and rise to 9.03 percent by December 1986. Similarly, CD rates were expected to be 8.08 percent in September 1985, and would rise to 9.76 percent by September 1986. Looking at the S&P 500 listings, participants

```
TREASURY BILLS (IMM)-$1 mil.; pts. of 100%
                                   Discount     Open
         Open  High   Low  Settle Chg  Settle Chg Interest
Sept    92.72 92.72 92.59 92.62 −  .07  7.38 +  .07  22,718
Dec     92.38 92.38 92.24 92.25 −  .11  7.75 +  .11  11,185
Mr86    91.98 91.98 91.87 91.88 −  .12  8.12 +  .12   2,552
June    91.61 91.61 91.54 91.55 −  .11  8.45 +  .11   1,073
Sept    91.29 91.30 91.24 91.24 −  .11  8.76 +  .11     420
Dec     91.06 91.06 90.97 90.97 −  .10  9.03 +  .10     206
  Est vol 4,927; vol Thur 6,301; open int 38,212, +208.
    BANK CDs (IMM)-$1 million; pts. of 100%
Sept    91.96 91.98 91.90 91.92 −  .09  8.08 +  .09   2,113
Dec     91.47 91.47 91.44 91.44 −  .11  8.56 +  .11     698
Mr86    .... .... .... 90.99 −  .10  9.01 +  .10     174
June    .... .... .... 90.60 −  .10  9.40 +  .10     154
Sept    .... .... .... 90.24 −  .10  9.76 +  .10     169
  Est vol 355; vol Thur 135; open int 3,395, +2.
   S&P 500 FUTURES INDEX (CME) 500 Times Index
Sept   192.80 192.80 191.75 191.85 − 1.25 198.00 158.10 57,427
Dec    195.35 195.35 194.25 194.45 − 1.20 200.85 175.40  2,547
Mar86  198.00 198.05 197.15 197.35 − 1.15 203.75 188.80    207
  Est vol 34,619; vol Thurs 52,790; open int 60,206, −406.
      S&P 500 STOCK INDEX (Prelim.)
      191.83  192.11 191.27 191.48 −  .63  ....  ....  ....
```

FIGURE 5–6   Futures Listing, *Wall Street Journal,* **August 5, 1985**

Source: Reprinted by permission of *The Wall Street Journal,* © 1985. World rights reserved.

[6] See L. C. Anderson, "A Monetarist Approach to Forecasting," in *Methods and Techniques of Business Forecasting*, ed. W. Butler, R. Kavesh, and R. Platt (Englewood Cliffs, N.J.: Prentice-Hall, 1974), and Michael Keran, "Expectations, Money, and the Stock Market," *Federal Reserve Bank of St. Louis Review*, January 1971.

in futures markets expected that the index would increase from 191.85 in September, 1985, (left-side settle column) to 197.35 in March, 1986.

Comprehensive Approach to Short-Term Economic Forecasting

We have discussed many different techniques that business economists employ to make economic forecasts. These techniques are by no means exclusive of one another. Actually, they complement each other. A well-known business economist and codeveloper of economic indicators, Geoffrey H. Moore, enumerated five principles that some forecasters follow to help them see ahead. These principles are:

1. Consider momentum. Pay close attention to what the rates of change of real GNP were in the last few quarters. Over a short interval, there is usually a close correlation between what has happened and what is to follow next.
2. Cyclical relationships among economic data usually persist.
3. Certain types of economic activities or processes usually anticipate other types (this is the *principle of economic indicators*).
4. Find out what businesspeople or consumers plan to spend or how they view their present situation.
5. In view of the importance of government policy in affecting the economic future, pay close attention to what steps the government has recently taken, what is likely to be done next, and what the effect of government actions will be.

These five principles, in essence, represent an endeavor to combine our knowledge about business cycles with available and ascertainable facts and information about the economy. The synthesis of theory and facts should form a good basis for a forecast.

Sources of Current Short-Term Forecasts

The principal function of our discussion on forecasting is to explain how economists derive their forecasts of the macroeconomy. Although most investors rely on the forecasts of those who specialize in that area, it is helpful to understand the strength and weaknesses of different methods. The investor may find that some forecasting methods produce more useful information than other techniques.

Many organizations, such as government agencies, investment advisory services, financial publications, banks, and some large business firms, make short-term economic forecasts. One good source of these forecasts is the monthly publication *Statistical Bulletin* put out by the Conference Board. It summarizes forecasts by well-known forecasting organizations. A sample of the information provided in the *Statistical Bulletin* is shown in Table 5–2. The data in this table is also available "on-line" through the Conference Board Data Base.

The short-term economic forecasts include quarterly projections of GNP in current dollars, GNP in constant dollars, GNP deflator, and the unemployment rate for a period of nine quarters. Investors who are interested in details of these forecasts can request from the respective organizations a copy of their full report.

CHANGES IN REAL GNP, CORPORATE PROFITS, AND STOCK PRICES

We have seen that stock prices in general are affected by the changes in business conditions, but we have not yet seen the relationships among the changes in real GNP, corporate profits, and stock prices in general. For that purpose, Table 5–3 has been prepared for the period from 1951 to 1984.

From the table we can observe several important findings. Fluctuations in the economy as measured by real GNP are amplified in fluctuations of corporate profits and stock prices. While the smallest decline in real GNP during the period was only 2.1 percent, corporate profits and stock prices fell as much as 16.2 percent and 22.9 percent, respectively. The largest increase in real GNP was 8.3 percent compared to 41.5 percent and 36.0 percent for profits and stock prices.[7]

The effect of economic recessions on profits and stock prices is examined in Table 5–4, which has been constructed with data from Table 5–3. In seven recession years (here specifically defined as years in which there was decline in real GNP) corporate profits were lower in six of those years. In 1975, the exception, the increase in profits took place in the months of that year after the recession had ended. While stock prices dropped during only three of the years, the market generally had already dropped in an anticipation of the recessions. The market generally declines during or preceding recession years (see Figure 5–1).

A similar relationship between corporate profits and stock prices may be observed in Figure 5–1. Sharp drops in stock prices are usually accompanied by significant declines in corporate profits. Likewise, during most periods of strong growth in profits, we tend to see a rising stock market. It should also be noted that other factors, such as interest rates and expectations of continued growth in the economy and in total corporate profits, have a major impact on stock prices. We now focus on the factors that underlie the growth in profits.

---

[7]These findings remain valid even if corporate profits and stock prices are expressed in constant dollars. In fact the declines of profits and stock prices are larger in real terms, but the increases in real terms are smaller than those shown.

TABLE 5-2   A Page from the *Statistical Bulletin:* Economic Forecasts

			U.C.L.A. Business Forecasting[1] Project		Merrill Lynch[1] Economics Inc.		E.I. duPont[1] de Nemours & Co.		Georgia State University[1]	
Date of Forecast			May, 1985		May, 1985		May, 1985		May, 1985	
			Level	*Percent Change*	*Level*	*Percent Change*	*Level*	*Percent Change*	*Level*	*Percent Change*
Gross National Product Billions of Current Dollars										
Actual	1985	I	$3817.1	6.4%	$3817.1	6.4%	$3817.1	6.4%	$3817.1	6.4%
		II	3882.3	7.0	3871.2	5.8	3837.8	2.2	3869.2	5.6
		III	3952.0	7.4	3937.6	7.0	3886.9	5.2	3944.9	8.1
		IV	4024.0	7.5	3997.9	6.3	3971.0	8.9	4012.2	7.0
	1986	I	4091.0	6.8	4069.1	7.3	4046.5	7.8	4085.0	7.5
		II	4160.8	7.0	4147.6	7.9	4129.9	8.5	4150.7	6.6
		III	4245.2	8.4	4229.0	8.1	4214.2	8.4	4187.1	3.6
		IV	4335.8	8.8	4315.0	8.4	4299.3	8.3	4213.5	2.5
	1987	I	4432.9	9.3			4366.5	6.4	4270.2	5.5
		II	4523.3	8.4			4448.2	7.7		
	1985	Annual	3918.9	7.0	3906.0	6.6	3878.2	5.9	3910.9	6.8
	1986	Annual	4208.2	7.4	4190.2	7.3	4172.5	7.6	4159.1	6.3
Gross National Product Billions of Constant (1972) Dollars										
Actual	1985	I	$1665.4	.7%	$1665.4	.7%	$1665.4	.7%	$1665.4	.7%
		II	1682.6	4.2	1675.6	2.5	1665.0	−.1	1674.1	2.1
		III	1699.9	4.2	1688.1	3.0	1679.0	3.4	1692.2	4.4
		IV	1714.6	3.5	1697.3	2.2	1697.0	4.4	1704.7	3.0
	1986	I	1725.8	2.6	1708.3	2.6	1711.0	3.3	1716.6	2.8
		II	1738.6	3.0	1723.4	3.6	1728.0	4.0	1724.7	1.9
		III	1755.6	4.0	1737.6	3.3	1745.0	4.0	1722.1	−.6
		IV	1773.3	4.1	1754.0	3.8	1762.0	4.0	1714.0	−1.9
	1987	I	1791.4	4.1			1775.0	3.0	1713.1	−.2
		II	1808.6	3.9			1790.0	3.4		
	1985	Annual	1690.6	3.1	1681.6	2.6	1676.6	2.3	1684.1	2.7
	1986	Annual	1748.3	3.4	1730.8	2.9	1736.5	3.6	1719.4	2.1
Gross National Product deflator Index, 1972 = 100										
Actual	1985	I	229.2	5.6%	229.2	5.6%	229.2	5.6%	229.2	5.6%
		II	230.7	2.7	231.0	3.2	230.5	2.3	231.1	3.4
		III	232.5	3.1	233.3	3.9	231.5	1.8	233.1	3.5
		IV	234.7	3.8	235.5	4.0	234.0	4.4	235.4	3.9
	1986	I	237.0	4.1	238.2	4.6	236.5	4.3	238.0	4.5
		II	239.3	3.9	240.7	4.2	239.0	4.3	240.7	4.6
		III	241.8	4.2	243.4	4.6	241.5	4.3	243.1	4.2
		IV	244.5	4.5	246.0	4.4	244.0	4.2	245.8	4.5
	1987	I	247.5	4.9			246.0	3.3	249.3	5.7
		II	250.1	4.3			248.5	4.1		
	1985	Annual	231.8	3.7	232.3	4.0	231.3	3.5	232.2	3.9
	1986	Annual	240.7	3.8	242.1	4.2	240.3	3.9	241.9	4.2

(*continued*)

TABLE 5–2,   continued

			U.C.L.A. Business Forecasting[1] Project		Merrill Lynch[1] Economics Inc.		E.I. duPont[1] de Nemours & Co.		Georgia State University[1]	
Date of Forecast			*May, 1985*		*May, 1985*		*May, 1985*		*May, 1985*	
			Level	*Percent Change*	*Level*	*Percent Change*	*Level*	*Percent Change*	*Level*	*Percent Change*
Unemployment Rate										
Actual	1985	I		7.3%		7.3%		7.3%		7.3%
		II		7.3		7.3		7.2		7.3
		III		7.2		7.4		7.1		7.1
		IV		7.2		7.5		6.9		7.1
	1986	I		7.2		7.5		6.9		7.0
		II		7.3		7.4		6.7		7.1
		III		7.2		7.2		6.8		7.3
		IV		7.2		7.1		6.9		7.5
	1987	I		7.1				6.9		7.8
		II		6.9				6.9		
	1985	Annual		7.3		7.4		7.1		7.2
	1986	Annual		7.2		7.3		6.8		7.2

			The Conference Board[1]		Chase Econometric[1] Associates, Inc.		Data Resources Inc.[1]		Wharton E.F.A. Inc.[1]	
Date of Forecast			*May, 1985*		*May, 1985*		*May, 1985*		*May, 1985*	
			Level	*Percent Change*	*Level*	*Percent Change*	*Level*	*Percent Change*	*Level*	*Percent Change*
Gross National Product **Billions of Current Dollars**										
Actual	1985	I	$3817.1	6.4%	$3817.1	6.4%	$3817.1	6.4%	$3817.1	6.4%
		II	3878.0	6.5	3880.5	6.8	3873.0	6.0	3874.4	6.1
		III	3929.0	3.4	3957.8	8.2	3929.7	6.0	3945.2	7.5
		IV	3964.0	3.6	4020.3	6.5	3985.1	5.8	4015.9	7.4
	1986	I	4029.0	6.7	4068.9	4.9	4038.3	5.4	4087.4	7.3
		II	4112.0	8.5	4124.6	5.6	4096.2	5.9	4153.4	6.6
		III	4203.0	9.2	4212.7	8.8	4172.5	7.7	4224.6	7.0
		IV	4282.0	7.7	4305.6	9.1	4257.1	8.4	4302.8	7.6
	1987	I			4403.6	9.4	4351.3	9.1	4393.8	8.7
		II			4494.0	8.5	4438.5	8.3	4485.4	8.6
	1985	Annual	3897.0	6.4	3918.9	7.0	3901.2	6.5	3913.2	6.8
	1986	Annual	4156.5	6.7	4178.0	6.6	4141.0	6.1	4192.1	7.1
Gross National Product **Billions of Constant (1972) Dollars**										
Actual	1985	I	$1665.4	.7%	$1665.4	.7%	$1665.4	.7%	$1665.4	.7%
		II	1676.2	2.6	1675.5	2.4	1678.8	3.3	1673.8	2.0
		III	1688.1	2.9	1691.4	3.9	1691.7	3.1	1687.9	3.4
		IV	1688.1	0.0	1702.5	2.7	1700.8	2.2	1700.6	3.0

TABLE 5–2,   continued

Date of Forecast			The Conference Board[1]		Chase Econometric[1] Associates, Inc.		Data Resources Inc.[1]		Wharton E.F.A. Inc.[1]	
			May, 1985		May, 1985		May, 1985		May, 1985	
			Level	Percent Change	Level	Percent Change	Level	Percent Change	Level	Percent Change
	1986	I	1698.2	2.4	1705.4	.7	1707.6	1.6	1710.6	2.4
		II	1713.3	3.6	1712.0	1.6	1716.9	2.2	1719.6	2.1
		III	1732.4	4.5	1729.8	4.2	1732.3	3.6	1730.4	2.5
		IV	1746.0	3.2	1748.3	4.3	1749.3	4.0	1743.7	3.1
	1987	I			1765.2	3.9	1767.0	4.1	1758.2	3.4
		II			1780.6	3.5	1782.9	3.6	1773.6	3.5
	1985	Annual	1679.5	2.4	1683.7	2.7	1684.2	2.7	1681.9	2.6
	1986	Annual	1722.5	2.6	1723.9	2.4	1726.5	2.5	1726.1	2.6

Gross National Product deflator
Index, 1972 = 100

			Level	Percent Change	Level	Percent Change	Level	Percent Change	Level	Percent Change
Actual	1985	I	$ 229.2	5.6%	229.2	5.6%	229.2	5.6%	229.2	5.6%
		II	231.4	3.8	231.6	4.3	230.7	2.6	231.5	4.0
		III	232.7	2.4	234.0	4.2	232.2	2.8	233.7	4.0
		IV	234.8	3.6	236.1	3.7	234.3	3.5	236.1	4.2
	1986	I	237.3	4.2	238.6	4.2	236.5	3.8	238.9	4.8
		II	240.0	4.7	240.9	4.0	238.6	3.6	241.5	4.4
		III	242.6	4.4	243.5	4.4	240.9	3.9	244.1	4.4
		IV	245.2	4.4	246.3	4.6	243.4	4.2	246.8	4.4
	1987	I			249.5	5.3	246.3	4.8	249.9	5.2
		II			252.4	4.8	248.9	4.4	252.9	4.9
	1985	Annual	232.0	3.9	232.7	4.2	231.6	3.7	232.6	4.1
	1986	Annual	241.3	4.0	242.3	4.1	239.8	3.5	242.8	4.4

Unemployment Rate

			Level	Percent Change	Level	Percent Change	Level	Percent Change	Level	Percent Change
Actual	1985	I		7.3%		7.3%		7.3%		7.3%
		II		7.3		7.2		7.4		7.4
		III		7.4		7.2		7.4		7.5
		IV		7.7		7.3		7.5		7.6
	1986	I		7.7		7.5		7.6		7.6
		II		7.7		7.7		7.7		7.6
		III		7.5		7.6		7.7		7.5
		IV		7.3		7.5		7.7		7.5
	1987	I				7.3		7.6		7.4
		II				7.1		7.5		7.3
Annual	1985			7.4		7.3		7.4		7.5
Annual	1986			7.6		7.6		7.7		7.5

Notes: Percentage changes represent compound annual rates of change from preceding period. Quarterly data are seasonally adjusted.

[1]Based on revised first quarter data.

Source: Conference Board. *Statistical Bulletin,* June 1985.

TABLE 5–3 Changes in Real GNP, Corporate Profits, and Stock Prices, 1951–1984

	GNP in 1972 Dollars (in billions)	Corporate[b] Profits (in billions)	S&P 500 Composite Index	Percent Change from Previous Year		
				GNP in 1972 Dollars	Corporate Profits	S&P 500 Composite Index
1951	579.4	38.7	22.34	8.3	14.2	21.4
52	600.8	36.1	24.50	3.7	−6.7	9.7
53	623.6	36.3	24.73	3.8	0.6	0.9
54R[a]	616.1	35.2	29.69	−1.2	−3.0	20.0
55	657.5	45.5	40.49	6.7	29.3	36.0
56	671.6	43.7	46.62	2.1	−4.0	15.1
57	683.8	43.3	44.38	1.8	−0.9	−4.8
58R	680.9	38.5	46.24	−0.4	−11.1	4.2
59	721.7	49.6	57.38	6.0	28.8	24.1
60	737.2	47.6	55.85	2.2	−4.0	−2.7
61	756.6	48.6	66.27	2.6	2.1	18.7
62	800.3	56.6	62.38	3.8	16.5	−5.9
63	832.5	62.1	69.87	4.0	9.7	12.0
64	876.4	69.2	81.37	5.3	11.4	16.5
65	929.3	80.0	88.17	6.0	15.6	8.4
66	984.8	85.1	85.26	6.0	6.4	−3.3
67	1011.4	82.4	91.93	2.7	−3.2	7.8
68	1058.1	89.1	98.70	4.6	8.1	7.4
69	1087.6	85.1	97.84	2.8	−4.5	−0.9
70R	1085.6	71.4	83.22	−0.2	−16.1	−14.9
71	1122.4	83.2	98.29	3.4	16.5	18.0
72	1185.9	96.2	109.20	5.7	16.1	11.1
73	1254.3	108.3	107.43	5.8	12.1	−1.6
74R	1246.3	94.9	82.85	−0.6	−12.4	−22.9
75R	1231.6	110.5	86.16	−1.2	16.4	4.0
76	1298.2	138.1	102.01	5.4	25.0	18.4
77	1369.7	167.3	98.20	5.5	21.1	−3.7
78	1438.6	192.4	96.02	5.0	15.0	−2.2
79	1479.4	194.8	103.01	2.8	1.2	7.3
80R	1475.0	175.4	118.78	−0.3	−10.0	15.3
81	1512.2	189.9	128.05	2.5	8.3	7.3
82R	1480.0	159.1	119.71	−2.1	−16.2	−6.5
83	1534.7	225.2	160.41	3.7	41.5	34.0
84	1639.0	284.5	160.46	6.8	26.4	0
Largest increase in a year				8.3	41.5	36.0
Largest decline in a year				−2.1	−16.2	−22.9

[a]R stands for recession year when real GNP was lower than in previous year.
[b]Corporate profits series includes inventory valuation and capital consumption and adjustments.
Source: Data from *Economic Report of the President,* February 1985.

TABLE 5–4   Changes in GNP, Corporate Profits, and Stock Prices during Recession Years, 1954–1982

	Percent Change from Previous Year		
Recession Years	GNP in Constant Dollar	Corporate Profits	S&P 500 Composite Index
1954	−1.2	− 3.0	20.0
1958	−0.4	−11.1	4.2
1970	−0.2	−16.1	−14.9
1974	−0.6	−12.4	−22.9
1975	−1.2	16.4	4.0
1980	−0.3	−10.0	15.3
1982	−2.1	−14.3	− 6.5

Determinants of Changes in Corporate Profits

The extent of changes in corporate profits is, of course, affected by the extent of changes in real GNP. However, the changes in real GNP are not the sole determinant of changes in corporate profits, as shown in Table 5–5.

The other determinant of corporate profits is profit margin. *Profit margin* can be defined as the ratio between corporate profits after tax and corporate sales, or simply the percentage of each sales dollar that becomes net profit.

The profit margin of manufacturing corporations is determined by three factors:

TABLE 5–5   Changes in Real GNP and Corporate Profits, for Selected Years, 1952–1984

Year	Percent Change in Real GNP	Percent Change in Corporate Profits
1952	3.7	−6.7
53	3.8	0.6
56	2.1	−4.0
60	2.2	−4.0
67	2.7	−3.2
69	2.8	−4.5
71	3.4	16.5
75	−1.2	16.4
83	3.7	41.5
84	6.8	26.4

1. The price at which manufactured goods can be sold.
2. Labor costs per unit of product, which in turn are determined by two factors:
   - Compensation per hour
   - Output per hour
3. The rate at which plant capacity is being utilized.

Out of these three factors affecting profit margin, the first two are more important under normal business conditions, whereas the third factor usually plays a dominant role in times of recession.

Assuming capacity utilization rates remain unchanged, if prices of manufactured goods and compensation of labor stay the same, while labor productivity (output per hour) increases, the result is increased profit margin. On the other hand, if compensation of labor increases faster than the increase in labor productivity, unit labor costs will increase. If the unit labor cost increases faster than the selling price of manufactured goods, the profit margin will suffer and decline, assuming the capacity utilization rates remain unchanged.

Figure 5–7, prepared by the Conference Board, shows profit margin and its determinants for nonfinancial corporations during the period from 1979 through the first quarter of 1985. From mid 1983 to mid 1984, profits went up 26.4 percent when real GNP increased only 6.8 percent (Table 5–3). The growth in profits was much higher than GNP growth because of an increase in profit margin. Price per unit grew more rapidly than unit labor costs during the period, and margins rose. However, between mid 1984 and the first quarter of 1985, margins leveled off, suggesting that there would be a much lower growth in profits between 1984 and 1985.

In summary, because stock prices are related to the change and level of corporate profits, security analysts and investors are interested in profit projections. Underlying such projections are estimates of real GNP growth and profit margin. Up-to-date reading of current statistics relating to these factors should prove helpful in assessing the future trend in stock prices.

SUMMARY

Both fixed-income securities and common stocks are affected by economic factors. One element of the economic environment, interest rates, has a direct impact on bond prices and strongly influences stock prices. Other economic factors, such as expectations of sales and profits, play a major role in the stock market and also affect the risk in holding corporate bonds.

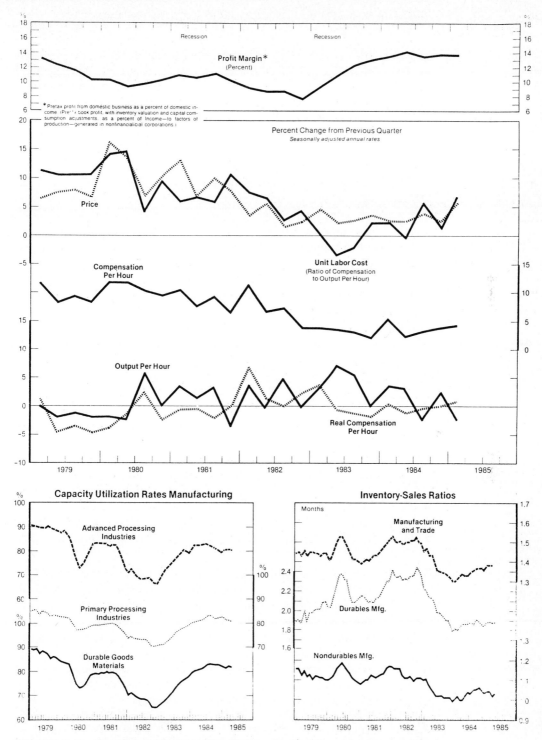

FIGURE 5–7   Key Determinants of Profit Margin, Nonfinancial Corporations

Source: Conference Board, *Statistical Bulletin,* June 1985.

Generally, the stock market starts to fall prior to the beginning of a recession and hits bottom prior to the end of the recession. This occurs because stock prices move in anticipation of future profits, and the market generally anticipates a recession or an economic expansion prior to its occurrence.

Economists use a variety of concepts and techniques in attempting to forecast business. Six frequently used approaches are

1. Economic indicators and diffusion indexes
2. Business and consumer surveys
3. National income and product accounts
4. Econometric models
5. Monetary measures
6. Futures markets

Given the stock market's sensitivity to expected profits, special attention is given to estimating future profits. Among the important variables that determine profitability are product prices, unit sales, labor cost per unit of product, and the rate at which capacity is being utilized.

QUESTIONS AND PROBLEMS

1. What kinds of investment policies protect against cyclical risks?
2. Obtain a forecast of GNP and national income prepared by a well-known public or private agency for the current year or next year. List their assumptions and evaluate their estimates of different components of GNP. Do you agree with their forecast? Why or why not?
3. What is your view of the current state of general business on the basis of the latest information published on leading economic indicators?
4. Gather some information on several diffusion indexes of key factors from the latest issue of *Business Conditions Digest*. Evaluate them and express your opinion of the current state of general business and its possible trend.
5. Using information from *Survey of Current Business, Federal Reserve Bulletin, Business Conditions Digest*, and similar publications, identify the present position of general business in the stages of the business cycle. Will business activity likely move up or down in the next six to twelve months?
6. What is your forecast of stock prices in the next twelve months? Why?
7. "Corporate earnings always follow the direction of sales. As sales

increase, corporate profits increase and vice versa." Do you agree with this statement? Why or why not?

8. What is the outlook for corporate profits in the current year or next twelve months? Why? Substantiate your arguments with tables of latest information or relevant factors.

9. What factors determine the future level and direction of corporate profits? Discuss these factors.

10. Name five leading indicators of general business. Explain why such economic series tend to lead the downturn and upturn of general business.

11. The leading indicators are widely followed. As soon as newspapers and radios report that the composite index of leading indicators is down, many people immediately come to the conclusion that recession is just around the corner. What dangers can you see for an investor who is formulating a judgment about future business conditions in this way?

12. If you are following the leading indicators approach to general business forecasting, how should you logically go about examining and evaluating the leading indicators so that you will more likely make a correct judgment about the outlook for general business?

REFERENCES

Bratt, E. C. *Business Cycles and Forecasting*, 5th ed. Homewood, Ill.: R. D. Irwin, 1961.

Brealy, R. A. *An Introduction to Risk and Return from Common Stocks*. Cambridge, Mass.: MIT Press, 1969.

Butler, William, Kavesh, Robert, and Platt, Robert, eds. *Methods and Techniques of Business Forecasting*. Englewood Cliffs, N.J.: Prentice-Hall, 1974.

Chambers, E. J., Scott, R. H., and Smith, R. S. *National Income Analysis and Forecasting*. Glenview, Ill.: Scott, Foresman, 1975.

Cohen, J., Zinbarg, E., and Zeikel, A. *Investment Analysis and Management*. Homewood, Ill.: R. D. Irwin, 1982.

Ehrbar, A. F. "Unraveling the Mysteries of Corporate Profits." *Fortune*, Aug. 27, 1979.

Financial Analysts Research Foundation. *The Economic Framework for Investors*, 1975.

Hafer, R. W. "Money, Debt and Economic Activity." *Review*, Federal Reserve Bank of St. Louis, June/July 1984.

Keran, Michael W. "Expectations, Money, and the Stock Market." *Review*, Federal Reserve Bank of St. Louis, January 1971.

Larsen, Robert A. "New Insight into Changes in Earnings Per Share." *Financial Analysts Journal*, March–April 1975.

Moore, Geoffrey. *Business Cycles, Inflation, and Forecasting*. Cambridge, Mass.: National Bureau of Economic Research, 1980.

Moore, Geoffrey H. and Shiskin, Julius. *Indicators of Business Expansions and Contractions*. Cambridge, Mass.: National Bureau of Economic Research, 1967.

Umstead, David A. "Forecasting Stock Market Prices." *The Journal of Finance*, 32, May 1977, pp.

U.S. Department of Commerce. *Handbook of Cyclical Indicators: A Supplement to the Business Conditions Digest*. Washington, D.C.: U.S. Government Printing Office, 1984.

Wolfe, Harry D. *Business Forecasting Methods*. New York: Holt, Rinehart and Winston, 1966.

6

Interest Rate Forecasting and Analysis

IMPORTANCE OF INTEREST RATE FORECASTS

Interest is the price paid to borrow funds for a period of time; the *interest rate* is typically expressed as a percent of principal for one year. In this chapter we extend our discussion of forecasting by looking closely at interest rate forecasting. Investors and security analysts carefully study forecasts of future interest rates for a number of reasons. First, as we have already noted, the prices of outstanding bonds vary inversely with interest rates. Second, changes in interest rates affect stock market behavior. When rates rise, bonds which provide those higher rates initially become more attractive compared to stocks, and stock prices usually respond by declining in order to eliminate the advantage to the bonds. The opposite behavior usually occurs when rates fall.

In their impact on general business conditions and profits, interest rates also affect stock prices. High interest rates increase the interest expense of companies, which tends to lower net profit margins. In addition, when rates are high, or if they are rising rapidly, the likelihood increases that an economic recession will occur. If the market anticipates a recession in response to upward movements in interest rates, stock prices will tend to decline. Finally, interest rates can be of particular importance to investments in specific sectors. The construction industry and many real estate investments are especially sensitive to changes in rates.

STRUCTURE OF INTEREST RATES

At any given time there is not a single interest rate but a host of interest rates. Differences in rates arise from differences in a variety of factors: degree of risk of default, duration of loan, marketability, repayment terms, tax treatment, and servicing costs.[1]

[1]The term basis point is often used in interest rate analysis. It represents $\frac{1}{100}$ of 1 percentage point. If the interest rate increases from 9.25 percent to 9.45 percent, the rate has risen by 20 basis points.

In Table 6–1 we list interest rates from 1929 to 1984 on U.S. government short-term and long-term securities, corporate bonds, municipal bonds, short-term bank loans, commercial paper, borrowings from Federal Reserve Banks, federal funds, and home mortgages. Economists often speak of "the" interest rate or the "basic" interest rate. When these terms are used, they are usually referring to the yields on taxable federal government secu-

TABLE 6–1   Bond Yields and Interest Rates, 1929–84 (percent per annum)

Year and month	U.S. Treasury securities				Corporate bonds (Moody's)		High-grade munici-pal bonds (Standard & Poor's)	New-home mortgage yields (FHLBB)[4]	Com-mercial paper, 6 months[5]	Prime rate charged by banks[6]	Discount rate, Federal Reserve Bank of New York[6]	Federal funds rate[7]
	Bills (new issues)[1]		Constant maturities[2]		Aaa[3]	Baa						
	3-month	6-month	3 years	10 years								
1929					4.73	5.90	4.27		5.85	5.50–6.00	5.16	
1933	0.515				4.49	7.76	4.71		1.73	1.50–4.00	2.56	
1939	.023				3.01	4.96	2.76		.59	1.50	1.00	
1940	.014				2.84	4.75	2.50		.56	1.50	1.00	
1941	.103				2.77	4.33	2.10		.53	1.50	1.00	
1942	.326				2.83	4.28	2.36		.66	1.50	*1.00	
1943	.373				2.73	3.91	2.06		.69	1.50	*1.00	
1944	.375				2.72	3.61	1.86		.73	1.50	*1.00	
1945	.375				2.62	3.29	1.67		.75	1.50	*1.00	
1946	.375				2.53	3.05	1.64		.81	1.50	*1.00	
1947	.594				2.61	3.24	2.01		1.03	1.50–1.75	1.00	
1948	1.040				2.82	3.47	2.40		1.44	1.75–2.00	1.34	
1949	1.102				2.66	3.42	2.21		1.49	2.00	1.50	
1950	1.218				2.62	3.24	1.98		1.45	2.07	1.59	
1951	1.552				2.86	3.41	2.00		2.16	2.56	1.75	
1952	1.766				2.96	3.52	2.19		2.33	3.00	1.75	
1953	1.931		2.47	2.85	3.20	3.74	2.72		2.52	3.17	1.99	
1954	.953		1.63	2.40	2.90	3.51	2.37		1.58	3.05	1.60	
1955	1.753		2.47	2.82	3.06	3.53	2.53		2.18	3.16	1.89	1.78
1956	2.658		3.19	3.18	3.36	3.88	2.93		3.31	3.77	2.77	2.73
1957	3.267		3.98	3.65	3.89	4.71	3.60		3.81	4.20	3.12	3.11
1958	1.839		2.84	3.32	3.79	4.73	3.56		2.46	3.83	2.15	1.57
1959	3.405	3.832	4.46	4.33	4.38	5.05	3.95		3.97	4.48	3.36	3.30
1960	2.928	3.247	3.98	4.12	4.41	5.19	3.73		3.85	4.82	3.53	3.22
1961	2.378	2.605	3.54	3.88	4.35	5.08	3.46		2.97	4.50	3.00	1.96
1962	2.778	2.908	3.47	3.95	4.33	5.02	3.18		3.26	4.50	3.00	2.68
1963	3.157	3.253	3.67	4.00	4.26	4.86	3.23	5.89	3.55	4.50	3.23	3.18
1964	3.549	3.686	4.03	4.19	4.40	4.83	3.22	5.82	3.97	4.50	3.55	3.50
1965	3.954	4.055	4.22	4.28	4.49	4.87	3.27	5.81	4.38	4.54	4.04	4.07
1966	4.881	5.082	5.23	4.92	5.13	5.67	3.82	6.25	5.55	5.63	4.50	5.11
1967	4.321	4.630	5.03	5.07	5.51	6.23	3.98	6.46	5.10	5.61	4.19	4.22
1968	5.339	5.470	5.68	5.65	6.18	6.94	4.51	6.97	5.90	6.30	5.16	5.66
1969	6.677	6.853	7.02	6.67	7.03	7.81	5.81	7.80	7.83	7.96	5.87	8.20
1970	6.458	6.562	7.29	7.35	8.04	9.11	6.51	8.45	7.71	7.91	5.95	7.18
1971	4.348	4.511	5.65	6.16	7.39	8.56	5.70	7.74	5.11	5.72	4.88	4.66
1972	4.071	4.466	5.72	6.21	7.21	8.16	5.27	7.60	4.73	5.25	4.50	4.43
1973	7.041	7.178	6.95	6.84	7.44	8.24	5.18	7.96	8.15	8.03	6.44	8.73
1974	7.886	7.926	7.82	7.56	8.57	9.50	6.09	8.92	9.84	10.81	7.83	10.50
1975	5.838	6.122	7.49	7.99	8.83	10.61	6.89	9.00	6.32	7.86	6.25	5.82
1976	4.989	5.266	6.77	7.61	8.43	9.75	6.49	9.00	5.34	6.84	5.50	5.04
1977	5.265	5.510	6.69	7.42	8.02	8.97	5.56	9.02	5.61	6.83	5.46	5.54
1978	7.221	7.572	8.29	8.41	8.73	9.49	5.90	9.56	7.99	9.06	7.46	7.93
1979	10.041	10.017	9.71	9.44	9.63	10.69	6.39	10.78	10.91	12.67	10.28	11.19
1980	11.506	11.374	11.55	11.46	11.94	13.67	8.51	12.66	12.29	15.27	11.77	13.36
1981	14.029	13.776	14.44	13.91	14.17	16.04	11.23	14.70	14.76	18.87	13.42	16.38
1982	10.686	11.084	12.92	13.00	13.79	16.11	11.57	15.14	11.89	14.86	11.02	12.26
1983	8.63	8.75	10.45	11.10	12.04	13.55	9.47	12.57	8.89	10.79	8.50	9.09
1984	9.58	9.80	11.89	12.44	12.71	14.19	10.15	12.38	10.16	12.04	8.80	10.22

Source: Economic Report of the President, 1985.

rities for which there is no risk of default. Specifically, the basic interest rate often refers to the yield on ninety-day Treasury bills for the short term and the yield on Treasury bonds for the long term.

Recent Pattern of Interest Rate Movements

See Figure 6–1 for how several different interest rate series have moved from 1959 to 1985. Note that rates were rising during most of the period from 1959 to 1981, but from 1981 to 1985 there was a major drop in rates. Much of this pattern can be explained by the relationship between inflation and interest rates (which will be discussed below). At this point we will examine the strong impact that the business cycle exerts on interest rates, which is seen in Figure 6–1 in the fluctuation of rates as the economy expands and contracts.

During periods of economic expansion, interest rates tend to rise for several reasons. First, there is an increase in loan demand caused by higher levels of spending by both consumers and businesses. Second, inflationary forces tend to become stronger as the economy continues to strengthen, and this adds upward pressure on rates. Finally, during the final stage of an expansion, policymakers in the Federal Reserve System generally become quite concerned about higher rates of inflation, and measures are taken to tighten credit. Their intent is to reduce spending growth and, in turn, dampen the rate of inflation. In the process of tightening credit, the Federal Reserve tends to cause interest rates to reach their peaks, but eventually spending growth does slow down, and interest rates also start to drop. During these periods, total spending in current dollars is usually still rising, but when measured in constant dollars, one frequently finds that real GNP is declining. If this situation persists for a few quarters, the economy is in a state of recession.

Interest rates drop during recessions because of lower borrowing and spending and also because the rate of inflation tends to drop. In addition, at some point in a recession the Federal Reserve usually takes steps to reverse the sluggishness of business conditions and the high level of unemployment. Eventually, an expansionary monetary policy is pursued that further pushes interest rates down. Soon the economy hits bottom, and a new business and interest rate cycle may begin.

THE FEDERAL RESERVE AND INTEREST RATES

The Federal Reserve System (Fed) is the central bank of the United States and is responsible for implementing monetary policy. In pursuing its policies, the Fed aims to promote a sustainable rate of economic growth, preventing high rates of unemployment and high rates of inflation. The Fed is also concerned about conditions in foreign exchange markets, and it assists

128

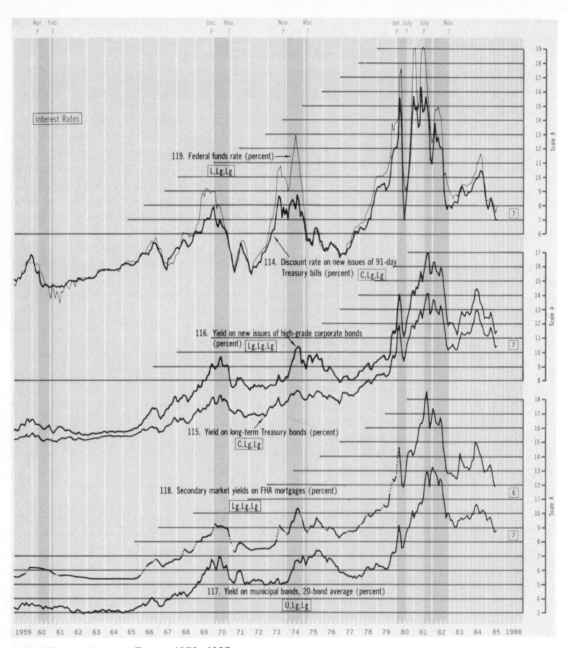

FIGURE 6-1 Interest Rates, 1959-1985

Source: U.S. Department of Commerce, *Business Conditions Digest,* July 1985.

the Treasury in obtaining borrowed funds for the federal government. Very often the Fed cannot achieve all of its objectives. For example, if the rate of inflation is high, the Fed may take actions to reduce the severity of the inflation but in doing so it may cause a recession and high unemployment.

In pursuing its policies, the Fed considers growth in several measures of money supply and the level of interest rates. It sets targets for the annual growth rates of M_1, M_2, and M_3. Of the three, M_1 is the most closely watched monetary measure. Its principal components are currency and deposits in checking accounts. M_2 primarily consists of M_1, plus savings accounts, plus deposits in money market accounts and money market mutual funds. M_3 is mainly M_2, plus negotiable certificates of deposits, plus some Eurodollar deposits.[2]

The details of how the Fed controls the money supply are discussed in virtually any introductory economics textbook. Here we will only provide a very brief overview. The principal tool of the Fed is the use of open market operations, which involves purchases and sales of government securities. The Federal Reserve holds a large quantity of Treasury securities, and if the money supply is growing too rapidly, the Fed sells some of those securities. These sales have several immediate effects. As the supply of securities on the market increases, their prices drop, and interest rates increase. In addition, when payment is made for the purchase of those securities, funds or reserves are transferred out of the banking system and into the Fed. As a result, banks have less money to lend, and this creates further upward pressure on rates. Federal Reserve purchases of securities have the opposite effects. Prices of securities rise, and rates drop. Payment for those securities increases bank reserves, and with more loanable funds available, lending rates tend to drop further.

Those who analyze and forecast the course of interest rates watch movements in the money supply. If M_1 grows beyond the Federal Reserve's target, the market may fear that a tight monetary policy will be implemented to push M_1 back into the bounds set by the Fed. Such anticipations tend to push up interest rates. Similarly, if M_1 falls below the Fed's target, the market may anticipate an easier monetary policy. This can cause interest rates to drop. In fact, on days when the Fed announces the latest M_1 statistics, interest rates usually adjust upward if M_1 unexpectedly increases. An unexpected decline in M_1 tends to cause a downward adjustment in rates.

One of the interest rates that analysts monitor is called the *federal funds rate* (see Table 6–1), the interest rate one bank charges another for an overnight loan of some of its reserves. While the Fed does not set this rate, its open market operations strongly influence movements in the rate. In implementing its policy, the Fed may attempt to keep the federal funds rate within certain bounds. If the rate rises or falls beyond certain limits, the

---

[2]For a more comprehensive discussion of M_1, M_2, and M_3, see an introductory economics text or the *Federal Reserve Bulletin*.

market may anticipate a change in policy. A second interest rate often cited in the business news is the *Federal Reserve discount rate*, the rate the Fed charges when it lends to member banks. Sometimes, though not always, changes in the discount rate are a signal that the Fed is moving policy in a particular direction. A decline might signal future easing, and an increase may mean future tightening.

Long-Term Effects of Monetary Policy

In describing how changes in monetary policy affect interest rates, we essentially focused on the initial effects of the policy. The initial effect of an easy monetary policy is to cause a drop in rates. However, if this expansionary policy continues, business activity will occur at a later point at higher levels. As spending and loan demand increase, interest rates will eventually begin rising. The higher level of spending may also increase the rate of inflation, and interest rates will rise still further. The opposite sequence of events would occur under a tight monetary policy.

The initial effect of monetary policy, the drop in rates, is sometimes called the *liquidity effect*. It lasts about six months until rates bottom out and begin to increase because of stronger business activity. After approximately twelve additional months (a total of eighteen months after initiation of the policy), the economy's growth causes interest rates to return to the level they held when the policy began. This upward movement caused by income growth is sometimes called the *income effect*. If, due to inflation, interest rates rise still further, we have a third stage that may be called the *price expectations effect*. Note, however, that the time spans cited above are subject to considerable variation, and in the mid 1980s the time spans appeared to be much longer. Nevertheless, in making an interest rate forecast, analysts take into account that monetary policy has immediate as well as longer-term implications.[3]

INFLATION AND INTEREST RATES

As stated above, continuous, higher rates of growth in money supply will generate a higher rate of inflation, and this in turn will cause higher market interest rates. The relationship between the expected rate of inflation and interest rates was described in 1930 by the economist Irving Fisher.[4] According to the Fisher equation,

$$i_m = i_r + P_e \tag{6.1}$$

[3]For an in-depth discussion of this topic, see Milton Friedman, "Factors Affecting the Level of Interest Rates," in *Money Supply, Money Demand, and Macroeconomic Models*, J. Boorman and T. Havrilesky, eds., (Boston: Allyn and Bacon, 1972).

[4]Irving Fisher, *The Theory of Interest* (New York: Macmillan, 1930).

where:

$$i_m = \text{the market interest rate}$$
$$i_r = \text{the real interest rate}$$
$$P_e = \text{the expected rate of inflation}$$

It is easiest to view the real interest rate as the rate of return investors would receive in an economy with neither expected nor actual inflation. The real rate of return would be a function of "real" economic forces, such as the productivity of the nation's capital stock and the real rate of return investors require in order to willingly lend funds to build plant and equipment. It is usually assumed that higher or lower expected rates of inflation will not affect the real productivity of capital nor the required real return of investors. Under these conditions, when expected inflation increases or decreases, there will be a corresponding change in market interest rates.

One of the principal factors underlying the expected rate of inflation is the actual rate of price increases. From 1959 to 1979, inflation (measured by the Consumer Price Index) increased from 1.5 percent to 13.3 percent. As we can see in Figure 6–1, interest rates rose substantially during that period. With the drop in inflation from 13.3 percent to 4 percent between 1979 and 1984, there was a significant decline in rates.

The Fisher equation may also be analyzed from a somewhat different point of view. If, instead of using the expected rate of inflation, we insert the actual rate of price increases (p), we obtain

$$i_m = i_r + p \tag{6.2}$$

Assume an investor wants a certain real rate of return, and the rate of inflation at the time is p. In this context, i_m represents the market interest rate required to achieve that objective. If an investor wants a real yield of 4 percent, and inflation occurs at a 10 percent rate, a market return of approximately 14 percent is necessary.[5]

METHODS OF FORECASTING INTEREST RATES

The forecasting methods discussed in Chapter 5 are applicable also to making interest rate forecasts. In the analysis below, we discuss in detail two often-used frameworks of analysis that are related to our discussion in Chapter 5.

---

[5] Equation 6.2 is not an exact relationship between inflation and required returns. To be precise, $1 + i_m = (1 + i_r)(1 + p)$ or

$$i_m = i_r + p + i_r p \tag{6.3}$$

As the rate of inflation increases $i_r p$ will become larger, and the discrepancy between Equations 6.2 and 6.3 will grow. If Equation 6.3 is used for the case described above, $i_m = 14.4$ percent.

One approach focuses on the factors underlying supply and demand for loanable funds. The second approach, which is applied in various ways, uses economic indicators that signal future interest rate movements.

Forecast of Interest Rates by Supply and Demand Analysis

Forecasters who use this method usually proceed according to the following steps:

1. Enumerate some basic assumptions under which the economy is expected to function in the coming period. The assumptions usually relate to peace or war, tax structure, strikes, and monetary policy.
2. Provide an economic projection for the economy in the form of GNP and its components.
3. On the basis of economic projections:
   a. Estimate demand for funds from business, federal government, state and local governments, home financing, consumer credit, and foreigners.
   b. Estimate supply of funds from savings, commercial bank credit, business corporations, government agencies, and foreigners.
   c. Calculate the difference between total estimated supply of funds and demand for funds.

Note in Figure 6–2 that if estimated supply exceeds estimated demand, the forecaster would project a drop in rates toward i_e. If estimated demand exceeds estimated supply, then a rise in interest rates from i_2 toward i_e would be forecasted. Only at rate i_e is there neither excess supply nor excess demand for funds. In order to estimate i_e the analyst would proceed to step 4.

4. a. Interpret the implications on interest rates of the total picture of financial demands and resources.

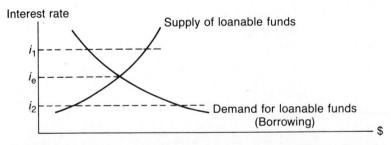

FIGURE 6–2 Supply and Demand for Loanable Funds as a Function of Interest Rates

b. Reassess the probable course of Federal Reserve policy in light of the above estimates and make a final judgment about possible movements and levels of interest rates.

In the financial community, Salomon Brothers, an investment banking firm, prepares a forecast of credit and capital markets for the coming year. Their forecasts include two sections. The first reviews developments in the credit markets of the previous year and sets forth their views of the current year. The second section contains many tables of statistics, including estimates on the uses and sources of funds for the economy and its various sectors. Let us discuss briefly the forecast of Salomon Brothers for 1985.

Salomon Brothers estimated that the total funds demanded for 1985 would be $796.7 billion, which was broken down as follows:

Privately held mortgages	$136.4 billion
Corporate and foreign bonds	45.3
Short-term business borrowing	153.2
Short-term consumer borrowing	120.7
Privately held federal debt	277.9
Tax-exempt notes and bonds	63.2
Total net demand for credit	$796.7 billion

The supply of funds was estimated to come from the following sources:

Thrift institutions	$171.7 billion
Insurance, pensions, and endowments	105.4
Investment companies	58.0
Other nonbank finance	41.3
Commercial banks	164.8
Nonfinancial corporations	23.1
State and local government	9.7
Foreign	30.8
Residual (household direct purchases)	191.9
Total net supply of credit	$796.7 billion

See Table 6–2 for the estimates of demand and supply of funds for 1985 and historical data going back to 1979. Also shown are percentages of total funds that were absorbed by the various demanders of funds between 1979 and 1985.

Before projecting the course of interest rates during the coming year, those who use the supply and demand for funds framework take into account the following factors:

1. Stage of the business cycle in which the economy lies at present.
2. Federal government finance.
3. Federal Reserve policy.

TABLE 6–2   Summary of Supply and Demand for Credit (annual net increases in amounts outstanding, dollars in billions)

	1979	1980	1981	1982	1983	1984E	1985P	Amt. Out. 31 Dec 84E	Table Refer.
Net Demand									
Privately Held Mortgages	$113.1	$84.2	$73.7	$15.9	$83.7	$148.5	$136.4	$1,485.5	2
Corporate and Foreign Bonds	35.7	40.2	34.9	39.1	37.9	50.5	45.3	656.9	3
Total Long-Term Private	148.8	124.3	108.6	54.9	121.7	199.0	181.7	2,142.4	
Short-Term Business Borrowing	98.0	67.1	117.3	47.5	60.1	141.6	153.2	1,006.7	8
Short-Term Other Borrowing	49.3	11.2	37.7	27.7	60.5	97.9	120.7	695.5	8
Total Short-Term Private	147.2	78.3	155.0	75.2	120.6	239.5	273.9	1,702.2	
Privately Held Federal Debt	76.2	118.7	123.0	214.1	241.0	257.3	277.9	1,728.1	6
Tax-Exempt Notes and Bonds	27.8	31.9	29.5	63.9	54.3	66.5	63.2	542.8	4
Total Government Debt	104.0	150.6	152.4	278.0	295.3	323.8	341.1	2,270.9	
Total Net Demand for Credit	**$400.0**	**$353.3**	**$416.0**	**$408.1**	**$537.6**	**$762.4**	**$796.7**	**$6,115.6**	▼
Net Supply[a]									
Thrift Institutions	$56.5	$54.5	$27.8	$31.3	$136.8	$155.8	$171.7	$1,117.1	9
Insurance, Pensions, Endowments	77.9	88.2	89.2	107.1	96.1	105.3	105.4	1,190.2	9
Investment Companies	29.3	15.9	72.4	52.4	6.0	49.9	58.0	261.3	9
Other Nonbank Finance	27.8	13.1	28.8	4.9	12.0	50.6	41.3	307.8	9
Total Nonbank Finance	191.4	171.7	218.1	195.6	250.9	361.5	376.5	2,876.3	
Commercial Banks	122.2	101.4	107.6	107.2	140.2	169.0	164.8	1,761.6	10
Nonfinancial Corporations	7.0	1.8	18.4	13.6	22.8	12.6	23.1	160.6	11
State and Local Governments	7.1	0.6	2.0	10.3	17.2	11.0	9.7	93.6	11
Foreign Investors	-4.6	23.2	16.3	18.1	28.5	30.7	30.8	283.2	11
Subtotal	323.1	298.7	362.4	344.8	459.5	584.8	604.8	5,175.3	
Residual: Households Direct	76.9	54.6	53.7	63.3	78.1	177.6	191.9	940.4	12
Total Net Supply of Credit	**$400.0**	**$353.3**	**$416.0**	**$408.1**	**$537.6**	**$762.4**	**$796.7**	**$6,115.6**	▲
Memo									
Net Issuance Corporate Stock	$-1.9	$18.2	$11.9	$19.5	$27.8	$-89.1	$-26.8	$2,030.0	
Total Credit and Stock	398.1	371.5	427.9	427.6	565.3	673.3	769.9	8,145.6	
Percentage of Total Absorbed by									
Households	56.2%	42.9%	40.1%	28.8%	40.6%	45.8%	44.3%		
Nonfinancial Business	24.3	25.3	25.1	18.5	15.0	9.6	15.2		
Financial Institutions	7.3	10.1	11.8	4.4	8.4	-2.7	5.1		
Government	7.9	15.6	17.6	45.7	33.5	46.4	34.2		
Foreigners	4.3	6.1	5.4	2.6	2.5	0.9	1.2		

[a] Excludes funds for equities and other demands not tabulated above.

E = Estimate
P = Preliminary

Source: Salomon Brothers, Inc., *1985 Prospects for Financial Markets.*

4. Current changes in some sensitive interest rates.
5. Expected rate of inflation.

Thus in presenting their analysis to investors, Salomon Brothers describes their assumptions regarding these factors and discusses how they expect interest rates to move from the beginning to the end of the coming year.

Forecasting with Economic Indicators

The use of the Index of Leading Indicators to forecast the economy was described in Chapter 5. We now extend that analysis and describe how indicator methodology can be applied to forecast turning points of interest rate movement. Basically, one can compare peaks and troughs in interest rates to peaks and troughs in a variety of series that lead movements in interest rates. In doing so, one can find a number of leading series that provide useful information in projecting the direction yields. In this section we briefly describe a study (by Randall, 1984) that uses this methodology.

The study focused on two interest rate series, the Treasury bill rate (short-term) and the yield on corporate bonds (long-term). Tables of monthly data covering the period from 1956 through 1982 were used to identify cyclical peaks and troughs.[6] Dates during which turning points occur are shown in Table 6–3.

The use of judgment is necessary in designating some of the dates, for several periods are characterized by multiple peaks and troughs. There are peaks in the Treasury bill rate in 1973 and 1974, and troughs occur in both 1970 and 1971. In these cases the second turning point is used as the date of reference because the latter point represents the beginning of a movement in a new direction.[7] A similar procedure has been utilized to estimate peaks

TABLE 6–3 Dates of Cyclical Peaks and Troughs in Interest Rate Movements, 1956–1982

Peaks		Troughs	
Treasury Bills	Corporate Bonds	Treasury Bills	Corporate Bonds
October 1957	August 1957	June 1958	June 1958
December 1959	October 1959	September 1961	January 1963
January 1970	June 1970	February 1972	January 1972
August 1974	September 1974	December 1976	December 1976
March 1980	March 1980	June 1980	June 1980
May 1981	September 1981		

[6]Statistics are available in selected issues of *Business Conditions Digest*.

[7]Another analyst with a different set of objectives might use other criteria in specifying turning points.

and troughs for a group of well-known economic series. In the majority of cases, turning points can be clearly specified. However, in a few instances, double peaks or troughs occur and, generally, the date of the second turning point is used. Six peaks and five troughs for each indicator have been identified, and they correspond to the cycles in Table 6–3.

For each peak and trough listed in Table 6–3 we count the number of months between the turning point of an indicator and the subsequent turning point of the interest rate. We then have a series of numbers such a those in Table 6–4. In 1957, real personal income peaked at the same time as corporate bond yields so that the lead time was zero. In 1959, 1973, 1980, and 1981 the peak in the income series preceded the peak in corporate bond yields by the number of months shown. In 1970, corporate bond yields peaked two months before the income series, which is indicated by −2. With these data we then compute a mean lead time of 2.3 months and a sample standard deviation of 4.1 months. The calculations are done separately for peaks and troughs using each series under consideration as an indicator.

Sequence of Turning Points

After examining a large number of series, nine were found to be particularly useful. In Table 6–5 we see the average number of months between the turning point in a series and the subsequent turning point in corporate bond yields. The first indicator to signal a peak is new housing starts, with a mean lead of 17.7 months and a standard deviation of 8.1 months. The shortest lead is associated with real personal income, which has a 2.3-month mean lead and a standard deviation of 4.1 months. An ideal indicator is one with a long lead and a small standard deviation. The longer the lead, the more time decision makers have to plan for the change in the movement of yields. A smaller standard deviation provides greater confidence about the accuracy of the mean lead. Thus the number of new housing starts is useful in providing an early signal, but its peaks have varied from eight to twenty-seven months prior to the peaks in bond yields. Industrial production figures have the desirable feature of peaking over a narrower range, but they sometimes provide a signal only shortly before the turning point in interest rates.

TABLE 6–4   Lead Times in Months of Real Personal Income at Corporate Bond Interest Rate Peaks, 1957–1981

	1957	1959	1970	1973	1980	1981	Mean (X)	Standard Deviation[b]
Real Personal Income[a]	0	3	−2	10	2	1	2.3	4.1

[a]Personal income less transfer payments, 1972 dollars.
[b]Sample Standard Deviation:

$$\sqrt{\frac{\sum_{i-1}^{n} (X_i - \overline{X})^2}{n-1}}$$

TABLE 6–5 Leads at Corporate Bond Turning Points

	Peaks		Troughs	
	Mean	Standard Deviation	Mean	Standard Deviation
1. New private housing units started (housing starts)	17.7	8.1	15.2	11.7
2. Money supply — M_1 — in 1972 dollars (real M_1)	14.7	7.3	13.6	11.5
3. Index of leading indicators (leading indicators)	13.5	7.5	14.2	10.6
4. Stock prices, 500 common stocks (stock prices)	10.8	7.7	15.6	11.1
5. Initial weekly state unemployment insurance claims (initial unemployment claims)	10.5	6.4	10.0	11.0
6. Sales of retail stores, 1972 dollars (real retail sales)	7.0	7.0	15.8	15.0
7. Percentage change of GNP implicit price deflator (inflation)	5.8	5.4	8.8	9.8
8. Index of industrial production (industrial production)	4.0	2.3	11.8	10.9
9. Personal income less transfer payments, 1972 dollars (real personal income)	2.3	4.1	12.2	11.4

The order of events and length of mean lead times at lower turning points is different than at upper turning points. Retail sales in constant dollars, with a mean lead of 7 months, is not among the earliest signals at the peaks. However, its mean lead of 15.8 months at the troughs is the longest of the group. Mean leads of other series also show sizable changes. For example, the mean lead in real personal income grew from 2.3 to 12.2 months, and the industrial production lead increased from 4.0 to 11.8 months. As we see in Table 6–5, mean lead times at the trough lie within a narrower interval. The lowest and highest values are 8.8 and 15.8 months, compared to 2.3 and 17.7 months at the peak. The standard deviations of lead times are also quite different at peaks and troughs, and in Table 6–6 we see similar findings during turning points of Treasury bill yields.

The high standard deviations in Table 6–5 and Table 6–6 illustrate the difficulties involved in forecasting interest rates. Leads at peaks and troughs vary widely from cycle to cycle. This is a major reason why those who forecast interest rates are frequently in error by substantial amounts. Despite the variability of relationships, however, the indicators can be helpful. Zarnowitz and Moore have suggested the following approach in using indicators: When the indicators with the longest leads begin to turn, the forecaster has ob-

TABLE 6–6   Leads at Treasury Bill Turning Points

		Peaks		Troughs	
		Mean	Standard Deviation	Mean	Standard Deviation
1.	Housing starts	16.7	9.5	12.2	10.8
2.	Real M_1	13.7	7.2	10.6	6.9
3.	Leading indicators	12.5	8.4	11.2	9.0
4.	Stock prices	9.8	6.9	12.6	9.3
5.	Initial unemployment claims	9.5	7.5	7.0	8.2
6.	Real retail sales	6.8	6.4	12.8	10.4
7.	Inflation	4.8	5.2	5.8	4.1
8.	Industrial production	3.0	3.2	8.8	9.1
9.	Real personal income	1.3	5.7	9.2	9.1

served a warning signal. As more indicators turn, there is increasing evidence that a cyclical change is in process, and a turn in rates can be predicted with greater probability.[8]

This technique can be applied using the series in Table 6–5 and Table 6–6. Consider the following example. Suppose interest rates have been falling, and an analyst wants to estimate when corporate bond rates will begin to rise. The analyst observes that stock prices and real M_1 begin to increase in early January of year $t = 0$. Referring back to the trough column of Table 6–5, we see that, on the average, corporate bond rates turned up 13.6 months after the bottom of real M_1 and 15.6 months after the trough in stock prices. Thus yields would be projected to rise approximately thirteen to sixteen months later, between February and May of year $t = 1$.

Next assume that real retail sales and new housing starts begin to rise in early February of year $t = 0$. These indicators suggest a turning point in fifteen to sixteen months, between May and June of year $t = 1$. Assume that more and more indicators start to move up, and near the end of year $t = 0$, the interval for the expected turn in interest rates has expanded to include January through July of year $t = 1$. At this point the analyst should carefully monitor movements in rates. If corporate bond yields begin to rise for a period of several weeks, it might well be the start of the anticipated upward interest rate cycle.

In summary, the use of indicators has several attractive features: First, it provides both forecasters and decision makers with relevant and understandable information of the economic and financial environment; second, it is not an expensive system to establish or maintain; and third, it helps in evaluating both forecasts and information provided by other analysts.

[8] Victor Zarnowitz and Geoffrey Moore, "Sequential Signals of Recession and Recovery." *Journal of Business*, January 1982, pp. 57–85.

SUMMARY

Both the level and changes of interest rates are very important to investors. Interest rates affect the course of the economy and the rates by which investors discount the future stream of benefits from securities to arrive at their values. Two major forces that have affected levels and movements of interest rates over the years have been the rates of inflation and cyclical factors. In addition, the Federal Reserve plays a major role through its control of monetary policy.

One common method used to project interest rates involves the estimation of the supply and demand conditions with respect to loanable funds for the coming year. The first step in this approach is to provide an economic projection of the economy in the form of GNP and its components. The second step is to estimate demand for funds from business, federal government, state and local governments, home financing, consumer credit, and foreigners. On the supply side, the forecasters will estimate the supply of funds from savings, commercial bank credit, business corporations, government agencies, and foreigners. Finally, the forecaster will evaluate the gap between supply and demand estimates and the possible role the Federal Reserve will play, and then render a judgment as to the possible direction and magnitude of interest changes in the coming year.

Another approach to forecasting involves the use of economic indicators to analyze movements in interest rates. In applying this approach, we showed how an analyst might find indicators that reach peaks and troughs prior to interest rate peaks and troughs. Based on the direction in which the indicators are moving, the analyst may be able to anticipate the direction that interest rates will follow in the future.

QUESTIONS AND PROBLEMS

1. Why should purchasers of equities be concerned with the analysis and forecast of interest rates?
2. Discuss the role of the Federal Reserve System in influencing the level and trend of interest rates.
3. Using data from *Business Conditions Digest*, prepare a table showing the changes in both long-term and short-term interest rates and their relation to stock prices and bond prices in the last three years. Discuss the implications of your table.
4. Discuss the changes in interest rates in relation to different stages of the two most recent business cycles.
5. Obtain a financial forecast using quotations of financial futures or from Salomon Brothers. Evaluate the forecast.

6. Gather enough relevant materials or information on key factors and discuss the outlook for interest rates in the next six to twelve months.
7. Distinguish between cyclical and long-term trends in interest rates.
8. List the borrowers of loanable funds in the order of importance.
9. What do current movements in economic indicators suggest regarding interest rates movements for the coming year?

REFERENCES

Board of Governors, Federal Reserve System. *The Federal Reserve System: Purposes and Functions*. Washington, D.C., 1974.

Boorman, J., and Havrilesky, T., eds. *Money Supply, Money Demand, and Macroeconomic Models*. Boston: Allyn and Bacon, 1979.

Campbell, Tim S. *Financial Institutions, Markets and Economic Activity*. New York: McGraw-Hill, 1982.

Carleton, W. T., and Cooper, I. A. "Estimation and Uses of the Term Structure of Interest Rates." *Journal of Finance*, Sept. 1976.

Darst, David M. *The Complete Bond Book*. New York: McGraw-Hill, 1975, Chapters 3–5.

Elliott, J. W., and Bair, Jerome R. "Econometric Models and Current Interest Rates: How Well Do They Predict the Future?" *Journal of Finance*, Sept. 1979.

Fama, E. and Schwert, G. W. "Asset Returns and Inflation." *Journal of Financial Economics*, Nov. 1977.

Fisher, Irving. *The Theory of Interest*. New York: Macmillan, 1930.

Freund, W. C., and Zinbarg, E. D. "Application of Flow of Funds to Interest Rate Forecasting." *Journal of Finance*, May 1963.

Hunt, Lacy. *Dynamics of Forecasting Financial Cycles*. Greenwich, Conn.: JAI Press, 1976.

Levi, M. D., and Makin, J. H. "Fisher, Phillips, Friedman and the Measured Impact of Inflation on Interest." *Journal of Finance*, March 1979.

Lintner, John. "Inflation and Security Returns." *Journal of Finance*, May 1975.

Moore, Geoffrey. *Business Cycles, Inflation, and Forecasting*. Cambridge, Mass.: National Bureau of Economic Research, 1980.

Palmer, Michael. "Money Supply, Portfolio Adjustments and Stock Prices." *Financial Analysts Journal*, July–Aug. 1970.

Salomon Brothers. *Prospects for the Credit Markets*, current issue.

Sprinkel, Beryl W. *Money and Markets, a Monetarist View*. Homewood, Ill.: R. D. Irwin, 1971.

Zarnowitz, Victor, and Moore, Geoffrey. "Sequential Signals of Recession and Recovery." *Journal of Business*, Jan. 1982.

7

Interest-Bearing Assets: Markets and Characteristics

There are many different types of interest-bearing assets available on financial markets. These instruments differ in terms of their yields, risk, liquidity, maturity, and tax features. In this chapter we will discuss the characteristics of these securities along with some of the mutual funds that purchase them. We will also briefly describe the markets on which they are bought and sold and the manner in which price information is reported in the financial press.

INSTRUMENTS OF THE MONEY MARKET

Money market instruments are short-term securities that are generally quite safe and are usually issued in large denominations. They have maturities of one year or less, but most actually mature within ninety days. Since these securities can be converted into cash quickly and with little or no loss in value, they are described as being *liquid assets*. Among the instruments that fall into the money market group are Treasury bills, commercial paper, negotiable certificates of deposit (CDs), bankers' acceptances, Eurodollar deposits, and short-term tax-exempt securities. Minimum denominations range from $10,000 for Treasury bills to over $200,000 for certain types of Eurodollar certificates.

Money Market Funds and Accounts

Many investors cannot or do not want to place between $10,000 and $100,000 into a money market instrument. But, if they have $1,000 or more for an initial deposit, they can open an account in a *money market mutual fund*. Managers of these funds pool the money of small savers and purchase money market instruments. Normally, shares in the fund are purchased at $1 per share, and through such purchases each investor will own a small slice of the fund's portfolio. Earnings after expenses are proportionately distributed to those who have invested in the fund based on the number of shares they own.

Usually, there are some check-writing privileges, and the investor may also be able to shift cash to other mutual funds linked to the money fund.

Among the alternatives to money funds are *money market accounts* at commercial banks or savings institutions. These accounts are similar to money market funds, but check-writing privileges may be more limited. Yields on these accounts vary among financial institutions with commercial banks usually paying slightly less than savings institutions. Normally, money market accounts are insured by federal agencies, while money market mutual funds do not have such insurance.[1] On the other hand, an investor can probably obtain a higher yield from a fund than an account at a financial institution.

Treasury Bills

The most important of the money market securities in terms of value outstanding are Treasury bills (T-bills). Most newly issued bills have maturities of either thirteen or twenty-six weeks, although some mature in fifty-two weeks. T-bills have a minimum denomination of $10,000 par (maturity) value, and they are sold at a discount. The interest is simply calculated as the difference between the price paid for the bill and the par value that the investor receives at maturity.

New Treasury bills are sold through an auction process administered by the Federal Reserve System. Investors can make competitive or noncompetitive bids. In a competitive bid, the individual states the price he or she will pay for a bill. A noncompetitive bidder will pay the average of the competitive bids accepted by the Federal Reserve. Normally, noncompetitive bidders will have their orders filled. However, competitive bids below the minimum price accepted by the Federal Reserve will not be filled. Generally, only very sophisticated investors make competitive bids. Individuals may purchase T-bills through banks, stockbrokers, or directly through a Federal Reserve Bank.

Every week a new group of Treasury bills mature, and a new group is auctioned. Usually the auctions occur on Monday and prices and yields are reported in Tuesday's *Wall Street Journal*. A portion of such a listing might appear as follows for a newly auctioned thirteen-week (ninety-one day) bill:

Price (Rate)   97.900 (8.31%)

The price number, 97.900, is the percentage of par value (assumed to be $10,000), and so the T-bill sold for $9,790. The rate, 8.31 percent, is

---

[1] Some money market funds invest exclusively in Treasury securities and are therefore at least as safe as bank money market accounts.

computed on a discount basis, using a 360-day year. The calculation is as follows:

$$\text{Discount} = 10{,}000 - 9{,}790 = 210$$

$$\text{Rate} = \left[\frac{210}{10{,}000} \times \frac{360}{91}\right]$$

$$= 8.31\%$$

Note that the Treasury bill rate understates the actual yield to the investor. The investor's (uncompounded) yield is based on the price paid and a 365-day year.

$$\text{Yield} = \frac{210}{9{,}790} \times \frac{365}{91}$$

$$= 8.60\%$$

In general, one can compute the Treasury bill rate and the associated yield with Equations 7.1 and 7.2:

$$\text{T-bill rate} = \frac{\text{Discount}}{10{,}000} \times \frac{360}{\text{Days to Maturity}} \quad \text{(7.1)}$$

$$\text{T-bill yield} = \frac{\text{Discount}}{\text{Price}} \times \frac{365}{\text{Days to Maturity}} \quad \text{(7.2)}$$

Secondary Market for Treasury Bills

One reason Treasury bills are very liquid is that there is a well-developed secondary market. If someone wants to buy or sell a previously issued bill, he or she may contact a stockbroker or a bank. The bank or broker would then ascertain the prices offered by dealers who "make a market" in Treasury securities. These dealers maintain inventories of Treasury securities, and they will provide quotes to either buy or sell. At any given time their selling or "asked" price will be greater than their buying or "bid" price.

Quotations for Treasury bills are available in the section "Treasury Bonds, Notes and Bills" in the *Wall Street Journal*. A sample listing is shown in the lower right corner of Figure 7–1. As an example, we will consider the following hypothetical entry ($t = 0$ represents year 0):

Listing for April 30, $t = 0$

Maturity Date	Bid Discount	Asked Discount	Yield
6/29	8.70	8.40	8.64

TREASURY BONDS, NOTES & BILLS

Wednesday, July 31, 1985

Representative mid-afternoon Over-the-Counter quotations supplied by the Federal Reserve Bank of New York City, based on transactions of $1 million or more.

Decimals in bid-and-asked and bid changes represent 32nds; 101.1 means 101 1/32. a-Plus 1/64. b-Yield to call date. d-Minus 1/64. k-Non U.S. citizens exempt from withholding taxes. n-Treasury notes. p-Treasury note; non U.S. citizens exempt from withholding taxes.

Treasury Bonds and Notes

Rate	Mat.	Date	Bid	Asked	Bid Chg.	Yld.
10⅝s,	1985	Jul n	99.31	100.3	....	0.00
8¼s,	1985	Aug n	100	100.4	....	4.59
9⅝s,	1985	Aug n	100.2	100.6	+ .1	4.21
10⅝s,	1985	Aug n	100.5	100.9	....	6.85
13⅛s,	1985	Aug n	100.6	100.10	....	4.16
10⅞s,	1985	Sep n	100.15	100.19	− .1	6.90
15⅞s,	1985	Sep n	101.9	101.13	....	6.70
10½s,	1985	Oct n	100.21	100.25	....	7.06
9¾s,	1985	Nov n	100.16	100.20	− .1	7.36
10½s,	1985	Nov n	100.25	100.29	− .1	7.53
11¾s,	1985	Nov n	101.2	101.6	− .1	7.37
10⅞s,	1985	Dec n	101.6	101.10	....	7.50
14⅛s,	1985	Dec n	102.20	102.24	....	7.14
10⅝s,	1986	Jan n	101.9	101.13	....	7.67
10⅞s,	1986	Feb n	101.18	101.22	....	7.84
13½s,	1986	Feb n	102.25	102.29	− .1	7.86
9⅞s,	1986	Feb n	100.29	101.1	....	7.88
14s,	1986	Mar n	103.22	103.26	− .1	7.99
11½s,	1986	Mar n	102.4	102.8	− .1	7.95
11¾s,	1986	Apr n	102.18	102.22	....	7.97
7⅞s,	1986	May n	99.25	99.29	− .1	8.00
9⅜s,	1986	May n	100.28	101	....	8.04
13s,	1986	Jun n	104.2	104.6	− .1	8.14
14⅞s,	1986	Jun n	106.2	106.6	....	7.72
12⅝s,	1986	Jul p	104	104.4	....	8.22
8s,	1986	Aug n	99.26	99.30	....	8.06
11⅜s,	1986	Aug n	102.29	103.1	....	8.26
12⅜s,	1986	Aug p	103.29	104.1	....	8.39
11⅞s,	1986	Sep p	103.20	103.24	+ .1	8.42
12¼s,	1986	Sep n	104	104.4	....	8.45
11⅝s,	1986	Oct p	103.15	103.19	....	8.53
6⅛s,	1986	Nov	97.13	98.13	....	7.45
10⅜s,	1986	Nov p	102.3	102.7	+ .1	8.57
11s,	1986	Nov n	102.25	102.29	....	8.57
13⅞s,	1986	Nov n	106.5	106.9	− .2	8.62
16⅛s,	1986	Nov n	109.6	109.10	− .2	8.35
9⅞s,	1986	Dec p	101.19	101.23	+ .1	8.56
10s,	1986	Dec n	101.24	101.28	....	9.56
9¾s,	1987	Jan p	101.10	101.14	+ .1	8.70
9s,	1987	Feb n	100.10	100.14	+ .1	8.69
10s,	1987	Feb p	101.18	101.22	+ .1	8.83
10⅞s,	1987	Feb n	102.27	102.31	+ .1	8.77
12¾s,	1987	Feb n	105.15	105.19	....	8.78
10¼s,	1987	Mar n	102	102.4	+ .2	8.85
10¾s,	1987	Mar p	102.24	102.28	+ .1	8.85
9¾s,	1987	Apr p	101.8	101.10	+ .2	8.92
9⅛s,	1987	May p	100.5	100.7	+ .2	8.99
12s,	1987	May n	104.26	104.30	+ .1	8.95
12½s,	1987	May n	105.15	105.19	+ .1	9.04
14s,	1987	May n	107.27	107.31	+ .1	9.07
8½s,	1987	Jun p	99.5	99.7	+ .2	8.95
10½s,	1987	Jun n	102.16	102.20	+ .2	8.98
8⅞s,	1987	Jul p	99.24	99.26	+ .2	8.98
12⅜s,	1987	Aug p	105.25	105.29	+ .1	9.13
13¾s,	1987	Aug n	108.14	108.18	+ .1	9.05
11⅛s,	1987	Sep n	103.24	103.28	+ .2	9.11
7⅝s,	1987	Nov n	97.18	97.26	+ .1	8.70
11s,	1987	Nov p	103.16	103.20	+ .2	9.21
12⅝s,	1987	Nov n	106.21	106.25	+ .3	9.27
11¼s,	1987	Dec n	104.4	104.8	+ .2	9.24
12⅜s,	1988	Jan n	106.15	106.19	+ .3	9.31
10⅛s,	1988	Feb n	101.17	101.21	+ .2	9.38
10⅜s,	1988	Feb p	102	102.2	+ .2	9.44
12s,	1988	Mar n	105.21	105.25	+ .1	9.49
13¼s,	1988	Apr n	108.15	108.19	+ .3	9.57
8¼s,	1988	May n	97.17	97.25	+ .3	9.17
9⅞s,	1988	May n	100.31	101.3	+ .3	9.42
10s,	1988	May p	101.14	101.18	+ .3	9.35
13⅝s,	1988	Jun n	109.28	110	+ .4	9.61
14s,	1988	Jul n	110.28	111.4	+ .2	9.58
10½s,	1988	Aug n	102.12	102.16	+ .3	9.53
15⅜s,	1988	Oct n	115.6	115.14	+ .5	9.66
11⅜s,	1988	Sep p	104.17	104.21	+ .4	9.63
8¾s,	1988	Nov n	98	98.8	+ .2	9.38
11¾s,	1988	Nov n	105.14	105.18	+ .4	9.73
10⅝s,	1988	Dec p	102.15	102.19	+ .4	9.71
14⅝s,	1989	Jan n	113.15	113.19	+ .3	9.88
11⅜s,	1989	Feb n	104.11	104.15	+ .4	9.85
11¼s,	1989	Mar p	104.3	104.5	+ .4	9.87
14⅜s,	1989	Apr n	113.7	113.15	+ .4	9.94
9¼s,	1989	May n	99.3	99.11	+ .5	9.46
11¾s,	1989	May n	105.14	105.18	+ .4	9.95
9⅝s,	1989	Jun p	99.16	99.18	+ .3	9.76
14½s,	1989	Jul n	114.5	114.13	+ .4	10.00

Rate	Mat.	Date	Bid	Asked	Bid Chg.	Yld.
10½s,	1990	Jan n	101.14	101.18	+ .4	10.06
3½s,	1990	Feb	92.8	93.8	+ .2	5.19
11s,	1990	Feb p	103.3	103.7	+ .4	10.10
10½s,	1990	Apr n	101.13	101.17	+ .6	10.08
8¼s,	1990	May	97.12	97.28	+ .11	8.80
11⅜s,	1990	May p	104.15	104.19	....	10.14
10¾s,	1990	Jul n	102.15	102.19	+ .4	10.07
9⅞s,	1990	Aug p	99.17	99.21	+ .5	9.96
10¾s,	1990	Aug n	102.14	102.18	+ .6	10.09
11½s,	1990	Oct n	104.31	105.3	+ .6	10.21
13s,	1990	Nov n	110.23	110.27	+ .7	10.29
11¾s,	1991	Jan n	105.26	105.30	+ .7	10.30
12⅜s,	1991	Apr	108.3	108.7	+ .7	10.43
14½s,	1991	May n	116.23	116.31	+ .8	10.51
13¾s,	1991	Jul n	113.24	113.28	+ .8	10.55
14⅞s,	1991	Aug n	118.28	119.4	+ .9	10.52
12¼s,	1991	Oct p	107.22	107.26	+ .10	10.50
14¼s,	1991	Nov n	116.23	116.31	+ .9	10.50
11⅝s,	1992	Jan p	105.1	105.5	+ .11	10.50
14⅝s,	1992	Feb n	118.24	119	+ .10	10.53
11¾s,	1992	Apr	105.31	106.3	+ .12	10.46
13¾s,	1992	May n	114.23	114.27	+ .9	10.63
10⅜s,	1992	Jul p	99.27	99.29	+ .15	10.39
4¼s,	1987-92	Aug	92.7	93.7	+ .3	5.42
7¼s,	1992	Aug	85.3	85.19	+ .12	10.17
10½s,	1992	Nov n	100.12	100.20	+ .15	10.38
4s,	1988-93	Feb	92.11	93.11	+ .3	5.07
6¾s,	1993	Feb	82.18	83.18	+ .3	9.90
7⅞s,	1993	Feb	86.26	87.10	+ .4	10.34
10⅞s,	1993	Feb n	101.28	102.4	+ .12	10.46
10⅛s,	1994	Nov	98.6	98.14	+ .11	10.59
11⅝s,	1994	Nov	105.18	105.22	+ .13	10.65
3s,	1995	Feb	92.13	93.13	+ .4	3.83
10½s,	1995	Feb	100.4	100.12	+ .13	10.44
11¼s,	1995	Feb p	103.18	103.22	+ .14	10.63
10⅜s,	1995	May	99.9	99.17	+ .15	10.45
11¼s,	1995	May p	104.3	104.7	+ .17	10.55
12⅝s,	1995	May	111.18	111.26	+ .18	10.65
11½s,	1995	Nov	105.13	105.21	+ .13	10.58
7s,	1993-98	May	75.12	75.28	+ .11	10.46
3½s,	1998	Nov	92.11	93.11	+ .4	4.16
8½s,	1994-99	May	84.10	84.26	+ .13	10.62
7⅞s,	1995-00	Feb	78.20	78.28	+ .15	10.79
8⅜s,	1995-00	Aug	81.19	82.3	....	10.81
11¾s,	2001	Feb	105.29	106.5	+ .17	10.92
13⅛s,	2001	May	115.16	115.24	+ .13	11.00
8s,	1996-01	Aug	78.30	79.14	+ .12	10.71
13⅜s,	2001	Aug	117.12	117.20	+ .11	11.01
15¾s,	2001	Nov	135.1	135.17	+ .23	11.01
14¼s,	2002	Feb	123.23	123.31	+ .15	11.06
11⅝s,	2002	Nov	104.24	105	+ .20	10.97
10¾s,	2003	Feb	98.4	98.12	+ .23	10.96
10¾s,	2003	May	98.4	98.12	+ .23	10.96
11⅛s,	2003	Aug	100.30	101.6	+ .18	10.97
11⅞s,	2003	Nov	106.21	106.29	+ .21	10.99
12⅜s,	2004	May	110.11	110.19	+ .23	11.03
13¾s,	2004	Aug	121.8	121.16	+ .20	11.03
11⅝s,	2004	Nov k	105.4	105.12	+ .23	10.95
10¾s,	2005	Aug k	98.28	99	+ .26	10.87
8¼s,	2000-05	May	79.20	80.4	+ .14	10.68
12s,	2005	May	108.4	108.12	+ .23	10.96
7⅝s,	2002-07	Feb	73.19	74.3	+ .19	10.73
7⅞s,	2002-07	Nov	75.28	76.12	+ .26	10.67
8⅜s,	2003-08	Aug	79.19	80.3	+ .27	10.72
8¾s,	2003-08	Nov	82.15	82.23	+ .24	10.79
9⅛s,	2004-09	May	85.17	85.25	+ .27	10.80
10⅜s,	2004-09	Nov	95.10	95.18	+ .23	10.90
11¾s,	2005-10	Feb	106.20	106.28	+ .27	10.89
10s,	2005-10	May	93.20	93.28	+ .24	10.71
12¾s,	2005-10	Nov	113.20	113.28	+ .28	11.02
13⅞s,	2006-11	May	123.4	123.12	+ .25	10.99
14s,	2006-11	Nov	124.6	124.14	+ .26	11.00
10⅜s,	2007-12	Nov	95.7	95.15	+ .27	10.90
12s,	2008-13	Aug	108.7	108.11	+ .26	11.00
13¼s,	2009-14	May	118.24	119	+ .19	10.98
12½s,	2009-14	Aug k	112.9	112.17	+ .30	11.01
11¾s,	2009-14	Nov k	107.1	107.5	+ .30	10.91
11¼s,	2015	Feb k	104.29	105.1	+ .25	10.69

U.S. Treas. Bills

Mat. date	Bid Discount	Asked Discount	Yield
-1985-			
8- 8	6.98	6.94	7.04
8-15	6.82	6.78	6.89
8-22	6.85	6.81	6.93
8-29	6.86	6.82	6.95
9- 5	6.96	6.92	7.06
9-12	6.95	6.91	7.06
9-19	6.91	6.87	7.03
9-26	6.94	6.88	7.05
10- 3	7.19	7.15	7.34
10-10	7.23	7.19	7.39
10-17	7.28	7.24	7.45

Mat. date	Bid Discount	Asked Discount	Yield
-1985-			
11-29	7.30	7.26	7.54
12- 5	7.31	7.27	7.56
12-12	7.31	7.27	7.57
12-19	7.28	7.24	7.55
12-26	7.26	7.22	7.54
-1986-			
1- 2	7.30	7.26	7.60
1- 9	7.35	7.31	7.66
1-16	7.41	7.37	7.74
1-23	7.45	7.41	7.79
1-86	7.42	7.40	7.79
2-20	7.45	7.41	7.81

FIGURE 7–1

Source: Wall Street Journal, August 1, 1985. Reprinted by permission of *The Wall Street Journal*, ©1985. World rights reserved.

The listing is for a T-bill that matures on June 29, $t = 0$. Note that unlike information on most other securities, quotations on Treasury bills are given in terms of rates and yields and not in terms of prices. The 8.70 percent represents the T-bill rate for the dealer based on an unstated underlying price offered by the dealer. The 8.40 percent is the T-bill rate the investor receives based on the price he or she pays. The 8.64 percent yield represents the investor's yield calculated with Equation 7.2 and is based on the investor's underlying purchase price.

The bid and asked rates can be converted into the underlying prices with the aid of Equation 7.1. To use that equation we must first note that there are sixty days between the listing date of April 30 and the maturity date June 29. From Equation 7.1:

$$.0870 = \frac{\text{Discount}}{10,000} \times \frac{360}{60}$$

$$\frac{\text{Discount}}{10,000} = .0145$$

$$\text{Discount} = 145$$

$$\text{Bid price} = 10,000 - \text{Discount}$$

$$= 9,855$$

Similarly, we can solve for the asked price with the same equation.

$$\text{Asked Price} = 9,860$$

Thus we see that the dealer's asked price exceeds the bid price as we would expect. It should also be noted that the spread between bid and asked prices becomes smaller for larger transactions. This is equivalent to the granting of a volume discount by the dealer.

Finally, to calculate the yield based on the asked price we use Equation 7.2:

$$\text{T-bill yield} = \frac{10,000 - 9,860}{9,860} \times \frac{365}{60}$$

$$= 8.64\%$$

Other Money Market Instruments

Negotiable certificates of deposit are issued by large commercial banks in denominations of $100,000 or more. Maturities on these securities range from a few weeks to twelve months. They differ from other time deposit certificates in that they are negotiable and can therefore be purchased or sold on a secondary market.

Commercial paper consists of unsecured promissory notes issued primarily by large creditworthy companies. These securities are similar to Treasury bills in that they are sold at a discount from par value. Risk is small, although there have been a few defaults in the past (for example, Penn Central, in 1970). Most maturities range from a few weeks up to nine months.

Bankers' acceptances are primarily generated from international trade transactions. A U.S. firm that sells to a foreign company may receive a draft stating a promise to pay a specified amount on a certain date. The U.S. selling firm may require that the foreign company find a commercial bank that will accept the draft and thereby guarantee that the foreign company will pay. If the draft is accepted by a bank, it becomes a bankers' acceptance, and it can be sold on a secondary market at a discount. The acceptance is backed both by the company that promises to make payment as well as the accepting bank. Maturities when issued usually range from thirty to 180 days.

A *repurchase agreement*, or *repo*, is an arrangement in which one party sells government securities to another party and promises to repurchase it at a later date and at a higher price. In other words, at the time of repurchase the second party receives the price paid plus some interest. In most cases the repurchase occurs within a few days, but longer time periods are also common. Government securities dealers are among the major participants in the repo market. They use repos as a source of financing to pay for a major portion of the inventories of government securities that they hold. While these transactions generally involve low risk, in 1985 two major dealers went bankrupt. Some of the holders of their repos, which included state and local governments and savings institutions, suffered major losses.

Eurodollar deposits refer to interest bearing deposits, denominated in dollars, that are held in banks located outside the U.S. The foreign banks that participate are primarily in Europe or Asia. The prominence of the dollar in international business has been a major factor in this market's growth.

Short-term tax-exempt securities consist of certain obligations issued by state and local governments. The interest on that group of securities is exempt from federal taxes, and if the investor resides in the state that issued them, the interest is also exempt from state taxation.[2] Additional details on tax-exempt securities are provided in the municipal bond section of this chapter.

Yields

The interest rates on the different money market instruments vary over time, but they all generally move in the same direction. At any particular time, short-term tax-exempt securities would have the lowest rates. The next highest rate would be on Treasury bills. Negotiable CDs, commercial paper, and

[2] Under the 1986 tax reform law, some state and local government securities are not exempt from federal income taxes. See section on municipal bonds in this chapter.

bankers' acceptances have yields that are quite close to each other, while Eurodollar rates tend to be a little higher. Individual issues, of course, will have different yields depending on the creditworthiness of the issuing institution. In Figure 7–2 is a listing of yields on some of these instruments. The information is obtained from the "Money Rates" column in the *Wall Street Journal*.

MONEY RATES

Friday, August 9, 1985

The key U.S. and foreign annual interest rates below are a guide to general levels but don't always represent actual transactions.

PRIME RATE: 9½%. The base rate on corporate loans at large U.S. money center commercial banks.

DISCOUNT RATE: 7½%. The charge on loans to member depository institutions by the New York Federal Reserve Bank.

FEDERAL FUNDS: 7¾% high, 7½% low, 7½% near closing bid, 7 9/16% offered. Reserves traded among commercial banks for overnight use in amounts of $1 million or more. Source: Prebon Money Brokers Inc., N.Y.

CALL MONEY: 8¾% to 9% to 270 days. The charge on loans to brokers on stock exchange collateral.

COMMERCIAL PAPER placed directly by General Motors Acceptance Corp.: 7.70% 30 to 59 days; 7.75% 60 to 270 days

COMMERCIAL PAPER: High-grade unsecured notes sold through dealers by major corporations in multiples of $1,000: 7.75% 30 days; 7.80% 60 days; 7.80% 90 days.

CERTIFICATES OF DEPOSIT: 7.55% one month; 7.60% two months; 7.70% three months; 8% six months; 8.20% one year. Typical rates paid by major banks on new issues of negotiable C.D.s, usually on amounts of $1 million and more. The minimum unit is $100,000.

BANKERS ACCEPTANCES: 7.70% 30 days; 7.70% 60 days; 7.70% 90 days; 7.70% 120 days; 7.70% 150 days; 7.70% 180 days. Negotiable, bank-backed business credit instruments typically financing an import order.

LONDON LATE EURODOLLARS: 8% to 7⅞% one month; 8 1/16% to 7 15/16% two months; 8 3/16% to 8 1/16% three months; 8¼% to 8⅛% four months; 8 5/16% to 8 3/16% five months; 8⅜% to 8¼% six months.

LONDON INTERBANK OFFERED RATES (LIBOR): 8⅛% three months; 8⅜% six months; 8 13/16% one year. The average of interbank offered rates for dollar deposits in the London market based on quotations at five major banks.

FOREIGN PRIME RATES: Canada 10½%; Germany 7.75%; Japan 5.70%; Switzerland 6%; Britain 11½%. These rate indications aren't directly comparable; lending practices vary widely by location. Source: Morgan Guaranty Trust Co.

TREASURY BILLS: Results of the Monday, August 5, 1985, auction of short-term U.S. government bills, sold at a discount from face value in units of $10,000 to $1 million: 7.30% 13 weeks; 7.52% 26 weeks.

FEDERAL HOME LOAN MORTGAGE CORP. (Freddie Mac): Posted yields on 30-year mortgage commitments for delivery within 30 days. 12.09%, standard conventional fixed-rate mortgages; 9.14%, one-year adjustable rate mortgages.

FEDERAL NATIONAL MORTGAGE ASSOCIATION (Fannie Mae): Posted yields on 30 year mortgage commitments for delivery within 30 days (priced at par). 11.80%, standard conventional fixed rate-mortgages; 10.40%, 5/2 rate capped one-year adjustable rate mortgages.

MERRILL LYNCH READY ASSETS TRUST: 6.80%. Annualized average rate of return after expenses for the past 30 days; not a forecast of future returns.

FIGURE 7–2

Source: Wall Street Journal, August 10, 1985.
Reprinted by permission of *The Wall Street Journal,* ©1985. World rights reserved.

FEATURES OF BONDS

Markets and Quotes for Corporate Bonds

Most corporate bonds are traded in the over-the-counter market among institutional investors, bond dealers, investment banking firms, wealthy individual investors, and foreign investors. However, many bonds are also listed and traded on the New York Stock Exchange. Quotations on these bonds appear in the *Wall Street Journal* under the heading "New York Stock Exchange Bonds."[3] Consider the following listing for one of the AT&T issues, which appeared on January 25, 1985.

		Current Yield	Vol.	High	Low	Close	Net Chg.
ATT	7s01	11	605	66	$65\frac{1}{8}$	66	$+\frac{7}{8}$

The entry 7s01 means that this bond has a coupon rate of 7 percent and matures in the year 2001. The coupon rate specifies the interest payments made to the investor. Since bonds ordinarily have a par value of $1,000, the annual interest payment on the listed bond would be .07 ($1,000) = $70. This bond, like many others, pays interest twice a year, and the $70 interest is paid in two semiannual installments of $35. The "s" after the 7 has no special significance. It merely means that these are the 7s of 2001. Investors who wish to know the exact payment dates on a bond can consult a source such as *Moody's Bond Record*.

The price information in the listing is the percentage of par value. The high price of the day was 66 percent of $1,000, or $660. The low price was $651.25, and the close was $660. This was an increase of $\frac{7}{8}$ of 1 percent of $1,000, which means the closing price was $8.75 higher than the previous day's close. The volume number indicates that 605 of these bonds were traded during the day.

In addition to paying the quoted price for a corporate bond, the investor will also have to pay any interest that has accrued. Maximum accrued interest would occur immediately before the issuing corporation is scheduled to make an interest payment. For example, the maximum accrued interest on the AT&T 7s01 bond would be $35, just before the scheduled semiannual payment. That $35 would be added to the quoted price plus the commission. Immediately after the date scheduled for the corporation's interest payment, accrued interest is zero, and the cost of the bond would be just the quoted price plus commission. The seller of a bond in which there is accrued interest would receive that interest plus quoted price less commission.

The current yield column is the ratio of the annual interest payment to the closing price: $70 divided by $660 equals (approximately) 11 percent.

---

[3] On the same page is a smaller and similar listing for the AMEX.

The current yield is sometimes a source of confusion. It represents the annual return the investor receives if there is no change in bond price. If this bond were held to maturity, the investor would receive a return called the *yield to maturity*, or YTM. In the case of our listing, the YTM (which is not given in the listing) is greater than the current yield because over time the value of the bond will approach $1,000 as we get closer and closer to the maturity date. If the bond is held to maturity, the investor will receive a capital gain of $1,000 − $660 = $340 spread over the time to maturity. In cases where a bond is selling above the par value, the current yield would exceed the yield to maturity because there will be a capital loss spread over the time to maturity (see Chapter 8).

There are two other types of bonds traded on the New York Stock Exchange:

		Current Yield	Vol.	High	Low	Close	Net Chg.
Eas A	5s92	cv	31	$45\frac{1}{2}$	$45\frac{1}{2}$	$45\frac{1}{2}$	$+\frac{1}{2}$
Alld C	zr92	—	8	44	$43\frac{7}{8}$	44	$+1\frac{1}{2}$

The Eastern Airlines issue (Eas A) is an example of a *convertible bond* (cv). Bonds of this type are discussed in detail in Chapter 14. The Allied Chemical issue (Alld C) is an example of a *zero coupon bond*. These bonds make no coupon interest payments. They are sold at a substantial discount, and the investor's return is based on the difference between the purchase price and the price received upon sale. If held to maturity, the owner receives the par value of $1,000.

Treasury Notes and Bonds

U.S. Treasury notes and bonds are available in minimum denominations of $1,000. They can be purchased through one of the Federal Reserve banks, a commercial bank, and through stockbrokers. Notes will mature one to seven years after being issued, and bonds usually mature within five to thirty years of the initial sale. Because the bonds have longer maturities than the notes, they usually have higher yields.

There is a secondary market for Treasury notes and bonds. From Figure 7–1 it can be observed that the manner of reporting quotes on transactions is slightly different from that just described for corporate bonds. As an example we will consider a hypothetical listing:

Rate	Maturity	Date	Bid	Asked	Bid Change	Yield
$9\frac{1}{4}$s	2004	May	94.22	94.30	+.9	10.76

Like the prices of the corporate bond, the prices of Treasury notes and bonds are expressed as a percentage of par or face value of the security. But the number after the decimal refers to thirty-seconds of 1 percent. In the current example, the asked price is $94\frac{30}{32}$. With a $1,000 bond or note, this amounts to $949.38. The asked price is the price the buyer of the security will pay to the bond dealer, and the bid price is the price the investor will receive if the bond is sold to the dealer.

Another difference is in yield. The quote on yield for Treasury notes and bonds refers to yield to maturity, rather than the current yield. In the example above, the yield to maturity is 10.76 percent. This means that if the buyer holds the security until maturity, he or she will receive a total annual return of 10.76 percent. The total annual return includes the return from both interest income and price change of the note.

U.S. Savings Bonds

Two types of savings bonds are currently available, Series EE and Series HH. Series EE are purchased at a 50 percent discount from face value and gradually increase in value with time. In 1985, the interest rate was 85 percent of the average return on marketable Treasury securities having a five-year maturity. At the same time, there was a floor of 7.5 percent on the rate. If the EE bonds are redeemed prior to the maturity date, the yield is reduced. These bonds may be purchased in a number of denominations, some as low as $50.

The HH bonds tend to have larger denominations and, unlike the EEs, they are not discount bonds. The HH securities pay interest on a semiannual basis. Both EE and HH bonds can be purchased at banks without paying a commission. However, investors can frequently get higher returns with the same degree of risk on other securities and savings programs.

Government Agency Securities

A large volume of securities are issued by agencies that have some relationship to the federal government. Three of the agencies, Federal Land Banks, Banks for Cooperatives, and Federal Intermediate Credit Banks, are components of the Federal Farm Credit Banks. When these agencies obtain funds from financial markets, they use the proceeds to support designated farm programs. Three other agencies, the Federal National Mortgage Association (FNMA or "Fannie Mae"), Federal Home Loan Banks, and the Government National Mortgage (GNMA or "Ginnie Mae"), also issue securities. They use the proceeds to purchase mortgages, thus supplying funds to the housing market. Information on prices and yields of these and related investments are published under the heading "Government Agency Securities" in the *Wall Street Journal*, shown in Figure 7–3.

Except for GNMAs, the securities described above are not U.S. government obligations. They are not in the same category as Treasury bonds,

GOVERNMENT AGENCY ISSUES

Wednesday, July 31, 1985

Mid-afternoon Over-the-Counter quotations usually based on large transactions, sometimes $1 million or more. Sources on request.

Decimals in bid-and-asked represent 32nds; 101.1 means 101 1/32. a-Plus 1/64. b-Yield to call date. d-Minus 1/64.

FNMA Issues

Rate	Mat	Bid	Asked	Yld
14.10	8-85	100.2	100.6	7.46
15.00	9-85	100.20	100.24	7.58
7.90	10-85	99.30	100.2	7.39
8.80	10-85	100.3	100.7	7.44
10.15	10-85	100.11	100.15	7.44
13.00	11-85	101.9	101.13	7.66
9.75	12-85	100.17	100.21	7.76
14.90	12-85	102.10	102.14	7.75
13.00	1-86	102.1	102.5	7.89
11.70	2-86	101.26	101.30	7.85
8.20	3-86	100	100.4	7.96
9.50	3-86	100.24	100.28	7.97
9.95	3-86	101	101.4	7.99
10.95	4-86	101.26	101.30	7.98
9.20	4-86	100.20	100.24	8.03
11.00	5-86	101.31	102.3	8.14
14.63	6-86	104.31	105.7	8.17
7.95	7-86	99.21	99.29	8.05
14.30	7-86	105.4	105.12	8.23
13.90	8-86	105	105.8	8.45
7.90	9-86	99.16	99.24	8.13
13.25	9-86	104.16	104.24	8.64
10.10	10-86	101.12	101.20	8.61
12.90	10-86	104.14	104.22	8.65
10.95	11-86	102.11	102.19	8.73
13.05	11-86	104.29	105.5	8.66
7.30	12-86	98.11	98.23	8.30
10.13	12-86	101.17	101.25	8.69
11.05	12-86	102.25	103.1	8.62
10.70	1-87	102.2	102.14	8.86
11.15	1-87	102.21	103.1	8.86
9.90	2-87	101.1	101.9	8.89
11.05	2-87	102.23	102.31	8.92
7.75	3-87	98.7	98.19	8.70
11.25	3-87	103.3	103.15	8.87
11.55	3-87	103.10	103.22	9.02
14.30	4-87	107.21	108.1	9.05
12.25	4-87	104.10	104.22	9.17
11.15	5-87	102.31	103.11	9.05
7.65	6-87	97.13	97.29	8.89
11.20	6-87	102.30	103.14	9.13
9.10	7-87	99.18	100.2	9.06
15.25	7-87	110	110.16	9.21
13.65	8-87	107.18	107.30	9.26
14.45	8-87	108.31	109.11	9.28
9.85	9-87	100.25	101.5	9.22
7.50	10-87	97	97.16	8.76
12.13	10-87	105	105.12	9.35
12.55	10-87	105.23	106.5	9.37
10.85	11-87	102.19	102.27	9.42
11.55	11-87	103.27	104.7	9.43
10.90	12-87	102.17	102.29	9.48
10.45	1-88	101.15	101.27	9.58
11.55	1-88	103.20	104	9.67
10.30	2-88	101.5	101.17	9.60
10.75	2-88	102.2	102.14	9.64
14.40	2-88	109.26	110.10	9.69
10.40	3-88	101.12	101.28	9.56
10.45	4-88	101.17	101.29	9.62
10.50	5-88	101.26	102.2	9.62
10.50	6-88	101.18	101.30	9.70
16.38	8-88	115.30	116.14	9.95
12.75	10-88	107.4	107.16	9.94
8.55	9-88	96.31	97.15	9.50
13.20	9-88	108.4	108.16	9.95
11.00	11-88	102.15	102.31	9.90
11.70	11-88	104.12	104.24	9.95
11.25	12-88	103.8	103.22	9.92
11.75	12-88	104.19	104.31	9.97
11.10	1-89	102.20	103	10.04
11.60	2-89	103.26	104.10	10.11
12.10	3-89	105.8	105.20	10.19
9.30	6-89	97.18	98.2	9.91
9.50	6-89	98.11	98.17	9.96
13.13	8-89	108.16	109	10.33
8.80	1-90	98.14	98.18	9.20
12.10	10-89	105.20	106.4	10.25
12.75	10-89	107.24	108.8	10.27
11.80	11-89	104.18	104.30	10.33
11.30	12-89	103.8	103.24	10.21
11.45	1-90	103.10	103.22	10.39
11.05	2-90	102	102.12	10.38
10.30	5-90	99.18	100.2	10.27
11.15	5-90	102.14	102.26	10.38
9.85	7-90	98.4	98.8	10.31
10.90	11-90	101.16	102	10.39
11.80	12-90	105.4	105.20	10.40
12.00	3-91	107	107.16	10.21
12.50	3-91	106.20	107.12	10.71
7.80	10-91	87.16	88	10.48

Fed. Home Loan Bank

Rate	Mat	Bid	Asked	Yld
9.35	8-85	100	100.4	7.25
11.95	8-85	100.5	100.9	7.49
11.70	9-85	100.14	100.18	7.60
14.15	9-85	100.25	100.29	7.66
11.20	10-85	100.21	100.25	7.57
8.10	11-85	100	100.4	7.58
10.13	11-85	100.19	100.23	7.66
14.70	12-85	102.17	102.21	7.79
9.20	1-86	100.16	100.20	7.86
12.75	1-86	102.16	102.20	7.44
13.85	1-86	103.1	103.5	7.47
9.55	2-86	100.24	100.28	7.92
15.30	2-86	103.27	103.31	7.97
10.20	3-86	101.7	101.11	8.00
15.75	3-86	104.22	104.26	7.95
9.15	4-86	100.19	100.23	8.09
10.25	4-86	101.11	101.15	8.11
11.70	4-86	102.12	102.16	8.08
8.75	5-86	100.10	100.14	8.16
15.50	5-86	105.15	105.23	8.12
15.35	7-86	106.10	106.18	8.26
14.60	8-86	105.28	106.4	8.46
16.40	9-86	108.11	108.19	8.37
12.25	9-86	103.25	104.1	8.47
10.80	10-86	102.15	102.23	8.42
11.00	11-86	102.24	103	8.52
11.30	11-86	103.3	103.11	8.54
9.88	12-86	101.14	101.22	8.57
13.25	12-86	105.23	105.31	8.65
10.10	2-87	101.19	101.21	8.93
10.45	2-87	101.31	102.11	8.81
11.05	2-87	102.24	103.4	8.86
11.05	3-87	102.22	103	9.04
11.10	3-87	102.23	103.3	9.02
11.25	3-87	102.31	103.11	9.01
7.65	5-87	97.25	98.9	8.68
9.63	5-87	100.26	101	9.00
13.00	5-87	106	106.16	9.03
8.45	6-87	98.29	99.1	9.01
10.30	6-87	101.26	102.10	8.94
11.35	7-87	103.22	104.2	9.07
13.30	7-87	107	107.12	9.16
7.60	8-87	97.18	97.30	8.71
12.63	8-87	105.30	106.10	9.19
12.05	10-87	105.10	105.22	9.16
12.15	10-87	105.16	105.28	9.17
10.65	11-87	102.7	102.19	9.36
11.30	11-87	103.18	103.30	9.36
10.63	1-88	102.1	102.13	9.51
10.20	3-88	100.30	101.14	9.56
11.90	3-88	105.5	105.17	9.48
10.15	4-88	101.1	101.13	9.54
10.38	4-88	101.11	101.23	9.63
10.15	5-88	101.1	101.13	9.56
8.80	6-88	97.31	98.5	9.53
10.80	6-88	102.18	102.30	9.61
9.15	7-88	98.22	98.24	9.64
11.63	8-88	104.9	104.25	9.78
11.40	10-88	103.20	104	9.91
14.20	11-88	111.14	111.26	9.92
10.70	12-88	102	102.12	9.86
11.38	1-89	103.20	104.4	9.94
10.80	2-89	102.2	102.18	9.92
15.10	2-89	114.2	114.18	10.13
14.25	4-89	111.30	112.10	10.19
10.20	5-89	100.12	100.24	9.95
14.13	7-89	112.2	112.18	10.21
12.50	9-89	107	107.16	10.23
14.55	9-89	113.20	114.4	10.27
11.55	11-89	104.8	105	10.08
11.20	1-90	102.30	103.10	10.26
11.90	3-90	105.10	105.18	10.35
9.50	6-90	97.6	97.18	10.14
9.75	7-90	98.6	98.10	10.19
12.50	9-90	107.20	108.4	10.41
13.70	11-90	112.28	113.12	10.36
10.90	12-90	101.24	102.8	10.34
11.88	2-91	105.20	106.4	10.39
11.10	8-91	102.4	102.20	10.50
11.75	9-91	104.28	105.12	10.53
11.40	12-91	102.28	103.12	10.65
11.45	2-92	103.2	103.14	10.70
11.70	4-92	103.28	104.12	10.76
10.85	10-92	100	100.16	10.74
11.10	11-92	101.8	101.24	10.74
10.70	1-93	99.4	99.20	10.77
10.75	5-93	99.12	99.28	10.77
11.70	7-93	104.12	104.28	10.77
11.95	8-93	105.24	106.8	10.77
7.38	11-93	82	82.16	10.59

Bank for Co-ops

Rate	Mat	Bid	Asked	Yld
7.75	1-86	99.25	100.1	7.63

Federal Farm Credit

Rate	Mat	Bid	Asked	Yld
9.00	9-85	100	100.4	7.32
9.30	9-85	100	100.4	7.43
12.75	9-85	100.10	100.14	7.41
14.90	9-85	100.16	100.20	7.37
8.80	10-85	100.1	100.5	7.47
9.25	10-85	100.4	100.8	7.50
8.45	11-85	100.1	100.5	7.65
8.65	11-85	100.1	100.5	7.68
7.80	12-85	99.27	99.31	7.80
9.25	12-85	100.8	100.12	7.81
14.30	12-85	101.30	102.2	7.82
17.00	12-85	102.26	102.30	7.81
7.63	1-86	99.25	99.29	7.81
9.55	1-86	100.15	100.19	7.84
10.90	1-86	101.6	101.10	7.97
15.80	1-86	103.13	103.17	7.96
8.70	2-86	100.8	100.12	7.76
7.95	3-86	99.26	99.30	7.96
13.95	3-86	103.6	103.10	8.04
7.80	4-86	99.24	99.28	7.95
10.85	4-86	101.24	101.28	8.09
14.00	4-86	103.30	104.2	8.05
13.13	6-86	103.21	103.29	8.16
15.10	6-86	105.7	105.15	8.16
15.15	7-86	106.2	106.10	8.25
11.63	7-86	102.26	103.2	8.28
13.35	9-86	104.15	104.23	8.68
14.50	9-86	105.21	105.29	8.66
9.95	10-86	101.5	101.13	8.69
10.75	10-86	101.30	102.6	8.79
12.00	10-86	103.11	103.19	8.80
10.00	12-86	101.5	101.13	8.84
9.90	1-87	101.3	101.11	8.90
13.20	1-87	105.6	105.18	9.07
14.63	1-87	107.3	107.15	9.07
11.45	3-87	103.7	103.19	8.96
12.40	3-87	104.12	104.24	9.10
14.38	4-87	107.20	108	9.21
14.40	4-87	107.21	108.1	9.22
10.63	7-87	101.24	102.8	9.17
10.55	6-87	102.3	102.15	9.22
10.13	9-87	101.7	101.19	9.26
10.45	10-87	101.21	102.1	9.40
10.55	10-87	101.29	102.5	9.44
10.30	12-87	101.9	101.21	9.48
10.65	12-87	102	102.12	9.48
9.45	1-88	99.13	99.19	9.61
10.90	3-88	102.6	102.18	9.75
11.35	3-88	103	103.12	9.83
12.65	4-88	106.6	106.18	9.83
11.50	7-88	103.26	104.10	9.79
11.70	7-88	104.9	104.25	9.80
12.88	9-88	107	107.12	10.03
11.50	10-88	103.28	104.8	9.91
11.65	1-89	104	104.12	10.12
13.05	1-89	107.30	108.10	10.15
12.50	4-89	106.10	106.22	10.28
13.70	7-89	110	110.16	10.40
7.75	9-89	92.8	92.24	9.94
10.60	10-89	100.8	101	10.29
15.65	10-89	116.16	117	10.55
12.45	10-89	106.8	106.24	10.42
10.95	1-90	101.12	101.28	10.41
11.15	1-90	102.6	102.18	10.42
10.85	2-90	101	101.16	10.42
11.35	4-90	102.22	102.30	10.53
14.10	6-90	112.24	113.8	10.52
9.55	7-90	97.4	97.8	10.27
10.40	7-90	99.16	100	10.40
12.50	9-90	106.20	107.4	10.64
10.60	10-90	100	100.16	10.46
14.10	4-91	112.6	112.18	10.42
9.10	7-91	92.28	93.12	10.62
14.70	7-91	115.12	115.28	11.00
10.60	10-91	99	99.16	10.70
13.65	12-91	111.12	111.28	10.99
11.50	1-92	102.18	102.26	10.88
15.20	1-92	118.26	119	11.01
13.75	7-92	112.16	113	11.03
10.63	1-93	98.8	98.24	10.90
11.80	10-93	104	104.16	10.95
12.35	3-94	106.28	107.12	11.00
14.25	4-94	116.24	117.8	11.10
13.00	9-94	110.14	110.30	11.06
11.45	12-94	102.2	102.14	11.02
11.90	10-97	105	105.24	11.03

Private Expt. Fndg. Corp.

Rate	Mat	Bid	Asked	Yld
14.125P	6-91	106	106½	13.21
12.35Q	11-90	103¾	104¼	11.25
10.75R	11-89	100½	101	10.44
11.25S	2-92	102¼	102⅝	10.68
11.25T	10-95	102¼	102½	10.83

World Bank Bonds

Rate	Mat	Bid	Asked	Yld
11.26	9-85	99.14	99.30	11.32
8.85	12-85	99.11	99.27	9.18
11.26	3-86	100.29	101.13	8.84
8.38	7-86	99	99.16	8.94
10.00	5-88	100.2	100.18	9.75
15.00	12-88	112.24	113.8	10.24
11.00	10-89	101.31	102.15	10.25
4.50	2-90	85.14	85.30	9.30
5.38	7-91	79.1	79.17	10.05
16.63	11-91	124.28	125.12	10.90
15.13	12-91	118.16	119	10.90
5.38	4-92	76.24	77.8	10.15
14.75	6-92	117.21	118.5	10.90
13.63	9-92	112.22	113.6	10.90
10.90	3-93	100.8	100.24	10.75
10.38	5-93	97.17	98.1	10.75
5.88	9-93	74.30	75.14	10.45
6.50	3-94	76.14	76.30	10.65
6.38	10-94	74.12	74.28	10.75
11.63	12-94	103.24	104.8	10.89
8.63	8-95	86.21	87.5	10.75
8.13	8-96	83.3	83.19	10.70
9.35	12-00	87.1	87.17	11.05
8.85	7-01	82.27	83.11	11.10
8.38	12-01	79.4	79.20	11.10
8.25	5-02	81.7	81.23	10.60
8.35	8-02	78.22	79.6	11.10
12.38	10-02	107.30	108.14	11.25

Federal Land Bank

Rate	Mat	Bid	Asked	Yld
7.95	10-85	100	100.4	7.22
8.80	10-85	100.4	100.8	7.47
7.60	4-87	97.27	98.7	8.73
7.25	7-87	96.31	97.11	8.74
7.85	1-88	96.18	96.30	9.26
8.20	1-90	92.28	93.12	10.07
7.95	4-91	89.18	90.2	10.28
7.95	10-96	80.22	81.14	10.85
7.35	1-97	76.22	77.14	10.83

Inter-Amer. Devel. Bk.

Rate	Mat	Bid	Asked	Yld
8.38	2-86	99.3	99.19	9.20
14.00	12-86	106	106.16	9.00
10.75	8-87	100	100.16	9.00
15.00	4-89	113.21	114.5	10.25
5.20	1-92	79.23	80.7	9.35
14.63	8-92	117.5	117.21	10.95
6.50	11-92	80.4	80.20	10.35
6.63	11-93	79.5	79.21	10.35
13.25	8-94	110.21	111.5	11.25
8.63	10-95	94.15	94.31	9.40
9.00	2-01	83.5	83.21	11.25
8.75	7-01	80.5	81.21	11.25
8.38	6-02	77.31	79.15	11.25
9.63	1-04	89.26	90.10	10.85

Asian Development Bank

Rate	Mat	Bid	Asked	Yld
8.63	8-86	98.16	99	9.70
	7-92	46.2	46.18	11.30
7.75	4-96	80.21	81.5	10.75
11.13	5-98	100.20	101.4	11.10

GNMA Issues

Rate	Mat	Bid	Asked	Yld
8.00		81.29	82.5	10.77
9.00		86.11	86.19	11.08
9.50		88.28	89.4	11.18
10.00		91.25	92.1	11.22
11.00		96.26	97.2	11.43
11.50		99.7	99.15	11.54
12.00		101.15	101.23	11.68
12.50		103.19	103.27	11.84
13.00		105.20	105.28	12.01
13.50		107.31	108.7	12.12
14.00		109.5	109.13	12.41
15.00		112.12	112.20	12.68
16.00		114.14	114.22	13.43

FIC Bank Debs.

Rate	Mat	Bid	Asked	Yld
7.95	4-86	99.23	99.31	7.97
6.95	1-87	97.26	98.6	8.32

Student Loan Marketing

Rate	Mat	Bid	Asked	Yld
11.25	10-87	103.15	103.27	9.24
10.10	1-88	100.17	100.29	9.67
9.63	5-88	99.18	99.26	9.69
11.70	7-88	104.10	104.22	9.81
12.85	9-89	107.24	108.8	10.32
10.90	2-90	101.10	101.26	10.39
10.50	4-93	97.20	98.4	10.86

FIGURE 7–3

Source: Wall Street Journal, August 1, 1985. Reprinted by permission of *The Wall Street Journal,* ©1985. World rights reserved.

notes, and bills. However, they are regarded as very safe investments, and even if there were danger of a default, the federal government would probably decide to back up the agencies.

GNMA Pass-Through

As stated above, the Government National Mortgage Association buys mortgages from institutions and organizations that make such loans. These purchases are financed with GNMA pass-through certificates that are backed by pools of those mortgages. The investor in a GNMA pass-through receives monthly payments that include both principal and interest, all guaranteed by the U.S. Government. The securities have stated maturities equal to the length of the mortgages that provide the cash flow. While the mortgages may run from twelve to forty years, there are frequently prepayments. Therefore, the actual maturity is usually less than what is stated, and the quoted yield on the GNMA may differ from the actual yield depending on the extent of prepayments.[4]

GNMA pass-through certificates are available in denominations of $100,000. Because of the high sums needed for certificates, many investors turn to GNMA unit trusts or mutual funds. Mutual funds are more diversified than unit trusts, but because of the government guarantee on interest and principal, there is no difference in the safety of the investments. Investors should keep in mind that the monthly payments received do contain repayment of principal. Therefore, they may want to reinvest that payment to prevent depletion of their capital.

Bearer and Registered Bonds

Bonds come in two forms: bearer and registered. For the bearer bond, the holder or the bearer is the owner. The issuer does not keep records of the transfer of ownership. If the bond is lost, there is no way to recover it. Therefore, the owner should guard the bond as carefully as cash. Interest coupons are attached to the bearer bond. When the interest comes due, usually every six months, the holder of the bond clips off the due portion and sends it in to the issuer or its agent, usually a commercial bank, for payment. In the case of a registered bond, the name of the owner is recorded in the books of the issuer or its agent. When the interest payment or principal is due, a check is automatically sent to the owner on record.

Ratings of Bonds

Corporate and municipal bonds are rated by agencies like Moody's Investors Service and Standard & Poor's Corporation. Various ratings appear in Table 7–1, and Tables 7–2 and 7–3 show the detailed definitions for these ratings by Moody's and Standard & Poor's. Bonds rated AAA or AA are high-quality bonds. They carry the smallest degree of investment risk. They are sometimes

---

[4] In 1985, yields on mortgages were generally quoted based on a ten- to twelve-year life.

TABLE 7–1 Bond Rating

Moody's Ratings	S&P's Ratings	Brief Description
Aaa	AAA	Highest quality
Aa	AA	High quality
A	A	Upper medium grade
Baa	BBB	Medium grade
Ba	BB	Speculative grade
B	B	Low grade
Caa	CCC-C	Default possible
Ca	C	In default or income bonds
C	DDD-D	Lowest rated grade

TABLE 7–2 Definition of Bond Ratings: Moody's Investors Service

Aaa Bonds which are rated Aaa are judged to be of the best quality. They carry the smallest degree of investment risk and are generally referred to as "gilt edge". Interest payments are protected by a large or by an exceptionally stable margin and principal is secure. While the various protective elements are likely to change, such changes as can be visualized are most unlikely to impair the fundamentally strong position of such issues.

Aa Bonds which are rated Aa are judged to be of high quality by all standards. Together with the Aaa group they comprise what are generally known as high grade bonds. They are rated lower than the best bonds because margins of protection may not be as large as in Aaa securities or fluctuation of protective elements may be of greater amplitude or there may be other elements present which make the long term risks appear somewhat larger than in Aaa securities.

A Bonds which are rated A possess many favorable investment attributes and are to be considered as higher medium grade obligations. Factors giving security to principal and interest are considered adequate but elements may be present which suggest a susceptibility to impairment sometime in the future.

Baa Bonds which are rated Baa are considered as lower medium grade obligations, i.e., they are neither highly protected nor poorly secured. Interest payments and principal security appear adequate for the present but certain protective elements may be lacking or may be characteristically unreliable over any great length of time. Such bonds lack outstanding investment characteristics and in fact have speculative characteristics as well.

Ba Bonds which are rated Ba are judged to have speculative elements; their future cannot be considered as well assured. Often the protection of interest and principal payments may be very moderate and thereby not well safeguarded during both good and bad times over the future. Uncertainty of position characterizes bonds in this class.

B Bonds which are rated B generally lack characteristics of the desirable investment. Assurance of interest and principal payments or of maintenance of other terms of the contract over any long period of time may be small.

Caa Bonds which are rated Caa are of poor standing. Such issues may be in default or there may be present elements of danger with respect to principal or interest.

Ca Bonds which are rated Ca represent obligations which are speculative in a high degree. Such issues are often in default or have other marked shortcomings.

C Bonds which are rated C are the lowest rated class of bonds and issues so rated can be regarded as having extremely poor prospects of ever attaining any real investment standing.

Source: Moody's Investors Service.

TABLE 7–3   Definition of Bond Ratings: Standard & Poor's Corporation

AAA   Bonds rated AAA are highest grade obligations. They possess the ultimate degree of protection as to principal and interest. Marketwise they move with interest rates, and hence provide the maximum safety on all counts.

AA   Bonds rated AA also qualify as high grade obligations, and in the majority of instances differ from AAA issues only in small degree. Here, too, prices move with the long term money market.

A   Bonds rated A are regarded as upper medium grade. They have considerable investment strength but are not entirely free from adverse effects of changes in economic and trade conditions. Interest and principal are regarded as safe. They predominantly reflect money rates in their market behavior, but to some extent, also economic conditions.

BBB   The BBB, or medium grade category is borderline between definitely sound obligations and those where the speculative element begins to predominate. These bonds have adequate asset coverage and normally are protected by satisfactory earnings. Their susceptibility to changing conditions, particularly to depressions, necessitates constant watching. Marketwise, the bonds are more responsive to business and trade conditions than to interest rates. This group is the lowest which qualifies for commercial bank investment.

BB   Bonds given a BB rating are regarded as lower medium grade. They have only minor investment characteristics. In the case of utilities, interest is earned consistently but by narrow margins. In the case of other types of obligors, charges are earned on average by a fair margin, but in poor periods deficit operations are possible.

B   Bonds rated as low as B are speculative. Payment of interest cannot be assured under difficult economic conditions.

CCC-CC   Bonds rated CCC and CC are outright speculations, with the lower rating denoting the more speculative. Interest is paid, but continuation is questionable in periods of poor trade conditions. In the case of CC ratings the bonds may be on an income basis and the payment may be small.

C   The rating of C is reserved for income bonds on which no interest is being paid.

DDD-D   All bonds rated DDD, DD and D are in default, with the rating indicating the relative salvage value.

Source: Standard & Poor's Corporation.

referred to as "money bonds," meaning that their market values fluctuate almost entirely in response to changes in interest rates.

Bonds rated A or BBB are medium-grade bonds. The market prices of these bonds are affected by changes in interest rates as well as economic conditions prevailing in the particular industry and in the general economy.

Bonds rated BB and lower are basically speculative low-grade bonds that entail considerable risk with respect to both interest and principal. These securities are sometimes referred to as "junk" bonds.

Limitations to Uses of Ratings

Bond ratings are designed to rank the probability of default in the payment of interest, or sinking fund, or principal. They have proved very useful in predicting the possibility of default in the past. Investors can use bond ratings as a simple screening device to eliminate the issues that are not up to the standard or quality desired. However, investors need to be aware that they should investigate and know much more about the bonds they finally select to purchase. Moody's Investors Service, for example, acknowledges that there are limitations to the uses of ratings:[5]

Bonds carrying the same rating are not claimed to be of absolutely equal quality. In a broad sense they are alike in position, but since there are only nine rating classes used in grading thousands of bonds, the symbols cannot reflect the fine shadings of risks that actually exist. Therefore, it should be evident to the user of ratings that two bonds identically rated are unlikely to be precisely the same in investment quality.

As ratings are designed exclusively for the purpose of grading bonds according to their investment qualities, they should not be used alone as a basis for investment operations. For example, they have no value in forecasting the direction of future trends of market price. Market price movements in bonds are influenced not only by the quality of individual issues but also by changes in money rates and general economic trends, as well as by the length of maturity, and so on. During its life even the best-quality bond may have wide price movements, while its high investment status remains unchanged.

The matter of market price has no bearing on the determination of ratings that are not to be construed as recommendations with respect to "attractiveness." The attractiveness of a given bond may depend on its yield, its maturity date, or other factors for which the investor may search, as well as on its investment quality, the only characteristic to which the rating refers.

Since ratings involve judgments about the future, on the one hand, and since they are used by investors as a means of protection, on the other, the effort is made when assigning ratings to look at "worst" potentialities in the "visible" future, rather than solely at the past record and the status of the present. Therefore, investors using the ratings should not expect to find in them a reflection of statistical factors alone, since they are an appraisal on long-term risks, including the recognition of many nonstatistical factors.

Analysis of Corporate Bonds

The analysis of corporate bonds usually includes the following four areas:

1. Economic significance of the company and the industry in which it operates
2. The quality of the management of the firm
3. Financial resources of the company
4. Indenture provisions

Economic Significance of the Firm

The economic significance of the firm depends on the following factors: What is the size of the firm? How long has it been in operation? Does it offer a broad and balanced group of products or services? Is it a leader in the

[5] Moody's Investors Service, *Moody's Bond Record*.

industry? How important is the industry? What is the growth prospect of the industry and the firm? Does the company have a satisfactory level of earnings? Is the company highly susceptible to fluctuations in general business?

The earning power of the company is the ultimate source of protection to the interests of the bondholders. To gauge how well interest charges are covered, two ratios are usually calculated:

1. *Interest Coverage Ratio.* This ratio is determined by dividing earnings before interest and income taxes by the interest charges:

$$\text{Interest coverage ratio} = \frac{\text{Income before taxes} + \text{Interest charges}}{\text{Interest charges}}$$

This ratio measures the extent to which operating profit can decline without affecting the firm's ability to pay interest charges.

2. *Fixed Charge Coverage Ratio.* Rentals on long-term leases are similar to interest charges on long-term debt—they both represent fixed charges to a corporation. The fixed charge coverage ratio includes both interest charges and rentals, and it may be calculated as follows:

$$\frac{\text{Fixed charge}}{\text{coverage ratio}} = \frac{\text{Income before taxes} + \text{Interest charges} + \text{Rentals on leases}}{\text{Interest charges} + \text{Rentals on leases}}$$

In examining these two ratios of a bond, it is obvious that the higher the ratios, the higher the quality and protection to bondholders. However, the level of the ratios, though important, is not as important as the stability of the ratios over time. If a bond has high but erratic ratios over time, the bond would not be rated as highly as a bond whose ratios are somewhat lower but stable over a number of years, including periods of recession.

SPECIFIC STANDARDS FOR COVERAGE RATIOS   What minimum coverage ratios must bonds possess to qualify for consideration by investors? Graham, Dodd, and Cottle suggest that in order to provide enough margin of safety, the average fixed-charge coverage ratios for a period of seven to ten years should equal at least the following multiple of fixed charges for three types of bonds:[6]

Types of Bonds	Before Taxes	After Taxes
Public utilities	4	2.4
Railroads	5	2.9
Industrials	7	3.8

[6] B. Graham, D. L. Dodd, and S. Cottle, *Security Analysis* (New York: McGraw-Hill, 1962), p. 348.

On the basis of their observations of the standards considered by large institutional investors, Cohen, Zinbarg, and Zeikel suggest that the average coverage ratios of fixed-income securities may be graded in accordance with the standards set as shown in Table 7–4.[7]

The Quality of the Management of the Firm

The second area of investigation and analysis of corporate bonds is the assessment and appraisal of the quality of management.

What are management's objectives and how does management plan to achieve them? What are management's financial and operating policies? To what degree have their objectives and policies been successful? One measure of the success of a company's management is, of course, the past performance of the company over a number of years, including periods of recession. Comparison of operating and profitability ratios with competitors within the industry provides important clues to management's ability to deal with competition and problems of rising costs.

Since bondholders are primarily interested in the long-run outlook of the company, they are particularly interested in future planning of the firm. This includes management training and succession, capital expenditure programs, planned areas of expansion, and research programs. Any sign of deterioration, either in market share or rate of return on invested capital, even in well-established companies, should be taken seriously by prospective buyers of their bonds, for the primary purpose in buying bonds is dependable income. There are many good bonds to choose from, and if investors have doubts about some of their bonds they should sell them and purchase others.

Financial Resources of the Firm

The third area of investigation and analysis of corporate bonds is the financial resources of the firm. Three groups of ratios are usually calculated to find out whether the firm has adequate liquidity, adequate assets to

TABLE 7–4   Standards for Grading Fixed-Income Securities

Average Coverage Ratio	Characteristic of the Issuer	Relative Quality of the Issue
6 and over	Cyclical	Very high
4 and over	Stable	Very high
3–6	Cyclical	Medium to high
2–4	Stable	Medium to high
Under 3	Cyclical	Low
Under 2	Stable	Low

[7] J. Cohen, E. Zinbarg, and A. Zeikel, *Investment Analysis and Portfolio Management*, 4th ed. (Homewood, Ill.: R. D. Irwin, 1982), p. 481.

protect bondholders, and adequate long-term capital in relation to long-term bonds outstanding. The ratios mentioned below are discussed in detail in Chapter 10.

1. *Liquidity.* To measure the liquidity of the bond-issuing company, several ratios are usually calculated, for example, current ratio, quick ratio, turnover of inventory, and turnover of accounts receivable. These ratios should indicate whether the company has sufficient working capital to meet day-to-day business requirements.

2. *Asset Protection.* To determine the degree of protection afforded by the company's assets, ratios relating total long-term debt to net plant and to net tangible assets of the corporation are usually calculated. In the calculation of these ratios, it is important to determine whether book values of these assets correspond to real market values.

3. *Capital Structure.* Bondholders are particularly interested in the relation between long-term debt outstanding and the total amount of long-term capital available to the corporation. Total long-term capital includes long-term debts, common equity, retained earnings, and preferred stock. The capital structure ratio (long-term debt divided by total capitalization) is also known as the *leverage ratio*. If this ratio is too high compared to the industry average, it means that the company has too much fixed financial burden, which can be very dangerous in time of severe recession.

Indenture Provisions

The rights of the bondholders and the obligations of the issuing company are spelled out in a legal contract known as a *bond indenture*. Although no combination of legal rights can substitute for the importance of economic performance of the firm, favorable provisions in the indenture can improve the quality of the issue. Some of the major provisions in which investors are particularly interested are examined below.

Collateral. Some bonds are secured by a lien on specific tangible assets, or a guarantee by the parent company. In the past, collateral used to be heavily stressed by bond buyers. But today, both analysts and investors realize that the best guarantee investors can possibly have is the long-run earning power of the firm. However, collateral, if independently valuable, remains an added favorable feature of the bond.

Sinking Funds. Sinking fund provisions usually require the debtor to make annual or semiannual payments to the trustee. The trustee may be authorized to buy the bonds in the open market or call up certain bonds at random for redemption. Investors generally like the sinking fund provision because it gives the lender greater assurance that the principal amount of the debt will be repaid by maturity date. However, early redemption can hurt the investor.

Call Provision. A call provision gives the issuing corporation the right to call in the bond for redemption before the date of maturity. The call provision generally states that the company will pay an amount over and above the par value of the bond; this additional sum is called a *premium*. The call provision is usually operated to the advantage of the corporation and against the interests of the bondholders. In the case of a bond issued when the market interest rate is high, the call provision will enable the company to call in the bond and issue a new bond at a much lower interest rate. The redemption price under these circumstances is usually much lower than the market price of an equivalent noncallable bond. When a call provision is included in the bond indenture, investors should determine the earliest date the corporation can begin to call in the bonds. In addition, they should find out whether the premium offered by the corporation on redemption is reasonable in relation to other issues available in the market.

Creation of Additional Debt. To protect the interests of bondholders there should be a provision in the indenture to restrict the creation of new long-term debt of equal or prior ranks. The restriction can be phrased in a number of ways. Most commonly, the restriction will be stipulated in the following manner:

1. Total long-term debt, new and old, cannot exceed a certain percentage of the total assets of the corporation.
2. Total interest payments on long-term debt, new and old, cannot exceed a certain percentage of earnings of the corporation over a specified period of past years.

Working Capital and Dividend Restrictions. Some protective provisions in bond indentures stipulate that the corporation cannot pay dividends to the extent that the working capital of the firm would fall below a specified amount. In addition, they may stipulate that the net current assets of the corporation bear a specified relation to the outstanding bonds.

Municipal Bonds

As we saw in Chapter 2, bonds issued by state and local governments, including counties, school districts, townships, and other special agencies, are known as municipal bonds. State and local government securities are of two categories: general obligation bonds and revenue bonds.

General obligation bonds are issued by state governments or municipal corporations chartered by the states and backed by the taxing power and the credit of the issuing governmental units.

Revenue bonds are bonds issued to finance specific capital projects, such as water systems, sewer systems, electric utilities, toll roads, bridges, and parking facilities, and so on. They are secured by the revenue to be generated by the specific project for which the bonds were issued.

Some General Features of Municipal Bonds

TAX EXEMPTION   The principal feature and attraction of municipal bonds is that the interest income from most of these bonds is exempt from federal income taxes.[8] In Chapter 8 we will see how the tax-exempt feature of municipal bonds has particular appeal to individuals in upper income brackets.

LEGAL OPINION   Numerous restrictions govern the issuance of municipal obligations. To avoid the possibility that a bond purchased may be later declared illegal, the buyer of municipal bonds should insist that a copy of legal opinion from qualified bond attorneys be provided to him together with the bond. The opinion usually states that the borrowing power does in fact exist and that all legal requirements and restrictions have been complied with.

MARKETS AND QUOTATIONS   Municipal obligations are bought and sold in the over-the-counter market. Dealers in municipal bonds usually carry an inventory of bonds for which they offer "bid" and "ask" prices. The municipal bond market is characterized by thousands of issuers and diversity of issues. The degree of marketability of each issue tends to vary with the size of the city and its general credit reputation.

In most instances the municipal bond market is dominated by institutional investors and wealthy individuals. It is usually difficult to market a small block— probably under $50,000—without a considerable yield sacrifice. Therefore, individual buyers of small blocks of municipal bonds should plan to hold the security until maturity. Otherwise, they must be prepared to accept considerable sacrifice in market yield when they resell the security in the open market.

Municipal securities are usually quoted on a yield basis. For example, a municipal bond with a 6 percent coupon maturing in ten years may be quoted as 6.50 percent bid and 6.40 percent offered. This means dealers will buy at a price yielding 6.5 percent to maturity, and they will sell the security at a price yielding 6.4 percent to maturity. The exact buying and selling prices can be found in a "basis book," which gives dollar prices if the yield is known.

In expressing yield and yield changes the term "basis point" is commonly used among bond traders. A *basis point* simply means one-hundredth of a percentage point, or 0.01 percent. A change of yield to maturity of 30 basis points means a change of yield of 0.3 percent.

---

[8] As previously noted in Chapter 2, under the 1986 tax reform law, all municipal bonds issued prior to 1986 have the federal tax exemption. Municipal bonds issued in 1986 and beyond which are used for essential government activities will continue to be federally tax exempt. However, under the 1986 law, new bonds used to finance what are considered to be nonessential government activities would not be federally tax exempt. In short, the investor should check on the tax status of a municipal bond before purchasing it.

Ratings of Municipal Bonds and Remedies in Cases of Default

Municipal bonds, like corporate bonds, are rated by agencies such as Moody's Investors Service and Standard & Poor's. Because of the great number and variety of municipal issues, it is expected that the rating agencies sometimes may not be up-to-date in revising their ratings. Therefore, investors should be aware that while the ratings are useful, one cannot always depend on them.

The legal remedies for holders of bonds issued by state and city governments differ considerably. Under the U.S. Constitution, individuals may not sue a state. Hence, if a state defaults, the bondholder may seek legal redress only with the state's own permission.

Individuals may sue a city or other political subdivision of a state for failure to meet its contractual obligations. The usual procedure is for the bondholders to bring suit in the appropriate court for a writ of mandamus ordering the municipal officials to levy and collect sufficient taxes to meet the obligations. The effectiveness of this right is limited by the fact that suits may be lengthy and costly. Moreover, the officials of city governments may either procrastinate or be unable to enforce the writ.

The difficulties in seeking legal remedies in case of default of municipal bonds point out the fact that investors should be careful in the quality of the issue they are buying. In fact, even if the rating at the time of purchase is correct, the bonds can subsequently fall sharply in quality. An example is a large number of bonds issued by Washington State Power Company. Initially, the bonds were regarded as being very safe, but ultimately they defaulted in the early 1980s. Thus one should carefully note any downward movements in ratings or other indications of declining quality.

Analysis of General Obligations

The analysis of general obligations of state and local governments can be roughly divided into four areas: (1) economic strength of the area or the community, (2) revenue-raising potential, (3) the relative magnitude of fixed charges, and (4) the attitudes and fiscal discipline of the officials in charge.

ECONOMIC STRENGTH OF THE COMMUNITY   The economic character of a community provides an indication of its long-term ability to service long-term debts. The economic makeup of the community depends on many factors, including location, climate, transportation facilities, diversity of industries, and so on. Some indication of the economic strength of the area can be obtained by comparing key economic data with that of other comparable states or cities. The important economic indexes are per capita income, rate of unemployment, population, electric power production, and retail sales. The trends in these economic indexes compared to those of the nation as a whole or certain geographical regions should indicate whether the economic strength of the community is improving or deteriorating.

REVENUE-RAISING POTENTIAL   Revenue-raising potential depends upon two factors: the economic strength of the community and the degree of taxation that has been already imposed. Some indication of the degree of taxation imposed by a community can be obtained by referring to several key ratios, such as revenue per capita, the proportion of revenue per capita to income per capita, and the tax rates on assessed value of properties.

If a community is relatively prosperous, but the proportion of taxes to income per capita is relatively high compared to that of other cities or states, the government unit will soon find out that voters' resistance will put a limit on the continued expansion of long-term debt financing.

The tax on real property is usually expressed as a certain percent of the assessed value of the property, and the percent levied is known as the tax rate. A rising trend in tax rates will mean that the community is moving toward a point beyond which no more rise will be feasible.

RELATIVE MAGNITUDE OF FIXED CHARGES   The relative magnitude of fixed charges can be gauged by a few ratios. They are (1) the ratio of debt services to operating expenses of the city or state, (2) the ratio of net debt to assessed valuation of real property, and (3) the per capita debt. Compared to those of other cities and states, these ratios would indicate whether the existing debt already constitutes an overload on the tax base of the community.

ATTITUDES AND FISCAL DISCIPLINE OF OFFICIALS   The attitudes and fiscal discipline of the officials of the government are no less important than the quantitative measures of the tax base and debt burden. If the government officials in charge are complacent about a continued deficit in the operating budget and imprudent in the planning of future expenditures, a city with a strong economic base can still run into trouble. A clear example was the near-bankruptcy of New York City in the 1970s.

Analysis of Revenue Bonds

Revenue bonds are intended to be self-liquidating. That is, the payment of interest and principal depends entirely on the revenues generated by the project for which the revenue bond was issued. The analysis of revenue bonds is similar to the analysis of corporate bonds. The important fact is that a project financed by revenue bonds needs to be well planned. The revenues to be generated by the project must be sufficient and stable to adequately cover the servicing requirements of the revenue bonds.

Individual Retirement Accounts (IRAs)

Tax-exempt municipal bonds represent one specific type of tax shelter. Another type of tax shelter is an IRA. These accounts can be opened through savings institutions, banks, insurance companies, mutual funds, and stock brokers. The accounts are particularly attractive to certain investors. If an investor's taxable income is below certain designated levels, he or she can contribute up to a specified amount into an IRA during a year and deduct the amount of the contribution from his or her taxable income. In addition, no taxes are paid on interest or dividends earned by the investments made into the account. Neither the principal nor interest and dividends can be withdrawn from the account without penalty if the investor has not reached a designated age. Withdrawals after that age, as well as withdrawals prior to that age, are treated as taxable income at the investor's tax rate when the withdrawals occur. Subject to some limitations, the investor can transfer funds from one IRA into another IRA. Investors should check into the latest rules and restrictions on these accounts with an accountant or a reliable organization that offers IRAs.

SUMMARY

Interest-bearing assets differ in terms of yields, risk, liquidity, maturity, and tax features. One group, money market instruments, are short-term, generally quite safe, and have relatively large denominations. These securities include Treasury bills, negotiable certificates of deposit, commercial paper, bankers' acceptances, repurchase agreements, Eurodollar deposits, and short-term tax-exempt securities.

Bonds and notes are longer-term securities and tend to be sold in denominations of $1,000. Bonds may be issued by corporations, by federal, state, or local governments, or by various government agencies. Most bonds have coupons, which means that interest payments are made on a regular basis, normally semiannually or annually. Zero coupon bonds make no regular interest payments but are sold at a discount from par value and mature at par value. Bonds vary in risk, and ratings of corporate and municipal bonds may be obtained from Moody's Investors Services and Standard & Poor's Corporation. Financial ratios relating to the firm, quality of management, financial resources, and indenture provisions are elements used in determining security ratings.

QUESTIONS AND PROBLEMS

1. Indicate the usefulness and limitations of bond ratings.
2. What provisions would investors of bonds like to have included in a bond indenture?
3. In the analysis of bonds, what factors do analysts emphasize?
4. In the analysis of bonds, analysts usually calculate a few ratios. What are some of these ratios? What do they indicate?

5. What is the difference between the valuation of a U.S. government bond and a corporate bond?
6. Find out the current yields on long-term government, industrial, and utility bonds of the top four ratings (AAA down to BBB).
7. In the analysis of general obligations of state and local governments, what areas should one examine?
8. Explain the difference between general obligation and revenue bonds.
9. What is the difference between the current yield and the yield to maturity?
10. A 180-day Treasury bill sold for a price listed as 96.000. Calculate the Treasury bill rate and Treasury bill yield.
11. A Treasury bill that matures in 180 days has the following listing:

Bid		Asked
	Discount	
8.96		9.30

Calculate the Treasury bill yield.

12. An investor bought and later sold a group of Treasury bonds with total par value of $5,000. The price listing on the purchase date was

Bid	Asked
101.8	101.20

On the date of sale the listing was:

Bid	Asked
99.16	99.28

Calculate the investor's loss on the group of bonds.

REFERENCES

Bellemore, Phillips, and Ritchie. *Investments*. Cincinnati: South-Western Publishing, 1979.

Cohen, J., Zinbarg, E., and Zeikel, A. *Investment Analysis and Portfolio Management*. Homewood, Ill.: R. D. Irwin, 1982.

Cook, T. Q. and Summers, B. J. eds. *Instruments of the Money Market*. Federal Reserve Bank of Richmond, 1981.

Darst, David M. *The Complete Bond Book*. New York: McGraw-Hill, 1975.

Fisher, D. and Jordan, R. *Security Analysis and Portfolio Management*, 2nd ed. Englewood Cliffs, N.J.: Prentice-Hall, 1979.

Fisher, Lawrence. "Determinants of Risk Premiums on Corporate Bonds." *The Journal of Political Economy*, June 1959.

Garbade, Kenneth. *Securities Markets*. New York: McGraw-Hill, 1982.

Garbade, K. D., and Hunt, J. F. "Risk Premiums on Federal Agency Debt." *Journal of Finance*, March 1978.

Graham, B., Dodd, D. L., and Cottle, S. *Security Analysis*. New York: McGraw-Hill, 1962, Part 3.

Gross, William H. "The Effect of Coupon on Yield Spreads." *Financial Analysts Journal*, July–Aug. 1979.

Latane, H., Tuttle, D., and Jones, C. *Security Analysis and Portfolio Management*. New York: Ronald, 1975.

Moody's Investors Service. *Moody's Bond Record*.

———. *Moody's Bond Survey.*

Phillips, Jackson. "Analysis and Rating of Corporate Bonds." *Financial Analyst's Handbook*. Homewood, Ill.: Dow Jones-Irwin, 1975.

—————. "Analysis and Rating of Municipal Bonds." *Financial Analyst's Handbook*. Homewood, Ill.: Dow Jones-Irwin, 1975.

Reilly, F. K., ed. *Readings and Issues in Investments*. Hinsdale, Ill.: Dryden Press, 1975, Part 7.

Salomon Brothers. *Prospects for the Credit Markets.*

Sharpe, William F. "Bonds Versus Stocks—Some Lessons from Capital Market Theory." *Financial Analysts Journal*, Nov.–Dec. 1973.

Sumutka, Alan R., and Randall, Maury R. "Some Tax Advantaged Investments—Part I." *CPA Journal*, February 1984.

Weinstein, Mark I. "The Seasoning Process of New Corporate Bond Issues." *Journal of Finance*, Dec. 1978.

8

Valuation and Yields of Bonds

In this chapter we examine in detail the relationship between prices of bonds and interest rates. Concepts that are analyzed include bond duration and term and risk structure of interest rates. In addition, various investment strategies relating to bonds are described.

BOND VALUE DETERMINATION

To understand the relationship between bonds and interest rates, one should know the basics of time value of money. Those who are unfamiliar with the concept of time value will find helpful the presentation in the Appendix to this chapter.

Since a bond is a promise to pay a series of interest payments and the par value at maturity, the price of a bond is just the present value of those future payments. First, let us consider a bond that pays interest, I, each year and the par value, Par, in year n. Its price, P_B, can be computed as:

$$P_B = \frac{I}{(1 + k_d)} + \frac{I}{(1 + k_d)^2} + \cdots + \frac{I}{(1 + k_d)^n} + \frac{\text{Par}}{(1 + k_d)^n}$$

$$= \sum_{t=1}^{n} \frac{I}{(1 + k_d)^t} + \text{Par}\frac{1}{(1 + k_d)^n} \qquad (8.1)$$

where:

k_d = interest rate applicable to the bond, which is also the yield to maturity

As noted in Chapter 7, I is calculated as the coupon rate times the par value. The value of k_d depends on a number of factors, including the riskiness of the bond, time to maturity, and the rate of inflation. If one prefers to use interest rate tables to perform calculations, Equation 8.2 can be derived from Equation 8.1.

$$P_B = I\left(\sum_{t=1}^{n} \frac{1}{(1 + k_d)^t}\right) + \text{Par}\frac{1}{(1 + k_d)^n}$$

or

$$P_B = I(\text{PVA}_{k_d,n}) + \text{Par}(\text{PVSP}_{k_d,n}) \qquad (8.2)$$

where:

$$\text{PVA}_{k_d,n} = \text{Present value of an annuity of \$1 per year at interest rate } k_d \text{ for } n \text{ years}$$

$$\text{PVSP}_{k_d,n} = \text{Present value of a single payment of \$1 to be received in } n \text{ years when } k_d \text{ is the interest rate}$$

Values of PVSP and PVA for different values of k_d and n are shown in Tables A–2 and A–3 in the Appendix at the end of this chapter.

As an example, consider a bond with a 10 percent coupon and $1,000 par value that matures in fifteen years. If the current interest rate for such bonds is 12 percent, we compute the price as follows:

$$P_B = 100 \text{ PVA}_{.12,15} + 1,000 \text{ PVSP}_{.12,15}$$

$$= 100(6.811) + 1,000(.183)$$

$$P_B = \$864.10$$

In cases when bonds pay interest semiannually, one must modify Equations 8.1 and 8.2. The investor receives $I/2$ twice a year. Payments are discounted every six months at interest rate $k_d/2$, and the number of interest payments doubles to $2n$. Thus we now have

$$P_B = \sum_{t=1}^{2n} \frac{I/2}{(1 + k_d/2)^t} + \frac{\text{Par}}{(1 + k_d/2)^{2n}} \qquad (8.3a)$$

$$P_B = (I/2)(\text{PVA}_{k_d/2,2n}) + \text{Par}(\text{PVSP}_{k_d/2,2n}) \qquad (8.3b)$$

Applying Equation 8.3b to the previous example, we see that the price of the bond is reduced slightly.

$$P_B = 50 \text{ PVA}_{.06,30} + 1,000 \text{ PVSP}_{.06,30}$$

$$= 688.25 + 174$$

$$= \$862.25$$

It is useful to know that when the coupon rate equals the current market yield to maturity, the bond price equals the par value. If market rates rise above the coupon rate, the bond will sell at a discount from par. Similarly, if interest rates fall below the coupon rate, the bond will sell at a premium above par. The fact that there is an inverse relationship between bond prices and interest rates is apparent in Equation 8.1. As k_d rises, the denominator increases, but I is constant and P_B must drop.

In Chapter 7 we described zero-coupon bonds as securities that make no annual interest payments and only pay the par value at maturity. Using Equation 8.2 we can evaluate those bonds by noting that $I = 0$, and therefore,

$$P_B = 0(\text{PVA}_{k_d,n}) + \text{Par}(\text{PVSP}_{k_d,n})$$

$$= \text{Par}(\text{PVSP}_{k_d,n}) \tag{8.4}$$

For example, consider a zero-coupon bond with a par value of $1,000 that matures in fifteen years. If the interest rate is 12 percent on this security,

$$P_B = 1,000 \text{ PVSP}_{.12,15}$$

$$= \$183$$

YIELD TO MATURITY

Up to this point we have been primarily concerned with determining the market value of bonds. However, what probably occurs more often is that the investor knows the price of a bond, the scheduled interest payments, and the maturity date but not the yield to maturity, k_d. In fact, the listings for New York Exchange Bonds cited in Chapter 7 provided all of the above information except yield to maturity.

Let us examine the following problem. A bond with a 10 percent coupon matures in ten years and is selling for $900. What is the yield to maturity, k_d?

One approach to this problem is to use a trial-and-error method to determine what discount rate comes sufficiently close to causing the present value of the cash flows from the bond to equal the price. Mathematically the problem is to find k_d so that

$$900 = 100 \text{ PVA}_{k_d,10} + 1,000 \text{ PVSP}_{k_d,10}$$

To solve this problem, one might use an electronic calculator or a computer with specialized software to do the trial-and-error calculations, given the price, coupon, and years to maturity. The answers provided are generally quite accurate.

A second method of estimating yields is less accurate than the use of calculators and computers. This method is arithmetically simple and involves the following equation to obtain an approximation.

$$k_d \approx \frac{\text{Annual interest} + \text{Average annual capital gain (or loss)}}{\text{Average value of bond}}$$

$$k_d \approx \frac{I + \left(\dfrac{\text{Par} - P_B}{n}\right)}{(P_B + \text{Par})/2} \tag{8.5}$$

In our example,

$$k_d \approx \frac{100 + \dfrac{1,000 - 900}{10}}{(900 + 1,000)/2} = \frac{110}{950}$$

$$= 11.6\%$$

A third method of obtaining a yield to maturity is to use a bond yield table. A page from such a table is shown in Table 8–1. The page refers to bonds with a 10 percent coupon. Going across price row 90 to the ten-year column, we find the yield to maturity on the bond is actually 11.72 percent.

In the case of zero-coupon bonds, a simple method using Equation 8.4 may be used to estimate yields. Details are in the Appendix to this chapter.

Note that the yield to maturity is the investor's return, assuming that all interest payments and principal are paid as scheduled. In bonds that have a high risk of default, the expected yield to maturity may be substantially less than the yields that we have been calculating.

Effects of Call Provisions

As we noted in Chapter 7, a minimum number of years must pass after issuance of a bond before it can be called. In addition, the firm normally pays a premium above the par value at the time of the call, but generally the premium declines if the firm redeems the bonds after the earliest possible call date.

If a callable bond is selling at a premium above the par value, it is useful for an investor to calculate the *yield to call*, which is the rate of return if the bond is called. Given that a bond is purchased above par value, the investor should be aware that the yield to call may be lower than the yield to maturity. For example, consider a bond with a 15 percent coupon that will mature in twenty-five years. Its price is currently $1,250, and it can be called for $1,150 in five years. First, we estimate the yield to maturity.

TABLE 8–1 Sample Page from a Bond Yield Table

10%

MATURITY PRICE	9½ YEARS	10 YEARS	10½ YEARS	11 YEARS	11½ YEARS	12 YEARS	12½ YEARS	13 YEARS
75	15.03	14.88	14.76	14.64	14.54	14.44	14.36	14.28
76	14.78	14.65	14.52	14.41	14.32	14.23	14.15	14.07
77	14.54	14.41	14.30	14.19	14.10	14.01	13.94	13.87
78	14.31	14.18	14.07	13.97	13.88	13.80	13.73	13.66
79	14.08	13.96	13.85	13.76	13.67	13.60	13.53	13.46
80	13.85	13.74	13.64	13.55	13.47	13.40	13.33	13.27
81	13.63	13.52	13.43	13.34	13.27	13.20	13.13	13.08
82	13.41	13.31	13.22	13.14	13.07	13.00	12.94	12.89
83	13.19	13.10	13.01	12.94	12.87	12.81	12.76	12.71
84	12.98	12.89	12.81	12.74	12.68	12.62	12.57	12.52
85	12.77	12.69	12.62	12.55	12.49	12.44	12.39	12.35
86	12.57	12.49	12.42	12.36	12.31	12.26	12.21	12.17
87	12.36	12.29	12.23	12.18	12.13	12.08	12.04	12.00
88	12.16	12.10	12.04	11.99	11.95	11.90	11.87	11.83
89	11.97	11.91	11.86	11.81	11.77	11.73	11.70	11.66
90	11.78	11.72	11.68	11.63	11.60	11.56	11.53	11.50
90½	11.68	11.63	11.59	11.55	11.51	11.48	11.45	11.42
91	11.59	11.54	11.50	11.46	11.43	11.39	11.37	11.34
91½	11.49	11.45	11.41	11.37	11.34	11.31	11.29	11.26
92	11.40	11.36	11.32	11.29	11.26	11.23	11.20	11.18
92½	11.31	11.27	11.23	11.20	11.17	11.15	11.13	11.10
93	11.22	11.18	11.15	11.12	11.09	11.07	11.05	11.03
93½	11.13	11.09	11.06	11.03	11.01	10.99	10.97	10.95
94	11.04	11.00	10.98	10.95	10.93	10.91	10.89	10.87
94½	10.95	10.92	10.89	10.87	10.85	10.83	10.81	10.80
95	10.86	10.83	10.81	10.79	10.77	10.75	10.74	10.72
95¼	10.81	10.79	10.77	10.75	10.73	10.71	10.70	10.68
95½	10.77	10.75	10.72	10.71	10.69	10.67	10.66	10.65
95¾	10.72	10.70	10.68	10.67	10.65	10.64	10.62	10.61
96	10.68	10.66	10.64	10.63	10.61	10.60	10.58	10.57
96¼	10.64	10.62	10.60	10.59	10.57	10.56	10.55	10.54
96½	10.59	10.58	10.56	10.55	10.53	10.52	10.51	10.50
96¾	10.55	10.53	10.52	10.51	10.49	10.48	10.47	10.46
97	10.51	10.49	10.48	10.47	10.45	10.44	10.44	10.43
97¼	10.46	10.45	10.44	10.43	10.42	10.41	10.40	10.39
97½	10.42	10.41	10.40	10.39	10.38	10.37	10.36	10.35
97¾	10.38	10.37	10.36	10.35	10.34	10.33	10.32	10.32
98	10.34	10.33	10.32	10.31	10.30	10.29	10.29	10.28
98¼	10.29	10.28	10.28	10.27	10.26	10.26	10.25	10.25
98½	10.25	10.24	10.24	10.23	10.22	10.22	10.22	10.21
98¾	10.21	10.20	10.20	10.19	10.19	10.18	10.18	10.18
99	10.17	10.16	10.16	10.15	10.15	10.15	10.14	10.14
99¼	10.12	10.12	10.12	10.11	10.11	10.11	10.11	10.10
99½	10.08	10.08	10.08	10.08	10.07	10.07	10.07	10.07
99¾	10.04	10.04	10.04	10.04	10.04	10.04	10.04	10.03
100	10.00	10.00	10.00	10.00	10.00	10.00	10.00	10.00
100¼	9.96	9.96	9.96	9.96	9.96	9.96	9.96	9.97
100½	9.92	9.92	9.92	9.92	9.93	9.93	9.93	9.93
100¾	9.88	9.88	9.88	9.89	9.89	9.89	9.89	9.90
101	9.84	9.84	9.85	9.85	9.85	9.86	9.86	9.86
101½	9.75	9.76	9.77	9.77	9.78	9.78	9.79	9.79
102	9.67	9.68	9.69	9.70	9.71	9.71	9.72	9.73
102½	9.59	9.61	9.62	9.63	9.64	9.64	9.65	9.66
103	9.51	9.53	9.54	9.55	9.56	9.57	9.58	9.59
103½	9.43	9.45	9.47	9.48	9.49	9.50	9.52	9.52

Source: High-Coupon Bond Yield Tables. Publication No. 354. Boston, Mass.: Financial Publishing Company, 1980. Copyright 1980 by Financial Publishing Company.

$$YTM \approx \frac{150 + \dfrac{1,000 - 1,250}{25}}{\dfrac{1,250 + 1,000}{2}}$$

$$\text{YTM} \approx \frac{140}{1,125} = 12.44\%$$

To calculate yield to call we use a similar equation:

$$\text{YTC} \approx \frac{\text{Interest} + \dfrac{\text{Call price} - \text{Current price}}{\text{Years to call}}}{\dfrac{\text{Current price} + \text{Call price}}{2}}$$

The average capital gain in the numerator is based on the difference between current price and call price, spread over the years to call. The average price of the bond in the denominator is also a function of the call price rather than the par value.

$$\text{YTC} \approx \frac{150 + \dfrac{1,150 - 1,250}{5}}{\dfrac{1,250 + 1,150}{2}} = \frac{130}{1,200}$$

$$\text{YTC} \approx 10.83\%$$

Thus, before purchasing this hypothetical bond, the investor should consider whether a call is likely and whether the 10.8 percent yield to call is a sufficient return to warrant the investment.

Taxable and Tax-Exempt Yields

The interest on corporate bonds is subject to federal tax and also to applicable state and local income taxes. Assume an investor is in a 35 percent marginal tax bracket on interest income.[1] In other words, for each additional dollar of interest received, the investor pays 35¢ in taxes. If $1,000 is invested in a corporate security with a one-year interest rate of 10 percent, there is a tax of $35 on the $100 of interest income. This leaves $65 of the interest for the investor, which means the after-tax return is $\frac{65}{1000} = 6.5$ percent.

Looked at from a slightly different point of view, the before-tax return is 10 percent, but 35 percent of that amount goes to taxes, while

---

[1]As previously noted in Chapter 1, it is possible that an investor's overall marginal income tax rate will be higher than 28 percent in 1988 and beyond. This could occur because of the added effect of state and local income taxes and because of a scheduled federal surtax which would be applicable in certain income ranges.

the remaining 65 percent stays with the investor. Thus the investor receives 6.5 percent on his or her investment, and the government receives 3.5 percent. In general, if the interest rate is i_c for a corporate security, and the marginal tax bracket of an investor is t, the portion of i_c paid as taxes is ti_c. The after-tax return to the investor, i_A is

$$i_A = i_c - ti_c \quad \text{or}$$

$$i_A = i_c(1 - t) \tag{8.6}$$

Next, consider a security that is completely tax-exempt and has a return i_M (with $i_M < i_c$).[2] Assume that the tax-exempt and corporate securities are comparable in other respects, such as in risk and maturity. If $i_M > i_A$, the investor would select the tax-exempt over the corporate security. For investors with sufficiently low values for t, $i_A > i_M$, and they would prefer the corporate security. To determine the tax bracket at which an investor would not have to decide between corporate and tax-exempt securities, set $i_M = i_A$ in Equation 8.6.

$$i_M = i_c(1 - t)$$

$$\frac{i_M}{i_c} = 1 - t$$

$$t = 1 - \frac{i_M}{i_c} \tag{8.7}$$

If $i_M = 7\%$ and $i_c = 10\%$, then $t = 1 - \frac{7}{10} = .30$, or 30 percent. Investors in the 30 percent tax bracket would be indifferent in deciding between the securities.

A similar problem that is often of interest is the following: What interest rate on a fully taxable security is equivalent to a tax-exempt rate for a particular investor? In this case we want to solve Equation 8.6 for i_c.

$$i_c = \frac{i_M}{1 - t} \tag{8.8}$$

An investor in a 35 percent tax bracket who can get 9.75 percent on a tax-exempt security would require a taxable rate of

$$i_c = \frac{9.75}{1 - .35} = 15\%$$

---

[2]Interest from most municipal bonds is exempt from federal taxation, and it is also exempt from state taxes in the state of issuance. Treasury securities are exempt from state and local taxes but not federal income taxes. Federal taxes normally comprise by far the largest portion of the investor's tax burden.

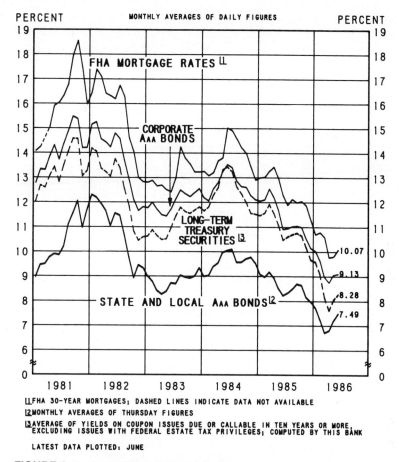

PERCENT   MONTHLY AVERAGES OF DAILY FIGURES   PERCENT

FIGURE 8–1   Long-Term Interest Rates
Source: Federal Reserve Bank of St. Louis, *Monetary Trends,* July 1986.

Because many investors are in relatively high income tax brackets, most municipal bonds, because of their tax benefits, provide lower interest rates than taxable securities. This fact is illustrated in Figure 8–1.

MATURITY, COUPON, AND PRICE FLUCTUATION OF BONDS

As we know, bond prices are sensitive to changes in interest rates. The extent of the sensitivity varies among different bonds and is strongly influenced by both time to maturity and the size of the coupon.

The effect of maturity can be illustrated with a simple example. Consider two different securities, each having a 10 percent coupon. The first is a one-year security that pays $1,000 in principal plus $100 interest, a total of $1,100 next year. If the interest rate is 10 percent, the price of this security is

$$P_{1YR} = \frac{1,100}{1.10} = \$1,000$$

The second security is a thirty-year bond with a 10 percent coupon rate. If the market interest rate is also 10 percent on this security, it will sell at its $1,000 par value.

Next, assume that interest rates rise from 10 percent to 11 percent. The price of the one-year security will drop only by $9:

$$P_{1YR} = \frac{1,100}{1.11} = \$991$$

The price of the thirty-year bond, however, falls by $87.

$$P_{30YR} = 100 \text{ PVA}_{.11, 30} + 1,000 \text{ PVSP}_{.11, 30} = 869 + 44$$
$$= 913$$

Measured in terms of percentage declines, the one-year security dropped by about 1 percent compared to almost 9 percent for the thirty-year bond.

Our next step is to analyze the relationship between price sensitivity and coupon. Consider two twenty-five-year bonds, one with a relatively low 6 percent coupon (L) and the other with a relatively high 11 percent coupon (H). If the interest rate is initially 10 percent, the prices are

$$P_L = 60 \text{ PVA}_{.10, 25} + 1,000 \text{ PVSP}_{.10, 25} = 545 + 92$$
$$= \$637$$
$$P_H = 110 \text{ PVA}_{.10, 25} + 1,000 \text{ PVSP}_{.10, 25} = 998 + 92$$
$$= \$1,090$$

Assuming the interest rate rises from 10 percent to 11 percent, the new prices are now:

$$P_L = 60 \text{ PVA}_{.11, 25} + 1,000 \text{ PVSP}_{.11, 25} = 505 + 74 = \$579$$
and
$$P_H = \$1,000 \text{ (since the coupon rate equals yield to maturity)}$$

The lower coupon bond's price has dropped by 9.1 percent compared to only 8.3 percent for the higher coupon bond.

TABLE 8–2 Price Fluctuations for Various Coupon Rates (twenty-year maturity bonds)

Coupon Rates (%)	Falling Securities Prices (Rising Interest Rates)			Rising Securities Prices (Falling Interest Rates)		
	Price at 7%	Price at 8%	% Change	Price at 7%	Price at 5%	% Change
4	68	$60\frac{3}{8}$	−11.3	68	$87\frac{1}{2}$	+28.7
5	$78\frac{5}{8}$	$70\frac{3}{8}$	−10.5	$78\frac{5}{8}$	100	+27.1
6	$89\frac{3}{8}$	$80\frac{1}{4}$	−10.0	$89\frac{3}{8}$	$112\frac{1}{2}$	+25.8
7	100	$90\frac{1}{8}$	−9.8	100	$125\frac{1}{8}$	+25.1
8	$110\frac{5}{8}$	100	−9.5	$110\frac{5}{8}$	$137\frac{5}{8}$	+24.4

Source: David M. Darst, *The Complete Bond Book* (New York: McGraw-Hill, 1975), p.30.

The reason why the 11 percent coupon bond is less price-sensitive than the 6 percent bond is because more of its value is attributable to the stream of interest payments rather than the par value at maturity. In other words, relatively more of the value of the 11 percent bond is derived from payments to the investor received prior to the maturity date in the twenty-fifth year. In a previous example we saw that other things being equal, a shorter maturity reduces price sensitivity to changes in interest rates. Similarly, given the maturity date, when more of the value of a bond comes from payments made in the early years, there is less price sensitivity.

Additional examples of the relationship between coupon and price sensitivity to interest rate changes are provided in Table 8–2. Price fluctuations are shown for various coupon rates of twenty-year bonds when the market interest rate rises from 7 percent to 8 percent and when it declines from 7 percent to 5 percent. The price of 4 percent coupon bonds fluctuated more than bonds of higher coupon rates in cases of both rising and declining interest rates. In summary, we see that the lower the coupon rate, the greater the impact on the price of a bond for a given change in interest rates.

DURATION

Since price sensitivity is a function of both coupon size and time to maturity, an overall measure of sensitivity should incorporate both of these factors. Such a measure does exist and is called the *duration of a bond*. The equation that defines duration (DUR) is the following:

$$\text{DUR} = \frac{\sum_{t=1}^{n} \frac{\text{PMT}_t(t)}{(1+i)^t}}{\sum_{t=1}^{n} \frac{\text{PMT}_t}{(1+i)^t}} \tag{8.9}$$

where:

$$PMT_t = \text{payment of interest and/or principal at time } t$$
$$n = \text{time period of maturity}$$
$$i = \text{yield to maturity of the security}$$

The denominator in Equation 8.9 is the present value of future payments from the bond discounted by the yield to maturity. That is, it is the price of the bond, P_B. The numerator is the present value of all payments from the security weighted by the number of periods (t) between the present time (0) and the period when the payment is to be received (t).

Substituting P_B into the denominator of Equation 8.9, we can obtain an equation in a slightly different form to compute duration:

$$\text{DUR} = \sum_{t=1}^{n} \left(\frac{\dfrac{PMT_t}{(1 + i)^t}}{P_B} \right)(t) \tag{8.10}$$

In using Equation 8.10 we calculate the present value of each cash flow received from that bond. Each present value is then used to compute a weight for the time required (t) to receive the cash flow. In short, Equation 8.10 shows duration as a weighted average of when cash flows arrive from the bond. The weights are based on the relative value each payment contributes to the price of the bond. As an illustration, consider a bond with a coupon rate of 10 percent that matures in four years and has a yield to maturity of 12 percent. Details are shown in Table 8–3.

In the upper panel of the table, the price of the bond is computed as $939.30. In the second column of the lower panel, we divide the present value of each payment by the bond's price. These weights are then multiplied by the number of years in Column 1, and we obtain the entries in Column 3. When we add up these entries, we have calculated the duration, which is slightly under 3.5 years.

Tables have been published that show bond duration for different securities, and a sample page is shown in Table 8–4. The page is applicable to a bond with a 12 percent coupon. If the current yield to maturity on such bonds is 11 percent, and if it matures in thirty years, the bond will have a duration of only 8.66 years.

At this point, some facts about duration of zero-coupon bonds and coupon paying bonds should be mentioned. The duration of a zero-coupon bond is equal to the term to maturity. This is because there is only one payment made, and that occurs at maturity. In contrast, bonds with coupons have a duration less than the term to maturity. This is because in the duration measure, weight is given to the periods prior to maturity when interest payments are made.

TABLE 8–3 Calculation of Duration of a Four-Year Bond with 10 Percent Coupon, 12 Percent Yield to Maturity

Bond Price:

Time (Years)	Payment	PVSP at 12%	Present Value[a] of Payment
1	100	.8929	89.30
2	100	.7972	79.70
3	100	.7118	71.20
4	1,100	.6355	699.10
		Price of Bond:	$939.30

Duration:

(1) Time (Years)	(2) Present Value of Payment/Price of Bond	(3) (1) × (2)
1	.0951	.0951
2	.0849	.1698
3	.0758	.2274
4	.7442	2.9768
	Sum: 1.0000	Duration: 3.4691 years

[a] Rounded to nearest 10¢.

Bonds with the same duration should have approximately the same percentage change in price when interest rates change. In the following equation we show a relationship between duration and movements in bond prices:[3]

$$\%\Delta P_B \approx -\text{DUR} \times \left[\frac{i_n - i_o}{1 + i_o}\right] \times 100\% \qquad (8.11)$$

where:

$\%\Delta P_B$ = percentage change in the bond's price
DUR = duration
i_n = new market interest rate
i_o = original market interest rate

To test this equation, assume that the market interest rate drops from 12 percent in our previous example to 10 percent. Since the coupon rate of

[3]See Bob Edwards, "Bond Analysis: The Concept of Duration." *AAII Journal*, March 1984, p. 37, or see Charles Jones, *Investments: Analysis and Management* (New York: Wiley, 1985), p. 204.

TABLE 8–4 Sample Page from a Duration Table

BOND DURATION	YEARS AND MONTHS										12%	
YIELD	21-0	22-0	23-0	24-0	25-0	26-0	27-0	28-0	29-0	30-0	35-0	40-0
4.00	11.47	11.82	12.16	12.49	12.82	13.13	13.44	13.74	14.03	14.31	15.64	16.81
4.20	11.36	11.70	12.03	12.36	12.67	12.97	13.27	13.56	13.84	14.12	15.38	16.50
4.40	11.26	11.59	11.91	12.22	12.52	12.82	13.11	13.38	13.66	13.92	15.13·	16.19
4.60	11.15	11.47	11.78	12.09	12.38	12.67	12.94	13.21	13.47	13.73	14.89	15.89
4.80	11.04	11.36	11.66	11.95	12.24	12.51	12.78	13.04	13.29	13.53	14.64	15.60
5.00	10.93	11.24	11.53	11.82	12.09	12.36	12.62	12.87	13.11	13.34	14.40	15.31
5.20	10.83	11.12	11.41	11.69	11.95	12.21	12.46	12.70	12.93	13.15	14.17	15.02
5.40	10.72	11.01	11.29	11.55	11.81	12.06	12.30	12.53	12.75	12.97	13.93	14.74
5.60	10.62	10.90	11.17	11.42	11.67	11.91	12.14	12.36	12.58	12.78	13.70	14.47
5.80	10.51	10.78	11.04	11.29	11.53	11.76	11.99	12.20	12.40	12.60	13.48	14.20
6.00	10.41	10.67	10.92	11.16	11.40	11.62	11.83	12.04	12.23	12.42	13.25	13.93
6.20	10.31	10.56	10.80	11.04	11.26	11.47	11.68	11.87	12.06	12.24	13.03	13.67
6.40	10.20	10.45	10.68	10.91	11.12	11.33	11.53	11.71	11.89	12.07	12.82	13.42
6.60	10.10	10.34	10.57	10.78	10.99	11.19	11.38	11.56	11.73	11.89	12.60	13.17
6.80	10.00	10.23	10.45	10.66	10.86	11.05	11.23	11.40	11.56	11.72	12.39	12.92
7.00	9.90	10.12	10.33	10.53	10.73	10.91	11.08	11.25	11.40	11.55	12.19	12.68
7.20	9.80	10.01	10.22	10.41	10.60	10.77	10.94	11.09	11.24	11.38	11.99	12.45
7.40	9.70	9.90	10.10	10.29	10.47	10.63	10.79	10.94	11.08	11.22	11.79	12.22
7.60	9.60	9.80	9.99	10.17	10.34	10.50	10.65	10.79	10.93	11.06	11.59	12.00
7.80	9.50	9.69	9.88	10.05	10.21	10.37	10.51	10.65	10.77	10.90	11.40	11.78
8.00	9.40	9.59	9.76	9.93	10.09	10.23	10.37	10.50	10.62	10.74	11.22	11.57
8.20	9.30	9.48	9.65	9.81	9.96	10.10	10.23	10.36	10.47	10.58	11.03	11.36
8.40	9.21	9.38	9.54	9.70	9.84	9.97	10.10	10.22	10.33	10.43	10.85	11.16
8.60	9.11	9.28	9.44	9.58	9.72	9.85	9.97	10.08	10.18	10.28	10.68	10.96
8.80	9.02	9.18	9.33	9.47	9.60	9.72	9.83	9.94	10.04	10.13	10.50	10.77
9.00	8.92	9.08	9.22	9.36	9.48	9.60	9.71	9.81	9.90	9.99	10.34	10.58
9.20	8.83	8.98	9.12	9.25	9.36	9.47	9.58	9.67	9.76	9.84	10.17	10.39
9.40	8.74	8.88	9.01	9.14	9.25	9.35	9.45	9.54	9.62	9.70	10.01	10.21
9.60	8.64	8.78	8.91	9.03	9.14	9.23	9.33	9.41	9.49	9.56	9.85	10.04
9.80	8.55	8.69	8.81	8.92	9.02	9.12	9.20	9.28	9.36	9.43	9.69	9.87
10.00	8.46	8.59	8.71	8.81	8.91	9.00	9.08	9.16	9.23	9.29	9.54	9.70
10.20	8.37	8.50	8.61	8.71	8.80	8.89	8.96	9.04	9.10	9.16	9.39	9.54
10.40	8.29	8.40	8.51	8.61	8.69	8.77	8.85	8.91	8.98	9.03	9.25	9.38
10.60	8.20	8.31	8.41	8.50	8.59	8.66	8.73	8.80	8.85	8.91	9.10	9.23
10.80	8.11	8.22	8.32	8.40	8.48	8.55	8.62	8.68	8.73	8.78	8.97	9.08
11.00	8.03	8.13	8.22	8.30	8.38	8.45	8.51	8.56	8.61	8.66	8.83	8.93
11.20	7.94	8.04	8.13	8.20	8.28	8.34	8.40	8.45	8.50	8.54	8.70	8.79
11.40	7.86	7.95	8.03	8.11	8.17	8.23	8.29	8.34	8.38	8.42	8.57	8.65
11.60	7.78	7.86	7.94	8.01	8.08	8.13	8.18	8.23	8.27	8.31	8.44	8.52
11.80	7.69	7.78	7.85	7.92	7.98	8.03	8.08	8.12	8.16	8.19	8.31	8.38
12.00	7.61	7.69	7.76	7.83	7.88	7.93	7.97	8.01	8.05	8.08	8.19	8.25
12.20	7.53	7.61	7.67	7.73	7.79	7.83	7.87	7.91	7.94	7.97	8.07	8.13
12.40	7.45	7.52	7.59	7.64	7.69	7.74	7.77	7.81	7.84	7.86	7.96	8.01
12.60	7.37	7.44	7.50	7.55	7.60	7.64	7.68	7.71	7.74	7.76	7.84	7.89
12.80	7.30	7.36	7.42	7.47	7.51	7.55	7.58	7.61	7.63	7.66	7.73	7.77
13.00	7.22	7.28	7.33	7.38	7.42	7.45	7.49	7.51	7.54	7.56	7.62	7.66
13.20	7.14	7.20	7.25	7.29	7.33	7.36	7.39	7.42	7.44	7.46	7.52	7.55
13.40	7.07	7.12	7.17	7.21	7.24	7.28	7.30	7.32	7.34	7.36	7.41	7.44
13.60	7.00	7.05	7.09	7.13	7.16	7.19	7.21	7.23	7.25	7.26	7.31	7.34
13.80	6.92	6.97	7.01	7.05	7.08	7.10	7.12	7.14	7.16	7.17	7.21	7.23
14.00	6.85	6.89	6.93	6.97	6.99	7.02	7.04	7.05	7.07	7.08	7.12	7.13
14.20	6.78	6.82	6.86	6.89	6.91	6.93	6.95	6.97	6.98	6.99	7.02	7.04
14.40	6.71	6.75	6.78	6.81	6.83	6.85	6.87	6.88	6.89	6.90	6.93	6.94
14.60	6.64	6.68	6.71	6.73	6.75	6.77	6.79	6.80	6.81	6.82	6.84	6.85
14.80	6.57	6.60	6.63	6.66	6.68	6.69	6.70	6.72	6.72	6.73	6.75	6.76
15.00	6.50	6.53	6.56	6.58	6.60	6.61	6.63	6.64	6.64	6.65	6.67	6.67

Source: Duration Tables. Publication No. 761. Boston, Mass.: Financial Publishing Company, 1980. Copyright 1979 Financial Publishing Company.

the bond described in Table 8–2 now equals the market interest rate, the price of the bond rises to $1,000.

$$\%\Delta P_B = \frac{1,000 - 939.3}{939.3}$$

$$= 6.46\%$$

From Equation 8.11 we obtain the following estimate:

$$\%\Delta P_B \approx -3.4691\frac{.10 - .12}{1.12} \times 100$$

$$= 6.19\%$$

Thus, while the formula is not exact, it does provide a reasonable approximation.

LEVEL OF YIELD EFFECT

Another factor that affects volatility of bond prices is the level of yield from which a given change in interest rates begins. Table 8–5 shows price fluctuations for a 10 percent coupon, thirty-year bond. From the table we see that equal interest rate increases of 1 percent have a different impact depending on the initial yield. When the initial yield is low, such as at 7 percent, there is a greater percentage decline in bond price compared to when the initial yield is at higher levels. The example in Table 8–5 illustrates a rule of thumb relating to bond prices. For a given change in yields, the percentage change in the price of a bond will be greater the lower the yield to maturity.[4]

TABLE 8–5   Price Fluctuations from Various Yield Levels*

Original Yield %	Price	New Yield	New Price	% Change
7.0	137.42	8.0	122.62	−10.8
8.0	122.62	9.0	110.32	−10.0
9.0	110.32	10.0	100.00	− 9.4
10.0	100.00	11.0	91.28	− 8.7
11.0	91.28	12.0	83.84	− 8.2
12.0	83.84	13.0	77.45	− 7.6

*For a 10 percent coupon, thirty-year bond with semiannual interest payments; in each case, the change in interest rates equals 1 percent.

[4]See G. O. Bierwag, G. Kaufman, and G. Toevs, "Duration: Its Development and Use in Bond Portfolio Management." *Financial Analysts Journal*, July/August 1983, p. 18.

Implications for Investment Strategy

We have described how three factors, maturity, coupon, and yield level, individually affect the extent of price change of a bond in response to a change in interest rate. Of the three factors, the investor can control or select two factors: maturity and coupon for a bond. The third factor, the level of yield, applies to a given moment in time and is beyond one's control. The investment implications of the discussion on volatility of bond price can be stated as follows:

1. If the investor anticipates a fall in interest rates, he or she should buy bonds, and if the investor foresees a rise in interest rates, he or she should sell bonds or sell bonds short, acting like a speculator rather than an investor, and he or she will have to borrow bonds from the brokerage firm for immediate delivery.

2. If the investor anticipates a fall in interest rates, he or she should buy long-term bonds rather than short-term bonds because the potential appreciation will be greater. If one foresees a rise in interest rates, one should refrain from buying bonds. If one has to buy bonds because of an inflow of cash funds, bonds that mature within a year or short-term maturity instruments like commercial paper, bankers' acceptances, or treasury bills should be purchased.

   If institutional investors managing diversified bond portfolios anticipate a rise in interest rates, they can sell some of the long-term bonds in the portfolio and replace them with short-term bonds or money market instruments. On the other hand, if they foresee a fall in interest rates, they should convert some of their short-term bonds into long-term bonds and also invest their current inflow of cash in long-term bonds.

3. For greater appreciation, investors should buy long-term and low-coupon bonds when they anticipate a fall in interest rates. On the other hand, to minimize price decline, they should buy short-maturity and high-coupon bonds when they anticipate a rise in interest rates. The reason for both strategies is that both maturity and coupon can affect price changes in bonds, and that a proper combination of the two factors will accentuate price appreciation and minimize price decline.

IMMUNIZATION OF INVESTMENTS IN BONDS

Some investors who purchase portfolios of bonds seek to accumulate a target value of wealth at the end of a certain period of time. These investors are said to be seeking to "immunize" their bond portfolio. They want to lock in that target value regardless of how interest rates may fluctuate in future periods.

The easiest way to accomplish this objective is with the use of zero-coupon bonds. Assuming they do not default, the future payment is known with certainty.

In some cases, however, zero-coupon bonds with the right mix of expected return, maturity date, and safety rating may not be available. At the same time, there may be some coupon-paying bonds that do fit the investor's needs with respect to yield to maturity and default risk, and the investor may also be able to achieve his or her immunization objectives using the coupon-paying bonds. In other words, it is possible to immunize portfolios of coupon bonds to a significant degree, although 100 percent immunization is not generally attained.

Two components of risk relate to obtaining a target future value using coupon bonds. First, if the investor's target date is prior to the maturity date of the bond, *price risk* exists. The price of the bond fluctuates as interest rates change. The second component of risk relates to the fact that the investor will have to reinvest the proceeds of coupons prior to the target date. *Coupon reinvestment risk* refers to the uncertainty of the accumulated value of coupon payments because of fluctuations in the rates at which the coupons are reinvested.

An interesting property of these two risks is that as interest rates change, one component at least partially offsets the other. An early general increase in interest rates will cause the security price on the target date to be lower than expected (we are still assuming the target date is prior to maturity). At the same time, higher reinvestment rates for coupons will result in a higher accumulated value for those funds. A drop in interest rates would have the opposite effect. The security price would be higher than expected at the target date, but the accumulated value of reinvested coupons would be lower. In a bond portfolio that was perfectly immunized, these two effects would be balanced so that one would exactly offset the other.

The measure of duration discussed above has been found to be useful in developing strategies to immunize bond portfolios. A considerable degree of immunization can be obtained if the investor's portfolio has a duration equal to the target holding period. In fact, Fisher and Weil have shown that under a set of quite restrictive conditions, it is possible to achieve perfect immunization if duration equals the target holding period. In addition, they empirically tested the use of duration to achieve immunization. They found it was quite effective and superior to alternative strategies that they tested, and subsequent studies have also verified the usefulness of duration in the effort to immunize.[5]

---

[5]See Lawrence Fisher and Roman Weil, "Coping with the Risk of Interest Rate Fluctuations: Returns to Bondholders from Naive and Optimal Strategies." *Journal of Business*, October 1971. In a more recent study (1983), Bierwag, Kaufman, and Toevs also report that duration performs reasonably well in comparison to more sophisticated approaches. See chapter References.

YIELD CURVE ANALYSIS: THE TERM STRUCTURE OF INTEREST RATES

We now turn to the examination of another aspect of bonds, the yield pattern of maturities, holding all other factors constant. This type of analysis is commonly known as *yield curve analysis*, or *term structure of interest rates*. In the examination of yield pattern, yields of different maturities are plotted on a graph with the horizontal scale representing maturity and the vertical scale representing yields. A smooth curve is then drawn through the various yields to form a yield curve. The empirical yield curves have generally approximated one of four forms, as shown in Figure 8–2.

1. *Ascending Curve.* The yield curve is sloping upward and is usually called an ascending yield curve. The yields on short-term maturities are lower and rise with longer maturity, but at a diminishing rate and flattening out at very long maturities. Historically, this type of yield curve is most common and is usually found in times of lower interest rates when the economy is recovering from a recession or when inflationary expectations are relatively low.

2. *Descending Yield Curve.* The yield on short-term maturities is higher than on long-term maturities. The yield curve is sloping downward. This type of yield curve is not as common as the previous type. It is usually found when interest rates are high and investors in general are expecting lower rates in the future. Because of this expectation, investors are willing to accept a lower yield on long-term bonds in order to lock in the current yield.

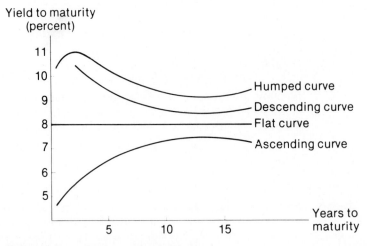

FIGURE 8–2 Types of Yield Curves

3. *Humpbacked Yield Curve.* The yield rises in the early maturities and then gradually declines for longer maturities. This type of yield curve is usually found when interest rates are very high during periods of stringent monetary conditions. The humpbacked yield curve bears a strong resemblance to the descending yield curve except for the short-term maturities of usually one to three years. As in the case of the descending yield curve, investors in general are expecting lower interest rates in the future.

4. *Flat Yield Curve.* The yields on short-term maturities are at about the same level as they are for longer-term maturities. Historically, this type of yield curve does not last long. It usually happens when the yield curve is in a period of transition, shifting from an upward sloping curve to a downward sloping one, or vice versa.

To estimate the yield curve as it currently exists, one needs only the section on Treasury bonds and notes in the *Wall Street Journal* (see Figure 7–1). All of the securities listed are equally safe with respect to default risk, and because there are data on many securities, we can draw a fairly detailed yield curve. The "Maturity Date" column shows the month and year of maturity, while the "Yld" column on the far right shows the yield to maturity. To graph the data we place yield to maturity on the vertical axis and time to maturity (or time of maturity) on the horizontal axis. This is essentially how Figure 8–3 is constructed. Note that the result is an ascending yield curve.

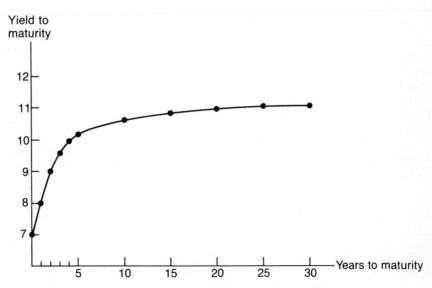

FIGURE 8–3   Treasury Yield Curve, July 31, 1985

Explanations for the Shape of the Yield Curve

Why should yield curves display different patterns at different points in time? Those who have studied this problem have offered three explanations: (1) the expectation theory, (2) the liquidity-premium theory, and (3) the segmented market theory. However, before we discuss these explanations we will provide some background details. The following timeline is used to define the concepts of spot and forward interest rates.

$$t_1 \qquad\qquad\qquad\qquad t_2$$

Time of   Time of

Investment   Maturity

Consider the term r_{t_1, t_2}. It refers to the interest rate on an investment in which the financial outlay is made at t_1, and principal plus interest are received at t_2. If $t_1 = 0$, we are referring to an investment made today, and we describe r_{0, t_2} as a *spot interest rate*. The term $r_{0, 2}$ refers to the current or spot interest rate on a two-year security, while $r_{0, 5}$ is the current rate on a five-year security.[6]

If $t_1 > 0$ we are talking about a *forward interest rate*. A forward rate may be viewed as the expected interest rate that the market believes will exist on a specified future date. For example, $r_{1, 3}$ is the rate the market expects on a two-year security to be purchased at $t = 1$ and to mature at $t = 3$. In the case of $r_{2, 7}$ we refer to the return on a security to be purchased two years from today and which will mature seven years from today (a five-year maturity).

Expectations Theory

The advocates of this theory assert that the interest rate or yield on a longer-term maturity tends to be a geometric average of expected short-term rates over the intervening period. For example, assume the current interest rate on a one-year security is $(r_{0, 1})$ 5 percent. Assume further that the market expects the one-year interest rate to be 6 percent next year $(r_{1, 2})$ and 7 percent for the year after that $(r_{2, 3})$. In this situation the interest rate on a three-year maturity $(r_{0, 3})$ should currently be approximately 6 percent. Only such a relationship would equalize the return between buying a three-year maturity and buying a one-year maturity each year for the next three years.

The expectations theory can be summarized with the approximation in Equation 8.12 or with the exact geometric relationship in Equation 8.13.

$$r_{0, n} \approx \frac{r_{0, 1} + r_{1, 2} + r_{2, 3} + \ldots r_{n-1, n}}{n} \qquad\qquad (8.12)$$

[6]It is best to think of these securities as zero-coupon bonds or savings certificates in which the interest is retained and compounded. The analysis to follow would only be an approximation if there are cash flows, such as coupon payments, that are reinvested at various rates.

$$(1 + r_{0,n}) = \sqrt[n]{(1 + r_{0,1})(1 + r_{1,2})(1 + r_{2,3})\ldots(1 + r_{n-1,n})} \qquad (8.13)$$

where:

n = time to maturity

Equation 8.13 follows directly from the expectations theory. If you invest \$1 in a three-year security today you will have $1(1 + r_{0,3})^3$. If you invest in three consecutive one-year securities, you will have

$$1(1 + r_{0,1})(1 + r_{1,2})(1 + r_{2,3}).$$

Under the expectations theory, market rates adjust so there is no net benefit on a three-year security versus rolling over consecutive one-year securities.

$$(1 + r_{0,3})^3 = (1 + r_{0,1})(1 + r_{1,2})(1 + r_{2,3})$$

$$1 + r_{0,3} = \sqrt[3]{(1 + r_{0,1})(1 + r_{1,2})(1 + r_{2,3})}$$

The expectations theory has been criticized as an explanation of the yield curve. If investors in general expect higher short-term rates in the future, the yield curve would have an upward slope. This should occur during periods when current rates are historically low. On the other hand, if investors expect lower rates in the future, the yield curve would slope downward. This should occur during times when current interest rates are historically high. One might expect that ascending and descending yield curves would be equally prevalent. In addition, the horizontal yield curve might also be quite common as a transition between ascending and descending patterns. However, this is not the case, for the ascending curve has clearly appeared most often. To explain this situation, the liquidity-premium theory, which is a variation of the expectations theory, has been advanced.

Liquidity-Premium Theory

The advocates of the liquidity-premium theory argue that investors are not indifferent to risk. Longer-term securities are more risky than short-term securities due to price fluctuations caused by changes in interest.[7] Therefore, the interest rate on long-term securities can be divided into two components: (1) an expected average of short-term rates and (2) a premium for risk. This can be stated as follows:

$$r_{n,LP} = r_{n,EX} + LP(n) \qquad (8.14)$$

[7]In addition, long-term, non-Treasury issues, which could conceivably default, have more years in which a default could occur than similar short-term securities.

where:

$r_{n,LP}$ = interest rate predicted by the liquidity-premium theory

$r_{n,EX}$ = interest rate predicted by expectations theory

$LP(n)$ = liquidity (risk) premium due to price risk which increases with the time to maturity, n

According to this theory, if short-term rates are expected to stay constant or rise, the long-term interest rate should be higher than the short-term rate. This would mean that the yield curve would show a positive slope. If future short-term rates are expected to fall, the interest rate predicted by the expectations theory, $r_{n,EX}$ would drop with higher values of n. However, because $LP(n)$ increases with n, the predicted rate, $r_{n,LP}$, could rise or fall as n increases. The outcome would depend on how rapidly $r_{n,EX}$ falls and $LP(n)$ rises. In other words, if future short-term rates are expected to fall, the yield curve would be positively sloping or negatively sloping, depending on how rapidly those future rates are expected to drop and also on the slope of $LP(n)$.

Segmented Market Theory

The advocates of this theory argue that short-term maturities are not perfect substitutes for long-term maturities. Some institutional investors, such as pension fund and life insurance companies, prefer to buy and own long-term bonds because their liabilities are basically long-term in nature. Commercial banks, on the other hand, prefer to own short- to intermediate-term bonds because their liabilities are mainly demand deposits. According to this theory, the market for short-term bonds is quite segregated from the markets for long-term bonds. Consequently, the yields on short-term and long-term bonds are determined separately by supply-and-demand conditions prevailing in these two markets.

Generally Accepted View

Various empirical studies have been conducted to test the validity of the three theories of yield curves.[8] Most of the empirical findings seem to confirm the generally accepted view that both investors' expectations of future interest rates and their preference for liquidity are the primary factors that determine the shape of the yield curve. The institutional factors, such as the preference of some institutional investors for certain lengths of maturities and transaction costs, are factors of only temporary or secondary importance.

[8]For more information on yield curve analysis, consult the following: Burton G. Malkiel, *The Term Structure of Interest Rates* (Princeton, N.J.: Princeton University Press, 1966); Joseph W. Conrad, *The Behavior of Interest Rates* (New York: National Bureau of Economic Research, 1966); Thomas F. Cargill, "The Term Structure of Interest Rates: A Test of the Expectation Hypothesis." *The Journal of Finance*, June 1975.

Applications of the Yield Curve

The analysis of yield curves can help investors in several ways. First, it points out the important fact that both the level and the shape of yield curves vary over time, and the change sometimes can be rather sharp and sudden. In addition, the level and shape of yield curves often have consistent relationships with different phases of the business cycle, and some analysts use these relationships in the forecasting of general business conditions. Another application of the yield curve is that it provides the consensus view of market participants about the future course of interest rates. This consensus may or may not be realized in the future. Nonetheless, it provides a framework against which one can compare one's own forecast of interest rates and future yield patterns. For example, let $r_{0,1} = 10$ percent and $r_{0,2} = 11$ percent. We can now calculate $r_{1,2}$ using the approximation equation under the expectations theory.[9]

$$r_{0,2} = 11 = \frac{10 + r_{1,2}}{2} \quad \text{and}$$

$$r_{1,2} = 12\%$$

If the investor expects interest rates to drop below 12 percent on a one-year security to be issued in period 1, he or she would earn more with the two-year security than with consecutive one-year securities. If the investor believes $r_{1,2}$ will exceed 12 percent, consecutive one-year securities would provide higher returns.

Using the previous interest rates, the analysis can be extended to three or more years. If $r_{0,3} = 11\frac{2}{3}$ percent, we can calculate $r_{2,3}$

$$r_{0,3} = 11\frac{2}{3} = \frac{10 + 12 + r_{2,3}}{3} \quad \text{and}$$

$$r_{2,3} = 13\%$$

In summary, once investors have firm views on the outlook of interest rates and yield patterns, they can proceed to identify the most attractive maturities and select the best course of action for their investment program.

YIELD SPREADS

In the section on yield curve analysis, we have seen the influence of maturity alone on yields of securities. But, at a given moment in time we are also confronted with a variety of yields on securities of the same maturity. What

---

[9]Some expected future rates can be found in the listings on financial futures.

are the causes? Numerous factors are responsible for the differences in yields among securities of the same maturity. The major factors are:

1. *Difference in quality or agency rating.* The degree of default risk is assessed by several rating agencies and conveyed in their ratings. The greater the risk, the greater the yield demanded by investors.

2. *Difference in marketability.* The liquidity or marketability of a fixed-income security influences its yields. Marketability refers to both (a) the volume of securities that can be sold at any time without significant price concession, and (b) the amount of time needed to complete a desired position. All factors being equal, the less marketable the security, the higher the yield. Of all fixed-income securities, Treasury securities are the most marketable.

3. *Tax factor.* The income from most securities of state and local governments is exempted from federal income tax and from the state and local taxes of the districts that issue the security. Consequently, these tax-exempts are selling at much lower yields than securities of comparable grade whose interest is fully taxable.

4. *Provisions of the bond indenture with respect to sinking-fund and call privilege of the issuer.* Investors generally prefer to have a sinking-fund provision included in the bond indenture. Securities without a sinking-fund provision tend to sell at higher yields than comparable issues. Investors generally do not like a call provision, which gives the issuer the right to call in the bond for redemption when market interest rates have fallen substantially. This deprives the bondholder of an opportunity for a capital gain on his bond. Other things being equal, securities without a call provision tend to sell at lower yields than securities with a call provision. The security with a deferred call provision (the call provision cannot be exercised for a specified period) tends to sell at a lower yield than a security with an unrestricted call provision.

5. *New issues versus existing issues.* The yields on new issues usually tend to be a little higher than on existing issues of the same grade or from the same issuer. Securities underwriters generally want to resell the underwritten securities quickly to the public for fear that interest rates may rise during the intervening period and make their securities unsalable at the original quote price. Consequently, they usually price the new issue at a yield slightly higher than an existing issue of comparable grade.

6. *Institutional factors.* Different sectors of the money and capital markets are interrelated, but they are also somewhat segregated because some institutional investors and issuers tend to operate more in one sector than another, or prefer one type of security more than another type of equal grade. For example, because of tax

consideration the commercial banks are big buyers of municipal bonds, but not corporate bonds. Pension funds, being tax-exempt, on the other hand, usually invest in the corporate bond sector where a higher yield is obtainable. Because some hindrance exists in the flow of funds between sectors, a given sector may be temporarily over- or undersupplied with funds (or securities). As a result, yields may be out of line with the rest of the credit markets, thus creating yield differentials between markets among securities of comparable features.

Trends and Yield Spreads of Corporate Bonds by Ratings, 1929–1985

See Figure 8–4 for bond yields by ratings from 1929 to 1985. The chart is drawn with the highest interest rates at the bottom rather than the top. This procedure has two desirable effects. First, when interest rates are rising, bond market prices are falling. Thus, we can clearly see the periods of a declining bond market. Second, yields on bonds with the highest rating are shown above the yields of lower-rated bonds. In other words, the top bonds are at the top of the chart.

An examination of the bond yields in Figure 8–4 shows the following movements.

1. A downward trend from 1932 to 1941
2. A level trend from 1942 to 1955
3. A moderate rising trend from 1956 to 1964
4. A sharp rising trend from 1965 to 1981
5. A falling trend from 1981 to 1985

In recession years like 1957, 1960, 1970, 1974–75, and 1980–82, yield differentials increased, especially between A and Baa bonds. By the same token, when the economy bounced back, the differentials between grades began to narrow.

The yield differentials between different grades of bonds do not stay unchanged over time. When the economy is progressing from recovery to booming business periods, many institutional investors (as well as individuals) are willing to switch a part of their bond portfolio into lower grades in order to increase overall yield return. This type of switch or swap can narrow the yield differentials among different grades of bonds. When the economy is moving into a recession, investors become more concerned about the quality of the issuing corporation. This greater concern for safety and the desire for high quality widens the differential between higher- and lower-rated securities.

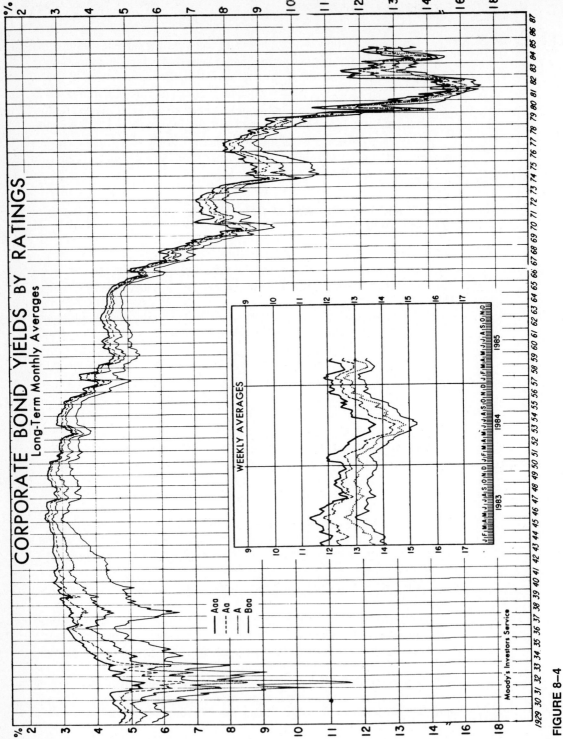

CORPORATE BOND YIELDS BY RATINGS
Long-Term Monthly Averages

Aaa
Aa
A
Baa

Moody's Investors Service

WEEKLY AVERAGES

1983   1984   1985

FIGURE 8–4

Source: Moody's Investors Service, *Moody's Bond Record*, May 1985.

BOND STRATEGIES

Strategies of Institutional Investors

In this discussion of bond strategies of both institutional and individual investors, let us begin with the bond strategies of institutional investors. We can classify the bond strategies of institutional investors roughly into three categories: (a) defensive, diversified approach, (b) very aggressive approach, and (c) moderately flexible approach.

Defensive, Diversified Approach
This approach may include most of the following ingredients:

1. Hold a diversified list of bonds.
2. Decide on certain grades and select issues accordingly.
3. Structure the portfolio with staggered maturities from, say, one to twenty years.
4. Invest new funds when available and select the most attractive bonds under the prevailing environment.
5. Usually hold the issues until maturity unless important unexpected changes take place with respect to the issuer.
6. Do not try to anticipate changes in interest rates or take advantage of them.

Very Aggressive Approach
The very aggressive approach to bond investment can include most or all of the following characteristics:

1. Make investment decisions on both new purchases and sales on the basis of:
   a. Forecast of interest rates
   b. Forecast of yield patterns among maturities
   c. A constant screening of yield differentials between grades and between sectors
2. Adjust risk exposure of the portfolio as expected investment environment changes.
3. Adjust average maturities of the portfolio in light of expected changes in interest rates.
4. Constantly look for opportunities to switch or swap.

Moderately Flexible Approach
This is a middle-of-the-road approach, the ingredients of which can be sketched as follows:

1. Maintain a diversified portfolio of bonds.

2. Moderately adjust the overall quality (grades) of the portfolio upward or downward based on the expected investment environment.
3. Structure the portfolio on a more or less staggered basis; however, make some adjustments from time to time on the basis of forecasts of interest rates.
4. Forgo the idea of concentration.
5. Make some swaps if opportunities are good.
6. Remain aware that interest rate forecasts may be wrong and, therefore, do not make portfolio changes solely on the basis of these forecasts.

Bond Strategies for Most Individual Investors

The bond markets are dominated by seasoned institutional investors and professional traders. They usually also employ experienced personnel on their staffs to keep a close watch on the developments in the credit and capital markets, and also to conduct their own forecasts of interest rates and yield patterns. Individual investors in general are, therefore, at a disadvantage to compete with institutional investors and professional traders in the bond markets.

However, bonds should constitute a part of the individual's portfolio. There are good reasons for that position. First, in mid-1986 the yield on high-grade bonds exceeded 10 percent, which was considerably greater than existing (or most historic returns) on money market instruments. Secondly, bonds in general are much safer than stocks in terms of both current return and price volatility. A portfolio composed of bonds, stocks, and reserve funds in liquid assets is better diversified than portfolios of either stocks or bonds alone. A better-diversified portfolio can reduce risks without losing expected return.

The bond strategy suitable to most individual investors should be the defensive or moderately flexible approach. Some of the ingredients of this approach are:

1. Hold a diversified set of bonds of good grades or purchase shares in a no-load bond fund.
2. Adjust to some extent the average maturity of the portfolio on the basis of the outlook of interest rates. Those in bond funds can switch some of their holdings into a money fund.
3. Adjust the proportion of the portfolio represented by bonds upward or downward on the basis of periodic assessment of the relative attractiveness of bonds and equity.
4. Forgo frequent trading or switches in bonds.

SUMMARY

The price of a bond can be calculated as the present value of both the interest payments and the par value to be paid to the bond holder. Bond prices fluctuate as interest rates change. These fluctuations are relatively greater for bonds with low coupons and long maturities. The concept of duration combines the effects of coupon and maturity and provides an index of bond price sensitivity to changes in interest rates.

Some bond investors seek to accumulate a target value of wealth at the end of a certain period of time and attempt to immunize their bond portfolio in that they want to lock in their target value regardless of interest rate movements. A considerable degree of immunization can be obtained if the investor's portfolio has a duration equal to the target holding period.

Analysis of the term structure of interest rate is concerned with the relationship between long-term and short-term interest rates. The dominant theories explaining the relationships are the expectations and liquidity-premium theories. A common ingredient in these theories is that long-term rates embody expectations on future short-term rates. The liquidity-premium theory also considers the greater price risk of longer-term bonds and the effect this has on the yields of longer-term securities.

QUESTIONS AND PROBLEMS

1. How might one go about determining the proper discount rate to use in evaluating a corporate bond?
2. An 11 percent coupon bond matures in fifteen years. It currently sells for $950. Find the current yield and approximate yield to maturity.
3. A 10 percent coupon bond matures in twelve years. The bond is selling at $950. Find the yield to maturity of the bond from the yield table.
4. A U.S. government bond with a 10.5 percent coupon matures in twenty years. You feel that the discount rate of the bond should be 12 percent. What should it sell for at that discount rate?
5. If you are anticipating a fall in interest rates, should you buy or sell bonds? Long-term or short-term?
6. A completely tax-exempt security pays 9 percent while a comparable taxable security pays 11 percent. At what tax bracket would an investor be indifferent between the two securities?
7. Calculate the duration of a five-year security with a 12 percent coupon and a 10 percent yield to maturity.

8. A bond is priced at $920, has a duration of ten years, and the yield on the bond is 13 percent. Calculate the approximate percentage change in price if yields on such bonds fall to 12 percent.

9. If an investor is anticipating a fall in interest rates, he or she should buy long-term and high-coupon bonds. Do you agree? Why or why not?

10. Describe some of the ingredients of an institutional investor's aggressive bond strategy.

11. Should individuals have bonds in their portfolios? Why?

12. What should a proper strategy be for most individuals?

13. What are some of the factors accounting for differentials in bond yields for the same maturities?

14. Describe several patterns of yield curves and indicate the circumstances under which each would occur.

15. What is a yield curve? What can the analysis of yield curves provide to an investor?

16. Using the latest Treasury security listings, draw the current yield curve.

17. What does it mean to immunize a bond portfolio, and how might it be done?

18. An investor has a three-year time horizon, and is considering a three-year security with $r_{0,3} = 11\%$ or a two-year security at $r_{0,2} = 10.6\%$, followed with a one-year security paying $r_{2,3}$. What value of $r_{2,3}$ will provide the same three-year return for both investment strategies?

19. Look up historical data on long-term and short-term government securities over the past seven years. Calculate the spread in interest rates and compare with the spread on current short- and long-term rates.

   a. Do you think the current spread will widen or narrow?

   b. What does your answer suggest for an investment strategy?

APPENDIX: The Time Value of Money

In this appendix we examine the basics of the *time value of money* that we apply in this textbook. For those who desire a more comprehensive analysis, most textbooks on financial management explore this subject more extensively.

FUTURE VALUES WITH COMPOUND INTEREST

Assume you have $1,000, which you invest at an interest rate of 10 percent. At the end of one year you will have

$$FV_1 = \underbrace{1,000}_{\text{Principal}} + \underbrace{1,000(.10)}_{\text{Interest}} = 1,000(1.10) = \$1,100$$

If the $1,100 is reinvested for another year at 10 percent, you will have

$$FV_2 = 1,100 = 1,100(.10) = 1,100(1.10)$$

$$= [1,000(1.10)](1.10)$$

$$= 1,000(1.10)^2$$

Similarly, at the end of a third year you have $FV_3 = 1,000(1.10)^3$. Also note that 1.10 is just 1 plus the interest rate, and we may also write $FV_3 = 1,000(1 + .10)^3$.

In general, if PV is invested for n years at interest rate k_d, the future value at the end of n years is

$$FV_n = PV(1 + k_d)^n \tag{A.1}$$

Values of $(1 + k_d)^n$ for different interest rates and investment periods are shown in Table A–1. Those values may be denoted as $FVF_{k_d, n}$, a future value factor at interest rate k_d for n periods. Thus, an alternative version of Equation A.1 is

$$FV_n = PV(FVF_{k_d, n}) \tag{A.2}$$

PRESENT VALUE OF A SINGLE PAYMENT

Assume an individual can buy a security that will pay $1,344 in one year. The current interest rate on a one-year investment is 12 percent. What is the fair market price of the security?

TABLE A–1 Future Value Factor, FVF: $(1 + k_d)^n$

Year	1%	2%	3%	4%	5%	6%	7%	8%	9%	10%
1	1.010	1.020	1.030	1.040	1.050	1.060	1.070	1.080	1.090	1.100
2	1.020	1.040	1.061	1.082	1.102	1.124	1.145	1.166	1.188	1.210
3	1.030	1.061	1.093	1.125	1.158	1.191	1.225	1.260	1.295	1.331
4	1.041	1.082	1.126	1.170	1.216	1.262	1.311	1.360	1.412	1.464
5	1.051	1.104	1.159	1.217	1.276	1.338	1.403	1.469	1.539	1.611
6	1.062	1.126	1.194	1.265	1.340	1.419	1.501	1.587	1.677	1.772
7	1.072	1.149	1.230	1.316	1.407	1.504	1.606	1.714	1.828	1.949
8	1.083	1.172	1.267	1.369	1.477	1.594	1.718	1.851	1.993	2.144
9	1.094	1.195	1.305	1.423	1.551	1.689	1.838	1.999	2.172	2.358
10	1.105	1.219	1.344	1.480	1.629	1.791	1.967	2.159	2.367	2.594
11	1.116	1.243	1.384	1.539	1.710	1.898	2.105	2.332	2.580	2.853
12	1.127	1.268	1.426	1.601	1.796	2.012	2.252	2.518	2.813	3.138
13	1.138	1.294	1.469	1.665	1.886	2.133	2.410	2.720	3.066	3.452
14	1.149	1.319	1.513	1.732	1.980	2.261	2.579	2.937	3.342	3.797
15	1.161	1.346	1.558	1.801	2.079	2.397	2.759	3.172	3.642	4.177
16	1.173	1.373	1.605	1.873	2.183	2.540	2.952	3.426	3.970	4.595
17	1.184	1.400	1.653	1.948	2.292	2.693	3.159	3.700	4.328	5.054
18	1.196	1.428	1.702	2.026	2.407	2.854	3.380	3.996	4.717	5.560
19	1.208	1.457	1.753	2.107	2.527	3.026	3.616	4.316	5.142	6.116
20	1.220	1.486	1.806	2.191	2.653	3.207	3.870	4.661	5.604	6.727
21	1.232	1.516	1.860	2.279	2.786	3.399	4.140	5.034	6.109	7.400
22	1.245	1.546	1.916	2.370	2.925	3.603	4.430	5.436	6.658	8.140
23	1.257	1.577	1.974	2.465	3.071	3.820	4.740	5.871	7.258	8.954
24	1.270	1.608	2.033	2.563	3.225	4.049	5.072	6.341	7.911	9.850
25	1.282	1.641	2.094	2.666	3.386	4.292	5.427	6.848	8.623	10.834
30	1.348	1.811	2.427	3.243	4.322	5.743	7.612	10.062	13.267	17.449
40	1.489	2.208	3.262	4.801	7.040	10.285	14.974	21.724	31.408	45.258
50	1.645	2.691	4.384	7.106	11.467	18.419	29.456	46.900	74.354	117.386

	1.110	1.120	1.130	1.140	1.150	1.160	1.170	1.180	1.190	1.200
1	1.110	1.120	1.130	1.140	1.150	1.160	1.170	1.180	1.190	1.200
2	1.232	1.254	1.277	1.300	1.322	1.346	1.369	1.392	1.416	1.440
3	1.368	1.405	1.443	1.482	1.521	1.561	1.602	1.643	1.685	1.728
4	1.518	1.574	1.630	1.689	1.749	1.811	1.874	1.939	2.005	2.074
5	1.685	1.762	1.842	1.925	2.011	2.100	2.192	2.288	2.386	2.488
6	1.870	1.974	2.082	2.195	2.313	2.436	2.565	2.700	2.840	2.986
7	2.076	2.211	2.353	2.502	2.660	2.826	3.001	3.185	3.379	3.583
8	2.305	2.476	2.658	2.853	3.059	3.278	3.511	3.759	4.021	4.300
9	2.558	2.773	3.004	3.252	3.518	3.803	4.108	4.435	4.785	5.160
10	2.839	3.106	3.395	3.707	4.046	4.411	4.807	5.234	5.695	6.192
11	3.152	3.479	3.836	4.226	4.652	5.117	5.624	6.176	6.777	7.430
12	3.498	3.896	4.334	4.818	5.350	5.936	6.580	7.288	8.064	8.916
13	3.883	4.363	4.898	5.492	6.153	6.886	7.699	8.599	9.596	10.699
14	4.310	4.887	5.535	6.261	7.076	7.987	9.007	10.147	11.420	12.839
15	4.785	5.474	6.254	7.138	8.137	9.265	10.539	11.974	13.589	15.407
16	5.311	6.130	7.067	8.137	9.358	10.748	12.330	14.129	16.171	18.488
17	5.895	6.866	7.986	9.276	10.761	12.468	14.426	16.672	19.244	22.186
18	6.545	7.690	9.024	10.575	12.375	14.462	16.879	19.673	22.900	26.623
19	7.263	8.613	10.197	12.055	14.232	16.776	19.748	23.214	27.251	31.948
20	8.062	9.646	11.523	13.743	16.366	19.461	23.105	27.393	32.429	38.337
21	8.949	10.804	13.021	15.667	18.821	22.574	27.033	32.323	38.591	46.005
22	9.933	12.100	14.713	17.861	21.644	26.186	31.629	38.141	45.923	55.205
23	11.026	13.552	16.626	20.361	24.891	30.376	37.005	45.007	54.648	66.247
24	12.239	15.178	18.788	23.212	28.625	35.236	43.296	53.108	65.031	79.496
25	13.585	17.000	21.230	26.461	32.918	40.874	50.656	62.667	77.387	95.395
30	22.892	29.960	39.115	50.949	66.210	85.849	111.061	143.367	184.672	237.373
40	64.999	93.049	132.776	188.876	267.856	378.715	533.846	750.353	1051.642	1469.740
50	184.559	288.996	450.711	700.197	1083.619	1670.669	2566.080	3927.189	5988.730	9100.191

Equation A.1 may be used to find the solution. $FV = 1,344$, $n = 1$, and $k_d = .12$. We are solving for the required investment PV or present value

$$1,344 = PV(1.12)$$

$$PV = \frac{1,344}{1.12} = \$1,200$$

The result makes sense because \$1,200 invested at the going interest rate of 12 percent would accumulate to \$1,344.

Next, consider the price of a similar security that will pay \$1,344 in two years rather than one year. Again, solving with Equation A.1,

$$PV = \frac{1344}{(1.12)^2} = \$1,071.43$$

TABLE A–2   Present Value of a Single Payment of \$1, $PVSP$: $1/(1 + k_d)^n$

Year	1%	2%	3%	4%	5%	6%	7%	8%	9%	10%
1	.990	.980	.971	.962	.952	.943	.935	.926	.917	.909
2	.980	.961	.943	.925	.907	.890	.873	.857	.842	.826
3	.971	.942	.915	.889	.864	.840	.816	.794	.772	.751
4	.961	.924	.888	.855	.823	.792	.763	.735	.708	.683
5	.951	.906	.863	.822	.784	.747	.713	.681	.650	.621
6	.942	.888	.837	.790	.746	.705	.666	.630	.596	.564
7	.933	.871	.813	.760	.711	.665	.623	.583	.547	.513
8	.923	.853	.789	.731	.677	.627	.582	.540	.502	.467
9	.914	.837	.766	.703	.645	.592	.544	.500	.460	.424
10	.905	.820	.744	.676	.614	.558	.508	.463	.422	.386
11	.896	.804	.722	.650	.585	.527	.475	.429	.388	.350
12	.887	.789	.701	.625	.557	.497	.444	.397	.356	.319
13	.879	.773	.681	.601	.530	.469	.415	.368	.326	.290
14	.870	.758	.661	.577	.505	.442	.388	.340	.299	.263
15	.861	.743	.642	.555	.481	.417	.362	.315	.275	.239
16	.853	.728	.623	.534	.458	.394	.339	.292	.252	.218
17	.844	.714	.605	.513	.436	.371	.317	.270	.231	.198
18	.836	.700	.587	.494	.416	.350	.296	.250	.212	.180
19	.828	.686	.570	.475	.396	.331	.277	.232	.194	.164
20	.820	.673	.554	.456	.377	.312	.258	.215	.178	.149
21	.811	.660	.538	.439	.359	.294	.242	.199	.164	.135
22	.803	.647	.522	.422	.342	.278	.226	.184	.150	.123
23	.795	.634	.507	.406	.326	.262	.211	.170	.138	.112
24	.788	.622	.492	.390	.310	.247	.197	.158	.126	.102
25	.780	.610	.478	.375	.295	.233	.184	.146	.116	.092
30	.742	.552	.412	.308	.231	.174	.131	.099	.075	.057
40	.672	.453	.307	.208	.142	.097	.067	.046	.032	.022
50	.608	.372	.228	.141	.087	.054	.034	.021	.013	.009

In general, when a security will provide a fixed single payment of FV_n, n years in the future, the fair market price of the security (from Equation A.1) is

$$PV = \frac{FV_n}{(1 + k_d)^n} = FV_n \left[\frac{1}{(1 + k_d)^n} \right] \qquad \text{(A.3)}$$

Values for $1/(1 + k_d)^n$ are shown in Table A–2. The values are denoted as $PVSP_{k_d, n}$, the present value of a single payment of \$1 to be received in n years when the interest rate is k_d. Equation A.3 may now be rewritten

$$PV = FV_n(PVSP_{k_d, n}) \qquad \text{(A.4)}$$

TABLE A–2, continued

Year	11%	12%	13%	14%	15%	16%	17%	18%	19%	20%
1	.901	.893	.885	.877	.870	.862	.855	.847	.840	.833
2	.812	.797	.783	.769	.756	.743	.731	.718	.706	.694
3	.731	.712	.693	.675	.658	.641	.624	.609	.593	.579
4	.659	.636	.613	.592	.572	.552	.534	.516	.499	.482
5	.593	.567	.543	.519	.497	.476	.456	.437	.419	.402
6	.535	.507	.480	.456	.432	.410	.390	.370	.352	.335
7	.482	.452	.425	.400	.376	.354	.333	.314	.296	.279
8	.434	.404	.376	.351	.327	.305	.285	.266	.249	.233
9	.391	.361	.333	.308	.284	.263	.243	.225	.209	.194
10	.352	.322	.295	.270	.247	.227	.208	.191	.176	.162
11	.317	.287	.261	.237	.215	.195	.178	.162	.148	.135
12	.286	.257	.231	.208	.187	.168	.152	.137	.124	.112
13	.258	.229	.204	.182	.163	.145	.130	.116	.104	.093
14	.232	.205	.181	.160	.141	.125	.111	.099	.088	.078
15	.209	.183	.160	.140	.123	.108	.095	.084	.074	.065
16	.188	.163	.141	.123	.107	.093	.081	.071	.062	.054
17	.170	.146	.125	.108	.093	.080	.069	.060	.052	.045
18	.153	.130	.111	.095	.081	.069	.059	.051	.044	.038
19	.138	.116	.098	.083	.070	.060	.051	.043	.037	.031
20	.124	.104	.087	.073	.061	.051	.043	.037	.031	.026
21	.112	.093	.077	.064	.053	.044	.037	.031	.026	.022
22	.101	.083	.068	.056	.046	.038	.032	.026	.022	.018
23	.091	.074	.060	.049	.040	.033	.027	.022	.018	.015
24	.082	.066	.053	.043	.035	.028	.023	.019	.015	.013
25	.074	.059	.047	.038	.030	.024	.020	.016	.013	.010
30	.044	.033	.026	.020	.015	.012	.009	.007	.005	.004
40	.015	.011	.008	.005	.004	.003	.002	.001	.001	.001
50	.005	.003	.002	.001	.001	.001	.000	.000	.000	.000

Using Equation A.4 for the two-year security described above, its price should equal

$$PV = 1,344 \; PVSP._{12,\,2}$$

$$= 1,344 \; (.797)$$

$$= \$1,017.17$$

This answer differs slightly from the previous one because table values have been rounded to the third decimal place.

PRESENT VALUE OF AN ANNUITY

An *annuity* is an equal stream of payments made at regular intervals of time. Analyses of annuities occur in problems involving bond analysis, mortgage payments, leasing situations, and pension plans. In this book we make use of present values of annuities. For example, assume a security will pay an amount A per period for n periods. What is the value of the security at the time of purchase in period 0?

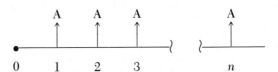

The value of the security is just the sum of the present values of the individual payments. The payment to be received in period 1 is worth $A/(1 + k_d)$. The value of the payment to be received in period 2 is $A/(1 + k_d)^2$, and so on until period n, whose payment is worth $A/(1 + k_d)^n$ in period 0.

When these values are added together, we obtain the fair market value of the security.

$$PV = \frac{A}{(1 + k_d)} + \frac{A}{(1 + k_d)^2} + \cdots + \frac{A}{(1 + k_d)^n}$$

$$= A\left[\frac{1}{1 + k_d} + \frac{1}{(1 + k_d)^2} + \cdots + \frac{1}{(1 + k_d)^n}\right]$$

The value of the sum in the brackets has been calculated for different values of k_d and n in Table A–3. We refer to these values as the *present value of an annuity factor*, PVA.

As an example, consider the case of a security that provides payments of $100 per year for fifteen years. What is the market value if the interest rate is 12 percent?

$$PV = 100 \ PVA_{.12, \ 15}$$

$$= 100 \ (6.811)$$

$$= \$681.10$$

ESTIMATION OF YIELDS FOR ZERO-COUPON BONDS

An approximate yield to maturity method for zero-coupon bonds, which is better than Equation 8.5, involves the use of Table A–2. Assume a ten-

TABLE A–3 Present Value of an Annuity Factor, $PVA = \sum_{t=1}^{m} 1/(1 + k_d)^t$

Year	1%	2%	3%	4%	5%	6%	7%	8%	9%	10%
1	.990	.980	.971	.962	.952	.943	.935	.926	.917	.909
2	1.970	1.942	1.913	1.886	1.859	1.833	1.808	1.783	1.759	1.736
3	2.941	2.884	2.829	2.775	2.723	2.673	2.624	2.577	2.531	2.487
4	3.902	3.808	3.717	3.630	3.546	3.465	3.387	3.312	3.240	3.170
5	4.853	4.713	4.580	4.452	4.329	4.212	4.100	3.993	3.890	3.791
6	5.795	5.601	5.417	5.242	5.076	4.917	4.767	4.623	4.486	4.355
7	6.728	6.472	6.230	6.002	5.786	5.582	5.389	5.206	5.033	4.868
8	7.652	7.326	7.020	6.733	6.463	6.210	5.971	5.747	5.535	5.335
9	8.566	8.162	7.786	7.435	7.108	6.802	6.515	6.247	5.995	5.759
10	9.471	8.983	8.530	8.111	7.722	7.360	7.024	6.710	6.418	6.145
11	10.368	9.787	9.253	8.760	8.306	7.887	7.499	7.139	6.805	6.495
12	11.255	10.575	9.954	9.385	8.863	8.384	7.943	7.536	7.161	6.814
13	12.134	11.348	10.635	9.986	9.394	8.853	8.358	7.904	7.487	7.103
14	13.004	12.106	11.296	10.563	9.899	9.295	8.746	8.244	7.786	7.367
15	13.865	12.849	11.938	11.118	10.380	9.712	9.108	8.560	8.061	7.606
16	14.718	13.578	12.561	11.652	10.838	10.106	9.447	8.851	8.313	7.824
17	15.562	14.292	13.166	12.166	11.274	10.477	9.763	9.122	8.544	8.022
18	16.398	14.992	13.754	12.659	11.690	10.828	10.059	9.372	8.756	8.201
19	17.226	15.679	14.324	13.134	12.085	11.158	10.336	9.604	8.950	8.365
20	18.046	16.352	14.878	13.590	12.462	11.470	10.594	9.818	9.129	8.514
21	18.857	17.011	15.415	14.029	12.821	11.764	10.836	10.017	9.292	8.649
22	19.661	17.658	15.937	14.451	13.163	12.042	11.061	10.201	9.442	8.772
23	20.456	18.292	16.444	14.857	13.489	12.303	11.272	10.371	9.580	8.883
24	21.244	18.914	16.936	15.247	13.799	12.550	11.469	10.529	9.707	8.985
25	22.023	19.524	17.413	15.622	14.094	12.783	11.654	10.675	9.823	9.077
30	25.808	22.397	19.601	17.292	15.373	13.765	12.409	11.258	10.274	9.427
40	32.835	27.356	23.115	19.793	17.159	15.046	13.332	11.925	10.757	9.779
50	39.197	31.424	25.730	21.482	18.256	15.762	13.801	12.234	10.962	9.915

(continued)

TABLE A–3, continued

Year	11%	12%	13%	14%	15%	16%	17%	18%	19%	20%
1	.901	.893	.885	.887	.870	.862	.855	.847	.840	.833
2	1.713	1.690	1.668	1.647	1.626	1.605	1.585	1.566	1.547	1.528
3	2.444	2.402	2.361	2.322	2.283	2.246	2.210	2.174	2.140	2.106
4	3.102	3.037	2.974	2.914	2.855	2.798	2.743	2.690	2.639	2.589
5	3.696	3.605	3.517	3.433	3.352	3.274	3.199	3.127	3.058	2.991
6	4.231	4.111	3.998	3.889	3.784	3.685	3.589	3.498	3.410	3.326
7	4.712	4.564	4.423	4.288	4.160	4.039	3.922	3.812	3.706	3.605
8	5.146	4.968	4.799	4.639	4.487	4.344	4.207	4.078	4.954	3.837
9	5.537	5.328	5.132	4.946	4.772	4.607	4.451	4.303	4.163	4.031
10	5.889	5.650	5.426	5.216	5.019	4.833	4.659	4.494	4.339	4.192
11	6.207	5.938	5.687	5.453	5.234	5.029	4.836	4.656	4.487	4.327
12	6.492	6.194	5.918	5.660	5.421	5.197	4.988	4.793	4.611	4.439
13	6.750	6.424	6.122	5.842	5.583	5.342	5.118	4.910	4.715	4.533
14	6.982	6.628	6.303	6.002	5.724	5.468	5.229	5.008	4.802	4.611
15	7.191	6.811	6.462	6.142	5.847	5.575	5.324	5.092	4.876	4.675
16	7.379	6.974	6.604	6.265	5.954	5.669	5.405	5.162	4.938	4.730
17	7.549	7.120	6.729	6.373	6.047	5.749	5.475	5.222	4.990	4.775
18	7.702	7.250	6.840	6.467	6.128	5.818	5.534	5.273	5.033	4.812
19	7.839	7.336	6.938	6.550	6.198	5.877	5.585	5.316	5.070	4.843
20	7.963	7.469	7.025	6.623	6.259	5.929	5.628	5.353	5.101	4.870
21	8.075	7.562	7.102	6.687	6.312	5.973	5.665	5.384	5.127	4.891
22	8.176	7.645	7.170	6.743	6.359	6.011	5.696	5.410	5.149	4.909
23	8.266	7.718	7.230	6.792	6.399	6.044	5.723	5.432	5.167	4.925
24	8.348	7.784	7.283	6.835	6.434	6.073	5.747	5.451	5.182	4.937
25	8.422	7.843	7.330	6.873	6.464	6.097	5.766	5.467	5.195	4.948
30	8.694	8.055	7.496	7.003	6.566	6.177	5.829	5.517	5.235	4.979
40	8.951	8.244	7.634	7.105	6.642	6.233	5.871	5.548	5.258	4.997
50	9.042	8.305	7.675	7.133	6.661	6.246	5.880	5.554	5.262	4.999

year zero-coupon bond is selling for $346. Substituting into Equation A.4 we obtain

$$346 = 1{,}000 \ PVSP_{k_d,\,10}$$

$$PVSP_{k_d,\,10} = .346$$

If we move across the $n = 10$ row of Table A–2, we see .346 lies between the 11 percent and 12 percent column, but is closer to 11 percent. Thus, the yield is approximately 11 percent.

To obtain a more accurate estimate, we use interpolation, as shown in the following diagram. The endpoints show the $PVSPs$ for $k_d = 11$ percent, and $k_d = 12$ percent. The interest rate for $PVSP = .346$ lies between 11 percent and 12 percent and is denoted by $11 + X$.

$$
\begin{array}{cccc}
k_d & 11\% & 11 + X & 12\% \\
\hline
PVSP & .352 & .346 & .322
\end{array}
$$

Note that the $PVSP$ "distance" between 11 percent and 12 percent is $.352 - .322 = .030$, and the distance between 11 and $11 + X$ is $.352 - .346 = .006$. The latter amount, $.006$, is $.006/.030 = 20$ percent of the total distance between 11 percent and 12 percent, and we, therefore, estimate k_d as 11.2 percent.

If one has a calculator that provides the nth root of a quantity, k_d can be directly obtained. From Equation A.1 we get:

$$FV_n = PV(1 + k_d)^n$$

$$(1 + k_d)^n = \frac{FV_n}{PV}$$

$$(1 + k_d) = \sqrt[n]{\frac{FV_n}{PV}}$$

and from Equation A.4:

$$k_d = \sqrt[n]{\frac{FV_n}{PV}} - 1$$

Using Equation A.4 in our zero-coupon bond example, we get

$$k_d = \sqrt[10]{\frac{1000}{346}} - 1$$

$$= 1.112 - 1$$

$$= .112 \text{ or } 11.2\%$$

In this case, our approximation and the exact method provided the same result to the nearest one tenth of one percent.

REFERENCES

Bierwag, G. O., Kaufman, G., and Toevs, A. "Duration: Its Development and Use in Bond Portfolio Management." *Financial Analysts Journal*, July/August 1983.

Billingham, Carol. "Strategies for Enhancing Bond Portfolio Returns." *Financial Analysts Journal*, May/June 1983.

Cargill, T. F. "The Term Structure of Interest Rates: A Test of the Expectations Hypothesis." *Journal of Finance*, June 1975.

Chua, Jess. "A Closed-Form Formula for Calculating Bond Duration." *Financial Analysts Journal*, May/June 1984.

Conrad, Joseph. *The Behavior of Interest Rates*. New York: National Bureau of Economic Research, 1966.

Edwards, Bob. "Bond Analysis: The Concept of Duration." *AAII Journal*, March 1984.

Fisher, Lawrence and Weil, Roman. "Coping with the Risk of Interest Rate Fluctuations: Returns to Bondholders from Naive and Optimal Strategies." *Journal of Business*, October 1971.

Garbade, Kenneth. *Securities Markets*. New York: McGraw-Hill, 1982.

Gross, William H. "The Effect of Coupon on Yield Spreads." *Financial Analysts Journal*, July/August 1979.

Jacob, N., and Pettit, R. *Investments*, Homewood, Ill.: C. D. Irwin, 1984.

Malkiel, Burton G. "Expectations, Bond Prices, and the Term Structure of Interest Rates," *Quarterly Journal of Economics*, May 1962.

———· *The Term Structure of Interest Rates*. Princeton, N.J.: Princeton University Press, 1966.

Reilly, Frank. *Investment Analysis and Portfolio Management*. Hinsdale, Ill.: Dryden, 1985.

Stevenson, Richard, and Jennings, Edward. *Fundamentals of Investments*. St. Paul, Minn.: West, 1984, Chapter 13.

Van Horne, James. *Financial Market Rates and Flows*. Englewood Cliffs, N.J.: Prentice-Hall, 1984.

III

Analysis of Variable Income Securities— Common Stocks

9

Industry Analysis

IMPORTANCE OF INDUSTRY ANALYSIS

When looking for investment opportunities, most individual investors adopt the common approach of directly examining the companies in which they may be interested or which may have been recommended. This approach may save some effort in research, but has its drawbacks. The security selected may be sound by itself. However, there may be better buys in that industry. More importantly, the industry itself may not be well situated at the moment.

If one finds that the overall economic picture looks good for the foreseeable future, this does not mean that all industries will benefit to the same extent. Each industry is governed by its own particular characteristics. For example, the airline industry is affected by these factors: fuel cost, price and routes competition, equipment replacement, and labor costs. The aerospace industry, on the other hand, is influenced mainly by the level of federal defense spending and the need for new commercial aircraft by the airline industry. A careful analysis of the special characteristics of different industries will reveal which industries will have a better future than others, and which industries will have problems that cannot be overcome within a short period of time.

Since an overview of different industries can help investors identify attractive industries and avoid those with continuing problems, investors should follow a decision process moving from macro to micro, that is, from economy to industries and from industries to companies.

CLASSIFICATION OF THE ECONOMY INTO INDUSTRIES

Industries are usually classified into several broad categories, such as industrials, financials, and public utilities. The New York Stock Exchange has classified all listed companies into four major categories: industrials, transportation, utilities, and finance and real estate. The category of industrials is further subdivided into twenty-nine groups. See Table 9–1 for the relative importance of each group in terms of market value at the end of 1984.

TABLE 9–1   Stocks Listed on the New York Stock Exchange, by Industry[a] (year-end, 1984)

Industry	No. Cos.	Common Stocks			All Stocks		
		No. Issues	No. Shares	Market Value	No. Issues	No. Shares	Market Value
Industrials	1,073	1,068	32,861	$1,140,786	1,328	33,366	$1,163,082
Aerospace	20	20	695	28,503	25	704	28,924
Business Supplies/Serv.	38	38	666	22,447	42	682	23,134
Chemicals	37	37	1,080	33,386	44	1,084	33,518
Computers, Data Process.	40	40	1,694	113,197	42	1,696	113,210
Construction	68	68	1,332	30,821	90	1,362	31,898
Electrical Equipment	18	18	992	43,844	18	992	43,844
Electronics	52	52	1,243	34,402	52	1,243	34,402
Environmental Control	6	6	115	3,851	6	115	3,851
Foods, Beverages	55	54	1,854	76,428	65	1,873	77,250
Health & Beauty Prods.	16	16	606	18,666	17	617	18,917
Health Care Services	25	25	967	24,264	26	967	24,287
Household Goods	36	36	850	30,099	41	853	30,173
Industrial Mach. & Equip.	75	75	1,107	27,267	87	1,120	27,651
Lodging, Restaurants	23	23	469	14,990	25	470	15,026
Mining, Refining, Fabric.	60	59	1,727	31,514	89	1,781	33,593
Motor Vehicles	26	26	994	42,773	34	1,027	44,198
Oil & Gas	89	89	6,031	188,832	128	6,115	193,566
Packaging	18	17	214	6,946	24	221	7,128
Paper Production	14	14	330	11,272	20	344	12,064
Pharmaceuticals	16	16	1,061	54,344	19	1,062	54,425
Publishing	18	18	496	21,089	19	496	21,091
Recreation Serv. & Prod.	39	39	911	31,099	44	926	31,335
Retail Trade	92	92	2,544	75,944	104	2,560	76,906
Textiles, Apparel	37	37	354	8,706	40	357	8,769
Tires, Rubber	7	7	259	5,972	10	260	6,034
Tobacco	6	6	233	13,750	11	251	14,679
Wholesalers, Distrib.	19	19	262	7,022	22	262	7,046
Multi-Industry	104	102	3,601	135,813	165	3,753	142,619
Other	19	19	173	3,544	19	173	3,544
Transportation	55	52	1,507	39,516	79	1,576	41,111
Utilities	196	174	8,910	233,174	600	9,318	245,425
Finance, Real Estate	219	217	4,610	127,137	312	4,831	136,480
Grand Total	1,543	1,511	47,888	$1,540,613	2,319	49,092	$1,586,098

[a] Shares and value in millions.

Source: The New York Stock Exchange, *1985 Fact Book*.

The *Value Line Investment Survey* classifies about 1700 stocks under their review into about ninety industries.

The Standard & Poor's Corporation, as shown in Table 9–2, classifies their selected 500 companies into four major groups: industrial (400), public utilities (40), transportation (20), and financial (40). The industrials category is subclassified into some seventy-five industry groups.

For the purpose of industry analysis, the most useful classification is that of Standard & Poor's, for several reasons. First, there is a price index for each industry group. Second, quarterly earnings and dividends are available to relate to each price index. Third, composite industry data on a per share basis, like sales, operating income, profit margin, depreciation, taxes, earnings, dividends, book value, working capital, and capital expenditures are published regularly in their *Industry Survey* and *Analysts Handbook*, with data going back to 1946.

Besides classification by nature of products, industries are often classified or grouped together in terms of secular growth and cyclical stability under four categories:

1. *Growth industry*. The growth of the industry is expected to persist and to exceed the average of the economy.
2. *Cyclical industry*. The industry is expected to move closely with the economy and to fluctuate cyclically.
3. *Defensive industry*. The industry is expected to grow steadily with the economy, but to decline less than the average in a cyclical downturn.
4. *Declining industry*. The industry is expected either to decline absolutely or to grow less than the average of the economy.

STAGES OF INDUSTRY DEVELOPMENT

The development of each industry, according to some economic theorists, can be likened to the life cycle of individuals.[1] There are four stages to the standard life cycle of industries (see Figure 9–1).

The pioneering stage represents the first phase of a new industry. The technology or the product is relatively new and still to be perfected. Demand expands rapidly. Opportunities of making big profits are great. Many venture capitalists enter the industry and organize their own firms. As a rule, competition is keen and mortality rates are high.

The second, fast-growing stage, arrives when the chaotic growth and competition is over, leaving only a number of surviving large corporations

---

[1] Edward S. Mead and Julius Grodinsky. *The Ebb and Flow of Investment Values* (New York: Appleton-Century-Crofts, 1939); Grodinsky. *Investments* (New York: The Ronald Press Co., 1953), Chapters 3, 4, and 5.

TABLE 9–2 Stocks in the S&P 500 Price Index

— 400 INDUSTRIALS —

AEROSPACE—Boeing; General Dynamics; Grumman; Lockheed Corp.; Martin Marietta; McDonnell Douglas; Raytheon; Rockwell Intl.; United Technologies.

ALUMINUM—Alcan Aluminium; Aluminum Co. of Amer.; Kaiser Aluminum; Reynolds Metals.

AUTOMOBILE—Amer. Motors; Chrysler; Ford; Gen. Motors.

AUTO PARTS (After Market)—Champion Spark Plug; Echlin Mfg.; Genuine Parts; Sealed Power Corp.

AUTO PARTS (Original Equip.)—Dana; Eaton; Lib.-Owens-Ford; TRW Inc.; Timken Corp.

AUTO TRUCKS & PARTS—Cummins Engine; Fruehauf; Paccar Inc.

BEVERAGES (BREWERS)—Anheuser-Busch; Coors (Adolph); Heileman (G) Brewing; Pabst Brew.

BEVERAGES (DISTILLERS)—Brown-Forman Distillers; Natl. Dist.; Seagram Ltd.; Walker.

BEVERAGES (SOFT DRINKS)—Coca-Cola; General Cinema; MEI Corp.; PepsiCo Inc.

BUILDING MATERIALS—American Standard; Crane; Fedders; Ideal Basic; Jim Walter; Kaiser Cement; Lone Star Ind.; Masco; Nat'l Gypsum; U.S. Gypsum.

CHEMICALS—Dow; Du Pont (E.I.); Hercules; Monsanto; Stauffer Chem.; Union Carbide.

CHEMICALS (MISC.)—American Cyanamid; Celanese Corp.; FMC Corp.; Grace (W.R.) & Co.; PPG, Inc.; Rohm & Haas.

COAL—Eastern Gas & Fuel; No. Amer. Coal; Pittston; Westmoreland.

COMMUNICATIONS—EQUIP./MFRS.—Andrew Corp.; Digital Switch; General Instrument; M/A-Com Inc.; Northern Telecom; Scientific Atlanta.

COMPUTER & BUSINESS EQUIPMENT—Apple Computer; Burroughs; Control Data; Data General; Datapoint Corp.; Digital Equip.; Intl. Bus. Mach.; NCR Corp.; Prime Computer; Sperry Corp.; Tandem Corp.; Wang Lab Cl B; Xerox Corp.

COMPUTER SERVICES—Automatic Data; Computer Sciences; Shared Medical Systems.

CONGLOMERATES—Gulf & Western; IC Indus.; ITT Corp.; Litton Indus.; Northwest Indus.; Teledyne; Tenneco Inc.; Textron.

CONTAINERS (METAL & GLASS)—Amer. Can; Ball Corp.; Crown Cork; Natl. Can; Owens-Ill.

CONTAINERS (PAPER)—Bemis Co.; Federal; Stone Container.

COPPER—ASARCO Inc.; Newmont Mining; Phelps-Dodge.

COSMETICS—Alberto-Culver; Avon; Chesebrough-Pond's; Gillette Corp.; Intl. Flavors & Fragrances; Noxell Corp.; Revlon.

DRUGS—Amer. Home; Bristol-Myers; Lilly (Eli); Merck; Pfizer; Schering-Plough; Searle (G.D.); SmithKline Beckman Corp.; Squibb Corp.; Sterling; Upjohn Co.; Warner-Lambert.

ELECTRICAL EQUIPMENT—Emerson Electric; Grainger (W.W.); McGraw Edison; Square D; Thomas & Betts.

ELECTRONICS MAJOR COS.—Gen. Elec.; RCA; Westinghouse Elec.

ELECTRONICS (INSTRUMENTATION)—Gould Inc.; Hewlett-Packard; Perkin-Elmer; Tektronix.

ELECTRONICS (SEMICONDUCTORS/COMPONENTS)—AMP Inc.; Advanced Micro Devices; Intel Corp.; Motorola; Nat'l Semiconductor; Texas Instruments.

ENTERTAINMENT—Disney (Walt); MCA; MGM/UA Entertainment Co.; Warner Communications.

FERTILIZERS—Beker Inds.; First Miss. Corp.; Intl. Minerals & Chem.; Williams Cos.

FOODS—Archer-Daniels-Midland; Beatrice Co.; Borden; CPC Int'l.; Campbell Soup; Carnation; ConAgra, Inc.; Consolidated Foods; Dart & Kraft Inc.; Gen. Foods; Gen Mills; Gerber Prod.; Heinz (H.J.); Hershey Foods; Kellogg; Nabisco Brands Inc.; Pillsbury; Quaker Oats; Ralston Purina; Wrigley (Wm.).

FOREST PRODUCTS—Boise Cascade; Champion Intl.; Georgia-Pacific; Louisiana-Pac.; Potlatch Corp.; Weyerhaeuser.

‡GAMING COS.—Caesars World; Circus Circus; Golden Nugget; Resorts Int'l (Cl. A)

GOLD MINING—ASA Ltd.; Campbell Red Lake; Dome; Homestake Mining.

HARDWARE AND TOOLS—Black & Decker; Snap-On-Tools; Stanley Works.

HOMEBUILDING—Centex Corp.; Kaufman & Broad; Pulte Home; Ryan Homes; U.S. Home Corp.

HOSPITAL MANAGEMENT—Amer. Med. Int'l.; Hospital Corp. of Amer.; Humana Inc.; Nat'l Med. Enter.

HOSPITAL SUPPLIES—Abbott Lab.; Amer. Hospital; Bard (C.R.); Baxter Travenol Lab.; Becton, Dickinson; Johnson & Johnson.

HOTEL-MOTEL—Hilton Hotels; Holiday Inns; Marriott Corp.; Ramada Inns.

HOUSEHOLD FURNISHING & APPLIANCES—Bassett Furniture Ind.; Maytag; Mohasco Corp.; Roper Corp.; Whirlpool; White Consolidated Inds.; Zenith.

LEISURE TIME—AMF Inc.; Brunswick; Coleman Co.; Handleman; Outboard Marine.

MACHINE TOOLS—Acme Cleveland; Brown & Sharpe; Cincinnati Milacron; Cross & Trecker; Monarch Machine Tool.

MACHINERY (AGRICULTURAL)—Allis Chalmers; Deere; Intl. Harvester; Massey Ferguson.

MACHINERY (CONSTRUCTION & MATERIALS HANDLING)—Bucyrus-Erie; Cater. Trac.; Clark Equip.; Rexnord Inc.

MACHINERY (INDUSTRIAL/SPECIALTY)—Briggs & Stratton; Chicago Pneumatic; Combustion Eng.; Cooper Indus.; Ex-Cell-O; Foster Wheeler; Ingersoll-Rand; Joy Mfg.

METALS MISC.—Amax Inc.; Engelhard Corp.; INCO Ltd.

MISCELLANEOUS—Allied Corp.; Amsted Industries; Armstrong World; Borg-Warner; Corning Glass; Diamond Shamrock; Donnelley (R.R.) & Sons; Eastman Kodak; Fluor Corp.; General Signal; Harris Corp.; Kerr-McGee; MCI Communications; Minnesota Mining; Owens-Corning; Phibro-Salomon; Polaroid; Sherwin-Williams; Singer.

MISC. (HIGH TECH.)—American Tel. & Tel'.; Computervision; Cullinet Software; Honeywell; Intergraph Corp.; Signal Cos.; Tandy.

MOBILE HOMES—Fleetwood Enterprises; Redman Inds.; Skyline.

OFFSHORE DRILLING—Global Marine; Reading & Bates; SEDCO; Western Co. of North America.

OIL (CRUDE PRODUCERS)—Louisiana Land & Exploration; Mesa Pet.; Texas Oil & Gas.

OIL (INTEGRATED-DOMESTIC)—Amerada Hess; Atl. Richfield; Occidental Petroleum; Pennzoil Co.; Phillips; Shell; Stand. Oil Ind.; Standard Oil Ohio; Sun Co.; Unocal Corp.

OIL (INTEGRATED-INTERNATIONAL)—Chevron Corp.; Exxon Corp.; Mobil Corp.; Royal Dutch; Texaco.

‡CANADIAN OIL & GAS EXPLORATION—Dome Petroleum; Gulf of Canada; Husky Oil; Imperial Oil Ltd.

OIL WELL EQUIPMENT AND SERVICES—Baker Intl.; Dresser; Halliburton; Hughes Tool; McDermott Int'l.; NL Industries; Schlumberger.

PAPER—Crown Zell.; Int'l Paper; Kimb-Clark; Mead; Scott; Union Camp; Westvaco.

POLLUTION CONTROL—Browning-Ferris; Peabody Int'l.; Waste Management Inc.; Zurn Ind.

PUBLISHING—Dun & Bradstreet; Harcourt Brace Jovanovich; Macmillan; McGraw-Hill; Meredith; SFN Cos.; Time Inc.

PUBLISHING (NEWSPAPERS)—Dow Jones; Gannett Co.; Knight Ridder Newspapers; New York Times Cl A; Times Mirror.

RADIO-TV BROADCASTERS—American; CBS Inc.; Capital Cities Comm.; Cox Communication Corp.; Storer Communications; Taft.

RESTAURANTS—Church's Fried Chicken; Denny's Inc.; McDonald's Corp.; Wendy's Int'l.

RETAIL STORES (DEPT. STORES)—Allied Stores; Associated; Carter Hawley Hale Stores; Dayton Hudson; Federated; Macy; May Dept.; Mercantile Stores.

RETAIL STORES (DRUG)—Eckerd (Jack); Revco D.S., Inc.; Rite Aid; Walgreen Co.

RETAIL STORES (FOOD CHAINS)—Albertson's; Amer. Stores Co.; Great A&P; Kroger; Lucky Stores; Safeway; Winn-Dixie.

RETAIL STORES (GEN. MDSE. CHAINS)—K mart; Penny (J.C.); Sears; Wal-Mart Stores; Woolworth.

RETAIL (MISCELLANEOUS)—Limited, Inc.; Lowe's Cos; Southland Corp.; Toys "R" Us.

SHOES—Brown Group; Genesco; Interco; Melville Corp.

SOAPS—Clorox; Colgate-Palmolive; Procter & Gamble; Unilever N.V.

STEEL—Armco; Beth.; Inland; Interlake; LTV Corp.; National Intergroup; U.S. Steel; Wheeling-Pittsburgh.

TEXTILES (APPAREL MFRS.)—Cluett, Peabody; Hartmarx Corp.; Levi Strauss; Liz Claiborne; Russell Corp.; V.F. Corp.

TEXTILE PRODUCTS—Burlington Indus.; Collins, Lowenstein; Springs Industries Inc.; Stevens; West Point-Pepperell.

TIRES & RUBBER GOODS—Firestone; Goodrich; Goodyear; Uniroyal.

TOBACCO—Amer. Brands Inc.; Philip Morris; Reynolds Indus.

TOYS—Coleco Inc.; Hasbro Bradley; Mattel, Inc; Tonka Corp.

— 40 PUBLIC UTILITIES —

ELECTRIC POWER—Amer. El. Pwr.; Balt. G. & E.; Cent. & So. West. Corp.; Comm. Ed.; Con. Ed.; Detroit Ed.; Dominion Resources; Duke Power; Fla. Power & Light; Middle So. Util.; Niagara Mohawk; No. States Pwr.; Ohio Ed.; Pac. G. & E.; Phila. Elec.; Pub. Serv. E. & G.; Public Service of Indiana; So. Calif. Ed.; Southern Co.; Texas Utils.

NATURAL GAS DISTRIBUTORS—Columbia; Consolidated Natural; ENSERCH Corp.; Oneok Inc.; Pac. Light; Peoples Energy.

NATURAL GAS PIPE LINES—Amer. Natural Resources; Houston Nat. Gas; InterNorth Inc.; Panhandle Eastern; Sonat Inc.; Texas East. Corp.

TELEPHONE (New)—Ameritech; Bell Atlantic; BellSouth; GTE Corp.; NYNEX; Pacific Telesis; Southwestern Bell; U.S. West.

— 20 TRANSPORTATION —

AIR FREIGHT—Emery Air Freight; Federal Express; Tiger International.

AIRLINES—AMR Corp.; Delta; Northwest; Pan Am; UAL, Inc.

RAILROADS—Burlington Northern Inc.; CSX Corp.; Chicago & Northwestern; Norfolk Southern Corp.; Santa Fe Southern Pac.; Union Pac. Corp.

TRUCKERS—Consol. Freightways; Overnite Transportation; Roadway Service; Yellow Freight Sys.

TRANSPORTATION (MISCELLANEOUS)—Leaseway Transportation; Ryder System.

— 40 FINANCIAL —

BANKS (NEW YORK CITY)—Bankers Trust New York; Chase Manhattan; Chemical; Citicorp; Manufacturers Hanover; Morgan (J.P.) & Co.

BANKS (OUTSIDE NEW YORK CITY)—BankAmerica; Bank of Boston Corp.; Barnett Banks of Florida; First Chic. Corp.; First Interstate Bancorp.; First Penn.; InterFirst Corp.; Mellon Natl.; NCNB Corp.; Norwest Corp.; Texas Commerce Bancshares.

LIFE INSURANCE—Capital Holding; Jefferson Pilot; Lincoln National Corp.; USLIFE Corp.

MULTI-LINE INSURANCE—Aetna Life & Cas.; American Int'l Group; American General; CIGNA Corp.; CNA Financial; Travelers.

PROPERTY-CASUALTY INSURANCE—Chubb Corp.; Continental Corp.; St. Paul; Safeco Corp.; USF & G Corp.

SAVINGS & LOAN HOLDING COS.—Ahmanson (H.F.); Financial Corp. of America; Great Western.

PERSONAL LOANS—Beneficial; Household Int'l Inc.

FINANCIAL-MISC.—American Express; Merrill Lynch; Transamerica Corp.

**BROKERAGE FIRMS—Donaldson Lufkin Jenrette; Edwards (A.G.); Hutton (E.F.) Group; Merrill Lynch; Paine Webber, Inc.

**INVESTMENT COMPANIES—Adams; Gen. Amer.; Lehman; Madison; Tri-Cont.

**INVESTMENT COS. (Bond Funds)—American Capital Bond; Intercapital Inc. Sec.; John Hancock Inc. Sec.; MassMutual Inc Inv.; Montgomery Str. Inc. Sec.

**REAL ESTATE INVEST.—First Union Real Estate; Lomas & Nettleton Mtge. Inv.; Mass-Mutual Mtge & Realty; Mony Mtg.; Wells Fargo Mortge & Equity.

‡Not included in 400 Industrials
**Not included in Financial composite
(Changes in S&P 500 on Preceding Page)

Source: The Outlook, Standard & Poor's Corporation, 1985.

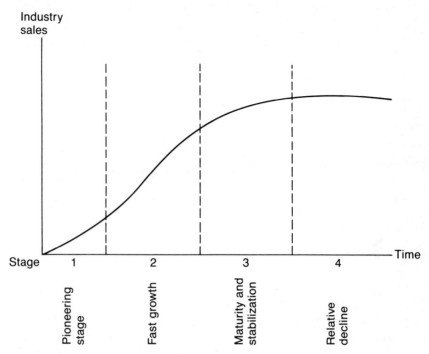

FIGURE 9–1   **Life Cycle of Industries**

dominating the industry. However, the demand is still growing faster than the economy. This is the stage of orderly, rapid growth.

During the third stage of maturity and stabilization the industry is fully developed and grows roughly at the same pace as the whole economy.

Eventually, the industry will grow old due to inroads from new products, new industries, changes in social habits, new technology, and changes in demand. In good times the industry will grow less than the economy, and in times of recession the industry will suffer sharp declines in demand. However, the industry may continue to exist for many years.

EVALUATION OF THE INDUSTRY LIFE-CYCLE THEORY

Several comments on the theory and its investment implications are offered here. First, the general description of the stages of development of industries by the life-cycle theory fits quite well with the past experience of many industries. Second, the theory offers a general description of the industry life cycle. Individual industries have varied substantially from the norm in the stage of developments as portrayed by the theory. What can be most safely said of the development of industries is the common trend toward *re-*

tardation in growth rates. Most industries mature and decline relatively, but do not die out. Not a few industries, after reaching the mature stage, often go through a long period of alternate prosperity and recession. In retrospect, it is often easy to define the stages a mature industry has gone through, but it is not easy to identify the current stage of many industries. Third, there are several important investment implications of the theory:

1. The risk of investments in the pioneering stage is very high. Investors should generally avoid commitments at this stage. If one insists on speculation in this early stage, he or she should spread funds over several leading companies, hoping that income from the ones that survive and prosper will more than offset the losses on the other companies that will be eliminated.
2. The investor should look for opportunities in an industry when the industry has gone through a shakeout period and has entered into the second stage of fast growth.
3. Industry selection should receive consideration prior to an investment decision.
4. Investors who are buying into companies in a fast-growing industry should beware of the price they are paying. Not infrequently, the prices of the shares of these attractive corporations are bid up much too high because of an impressive past record and bright prospects. Purchases at such high price levels can easily turn into substantial losses for a long period of time, and there is a good possibility that the investor may be disillusioned and sell out after a while. What happened to home computer stocks, like Apple, Commodore, and Coleco in 1983 is a clear reminder of the dangers that face investors when they purchase seemingly attractive stocks with bright futures (Apple: 1983 high 63, low 17; Commodore: 1983 high 61, low 29; Coleco: 1983 high 65, low 16).

STRUCTURE AND OPERATIONAL CHARACTERISTICS

Each industry is unique. A careful review of these unique features should always form an important part of an industry study. They include:

1. The state of competition in the industry.
2. The nature and prospect of demand for the product and services of the industry.
3. Cost conditions and profitability.
4. Technology and research.
5. Immediate and long-term outlook for sales and profits.

State of Competition

With respect to the state of competition, the investor is interested in these questions:

1. What are the price policies of the firm? Do they compete in price? Do they "follow the leader" in announcing price changes?
2. Are products of the industry relatively homogeneous in nature or highly differentiated?
3. Do firms compete actively and in advertising in offering supplementary services?
4. With which domestic industries is the industry in competition? How are the products of the industry compared with substitutes in terms of quality, price, appearance, and other features?
5. What is the state of competition with foreign producers in domestic and foreign markets? Is the industry losing or gaining in the competition with foreign producers?

The pertinent questions to be raised in the inquiry of the nature and prospect of demand for the industry are:

1. Which classification does this industry fall into: growth, cyclical, defensive, or relative decline industry?
2. What are the major markets by customers? What is the distribution of markets by geographical areas, including foreign demand?
3. What are the determinants of demand?
4. What factors will likely affect the demand from each major group of customers?
5. What is the immediate and long-run outlook of demand, taking into consideration both the secular and cyclical prospects of general business?

Cost Conditions and Profitability

The intrinsic value, or normal worth, of a security is determined by the profitability, current and prospective, that it represents. Fast-growing demand for an industry does not automatically guarantee high profits for the industry as a whole or for individual companies in the industry. Profitability depends no less on cost control and state of competition than on growth in demand. The cost factors and concepts the investor should examine in an industry study are:

1. Distribution of costs for the industry among wages, raw materials, and overhead.
2. The rate of increase of labor costs per hour and labor productivity.

3. Rate of increase of prices for finished products.
4. Extent and control of excess capacity.
5. Requirements for new capital expenditures to maintain productive efficiency and keep up competition with producers outside the industry.
6. Turnover of invested capital.

To measure profitability, the following ratios should be computed, compared over time, and analyzed for indications of the causes of changes:

1. Gross profit margin, which relates gross income (sales less cost of goods sold) to sales to indicate profitability at the manufacturing level.
2. Operating profit margin, which relates income before income taxes to sales.
3. Rate of return on equity, which relates net income after income taxes to stockholders' equity.
4. Rate of return on total capital, which relates net income after income taxes plus interest charges to total capital invested, including loans from creditors.

Technology and Research

Changes in technology often have an important impact on the prospects of an industry. Advances in technology can either broaden and accelerate the growth of an already fast-growing industry or rejuvenate an industry that is on the decline. As far as information is available, the analyst should try to answer a few pertinent questions:

1. Is the technology of the industry relatively stable and mature, or is it still in a stage of rapid change?
2. Are there any important technological changes on the horizon? What will their effects be?
3. What percentage of sales growth of the industry can be attributed to introduction of new products?
4. What has been the relationship between capital expenditures and sales?
5. What percentage of industry sales has been spent on research and development?

Immediate and Long-Run Outlook for Sales and Profits for the Industry

The investor should assess the findings on the various factors mentioned above and translate them into two basic statistics for two time periods.

They are:

1. Estimate of rate of growth of sales for the industry
   a. in the year ahead
   b. in the next three to five years
2. Estimate the rate of growth of profits after taxes
   a. in the year ahead
   b. in the next three to five years

For short-term investors, the year-ahead figures for sales and profits growth are likely given more weight, whereas the long-run-oriented investors would probably treat the three- to five-year estimates as no less important than the year-ahead estimates.

If the investor has compiled estimates of growth for the whole economy for the two time periods, a comparison should be made between the industry and the economy to see how much better or worse the relative position of the industry will be in the year ahead and in three to five years.

INPUT-OUTPUT ANALYSIS

For the purpose of developing forecasts of industry sales, many analysts have turned to a type of interindustry analysis known as *input-output analysis*. Input-output analysis was developed by Wassily Leontief of Harvard University, who developed and published the first input-output table for the economy of the United States in an article "Quantitative Input-Output Relations in the Economic System of the United States," in *The Review of Economics and Statistics* in August, 1936. The purpose of his approach is to show empirically the structure and the working of the national economy, highlighting the interdependence of the different sectors in the economy.

Following his lead, the United States government has undertaken the job of compiling and publishing input-output tables for the economy; the latest table published was for the year 1977.[2] Although input-output analysis is still in its developmental stage in terms of both content of information and frequency of publication, the approach seems to possess much potential and will likely constitute an important tool in economic forecasts, especially of interindustry relationships, in future years.

The Input-Output Table

A highly simplified hypothetical input-output relationship is shown in Table 9–3. The processing sector of the economy is divided into six basic

---

[2] Interindustry Economics Division of the Commerce Department. "The Input-Output Structure of the U.S. Economy, 1977." *Survey of Current Business*, May 1984.

TABLE 9–3   Hypothetical Transactions Table

									Final Demand			
Outputs* Inputs†	(1)	(2)	(3)	(4)	(5)	(6)	(7) Gross Inventory Accumulation (+)	(8) Exports to Foreign Countries	(9) Government Purchases	(10) Gross Private Capital Formation	(11) Households	(12) Total Gross Output
	A	B	C	D	E	F						
(1) Industry A	10	15	1	2	5	6	2	5	1	3	14	64
(2) Industry B	5	4	7	1	3	8	1	6	3	4	17	59
(3) Industry C	7	2	8	1	5	3	2	3	1	3	5	40
(4) Industry D	11	1	2	8	6	4	0	0	1	2	4	39
(5) Industry E	4	0	1	14	3	2	1	2	1	3	9	40
(6) Industry F	2	6	7	6	2	6	2	4	2	1	8	46
(7) Gross inventory depletion (–)	1	2	1	0	2	1	0	1	0	0	0	8
(8) Imports	2	1	3	0	3	2	0	0	0	0	2	13
(9) Payments to government	2	3	2	2	1	2	3	2	1	2	12	32
(10) Depreciation allowances	1	2	1	0	1	0	0	0	0	0	0	5
(11) Households	19	23	7	5	9	12	1	0	8	0	1	85
(12) Total gross outlays	64	59	40	39	40	46	12	23	18	18	72	431

Industry Purchasing spans the full table header; *Processing Sector* spans columns (1)–(6). At the left margin: *Processing Sector Industry Producing*, *Payments Sector*, *Processing Sector*.

* Sales to industries and sectors along the top of the table from the industry listed in each row at the left of the table.

† Purchases from industries and sectors at the left of the table by the industry listed at the top of each column.

Source: From *The Elements of Input-Output Analysis* by William H. Miernyk. Copyright © 1957 by Northeastern University. Copyright © 1965 by Random House, Inc. Reprinted by permission of the publisher.

industries labeled A to F. They can be agriculture, mining, manufacturing, transportation, wholesale and retail trade, and so on. In addition, there is a payments sector composed of inventory changes, import or exports, governments, private capital formation, and households. Altogether, there are eleven departments for the economy into which all transactions representing production, distribution, transportation, and consumption are grouped.

Each horizontal row of figures in the table shows the distribution of the output of one sector among other sectors of the economy, including itself. The vertical columns show how each sector obtains its inputs from other sectors. Take industry B, for example. The total output is 59 units, or dollars, worth of goods or services. They are distributed as follows: 4 for intraindustry consumption, 5 for A, 7 for C, 1 for D, 3 for E, 8 for F, 1 for addition to inventory, 6 for exports to foreign countries, 3 for governments, 4 for private capital formation, and 17 for consumption by households. In order to enable industry B to produce 59 units of goods, it obtains inputs from other sectors as follows: 15 from A, 4 from intraindustry firms, 2 from C, 1 from D, 6 from F, 2 from depletion of inventory, 1 from imports, 3 from government services, 2 from wear and tear of equipment, and 23 from services rendered by households.

As shown in the table, the total inputs of each industry in the processing sector must equal its total outputs. For the payments sector, however, receipts and expenditures of each department can vary. For example, the households received a total of 85 units but spent only 72 units. Of course, the total receipts of all departments in the payments sector must be the same as their total expenditures for the whole payments sector.

Possible Application of the Input-Output Table
The possibilities for applications of input-output analysis are not yet fully developed. They depend not only on the ingenuity of the user but also on the table's amount of desegregation of industries and on its timeliness. However, several obvious uses can be noted:

1. To indicate the amount of direct purchases required from other industries per dollar of output for each industry.
2. To estimate not only the distribution of output of one sector but probably also the types of uses the product enters into.
3. To help avoid some inconsistencies that may otherwise develop in economic projections, both long-term and short-term.
4. To evaluate market prospects for established products, to identify potential markets for new products, to spot prospective shortages in supplies, and to enable analysts to evaluate investment prospects in various industries.
5. To help make a forecast of the total sales of an industry. The analyst can estimate the demands from individual sectors and then the total demand for the industry. One can also start from an assumed level of GNP for the economy and work backward to individual industries.

RESEARCHING AN INDUSTRY

Most individual investors cannot be expected to be forecasters of general business or interest rates. Neither can we expect that investors will conduct industry studies themselves. This is not really necessary because at any time many investment materials, including analyses prepared by professional analysts on individual industries, are available.

What investors do need is to know where to look for the relevant materials and, more importantly, to understand them and their investment implications. If they feel some aspects of the materials and studies gathered are still deficient, they can do a little more research on their own.

For example, let us consider the chemical industry. Assume that you are interested in some chemical stocks because they are recommended to you. Before you look at some individual companies, you should examine the chemical industry as a whole to see whether or not there are problems in the industry. Among the many investment materials available on an industry, some materials are particularly useful.

Forbes

In the mid-January issue, *Forbes* evaluates over 1000 major firms in forty-two basic industry groups and eighty-two subgroups by two management performance yardsticks. See Table 9–4 for degree of profitability and rate of growth of the chemical industry. *Forbes* also has two other columns in the table on performance. One column shows the percentages of corporate sales and profits of each firm that originate from the industry group. The second column shows Forbes' estimates of earnings predictability of each firm. They arrive at the estimates through a statistical measure called the *coefficient of determination,* which measures how much earnings fluctuate from the five-year growth rate. Companies with predictability ratings in the top 20 percent are designated "very high," those in the next 20 percent, "high," and so on.

In Table 9–4 we see the performance of two chemical industry groups, diversified chemicals and specialized chemicals. In the last twelve months, the diversified group earned a return on equity of 12.7 percent. The net profit margin was 3.4 percent, and sales growth rate was 10.1 percent. The specialized group during the same period earned a rate of return on equity of 13.8 percent. The net profit margin was 3.9 percent, and sales growth rate was 10.7 percent. The all-industry median, on the other hand, showed a 13.4 percent rate of return on equity, 3.7 percent net profit margin, and 11.5 percent sales growth rate.

Standard & Poor's *Analysts Handbook*

One of the best sources of statistical data on an industry is the *Analysts Handbook* published annually by the Standard & Poor's Corporation with quarterly supplements. See Tables 9–5 and 9–6 for the statistics on the chemical industry. See Table 9–7 for per share data for the chemical industry in the form of income statements and balance sheets plus various financial ratios.

Value Line Investment Survey

The *Value Line Investment Survey* includes two parts: (1) reports on individual companies, and (2) reports on individual industries. Preceding reports on individual companies in a given industry, there is a brief section of a few pages highlighting the developments and trends in that industry.

The reports on individual industries include some basic statistics for the industry such as sales, operating margin, depreciation, net profit, income tax rate, net profit margin, working capital, long-term debt, net worth, percent earned on total capital, percent earned on net worth, average annual price-earnings ratio, and average annual dividend yield. Also included are *Value Line's* estimates for the current year.

TABLE 9–4

Chemicals

Yardsticks of management performance

Company	% in —segment— sales/profits	Profitability — Return on equity: rank	Profitability — Return on equity: 5-year average	Profitability — Return on equity: latest 12 months	debt/ equity ratio	net profit margin	Growth — Sales: rank	Growth — Sales: 5-year average	Growth — Sales: latest 12 months	Growth — Earnings per share: rank	Growth — Earnings per share: 5-year average	Growth — Earnings per share: latest 12 months	predictability
Diversified													
Allied Corp	23/ 17	1	35.4%	2.7%	0.4	0.6%	2	21.5%	19.3%		NM	−78.2%	NM
Rohm & Haas		2	14.7	19.4	0.3	7.3	6	7.5	10.7	1	12.8%	31.7	average
E I du Pont	33/ 45	3	14.7	13.0	0.4	3.2	1	30.9	4.6	10	−5.9	47.8	low
Hercules	65/ 66	4	14.2	15.8	0.3	6.6	8	5.1	6.0	8	−1.1	28.5	very low
Borg-Warner	23/ 35	5	14.1	14.0	0.2	5.2	5	7.8	14.6	3	5.4	16.9	average
Dow Chemical	83/111	6	13.9	10.8	0.6	2.7	4	8.5	10.1	14	−17.7	122.2	average
FMC	37/ 61	7	13.1	15.6	0.2	4.8	13	3.1	4.9	6	2.5	46.1	average
Univar	57/ 66	8	13.1†	17.3	0.6	0.8	14	2.3‡	12.6	12	−12.3‡	131.0	average
Borden	30/ 37	9	12.9	13.8	0.3	4.4	16	1.1	9.8	2	9.1	11.7	very high
Pennwalt	61/ 58	10	12.3	12.2	0.4	4.6	19	−0.6	8.6	11	−11.7	75.0	average
Stauffer Chemical	80/104	11	12.2	1.8	0.3	def	17	0.7	12.4		NM	D-P	NM
American Cyanamid	48/ 36	12	11.7	13.7	0.3	4.7	9	4.5	10.0	7	−0.9	45.6	very low
Diamond Shamrock	23/ 7	13	11.3	1.5	0.7	def	3	16.5	27.1		NM	P-D	NM
Monsanto	63/ 49	14	10.9	12.7	0.3	5.9	10	3.7	11.0	4	3.3	43.2	very low
Natl Distillers	34/ 41	15	10.6	6.4	0.3	2.6	7	6.5	88.2	13	−12.7	47.4	average
Union Carbide	43/ 40	16	10.6	4.0	0.5	0.9	15	1.9	6.2	15	−25.7	−9.9	low
Celanese	51/ 29	17	9.9	16.4	0.7	3.4	12	3.3	7.4		NM	500.0 +	NM
Olin	57/ 48	18	8.6	10.4	0.5	3.7	11	3.5	10.2	5	2.6	60.2	very low
Reichhold Chemicals		19	6.9	12.3	0.2	2.9	18	−0.5	3.7	9	−3.7	49.8	very low
Medians			12.3	12.7	0.3	3.4		3.7	10.1		−5.9	45.9	

Company	% in —segment— sales/profits	Profitability — Return on equity: rank	Profitability — Return on equity: 5-year average	Profitability — Return on equity: latest 12 months	debt/ equity ratio	net profit margin	Growth — Sales: rank	Growth — Sales: 5-year average	Growth — Sales: latest 12 months	Growth — Earnings per share: rank	Growth — Earnings per share: 5-year average	Growth — Earnings per share: latest 12 months	predictability
Specialized													
Freeport-McMoran	56/ 47	1	24.4%	12.5%	0.4	11.9%	1	19.6%	6.4%	4	10.0%	67.1%	very low
Nalco Chemical		2	24.2	21.7	0.1	10.8	13	6.0	8.1	5	8.3	23.7	low
Cabot	29/ 26	3	21.5	14.4	0.4	4.1	2	15.7	12.5	7	4.7	51.0	very low
Intl Flavors		4	21.4	19.9	0.0	14.8	16	4.2	2.6	8	3.3	3.3	high
Morton Thiokol	50/ 57	5	20.5	19.4	0.2	5.5	3	13.7	13.3	1	19.8	23.6	average
Lubrizol		6	20.4	14.2	0.1	8.1	14	5.1	6.8	17	−8.4	31.5	low
Vulcan Materials	31/ 16	7	19.2	17.2	0.2	6.6	19	3.1	26.8	13	−0.1	78.3	very low
Universal Leaf	35/ 20	8	19.0	19.3	0.1	3.8	12	6.0	5.3	2	12.7	17.9	very high
Dexter	47/ 40	9	17.1	15.1	0.4	4.9	10	7.4	15.1	9	3.1	1.7	average
Big Three Inds	43/ 67	10	17.0	8.4	0.3	6.8	6	11.1	13.4	12	0.0	4.2	very low
Air Products		11	17.0	13.4	0.4	6.7	8	9.2	13.1	6	4.8	31.1	low
Witco Chemical		12	16.3	18.6	0.4	3.8	5	12.3	11.8	11	0.9	37.3	very low
Sun Chemical	61/ 60	13	15.7	7.0	0.8	1.3	4	13.4	19.3	19	−29.3	−25.8	average
W R Grace	44/ 62	14	15.4	8.9	0.6	2.6	11	7.0	9.9	14	−0.6	23.5	very low
Intl Minerals	70/ 83	15	15.1	8.8	0.4	5.3	21	1.8	8.3	15	−4.0	5.0	very low
NL Industries	33/NM	16	14.7	0.9	0.4	def	23	−2.2	−10.0		NM	D-P	NM
Ethyl	47/NA	17	14.6	14.6	0.3	6.1	20	2.8	3.8	10	2.5	31.3	average
Liquid Air	84/104	18	14.1	9.7	0.5	5.2	9	8.0	7.4	16	−5.7	10.0	low
Ferro		19	11.8	10.6	0.3	3.1	17	3.4	12.0	18	−11.7	28.9	average
Williams Cos	34/ 58	20	9.7	14.3	1.5	2.5	15	4.5	228.1	3	12.0	500.0 +	very low
Koppers	35/ 8	21	5.8	5.6	0.4	1.6	22	−1.2	19.9		NM	D-P	NM
B F Goodrich	35/ 36	22	4.5	6.3	0.6	0.6	18	3.2	11.4		NM	D-P	NM
Uniroyal	29/ 40	23	0.2	15.0	0.5	2.6	25	−6.3	12.2		NM	194.0	NM
Gulf Resources	42/ 33	24	def	19.1	2.2	3.3	24	−4.6	6.2		NM	169.7	NM
GAF	46/115	25	def	def	0.5	def	26	−11.0	8.9		NM	D-D	NM
Inspiration Res	31/DD	26	def	def	0.7	def	7	9.2	12.3		NM	D-D	NM
Medians			15.6	13.8	0.4	3.9		5.5	10.7		−0.4	23.7	
Industry medians			14.1	13.0	0.4	3.8		4.5	10.1		−3.7	31.3	
All-industry medians			15.1	13.4	0.4	3.7		10.2	11.5		−0.6	15.8	

DD: Segment deficit, total deficit **DP:** Segment deficit, total profit **PD:** Segment profit, total deficit **E:** Estimated. D-D: Deficit to deficit. D-P: Deficit to profit. P-D: Profit to deficit. def: Deficit. NA: Not available. NE: Negative equity. NM: Not meaningful. For further explanation, see p 46.

Sources: Media General Financial Services, Inc. Forbes

Source: Forbes, January 14, 1985.

TABLE 9-5

CHEMICALS

Per Share Data—Adjusted to stock price index level. Average of stock price indexes, 1941-1943=10

	Sales	Oper. Profit	Profit Margin %	Depr.	Income Taxes	Earnings Per Share	Earnings % of Sales	Dividends Per Share	Dividends % of Earn.	Price 1941-1943=10 High	Price Low	Price/Earn. Ratio High	Price/Earn. Ratio Low	Div. Yields % High	Div. Yields % Low	Book Value Per Share	% Return	Working Capital	Capital Expenditures
1953	13.84	3.92	28.32	0.94	1.88	1.34	9.68	0.95	70.90	26.79	23.35	19.99	17.43	4.07	3.55	9.31	14.39	4.40	1.74
1954	13.79	3.73	27.05	1.06	1.35	1.60	11.60	1.16	72.50	37.44	26.23	23.40	16.39	4.42	3.10	9.91	16.15	4.82	1.36
1955	16.14	4.77	29.55	1.17	1.82	2.13	13.20	1.39	65.26	50.25	35.54	23.59	16.69	3.91	2.77	11.15	19.10	5.13	1.21
1956	16.83	4.44	26.38	1.22	1.62	1.98	11.76	1.38	69.70	52.30	41.55	26.41	20.98	3.32	2.64	12.29	16.11	5.01	1.95
1957	17.38	4.44	25.55	1.28	1.59	1.95	11.22	1.43	73.33	47.21	37.97	24.21	19.47	3.77	3.03	13.11	14.87	5.18	2.36
1958	16.89	4.01	23.74	1.36	1.25	1.69	10.01	1.36	80.47	49.76	38.27	29.44	22.64	3.55	2.73	13.81	12.24	5.14	1.79
1959	19.34	5.16	26.68	1.40	1.90	2.23	11.53	1.47	65.92	61.60	48.57	27.62	21.78	3.03	2.39	14.75	15.12	5.76	1.62
1960	19.97	4.82	24.14	1.50	1.65	2.08	10.42	1.46	70.19	60.80	44.15	29.23	21.23	3.31	2.40	15.79	13.17	5.67	2.29
1961	20.67	4.96	24.00	1.66	1.64	2.08	10.06	1.55	74.52	56.69	47.55	27.25	22.86	3.26	2.73	16.66	12.48	5.68	2.17
1962	23.55	5.92	25.14	1.88	2.01	2.42	10.28	1.67	69.01	54.31	39.16	22.44	16.18	4.26	3.07	17.34	13.96	6.75	2.33
1963	26.69	6.60	24.73	2.10	2.22	2.75	10.30	1.83	66.55	62.36	52.50	22.68	19.09	3.49	2.93	18.61	14.78	7.77	2.71
1964	31.88	7.99	25.06	2.41	2.58	3.34	10.48	1.99	59.58	72.87	62.96	21.82	18.85	3.16	2.73	20.09	16.63	8.99	3.85
1965	34.52	8.59	24.88	2.64	2.55	3.41	9.88	1.89	55.43	76.78	68.78	22.52	20.17	2.75	2.46	21.94	15.54	9.90	4.88
1966	38.18	8.97	23.49	2.88	2.58	3.50	9.17	1.94	55.43	75.38	49.82	21.54	14.23	3.89	2.57	23.51	14.89	9.93	5.41
1967	38.63	8.12	21.02	3.15	1.99	2.84	7.35	1.87	65.85	60.53	50.87	21.31	17.91	3.68	3.09	24.40	11.64	10.21	5.07
1968	43.96	9.37	21.31	3.51	2.56	3.16	7.19	2.00	63.29	61.43	50.20	19.44	15.89	3.98	3.26	26.25	12.04	11.21	4.59
1969	47.18	9.55	20.24	3.70	2.52	3.17	6.72	1.94	61.20	57.95	40.08	18.28	12.64	4.84	3.35	27.17	11.67	11.79	5.40
1970	47.51	8.89	18.71	3.90	1.95	2.70	5.68	1.90	70.37	47.11	36.93	17.45	13.68	5.14	4.03	27.77	9.72	11.75	5.95
1971	49.55	9.36	18.89	3.99	2.07	2.93	5.91	1.90	64.85	58.71	47.56	20.04	16.23	3.99	3.24	29.48	9.94	12.97	5.25
1972	54.18	10.77	19.88	4.15	2.66	3.61	6.66	1.97	54.57	67.13	56.40	18.60	15.62	3.49	2.93	30.64	11.78	14.51	5.00
1973	64.00	13.54	21.16	4.23	3.91	5.10	7.97	2.08	40.78	72.95	55.46	14.30	10.87	3.75	2.85	33.84	15.07	16.39	6.39
1974	85.47	17.01	19.90	4.76	5.10	6.79	7.94	2.21	32.55	68.80	47.20	10.13	6.95	4.68	3.21	38.34	17.71	18.71	10.26
1975	80.33	15.24	18.97	4.92	4.18	5.51	6.86	2.18	39.56	74.63	48.76	13.54	8.85	4.47	2.92	39.26	14.03	17.59	11.95
1976	91.16	17.47	19.17	5.49	4.52	6.59	7.23	2.48	37.63	89.70	67.27	13.61	10.21	3.69	2.76	43.27	15.23	18.93	12.97
1977	101.01	18.44	18.26	6.37	4.31	6.16	6.10	2.78	45.13	72.45	52.70	11.76	8.56	5.28	3.84	46.55	13.23	19.77	12.10
1978	112.76	20.82	18.46	7.21	5.07	7.16	6.35	3.10	43.30	59.62	46.05	8.33	6.43	6.73	5.20	50.65	14.14	22.27	12.13
1979	129.30	22.59	17.47	7.51	5.13	9.17	7.09	3.38	36.86	61.04	51.75	6.66	5.64	6.53	5.54	54.58	16.80	24.87	12.48
1980	140.37	20.86	14.86	7.73	4.03	8.07	5.75	3.56	44.11	64.88	49.70	8.04	6.16	7.16	5.49	60.53	13.33	25.83	15.11
1981	143.65	21.09	14.68	7.72	R4.79	7.71	5.37	3.37	43.71	73.84	52.81	9.58	6.85	6.38	4.56	65.84	11.71	29.45	15.26
1982	159.01	21.85	13.74	9.56	5.52	5.21	3.28	3.57	68.52	63.30	45.44	12.15	8.72	7.86	5.64	65.63	7.94	26.03	15.89
1983	161.68	23.41	14.48	10.18	6.66	4.98	3.08	3.66	73.49	81.75	57.95	16.41	11.64	6.32	4.48	66.32	7.51	22.60	12.06

Stock Price Indexes for this group extend back to 1926.
•Dow Chemical (7-30-47)
•du Pont de Nemours (1-16-35)
•Hercules Inc. (9-17-30)
•Monsanto Co. (1-16-35)
•Stauffer Chemical Co. (7-25-79)
•Union Carbide Co. (12-31-25)
Airco Inc. (Formerly Air Reduction) (1-2-18 to 2-5-75)

Allied Chemical Corp. (1-2-18 to 7-25-79)
American Cyanamid (9-17-30 to 7-25-79)
American Potash & Chem. (2-14-62 to 1-3-68)
Atlas Powder (1-16-35 to 7-23-47)
Chemetron Corp. (Formerly Nat'l Cylinder Gas) (4-16-58 to 2-5-75)
Columbian Carbon (12-31-25 to 2-7-62)
Commercial Solvents (12-31-25 to 6-16-65)

GAF Corp. (Formerly General Aniline & Film) (6-16-65 to 2-5-75)
Hooker Chemical (1-3-68 to 7-30-68)
Olin Corp. (1-2-18 to 2-5-75) (Formerly Olin-Mathieson Chemical)
United Carbon (1-16-35 to 7-23-47)
U.S. Industrial Chemicals (5-11-38 to 8-1-51)

Source: ©Standard & Poor's Corporation.

TABLE 9–6

CHEMICALS

Quarter	Sales Qtr'ly	Sales 4 Qtrs. Total	Earnings Qtr'ly	Earnings 4 Qtrs. Total	% of Sales	Prices 1941-1943=10 High	Prices Low	Prices Close	Price/Earn. Ratio High	P/E Low	P/E Close	Dividends Qtr'ly	Dividends 4 Qtrs. Total	% of Earn.	Yield % High	Yield Low	Yield Close
1981																	
3rd	45.23	157.50	1.88	8.42	5.35	70.27	53.81	53.81	8.3	6.4	6.4	0.90	3.77	44.77	7.01	5.37	7.01
4th	41.05	162.11	1.83	8.48	5.23	58.13	52.81	56.26	6.9	6.2	6.6	1.10	3.73	43.99	7.06	6.42	6.63
1982																	
1st	41.69	165.61	1.74	7.79	4.70	54.76	47.54	50.20	7.0	6.1	6.4	0.90	3.79	48.65	7.97	6.92	7.55
2nd	40.77	168.74	1.73	7.18	4.26	53.88	46.95	47.15	7.5	6.5	6.6	0.90	3.80	52.92	8.09	7.05	8.06
3rd	38.64	162.15	1.02	6.32	3.90	55.56	45.44	51.94	8.8	7.2	8.2	0.90	3.80	60.13	8.36	6.84	7.32
4th	39.31	160.41	0.79	5.28	3.29	63.30	54.46	56.59	12.0	10.3	10.7	0.90	3.60	68.18	6.61	5.69	6.36
1983																	
1st	39.62	158.34	1.12	4.66	2.94	66.56	57.95	64.11	12.6	11.0	12.1	0.90	3.60	77.25	6.21	5.41	5.62
2nd	40.76	158.33	1.46	4.39	2.77	76.37	62.83	73.03	17.4	14.3	16.6	0.91	3.61	82.23	5.75	4.73	4.94
3rd	40.86	160.55	1.41	4.78	2.98	81.75	71.11	78.67	17.1	14.9	16.5	0.91	3.62	75.73	5.09	4.43	4.60
4th	41.76	163.00	0.99	4.98	3.06	79.82	74.54	75.49	16.0	15.0	15.2	0.97	3.69	74.10	4.95	4.62	4.89
1984																	
1st	42.75	166.13	2.03	5.89	3.55	75.82	63.32	69.96	12.9	10.8	11.9	0.97	2.79	47.37	4.41	3.68	3.99
2nd	42.68	168.05	2.37	6.80	4.05	72.12	62.44	63.82	10.6	9.2	9.4	0.98	3.83	56.32	6.13	5.31	6.00
3rd	40.67	167.86	1.67	7.06	4.21	71.02	61.85	66.93	10.1	8.8	9.5	1.01	3.93	55.67	6.35	5.53	5.87
4th	40.68	166.78	1.20	7.27	4.36	67.30	61.58	63.99	9.3	8.5	8.8	1.01	3.97	54.61	6.45	5.90	6.20
1985																	
1st	.....	.....	.....	.....	.....	69.20	63.14	67.02	9.5	8.7	9.2	1.01	4.01	55.16	6.35	5.79	5.98
'2nd	.....	.....	.....	.....	.....	70.71	66.73	70.71	9.7	9.2	9.7	.....	.....		6.01	5.67	5.67
1985 Earnings E7.85(1984- P7.29)					+7.7%			70.71			9.0		3.89				5.50

Source: ©Standard & Poor's Corporation.

Value Line classifies the chemical industry into three subgroups:

1. Chemical (Basic) Industry
2. Chemical (Specialty) Industry
3. Chemical (Diversified) Industry

See Table 9–8 for industry statistics for the three subgroups of the chemical industry by Value Line.

U.S. Industrial Outlook

The *U.S. Industrial Outlook* is published annually by the Bureau of Domestic Commerce of the Department of Commerce. It is a product of more than 100 industry specialists. It reviews recent trends in each industry and presents a five- to ten-year projection. Most analysts consider it an important reference in their forecasting of future industry demand.

Quarterly Financial Report for Manufacturing, Mining, and Trade Corporations

This report, which is published jointly by the Federal Trade Commission and Securities & Exchange Commission, reports up-to-date information on each individual industry in the United States. It reports quarterly sales, operating profit, net profit, and profit margin for each major industry.

TABLE 9-7

CHEMICALS

Per Share Data - Adjusted to Stock Price Index Level
Average of Stock Price Indexes, 1941 - 1943 = 10

Income Account —

	1983	1982	1981	1980	1979	1978
Sales	161.68	159.01	143.65	140.37	129.30	112.76
Costs & expenses	138.54	137.16	122.57	119.51	106.71	91.95
Operating income	23.14	21.85	21.09	20.86	22.59	20.82
Other income	NA	NA	3.75	2.69	2.18	1.29
Total income	NA	NA	24.84	23.55	24.78	22.10
Depreciation	9.91	9.56	7.72	7.73	7.51	7.21
Interest	4.57	5.31	4.36	3.42	2.71	2.48
Minority interest	NA	NA	0.25	0.28	0.23	0.15
Income taxes	6.66	5.52	4.79	4.03	5.13	5.07
Net income	5.00	5.23	7.73	8.09	9.19	7.18
Preferred dividends	0.03	0.03	0.01	0.01	0.03	0.03
Savings fr. com. stk. equiv.	0.01	0.01	0.01	0.01	0.01	0.01
Common earnings	4.98	5.21	7.71	8.07	9.17	7.16
Common dividends	3.66	3.57	3.37	3.56	3.38	3.10
Balance after dividends	1.33	1.64	4.34	4.51	5.79	4.07

Financial Ratios —

	1983	1982	1981	1980	1979	1978
Current ratio	1.8	2.0	2.0	2.0	2.0	2.0
Quick ratio	1.0	1.2	1.1	1.1	1.2	1.2
Debt to total assets (%)	24	26	29	26	25	27
Times interest earned	3.6	3.0	3.9	4.5	6.3	5.9
Inventory turnover	7.6	7.3	5.6	6.2	6.3	6.3
Total assets turnover	1.1	1.1	1.0	1.1	1.1	1.0
Profit margin (%)	14.31	13.74	14.68	14.86	17.47	18.46
Return on total assets (%)	3.53	3.64	5.31	6.38	7.83	6.56

Balance Sheet

Assets —

	1983	1982	1981	1980	1979	1978
Cash & equivalent	NA	4.85	4.22	2.97	4.58	4.66
Receivables	23.09	22.46	25.52	24.58	23.42	20.73
Income tax refund	0.00	0.00	0.00	0.00	0.00	0.00
Inventories	21.26	21.67	25.81	22.77	20.89	17.97
Other current assets	1.78	3.18	2.02	2.31	1.34	1.49
Total current assets	51.94	52.16	57.56	52.63	50.23	44.85
Net property, plant, & equipment	77.50	79.60	76.50	63.42	57.52	56.78
Inv. & adv. to uncons. subs.	5.65	5.54	5.54	5.76	5.09	3.92
Intangibles	0.69	0.70	0.78	0.61	0.79	0.78
Other assets	NA	NA	NA	NA	NA	NA
Total assets	141.36	142.96	145.21	126.42	117.03	109.24

Liabilities —

	1983	1982	1981	1980	1979	1978
Notes payable	4.58	2.52	3.30	5.36	4.29	3.79
Current portion of long term debt	1.04	0.70	0.74	1.24	0.66	0.83
Accounts payable	10.39	9.76	11.32	8.42	9.24	7.68
Income tax payable	2.84	1.83	1.68	1.86	2.11	2.52
Accrued expenses	7.41	7.61	7.62	NA	6.22	5.62
Other current liabilities	3.07	3.71	3.47	4.92	2.84	2.15
Total current liabilities	29.33	26.13	28.11	26.80	25.35	22.58
Long term debt	28.46	34.24	37.39	26.51	24.58	25.05
Deferred income tax	8.59	8.28	7.40	7.35	5.93	4.76
Minority interest	1.47	1.67	1.73	2.01	1.89	1.25
Other liabilities	5.87	5.70	4.13	2.46	3.15	3.45
Preferred stock	0.63	0.60	0.61	0.74	0.75	0.70
Common stock	4.45	4.45	4.31	4.54	4.40	5.61
Capital surplus	14.97	14.71	14.27	4.18	3.85	3.35
Retained earnings	47.60	47.18	47.27	51.83	47.13	42.49
Total liabilities	141.36	142.96	145.21	126.42	117.03	109.24

NA - Not Available
NM - Not Meaningful

Source: ©Standard & Poor's Corporation.

TABLE 9–8   Composite Statistics: Chemical (Basic) Industry

1980	1981	1982	1983	1984	1985	©Value Line, Inc.	87-89E
50409	62328	68678	71498	73714	72650	Sales ($mill)	102600
14.3%	16.3%	16.7%	17.3%	19.0%	17.0%	Operating Margin	17.5%
2914.2	3235.5	3910.3	4127.2	4206.4	4150	Depreciation ($mill)	5400
2712.0	3213.7	1970.3	2432.6	3345.2	3035	Net Profit ($mill)	5200
33.4%	37.4%	50.3%	52.8%	51.2%	51.0%	Income Tax Rate	51.0%
5.4%	5.2%	2.9%	3.4%	4.5%	4.2%	Net Profit Margin	5.1%
9237.0	12456	11171	10184	9643.2	9600	Working Cap'l ($mill)	15000
9379.1	16373	14637	12655	11129	11300	Long-Term Debt ($mill)	12500
21308	27814	28402	29367	30197	31300	Net Worth ($mill)	39300
10.1%	8.7%	6.6%	7.5%	9.5%	8.5%	% Earned Total Cap'l	11.0%
12.7%	11.6%	6.9%	8.3%	11.1%	9.5%	% Earned Net Worth	13.0%
7.2%	6.6%	1.7%	3.0%	5.5%	4.5%	% Retained to Comm Eq	7.5%
45%	44%	77%	65%	51%	53%	% All Div'ds to Net Prof	44%
7.3	8.2	10.7	14.1	9.0		Avg Ann'l P/E Ratio	11.0
.97	1.00	1.18	1.19	.83		Relative P/E Ratio	.90
6.1%	5.3%	6.8%	5.0%	5.8%		Avg. Ann'l Div'd Yield	3.7%

Composite Statistics: Chemical (Specialty) Industry

1980	1981	1982	1983	1984	1985	©Value Line, Inc.	87-89E
12718	13626	13315	14597	15700	17000	Sales ($mill)	24000
12.7%	12.3%	11.4%	12.3%	12.5%	12.5%	Operating Margin	13.0%
299.0	346.7	374.3	424.8	460	510	Depreciation ($mill)	650
773.2	744.5	621.3	756.3	850	920	Net Profit ($mill)	1400
40.7%	40.9%	40.9%	42.5%	42.5%	42.5%	Income Tax Rate	42.0%
6.1%	5.5%	4.7%	5.2%	5.4%	5.4%	Net Profit Margin	5.8%
2866.7	2906.8	2878.7	3030.0	3100	3400	Working Cap'l ($mill)	4600
1297.2	1330.2	1370.5	1330.1	1300	1300	Long-Term Debt ($mill)	1200
4626.2	5005.5	4898.2	5452.1	5900	6450	Net Worth ($mill)	9250
14.1%	12.9%	11.1%	12.3%	12.5%	12.5%	% Earned Total Cap'l	14.0%
16.7%	14.9%	12.7%	13.9%	14.5%	14.5%	% Earned Net Worth	15.0%
11.1%	8.8%	6.3%	7.8%	8.5%	8.5%	% Retained to Comm Eq	9.5%
36%	43%	52%	45%	43%	42%	% All Div'ds to Net Prof	38%
10.0	11.3	12.4	15.1	Bold figures are		Avg Ann'l P/E Ratio	15.0
1.33	1.37	1.37	1.28	Value Line		Relative P/E Ratio	1.25
3.5%	3.7%	4.3%	3.1%	estimates		Avg Ann'l Div'd Yield	2.7%

(continued)

TABLE 9–8, continued

Composite Statistics: Chemical/Diversified Industry

1980	1981	1982	1983	1984	1985	©Value Line, Inc.	87-89E
39413	41103	38426	44315	46434	48000	Sales ($mill)	58000
16.6%	16.3%	14.9%	14.6%	15.7%	14.5%	Operating Margin	15.5%
1576.1	1814.2	2034.3	2273.3	2320.0	2500	Depreciation ($mill)	3200
2224.1	2626.5	1968.7	2106.9	2413.0	2400	Net Profit ($mill)	3100
46.5%	44.5%	41.8%	43.3%	42.7%	43.0%	Income Tax Rate	41.0%
5.6%	6.4%	5.1%	4.8%	5.2%	5.0%	Net Profit Margin	5.3%
6576.1	6715.2	6327.9	6108.5	6061.2	6000	Working Cap'l ($mill)	8500
6026.9	6210.8	6212.0	7936.7	8157.3	8100	Long-Term Debt ($mill)	11000
15439	17144	19072	19083	18543	19500	Net Worth ($mill)	24000
11.6%	12.5%	9.0%	9.2%	10.7%	10.0%	% Earned Total Cap'l	10.5%
14.4%	15.3%	10.3%	11.0%	13.0%	12.5%	% Earned Net Worth	13.0%
8.8%	9.7%	5.0%	5.0%	7.1%	6.5%	% Retained to Comm Eq	7.5%
42%	40%	58%	57%	48%	49%	% All Div'ds to Net Prof	45%
9.2	8.2	10.0	16.3	10.6		Avg Ann'l P/E Ratio	11.0
1.22	1.00	1.10	1.38	.97		Relative P/E Ratio	.90
4.4%	4.7%	5.5%	4.2%	4.3%		Avg Ann'l Div'd Yield	3.8%

Source: Value Line Investment Survey: Chemical Specialty Industry, Apr. 12, 1985; Chemical Basic Industry, May 17, 1985; and Chemical Diversified Industry, June 14, 1985. ©1985 Value Line, Inc. Reprinted by permission.

Business Week's Quarterly Corporate Scoreboard

For current information on how major firms are performing in their respective industries, *Business Week* publishes a Corporate Scoreboard that provides data on quarterly sales, profits, profit margin and their changes, price-earnings ratio, return on common equity, and earnings per share in the last twelve months. In addition, industry composite data is also provided for comparison.

Advice by Industry Experts

Experienced industry experts have invaluable experience and insight. Whenever possible, investors should seek the views and suggestions of these experienced analysts as to how the industry should be analyzed. For example, *The Paine Webber Handbook of Stock & Bond Analysis*, edited by Kiril Sokoloff (New York: McGraw-Hill, 1979), contains articles by industry experts on thirty-one industries, including chemicals.

SUMMARY

Most analysts and investment managers agree that the best approach to investment decision making is to move from macro to micro, namely, from economy to industries and from industries to individual companies.

The life-cycle theory of industry development argues that most industries go through definable stages:

1. Pioneering stage
2. Fast-growing stage
3. Maturity and stabilization stage
4. Relative decline stage

Many proponents of this theory believe in investing in fast-growing industries. However, when an industry is well known for its growth potentials, the investor may pay too high a price for the popular stock. Investors should beware of this type of risk.

A thorough analysis of an industry should cover the following areas:

1. The structure and the state of competition in the industry
2. The nature and prospect of demand for the products and services of the industry
3. Cost conditions and profitability
4. Technology and research
5. Immediate and long-term outlook of sales and profits

Individual investors are not expected to be industry experts, but they should know where to look for relevant materials and studies on a given industry and also be able to understand their investment implications.

QUESTIONS AND PROBLEMS

1. In seeking to make a long-term commitment of funds, is it important to seek a growth industry?
2. Despite the fact that investors are ultimately concerned with earnings and dividends, why do security analysts place so much emphasis on the sales of the firm and growth prospects for the industry?
3. Discuss the life-cycle theory of industry selection. What arguments are there for and against placing primary emphasis on this consideration when selecting investments?
4. Select five growth industries and defend your selection.

5. What are some of the reasons why industries show differing rates of growth?

6. Under what categories of industries — growth, cyclical, defensive, declining — do you place the following industries: steel, shipbuilding, chemical, motion pictures, automobile, air transportation, drugs, and food? Why?

7. Why must an analyst always investigate the industry when looking at a particular security?

8. Select an industry and prepare a study of cost conditions and profitability in that industry.

9. What kind of information about a given industry can be usually found in the *Industry Survey* and *Analysts Handbook* published by Standard & Poor's Corporation?

10. Prepare an industry analysis from appropriate source material, including all information that can be used as a guide to appraise the record of the leading firms in the industry.

11. What is an input-output table? Why is it useful in industry forecast?

12. Industries differ in sensitivity to variation in general business. Classify the following industries into four groups: (1) very sensitive, (2) sensitive, (3) less sensitive, and (4) not so sensitive. Explain also your reasoning.

Building Materials	Computer and Business Machines
Airlines	Grocery
Food Processing	Chemicals
Insurance	Electric Utilities
Machinery	Banks

REFERENCES

"*Annual Report on American Industry.*" *Forbes,* January issue, current year.

Bossong, Elizabeth A. "The Steel Industry — Stagnation, Decay or Recovery?" *Business Economics,* July 1985.

Bureau of Domestic Commerce, U.S. Department of Commerce. *U.S. Industrial Outlook,* current edition.

Butler, Peter E. "The Chemical Industry." *The Paine Webber Handbook of Stock & Bond Analysis,* edited by Kiril Sokoloff. New York: McGraw-Hill, 1979.

Cohen, Jerome B., Zinbarg, Edward D., and Zeikel, Arthur. *Investment Analysis & Portfolio Management,* 4th Edition. Homewood, Ill.: R. D. Irwin, 1982, Chapter 11.

Feldman, Stanley J., and Palmer, Karen. "Structural Change in the United States: Changing Input-Output Coefficient." *Business Economics,* Jan. 1985.

Levine, Summer N., ed. *Financial Analysts' Handbook*. New York: Dow Jones-Irwin, 1975, Vol. 2.

Livingston, Miles. "Industry Movements of Common Stocks." *The Journal of Finance*, June 1977.

Porter, Michael E. *Competitive Strategy: Techniques for Analyzing Industries and Competitors*. New York: The Free Press, 1980.

Sokoloff, Kiril, ed. *The Paine Webber Handbook of Stock and Bond Analysis*. New York: McGraw-Hill, 1979.

Standard & Poor's Corporation. *Industry Survey; Analysts Handbook*, current issues.

Value Line, Inc., *Value Line Investment Survey*, current issues.

10

Financial Statement Analysis

In Chapters 5, 6, and 9 we discussed the macroeconomic environment for investment. An examination of the general business outlook and trends in interest rates can tell us whether it is a good time to invest and what types of securities to invest in. Industry analysis helps us look for attractive industries from which we may select stocks of individual companies.

With the completion of macroeconomic analysis, we now begin microeconomic analysis, namely, the analysis of individual companies. We divide the analysis of an individual company into four parts:

1. Understanding and analysis of financial statements
2. Growth analysis
3. Risk analysis
4. Valuation of common stock of an individual company

In this chapter we take up the analysis of financial statements and in the following chapters we will discuss the other three topics.

FINANCIAL STATEMENTS

The basic financial statements each corporation issues quarterly and annually are the *balance sheet* and the *income statement*. Because quarterly financial statements are usually brief and not audited by certified public accountants, they are not as useful as annual statements for the purpose of investment analysis. The quarterly financial reports have value, however, because they report current financial conditions and operational progress of the firm.

The Balance Sheet

The balance sheet is a "snapshot" of the financial condition of a firm at a certain time (see Table 10–1). The left side of a balance sheet lists resources the firm owns. The right side of a balance sheet lists claims on the cor-

TABLE 10–1   Key Elements of Typical Balance Sheet

Assets	*Liabilities and Net Worth*
Current assets	Current liabilities
Cash and securities	Trade obligations
Accounts receivable	Accrued items
Inventories	Accrued taxes
Other assets	Current debt due
Fixed assets	Other liabilities
Land and improvements	Deferred taxes
Building & equipment	Contingencies
Less: Accumulated depreciation	Long-term liabilities
Net fixed assets	Mortgages, other contracts
Other assets	Bonds and similar obligations
Accrued items	Net worth
Goodwill	Preferred stock
Prepaid items	Common stock
	Paid-in surplus
	Retained earnings

poration. Claims on the corporation must equal resources of the corporation; therefore the statement is called a balance sheet.

The resources the corporation owns include properties and property rights. They are called *assets of the corporation*. Assets are usually classified as current assets, fixed assets, and other assets. *Current asset* items are expected to be converted into cash within a year from the normal operation of the business. *Fixed assets* might include land, plant, equipment, tools, furniture, fixtures, and vehicles. Other assets usually include property rights, such as accrued items, prepaid expenses, and goodwill.

The claims on the corporation belong to two groups: creditors and owners. Claims by creditors are called *liabilities*. Short-term liabilities are expected to be paid within a year. The claims by owners are called *net worth* or *stockholders' equity*.

The net worth of a firm includes preferred stock, common stock, paid-in surplus, and retained earnings.

The Income Statement

The income statement is a financial summary covering the revenues and expenses of a firm for a given period of time. Revenues are derived from selling goods and services. Expenses are usually classified into: manufacturing costs (costs of goods sold) and operating expenses. Operating expenses include selling, general, and administrative expenses.

The key elements of a typical income statement appear in Table 10–2.

TABLE 10–2   Key Elements of Typical Income Statement

Revenue (net of adjustment)
Cost of goods, services
Gross profit (margin)
Operating expenses (salaries, general & administrative, etc.)
Operating income
Nonoperating income, expenses
Interest income, expenses
Income before taxes
Income taxes
Net income

BASIC ACCOUNTING CONCEPTS

Over the years, a number of fundamental concepts have been established by the accounting profession. These basic premises are regarded as generally accepted accounting principles (GAAP). They are generally followed by accountants in the preparation of financial statements. Some of the more important concepts are briefly explained below so that the nature of financial statements can be more fully understood.[1]

The Going Concern. In accounting, the assumption is made that a business will continue to operate into the foreseeable future.

Historical Costs. Accounting transactions are measured and recorded in terms of costs at the time the transaction is consummated, to avoid unsubstantiated judgmental values; and no updating to higher values is permitted, only reductions (write-downs) when significant.

Consistency. Accounting requires that similar transactions be treated in a consistent manner from period to period for a given company.

Matching. Accounting requires that in determining profit over a given period the applicable cost must be related to the revenues recorded for the period.

Realization. Revenues from the sales of goods and services are regarded as realized (recognized) when there is a high probability of receipt of payment when the conditions of the sales are fulfilled. Four categories of realization are recognized:

1. Recognition at the time of shipping and invoicing when the credit status of the customer leaves little doubt as to payment.
2. Recognition at the time of payment of the sales price—the so-called installment method.
3. Recognition when production is completed but sales have not yet been made—the so-called production method.

[1]Source: Erich A. Helfert, "Analysis of Financial Statements," *Financial Analyst's Handbook,* Vol. I (New York: Dow Jones-Irwin, 1975).

4. Recognition with long-term contracts either under the percentage of completion method, with income reflected proportionately as the work progresses, or under the completed contract method, with revenue reflected on completion of contract.

Convervatism. This concept holds that when there is a high degree of uncertainty in accounting measurements, preference will be given to those that result in lower current income and asset values.

Disclosure. Accounting statements must disclose sufficient information so that they are not misleading.

DEFICIENCIES OF FINANCIAL STATEMENTS

Generally accepted accounting principles are simply standards or guidelines in financial reporting. They do not constitute a uniform set of rules or procedures. The accounting profession sanctions a variety of alternative principles or methods in the valuation of assets, computation of costs and expenses, recognition of revenues, accounting of mergers and acquisitions, and in the estimation of liabilities.

See Table 10–3 for some generally accepted alternative accounting methods of handling transactions that would significantly affect earnings of a company.

To show the problems that investors will face in connection with earnings reported by corporations, let us now review some of the other acceptable accounting methods that a firm's management can choose.

Recognition of Revenue

As mentioned previously, there are four ways to recognize revenue: (1) at the time of shipping and invoicing; (2) at the time of payment of the sales price; (3) at the time when production is completed; (4) using either the percentage method or the completed contract method in dealing with long-term contracts.

Obviously the choice of a particular method in recognizing revenues will significantly affect the amount of gross revenue to be included in the income statement for a given year, thereby affecting earnings of the firm for that year.

Inventory Valuation

Accounting convention permits different methods in the valuation of inventory. The most widely used methods are LIFO (last-in, first-out) and FIFO (first-in, first-out). LIFO assumes that the last units produced are the first

TABLE 10–3 Some Generally Accepted Methods of Handling Transactions

Revenue Recognition
  Before sale (precious metals)
  At sale
  After sale:
    Completed contract
    Percentage of completion
Inventory Methods
  Specific identification
  Weighted average
  Last-in, first-out
  First-in, first-out
  Standard costs
  Simple average (not commonly)
    used)
Depreciation Methods[b]
  Straight line
  Fixed percentage declining balance
  Sum of the year's digits
  Units of output

Subsidary Operations
  Consolidate
  Do not consolidate:
    Equity basis[a]
    Cost basis
Treasury Stock
  Cost
  Par

Investment Credit
  Year of acquisition
  Throughout life of asset
Pensions
  Current costs
  Current costs plus past
    service
  Ten percent of past
    service
  Interest on past
    service only
Purchases
  Net method
  Gross method
Business Combinations
  Purchase
  Pooling of interests

Intangibles
  Either capitalize and write off
    over a period of up to 40
    years of expense:
  Organization costs
  Goodwill
  Patents
  Copyrights
Leases
  Capitalize
  Expense

[a] If the equity basis is used, EPS is the same whether the firm consolidates or not.

[b] The Accelerated Cost Recovery System (ACRS) in the current tax code defines how depreciation can be taken for capital assets.

Source: Latané, Tuttle, and Jones, *Security Analysis and Portfolio Management,* 2d ed. (New York: Ronald, 1975), p. 98.

sold; FIFO assumes that older units are sold first. When prices are stable, both methods give the same value for inventory. However, in a period of rising prices, the two methods yield different inventory figures, thereby affecting cost of goods sold and profits of the firm.

For example, a firm had the following transactions:

Beginning inventory	10 units	$10 each
Purchases:		
1st	10 units	12
2nd	10 units	14
3rd	10 units	15
Ending inventory	20 units	
Sales for the period	20 units	18

What are the profits and inventory value of the firm under LIFO and FIFO methods?

		LIFO		FIFO
Sales (20 × 18)		$360		$360
Cost of sales:				
Beginning inventory	100		100	
Purchases	410		410	
Total goods available	510		510	
Less: Ending inventory	220		290	
Total cost of sales		290		220
Profits before tax		70		140
Ending inventory		220		290

As shown in these calculations, the LIFO method yields lower inventory value, lower profits, and therefore, less income tax, whereas the FIFO method yields higher figures for both inventory and profits, and, therefore, more taxes.

In recent years of high inflation, many companies have switched from FIFO to LIFO in order to avoid paying income taxes on inventory profits. This creates a problem for investors in that unless the profits of prior years were adjusted on a LIFO basis, the year-to-year figures concerning profits are not comparable.

Depreciation Accounting

The Accelerated Cost Recovery System (ACRS) in the 1981 Tax Act defines how depreciation can be taken for capital assets. The ACRS classifies all capital into four classes of life: three-year, five-year, ten-year and eighteen-year.

In Table 10–4 we include the essential elements of the ACRS. In the first column are the four classes of life of capital assets. The second column of the table describes the types of property that fall into each category of class life. The last column indicates the optional recovery periods the firm can choose to depreciate its property with straight-line depreciation method.

See Table 10–5 for the allowable percentages of depreciation taken in each year by the firm for four classes of property life.

In general, the prescribed percentages provide faster depreciation than the optional straight-line method.

The Tax Reform Act of 1986

The new tax act passed recently by Congress was signed into law. The new tax act will modify the Accelerated Cost Recovery System as passed in 1981. In general, depreciation periods will be longer under the new law. Business

TABLE 10–4   Classes and Asset Lives under ACRS

Class	Type of Property	Optional Recovery Period for Straight Line Depreciation
3-year	Automobiles, tractor units, light-duty trucks, and certain special manufacturing tools.	3, 5, or 12 years
5-year	Personal property that is not 3-year or 10-year property. Includes most equipment, office furniture, and fixtures.	5, 12, or 25 years
10-year	Certain real property, certain public utility property, and theme park structures. Includes manufactured homes and mobile homes.	10, 25, or 35 years
18-year[a]	All real property, such as buildings, other than any designated as 10-year property.	18, 35, or 45 years

[a] Some low-income housing is depreciated over 15 years rather than 18 years. Also, note that land cannot be depreciated.

Source: 1981 Tax Act.

plants, machinery, and equipment would be subject to depreciation periods of three, five, seven, ten, fifteen and twenty years. For example, automobiles and light trucks would have to be depreciated over five years, instead of three years under the old law.

TABLE 10–5   Recovery Allowances for Property Placed in Service after December 31, 1980

Ownership Year	3-Year	5-Year	10-Year	18-Year
1	25%	15%	8%	4%
2	38	22	14	8
3	37	21	12	7
4		21	10	7
5		21	10	6
6			10	6
7			9	6
8			9	6
9			9	5
10			9	5
11				5
12				5
13				5
14				5
15				5
16				5
17				5
18				5
	100%	100%	100%	100%

Source: 1981 Tax Act.

Residential real estate would have to be written off over twenty-seven-and-a-half years using a straight-line formula, versus nineteen years under the old law, which allows larger write-offs in the earlier years. Commercial real estate would be depreciated under a thirty-one-and-a-half-year schedule.[2]

Pension Costs

Pension obligations of a firm usually comprise two parts: current service liability and past service liability.

The past service liability is created because when the pension fund is adopted, some employees may have been with the company for many years. Their past service has to be taken into account and funded.

The Employee Retirement Income Security Act of 1974 requires that, at a minimum, the account must charge (a) the current service cost plus (b) interest on the unfunded past service cost. The maximum that a company may charge in a given year is the minimum plus 10 percent of the past service cost.

Since there is a broad range between the maximum and minimum charge, companies have considerable leeway in determining their yearly contributions to pension funds. Some companies, for example, may try to use the pension fund contribution as a vehicle to smooth out to some extent the yearly fluctuations in the earnings of the corporation.

Consolidation with Subsidiaries

If Company A owns more than 50 percent of the common stock of Company B, Company B is regarded as a *subsidiary* of the parent Company A. If Company A owns less than 50 percent of Company C, Company C is referred to as an *affiliate* of Company A.

Accounting convention requires that, in financial reporting, subsidiaries be combined with the parent company in a consolidated statement. Subsidiaries are treated as if they were divisions of the parent company.

In the case of an affiliate, the parent company's investments in an affiliate can be accounted for in two ways: the cost method and the equity method. Under the cost method, the investments in affiliates are carried at cost on the books of the parent company. Dividends received from affiliates are to be included in the income statement. Under the equity method, the parent company's share of profit or loss in its affiliate is recognized as earned, and dividends are considered to be a return of investment. The parent

---

[2]Source: *Tax Reform Act of 1986, Conference Agreement*, Peat, Marwick, Mitchell & Co., 1986.

company's investment, then, is carried at cost adjusted for changes in the affiliate's net assets resulting from profits, losses, and dividends.

Most parent companies consolidate their statements with subsidiaries. But for one reason or another, many choose not to consolidate one or more subsidiaries. In such cases, investment in nonconsolidated subsidiaries is often carried at cost in the statement of the parent company. The parent company's share of profit or loss in subsidiaries is revealed only in the footnotes to the financial statements of the parent company. Unless investors read the footnotes to financial statements and make adjustments in the earnings of the parent company, they may be led to believe that the company is actually more profitable than the case may be.

Investment Tax Credit

To encourage business spending on capital expenditures, Congress periodically passes laws to provide tax credit for the purchase of new capital equipment. The old law allowed a 10 percent tax credit for the purchase of new capital equipment.[3] This meant that, if a firm bought new capital equipment for $1 million, it was entitled to reduce income taxes by the amount of $100,000 (.10 × $1,000,000).

The accounting profession sanctions two ways to take the tax credit: the flow-through method and the deferred method. Under the flow-through method, the whole sum of the tax credit is taken in the current year to offset income taxes. This will increase the profits of the firm by the total amount of the tax credit. Under the deferred method, the total tax credit is spread over the life of the new machinery. If the equipment is expected to last ten years, each year for ten years the firm can take one tenth of the total tax credit. This subjects corporate profits to an additional variable at the discretion of the management of a corporation.

MANIPULATING INCOME BY MANAGEMENT

The previous discussion of deficiencies in financial statements has served to emphasize that the financial statements are simply summaries of *estimates* of revenues, costs, expenses, assets, and liabilities. All of these elements are subject more or less to the discretion of the firm's management. Part of the problem is that the accounting profession allows many alternative principles or methods of handling and reporting transactions. Consequently, the income of a corporation can be manipulated to some extent by the management, if it chooses to do so.

---

[3]The new tax law effective January 1, 1987, eliminates the 10 percent tax credit. However, it is conceivable that tax credit will be reinstated later on.

Some of the practices designed to puff up current earnings are:[4]

1. Recognize sales as having occurred long before final delivery has been made to the customer's satisfaction and before the invoice is paid.
2. Select inventory valuation methods that minimize cost of goods sold.
3. Assume pension expenses at the lowest possible rates, and vary the rates to smooth reported earnings.
4. Charge depreciation and amortization at the lowest permitted rates.
5. Capitalize some expenses that can be either charged against current income or interpreted as creating assets or future benefits to the company.
6. Classify numerous outlays as extraordinary expenses.
7. Flow through to earnings all available income tax benefits.
8. Alter the timing of expenses.
9. Take the nonrecurrent profits in poor years.

QUALITY OF EARNINGS

To analysts, total earnings and earnings per share reported by a corporation are not numbers that can be safely used as one of the important factors determining the value of a stock. They know that the reported earnings are often the product of deliberate choices between various accounting treatments and business options. In order to determine the true performance of a corporation, they employ additional analysis. One additional input comes from the assessment of *quality of earnings*. Professor Joel Siegel has found that the quality of earnings concept is widely used among analysts, financial managers, and accountants.[5]

The elements that comprise earnings quality can be grouped into three categories:

1. Alternative accounting principles and procedures selected — the quality of earnings is low if management chooses such practices to boost earnings as premature recognition of revenue, changes of accounting policy, and minimizing or underestimating expenses.

---

[4]J. B. Cohen, E. D. Zinbarg, and A. Zeikel, *Investment Analysis and Portfolio Management*, 4th ed. (Homewood, Ill.: R. D. Irwin, 1982), p. 358; Ford S. Worthy, "Manipulating Profits: How It is Done," *Fortune*, June 25, 1984.

[5]Joel Siegel, "The 'Quality of Earnings' Concept — A Survey," *Financial Analysts Journal*, March–April 1982.

2. Management decisions to raise or lower discretionary expenses—the quality of earnings is low if management deliberately raises earnings by failing to replace obsolete fixed assets, neglecting necessary repairs, excessive cutting of advertising, personnel training, and research and development budget.
3. External factors—the quality of earnings is low if the company is situated in a cyclical industry, a substantial portion of earnings is coming from abroad, or the company is importantly affected by the uncertainty of the regulatory environment.

In order to have a reasonable assessment of the above factors, and, therefore, the quality of earnings of the firm, professional analysts examine carefully the following sections of the firm's annual report.

1. The analyst will check the Auditor's Report to see if there are qualifying statements like "except for" or "subject to" in the opinion paragraph of the auditing report.
2. Summary statements on changes of accounting policies. Were changes in policies made in order to conform with the current opinion issued by FASB (Financial Accounting Standard Board) or rather for the favorable result of increasing profits for the firm?
3. Notes to financial statements are examined to find out how accounting data are determined, their reasonableness in calculation, pension plan and its accumulated unfunded liabilities, future contingent liabilities, and overall impression of the accounting model in use.

Analysts also need to examine several other aspects of a firm. These include:

1. A review of operations, including:
    Plants—age and rate of operation.
    Products—quality, price, service compared to competitors; types of products, geographical distribution, and profit contribution.
    Research and Development—effectiveness in bringing out new products, percent of sales spent on research and development.
    Personnel—background and quality of top management, training programs, turnover rate, and general morale of employees.
2. A review of industry characteristics of the firm.
3. Trends in sales, earnings, dividends, and book value per share; level and variation of profit margin over time; price performance of stock by itself and relative to market index.

The result of this careful study by the analyst is to enable him or her (1) to adjust earnings reported by the firm to a level to indicate the true performance of the firm and (2) to form a general impression as to the quality of earnings of the firm, which will be one of the important factors determining the selection of a "right P/E ratio" for the stock for purposes of valuation.

ANALYSIS OF DOW CHEMICAL STATEMENTS

To explain various aspects of financial statement analysis, we will use the financial data of a large chemical firm, Dow Chemical, for illustration.

See Table 10–6 for the consolidated income statements of Dow Chemical for 1984, 1983, and 1982, and Table 10–7 for the consolidated balance sheet for 1984 and 1983.

To analyze the financial statements of the Dow Chemical Co., we will go through three steps:

1. Assess the quality of earnings as reported by the company.
2. Common-size financial statement analysis.
3. Ratio analysis.

Assessing the Quality of Earnings of the Company

To assess the quality of earnings, the analyst must examine carefully the auditors' report, changes in accounting policy and procedures, notes to financial statements, management's discretionary decisions, and industry characteristics of the company.

The auditor's report by Deloitte Haskins & Sells, independent public accountant, was a "clean" report, that is, containing no qualifying statements. There was a summary of significant accounting policies. Topics included in the summary were: consolidation, nonconsolidated equity investments, foreign currency transactions, inventories, plant, property and depreciation, goodwill, retirement plans, taxes on income and investment credits, and earnings per common share. We found no important changes in accounting policies dealing with these items.

There were nine pages of footnotes to financial statements, mostly tables and explanations of how each item was derived. We found no item that can be construed as irregular or unconventional in relation to current accounting practice. There was also no sign that management is deliberately postponing necessary, but discretionary, expenditures.

In terms of product mix, two-thirds of Dow Chemical's sales were in basic chemicals; the remaining one-third was in specialty chemicals. In terms of earnings source, over 50 percent of earnings came from foreign sales. Dow Chemical's business is, therefore, affected importantly by general business expansion and contraction, both in the U.S. and abroad.

TABLE 10–6   Consolidated Statement of Income

Years Ended December 31 (in millions, except per share amounts)	1984	1983	1982
Net Sales	$11,418	$10,951	$10,618
Operating costs and expenses			
Cost of sales	9,516	9,446	9,310
Selling and administrative	1,054	989	952
	10,570	10,435	10,262
Operating income	848	516	356
Other income (expense)			
Equity in earnings:			
Nonconsolidated subsidiaries (excluding translation)	23	12	14
Losses on translation — nonconsolidated subsidiaries			(10)
20%–50% owned companies	50	84	140
Interest income	94	113	108
Interest and amortization of debt discount and expense	(437)	(431)	(514)
Gains on exchange and translation — consolidated subsidiaries	14	66	47
Gains on sale of investments	183	101	214
Provision for plant closings and cancelled projects	(157)	(58)	(102)
Sundry income — net	57	43	60
Income before provision for taxes on income	675	446	313
Provision for taxes on income	126	153	(29)
Income before extraordinary items	549	293	342
Extraordinary items:			
Tax benefit from realization of foreign tax loss carryforwards	36		
Gain on redemption of long-term debt		41	57
Net income	$585	$334	$399
Earnings per common share			
Income before extraordinary items	$2.83	$1.50	$1.77
Extraordinary items:			
Tax benefit from realization of foreign tax loss carryforwards	.19		
Gain on redemption of long-term debt		.21	.30
Net income	$3.02	$1.71	$2.07

Source: 1984 Annual Report of Dow Chemical Co.

We can summarize our findings from the examination of the financial statements of Dow Chemical. From an accounting perspective, the quality of earnings was good. However, the company is situated in a cyclical industry. Taking this factor into account, the overall rating of the quality of earnings of the company is *fair*.

TABLE 10–7   Consolidated Balance Sheet

Assets

December 31 (in millions)	1984	1983
Current assets		
Cash	$ 19	$ 12
Marketable securities and interest-bearing deposits (at cost, approximately market)	102	166
Accounts and notes receivable:		
Trade (less allowance for doubtful receivables—1984, $37; 1983, $53)	1,380	1,661
Other	503	605
Inventories:		
Finished and work in process	1,426	1,291
Materials and supplies	501	670
Total current assets	3,931	4,405
Investments		
Capital stock of related companies—at cost plus equity in accumulated earnings:		
Banking and insurance subsidiaries	214	191
Associated companies (50% owned)	833	687
20%–49% owned companies	105	153
Other investments (at cost)	413	186
Noncurrent receivables	384	298
Total investments	1,949	1,515
Plant properties	11,256	11,524
Less—Accumulated depreciation	6,083	5,829
Net plant properties	5,173	5,695
Goodwill	202	196
Deferred charges and other assets	164	170
Total	$11,419	$11,981

Liabilities

December 31 (in millions)	1984	1983
Current liabilities		
Notes payable	$ 250	$ 694
Long-term debt due within one year	234	70
Accounts payable:		
Trade	947	1,056
Other	203	257
United States and foreign taxes on income	305	294
Accrued and other current liabilities	737	767

(continued)

TABLE 10–7, continued

Total current liabilities	2,676	3,138
Long-term debt	2,745	2,803
Deferred taxes and other liabilities		
Deferred income taxes	576	683
Deferred employee benefits	62	68
Other noncurrent obligations	277	209
Total deferred taxes and other liabilities	915	960
Minority interests in subsidiary companies	21	33
Stockholders' equity		
Common stock (authorized 500,000,000 shares of $2.50 par		
value each; issued—1984, 208,613,652; 1983, 206,549,098)	522	516
Additional paid-in capital	597	552
Retained earnings	4,361	4,123
Cumulative translation adjustments	(35)	9
Treasury stock, at cost (1984, 18,521,367; 1983, 10,703,412 shares)	(383)	(153)
Net stockholders' equity	5,062	5,047
Total	$11,419	$11,981

Source: 1984 Annual Report of Dow Chemical Co.

Common-Size Financial Statement Analysis

In the analysis of financial statements it is often instructive to find out the proportion of a total group that a single item within it represents. In the case of the balance sheet, we treat either total assets or the sum of liabilities and net worth as 100 percent, and then convert each item in the balance sheet as a percent of total assets. Similarly, in the income statement, net sales are set as 100 percent, and every item in the statement is expressed as a percent of net sales.

This approach has the advantage of showing at a glance the relationships between:

> each asset item and total assets;
> each liability/capital item and total sources of funds; and
> each item in income statement and net sales.

If statements of several years are examined together, we can readily spot the changes in relationships between each item and its total that took place in particular years.

See Table 10–8 for the common-size income statements of Dow Chemical for 1984 and 1983. In Table 10–9 are the common-size balance sheets for

1984 and 1983. Looking over the common-size income statements and balance sheets of the Dow Chemical Co., we notice the following changes between 1984 and 1983:

1. Net sales increased 4.3 percent to $11,418 million in 1984.
2. Cost of sales as a percentage of net sales was reduced from 86.3 percent to 83.3 percent in 1984.
3. As a result, operating income as a percent of net sales increased from 4.7 percent to 7.4 percent in 1984.

TABLE 10–8   Common-Size Consolidated Income Statements of Dow Chemical Co., 1983 and 1984

	1984 (in millions)	As % of Sales	1983 (in millions)	As % of Sales
Net sales	$11,418	100.0%	$10,951	100.0%
Operating costs and expenses				
Cost of sales	9,516	83.3%	9,446	86.3%
Selling and administrative	1,054	9.2%	989	9.0%
Total operating costs	10,570	92.6%	10,435	95.3%
Operating income	848	7.4%	516	4.7%
Other income (expenses)				
Equity in earnings:				
Nonconsolidated subsidiaries	23		12	
Losses on translation (20%–50% owned companies)	50		84	
Interest income	94		113	
Interest, amortization of debt discount and expenses	(437)		(431)	
Gains on exchange and translation	14		66	
Gains on sales of investments	183		101	
Provision for plant closings and cancelled projects	(157)		(58)	
Sundry income	57		43	
Income before taxes on income	675	5.9%	446	4.1%
Provision for taxes on income	126	1.1%	'153	1.4%
Income before extraordinary items	549	4.8%	293	2.7%
Extraordinary items:				
Tax benefit from foreign tax loss carry-forwards	36			
Gain on redemption of long-term debt			41	
Net income, including extraordinary items	$ 585	5.1%	$ 334	3.0%

	1984	1983
Earnings per common share before extraordinary items	$ 2.83	$ 1.50
Extraordinary items:		
Tax benefit from foreign tax loss carry-forwards	.19	
Gain on redemption of long-term debt		.21
Earnings per share, including extraordinary items	$ 3.02	$ 1.71

Source: 1984 Annual Report of Dow Chemical Co.

TABLE 10–9 Common-Size Consolidated Balance Sheets of Dow Chemical Co.

	1984 (in millions)	As % of Total Assets	1983 (in millions)	As % of Total Assets
Assets				
Current assets				
Cash	$ 19	1.1%	$ 12	1.5%
Marketable securities	102		166	
Accounts and notes receivable	$ 1,883	16.5%	$ 2,266	18.9%
Inventories				
Finished and work in process	1,426	16.9%	1,291	16.4%
Materials and supplies	501		670	
Total current assets	3,931	34.4%	4,405	36.8%
Investments				
Equity in banking and Ins. subsidiaries	214		191	
Equity in associated companies (50% owned)	833		687	
20%–49% owned companies	105		153	
Other investments	413		186	
Nonrecurrent receivables	384		298	
Total investments	1,949	17.1%	1,515	12.6%
Plant properties	11,256		11,524	
Accumulated depreciation	(6,083)		(5,829)	
Net plant properties	5,173	45.3%	5,695	47.5%
Goodwill	202	1.8%	196	1.6%
Deferred charges and other assets	164	1.4%	170	1.4%
Total assets	11,419	100.0%	11,981	100.0%
Liabilities				
Current Liabilities				
Notes payable	250		694	
Debt due within one year	234		70	
Accounts payable	1,150		1,313	
Income taxes payable	305		294	
Other current liabilities	737		767	
Total current liabilities	2,676	23.4%	3,138	26.2%
Long-term debt	2,745	24.0%	2,803	23.4%
Deferred taxes and other liabilities	915	8.0%	960	8.0%
Minority interest in subsidiaries	21	0.2%	33	0.3%
Equity				
Common stock (issued 208,613,652 in 1984 and 206,549,098 in 1983)	522		516	
Paid-in capital	597		552	
Retained earnings	4,361		4,123	
Treasury stock (18,521,367 in 1984, 10,703,412 shares in 1983)	(383)		(153)	
Cumulative translation adjusted	(35)		9	
Total stockholders' equity	5,062	44.3%	5,047	42.1%
Total liabilities and net worth	11,419	100.0%	11,981	100.0%

Source: 1984 Annual Report of Dow Chemical Co.

4. Net income, excluding extraordinary items, as a percent of net sales increased from 2.7 percent to 4.8 percent.
5. Earnings per share, excluding extraordinary items, increased from $1.50 to $2.83 in 1984.
6. In the balance sheet, investments in subsidiary and others as a percent of total assets increased from 12.6 percent to 17.1 percent in 1984.
7. Current liabilities as a percent of total liabilities and net worth was reduced from 26.2 percent to 23.4 percent in 1984.

In all, 1984 was a good year for the company.

Ratio Analysis

Ratios are among the best known and most widely used tools of financial analysis. Ratio analysis and common-size statement analysis are complementary to each other.

There are, basically, four types of ratios:

1. Liquidity ratios measure the firm's ability to meet its short-term obligations.
2. Leverage ratios measure the extent to which the firm has been financed by debt.
3. Activity ratios measure how effectively the firm is using its resources.
4. Profitability ratios measure management's overall effectiveness as shown by the returns generated on sales and investment.

Liquidity Ratios

Liquidity ratios are designed to find out whether or not the corporation under study is having problems meeting its short-term obligations. Major corporations are not expected to have problems in this area. Consequently, liquidity ratios are not the main concern of investors, but we will calculate two commonly used liquidity ratios, the current ratio and the quick ratio (or acid test).

CURRENT RATIO   The current ratio is computed by dividing current assets by current liabilities. The current ratios of Dow Chemical at year-end 1984 and 1983 were:

$$\text{Current ratio} = \frac{\text{Current assets}}{\text{Current liabilities}} = \frac{\$3931}{2676} = 1.47 \quad (1984)$$

$$= \frac{\$4405}{3138} = 1.40 \quad (1983)$$

QUICK RATIO OR ACID TEST   Inventories are typically the least liquid item in current assets. The quick ratio is calculated by deducting inventories from current assets and dividing the remainder by current liabilities. Normally, a quick ratio of over one is considered satisfactory. The quick ratios of Dow Chemical at year-end 1984 and 1983 were:

$$\text{Quick ratio} = \frac{\text{Current assets} - \text{Inventory}}{\text{Current liabilities}} = \frac{\$3931 - 1927}{\$2676} = 0.75$$

$$(1984)$$

$$= \frac{\$4405 - 1961}{\$3138} = 0.78$$

$$(1983)$$

From Table 9–6, which contains data of the chemical industry, we know that the current ratio was 1.8, and the quick ratio was 1.0 at year-end 1983 for the industry as a whole. On the basis of the ratios just calculated, Dow Chemical seemed slightly deficient in liquidity.

Leverage Ratios

Leverage ratios measure the extent to which a corporation is financing its assets with debt. Excessive use of debt by a corporation is not looked upon favorably by either creditors or investors. Creditors look for protection of stockholders' equity. Excessive debt means a lower percentage of assets are financed by equity, and, therefore, there is less protection for creditors. Investors in general are averse to risks. Debt represents fixed obligations for the payment of interest and principal. The more debt outstanding, the greater is the amount of fixed obligations. In times of adverse business conditions, high debt can mean financial risk to a corporation.

In practice, leverage ratios are usually computed in two ways. One approach uses balance sheet ratios and determines the extent to which borrowed funds have been used to finance the firm. The other approach measures the risks of debt by relating operating profits in the income statement to fixed charges to determine the number of times these fixed charges are covered. The two leverage ratios complement each other, and most analysts examine both leverage ratios.

TOTAL DEBT TO TOTAL ASSETS   The ratio of total debt to total assets, generally called the *debt ratio*, measures the percentage of total assets financed by creditors. Debt includes both short-term and long-term liabilities.

The debt ratios of Dow Chemical for 1984 and 1983 were:

$$\text{Debt ratio} = \frac{\text{Total debt}}{\text{Total assets}} = \frac{2676 + 2745 + 915 \text{ mil.}}{11,419 \text{ mil.}} = 55.5\%$$

$$(1984)$$

$$= \frac{3138 + 2803 + 960 \text{ mil.}}{11,981 \text{ mil.}} = 57.6\%$$

$$(1983)$$

From Table 9–6 we calculated the debt ratio for the chemical industry in 1983 at 52.2 percent, which was slightly lower than the debt ratio of Dow Chemical for the same year.

TIMES-INTEREST-EARNED   The times-interest-earned ratio is determined by dividing earnings before interest and income taxes by the interest charges. This ratio measures the extent to which operating profit can decline without affecting the firm's ability to pay interest charges. The times-interest-earned ratios for Dow Chemical for 1984 and 1983 were:

$$\text{Times-interest-earned} = \frac{\text{Income before taxes + Interest charges}}{\text{Interest charges}}$$

$$= \frac{675 + 437 \text{ mil.}}{437 \text{ mil.}} = 2.5 \text{ times (1984)}$$

$$= \frac{446 + 431}{431} = 2.0 \text{ times (1983)}$$

Compared to the industry average of 3.6 times in 1983 as shown in Table 9–6, Dow Chemical's ratios were much lower, which means inferior than industry average.

FIXED-CHARGE COVERAGE   Rentals on long-term leases are similar to interest charges on long-term debt in that they both represent fixed charges to a corporation. The fixed-charge coverage ratio includes both interest charges and rentals in the calculation. The formula for the calculation of the fixed-charge ratio is:

$$\text{Fixed-charge coverage} = \frac{\text{Income before taxes + Interest charges + rentals on lease}}{\text{Interest charges + rentals on lease}}$$

In the footnotes to Dow Chemical's financial statement, we found that rental expense was \$216 million for 1984, and \$207 million for 1983. The fixed-charge coverage ratios for Dow Chemical for 1984 and 1983 were:

$$\text{Fixed-charge coverage} = \frac{\$675 + 437 + 216 \text{ mil.}}{\$437 + 216 \text{ mil.}} = 2.0 \text{ times (1984)}$$

$$= \frac{\$446 + 431 + 207 \text{ mil.}}{\$431 + 207 \text{ mil.}} = 1.7 \text{ times (1983)}$$

Because of lack of data on rentals, we are unable to calculate a fixed-charge coverage ratio for the chemical industry with which to compare Dow's ratio.

Activity Ratios

Activity ratios are designed to measure how effectively the firm is utilizing its resources. Activity ratios involve the comparison between the level of sales on the one hand and the investment in assets on the other. The activity ratios include three basic ratios: inventory turnover, fixed-assets turnover, and total assets turnover. The three ratios for Dow Chemical for 1984 were:

$$\text{Inventory turnover} = \frac{\text{Sales}}{\text{Inventory}} = \frac{\$11,418 \text{ mil.}}{1927 \text{ mil.}} = 5.9$$

$$\text{Fixed-assets turnover} = \frac{\text{Sales}}{\text{Net fixed assets}} = \frac{\$11,418 \text{ mil.}}{5173 \text{ mil.}} = 2.2$$

$$\text{Total assets turnover} = \frac{\text{Sales}}{\text{Total assets}} = \frac{\$11,418 \text{ mil.}}{11,419 \text{ mil.}} = 1.0$$

We do not have comparable data for the chemical industry for 1984. However, in Table 9–6 we have industry data for 1983. The three comparable ratios for the chemical industry for 1983 were:

$$\text{Inventory turnover} = \frac{\text{Sales}}{\text{Inventory}} = \frac{161.68}{21.26} = 7.6$$

$$\text{Fixed-assets turnover} = \frac{\text{Sales}}{\text{Net fixed assets}} = \frac{161.68}{77.5} = 2.1$$

$$\text{Total assets turnover} = \frac{\text{Sales}}{\text{Total assets}} = \frac{161.68}{141.36} = 1.1$$

The activity ratios seem comparable between Dow Chemical and the chemical industry composite except that the inventory turnover of Dow Chemical was slightly lower.

Profitability Ratios

Investors in general are most interested in profitability ratios, which are usually computed in two ways. One approach is to relate profit to sales. The profit figure can be either gross profit, operating profit, or net profit. Another approach is to relate profits to balance sheet items, such as common equity, net worth, or total assets. We will calculate four profit ratios for Dow Chemical.

OPERATING PROFIT MARGIN   Operating profit margin is obtained by dividing operating profit of a corporation by its sales. This ratio shows operating profit per dollar of sales.

$$\text{Operating profit margin} = \frac{\text{Sales} - \text{Cost of goods sold} - \text{Selling,}}{\text{Sales}}$$

$$= \frac{\$848 \text{ mil.}}{\$11,418 \text{ mil.}} = 7.4\% \ (1984)$$

$$= \frac{\$516 \text{ mil.}}{\$10,951 \text{ mil.}} = 4.7\% \ (1983)$$

NET PROFIT MARGIN   Net profit margin is obtained by dividing net profit after taxes by sales. This ratio indicates net profit per dollar of sales.

$$\text{Net profit margin} = \frac{\text{Net profit after taxes}}{\text{Sales}} = \frac{\$549 \text{ mil.}}{\$11,418 \text{ mil.}} = 4.8\%$$
$$(1984)$$

$$= \frac{\$293 \text{ mil.}}{\$10,951 \text{ mil.}} = 2.7\%$$
$$(1983)$$

RATE OF RETURN ON TOTAL ASSETS   This ratio is obtained by dividing total assets into net profits after taxes and indicates the rate of return obtained by the corporation per dollar of assets invested.

$$\text{Rate of return on total assets} = \frac{\text{Net profits after taxes}}{\text{Total assets}}$$

$$= \frac{\$549 \text{ mil.}}{\$11,419 \text{ mil.}} = 4.8\% \ (1984)$$

$$= \frac{\$293 \text{ mil.}}{\$11,981 \text{ mil.}} = 2.4\% \ (1983)$$

RATE OF RETURN ON NET WORTH   Rate of return on net worth is obtained by dividing net profit after taxes by net worth. This ratio indicates the rate of return per dollar of equity, both common and preferred.

$$\text{Rate of return on net worth} = \frac{\text{Net profit after taxes}}{\text{Net worth}}$$

$$= \frac{\$549 \text{ mil.}}{\$5,062 \text{ mil.}} = 10.8\% \ (1984)$$

$$= \frac{\$293 \text{ mil.}}{\$5,047 \text{ mil.}} = 5.8\% \ (1983)$$

Since we do not have industry data for 1984, we calculate the four comparable profit ratios for the chemical industry for 1983 (see Table 9–6):

$$\text{Operating profit margin} = \frac{\text{Operating profit}}{\text{Sales}} = \frac{23.14}{161.68} = 14.3\%$$

$$\text{Net profit margin} = \frac{\text{Net profit after taxes}}{\text{Sales}} = \frac{5}{161.68} = 3.1\%$$

$$\text{Rate of return on total assets} = \frac{\text{Net profit after taxes}}{\text{Total assets}} = \frac{5}{141.36} = 3.5\%$$

$$\text{Rate of return on net worth} = \frac{\text{Net profit after taxes}}{\text{Net worth}} = \frac{5}{67.65} = 7.4\%$$

All the calculated profit ratios indicate that Dow Chemical Co. compared quite poorly with the average of the chemical industry in 1983.

In 1984, Dow Chemical did substantially better. For a comparison with the industry, we refer to the Corporate Scoreboard for the chemical industry in *Business Week*. The comparison between Dow Chemical and the chemical industry composite in 1984 can be summarized as follows:

	Percent Growth of Sales 1984/1983	Percent Increase in Net Profit 1984/1983	Net Profit Margin	Return on Common Equity
Dow Chemical	4%	87%	4.8%	10.7%
Chemical industry	5%	34%	4.6%	11.5%

Overall, Dow Chemical seems to have performed as well as the industry average in 1984.

Comparison of Ratios over Time and Comparison with Competitors and the Industry Average

The ratio analysis of financial statements can reveal a great deal about a corporation: its liquidity, degree of leverage, efficiency, and profitability.

However, investors need more than one year's analysis. What investors really want to know are answers to three basic questions:

1. Is the corporation improving in its overall performance?
2. How serious was the impact of past business recessions on this corporation? In other words, to what extent is the corporation vulnerable to recession?
3. Is the corporation moving ahead of its close competitors? Is it performing better than the industry average?

To answer these important questions, financial ratios of the firm must be examined over a period of years with close competitors and industry averages.

Since most of these financial ratios, both current and historical, are available in publications such as Standard & Poor's *Industry Survey, Analysts Handbook, Value Line Investment Survey, Forbes,* "Quarterly Corporate Scoreboard" of *Business Week,* and the historical section of financial statements of individual corporations, investors need not calculate the ratios themselves. What investors do need is to understand the meaning of these ratios, know where to get them, and how to compare and evaluate them.

The Z Scores

Sometimes the financial ratios computed can be confusing. For instance, one group of ratios indicates the company is doing well, while a second group suggests that the company is doing poorly. In evaluating a company's position, these ratios must be considered carefully with other data about a company's performance. However, even if most ratios indicate a firm is encountering some problems, how can one ascertain if these problems are, in fact, serious?

The Altman Model[6]

The problem of determining which ratios predict whether a firm is in financial trouble has received considerable attention. Much of the work in this area has been done by Professor Edward Altman of New York University. Using a method called *Multiple Discriminant Analysis,* Professor Altman obtained an equation that is useful in predicting potential bankruptcy. Most of the information required by the equation is easily calculated from numbers on income statements and balance sheets. The equation is as follows:

$$Z = 1.2X_1 + 1.4X_2 + 3.3X_3 + .6X_4 + 1.0X_5$$

---

[6]Edward Altman, "Financial Ratios, Discriminant Analysis, and the Prediction of Corporate Bankruptcy," *Journal of Finance,* Sept. 1968.

where:

> Z = a score that indicates the financial strength of the company.
>
> X_1 = net working capital (that is, current assets less current liabilities) divided by total assets.
>
> X_2 = accumulated retained earnings (from the balance sheet) divided by total assets.
>
> X_3 = earnings before interest and taxes (EBIT) divided by total assets.
>
> X_4 = market value of common and preferred stock divided by book value of total liabilities.
>
> X_5 = sales divided by total assets.

The meanings of X_3 and X_5 were discussed above and, as explained, higher values indicate a stronger company. X_1 is a measure of liquidity relative to size of the company. It will be low if a firm is experiencing difficulties in raising cash to pay its bills. Companies that are having no problems in paying creditors usually have high values of X_1.

X_2 is an index of the amount of profits reinvested into the company over the years. A high level of accumulated retained earnings implies that the company has a history of profitable activity. Such established firms have a lower failure rate than newly created firms, and X_2 recognizes this factor.

The purpose of X_4 is to measure the burden of debt carried by a firm. As debt increases relative to equity, the ratio declines. Large quantities of debt imply an obligation to pay substantial sums in principal and interest. If X_4 is low and business conditions deteriorate, a firm may find it quite difficult to make the required payments. The Braniff Airlines example is a case in point. The company borrowed heavily to expand its operations, but the expected increase in revenues did not materialize. Braniff did not have sufficient funds to pay lenders and suppliers the amounts that were due, and bankruptcy followed.

Evaluating Z Scores

In a study of manufacturing companies, Altman found that the Z scores frequently predicted bankruptcy. Companies with scores below 1.8 generally went bankrupt within one year. Companies with Z scores above 3.0 were found to be healthy. All the companies in the original study survived and were still in existence at the end of one year. Scores between 1.8 and 3.0 fall within a grey area, and their survival is uncertain. Tests performed since Altman developed the model have shown it is still useful, and its accuracy in predicting bankruptcy has been over 80 percent.

It should be stressed that the bankruptcy predictions are for manufacturing firms, and the Z limits described above do not necessarily apply to other types of companies. However, movements in the Z scores over time would generally be of interest to any firm. In using the Altman model, a company should compute its Z score over recent years. If the Z value had been greater than 3.0, but has since dropped below that level, there may be some cause for concern. If it has fallen below 1.8, the signs are more ominous. In general, while the absolute Z score is important in indicating degree of financial distress of a firm, the *trend* in Z is even more important.[7]

The Z Score of Dow Chemical

$$X_1 = \frac{CA - CL}{TA} = \frac{3,931 - 2,676}{11,419} = 0.11$$

$$X_2 = \frac{RE}{TA} = \frac{4,361}{11,419} = 0.38$$

$$X_3 = \frac{EBIT}{TA} = \frac{1,112}{11,419} = .097$$

$$X_4 = \frac{Mkt\ value\ of\ equity}{TL} = \frac{6843.32}{6357}$$

$$= 1.08 \quad \text{(Price of common stock: \$ 36 per share, 7/15/85)}$$

$$X_5 = \frac{Sales}{TA} = \frac{11,418}{11,419} = 1$$

$$Z = 1.2X_1 + 1.4X_2 + 3.3X_3 + .6X_4 + 1X_5$$

$$= 1.2(.11) + 1.4(.38) + 3.3(.097) + .6(1.08) + 1(1)$$

$$= .132 + .532 + .320 + .648 + 1$$

$$= 2.63$$

The Z score of Dow Chemical for 1984 was 2.63, which is one-third of a point less than 3.0, a healthy financial condition. The Z score indicates that there is some financial risk for Dow Chemical Corp. This is confirmed by the fact that in the ratios computed earlier, we found some ratios were not satisfactory, namely:

1. The current ratio of 1.47 for 1984 was too low.
2. The debt ratio at 55.5 percent for 1984 was higher than the industry average of 52.2 percent.
3. Inventory turnover ratio at 5.9 for 1984 was lower than the industry average of 7.6.

---

[7]Edward Altman and Joseph Spivack, "Predicting Bankruptcy: The *Value Line* Relative Financial Strength vs. the Zeta Bankruptcy Classification Approach," *Financial Analysts Journal*, Nov.–Dec. 1983.

Besides, two-thirds of the business of Dow Chemical was in basic chemicals, which are affected importantly by general business expansion or contraction.

SUMMARY

The balance sheet and income statement are the two basic financial statements reporting a corporation's status of financial conditions as of a given date and its performance over a given year or quarter. Accountants prepare these statements on the basis of several generally accepted accounting principles or conventions: the going concern, historical costs, consistency, matching, realization, conservatism, and disclosure.

The accounting profession allows a number of alternative acceptable accounting methods in respect to recognition of revenue, inventory valuation, depreciation, pension costs, investment tax credit, and merger and acquisitions. Consequently, the figures in the financial statements depend partly on the accounting methods chosen by the corporation. Analysts have thus introduced the concept of quality of earnings. They examine the auditor's report, changes in accounting policies, notes of financial statements, and management discretionary decisions in order to determine the quality of earnings of a corporation, which will be used as an important factor in determining the value of its stock. Individual investors must realize that the notes to financial statements are an integral part of financial statements.

On the basis of the figures in the financial statements, investors usually calculate four types of ratios: liquidity ratios, leverage ratios, activity or efficiency ratios, and profitability ratios. Ratios of only one year are usually not very useful. To have a good perspective on the weakness and strength of a corporation and its future potential, the investor must compare the ratios of a corporation over a period of at least five years and compare those figures with close competitors or the industry average over the same period.

QUESTIONS AND PROBLEMS

1. Illustrate the impact of LIFO and FIFO inventory accounting on inventory values and profits of a corporation in a period of rising prices.
2. What problems of financial statement analysis are created by pension plans?
3. Indicate a few ratios designed to measure the profitability of a corporation.
4. Can a corporation "manipulate" its income? How?
5. It is recommended that investors never ignore the footnotes to financial statements. Why?

6. Why are earnings per share of different corporations often not strictly comparable?

7. As a prospective investor in the stocks of a corporation, which ratios do you consider most important?

8. Name a few deficiencies of financial statements.

9. Explain a few accounting concepts or principles.

10. Since financial statements are subject to much management discretion, what should investors do?

11. What is meant by quality of earnings?

12. Explain how analysts determine the quality of earnings of a given stock.

13. Find the statistics from pertinent sources to compare General Motors, Ford, and Chrysler in terms of leverage, efficiency in utilization of assets, and profitability in the last five years.

14. Find the necessary information from pertinent sources to calculate the Z score for the following companies:
   a. Squibb Corp.
   b. J.C. Penney
   c. U.S. Steel

REFERENCES

Altman, Edward. "Financial Ratios, Discriminant Analysis, and the Prediction of Corporate Bankruptcy." *Journal of Finance*, Sept. 1968.

Altman, Edward, and Spivack, Joseph. "Predicting Bankruptcy: The *Value Line* Relative Financial Strength vs. the Zeta Bankruptcy Classification Approach." *Financial Analysts Journal*, Nov.–Dec. 1983.

Anthony, Robert N. and Reece, James S. *Accounting Principles*, 5th ed. Homewood, Ill.: R. D. Irwin, 1983.

Bernstein, Leopold A. *Financial Statement Analysis: Theory, Application, and Interpretation*, 3rd Ed. Homewood, Ill.: R. D. Irwin, 1983.

Bernstein, Leopold A. and Siegel, Joel G. "The Concept of Earning Quality." *Financial Analysts Journal*, July–Aug. 1979.

Branch, Ben. "Misleading Accounting: The Danger and the Potential." *American Association of Individual Investors Journal*, Oct. 1984.

Cohen, Jerome B., Zinbarg, Edward D., and Zeikel, Arthur. *Investment Analysis & Portfolio Management*, 4th Ed. Homewood, Ill.: R. D. Irwin, Chapt. 9.

Hale, David D. "The Financial Analyst's Approach." *Handbook of Accounting and Auditing*, Edited by Buton, Palmer, and Kay. Boston, Mass.: Warren, Gorham, & Lamont, 1981.

Helfert, Erich A. "Analysis of Financial Statements," "Evaluation of Financial Statements." *Financial Analysts Handbook I*. New York: Dow Jones-Irwin, 1975.

Katz, Steven, Lilien, Steven, and Nelson, Bert. "Stock Market Behavior Around Bankruptcy Model Distress and Recovery Predictions." *Financial Analysts Journal*, Jan.–Feb. 1985.

Latané, H., Tuttle, D., and Jones, C. *Security Analysis and Portfolio Management*. New York: Ronald, 1975, Chap. 5.

Mortimer, Terry. "Reported Earnings: A New Approach." *Financial Analysts Journal,* Nov.–Dec. 1979.

Olstein, Robert. "Quality of Earnings: The Key to Successful Investing." *Barron's,* July 2, 1984.

Siegel, Joel G. "The 'Quality of Earnings' Concept — A Survey." *Financial Analysts Journal,* March–April 1982.

Tevelow, Rosemarie. "How a Security Analyst uses the Annual Report." *Financial Executive,* Nov. 1971.

Worthy, Ford S. "Manipulating Profits: How It's Done." *Fortune,* June 25, 1984.

11

Growth Analysis

IMPORTANCE OF GROWTH OF EARNINGS PER SHARE

Investors in general are very much interested in the potential earnings of a corporation, especially on a per-share basis. The reason is quite obvious: Growth of earnings per share (EPS) is the foundation for increases in dividends if the corporation maintains a given dividend payout ratio (dividend divided by earnings per share). In practice, most corporations do declare more dividends when earnings per share are rising.

Investors should distinguish between two types of increases in earnings of a corporation. One type of increase is due to the cyclical recovery in general business. This is a short-term phenomenon that may last a few years depending on the length of the recovery phase of the economy. The other type of increase in earnings represents a long-term trend of growth that will likely persist into the future. What investors are most interested in is not the temporary recovery of earnings (which will fall back when the economy slides into recession), but the long-term growth potential of total earnings and earnings per share of a corporation.

The increase in earnings of corporations can assume different patterns. A few common patterns are illustrated in Figure 11–1. Corporation A experiences only a cyclical increase and decline in earnings. It has no growth potential. Corporation B has a secular growth trend in EPS. It has never

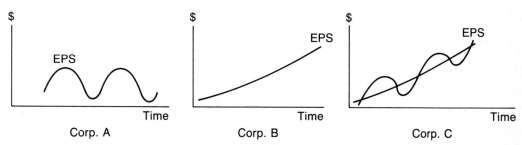

FIGURE 11–1 Three Patterns of Increase in Corporate Earnings

experienced a decline in earnings, even during a recession. Corporation C shows a growth trend of EPS as well as cyclical variation.

Because most corporations are like Corporation C for which the secular growth of EPS is intertwined with cyclical variation, it is important for investors to recognize the differences between secular growth and cyclical variation of EPS, and to correctly measure the growth rate of EPS and the normal level of EPS of a corporation at a given moment in time.

As we see in Figure 11–2, the cyclical high of EPS of a corporation should not be mistaken by the investor for the normal earning power of the corporation. The normal earning power would be better measured by the average of EPS over the whole business cycle.

Internal versus External Growth of Earnings

To expand the operation of a business and to increase its total earnings and earnings per share, a corporation can rely on internal growth, external growth, or a combination of both.

Most corporations grow internally. They plow back part or all of their net earnings for reinvestment. Some corporations, on the other hand, choose to acquire other businesses to grow. There are advantages and disadvantages to both methods. Internal growth usually takes longer than external growth, but is usually less risky. The most successful example of a corporation using internal growth is the IBM Corporation. Expansion through acquisition has the advantages of getting into a new field fast, and acquiring the expertise, organization structure, and management of an existing corporation. However, acquisition can produce many unanticipated problems. *Business Week*[1] recently reported that the overall record of company mergers in recent years is not encouraging. One out of three acquisitions is later undone.

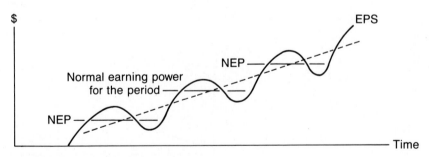

FIGURE 11–2   NEP versus EPS

[1] *Business Week*, "Do Mergers Really Work?" June 3, 1985.

Because external growth has been more risky, the analyst should find out what has been the company's policy in terms of growth and to what extent past growth has been dependent on acquiring external firms.

Problems in Extending a Past Trend

One of the common mistakes both professional analysts and individual investors often make is to assume that the past trend of sales and profit growth of a successful company or an industry will continue. The trouble encountered by many computer firms and their suppliers in 1985 points out clearly the danger of this assumption. If extending past trends is not dependable, what should be the logical method in estimating the growth potential of the firm? One method consists of examining the factors that explain the past trend of earnings growth of the firm, determining if these factors remain operating, and if they will likely continue to operate in the near future.

DETERMINANTS OF EARNINGS PER SHARE

The level of EPS of a corporation is determined by a number of factors, some of which are financial, and others operational. Some factors are within the control of the management, and others are beyond its influence.

The best way to analyze EPS is probably through using the following framework:

$$\text{EPS} = \text{Book value per share} \times \text{rate of return on common equity, or}$$

$$\text{EPS} = \frac{\text{Common equity}}{\text{Number of common shares}} \times \frac{\text{Net profits}^2}{\text{Common equity}}$$

As shown, the EPS is determined by two factors: the amount of capital per common share and the degree of profitability, or the rate of return obtained on common equity. For example, if the capital contributed per common share was $10 at the beginning of 1986, and the rate of return on common equity was 12 percent for the year, then multiplying the two factors results in an EPS of $1.20 for the year 1986.

Book Value per Common Share

The book value per common share of a corporation changes from year to year. In most successful corporations, book value per share usually increases, and

---

[2] Net profits are profits after income taxes and after dividends on preferred stock, if there are preferred stocks in the capital structure of the company.

can be attributed to one of two factors. The most common reason for the increase in book value is that a part of the EPS is usually retained and reinvested in the business.

For example, our hypothetical corporation earned $1.20 per common share in 1986. If 60 percent of the EPS was paid out in the form of dividends, the corporation retained 40 percent × $1.20, or $.48. The book value at the beginning of 1987 would be $10.48, an increase of $.48 per share.

Another source for the increase of book value per share is available to only a few corporations. When corporations are very successful, such as IBM and Johnson & Johnson, the market prices of these stocks are usually much higher than their book values.

Assume IBM issues one million new common shares in the market at $120 per share. The book value per share of IBM at the end of 1984 was $43.23. The total difference between issuing price and book value amounts to ($120 − $43.23) × 1 million = $76.77 million. This difference is called *capital surplus* in accounting and belongs to all common shares outstanding. Thus it will raise the book value of every share of common stock.

Rate of Return on Common Equity

Rate of return on common equity measures the profitability per dollar of capital contributed by common-stock holders. Note in Figure 11–3 that the rate of return on common equity is determined by two factors: turnover of common equity (Sales divided by Common equity), and net profit margin (Net profit divided by Sales).

The relationships between profitability of common equity, turnover of common equity, and net profit margin can be also shown in equation form:

$$\text{Rate of return on common equity} = \text{Turnover of common equity} \times \text{net profit margin}$$

$$= \frac{\text{Sales}}{\text{Common equity}} \times \frac{\text{Net profit}}{\text{Sales}}$$

$$= \frac{\text{Net profit}}{\text{Common equity}}$$

Improvement of Net Profit Margin

Net profit margin can be improved in two ways. The most common way is through increasing operating efficiency, which can be achieved through various measures, such as better cost control, increasing labor efficiency, and increasing selling prices. At certain times, some corporations could improve net profit margin by increasing financial leverage (the use of more debt) when the corporation earns a rate of return much higher than the rate of interest

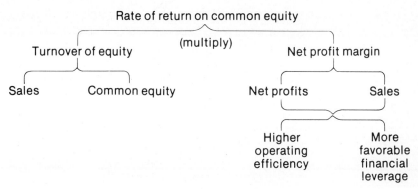

FIGURE 11–3   Rate of Return on Common Equity

on borrowing. The excess of return over interest costs can boost the net profit margin. However, in reality, this method is only occasionally used by some corporations, because most firms find themselves already operating at a leverage ratio close to the upper limit. Further increase in this ratio may alarm creditors and stockholders. Negative market reaction may more than offset any benefit achieved from additional borrowing.

The Complete Framework for Analysis of EPS

The different components of the framework for the analysis of EPS appears in Figure 11–4, where:

$$rr(\text{CE}) = \text{Rate of return on common equity}$$
$$\text{BVPS} = \text{Book value per common share}$$
$$\text{T(CE)} = \text{Turnover of common equity}$$
$$\text{NPM} = \text{Net profit margin}$$
$$\text{NP} = \text{Net profit}$$
$$\text{R/E} = \text{Retained earnings}$$

Alternative Framework for the Analysis of EPS

Another useful framework in the analysis of EPS can be seen in the following, where EPS is related to two basic factors: sales per common share, and the net profit margin (Net profit/Sales).

EPS

Sales P.S. (Sales/No. of Shares)   NPM (NP/Sales)

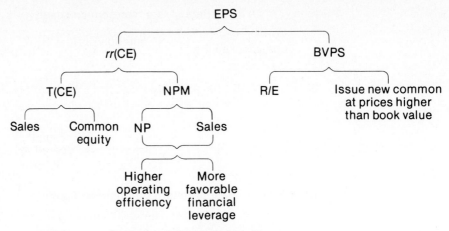

FIGURE 11–4   Analysis of Earnings Per Share

The relationships among the factors can be expressed as:

EPS = Sales per common share × Net profit margin

$$= \frac{\text{Sales}}{\text{Number of shares}} \times \frac{\text{Net profits}}{\text{Sales}}$$

$$= \frac{\text{Net profits}}{\text{Number of shares}}$$

Under this framework, the sales per common share is emphasized as one of the key determinants of EPS, whereas in the previous framework, the book value per share (the capital base) was emphasized as one of the two key determinants of EPS.

It is obvious that sales per common share is actually related to the amount of capital put in common share. Hence the two frameworks are alternative expressions of the basic relationships among factors determining EPS. As a matter of fact, the frameworks are complementary.

THREE APPROACHES TO ESTIMATING GROWTH POTENTIAL OF EPS

Book Value Times Rate of Return

The first framework discussed for the analysis of EPS was:

EPS = Book value per common share
        × Rate of return on common equity

In our example, if the book value per share was $10 at the beginning of 1986, and the rate of return on common equity was 12 percent in 1986, then the EPS was $10 \times 12\% = \$1.20$ for 1986.

If there will be an increase in EPS in 1987, it must come from an increase in either book value or rate of return, or both (or an increase in one factor large enough to more than offset a decline in another factor). So the growth potential of EPS for 1987 can be calculated from the following formula:

$$\text{Growth potential of EPS} = \frac{\text{BVPS}_t}{\text{BVPS}_{t-1}} \times \frac{rr(\text{CE})_t}{rr(\text{CE})_{t-1}}$$

where:

$$\text{BVPS}_t = \text{Book value per share in year } t$$
$$\text{BPVS}_{t-1} = \text{Book value per share in year } t - 1$$
$$rr(\text{CE})_t = \text{Rate of return on common equity in year } t$$
$$rr(\text{CE})_{t-1} = \text{Rate of return on common equity in year } t - 1$$

Assume that in 1986 the corporation paid out 60 percent of EPS in dividends and retained 40 percent of EPS in the corporation, and that the rate of return on common equity will be a little higher at 12.6 percent in 1987. What will the EPS and the growth rate of EPS be for 1987?

First, we must calculate the book value per share at the beginning of 1987. It was $\$10 + 40\%(1.20) = \$10.48$. Then we can proceed to calculate the growth rate of EPS in 1987 as:

$$\text{Growth of EPS in 1987} = \frac{10.48}{10} \times \frac{12.6\%}{12\%} - 1 = 1.048 \times 1.05 - 1$$

$$= 1.1004 - 1 = .1004 = 10.04\%$$

We know the growth rate of EPS would be 10.04 percent in 1987, which was caused by an increase of 4.8 percent in the book value per share and a 5 percent increase in the rate of return on common equity.

We can check the results in another way:

1987 EPS $= \$10.48 \times 12.6\% = \$1.32048$

1986 EPS $= \$10 \times 12\% = \$1.20$

$$\frac{1987 \text{ EPS}}{1986 \text{ EPS}} = \frac{\$1.32048}{\$1.20} = 1.1004$$

The percentage increase of EPS in 1987 $= 1.1004 - 1 = .1004$
$$= 10.04\%$$

Later in this chapter, we will illustrate the estimate of growth potential of EPS in two companies: IBM and Dow Chemical.

Sales per Share Times Net Profit Margin

Another approach to the estimate of growth potential of EPS of a corporation is based on the alternative framework discussed in the analysis of EPS, which was:

$$\text{EPS} = \text{Sales per common share} \times \text{Net profit margin}$$

$$= \frac{\text{Sales}}{\text{Number of common shares}} \times \frac{\text{Net profits}}{\text{Sales}}$$

$$= \frac{\text{Net profits}}{\text{Number of common shares}}$$

On the basis of this framework, the growth potential of EPS of a corporation can be calculated using the following formula:

$$\text{Growth rate of EPS} = \frac{\text{Sales per share}_t}{\text{Sales per share}_{t-1}} \times \frac{\text{Net profit margin}_t}{\text{Net profit margin}_{t-1}}$$

where:

t stands for year t

Rate of Return Times Earnings Retention Ratio

The increase in book value per common share for most corporations (probably over 90 percent of the companies listed on the NYSE) is a result of their retaining a part of their earnings for reinvestment. For these corporations, market prices are usually either around or under the book value per share. Hence, increasing book value through issuing stocks at prices higher than book value is not possible.

If the rates of return of these corporations are relatively stable over time (from one business cycle to another), then a general formula is available for estimating the earnings growth rate. The formula is:[3]

[3] This formula can be proved by a hypothetical example: ABC Corp. on Jan. 1, 1983, had a book value per share of $20. It earned $3 per share for the year, giving a rate of return on common equity of 15 percent ($3/$20). It paid out 60 percent of earnings as dividend, and retained the remaining 40 percent for capital expansion within the corporation. If the rate of return on common equity is assumed to be unchanged in the following year, 1984, the corporation will earn ($20 + .4 × $3) × 15% = $3.18. The earnings growth rate (EGR) was 6 percent ($3.18/$3 − 1). We can obtain the same result by applying the formula:

$$\text{EGR} = \text{Rate of return on common equity} \times (1 - \text{dividend payout ratio})$$
$$= 15\% \times (1 - 60\%)$$
$$= 6\%$$

$$\text{Earnings growth rate} = \text{Rate of return on common equity}$$
$$\times \ (1 - \text{Dividend payout ratio})$$

The rate of return on common equity and the dividend payout ratio (Dividend/EPS) of a corporation change somewhat from year to year. In applying the equation to estimate the long-term growth potential of a corporation's EPS, one should use averages of rates of return and dividend payout ratios over a period of time (perhaps five to seven years — long enough to cover at least one business cycle).

Estimating Growth Potential of a Growth Stock: IBM

Analysts usually define a growth stock as a stock whose earnings have been growing year after year without interruption for at least five years at an annual rate exceeding, perhaps, 10 percent.

In Figure 11–5 we see some of IBM's significant statistics from 1968 to 1983 with estimates for 1984 and 1985 by the *Value Line Investment Survey*. Before we estimate the growth potential of EPS of this company, we should first review its historical record.

Past Growth Rate of Sales Per Share

The growth of sales per share is one of the key factors that causes earnings per share to increase. Hence we will review the sales record of the company first.

For the calculation of past growth rate of sales or earnings per share, a proper past period should probably cover five to ten years. Too short a period will not sufficiently reflect the vagaries of the business cycle. A period too distant in the past could reflect factors that may no longer be relevant now and in the near future. In the calculation of past growth rate of sales and earnings per share of IBM, we arbitrarily select a period of nine years.

In Table 11–1 we show two methods for calculating growth rates. In the first, we compute first the year-to-year percentage increase and then take an average of these yearly percentage changes to get an average annual growth rate for the period. The result was 13.6 percent for the whole period 1976–84, and 13.9 percent for the years 1980–84.

The second method uses a compound-interest table (see Table 11–2). First we divide the sales of 1984 (terminal year) by the sales of 1976 (beginning year) to get a ratio of 2.77. Then we read along the row for eight years (1984–76), looking for a figure close to 2.77. We find a figure of 2.66 under the column head of 13% and another figure of 2.85 under the column of 14%. Since the figure of 2.77 is at the midpoint of 2.66 and 2.85, the average annual growth rate for the whole period 1976–84 was about 13.5 percent. This figure is almost the same as we get under the first method. With the second method, it is important to select beginning and terminal years of comparable

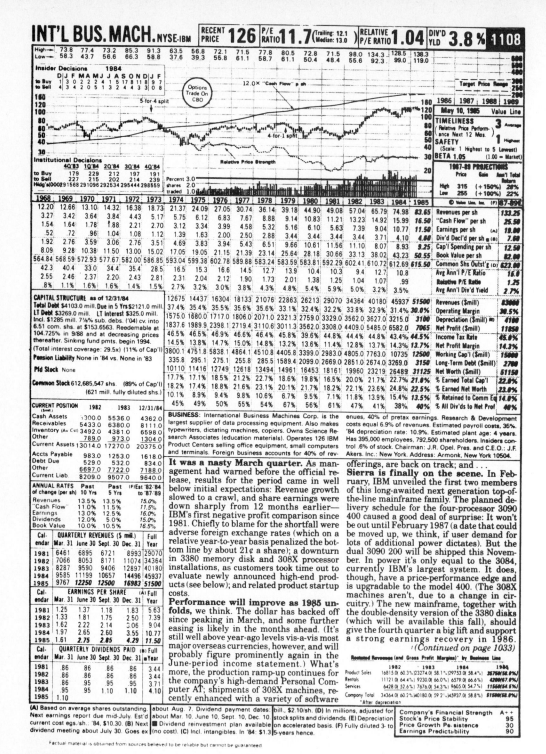

FIGURE 11–5

Source: Value Line Investment Survey, 1985. ©1985 Value Line, Inc. Reprinted by permission.

TABLE 11–1 Computation of Growth of Sales of IBM by Two Methods

Year	IBM Sales per Share	Annual Increase	Method 2	
1984	74.98	14.0%	1984 Sales per share	74.98
83	65.79	15.3	1976 Sales per share	27.05
82	57.04	16.2	1984 Sales/1976 sales	2.77
81	49.08	9.3	(over eight years)	
80	44.90	14.6		
79	39.18	8.4		
78	36.14	17.6		
77	30.74	13.6		
76	27.05			

Average annual growth rate
1976–84   13.6%
1980–84   13.9%

Average annual growth rate
from compound-interest table
1976–84   13.5%

Source: Data from *Value Line Investment Survey,* 1985.

general business conditions. Otherwise, if the beginning year is a recession year and the terminal year one of prosperity, the growth rate obtained would be higher than was actually the case.

Past Growth Rate of Earnings per Share

Investors are keenly interested in the historical growth rate of EPS of a corporation because it could indicate to some extent the potential future growth of EPS.

See Table 11–3 for the computation of growth rates of EPS of IBM during 1976–84 by two different methods as we did in the calculation of growth rates of sales per share.

The method of averaging yearly percentage changes shows a growth rate in EPS of IBM at 13.9 percent during 1976–84. The method using the compound-interest table gives us a slightly lower growth rate at 13.2 percent for the same period.

Estimating the Future Growth Potential of the EPS of IBM

We have reviewed the historical record of sales and earnings per share of IBM by calculating their growth rates. Now we turn to the task of estimating the future growth potential of EPS of this company on the basis of the different approaches discussed above.

The first framework for the estimate of the future growth rate of EPS was:

$$\text{Growth potential of EPS} = \frac{\text{BVPS}_t}{\text{BVPS}_{t-1}} \times \frac{rr(\text{CE})_t}{rr(\text{CE})_{t-1}}$$

TABLE 11–2 Condensed Compound-Interest Table: 3% to 24% Rates

Years	3%	4%	5%	6%	7%	8%	9%	10%	11%	12%	13%	14%	16%	18%	20%	22%	24%
1	1.03	1.04	1.05	1.06	1.07	1.08	1.09	1.10	1.11	1.12	1.13	1.14	1.16	1.18	1.20	1.22	1.24
2	1.06	1.08	1.10	1.12	1.14	1.17	1.19	1.21	1.23	1.25	1.28	1.30	1.35	1.39	1.44	1.49	1.54
3	1.09	1.12	1.16	1.19	1.23	1.26	1.30	1.33	1.37	1.40	1.44	1.48	1.56	1.64	1.73	1.82	1.91
4	1.13	1.17	1.22	1.26	1.31	1.36	1.41	1.46	1.52	1.57	1.63	1.69	1.81	1.94	2.07	2.22	2.36
5	1.16	1.22	1.28	1.34	1.40	1.47	1.54	1.61	1.69	1.76	1.84	1.93	2.10	2.29	2.49	2.70	2.93
6	1.19	1.27	1.34	1.42	1.50	1.59	1.68	1.77	1.87	1.97	2.08	2.19	2.44	2.70	2.99	3.30	3.64
7	1.23	1.32	1.41	1.50	1.61	1.71	1.83	1.95	2.08	2.21	2.35	2.50	2.83	3.19	3.58	4.02	4.51
8	1.27	1.37	1.48	1.59	1.72	1.85	1.99	2.14	2.30	2.48	2.66	2.85	3.28	3.76	4.30	4.91	5.59
9	1.30	1.42	1.55	1.69	1.84	2.00	2.17	2.36	2.56	2.77	3.00	3.25	3.80	4.44	5.16	5.98	6.93
10	1.34	1.48	1.63	1.79	1.97	2.16	2.37	2.59	2.84	3.11	3.39	3.71	4.41	5.23	6.19	7.30	8.59
11	1.38	1.54	1.71	1.90	2.10	2.33	2.58	2.85	3.15	3.48	3.84	4.23	5.12	6.18	7.43	8.91	10.66
12	1.43	1.60	1.80	2.01	2.25	2.52	2.81	3.14	3.50	3.90	4.33	4.82	5.94	7.29	8.92	10.87	13.21
13	1.47	1.67	1.88	2.13	2.41	2.72	3.07	3.45	3.88	4.36	4.90	5.49	6.89	8.60	10.70	13.26	16.39
14	1.51	1.73	1.98	2.26	2.58	2.94	3.34	3.80	4.31	4.89	5.53	6.26	7.99	10.15	12.84	16.18	20.32
15	1.56	1.80	2.08	2.40	2.76	3.17	3.64	4.18	4.78	5.47	6.25	7.14	9.27	11.97	15.41	19.74	25.20
16	1.60	1.87	2.18	2.54	2.95	3.43	3.97	4.59	5.31	6.13	7.07	8.14	10.75	14.13	18.49	24.09	31.24
17	1.65	1.95	2.29	2.69	3.16	3.70	4.33	5.05	5.90	6.87	7.99	9.28	12.47	16.67	22.19	29.38	38.74
18	1.70	2.03	2.41	2.85	3.38	4.00	4.72	5.56	6.54	7.69	9.02	10.58	14.46	19.67	26.62	35.85	48.03
19	1.75	2.11	2.53	3.02	3.62	4.32	5.14	6.12	7.26	8.61	10.20	12.06	16.78	23.21	31.95	43.74	59.57
20	1.81	2.19	2.65	3.21	3.87	4.66	5.60	6.73	8.06	9.65	11.52	13.74	19.46	27.39	38.34	53.36	73.86

TABLE 11–3   Computation of Growth Rates of EPS of IBM by Two Methods

	Method 1		Method 2	
Year	IBM Earnings per Share	Annual Increase		
1984	10.77	19.1%	1984 Earnings per share	10.77
83	9.04	22.3	1976 Earnings per share	3.99
82	7.39	31.3	1984 EPS/1976 EPS	2.70
81	5.63	−7.7		
80	6.10	18.2		
79	5.16	−3.0		
78	5.32	16.2		
77	4.58	14.8		
76	3.99			

Average annual growth rate:

1976–84   13.9%

1980–84   16.6%

Average annual growth rate from compound-interest table

1976–84   13.2%

Source: Data from Value Line Investment Survey, 1985.

In Table 11–4 we analyze the causes for increases in EPS in terms of two factors: changes in book value and changes in profitability.

From the table, the increase in earnings of IBM in 1977 was 16.2 percent, which was caused by a 1.1 percent increase in book value and an increase in profitability of 14.9 percent.

Over the period 1976–84, IBM had an average annual increase of EPS of 13.9 percent, which was caused by an average annual increase of book value of 9.4 percent and an increase in profitability of 4.3 percent.

In the last four years, 1981–84, the average rate of return on net worth was 22.2 percent, as against 21.6 percent for the whole period, and the average annual increase in book value was 11.4 percent, as against 9.4 percent for the whole period 1976–84. In other words, on the basis of the historical performance we have analyzed, we find no evidence suggesting that the past earnings trend will slow down.

The second framework for the estimate of the future growth rate was:

$$\text{Growth potential of EPS} = \frac{\text{Sales per share}_t}{\text{Sales per share}_{t-1}}$$
$$\times \frac{\text{Net profit margin}_t}{\text{Net profit margin}_{t-1}}$$

With this formula, the key determinants of changes in EPS are attributable to changes in sales per share and changes in net profit margin. In Table 11–5 we analyze the record of EPS of IBM in terms of these factors.

Over the whole period 1976–84, the EPS of IBM grew at an average annual rate of 13.9 percent, which was caused by an average annual sales

TABLE 11–4 Analysis of Causes of Earnings Growth of IBM, 1976–1984

	1976	1977	1978	1979	1980	1981	1982	1983	1984	Average 1976–1984
Book value per share	21.15	21.39	23.14	25.64	28.18	30.66	33.13	38.02	43.23	
Rate of return on net worth (%)[a]	18.8	21.6	23.1	20.1	21.7	18.2	22.1	23.6	24.8	21.6%
$BVPS_t/BVPS_{t-1}$		1.011	1.082	1.108	1.099	1.088	1.081	1.148	1.137	1.094
$rr(CE)_t/rr(CE)_{t-1}$		1.149	1.069	0.87	1.08	0.839	1.214	1.068	1.051	1.043
$\left[\dfrac{BVPS_t}{BVPS_{t-1}} \times \dfrac{rr(CE)_t}{rr(CE)_{t-1}}\right]^{\text{b}} = EGR$		.162	.157	−.04	.187	−.09	.312	.226	.195	.139

[a] Since IBM did not have preferred stock outstanding, the rate of return on net worth was the same as the rate of return on common equity.
[b] BVPS and $rr(CE)$ came from Table 11–1.
Source: Data from *Value Line Investment Survey,* 1985.

TABLE 11–5 Analysis of Causes of Earnings Growth of IBM, 1976–1984

	1976	1977	1978	1979	1980	1981	1982	1983	1984	Average 1976–1984
Sales per share	27.05	30.74	36.14	39.18	44.90	49.08	57.04	65.79	74.98	
Net profit margin (%)	14.7	15.0	14.8	13.2	13.6	11.4	12.8	13.7	14.3	13.7%
SPS_t/SPS_{t-1}		1.136	1.176	1.084	1.146	1.093	1.162	1.153	1.140	1.136
NPM_t/NPM_{t-1}		1.020	.987	.892	1.030	.838	1.123	1.070	1.044	1.0005
$\left[\dfrac{SPS_t}{SPS_{t-1}} \times \dfrac{NPM_t}{NPM_{t-1}}\right]^{\text{a}} = EGR$		.159	.161	−.033	.180	−.084	.305	.234	.190	.139

[a] SPS and NPM came from Table 11–1.
Source: Data from *Value Line Investment Survey,* 1985.

increase of 13.6 percent. The net profit margin for the whole period remained the same.

In the four years 1981–84, the average annual increase of sales per share was 13.7 percent, about the same as the average for the whole period. The net profit margin in the years 1981–84 was 13.1 percent, which was slightly lower than the average for the whole period at 13.7 percent. In other words, both determinants of EPS remained quite strong in the most recent period compared to the average of the whole period. The evidence seems to suggest again that IBM can continue its past growth rate of EPS into the foreseeable future.

Estimating Growth Potential of the EPS of an Established Company: Dow Chemical

Now, we turn to the estimate of growth potential of EPS of another large established company, Dow Chemical. In Figure 11–6 we see some of Dow Chemical's significant statistics from 1968 to 1984 with estimates for 1985 by the *Value Line Investment Survey*.

Past Growth Rate of Sales per Share

In Table 11–6 we compute the growth rate of sales per share of Dow Chemical by two methods. The first method of averaging annual percentage changes of sales per share provides an average annual growth rate of 9.5 percent for the period 1976–84. The second method using the compound-interest table yields a slightly lower growth rate of 8.9 percent.

TABLE 11–6   Computation of Growth of Sales of Dow Chemical by Two Methods

	Method 1		Method 2	
Year	Dow Chemical Sales per Share	Annual Increase		
1984	60.07	7.4%	1984 Sales per share	60.07
83	55.91	2.2	1976 Sales per share	30.48
82	54.68	−12.8	1984 Sales/1976 sales	1.97
81	62.69	7.8	(over eight years)	
80	58.16	13.9		
79	51.08	34.4		
78	38.02	11.4		
77	34.13	12.0		
76	30.48			
Average annual growth rate			Average annual growth rate	
1976–84	9.5%		from compound-interest table	
1980–84	3.7%		1976–84 8.9%	

Source: Data from *Value Line Investment Survey,* 1985.

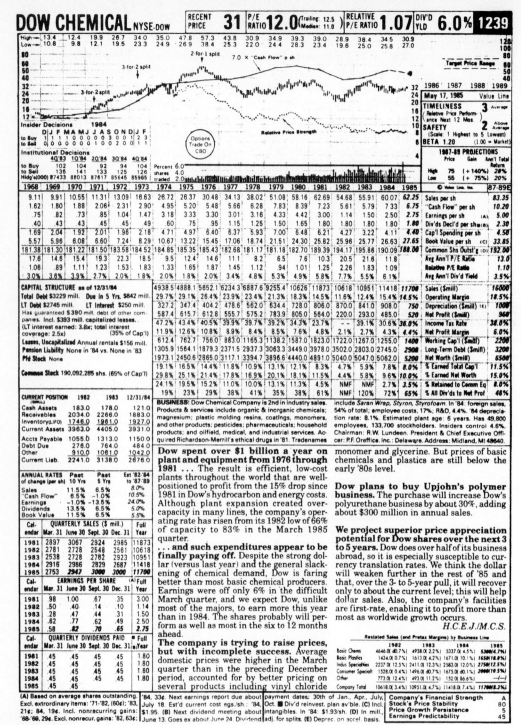

FIGURE 11–6

Source: Value Line Investment Survey, 1985. ©1985 Value Line, Inc. Reprinted by permission.

Past Growth Rate of Earnings per Share

In Table 11–7 we compute the growth rate of EPS by two methods. The method of averaging annual percentage changes of EPS provides an annual growth rate of 4.9 percent for the period 1976–84. However, by using the compound-interest table we find no growth in earnings per share during the period 1976–84. The difference between the two methods lies in the fact that the first method was based on year-to-year changes, and with the second method we look at the whole period for indication of a trend.

Estimating the Future Growth Potential of EPS of Dow Chemical

In Table 11–8 we analyze the causes of earnings growth of Dow Chemical during 1976–84 by the framework:

$$\text{Earnings growth rate} = \frac{\text{BVP}_t}{\text{BVP}_{t-1}} \times \frac{rr(\text{CE})_t}{rr(\text{CE})_{t-1}}$$

The growth in earnings during 1976–84 was at an annual rate of 5.3 percent, which was caused by an annual growth rate of book value of 7.2 percent and an average annual reduction in profitability of 1.7 percent.

The performance of the company in the years 1981–84 was not as good as the average for the whole period. The average rate of return on net worth was 7.8 percent, compared with the average of the whole period at 14 percent. The average annual increase in book value per share in the years 1981–84 was 2.4 percent, compared with 7.2 percent, the average for the whole period 1976–84.

As we mentioned in Chapter 10, two-thirds of the business of Dow Chemical is in basic chemicals, which is a cyclical business and also one of low

TABLE 11–7   Computation of Growth Rate of EPS of Dow Chemical by Two Methods

	Method 1		Method 2	
Year	Dow Chemical Earnings per Share	Annual Increase		
1984	2.50	66.7%	1984 Earnings per share	2.50
83	1.50	31.6	1976 Earnings per share	3.30
82	1.14	−62.0	1984 EPS/1976 EPS	0.76
81	3.00	−32.1		
80	4.42	2.1		
79	4.33	37.0		
78	3.16	5.0		
77	3.01	− 8.8		
76	3.30			
Average annual growth rate			Average annual growth rate	
1976–84	4.9%		from compound-interest table	
1980–84	1.3%		1976–84 0%	

Source: Data from *Value Line Investment Survey,* 1985.

TABLE 11–8 Analysis of Causes of Earnings Growth of Dow Chemical, 1976–1984

	1976	1977	1978	1979	1980	1981	1982	1983	1984	Average 1976–1984
Book value per share	15.45	17.06	18.74	21.51	24.30	25.82	25.96	25.77	26.63	
Rate of return on net worth (%)	21.4	17.8	16.9	20.1	18.1	11.5	4.4	5.8	9.6	14%
$BVPS_t/BVPS_{t-1}$		1.104	1.098	1.148	1.130	1.063	1.005	.993	1.033	1.072
$rr(CE)_t/rr(CE)_{t-1}$		.832	.949	1.189	.900	.635	.383	1.318	1.655	.983
$\left[\dfrac{BVPS_t}{BVPS_{t-1}} \times \dfrac{rr(CE)_t}{rr(CE)_{t-1}}\right] = EGR$		−.081	.042	.365	.017	−.325	−.615	.309	.710	.053

Source: Data from Value Line Investment Survey, 1985.

profit margin. On the basis of our analysis of its performance in the nine years 1976–84, and based also on our understanding of its basic business, it seems that the earnings growth potential in the foreseeable future will not exceed 5 percent to 6 percent.

Computation of Earnings Growth Potential of Dow Chemical by Another Framework

The market price of Dow Chemical (mean of high and low for the year) has been selling at about one-third higher than its book value since 1978. From the financial statements of the company we know that they did not try to sell new shares to increase capital surplus and book value. In other words, the increase in book value per share during 1976–84 was all derived from retention of earnings. For corporations like Dow Chemical where the increase in book value comes only from retention of earnings, we have indicated previously a simpler framework for the estimate of future growth of earnings:

$$\text{Growth potential} = \text{Average rate of return on common equity}$$
$$\times (1 - \text{Average divided payout ratio})$$

See Table 11–9 for the computations of earnings growth potential of Dow Chemical in accordance with the framework just given. The estimated growth potential of EPS will be about 4.8 percent.

These two frameworks provide us with two similar estimates of potential earnings growth for Dow Chemical in the area of 5 percent to 5.5 percent.

How Accurate Are Estimates of Earnings by Analysts?

Why should we pay so much attention to determining the quality of earnings and earnings growth potential of a firm? After all, analysts of different brokerage firms estimate earnings of different corporations, and these estimates are usually available to clients and in different publications such as *S&P's Earnings Forecast, Money, Business Week, Forbes,* and others.

There are several good reasons why we must analyze and evaluate such important questions regarding earnings. First, analysts provide only earnings estimates for the current year, and these estimates vary over a wide range.[4] Nowhere can we obtain an indication of the quality of earnings of a firm. Second, we are interested in not simply the earnings estimate for the current year, but rather the earnings growth potential for the next few years. Third, sometimes the earnings estimates by analysts can be completely wrong. A case in point is Baldwin United. Baldwin United was a large insurance and

---

[4] Anne B. Fisher, "How Good are Wall Street's Security Analysts?" *Fortune,* Oct. 1984.

TABLE 11-9   Computation of Earnings Growth Rate Potential of Dow Chemical

	1976	1977	1978	1979	1980	1981	1982	1983	1984	Average 1976–84
Rate of return on net worth (%)	21.4	17.8	16.9	20.1	18.1	11.5	4.4	5.8	9.6	14%
Dividend payout ratio (%)	29	38	41	35	38	61	158	120	72	65.8%
Dividend retention ratio										34.2%

Growth potential of EPS = Average rate of return on common equity × (1 − Average dividend payout ratio)

= 14% × (1 − 65.8%)

= 4.8%

Source: Data from *Value Line Investment Survey,* 1985.

financial services firm, growing very rapidly in both revenue and earnings up to 1982. Many well-known analysts and fund managers on Wall Street considered it a super growth stock and recommended it very highly to investors in 1982.

A young analyst, Mr. James S. Chano, was told by his boss to look over the company. He was a thorough analyst, digging into piles of financial documents and trying to find out how Baldwin United had produced its fast-growing earnings. To his surprise, he found the earnings were not genuine. They came from accounting gimmicks, questionable tax credits, and complex asset-shuffling. Mr. Chano's firm cited his study and recommended to their clients to sell the stock. Few on Wall Street believed him, and those analysts who recommended the stock earlier continued to offer a variety of reasons why this stock was a strong buy.

However, six months later the signs of financial difficulty began to surface bit by bit, and the stock began to fall. In another six months, the company went into bankruptcy.[5] This serves to remind us that even the consensus among well-known analysts was not totally dependable.

SUMMARY

Investors in general are keenly interested in the growth potential of a corporation. It is important to distinguish between two types of increases in earnings of a corporation. One type is due to cyclical recovery and it is short-term. The other type of increase represents a long-term trend of growth that will likely persist into the future.

The determinants of earnings per share were traced in two frameworks:

1. EPS = Book value per share $\times$ Rate of return on common equity

$$= \frac{\text{Common equity}}{\text{Number of common shares}} \times \frac{\text{Net profits}}{\text{Common equity}}$$

2. EPS = Sales per share $\times$ Net profit margin

$$= \frac{\text{Sales}}{\text{Number of common share}} \times \frac{\text{Net profits}}{\text{Sales}}$$

On the basis of the two frameworks, three alternative formulas were derived and illustrated for the estimate of earnings growth potential of a corporation:

1. Earnings growth rate $= \dfrac{\text{BVPS}_t}{\text{BVPS}_{t-1}} \times \dfrac{rr(\text{CE})_t}{rr(\text{CE})_{t-1}} - 1$

---

[5] Damon Darlin, "Picking a Loser: Young Analyst Defied Experts and Foresaw Baldwin United's Ills," *Wall Street Journal*, Sept. 28, 1983.

2. Earnings growth rate $= \dfrac{\text{Sales PS}_t}{\text{Sales PS}_{t-1}} \times \dfrac{\text{NPM}_t}{\text{NPM}_{t-1}} - 1$

3. Earnings growth rate $=$ Average rate of return on common equity
    $\times$ (1 $-$ Average divided payout ratio)

The third formula is based on two assumptions. First, the increase in book value per share is assumed to come only from retention of earnings. Second, the rate of return on common equity of the corporation is relatively stable over time, that is, from one business cycle to another.

In this chapter we have discussed the methodologies that one can follow in estimating the earnings growth rate of a stock based on financial analysis. For professional analysts, this method should be supplemented by an analysis of the operations of the firm and its management, because analysts have the opportunity to visit the firm and interview its management. However, for the general public the methodologies described here provide perhaps the only reasonable framework to use to estimate the potential earnings growth rate of a firm.

QUESTIONS AND PROBLEMS

1. Choose a growth stock, analyze its record of earnings in the last seven years in terms of causal factors, and estimate its earnings growth potential.

2. Select a large established company, analyze its record of sales and earnings per share in the last seven years, and estimate its earnings growth potential.

3. Compute the growth rate of EPS of the General Motors Corporation in the last ten years using two different methods: (a) averaging annual percentage changes and (b) using the compound-interest table.

4. What procedure will you use in estimating earnings per share of a corporation in the next two years?

5. How important do you consider the factor of management in the evaluation of an enterprise for investment purposes? How do you appraise the quality of management?

6. What is the influence of a company's dividend policy on its growth of earnings per share?

7. Discuss the interrelationships between the growth rate of sales per share and the growth rate of earnings per share.

8. Explain the interrelationships among factors determining EPS in Figure 11–4.

9. Investors in general expect that most corporations will achieve some growth in EPS in the years ahead. Why?

10. As shown below in Figure 11–7, *Value Line* established that the potential earnings growth rate of RCA from 1982–84 to 1987–89

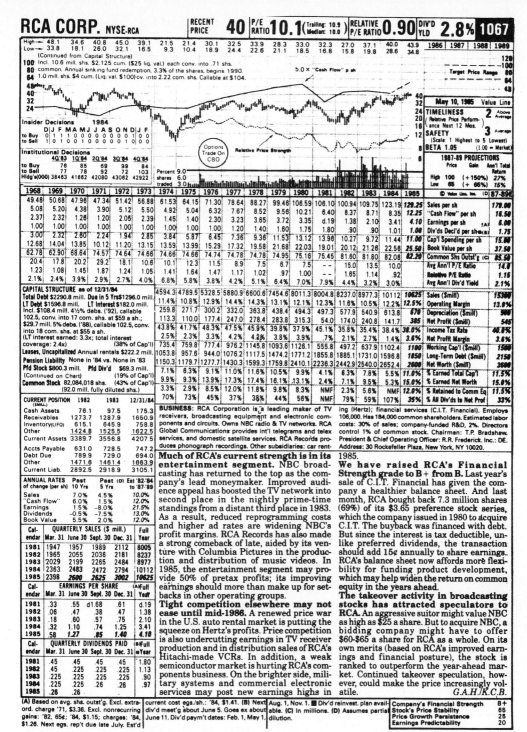

FIGURE 11-7

Source: Value Line Investment Survey, 1985. ©1985 Value Line, Inc. Reprinted by permission.

will be about 21.5 percent annually. Do you agree with this estimate? Substantiate your answer with your own analysis and calculations.

REFERENCES

Babcock, Guilford C. "The Concept of Sustainable Growth." *Financial Analysts Journal,* May–June 1970.

Business Week. "Do Mergers Really Work?" June 3, 1985; "The Computer Slump." June 24, 1985.

Darlin, Damon, "Picking a Loser: Young Analyst Defied Experts and Foresaw Baldwin United's Ills." *Wall Street Journal,* Sept. 28, 1983.

Fisher, Anne B. "How Good are Wall Street's Security Analysts?" *Fortune,* Oct. 1984.

Givoly, Dan, and Lakonishok, Joseph. "The Quality of Analysts' Forecast of Earnings." *Financial Analysts Journal,* Sept.–Oct. 1984.

Goodman, Sam R. *Techniques of Profitability Analysis.* New York: John Wiley & Sons, 1970.

Hawkins, Eugene A., Chamberlin, Stanley C., and Daniel, Wayne E. "Earnings Expectations and Security Prices." *Financial Analysts Journal,* Sept.–Oct. 1984.

Kisor, Manown, Jr. "The Financial Aspects of Growth." *Financial Analysts Journal,* March–April 1964.

Larsen, Robert A., and Murphy, J. E. Jr. "New Insight into Changes in Earnings per Share." *Financial Analysts Journal,* March–April 1975.

Makridakis, Spyros, Wheelwright, Steven C., and McGee, Victor E. *Forecasting: Methods & Applications.* New York: John Wiley & Sons, 1983.

Niederhoffer, Victor and Reagen, P. J. "Earnings Changes, Analysts Forecasts and Stock Prices." *Financial Analysts Journal,* May–June 1972.

O'Higgins, Michael B. "All-Star Strikeouts — Analysts' Earnings Projections are Way Off the Mark." *Barron's,* June 4, 1984.

Pakkala, A. L. "Fixed Costs and Earnings Predictions." *Financial Analysts Journal,* Jan.–Feb. 1979.

Zacks, Leonard. "EPS Forecasts — Accuracy is not Enough." *Financial Analysts Journal,* March–April 1979.

12

Analysis and Measurement of Uncertainty of Return of Common Stocks

The outstanding feature of common stocks is the uncertainty of their returns—both positive and negative. The factors contributing to the uncertainty of returns from common stocks can be classified into two categories: macroeconomic and microeconomic.

1. Macroeconomic:
   a. Fluctuation in general business conditions
   b. Changes in inflation
   c. Changes in market interest rates
   d. Changes in technology, taste, and in political and social areas
   e. Changes in expectation and psychology of market participants
2. Microeconomic:
   a. Industrywide
      Changes in demand due to new substitutes and/or other factors
      Changes in industry capacity
      Changes in price competition
      Emergence or resolution of labor problems
      Changes in government regulations
   b. Company
      Success or failure in introducing new products
      Effective or inadequate cost control
      Optimum or excessive financial leverage
      Changes in quality of management

It is, of course, important to know the different factors contributing to the uncertainty of returns from common stocks. However, when investors consider the purchase or sale of a stock, they want to know a lot more: What is the possibility of dividend increase or reduction and how much will it be for the next period? To what extent is the current price of a stock vulnerable if recession comes? If worse comes to worst, what percentage decline can one expect in price? In other words, investors want a quantitative measurement to indicate the degree of uncertainty of returns from the stock so that they can evaluate the current price of the stock and compare it with others.

HOW TO DEAL WITH UNCERTAINTY

There is a continuing controversy among economists, statisticians, investment theorists, investment professionals, and others on how best to deal with problems of uncertainty in decision making. Since this question is of critical importance in investing, we will cite below the views of several scholars.

Frank H. Knight

Professor Knight's book, *Risk, Uncertainty and Profit* (1921), is a classic in economics. In his text he distinguishes between the concept of risk and the concept of uncertainty. He states that risk pertains to situations like insurance where empirical evidence can be relied upon to formulate probabilities of, say, how long an average person aged 21 can expect to live in the U.S. Uncertainty, on the other hand, pertains to situations where one can only estimate the probable outcome, but the situation is unique in that the past experience of the decision maker cannot be used to formulate frequency probability as in the case of risk. He concludes that entrepreneurial decisions and profits belong in the theory of uncertainty, not in that of risk. The following quotation illustrates his thinking.

> The theoretical difference between the probability connected with an estimate and that involved in such phenomena as are dealt with by insurance is, however, of the greatest importance, and is clearly discernible in nearly any instance of the exercise of judgment. Take as an illustration any typical business decision. A manufacturer is considering the advisability of making a large commitment in increasing the capacity of his works. He "figures" more or less on the proposition, taking account as well as possible of the various factors more or less susceptible of measurement, but the final result is an "estimate" of the probable outcome of any proposed course of action. What is the "probability" of error (strictly, of any assigned degree of error) in the judgment? It is manifestly meaningless to speak of either calculating such a probability *a priori* or of determining it empirically by studying a large number of instances. The essential and outstanding fact is that the "instance" in question is so entirely unique that there are no others or not a sufficient number to make it possible to tabulate enough like it to form a basis for any inference of value about any real probability in the case we are interested in. The same obviously applies to the most of conduct and not to business decisions alone.[1]

[1]Frank H. Knight, *Risk, Uncertainty and Profit* (Boston, Mass.: Houghton Mifflin Co., 1921), p. 226.

Frank Ramsey and Leonard J. Savage

Ramsey and Savage, two famous statisticians, represent a more recent school of thought on how to deal with problems of uncertainty. They argued that in problems of uncertainty, intelligent individuals should in general attach to prospective events weights that obey the laws of probability theory, regardless of how their degree of beliefs concerning these events are derived. In other words, personal beliefs concerning future events, in their view, can be formulated in the form of probabilities, and these subjective probabilities should apply to problems of uncertainty such as forecasting future stock prices, outcomes of elections, and other entrepreneurial decisions.[2]

John M. Keynes and William Fellner

The famous economist, John M. Keynes, authored *A Treatise on Probability* (1921) in which he expresses his view that subjective probability is of less quality than objective probability and, therefore, should be discounted when it is used in decision making. However, he did not specify how to discount subjective probability.[3]

Professor Fellner, author of *Probability and Profit* (1965), discusses at length the differences between subjective and objective probabilities and their relation to the theory of profit. While he is sympathetic to the growing discussions on subjective probability as a concept and tool in decision making, he, like Keynes before him, expresses his reservations. He indicates that his views may be described as semiprobabilistic views:

> In my view, subjective degrees of beliefs of all sorts — degrees of belief relating to events of various kinds — should be regarded as probabilities. And yet, I shall now add to this statement an explanation which in a sense qualifies the statement.
>
> **A Semiprobabilistic Position**
>
> While the view which this book will take of the concept of probability is subjectivistic, the writer's views about the central problems of decision theory may be described as semiprobabilistic views. By this I mean to say that in my opinion the directly observable weights which reasonable and consistent individuals attach to specific types of prospects are not necessarily the genuine (undistorted) subjective probabilities of the prospects, although these *decision weights* of consistently acting individuals do bear an understandable relation to probabilities, i.e., to weights that do satisfy the rules of probability theory.
>
> A good many reasonable decision makers — though by no means all — seem to act differently depending on whether they act under the influence of shaky degrees of belief, i.e., of probabilities the numerical values of which are highly unstable in their minds, or act under the guidance of firm and stable degrees

---

[2]Frank Ramsey, *The Foundations of Mathematics and Other Logical Essays* (New York: Humanities Press, 1950); Leonard Savage, *The Foundations of Statistics* (New York: John Wiley & Sons, Inc., 1954); William Fellner, *Probability and Profit* (Homewood, Ill.: Irwin, 1965), pp. 31–32.

[3]John M. Keynes, *A Treatise on Probability* (New York: Macmillian & Co., 1921).

of belief. Degrees of belief that are highly unstable are appreciably influenced by what a few pages further on will be defined as "elusive hypotheses." These beliefs usually also have the property of being interpersonally controversial even among the well informed and even among individuals who exchange their information. Such degrees of belief are apt to become unconvincing in retrospect, a fact of which individuals are well aware in advance. There is little observable difference between the content of the statement that many reasonable decision makers are influenced by whether their degrees of belief are or are not *shared* by groups of other individuals, and the content of the statement that these decision makers are influenced by whether their degrees of belief are or are not expected to stay *stable in their own minds*. It seems to me that both these statments make good sense.[4]

Jerry Felsen

Professor Felsen, who wrote *Cybernetic Approach to Stock Market Analysis* (1975), is dissatisfied with the existing capital market theories. He noted their deficiencies as follows:

Almost all works relevant to the capital asset pricing model pertain to the analysis of Alpha and Beta. Very few attempts have been made to analyze γ and R_M as functions of available information. These tasks, of course, correspond to investment selection and timing which have been generally ignored by many academicians. The task of selecting and managing an investment portfolio is a dynamic sequential process, but the time dimension is largely neglected by conventional approaches to portfolio management. The investment-decision problem is clearly a dynamic one, and portfolio theory is defective as long as it does not incorporate the time element into its basic structure.

Contemporary CMT [Capital Market Theory] has two other defects. First, present CMT makes use of techniques developed for decision analysis under conditions of risk, but the stock market is so poorly understood that investment analysis really involves decision making under uncertainty rather than risk because the relevant probabilities and statistics are usually not known in advance. Thus, the design of investment-decision systems should be based on principles for decision making under uncertainty rather than risk (cf. Felsen 1975).

Second, conventional methods seem to yield many decisions that are satisfying rather than optimal: There are no formal methods for analysis of past investment decisions in an attempt to improve on future decisions. In other words, there seems to be very little learning from past experiences with the aim of improving the investment-decision system's future performance.

There are two reasons why the usefulness of existing CMT is rather limited. First, it has been developed within a statistical framework, but statistical tools seem to be inadequate for the synthesis of investment-decision systems. Second, present CMT is based on the assumption that the efficient market

---

[4]William Fellner, *Probability and Profit* (Homewood, Ill.: Irwin, 1965), pp. 4–5.

model is a very accurate representation of reality. This assumption may be questioned.[5]

Professor Felsen also argues that "investment analysis, if it is to succeed, requires simultaneous processing of very complicated information patterns. The investment policy must reflect fundamental, psychological, technical, and other factors affecting the market."[6] To contend with a very complicated investment problem, he proposes a *cybernetic approach* to stock market analysis, which aims at the integration of several elements: (1) cybernetic concepts and artificial intelligence, (2) modern computer technology in programming the human judgment process, and (3) the original ideas of the analyst or the investor. He explains his cybernetic approach in these words:

> Thus we design our cybernetic investment-decision systems as man-machine interactive systems, where each partner performs those tasks of which the other is not capable. Usually the man provides creativity and originality, makes intuitive judgments and performs inductive reasoning, or generates new ideas and concepts. The machine's main task is reliable processing of extremely complex information patterns and synthesizing them into optimal investment decisions—this it can often do better than the human analyst. In this way the machine amplifies human intellect. A coupling of the creativity of the human being with the large information-processing capacity of the computer may then result in *man-machine synergism* which will enable the combined decision system to solve problems that neither partner could successfully handle alone. Thus, although neither the human analyst alone nor the computer alone can consistently outperform market averages, a cybernetic (man-machine) investment-decision system may be able to do so.[7]

SUBJECTIVE PROBABILITY — THE MARKOWITZ APPROACH

From these different views on problems of uncertainty, we can see that the controversy about which is the better, more appropriate method to deal with problems of uncertainty is by no means settled.

Harry Markowitz, the pioneer of modern portfolio theories, adopted the *subjective probability approach* to deal with the uncertainty of returns of common stocks. Following Markowitz, the authors of most texts on investments who are currently discussing the uncertainty of returns from common stocks do so also in terms of the subjective probability approach.

We shall discuss Markowitz's portfolio theories in detail in Chapter 18. At this point, however, we will examine his system of portfolio theories,

---

[5]Jerry Felsen, *Cybernetic Approach to Stock Market Analysis* New York: CDS Publishing Co., 1975.

[6]Ibid., p. xviii.

[7]Ibid, p. xix.

especially those parts dealing with risk and return of individual securities and portfolios.

Markowitz was a master theoretician. He built a theoretical, quantitative model of portfolio theory in successive steps as follows:

1.   Expected return and risk of an individual security
2.   Expected return and risk of a portfolio
3.   Efficient portfolios and frontier
4.   Indifference curve of return and risk of individual investors
5.   Optimum portfolio for a given investor[8]

Risk and Return of an Individual Security in the Markowitz Approach

Following the lead of Ramsey and Savage, Markowitz suggested that individual investors are rational and can use personal or subjective probabilities for the estimates of expected return and risk of an individual stock. We illustrate his approach with an example below.

Rate of Return on Common Stocks

The return on common stock includes both dividend payments and changes in the price of the stock, resulting in capital gain or loss. The rate of return on common stock is usually expressed as a percent of the original cost of investment on an annual basis. The formula for the rate of return is:

$$\text{Annual rate of return} = \frac{D + (P_1 - P_0)}{P_0}$$

where:

D = dividend for the year
P_0 = the price of the stock at the beginning of the year
P_1 = the price of the stock at the end of the year

For example, you bought ABC stock at \$40 a year ago. During the last 12 months you received a dividend of \$2, and the price of the stock is now \$46. The annual rate of return (before taxes) is:

$$\text{Annual rate of return} = \frac{\$2 + (\$46 - \$40)}{\$40} = \frac{\$8}{\$40} = 20\%$$

[8]Harry M. Markowitz, "Portfolio Selection." *The Journal of Finance*, March 1952; *Portfolio Selection* (New Haven, Conn.: Cowles Foundation for Research in Economics, Yale University, 1959).

Expected Return

Assume that you are now considering the purchase of General Motors stock. As an intelligent investor you must first estimate the expected return as well as the expected risk of the stock, and then decide whether or not it pays to incur the risk for the expected level of return.

To obtain an estimate of expected return and risk of GM stock, you need to:

1. Estimate and list the realistically possible returns that you can obtain from the investment in GM stock.
2. Estimate the likelihood of occurrence of each possible return.

In other words, you have to formulate a probability distribution of possible returns from the investment. The expected return will be the weighted average of the probability distribution. In equation form, the expected return can be expressed as:

$$E(r_i) = \sum P_i r_i$$

where:

$E(r_i)$ = expected return
r_i = each possible return
P_i = the probability of each possible return

Table 12–1 shows the calculations of expected return on GM stock. The first column of the table lists your estimates of seven possible returns on GM stock. The second column lists your estimates of the probability of occur-

TABLE 12–1   Expected Return Calculations for General Motors Stock

Possible Return r_i	Probability P_i	Possible Return × Probability $r_i P_i$
20%	.05	1.00%
15	.15	2.25
10	.30	3.00
5	.20	1.00
0	.15	0
−5	.10	−0.50
−10	.05	−0.50
	1.00	$E(r_i)$ = 6.25%

rence for each possible return. The second column must add up to 1, meaning that all possible outcomes have been included. The third column shows possible returns weighted by their probabilities. The sum of the third column is the expected return. The expected return on GM stock in this case is 6.25 percent.

RISK OF INVESTMENT MEASURED BY STANDARD DEVIATION

The risk of investment in GM stock rests on the fact that the actual return to be realized can be different from the expected return. The best statistical method to measure the degree of variability or dispersion of possible returns from the expected return is the *standard deviation,* which measures the deviation of each possible return from the weighted mean of the possible return. The formula is:

$$\sigma = \sqrt{\sum_{i}^{n} P_i [r_i - E(r_i)]^2}$$

where:

σ = standard deviation of the expected return
P_i = probability of each possible return
r_i = possible rate of return
$E(r_i)$ = expected return

See Table 12–2 for the calculation of the risk of GM stock as measured by the standard deviation.

TABLE 12–2   Calculations of the Risk of GM Stock as Measured by Standard Deviation

Possible Return r_i	Expected[a] Return $E(r_i)$	Deviation from $E(r_i)$ d_i	(Deviation)^2 d_i^2	Probability P_i	(Deviation)^2 × Probability $P_i d_i^2$
20%	6.25%	13.75%	.01891	.05	.00095
15	6.25	8.75	.00766	.15	.00115
10	6.25	3.75	.00141	.30	.00042
5	6.25	− 1.25	.00016	.20	.00003
0	6.25	− 6.25	.00391	.15	.00059
− 5	6.25	−11.25	.01266	.10	.00127
−10	6.25	−16.25	.02641	.05	.00132
				Variance σ^2 =	.00573

[a] Expected return is calculated in Table 12–1.

The risk of GM stock as measured by standard deviation is 7.6%.

$$\sigma = \sqrt{.00573} = .0757 = 7.6\%$$

Standard Deviation and Normal Distribution

In statistics, if a probability distribution is bell-shaped and symmetrical, it is known as a *normal distribution*. The standard deviation of a normal distribution has some interesting relationships with the area under the normal curve. See Figure 12–1.

Although the probability distribution of returns of GM stock or other stocks does not strictly qualify as a normal distribution, we assume at this point that they can be approximated with the normal distribution. Therefore, the characteristics of a standard deviation for a normal distribution can be used for investments in common stocks. The expected return and standard deviation of GM stock are calculated at 6.25 percent and 7.6 percent, respectively.

Treating the probability distribution of GM stock as if it were a normal distribution, our calculations indicate that the actual return of GM stock will fall into the range from −1.35 percent to 13.85 percent (6.25% ± 7.6% = −1.35% to 13.85%), 68.3 percent of the time. The probability distribution of GM stock is charted with values for $E(r)$ and σ in Figure 12–2.

Observation within the range	Percent of area under the normal curve
$E(r) \pm 1\sigma$	68.3%
$E(r) \pm 2\sigma$	95.5%
$E(r) \pm 3\sigma$	99.7%

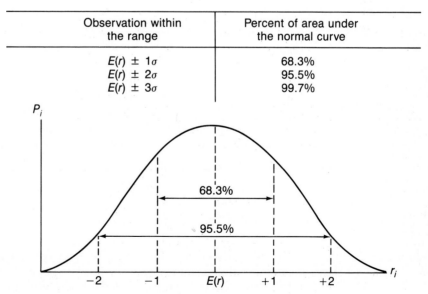

FIGURE 12–1   The Standard Deviation of a Normal Distribution

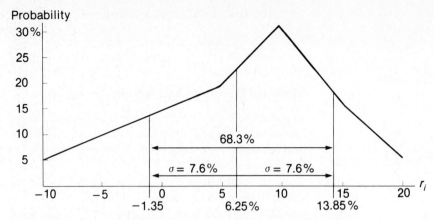

FIGURE 12–2   Probability Distribution of Return on GM Stock

Using the Markowitz Approach to Determine Probabilities of Outcomes of a Stock

What we have discussed above on calculations of rate of returns, expected returns, and standard deviation of possible returns from the expected return represents the Markowitz approach to the estimates of the expected return and risk of an individual stock, and this approach is adopted currently by most authors of texts on investments.

We proceed to discuss methods for the formulation of probabilities of outcomes of an individual stock as envisaged by Markowitz. Markowitz discussed this problem in relation to institutions that employ security analysts and fund managers. In his view, security analysts can develop the probability distribution in three ways:

1. Security analysts examine the past experience of the company and use the findings for the formulation of a probability distribution. Analysts assume that past rates of return and their variability of the stock are good estimates for the future.
2. Analysts form independent opinions about the future of the company and the stock without going through analysis of past experience of the company.
3. Analysts can combine approaches (1) analysis of past experience and (2) forming independent opinions about the future of the stock, and arrive at a synthesis.

The following quotation illustrates Markowitz's view as to what factors a careful analyst should review and analyze before he formulates his probability distribution of outcomes for the future of a stock.

The Security Analyst is the meteorologist of stocks and bonds. If he is thorough, his statements about the future of a security will be based on general conditions and prospects for the economy and the market; the nature of possible new developments in the industry; the past performance, financial structure, and other matters relating to the opportunities and dangers confronting the corporation; and, finally, the position of the particular security vis-a-vis others of the corporation.[9]

CALCULATING RISK AND RETURN OF PORTFOLIOS USING THE MARKOWITZ APPROACH

Having completed the risk and return analysis of individual security, Markowitz went on to show how to estimate the expected return and risk of a portfolio.

Expected Return of a Portfolio

The expected return of a portfolio is simply a weighted average of the expected return of individual stocks in the portfolio. The formula for its calculation is:

$$E_p = \sum_{i=1}^{N} X_i E_i$$

where:

E_p = expected return of a portfolio
X_i = proportion of total portfolio invested in security i
E_i = expected return of security i
N = number of securities in the portfolio

Expected Risk of a Portfolio

The expected risk of a portfolio, Markowitz stated, depends on three factors:

1. The standard deviation of possible returns of each security.
2. The correlation between each pair of securities in the portfolio.
3. The proportion of each security represented in the portfolio.[10]

In general, the lower the correlation among securities in the portfolio, the lower is the expected risk of the portfolio. Therefore, for reduction of risk

[9]Harry M. Markowitz, "Portfolio Selection," p. 28.
[10]Ibid., p. 19.

of a portfolio, the investor should include securities with low or no correlation to one another, or even better, include securities having negative correlations. But in real life, there are few stocks (with the exception of gold stocks) that are negatively correlated with the overall market performance because most issues are influenced by the general business conditions.

Other Aspects of the Markowitz Portfolio Theories

Markowitz's portfolio theories are fully discussed in Chapter 18. Readers who are interested, at this point, in seeing the whole body of Markowitz's theories can proceed to that chapter after finishing this chapter.

OUR VIEWS ON HOW BEST TO DEAL WITH PROBLEMS OF UNCERTAINTY

Philosophically, we lean toward the position of Keynes and Fellner. We believe objective probabilities are very different from personal beliefs expressed in the form of probabilities. The former is derived from equally likely principles or long-run frequencies, whereas the latter is based on personal beliefs that vary from person to person.[11] If subjective probabilities are used in problems dealing with uncertainty, they need to be discounted or qualified, but we do not know how.

We are not objecting to others who are more quantitative-oriented and wish to use subjective probabilities to deal with problems of uncertainty. However, they need to realize fully the difficulties and limitations of this approach. For instance, using subjective probabilities in the Markowitz approach to estimate the expected return and risk of a security, the investor is called on to estimate (a) all possible returns and (b) the likelihood of occurrence of each possible return. For indications of possible returns, the investor can review the historical record of quarterly, semiannual, or annual rates of return obtained by owners of the stock in the last five to ten years. However, it is much more difficult to obtain some idea of the probabilities for all possible rates of return. Historical frequency distributions of actual returns may provide only limited help in this respect.

To estimate the degree of uncertainty of returns from a stock, we propose three steps as follows:

1. To analyze the historical record of the stock for the past seven to nine years in terms of key variables such as price of stock, rate of return, earnings per share, and so forth.
2. To adjust the measurements derived from the historical record when current developments suggest that some basic changes in the company are taking place.

[11]Gary Smith, *Statistical Reasoning* (Boston, Mass.: Allyn & Bacon, Inc., 1985), p. 68.

3. To adjust the measurements thus derived in the light of the projected investment environment for the forthcoming period.

In the rest of this chapter, we will show how the historic record of a stock can be analyzed as a first step to help the investor formulate estimates of returns and their degree of uncertainty concerning a stock.[12]

Analysis of the Historic Record in Estimating Future Returns and Their Degree of Uncertainty

The most relevant past period of historical record of a stock is probably the most recent five to ten years. Any period beyond that may contain factors that are no longer pertinent to the foreseeable future. The degree of uncertainty of returns of a stock can be measured in a number of ways, based on the historical record of the stock.

Variation in Price of Stock Plus Price Trend of Stock

Price changes that cause capital gain or loss to the owner constitute the major portion of the rate of return of a stock (both positive and negative rates of return). The degree of risk of a stock can be measured by two factors: annual variation in price of stock and trend of stock prices over a number of years.

The variation in price can be measured by the formula:

$$\text{Annual percent variation in price} = \frac{\text{Yearly high} - \text{Yearly low}}{(\text{Yearly high} + \text{Yearly low}) \div 2}$$

In other words, the variation in price is computed by dividing the range of prices for the year by the mean price of the year's high and low.

The risk of the stock cannot be determined solely by the annual percentage variation in the price of the stock. The price trend of the stock must also be considered. For instance, in Figure 12–3, the three stocks had identical price variations, say, 15 percent per year, but their price trends were different. Obviously they are not identical in degree of risk. Out of three, Stock C is the most risky and Stock A the least risky.

In Table 12–3 we see the calculations of annual price variation of GM stock during the period 1976–84. The average annual price variation was 36.1 percent, which was quite high. The price trend of the stock over the nine years was almost flat. Therefore, we can conclude that, based on historical record, the GM stock seems to possess a substantial degree of risk.

---

[12]In the following examples, for the purpose of convenience we use absolute deviation instead of standard deviation for the calculation of variation. From here on, whenever the word "risk" is used, it is meant as the degree of uncertainty of returns from the stock.

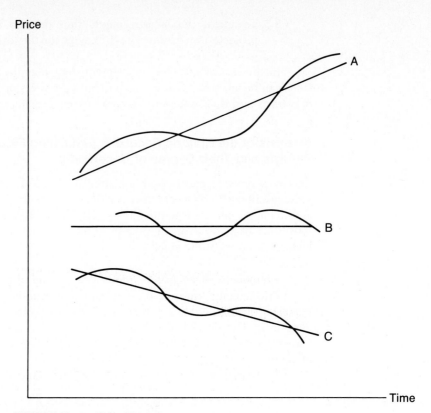

FIGURE 12–3   Price Trends

TABLE 12–3   Annual Percentage Variation of GM Stock, 1976–1984

Year	Price High	Price Low	Range $H - L$	Mean $(H + L)/2$	Annual % Variation Range/Mean
1976	78.9	57.8	21.1	68.4	30.8
77	78.5	61.1	17.4	69.8	24.9
78	66.9	53.8	13.1	60.4	21.7
79	65.9	49.4	16.5	57.7	28.6
80	58.9	39.5	19.4	49.2	39.4
81	58.0	33.9	24.1	46.0	52.4
82	64.5	34.0	30.5	49.3	61.9
83	80.0	56.0	24.0	68.0	35.3
84	82.8	61.0	21.8	71.9	30.3
Average 1976–84				60.1	36.1%

Source: Data from *Value Line Investment Survey,* 1985.

Variation and Level of Rate of Return on Stock

Another way to measure the risk of a stock is to examine the variations in and levels of rates of return experienced in the last five to ten years. The rate of return on a stock includes the dividend and price changes of the stock.

The variations in rate of return on a stock can be measured by either the standard deviation or average deviation. The average deviation is simpler to compute. It is obtained by dividing the sum of the absolute deviations of returns from the mean by the number of observations. The formula for the average deviation is:

$$\text{Average deviation} = \frac{\Sigma |d|}{n}$$

where:

$|d|$ = the absolute deviation of each return from the arithmetic mean

n = number of observations

See Table 12–4 for the calculations of risk for a hypothetical stock. The mean rate of return was 6 percent, and the mean deviation was 12.44 percent.

In considering the risk of a stock, besides the variation in rates of return, the average level of rates of return experienced should also be considered. Two stocks having identical mean deviations but different average rates of return are not identical in risk. The stock that experiences a higher average rate of return is, obviously, less risky than the one with a lower average rate of return.

TABLE 12–4   Variation of Rate of Return of ABC Stock

Year	Annual Rate of Return	Absolute Deviation from the Mean	
1976	15%	9%	
77	5	1	Mean rate of return $= \dfrac{54\%}{9} = 6\%$
78	10	4	
79	15	9	
80	10	4	Mean deviation $= \dfrac{112\%}{9} = 12.44\%$
81	−18	24	
82	−25	31	Variation of rate of return
83	25	19	$= \dfrac{\text{mean deviation}}{\text{mean rate of return}} = \dfrac{12.44}{6} = 2.07$
84	17	11	
Total	54%	112%	

To bring the level of return into consideration, we can divide the mean deviation by the mean rate of return. In the example, we get a figure of 2.07 (12.44/6), which means that the variation in rate of return was 2.07 percent for each percent of rate of return obtained.

Variation and Level of Rate of Return on Net Worth

The method just described measures the total risk of a stock. If we are interested only in the variation in performance of the company itself, we should examine the variation in the level of rate of return on net worth of the stock. (The statistical method is the same as explained in the previous method.)

In Table 12–5 we see the calculation of risk of Ford Motor stock as measured by the variation of its profitability on net worth. The average rate of return on net worth over the nine years 1976–84 was 8.03 percent, and the average deviation was 14.98 percent. The relative variation in rate of return on net worth was 1.87, which means that the variation in rate of return on net worth was 1.87 percent for each percent of rate of return on net worth obtained. Therefore, we can conclude that the risk of Ford stock was tremendous, as measured by variation in profitability on net worth.

Variation in Earnings per Share (EPS)

Earnings per share is an important measure of the performance of a corporation, and variation of EPS is a useful measure of risk.

Some suggest that the way to measure variation of EPS includes two steps: (1) to fit a trend line through the observations of EPS of different years in a chart, and (2) to calculate a standard deviation or an average deviation from the trend line. The resulting deviation represents the risk of the stock.

On the surface, this method appears to be a reasonable approach. However, when applied, it can produce erroneous results. In Figure 12–4

TABLE 12–5   Variation of Rate of Return on Net Worth of Ford Motor Co., 1976–1984

Year	Rate of Return on Net Worth	Absolute Deviation from the Mean	
1976	13.9%	5.87	Average rate of return on
77	19.8	11.77	net worth $= \dfrac{72.3\%}{9} = 8.03\%$
78	16.4	8.37	
79	11.2	3.17	Average deviation $= \dfrac{134.81}{9}$
80	−18.1	26.13	
81	−14.4	22.43	$= 14.98\%$
82	−10.8	18.83	Variation in rate of return on
83	24.7	16.67	net worth $= \dfrac{14.98}{8.03} = 1.87$
84	29.6	21.57	

Source: Data from *Value Line Investment Survey,* 1985.

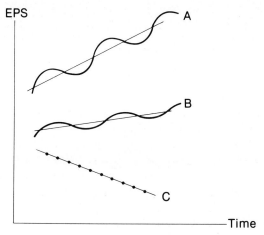

FIGURE 12–4   EPS Curves and Trend Lines

we draw the EPS curves and trend lines of three hypothetical stocks A, B, and C. A has the largest standard or average deviation, C has the least, and B is in between. Can we, therefore, conclude that A is the most risky; C, the safest; and B, in between? The answer is, of course, no. The correct answer based on earnings variation as well as earnings trend should be that A is the least risky; C, most risky; and B, in between.

The method we propose for measuring the variability of earnings per share also consists of two steps:

1. To draw a trend line of earnings growth that was *expected* of the corporation,
2. To calculate a standard or average deviation of actual EPS from the *expected* trend line of EPS.

If this procedure is followed for the three hypothetical stocks, A, B, and C, it would be as correctly shown in Figure 12–5 that stock C was the most risky; A, the least risky; and B, in between.

The expected growth trend of earnings of a stock can be obtained from applying the methods we discussed in Chapter 11. For most corporations, retained earnings is the only source for the increase in book value per share. For these corporations, the expected earnings growth rate can be obtained by simply applying the following formula:

Growth rate potential of EPS = Average rate of return on common equity (or net worth)

× (1 − average dividend payout ratio)

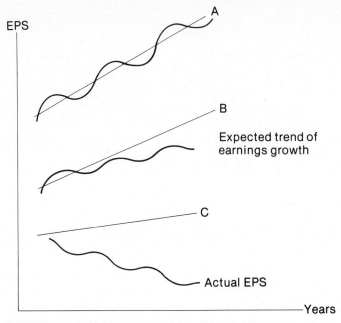

FIGURE 12–5   Expected Earnings Trend Compared to Actual Earnings per Share

In Table 12–6 we have applied this method to Dow Chemical stock. The statistical procedures were:

1. List EPS in the last five to ten years, and calculate the average EPS for the period. The average EPS of Dow Chemical was $2.93 for the period 1976–84.
2. Calculate the expected earnings growth rate for the stock, using methods discussed in Chapter 11. From Chapter 11, we know that

TABLE 12–6   Risk of Stock Measured by Actual EPS Compared to their Expected Level, Dow Chemical

Year	1976	1977	1978	1979	1980	1981	1982	1983	1984	Average 1976–84
Earnings per share	3.30	3.01	3.16	4.33	4.42	3.00	1.14	1.50	2.50	2.93
Expected EPS on basis of 5% growth rate	2.41	2.53	2.66	2.79	2.93	3.08	3.23	3.39	3.56	
Absolute deviation	0.89	0.48	0.50	1.54	1.49	0.08	2.09	1.89	1.06	1.11

$$\text{Relative Risk} = \frac{\text{Average deviation}}{\text{Average EPS}} = \frac{\Sigma |d|/n}{\text{Average EPS}} = \frac{1.11}{2.93} = 37.9\%$$

Source: Data from *Value Line Investment Survey,* 1985.

the expected earnings growth rate for Dow Chemical will most likely be around 5 percent to 5.5 percent. We used the 5 percent figure.

3. Place the average EPS ($2.93) at the middle of the period (1980) and then extrapolate the other years at the expected growth rate of 5 percent for Dow Chemical.[13]

4. Find the deviation of actual EPS from the expected level, and find an average deviation for the period. We found it was $1.11 for Dow Chemical.

5. Obtain the relative risk of the stock by dividing the average absolute deviation by the average EPS for the period.

In the case of Dow Chemical, we divide the average deviation of $1.11 by the average EPS of $2.93 and get a relative risk of .379, which means that the EPS varies as much as 37.9 percent from the expected level of EPS. Therefore, we can conclude that the risk of Dow Chemical stock was substantial as measured by variation of EPS.

Measurement of Risk on the Basis of Selected Financial Ratios

The risk of a stock can also be evaluated on the basis of trend and level of some selected financial ratios. Stockholders in general are particularly interested in three types of ratios: leverage ratios, profitability ratios, and return on investment ratios.

The leverage ratios indicate whether or not the company is exposed to excessive financial leverage. The various profitability ratios indicate whether or not the firm is maintaining or improving its ability to make profits. The dividend yield indicates what percentage of return the stockholder is getting in the form of dividends. The earnings yield (earnings divided by price of stock) indicates what percentage the corporation earns per dollar of market price of the stock. The earnings yield may be considered as the gross yield to the stockholder, even though a part of it will be retained in the corporation. In general, stockholders are looking for lower financial leverage, higher profitability, and higher return ratios on their investment.

In Table 12–7, the Dow Chemical stock was analyzed on the basis of leverage, profitability, and return ratios. The year 1984 was a recovery year for Dow Chemical. During the year the debt ratio was reduced and the profit ratio improved. However, the company had not yet achieved the average level of profitability over the period 1979–83. The company's performance in 1984 was still a little behind the industry average. In sum, while the company had achieved some improvements in both leverage and profitability in the years 1983–84, the stock still carries some risk.

---

[13]An alternative procedure would be to extrapolate the EPS from the base year 1975 at a 5 percent growth rate. But the base year 1975 may not have been a normal business year. If that is the case, we would need to adjust the EPS.

TABLE 12–7 Selected Financial Ratios of Dow Chemical and the Chemical Industry[a]

	1979	1980	1981	1982	1983	Average 1979–1983	1984	1984 vs. Historical Average	Industry 1984	Dow vs. Industry
Leverage:										
Long-term debt/Net worth	78.6	77.7	81.3	69.5	55.5	72.5	54.2	F	36.9	NF
Profitability:										
Operating profit margin	21.3	18.3	14.5	11.6	12.4	15.6	15.4	C	19	NF
Net profit margin	8.5	7.6	4.8	2.1	2.7	5.1	4.3	NF	4.5	C
Rate of return on net worth	20.1	18.1	11.5	4.4	5.8	12.0	9.6	NF	11.1	NF
Return to stockholders:										
Dividend yield D/P	5.3	4.9	5.8	7.7	5.5	5.8	6.1	C	5.8	C
Earnings Yield E/P	15.4	13.2	9.8	4.9	4.6	9.6	8.5	NF	11.1	NF

[a]Data from *Value Line Investment Survey* (see Table 9–7 and Table 11–7). F stands for favorable, NF stands for not favorable, C for comparable.

Risk Measurements on the Basis of Comparison with the Industry Average and the S&P 400 Industrials

While the risk measurement of a stock by its own record is useful and important in investment decisions, its usefulness is limited if it is not compared with the industry average or with the larger investment world, as represented by the S&P 400 Industrials, because investment decisions are generally based on relative risk rather than solely on the absolute risk of a given stock.

The relative risk of a stock can be measured in a number of ways, as was the case in measuring the risk of a given stock by itself. In Tables 12–8 and 12–9 we illustrate one possible way to measure relative risk. In this example, we compared Dow Chemical to the chemical industry and to the S&P 400 Industrials with respect to four factors:

1. Year-to-year percentage change in sales per share
2. Year-to-year percentage change in EPS
3. Average annual dividend yield
4. Average annual price-earnings ratio (P/E)

Increasing sales per share is, of course, important to the health of a firm. Increase in EPS represents the end result of the corporation's performance and the source of dividend payments. The price-earnings ratio together with the earnings growth rate should indicate to some extent whether the stock is reasonably priced in the marketplace. In general, investors prefer stocks of low P/E to stocks of high P/E for a given earnings growth rate.

In Table 12–8 we compare Dow Chemical with the S&P composite figures for the basic chemical industry, which includes twenty large chemical companies. Over the period 1976–84, Dow Chemical had an average increase in sales per share of 10.2 percent compared with the industry average of 8.57 percent. The average growth in EPS over the same period was 4.4 percent for Dow Chemical, compared with 5.6 percent for the industry.

Dow Chemical's average dividend yield was 5.06 percent, which was slightly lower than the industry average of 5.54 percent. Dow Chemical tended to sell at a higher P/E than the industry, which was also true in 1984. Based on the overall evidence, Dow Chemical stock seems to possess slightly higher risk than the industry average.

In Table 12–9 we compare Dow Chemical stock with the S&P 400 Industrials whose per-share data are shown in Table 12–10. Over the period 1976–84, Dow Chemical's growth of sales was a little higher than the 400 Industrials. However, Dow Chemical did not perform very well in growth of EPS, obtaining an average annual growth of 4.4 percent, against 9.5 percent for the 400 Industrials. Dividend yield on Dow Chemical stock was slightly higher than that of the 400 Industrials.

TABLE 12–8 Comparison between Dow Chemical Stock and the S&P's Chemical Industry[a]

	1984	1983	1982	1981	1980	1979	1978	1977	1976	Average % Change 1976–1984
Annual % change of sales per share										
Chemical industry	3.2	1.7	10.7	2.3	8.6	14.7	11.6	10.8	13.5	8.57%
Dow Chemical	7.4	2.2	−12.8	7.8	13.9	34.3	11.4	12.0	15.6	10.20%
Annual % change of earnings per share										
Chemical industry	46.0	−4.4	−32.4	−4.5	−12.0	28.1	16.2	−6.5	19.6	5.6%
Dow Chemical	66.7	31.6	−62.9	−32.1	2.1	37.0	5.0	−8.8	−0.1	4.4%
Average dividend yield										
Chemical industry	6.2	5.4	6.75	5.47	6.33	6.0	5.97	4.56	3.23	5.54%
Dow Chemical	6.1	5.5	7.7	5.8	4.9	5.3	4.8	3.4	2.0	5.06%
Average price-earning ratio (P/E)										
Chemical industry	8.8	14.0	10.4	8.2	7.1	6.2	7.4	10.2	11.9	9.4
Dow Chemical	11.8	21.6	20.5	10.3	7.6	6.5	8.2	11.1	14.6	12.5
P/E of company as % of industry average	134%									133%

[a] Computed from per-share data of S&P's chemical industry (see Table 9–5) and from data in *Value Line Investment Survey* (see Table 11–7).

TABLE 12–9 Comparison between Dow Chemical and the S&P 400 Industrial Average[a]

	1984	1983	1982	1981	1980	1979	1978	1977	1976	Average % Change 1976–1984
Annual % change of sales per share										
S&P 400 Industrials	16.5	2.2	– 3.0	5.2	12.0	16.3	12.1	10.6	9.5	9.0%
Dow Chemical	7.4	2.2	–12.8	7.8	13.9	34.3	11.4	12.0	15.6	10.2%
Annual % change of earnings per share										
S&P 400 Industrials	21.4	12.0	–21.1	3.8	– 1.0	24.9	13.9	7.1	24.6	9.5%
Dow Chemical	66.7	31.6	–62.0	–32.1	2.1	37.0	5.0	– 8.8	– 0.1	4.4%
Average dividend yield										
S&P 400 Industrials	4.1	4.24	5.36	5.0	4.9	5.1	5.1	4.56	3.82	4.67%
Dow Chemical	6.1	5.5	7.7	5.8	4.9	5.3	4.8	3.4	2.0	5.06%
Average price-earnings ratio										
S&P 400 Industrials	10.6	11.83	10.37	8.45	8.44	7.1	8.22	9.56	10.41	9.4
Dow Chemical	11.8	21.6	20.5	10.3	7.6	6.5	8.2	11.1	14.6	12.5
P/E of company as % of S&P 400 Industrials	113%									133%

[a] From per-share data of the S&P 400 Industrials (see Table 12–10) and from data in *Value Line Investment Survey*.

TABLE 12–10 400 Industrials* (per Share Data—Adjusted to stock price index level. Average of stock price indexes, 1941–1943 = 10)

	Sales	Oper. Profit	Profit Margin %	Depr.	Income Taxes	Earnings Per Share	Earnings % of Sales	Dividends Per Share	Dividends % of Earn.	Price 1941–1943 = 10 High	Price Low	Price-Earn. Ratio High	Price-Earn. Ratio Low	Div. Yields % High	Div. Yields % Low	Book Value Per Share	Book Value % Return	Working Capital	Capital Expenditures
1953	49.50	6.99	14.12	1.53	2.95	2.57	5.19	1.34	52.14	26.99	22.70	10.50	8.83	5.90	4.96	20.76	12.38	11.70	2.77
1954	46.19	6.50	14.07	1.66	2.29	2.69	5.82	1.45	53.90	37.24	24.84	13.84	9.23	5.84	3.89	22.09	12.18	12.19	2.77
1955	54.14	8.58	15.85	1.92	3.23	3.58	6.61	1.74	48.60	49.54	35.66	13.84	9.96	4.88	3.51	25.09	14.27	14.03	3.03
1956	54.73	8.36	15.27	2.04	2.96	3.50	6.40	1.84	52.57	53.28	45.71	15.22	13.06	4.03	3.45	26.35	13.28	13.91	4.14
1957	55.81	8.79	15.75	2.41	2.87	3.53	6.33	1.94	54.96	53.25	41.98	15.08	11.89	4.62	3.64	29.44	11.99	13.50	4.84
1958	53.48	7.70	14.40	2.38	2.40	2.95	5.52	1.86	63.05	58.97	43.20	19.99	14.64	4.31	3.15	30.66	9.62	14.27	3.58
1959	57.83	8.84	15.29	2.47	2.99	3.47	6.00	1.95	56.20	65.32	57.02	18.82	16.43	3.42	2.99	32.26	10.76	14.93	3.65
1960	59.47	8.73	14.68	2.56	2.87	3.40	5.72	2.00	58.82	65.02	55.34	19.12	16.28	3.61	3.08	33.74	10.08	15.29	4.23
1961	59.51	8.75	14.70	2.66	2.80	3.37	5.66	2.07	61.42	76.69	60.87	22.76	18.06	3.40	2.70	34.85	9.67	15.84	3.97
1962	64.63	9.81	15.18	2.89	3.16	3.83	5.93	2.20	57.44	75.22	54.80	19.64	14.31	4.01	2.92	36.37	10.53	16.85	4.41
1963	68.50	10.73	15.66	3.04	3.51	4.24	6.19	2.36	55.66	79.25	65.48	18.69	15.44	3.60	2.98	38.17	11.11	17.64	4.41
1964	73.19	11.67	15.94	3.24	3.70	4.85	6.63	2.58	53.20	91.29	79.74	18.82	16.44	3.24	2.83	40.23	12.06	18.07	5.71
1965	80.69	13.11	16.25	3.52	4.14	5.50	6.82	2.82	51.27	98.55	86.43	17.92	15.71	3.26	2.86	43.50	12.64	18.80	6.87
1966	88.46	14.48	16.37	3.87	4.35	5.87	6.64	2.95	50.26	100.60	77.89	17.14	13.27	3.79	2.93	45.59	12.88	19.48	8.26
1967	91.86	14.28	15.55	4.25	4.11	5.62	6.12	2.97	52.85	106.15	85.31	18.89	15.18	3.48	2.80	47.78	11.76	20.74	8.35
1968	101.49	16.08	15.84	4.56	5.14	6.16	6.07	3.16	51.30	118.03	95.05	19.16	15.43	3.32	2.68	50.21	12.27	21.08	8.65
1969	108.53	16.63	15.32	4.87	5.14	6.13	5.65	3.25	53.02	116.24	97.75	18.96	15.95	3.32	2.80	51.70	11.86	21.05	9.70
1970	109.85	15.54	14.15	5.17	4.23	5.41	4.92	3.20	59.15	102.87	75.58	19.01	13.97	4.23	3.11	52.65	10.28	20.70	10.25
1971	118.23	17.22	14.56	5.45	4.98	5.97	5.04	3.16	52.93	115.84	99.36	19.40	16.64	3.18	2.73	55.28	10.80	22.61	9.96
1972	128.79	19.39	15.06	5.76	5.90	6.83	5.30	3.22	47.14	132.95	112.19	19.47	16.43	2.87	2.42	58.34	11.71	24.41	10.08
1973	149.22	23.64	15.84	6.25	7.59	8.89	5.96	3.46	38.92	134.54	103.37	15.13	11.63	3.35	2.57	62.84	14.15	26.49	11.65
1974	182.10	27.97	15.36	6.86	10.22	9.61	5.28	3.71	38.61	111.65	69.53	11.62	7.24	5.34	3.32	67.81	14.17	28.47	14.65
1975	185.16	26.63	14.38	7.36	9.40	8.58	4.63	3.72	43.36	107.40	77.71	12.52	9.06	4.79	3.46	70.84	12.11	30.47	14.43
1976	202.66	29.23	14.42	7.58	10.21	10.69	5.27	4.22	39.48	120.89	101.64	11.31	9.51	4.15	3.49	76.26	14.02	31.89	14.92
1977	224.24	32.20	14.36	8.53	11.14	11.45	5.11	4.95	43.23	118.92	99.88	10.39	8.72	4.96	4.16	82.21	13.93	33.28	17.02
1978	251.32	36.19	14.40	9.64	12.14	13.04	5.19	5.37	41.18	118.71	95.52	9.10	7.33	5.63	4.53	89.34	14.60	34.88	19.70
1979	292.38	42.01	14.37	10.82	14.02	16.29	5.57	5.92	36.34	124.49	107.08	7.64	6.57	5.53	4.76	98.71	16.50	36.32	26.44
1980	327.36	43.08	13.16	12.37	13.67	16.12	4.92	6.49	40.26	160.96	111.09	9.99	6.89	5.84	4.03	108.33	14.88	36.52	29.86
1981	344.31	44.50	12.92	13.82	12.95	16.74	4.86	7.01	41.88	157.02	125.93	9.38	7.52	5.57	4.46	116.06	14.42	35.98	30.03
1982	333.86	42.67	12.78	15.30	10.95	13.20	3.95	7.13	54.02	159.66	114.08	12.10	8.64	6.25	4.47	118.60	11.13	34.41	31.30
1983	334.58	45.81	13.69	16.16	12.13	14.78	4.42	7.32	49.53	194.84	154.95	13.18	10.48	4.72	3.76	121.66	12.15	36.74	24.86
1984	389.75					17.95	4.61	7.43	41.39	191.48	167.75	11.80	9.40	4.39	3.85				

NOTE: 1983 data incls. results of 'old' A.T.; excls. $5.5 bil. charge
*Based on 68 individual groups.
Stock Price Indexes for this group extend back to 1918.
Source: Analysts Handbook, Standard & Poor's Corporation, 1985.

Dow Chemical has usually been selling at a higher P/E than the S&P 400 Industrials. This was also true in 1984, but at a lower premium than before. In 1984, Dow Chemical began to catch up with the average of the 400 Industrials, and the stock does not appear to be any riskier than the average of the S&P 400 Industrials.

VALUE LINE SYSTEM OF MEASURING RISKS OF A STOCK

The *Value Line Investment Survey* measures the risk of a stock in a number of ways. The different measures are:

1. Company's financial strength
2. Stock price stability
3. Price growth persistence
4. Earnings predictability
5. Rank of safety[14]

The *Value Line Investment Survey* rates the financial strength of each stock under their review (about 1700 stocks) with a system of classifications, including A^{++}, A^+, A, B^{++}, B^+, B, C^{++}, C^+, and C.

The price stability index is based on a ranking of the standard deviation of weekly percent changes in price of a stock over the last five years. The lower the standard deviation, the more stable the stock. The top 5 percent (lowest standard deviation) carry a price stability index of 100; the next 5 percent, 95; and so on down to 5.

The index of growth persistence is a measurement of the consistency of relative price growth. Using each year of the past ten (or fewer) years as a base, a count is made of the number of subsequent years in which the relative price of the stock was higher than in the base period. The sum of these counts is the base for the index. Growth persistence indexes range from 100 (highest) to 5 (lowest).

Earnings predictability is a measurement of the reliability of an earnings forecast. Predictability is based on the stability of year-to-year quarterly earnings comparisons. The earnings stability is based on the standard deviation of percent changes in quarterly earnings over a ten-year period. Special adjustments are made for comparisons around zero and from plus to minus.

The *Value Line* safety rank is presented in five grades from 1 (highest) to 5 (lowest). The safety rank is derived by averaging two variables: the stock's index of price stability, and the financial strength rating of the company.

In Table 12–11 we see how the *Value Line Investment Survey* (as of July, 1985) rates several selected stocks by the five measurements. GE and

---

[14]Arnold Bernhard, "Value Line Methods of Evaluating Common Stocks." *Value Line Investment Survey*, 1979, pp. 56–60.

TABLE 12–11   Ranking of Seven Selected Stocks by the *Value Line Investment Survey*

Measurements of Risk	IBM	Dow Chemical	GM	Ford	Chrysler	GE	U.S. Steel
Company's financial strength	A++	A	A+	B++	B	A++	B
Stock price stability	95	80	80	50	15	95	65
Price growth persistence	30	5	25	25	35	45	10
Earnings predictability	90	45	10	5	20	100	5
Rank of safety	1	2	2	3	4	1	3

Source: Data from *Value Line Investment Survey,* 1985.

IBM are rated the highest among the seven stocks in terms of both stock price stability and earnings predictability, while Ford and U.S. Steel are rated the poorest by the two standards.

For the purpose of measuring the risk of stocks, in our view the *Value Line's* five measurements can be ranked, in order of importance, as follows:

1. Earnings predictability
2. Price growth persistence
3. Company's financial strength
4. Stock price stability
5. Safety

The measurement of safety is derived by averaging the stock's Price Stability and the company's Financial Strength and, therefore, does not add any new information.

Risk of Individual Security versus Portfolio Risk

At the beginning of this chapter we mentioned that the sources of the risks of owning an individual stock can be classified into two categories: macroeconomic and microeconomic.

The macroeconomic risks stem from changes in factors that affect the whole economy. For instance, when an economic recession begins, most stocks decline in price regardless of individual quality. Similarly, in times of rising interest rates, prices of stocks and bonds generally fall no matter what the quality of the individual security. The microeconomic risks, on the other hand, are specific risks arising from problems in a particular industry or a particular company.

In a large and efficient portfolio, the individual fortunes or misfortunes from individual companies and industries (microeconomic risks) tend to by and large cancel out. However, the macroeconomic risks arising from changes in factors affecting the whole economy would remain, even if the portfolio were well diversified. We know very well from experience that when the general economy slides into recession, very few businesses escape its adverse impact. Hence, the macroeconomic risks are often referred to as undiversifiable risks, meaning that they cannot be eliminated through diversification of a portfolio. The microeconomic risks, on the other hand, are known as diversifiable risks, because they can be eliminated if the portfolio is well diversified.

The contribution to the risk of a portfolio by an individual security depends not only on the risk of the security itself, but also on its relationships or covariation with other securities in the portfolio as well as the proportion of the security represented in the portfolio. The important literature on modern portfolio theory and portfolio risk will be examined in detail in Chapters 18 and 19. Readers who would prefer to examine modern portfolio theories at this point can proceed to Chapters 18 and 19 after reading this chapter.

SUMMARY

The returns from common stock, consisting of dividend and change in the price of a stock, are basically uncertain. The uncertainty of returns are caused by many factors, which can be classified into two types: macroeconomic and microeconomic. The macroeconomic factors are cyclical variations in general business conditions, inflation, changes in market interest rates, as well as changes in public taste, political shifts, and social trends. The microeconomic factors can be divided into industrywide factors and company factors.

The question concerning how best to deal with problems of uncertainty is controversial. Some statisticians like Ramsey and Savage are of the view that subjective probabilities based on personal beliefs can apply to problems of uncertainty. Many other statisticians and economists are not comfortable with this approach. Markowitz, following the lead of Ramsey and Savage, suggests using subjective probabilities to estimate the expected return and risk of a security. Some academicians are adopting Markowitz's suggestion, but others, including many professional analysts and money managers, remain to be convinced.

The authors of this book feel that regardless of the approach one may prefer to follow to deal with problems of uncertainty, in investing it is essential that the historical record of a stock be carefully analyzed. In this chapter we illustrate a number of ways to analyze the historic record of a stock:

1. Variation in price of a stock plus price trend of the stock.
2. Variation and level of rate of return on a stock.
3. Variation and level of rate of return on net worth.
4. Variation in earnings per share of a stock.
5. Measurement of risk on basis of selected financial ratios.

To get a proper perspective, the risk of a security should be compared with its competitors or industry average for a number of years.

The risk of a security by itself is different from its contribution of risk to a portfolio. The risk of a security to a diversified portfolio will be discussed later in chapters on "Efficient Portfolio" and "The Efficient Market Hypothesis and the Capital Market Theory."

Understanding the degree of riskiness of individual stocks is very important for several reasons. They are: First, the risk of individual securities is one of the elements of determining the risk of a portfolio. Second, many individual investors only own a few securities. The riskiness of these securities themselves would be the overwhelming factor in determining the total risk of the portfolio. Third, many investors, though they own a number of securities constituting a somewhat diversified portfolio, are still interested in knowing the degree of riskiness of a security by itself when that security is evaluated for possible purchase. Fourth, understanding the degree of riskiness of a given security should be helpful in appraising the market price and P/E multiple of the security. Fifth, understanding the riskiness of a security by itself will help explain why a given security is more or less sensitive to the variation in the general level of stock prices.[15]

QUESTIONS AND PROBLEMS

1. What are some of the risks that investors will incur when they buy a common stock?
2. What risks are known as diversifiable risks? Why?
3. Can you compare the degree of risk of two stocks by their standard deviation of expected return?
4. Explain two methods whereby you may estimate the degree of risk of a stock on the basis of its past record.
5. Explain the *Value Line* system of measuring the risk of a stock.
6. Enumerate some of the risks of a stock that can be classified as microeconomic risks.
7. Is it always better to buy stocks with low risk?
8. How do you formulate probability distribution of returns of a stock?
9. Do you think you can formulate the probability distribution of a stock, say, Ford? Why or why not?
10. Do you think we should formulate an independent opinion about a stock without going through the analysis of its historic record? Why?

[15]Robert A. Haugen, "Common Stock Quality Ratings and Risks." *The Financial Analysts Journal,* March–April 1979.

TABLE 12–12 Selected Statistics on the Common Stock of Monsanto, Texas Instruments, and Johnson & Johnson

	1976	1977	1978	1979	1980	1981	1982	1983	1984
Monsanto									
Earnings per share	$ 5.03	3.73	4.15	4.56	2.05	5.75	4.24	4.72	5.42
Rate of return on net worth (%)	16.3	11.5	11.7	11.9	5.3	13.4	9.1	10.6	12.1
Stock price: High	$ 50	44.5	30.2	31	35.2	43.8	44.5	58.2	53.9
Low	$ 38	26	22.1	22.5	21.2	29.8	28.3	37.1	40.6
Texas Instruments									
Earnings per share	$ 4.25	5.11	6.15	7.58	9.22	4.62	6.10	d6.09	12.72
Rate of return on net worth (%)	14.8	15.7	16.6	18.1	18.2	8.6	10.6	–12.1	20
Stock price: High	$129.8	102.2	92.5	101	105.8	126.3	152.5	176	149.5
Low	$ 93.1	68.6	61.4	78	78.6	75	70.5	101	111.8
Johnson & Johnson									
Earnings per share	$ 1.18	1.41	1.67	1.92	2.17	2.51	2.79	2.88	2.75
Rate of return on net worth (%)	15.8	16.7	17.6	17.7	17.7	18.5	18.7	18.1	17.6
Stock price: High	$ 32.2	26	29.7	26.8	33.8	39.4	51.3	51.5	42.9
Low	$ 23.8	20.7	21.8	21.6	22	28.3	32.5	39	28

d = deficit.

Source: Data from *Value Line Investment Survey,* 1985.

11. Table 12–12 shows statistics for three corporations on EPS, rate of return on net worth, and yearly high and low of stock prices during 1976–84.

    a. Measure the degree of risk of the stock of Monsanto in terms of (1) stock price fluctuation, (2) variation and trend of EPS, and (3) variation and level of rate of return on net worth.

    b. Measure the degree of risk of the stock of Johnson & Johnson the same way as in problem (a).

    c. Measure the degree of risk of the stock of Texas Instruments the same way as in problem (a).

    d. Compare the three stocks in terms of degree of riskiness. Which stock is least risky? Which is most risky?

    e. Evaluate the risk of General Electric and RCA stocks using the method described in the text for calculating risk in terms of variations of EPS from their expected levels.

    f. An investor has estimated the potentials of a stock as follows:

Possible Return	Probability
−5%	.10
0%	.20
5%	.20
10%	.20
15%	.10
20%	.10

Find (1) the expected return and (2) the standard deviation.

REFERENCES

Bernhard, Arnold. "Investing in Common Stocks," *The Value Line Investment Survey*, 1975.

———. *Value Line Methods of Evaluating Common Stocks*, 1979.

Cohen, Jerome B. "Analysis of Common Stock." *Financial Analysts Handbook*. Homewood, Ill.: Dow Jones-Irwin, 1975.

Crowell, Richard A. "Risk Measurement: Five Applications." *Financial Analysts Journal*, July–Aug. 1973.

D'Ambrosio, Charles A. "Truth, Reality and Financial Analysis." *Financial Analysts Journal*, July–Aug. 1982.

Farrell, James L., Jr. *Guide to Portfolio Management*. New York: McGraw-Hill, 1983.

Fellner, William. *Probability and Profit*. Homewood, Ill.: Irwin, 1965.

Felsen, Jerry. *Cybernetic Approach to Stock Market Analysis*. New York: Exposition Press, 1975.

Fouse, W. L., Jahnke, W. W., and Rosenberg, B. "Is beta Phlogiston?" *Financial Analysts Journal*, Jan–Feb. 1974.

Good, Walter R. "Interpreting Analysts' Recommendations." *The Financial Analysts Journal*, May–June 1975.

Gooding, Arthur E. "Perceived Risk and Capital Asset Pricing." *The Journal of Finance*, Dec. 1978.

———. "Quantification of Investors' Perceptions of Common Stocks: Risk and Return Dimensions." *Journal of Finance*, Dec. 1975.

Graham, B., Dodd, D. L., and Cottle, S. *Security Analysis*. New York: McGraw-Hill, 1962, Chapters 7, 17, 33, and 34.

Gropper, Diane Hal. "How John Neff Does It." *Institutional Investors*, May 1985.

Haugen, Robert A. "Common Stock Quality Ratings and Risk." *The Financial Analysts Journal*, March–April 1979.

Knight, Frank H. *Risk, Uncertainty and Profit*. Boston, Mass.: Houghton Mifflin Co., 1921.

Markowitz, Harry M. *Portfolio Selection*. New Haven, Conn.: Cowles Foundation for Research in Economics, Yale University, 1959.

Olstein, Robert. "Quality of Earnings — The Key to Successful Investing." *Barron's*, July 2, 1984.

Porter, Michael E. *Competitive Strategy: Techniques for Analyzing Industries and Competitors*. New York: The Free Press, 1980.

13

Valuation of Common Stock

Whenever we purchase anything we always ask ourselves whether the item is worth the price. Buying common stocks is no different from buying any other object. We want to pay a price that is fair or better than fair. The process of determining the value of a security is, therefore, an essential step in investment decision making. In this chapter we discuss two approaches to valuation: expected dividend valuation and price-earning ratios.

EXPECTED DIVIDEND VALUATION[1]

Securities are not consumable. We buy them because we expect them to provide future returns. Were it not for this expectation, they would be worthless. The intrinsic value of a security is equal to the present value of the future stream of expected returns from the security, discounted at an appropriate rate.

We know that a dollar received today is worth more than one received a year from today because the dollar today can be invested at a risk-free interest rate to generate an amount greater than a dollar a year from today. Therefore we cannot simply add up the expected future stream of returns from a security to arrive at its value. Instead, we must first convert each future return into an equivalent present amount, and then sum up these equivalent amounts of future returns to get a total present value.

The value of a stock today can be expressed mathematically as the present value of an infinite stream of dividends:

Value of stock = PV of expected future dividends

$$V_0 = \frac{D_1}{(1 + K_s)^1} + \frac{D_2}{(1 + K_s)^2} + \cdots + \frac{D_\infty}{(1 + K_s)^\infty} \tag{13.1}$$

---

[1]This model was first developed by J. B. Williams in *The Theory of Investment Value* (Cambridge: Harvard University Press, 1938). The theory was later expanded by Myron J. Gordon in *The Investment, Financing, and Valuation of the Corporation* (Homewood, Ill.: R. D. Irwin, 1962).

where:

V_0 = the value of the security
K_s = the required rate of return on the stock
D = the dividend expected at end of period

Alternately, if we assume the more typical case of holding a stock for a few years, and then selling it, the valuation model is:

$$V_0 = \frac{D_1}{(1 + K_s)^1} + \frac{D_2}{(1 + K_s)^2} + \cdots + \frac{D_n}{(1 + K_s)^n} + \frac{SP_n}{(1 + K_s)^n} \quad (13.2)$$

where SP = the expected selling price at the end of period n.

Suppose you are considering the purchase of Transamerica stock, which is now selling at $30 a share and which paid a dividend of $1.60 in the last twelve months. After careful study of the stock, you have the following estimates of the stock:

Expected dividend growth rate (annually)	7%
Expected price/dividend ratio, three years from now	20
Expected discount rate (your required rate of return)	11%

You plan to hold this stock for three years and then sell it at the estimated price/dividend ratio of 20. What is the present value of Transamerica stock on the basis of your estimates?

Table 13–1 is a present value table,[2] and Table 13–2 shows the calculations for the present value of the Transamerica stock. First, we calculate

[2]The present value table is derived from the application of the basic formula:

$$S = P(1 + i)^n \text{ or } P = \frac{S}{(1 + i)^n} = S \times \frac{1}{(1 + i)^n}$$

where:

S = future sum of the investment
P = principal or original investment
i = annual interest rate
n = number of years

For example, the present value of a dollar to be received two years from now at 5 percent interest is:

$$P = S \times \frac{1}{(1 + i))^n} = \$1 \times \frac{1}{(1 + .05)^2} = \$1 \times \frac{1}{1.1025} = \$1 \times .907$$

$$= \$.907$$

Alternatively, the same answer can be obtained by simply referring to the present worth table, Table 13–1.

TABLE 13–1   Present Value of One Dollar at the End of *n* Years

Year (n)	5%	6%	7%	8%	9%	10%	11%	12%	13%	14%	15%
1	0.952	0.943	0.935	0.926	0.917	0.909	0.901	0.893	0.885	0.877	0.870
2	0.907	0.890	0.873	0.857	0.842	0.826	0.812	0.797	0.783	0.769	0.756
3	0.864	0.840	0.816	0.794	0.772	0.751	0.731	0.712	0.693	0.675	0.658
4	0.823	0.792	0.763	0.735	0.708	0.683	0.659	0.636	0.613	0.592	0.572
5	0.784	0.747	0.713	0.681	0.650	0.621	0.593	0.567	0.543	0.519	0.497
6	0.746	0.705	0.666	0.630	0.596	0.564	0.535	0.507	0.480	0.456	0.432
7	0.711	0.665	0.623	0.583	0.547	0.513	0.482	0.452	0.425	0.400	0.376
8	0.677	0.627	0.582	0.540	0.502	0.467	0.434	0.404	0.376	0.351	0.327
9	0.645	0.592	0.544	0.500	0.460	0.424	0.391	0.361	0.333	0.308	0.284
10	0.614	0.558	0.508	0.463	0.422	0.386	0.352	0.322	0.295	0.270	0.247
11	0.585	0.527	0.475	0.429	0.388	0.350	0.317	0.287	0.261	0.237	0.215
12	0.557	0.497	0.444	0.397	0.356	0.319	0.286	0.257	0.231	0.208	0.187
13	0.530	0.469	0.415	0.368	0.326	0.290	0.258	0.229	0.204	0.182	0.163
14	0.505	0.442	0.388	0.340	0.299	0.263	0.232	0.205	0.181	0.160	0.141
15	0.481	0.417	0.362	0.315	0.275	0.239	0.209	0.183	0.160	0.140	0.123
16	0.458	0.394	0.339	0.299	0.252	0.218	0.188	0.163	0.141	0.123	0.107
17	0.436	0.371	0.317	0.270	0.231	0.198	0.170	0.146	0.125	0.108	0.093
18	0.416	0.350	0.296	0.250	0.212	0.180	0.153	0.130	0.111	0.095	0.081
19	0.396	0.331	0.277	0.232	0.194	0.164	0.138	0.116	0.098	0.083	0.070
20	0.377	0.312	0.258	0.215	0.178	0.149	0.124	0.104	0.087	0.073	0.061
21	0.359	0.294	0.242	0.199	0.164	0.135	0.112	0.093	0.077	0.064	0.053
22	0.342	0.278	0.226	0.184	0.150	0.123	0.101	0.083	0.068	0.056	0.046
23	0.326	0.262	0.211	0.170	0.138	0.112	0.091	0.074	0.060	0.049	0.040
24	0.310	0.247	0.197	0.158	0.126	0.102	0.082	0.066	0.053	0.043	0.035
25	0.295	0.233	0.184	0.146	0.116	0.092	0.074	0.059	0.047	0.038	0.030
30	0.231	0.174	0.131	0.099	0.075	0.057	0.044	0.033	0.026	0.020	0.015

the dividends for years 1, 2, and 3, and the estimated selling price of Transamerica stock three years from now. Second, we determine the present value of the dividends and selling price. Third, we sum the present values to get the total present value of the stock, which is $33.12.

The present value of Transamerica stock, $33.12, is based on estimates of the stock. If the estimates are wrong, obviously the answer is also wrong.

TABLE 13–2   Calculating Present Value of Transamerica Stock

Dividend and Selling Price			P.V. of $1 at 11%	Present Value
Dividend in yr. 1	$1.60(1 + .07)^1 =$	1.712	.901	$ 1.543
Dividend in yr. 2	$1.60(1 + .07)^2 =$	1.832	.812	1.488
Dividend in yr. 3	$1.60(1 + .07)^3 =$	1.960	.731	1.433
Selling price in yr. 3	$1.96 \times 20 =$	39.20	.731	28.655
Present value of dividend and sales proceeds				$33.12

The critical question is whether or not one is able to formulate reasonable estimates of the factors involved.

How did we arrive at estimates about Transamerica stock? For the dividend growth rate, we may answer that, on the basis of the text in Chapter 11, we are confident that one may estimate the earnings growth rate of the company as 7 percent. Since most companies usually maintain a given level of dividend payout ratio, we can also estimate the dividend growth rate of the company.

What about the price/dividend ratio three years from now? You will probably want to look at the history of the stock for an indication, but in most cases we will find that price/dividend ratios fluctuate widely from year to year because the prices of most common stocks are very volatile. Because of this difficulty, most practicing analysts prefer to use other methods to evaluate whether a stock is fairly priced. These methods will be discussed later in this chapter.

The Present Value Model with Constant Dividend Growth

If the dividend of a stock can be assumed to increase at a constant, or normal, rate, g, and the discount rate is larger than g, then Equation 13.1 can be simplified to:[3]

$$V_0 = \frac{D_1}{K_s - g} \text{ or } \frac{D_0(1 + g)}{K_s - g} \tag{13.3}$$

where:

V_0 = present value of the stock
D_0 = dividend of the last twelve months
D_1 = expected dividend income at the end of period 1
K_s = the discount rate (or the rate of return required by the investor)
g = the long-run expected constant growth rate of dividends

Before we illustrate an application of Equation 13.3, let us discuss the variables in the equation and also the two assumptions of this equation.

The Discount Rate

The *discount rate* is the rate that an investor uses to discount future incomes from the stock. It represents the minimum rate of return an investor requires from the purchase of this stock.

[3]The proof of Equation 13.3 is given in the Appendix to this chapter.

The discount rate is affected by the long-run real growth rate of the economy, the expected rate of inflation, and the risk premium of the stock. The long-run growth rate of the economy depends on such economic factors as labor productivity, technology, changes in capital stock, and changes in labor time worked. The long-run growth rate in the U.S. has been between 2.5 percent and 3 percent per year.

The expected rate of inflation is affected by the actual rate of inflation over the last five to ten years, and the investor's own judgment as to the probable average rate of inflation in the foreseeable future.

The risk premium of a stock depends on the perceived business and financial risk of the firm and the volatility of the stock. To gauge the appropriate premium assigned to a stock, the investor can use the risk measures, such as beta, and quality ratings of stocks by Standard & Poor or *Value Line*. However, it is much more meaningful if one develops one's own risk measures of a stock. The discussion in the previous chapter on measuring degree of uncertainty of returns from stocks should be helpful.

The Long-Run Growth Rate of Dividend (g)

Most firms follow established dividend policies, paying out a certain percentage of normal earnings (or average earnings) to stockholders as dividends. Consequently, the long-run growth rate of dividends is very similar to the long-run growth rate of earnings per share (EPS).

The growth rate of the EPS for most corporations, as we discussed in Chapter 11, depends on the rate of return on common equity, and the percentage of EPS retained in the business. For most corporations, the rate of growth of EPS and, therefore, for dividends per share can be estimated by using the following formula:

EGR = Average rate of return on common equity

$\times$ (1 − Average dividend payout ratio)

The Assumption that K is Larger than g

Buyers of common stocks look for returns composed of both dividend and capital appreciation. The required rate of return of a stock can be expressed mathematically as follows:

$$K_s = \frac{D_0}{P_0} + g$$

where:

D_0 = current annual dividend

P_0 = current price of a stock

g = long-run dividend growth rate

Therefore, for dividend paying stocks r must be larger than g; the assumption is necessarily true.

The Assumption that the Dividend Grows at a Constant Rate

For most corporations, dividend growth from year to year varies. The most important reason is, of course, the changes in tempo of general business. Over a long period of time, however, the growth rates of EPS and dividends of large and mature corporations are quite stable. Therefore, the assumption that dividends will grow at a constant rate does not seem unreasonable, especially in the case of large and mature corporations.

Application of the Constant Dividend Growth Model

We shall calculate the present value of Dow Chemical stock as of the end of July, 1985. The stock paid a dividend of $1.80 during the previous twelve months, and the market price of the stock was $36.

Investor A was considering the stock. He figured that he required a rate of return from the stock of 11 percent, which was made up of the following:

Long-run real growth rate of the economy	3%
Expected rate of inflation	5%
Risk premium for the stock	3%
Total	11%

Investor A also felt that the long-run expected constant dividend growth rate would be about 5.5 percent. The present value of the Dow Chemical stock based on these estimates was:

$$V_0 = \frac{D_0(1 + g)}{K - g} = \frac{1.80(1 + .055)}{.11 - .055} = \frac{1.899}{.055} = \$34.50$$

Compared with the market price of $36, the stock's present value of $34.50 indicated the stock was fairly priced.

Valuation of Growth Stock and Price/Dividend Tables

Stocks that achieve consistently high growth rates of EPS (in excess of 10 percent over a long period, at least five years) are generally referred to as *growth stocks*. These stocks consistently earn a rate of return on common equity much higher than their cost of capital.

The present value model with a constant dividend growth rate is not applicable to growth stocks because the high growth rate for dividends may exceed the discount rate, r, and the high growth rate in EPS and dividend per share (DPS) is expected to decline in the future. Therefore there will be different growth rates of dividends for different periods of time.

To value growth stocks using the present value of dividend model, we first need to estimate the pattern of dividend growth for the stock, taking into account the decline in rate of growth at some point in the future. Then we discount the future dividends and finally add up the present values into the present value of the stock. The whole procedure can be quite laborious.

Hayes and Bauman Approach

Fortunately, tables of price/dividend and price-earnings ratios are available that greatly facilitate the application of present value analysis in practical investment decisions.[4] The tables of price/dividend ratios constructed by Hayes and Bauman are particularly interesting. Their tables (see Table 13–3) include five items:

1. Initial growth rate of dividend (first column on the left)
2. Terminal growth rate of dividend (at the head of the table)

TABLE 13–3   11% Discount Rate — Terminal Growth Rate 5% Dividend Multipliers

Initial Growth Rate (percent)	Number of Years in the Transition Period								
	2	4	6	8	10	12	15	20	25
4	17.3	17.1	17.0	16.8	16.7	16.6	16.5	16.3	16.1
5	17.5	17.5	17.5	17.5	17.5	17.5	17.5	17.5	17.5
6	17.7	17.9	18.0	18.2	18.3	18.4	18.6	18.8	19.0
8	18.2	18.7	19.2	19.6	20.0	20.4	21.0	21.8	22.6
10	18.7	19.6	20.3	21.1	21.8	22.6	23.6	25.3	26.9
12	19.3	20.4	21.6	22.7	23.8	25.0	26.6	29.4	32.1
14	19.8	21.3	22.9	24.4	26.0	27.6	30.0	34.2	38.4
16	20.3	22.2	24.2	26.3	28.4	30.5	33.9	39.7	46.0
20	21.4	24.2	27.1	30.3	33.7	37.2	43.0	53.8	66.4
25	22.7	26.7	31.2	36.1	41.5	47.6	57.9	78.8	105.7
30	24.1	29.5	35.7	42.8	51.1	60.6	77.6	115.2	168.6
35	25.5	32.4	40.7	50.6	62.5	76.8	103.7	168.1	268.7
40	27.0	35.6	46.3	59.7	76.3	97.0	138.0	244.4	427.0
50	30.1	42.6	59.4	81.9	112.3	153.0	241.4	509.3	1062.4
60	33.3	50.5	75.3	111.1	162.8	237.3	414.7	1038.6	2577.1
70	36.6	59.4	94.5	148.9	232.9	362.4	699.3	2069.7	6076.8

Source: D. A. Hayes and W. S. Bauman, *Investments: Analysis & Management* (New York: Macmillan, 1976), p. 523. Reprinted with permission of Macmillan Publishing Company.

[4]Soldofsky and Murphy, *Growth Yields on Common Stock — Theory and Tables* (State University of Iowa, 1961); W. Scott Bauman, *Estimating the Present Value of Common Stocks by the Variable Method* (University of Michigan, 1963); Modolovsky, May, and Cnottiner, "Common Stock Valuation: Theory & Tables," *Financial Analysts Journal*, March–April 1965.

3. Transition period
4. Discount rate (at the head of the table)
5. Price/dividend ratios (body of the table)

Hayes and Bauman assume that a high-growth stock cannot continue its growth indefinitely. There will be a transition period during which the initial high growth rate of earnings and dividends will gradually decline to a sustainable long-term growth rate, which they call the *terminal growth rate*. This pattern of growth of a high-growth stock is depicted in Figure 13–1.

To illustrate this point, we will calculate the present value of a famous growth stock, IBM, using the Hayes and Bauman tables. Between 1980 and 1985, IBM had an earnings growth rate of about 13.5 percent per year, and it paid an annual dividend of $4.40. Assume it is July, 1985, and that we have made these estimates for IBM:

1. Initial growth rate of dividend   12%
2. Terminal growth rate of dividend   5%
3. Transition period   15 years
4. Discount rate   11%

What is the present value of IBM stock? Using Table 13–3, we determine a price/dividend ratio of 26.6. Therefore the present value of the IBM stock is:

26.6 × $4.4 = $117.04

The market price of IBM in July, 1985, was $130. Compared with the present value we just calculated ($117) the stock was not an attractive investment.

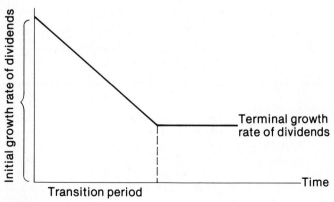

FIGURE 13–1 Assumed Pattern of Growth of a High-Growth Stock

Limitations of the Expected Dividend Valuation Approach

The expected dividends valuation approach is certainly logical. It includes the basic elements: dividend, dividend growth, and discount rate, all of which determine the value of a stock. However, there are several assumptions in this approach: investors are rational and able to evaluate available information; the stock market is efficient; and there are no other factors important enough to affect the determination of prices.

Many Wall Street professionals and experienced investors hold a different view. They feel that the stock market is only moderately efficient; that investors are not always rational, and that psychology plays an important role in determining stock prices. One economist, Robert Shiller, suggests that stock prices are importantly affected by "social dynamics," that is, social movements, fads, or fashions.

> The most important reason for expecting that stock prices are heavily influenced by social dynamics comes from observations of participants in the market and of human nature as presented in the literature on social psychology, sociology, and marketing. A study of the history of the U.S. stock market in the postwar period suggests that various social movements were under way during this period that might plausibly have major effects on the aggregate demands for shares. Must we rely on such evidence to make the case against market efficiency? Yes; there is no alternative to human judgment in understanding human behavior.[5]

Our views on the present value of dividend approach can be summarized in a few statements:

1. The valuation by present value of dividends approach can only represent long-run tendencies.
2. The stock market is importantly affected by prevailing psychology, which can be subjected to extreme and sudden changes.
3. An intelligent investor should carefully examine the reasons for any discrepancy between his or her valuation and the market price of a stock under consideration.

THE PRICE-EARNINGS RATIO

According to a survey by a noted security analyst, Ralph A. Bing, more than 75 percent of the analysts surveyed reported that they use the price-earnings

---

[5]Robert J. Shiller, "Stock Prices and Social Dynamics." *Brookings Papers on Economic Activity, II,* edited by Brainard and Perry (New York: Brookings Institution, 1984) p. 497.

approach in the valuation of common stocks.[6] There are different variations, but basically the methods can be classified as follows:

Method 1. Divide the current price of stock by normalized earnings (the earnings in normal business years) or average earnings to get a price-earnings (P/E) ratio and compare this ratio with what the analyst considers a normal P/E ratio for the stock in question.

Method 2. Divide the current price of stock by estimated future earnings (one to three years out) to get a P/E ratio and compare this ratio with what the analyst considers a normal P/E for the stock in question.

Method 3. Compare the P/E ratio and growth rate of earnings of individual stock with the P/E and growth rate of earnings of the industry average.

The first two methods of the P/E approach include the concept of the normal P/E ratio of a stock.

In recent years, many researchers have endeavored to isolate the factors that seem to determine the P/E level of an individual stock. Among the many factors determining the P/E level of individual stocks, four factors seem to be dominant:

1. Expected growth rate of earnings per share of the stock.
2. Degree of confidence in the realization of the expected earnings growth rate of the stock.
3. Level of market interest rate.
4. Earnings growth rate of the stock in the last five to seven years.

The reason why these factors are important can be seen from Equation 13.3:

$$V_0 = \frac{D_0(1 + g)}{K - g}$$

Substituting a constant dividend payout ratio (d) into the equation, we get

$$V_0 = \frac{EPS_0 \times d(1 + g)}{K - g}$$

Assuming $V_0 = P_0$ and dividing both sides of the equation by EPS_0, we obtain

$$\frac{P_0}{EPS_0} = \frac{d(1 + g)}{K - g} \tag{13.4}$$

[6]Ralph A. Bing, "Survey of Practitioners' Stock Evaluation Methods." *Financial Analysts Journal,* May–June 1971.

From Equation 13.4 we see that price-earnings ratios are determined by three factors: expected earnings growth rate (g), the required rate of return (K), and the dividend payout ratio (d).

Now we examine each of the four factors mentioned above in relation to Equation 13.4. The relationship between the first factor and P/E of a stock is positive, that is, the higher the expected earnings growth rate, the higher the P/E level of the stock. This is because when g is higher, the divisor ($K - g$) is smaller, resulting in higher P/E.

The relationship between the second factor and the P/E of a stock is also positive. A higher degree of confidence in the realization of the expected earnings growth rate of a stock means less risk is associated with the stock, which means a smaller K. Therefore, the higher the confidence in the estimated earnings growth rate, the higher the P/E of the stock.

The third factor bears an inverse relationship with the P/E of a stock. Higher market interest rates, causing a higher required rate of return, usually push prices of common stocks down, resulting in lower P/E ratios for individual stocks.

The fourth factor, the actual earnings growth rate in the past five to seven years, is not as important as the first three factors in determining the P/E level of a stock. However, when the expected future earnings growth rate is high but the past earnings growth rate is low, the past earnings growth rate has a restraining effect on the P/E multiple of the stock. On the other hand, if the expected future earnings growth rate is low but the past earnings growth rate is high, the past earnings rate will have little favorable impact on the P/E of the stock.[7]

To show how the current P/E (price divided by earnings of the last twelve months) of stocks is influenced by these factors, refer to Table 13–4, in which the P/E of thirty-one stocks selected at random are related to the four factors:

1. Expected earnings growth rate, taken from *Value Line's* estimates of growth of the stock from 1982–84 to 1987–89.
2. Earnings predictability, as estimated by *Value Line*.
3. Actual earnings growth rate in the last five years, as calculated by *Value Line*.
4. Price growth persistence (an index of consistency of relative price growth in the last ten years) as calculated by *Value Line*.

We can make several observations:

Ignoring Ford and Chrysler (whose P/E were very low for special reasons of their own), the median P/E of the twenty-nine stocks in the list

---

[7]Stanley S. C. Huang, *Techniques of Investment Analysts* (New York: Intext Educational Publishers, 1972), Chapter 8.

TABLE 13–4 P/E Compared with Expected Earnings Growth Rate, Earnings Predictability, Actual Earnings Growth Rate, and Price Growth Persistence[a]

Stocks	P/E 8-3-85	Expected Annual Earn. Growth Rate 1982–1984 to 1987–1989	Earnings Predictability	Actual Earnings Growth Rate Last Five Years	Price Growth Persistence
Merk & Co.	16	12%	95	7.5%	15
Bristol Myers	16	15	100	14	55
Motorola	16	19	65	9.5	55
Am. Hospital Supply	15	9	100	12	40
Pfizer	15	13.5	80	13	65
Coca Cola	15	11	100	7	20
Xerox	15	13.5	75	−8.5	5
Johnson & Johnson	15	10	95	11	25
Procter & Gamble	14	10	100	9.5	20
Dow Chemical	14	24	45	−13.5	5
Honeywell	14	13.5	70	4	75
Texas Instruments	14	39	5	−8	20
IBM	13	16	90	12.5	30
Eastman Kodak	13	1	65	1	10
General Electric	13	13	100	10.5	45
Union Carbide	13	19	50	−9.5	10
Monsanto	13	11	50	3	35
Am. Home Products	12	12.5	100	12	35
Burroughs	12	19	35	−8.5	5
U.S. Tobacco	12	15.5	100	18	80
General Foods	12	14	80	6.5	30
Avon	11	6.5	80	−3	5
American Can	11	26	40	−12.5	15
Sears Roebuck	10	12	70	5	30
Owens-Illinois	10	26	30	0	30
General Dynamics	9	16	25	31	95
Allied Co.	9	13.5	25	15.5	15
Goodyear	8	3.5	60	5	30
General Motors	7	23.5	10	−14	25
Ford	3	6	5	−2	25
Chrysler	3	20.5	20	—	35

[a] Data on P/E from the *New York Times;* other data from *Value Line Investment Survey.*

is 11.5, which is almost identical to the median P/E of *Value Line's* stocks of 11.8

The actual earnings growth rate in the last five years is closely related to price growth persistence. This is logical, because both factors relate to past experience, one on earnings and the other on relative price growth of the stock.

Among the four determining factors selected, earnings predictability seems to have the most influence on the level of P/E of the stock.

A high P/E stock seems to require (a) a high expected earnings growth rate, (b) a high degree of confidence by investors in the realization of the expected earnings growth rate, and (c) a good earnings growth rate in the past period.

A low P/E stock, on the other hand, is usually associated with low earnings predictability and a poor record of earnings performance in the past period.

The medium P/E stocks are stocks whose overall showing on the four factors is fairly good, but may be weak on either earnings predictability or actual earnings growth in the past period.

The expected earnings growth rates by *Value Line* for different stocks, unfortunately, may not be very meaningful because first of all, we do not know the basis upon which *Value Line* formulates its estimates, and secondly, we believe that our own estimates, if performed in accordance with the framework discussed earlier in Chapter 11, could be in some cases quite different from *Value Line's* estimates.

Despite the drawbacks just mentioned about earnings growth estimates, the approach in Table 13–4 in our view serves well to indicate how to select a normal P/E for a stock, if one plans to use the P/E approach (as many practicing analysts do) in the valuation of common stock.

If we develop our own estimates of the earnings growth rate and the degree of riskiness of a stock using procedures discussed in previous chapters, and at the same time use *Value Line's* estimates for reference, we can estimate what normal P/E should be assigned to a given stock.

The Ratio of Price to Earnings Reinvested

Price-earnings ratios are widely used by investors to compare individual stocks for relative values. The price-earnings ratio, however, has an important drawback in that it does not take into account the percentage of earnings paid out in dividends.

A well-known analyst, Peter L. Bernstein, suggests that we should compute another ratio indicating how much is being paid by investors for $1 earnings reinvested in a business.[8] The procedures of the computation are:

1. Capitalize the current dividend paid by a stock by the current AAA bond yield.
2. Subtract the capitalized value of the dividend from the price of the stock to get a net price.
3. Subtract the dividend from earnings per share to get earnings per share reinvested.
4. Divide the net price of the stock by earnings per share reinvested to get a ratio; this ratio indicates how much is being paid by investors for $1 of earnings reinvested in the company.

---

[8]Robert Metz, "Calculating Price of Growth." *New York Times*, April 16, 1981.

For example, the current data for GE stock are these:

Market price (8/6/85)	$64.00
Dividend (last four quarters)	$ 2.20
Earnings per share (last four quarters)	$ 5.10
Price-Earnings ratio	12.5

1. Current AAA bond yield is about 12 percent, so the annual dividend is worth $2.20/.12 = $18.30. If an investor could buy an $18.30 bond, he or she would receive interest income of $2.20 a year.
2. Net price paid for retained earnings: $64.00 − $18.30 = $45.70
3. Net earnings reinvested per share: $5.10 − $2.20 = $2.90
4. Price paid by investors for $1 earnings reinvested by GE: $45.70/$2.90 = $15.80

The advantages of this ratio (net price to reinvested earnings) are:

- The ratio can be related to expected earnings growth rate to see whether it is high, low, or reasonable.
- This ratio can be compared with the ratio of other stocks to indicate how much more or less investors paid for a dollar of earnings reinvested in their respective firms.

In Table 13–5 are calculations for several stocks and for the Dow Jones Industrial Average (DJIA) index. From the table, it appears the price paid for $1 of earnings reinvested in Dow Chemical was too high. Currently the ratio of net price to earnings reinvested for the DJIA is about 18, which is somewhat high relative to IBM, Johnson & Johnson, or RCA.

Valuation of Stock by Comparison with Industry Average or General Market Index

Another useful way to evaluate common stocks is by comparing the stock with the industry average or the general market index, such as the S&P 400 Industrials or the Dow Jones Industrial Average.

The *Value Line Investment Survey* publishes a statistical series, the relative P/E ratio. The relative P/E is arrived at by dividing the current P/E of a stock by the median P/E of all stocks under *Value Line* review.

The advantages of having relative P/E data over a period of time are:

- One can determine when the stock has been traded at a discount or at a premium to the market and which way the trend has been moving in recent years.

TABLE 13–5 Ratio of Net Price to Earnings per Share Reinvested

Stocks	Stock Price	Annual Dividend[a]	Earnings per Share	P/E	Worth of Dividend Div./Bond Yield	Stock Price Less Dividend Worth	Earnings per Share Retained	Net Price to Earnings Retained
General Electric	64	2.20	5.1	12.5	18.30	45.7	2.9	15.8
Burroughs	64.50	2.60	5.41	11.9	21.70	42.8	2.81	15.2
Monsanto	53.25	2.50	4.24	12.6	20.80	32.45	1.74	18.6
Johnson & Johnson	45	1.30	3.13	14.4	10.80	34.20	1.83	18.7
Dow Chemical	36.50	1.80	2.50	14.6	15	21.50	0.70	30.7
RCA	44	1.04	3.93	11.2	8.70	35.30	2.89	12.2
IBM	131	4.40	10.06	13	36.70	94.30	5.66	16.7
DJIA (30 stocks)	1347	61.53	107.90	12.50	512.80	834.20	46.37	18.0

[a] Dividend capitalized at current AAA Bond Yield at 12%.

TABLE 13–6 P/E and Relative P/E for Six Computer Firms[a]

	IBM		Digital		Hewlett-Packard		Honeywell		Burroughs[b]		Sperry	
	P/E	Relative P/E	P/E	Relative P/E	P/E	Relative P/E	P/E	Relative P/E	P/E	Relative P/E	P/E	Relative P/E
1985	13.0	1.1	13.0	1.1	18.0	1.53	13.0	1.1	12.0	1.02	9.0	.76
1984	10.8	.99	15.4	1.39	17.7	1.65	9.0	.83	9.7	.89	10.9	1.0
1983	12.7	1.07	20.4	1.72	24	2.03	11.2	.95	10.9	.92	10.9	.92
1982	9.4	1.04	11.4	1.26	14.6	1.61	8.3	.91	16.7	1.84	10.8	1.19
1981	10.3	1.25	13.5	1.64	17.8	2.16	7.9	.96	11.3	1.37	7.3	.89
1980	10.4	1.38	11.9	1.58	14.6	1.94	7.0	.93	32.7	4.34	7.1	.94
1979	13.9	2.01	12.5	1.81	14	2.03	6.6	.95	9.6	1.39	7.1	1.03
1978	12.7	1.73	13.3	1.81	14.5	1.98	6.8	.93	11.5	1.57	7.7	1.05
Average 1978–84	11.5	1.35	14.1	1.60	16.7	1.91	8.1	.92	11.6	1.33	8.8	1.0

[a] Data on P/E from the *New York Times*, August 6, 1985. Data on relative P/E from *Value Line Investment Survey*.
[b] 1980 was an abnormal year for Burroughs Co., and, therefore, not included in the average for 1978–84.

- One can also judge whether the current relative P/E of a stock is reasonable (a) terms of historical experience and (b) in relation to the expected earnings growth rate of the stock.

See Table 13–6 for the P/E and relative P/E for six major computer firms. A careful examination of the table enables us to make some judgments as to:

1. Whether these stocks are overpriced or underpriced relative to the market, and relative to their own experience in the last seven years.
2. Which stock seems most under- or overpriced.
3. If we have developed expected earnings growth rates for these stocks for comparison, we may be able to formulate some informed opinion about these stocks.

The P/E of a stock, instead of being related to a market aggregate as in the case of the *Value Line* approach, can be usefully related to the average or median P/E of the industry. Goodman and Peavy report that their strategy of buying stocks of large companies with relatively low P/E to the industry average produced excess returns over the period 1969 to 1980.[9]

VALUATION OF STOCKS ON THE BASIS OF CASH FLOW[10]

As we mentioned in Chapter 10, corporate management has considerable leeway in estimating and charging costs against current revenues, thereby affecting profits reported. Among the cost items, depreciation expense is an important item. Consequently, some analysts suggest that cash flow be substituted for earnings as the basis for valuation of a stock. The term *cash flow* is used to denote the amount of funds generated from operations that remain after all other cash expenses have been met. It indicates the amount of funds available to management for whatever corporate purposes deemed appropriate. These corporate purposes would include replacement and expansion of corporate facilities, reduction of debt, increase in working capital, and disbursement of dividends.

Cash flow is usually calculated by adding all non-cash expenditures to net earnings after taxes. The two most important items are depreciation and depletion. For most companies (except industries in natural resources), depreciation is usually the only item of any significance.

[9]David A. Goodman and John W. Peavy, III, "Industry Relative Price-Earnings Ratios as Indicators of Investment Returns." *Financial Analysts Journal,* July–Aug. 1983.
[10]Stanley S. C. Huang, *Corporate Earning Power and Valuation of Common Stock.* (Larchmont, N.Y.: Investors Intelligence, Inc., 1966), Chapter 7.

The Proper Use of the Concept of Cash Flow

A close examination of current and past cash flow data of a stock can shed much light on these questions:

- Will the existing dividend policy likely be maintained?
- Does the firm have the ability to modernize its facilities and thereby create the future ability to earn?
- Do the reported earnings of the firm require adjustments because of wide fluctuation in depreciation charges?
- Can a reasonable comparison of earnings performance of firms in the same industry be obtained by comparing reported earnings? If not, what adjustments are necessary to achieve the objective?

Cash Flow as a Base for Capitalization

Because of the relative stability of the price/cash flow ratio compared with P/E, and the obvious connection between the magnitude of cash flow and the ability to modernize productive facilities, some analysts suggest using cash flow as a base for capitalization.

Cash flow can be used as a supplementary basis for capitalization or as a qualitative factor in the evaluation of P/E, but cash flow should not be substituted for earnings as a basis for capitalization. Cash flow is a *mixed* concept composed of both profits on capital and return of capital itself. It represents neither the income accruing to the owner nor the amount of profit the corporation is making. While the concept has special uses as mentioned above, it cannot replace the concept of earnings as a base for valuation. Furthermore, while cash flow may be more stable than earnings over time, the forecast of cash flow consists of a forecast of earnings as well as non-cash expenses and, therefore, does not appear to be any easier than forecasting earnings alone.

Cash flow is a valuable input, and should be analyzed not only in its entirety but also in its components. The analysis of current and past cash flow of a stock can help establish the real changes in earning power and thus can help select a "proper" P/E multiplier to be applied to the earnings base.

PRICE/SALES PER SHARE RATIO (P/S)

Price-earnings ratios are widely used by both analysts and investors as a tool in the evaluation of stocks. However, the tool does have some limitations. When a firm's earnings are negative, a P/E ratio is meaningless. When the P/E of a stock is high, investors usually consider it a growth stock and assume there will be a high earnings growth rate in the future. If future earnings fail to live up to expectations, the price of the stock can decline precipitously.

The P/E ratio is a quotient of two factors, both of which can change quickly over a business cycle. As a result, it can swing widely over a business cycle.

An interesting alternative to the P/E ratio is the price/sales per share ratio.[11] Advocates argue that sales per share is a better measure because sales tend to be more stable than EPS. Furthermore, P/E ratios are unreliable as value indicators because both price and earnings tend to move in tandem. For example, a stock might sell at eighteen times earnings for $60, and a year later still sell at eighteen times earnings for $11 a share because profits collapsed.

A study in 1984 of the P/S and P/E of the DJIA for 1983 produced the results shown in Table 13–7. For 1983, the stocks with the seven lowest price/sales ratios averaged gains of 63.6 percent, while the stocks with the nine lowest price-earning ratios averaged gains of 28.7 percent. The DJIA at the same time averaged a gain of 20.3 percent. The low price/sales ratio stocks outperformed the low P/E stocks by a wide margin, but the low P/E stocks also outperformed the DJIA as a whole.

Comments on the Price/Sales Approach

Sales are the foundation of any business, and are also more stable than earnings. The P/S complements the P/E ratio in the assessment of the performance and outlook of a corporation. However, it should not be used in isolation. When the price/sales ratio is very low, a corporation might face bankruptcy if it has some basic problems such as excessive leverage, a burdensome cost structure, or a severe liquidity problem.

GRAHAM'S INTRINSIC VALUE APPROACH TO COMMON STOCKS

Benjamin Graham is the coauthor of *Security Analysis*, which has gone through four editions since 1934. For many years, the book was considered by many practicing analysts as the bible for security analysis. He also wrote *The Intelligent Investor*, which has gone through many editions since 1949. Graham suggests that there are three different approaches to the analysis of common stock:

1. The anticipation approach
2. The absolute value approach
3. The relative value approach

The anticipation approach assumes that the current market price is, by and large, an appropriate reflection of the present situation of a stock. But

[11]Lawrence Minard, "The Case Against Price/Earnings Ratios." *Forbes*, Feb. 13, 1984; Kenneth L. Fisher, "Price-Sales Ratios: A New Tool for Measuring Stock Popularity." *American Association of Individual Investors Journal*, June 1984.

TABLE 13–7 1983 Percentage Gains, P/Ss, and P/Es of the Dow Industrials

	1983 Gains (%)	1/1/83 P/S	1/1/83 P/E
International Harvester	177%	0.03*	deficit
Allied Corp.	72	0.17*	5*
American Can	52	0.13*	25
Bethlehem Steel	47	0.14*	deficit
U.S. Steel	45	0.12*	deficit
DuPont (E.I.)	45	0.25	9
Aluminum Co. of America	45	0.52	deficit
Westinghouse	41	0.35	8*
Woolworth	36	0.14*	10
Owens-Illinois	32	0.21	8*
General Foods	30	0.24	8*
American Brands	29	0.39	7*
United Technologies	28	0.23	9
IBM	27	1.79	13
Exxon	26	0.25	6*
Inco	26	0.76	deficit
General Electric	24	0.81	12
Sears Roebuck	23	0.36	13
International Paper	22	0.59	16
General Motors	19	0.31	18
Union Carbide	19	0.40	12
Texaco	16	0.15*	7*
Minnesota Mining & Manufacturing	10	1.33	14
Merck	9	2.07	15
SOCAL	9	0.29	8*
AT&T	3	0.81	7*
American Express	1	0.79	11
Procter & Gamble	−4	0.81	12
Eastman Kodak	−11	1.39	12
Goodyear Tire	−14	0.29	11
Average	**20**	**0.54**	**N/A**

*Seven lowest P/S stocks and nine lowest P/E stocks.
Source: Kenneth L. Fisher, "Price-Sales Ratios: A Tool for Measuring Stock Popularity." *American Association of Individual Investors Journal*, June 1984.

the price of the stock will be different a year or two from now and will correspond to the new conditions then. The function of the security analyst is to anticipate the new situation, to select stocks that will benefit most, and to reject those that will fare badly.

The absolute value approach attempts to value a stock independently of its current market price. The independent value has a variety of names: intrinsic value, indicated value, central value, normal value, investment value, or fair value.

The third approach is concerned with relative rather than intrinsic value. In estimating relative value, the analyst more or less accepts the prevailing market level and seeks to determine the value of a stock in terms of it. He tries to appraise the relative attractiveness of the individual issues in terms of the existing level of stock price, rather than determine the fundamental worth of a stock.

Graham favored the second approach — absolute value or "intrinsic value" approach. He defined the intrinsic value as that value that is justified by the facts, for example, assets, earnings, dividends, or definite prospects, including the factor of management.[12]

Graham's Rules for Purchases of Common Stocks

Graham believed in the overall efficiency of security markets, but he also believed that from time to time there are areas of market inefficiency and mispricing of individual securities. Superior returns can be obtained if individuals pay close attention to investment fundamentals. Over the years, Graham offered various stock selection criteria. They are:[13]

1. An earnings-to-price yield at least twice the AAA bond yield.
2. A price-earnings ratio less than 40 percent of the highest price-earnings ratio the stock has had over the past five years.
3. A dividend yield of at least two-thirds the AAA bond yield.
4. A stock price below two-thirds of tangible book value per share.
5. A stock price below two-thirds "net current asset value."
6. A total debt less than book value.
7. A current ratio greater than two.
8. A total debt less than twice "net current asset value."
9. An earnings growth of the prior ten years of at least a 7 percent annual (compound) rate.
10. Stability of growth of earnings in that no more than two declines of 5 percent or more in year-end earnings in the prior ten years are permissible.

Henry Oppenheimer studied selected issues on the New York and American Exchanges that met various sets of Graham's criteria and measured the performances of portfolios formed from these issues over the years 1974 through 1981. He found that these portfolios did provide superior returns even after risk adjustment and adjustment for firm size effects.[14]

---

[12]Graham, Dodd, and Cottle, *Security Analysis,* 4th ed. (New York: McGraw-Hill, 1962), Chapter 2.

[13]Henry R. Oppenheimer, "A Test of Ben Graham's Stock Selection Criteria." *Financial Analysts Journal,* Sept.–Oct. 1984.

[14]Ibid., pp. 68–73.

VALUATION OF THE GENERAL MARKET

In addition to the valuation of individual stocks that are attractive at the moment, the investor should also put a "value" on the general market. The purpose of the valuation of the general market is to determine if the general level of stock prices is relatively high or low in terms of past and prospective earnings, so that the investor can decide whether he or she should pursue a relatively aggressive, neutral, or defensive investment strategy.

The general level of stock prices is most frequently measured by two well-known indexes, the Dow Jones Industrial Average and the Standard & Poor's Index of 500 Common Stocks.

Valuation of the General Market by the Present Value Approach

One approach is to use the present value formula with a constant dividend growth rate. The formula, which we discussed before, is:

$$V_0 = \frac{D_1}{K - g} \quad \text{or} \quad \frac{D_0(1 + g)}{K - g} \tag{13.3}$$

where:

K = the required rate of return desired

g = the constant growth rate of the dividend

D_1 = the annual dividend one year from now

For example, we use the DJIA to represent the general market and assume that the investor is demanding a return of 11 percent on DJIA stocks. The constant dividend growth rate of DJIA stocks is assumed to be 5.5 percent, and the aggregate dividend of the DJIA in the last four quarters is assumed to be $61.53. The present value of DJIA is:

$$V_0 = \frac{D_1}{K - g} = \frac{\$61.53(1 + .055)}{11\% - 5.5\%} = \frac{\$64.91}{.055} = 1180.20$$

The DJIA was around 1302 on August 9, 1985. According to the valuation, on this date the market as represented by the DJIA seemed overpriced.

The other approach to valuation of the general market is to use the preconstructed multiplier table of Hayes and Bauman. If the initial growth rate and the terminal growth rate of the DJIA are assumed at 5.5 percent and 5 percent, respectively, and the investor is demanding an 11 percent return, one can find the P/D ratio (dividend multiplier) to be $(17.5 + 19)/2 = 18.25$

in Table 13–3. The current dividend of the DJIA in the last four quarters was $61.53. So the present value of the DJIA is:

$$61.53 \times 18.25 = 1122.9$$

Compared to the August, 1985, level of 1302, the general market represented by the DJIA again seems overpriced.

DJIA Five Months Later at the End of 1985

Despite our valuation indicating that the general market as represented by DJIA seemed overpriced at the beginning of August, 1985, the stock prices continued to move up in the following months, and the DJIA reached 1547 by December 31, 1985, and over 1800 early in 1986. Does this mean our valuation techniques are useless? Here we have a good case to illustrate both the usefulness and the limitation of valuation.

During the five months from August to December, 1985, there were two important developments affecting the stock market. First, being worried by the possibility that the economy might slide into a recession by the end of 1986, as many business economists predicted, the Federal Reserve decided to ease its monetary policy and reduce interest rates. As a result, short-term and long-term interest rates declined 1 percent to 1.25 percent from August to December, 1985. Second, in December, 1985, Congress passed an important law, the Gramm-Rudman Act, which will force the government to gradually reduce the federal deficit and have a balanced budget by 1992. This law created a favorable impact on investor psychology. The two developments created a powerful impact on the stock market, resulting in an approximately 17 percent rise in stock prices during the last five months of 1985. This illustrates vividly how the investment environment and investor psychology can change quickly. The lesson is that valuation is useful, but it is only a reference point and, most important of all, it needs updating when the investment environment changes.

Valuation of the General Market by Capitalizing Average Past Earnings

Graham, Dodd, and Cottle, in their 1962 edition of *Security Analysis*, propose to value the general market by the following formula:

$$\text{DJIA central value} = \frac{\text{Average DJIA earnings for the past ten years}}{1\tfrac{1}{3} \text{ times the average yield on Aaa bonds in the last three years}}$$

Their formula is based on the rationale that investors are constantly comparing the yield on bonds and the returns on common stocks. Since earnings are not all distributed in the form of dividends, and since stocks are riskier than bonds, they feel that the discount rate should be higher than the yield on Aaa bonds.

See Table 13–8 for the valuation of the S&P 400 Industrials on the basis of their formula. The valuation of the general market as represented by the S&P 400 Industrials was lower than the average of the annual high and low of the market index for each year since 1962. In the years 1981–1984, the valuation was as low as 42 percent to 53 percent of the market index. Why? First, the average earnings of the past ten years understated the earnings power of the 400 stocks in the index. Second, the discount rate, at $33\frac{1}{2}$ percent higher than the bond yield, may be a little too high.

For investors interested in this approach of valuing the overall market, we propose the following modified formula:

$$\text{Normal value of market index} = \frac{\text{Average earnings for the last five years}}{1.15 \text{ times the average yield on AAA bonds in the last three years}}$$

Average earnings for the past five years is a better approximation of the earning power of stocks in the market index. However, it does understate the earning power of these stocks to some extent. To offset this, we lower the discount rate to 1.15 times the average bond yield of the last three years. The valuation of the S&P 400 Industrials on the basis of our modified formula appears in Table 13–9.

Using the modified formula, the overall valuation of the S&P 400 Industrials from 1967 to 1980 seems to fit quite well with actual market developments. The valuation for the recent period 1981–1984, on the other hand, does not fit with actual market developments. While the valuation was indicating the market level was relatively high, the general level of stock prices continued to move up. As we said earlier, stock prices are importantly affected by investors' *expectations* of the economy, corporate profits, inflation, and interest rates. These factors were left out of the formula. Finally, while the results of valuing the general market level by our suggested modified version of Graham's formula were only fair, they did provide a *historic perspective*. We all know that the stock market is famous for the gyration of emotions among participants from time to time. A valuation based on average realized earnings in the past can help restrain the overenthusiasm or overpessimism of the investor in the stock market.

Valuation of the General Market by Multiple Regression and Correlation Analysis

The general level of common stock prices is determined by a number of factors, such as the expected level of corporate profits, dividends, real GNP,

TABLE 13–8 Valuation of S&P 400 Industrials on the Basis of Graham, Dodd, and Cottle's Formula

Year	Earnings per Share, S&P 400	Average Earnings Last Ten Years	Yield on Aaa Corporate Bonds	Average Bond Yields Last Three Years	Average Bond Yield × $1\frac{1}{3}$	Average Earnings/ $1\frac{1}{3}$ × Bond Yield	Average of High and Low, S&P 400	Valuation as % of High and Low
1953	2.57		3.20%					
4	2.69		2.90					
5	3.58		3.06					
6	3.50		3.36					
7	3.53		3.89					
8	2.95		3.79					
9	3.47		4.38					
60	3.40		4.41					
1	3.37		4.35					
2	3.83	3.29	4.33	4.36%	5.81%	56.62	65.01	87%
3	4.24	3.46	4.26	4.31	5.75	60.17	72.37	83
4	4.85	3.67	4.40	4.33	5.77	63.60	85.52	74
5	5.50	3.86	4.49	4.38	5.84	66.10	92.49	71
6	5.87	4.10	5.13	4.67	6.23	65.81	89.25	74
7	5.62	4.31	5.51	5.04	6.72	64.14	95.73	67
8	6.16	4.63	6.18	5.61	7.48	61.90	106.54	58
9	6.13	4.90	7.03	6.24	8.32	58.89	107.00	55
70	5.41	5.10	8.04	7.08	9.44	54.02	89.23	61
1	5.97	5.36	7.39	7.49	9.98	53.71	107.60	50
2	6.83	5.66	7.21	7.55	10.06	56.26	122.57	46
3	8.89	6.12	7.44	7.35	9.80	62.45	118.96	53
4	9.61	6.60	8.57	7.74	10.32	63.95	90.59	71
5	8.58	6.91	8.83	8.28	11.04	62.59	92.56	68
6	10.69	7.39	8.43	8.61	11.48	64.37	111.27	58
7	11.45	7.97	8.02	8.43	11.24	70.91	109.40	65
8	13.04	8.66	8.73	8.39	11.18	77.46	107.12	72
9	16.29	9.68	9.63	8.79	11.72	82.59	115.79	71
80	16.12	10.75	11.94	10.10	13.46	79.87	136.03	59
1	16.74	11.82	14.17	11.91	15.88	74.43	141.48	53
2	13.20	12.46	13.79	13.30	17.73	70.28	136.87	51
3	14.78	13.05	12.04	13.33	17.77	73.44	174.90	42
4	17.95	13.88	12.71	12.85	17.13	81.03	179.62	45

Source: Data from the *S&P Analysts Handbook* and the *Economic Report of the President,* 1985.

TABLE 13–9 Valuation of the S&P 400 Industrials on the Basis of the Modified Formula of Normal Value

Year	Earnings per Share, S&P 400	Average Earnings, Last Five Years	Yield on Aaa Corporate Bonds	Average Bond Yields, Last Three Years	Average Bond Yield × 1.15	Average Earnings/ 1.15 × Bond Yield	Average of High and Low, S&P 400	Valuation as % of High and Low
1953	2.57		3.20%					
4	2.69		2.90					
5	3.58		3.06					
6	3.50		3.36					
7	3.53	3.17	3.89	3.44%	3.96%	80.1	47.6	168%
8	2.95	3.25	3.79	3.68	4.23	76.8	51.1	150
9	3.47	3.41	4.38	4.02	4.62	73.8	61.2	121
60	3.40	3.37	4.41	4.19	4.82	69.9	60.2	116
1	3.37	3.34	4.35	4.38	5.04	66.3	68.8	96
2	3.83	3.40	4.33	4.36	5.01	67.9	65.1	104
3	4.24	3.66	4.26	4.31	4.96	73.79	72.37	102
4	4.85	3.94	4.40	4.33	4.98	79.12	85.52	93
5	5.50	5.45	4.49	4.38	5.04	108.13	92.49	117
6	5.87	5.46	5.13	4.67	5.37	101.68	89.25	114
7	5.62	5.22	5.51	5.04	5.80	90.0	95.73	94
8	6.16	5.60	6.18	5.61	6.45	86.8	106.54	81
9	6.13	5.86	7.03	6.24	7.18	81.6	107.0	76
70	5.41	5.84	8.04	7.08	8.14	71.7	89.23	80
1	5.97	5.86	7.39	7.49	8.61	68.1	107.6	63
2	6.83	6.10	7.21	7.55	8.68	70.28	122.57	57
3	8.89	6.65	7.44	7.35	8.45	78.7	118.96	66
4	9.61	7.34	8.57	7.74	8.90	82.47	90.59	91
5	8.58	7.98	8.83	8.28	9.52	83.82	92.56	91
6	10.69	8.92	8.43	8.61	9.90	90.1	111.27	81
7	11.45	9.84	8.02	8.43	9.69	101.5	109.4	93
8	13.04	10.67	8.73	8.39	9.65	110.6	107.12	103
9	16.29	12.01	9.63	8.79	10.11	118.8	115.79	103
80	16.12	13.52	11.94	10.10	11.62	116.35	136.03	86
1	16.74	14.73	14.17	11.91	13.70	107.52	141.48	76
2	13.20	15.08	13.79	13.30	15.30	98.56	136.87	72
3	14.78	15.43	12.04	13.33	15.33	100.65	174.9	58
4	17.95	15.76	12.71	12.85	14.78	106.63	179.62	59

Source: Data from the S&P *Analysts Handbook* and the *Economic Report of the President,* 1985.

interest rates, and rate of inflation. Multiple regression analysis, one of the most widely used of all statistical tools, measures the effect of two or more independent variables on the dependent variable. The multiple regression model can be written in linear form as:

$$Y_c = a + b_1 x_1 + b_2 x_2 + b_3 x_3$$

where Y_c is the computed or estimated value of the dependent variable Y, and x_1, x_2, x_3 are the independent variables. The term a is the value of Y_c when all the x's are zero. The terms b_1, b_2, b_3, . . . are the regression coefficients. Each measures the change in Y per unit change in that particular independent variable. For instance, b_1 measures the change in Y when x_1 changes by 1 unit.

Multiple regression analysis has wide application in many areas because most economic and noneconomic phenomena are caused by or related to a number of factors (independent variables). The availability of computers and computer programs makes it relatively easy to apply multiple regression analysis in actual problems.

Since the general price level of stocks is determined by a number of factors, the multiple regression method may be one method to evaluate and forecast the general level of stock prices. Let us see how *Value Line* uses multiple regression to forecast stock price levels.

The *Value Line* Approach

A multiple regression model is used by the *Value Line Investment Survey* to forecast the general level of stock prices. The equation they used for the year 1986 was:[15]

$$P_t = 1.019 P_{t-1} \times \left(\frac{\text{Dividends}_t}{\text{Dividends}_{t-1}} \right)^{.273} \times \left(\frac{\text{Earnings}_t}{\text{Earnings}_{t-1}} \right)^{.242}$$

$$\times \left(\frac{\text{Aaa Bond Yield}_t}{\text{Aaa Bond Yield}_{t-1}} \right)^{-.268}$$

where:

P_t = the DJIA in the current year

P_{t-1} = the DJIA a year ago

Dividend_t = the dividend amount on the DJIA in the current year

Dividend_{t-1} = the dividends on the DJIA a year ago

See Figure 13–2 for *Value Line*'s computed values of the DJIA on the basis of the regression equation and the actual range of the DJIA during the

[15]*Value Line Investment Survey*, Part II, Section & Opinion, Dec. 27, 1985.

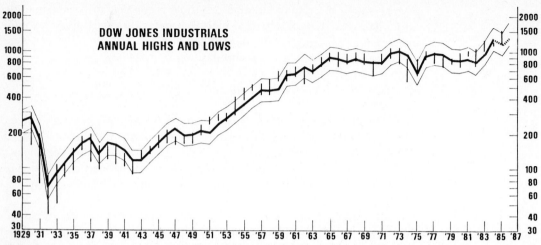

FIGURE 13–2   Computed Values of the DJIA Compared with the Actual Range of DJIA, 1929–1985

Regression Formula: $P_t = 1.019\, P_{t-1} \times \left[\dfrac{\text{Dividends}_t}{\text{Dividends}_{t-1}}\right]^{.273} \times \left[\dfrac{\text{Earnings}_t}{\text{Earnings}_{t-1}}\right]^{.242} \times \left[\dfrac{\text{Aaa Bond Yld}_t}{\text{Aaa Bond Yld}_{t-1}}\right]^{-.268}$

In three parts: Part I is the Summary & Index. This is Part II, Selection & Opinion. Part III is Ratings & Reports. Volume XLI, No. 14.

Source: Value Line Investment Survey, Dec. 27, 1985. ©1985 Value Line, Inc. Reprinted by permission.

period 1929–1985. The vertical bars in the chart indicate the actual range of DJIA in each year. The dark center curve across the chart indicates the computed value of the DJIA for each year on the basis of the regression equation. Notice that the computed values of the DJIA for most years were within the actual range of high and low of the DJIA. However, for a few years the computed value of the DJIA was either too high or too low compared with the actual range of the DJIA in these years.

A good forecast of the general level of stock prices on the basis of the regression equation requires two conditions. Obviously, the multiple regression model must identify the appropriate independent variables that affect the general level of stock prices. Then, the forecaster must have reasonably accurate estimates of the independent variables in the equation for the forthcoming period.

For 1986, *Value Line* explained its forecast as follows:

Value Line's model of the Dow Jones Industrials calls for that index to average 1435 in 1986—about 7% below its closing price of 1544 on Thursday, December 19th. This forecast, however, represents the midpoint of a wide range, from 1150 to 1800. Based on the formula at the bottom of this page, there are 95 chances out of 100 that the Dow's 1986 average will be in this range. Since this range still leaves open considerable possibility of price appreciation from the current level, the model's results have not led us to abandon our "full invested" stance. Since 1981, the Dow has shown a preference for the upper half of the model's projection band.[16]

As shown in Figure 13–2, the actual range of the DJIA from 1977 to 1979 was below the computed value by *Value Line,* but since 1981 the actual range of the DJIA has been above the computed value by *Value Line.*

Value Line felt that the reason the valuation tends to over- or under-shoot the mark is probably because a key missing variable, investor psychology, cannot be quantified.

The investment environment often changes quickly. Statistical analysis on the basis of annual data cannot capture such changes.

The Analysts' View

Analysts, as appraisers of securities, play an important role in the decision making of both individual and institutional investors. It is, therefore, important and instructive to learn how analysts view the stock valuation process.

Chugh and Meador conducted a survey of 2000 security analysts in 1984, inquiring about their views on stock valuation.[17] The variables emphasized most by the analysts are about the same for both the short term and longer term. They are: prospects of the relevant industry; expected change in earnings per share; expected return on equity; and general economic conditions.

The analysts reported that qualitative factors are as important as quantitative financial and economic variables in stock valuation. They look at the qualitative factors as a means to validate or modify quantitative findings about a stock. The key qualitative factors are the quality and depth of management, market dominance of the company, the quality of a company's strategic plans and planning system, and strategic credibility (ability to achieve stated goals).

The consensus valuation process included these factors:

1. A quantitative analysis of the performance and outlook of the company, its industry, and the economy.
2. An analysis of qualitative factors of the company as a means to validate or modify quantitative findings about the company.
3. A forecast of rate of return on equity, earnings growth rate, and earnings per share for the foreseeable future.
4. An estimate of the value of the stock on the basis of forecasted earnings of the company and its quality rating in the opinion of the analyst.

---

[16]Ibid.

[17]Lal Chugh and Joseph Meader, "The Stock Valuation Process: The Analysts' View." *Financial Analysts Journal,* Nov.–Dec. 1984.

SUMMARY

In this chapter we have discussed various methods and procedures for the valuation of individual stocks as well as the valuation of the general level of stock prices. Valuation is an indispensable part of investment analysis. The purpose of valuation is to find out whether the security under consideration is fairly priced on the basis of historical performance and definable prospects of the company.

Stock prices are determined by the expectations of buyers and sellers. Expectations are greatly influenced by current developments and "crowd" thinking at the moment. General expectations are frequently found to be very different from reality. Consequently, stock prices can differ substantially from "normal value" and sometimes for a prolonged period of time.

The fact that many professional investment managers place a great deal of emphasis on short-term gains and turnover of their portfolios does not alleviate, but rather tends to accentuate, the volatility of the stock market. J. M. Keynes commented on the behavior of professional money managers and the vagaries of the stock market:

> A conventional valuation which is established as the outcome of the mass psychology of a large number of ignorant individuals is liable to change violently as the result of a sudden fluctuation of opinion due to factors which do not really make much difference to the prospective yield; since there will be no strong roots of conviction to hold it steady. In abnormal times in particular, when the hypothesis of an indefinite continuance of the existing state of affairs is less plausible than usual even though there are no express grounds to anticipate a definite change, the market will be subject to waves of optimistic and pessimistic sentiment, which are unreasoning and yet in a sense legitimate where no solid basis exists for a reasonable calculation.
>
> But there is one feature in particular which deserves our attention. It might have been supposed that competition between expert professionals, possessing judgment and knowledge beyond that of the average private investor, would correct the vagaries of the ignorant individual left to himself. It happens, however, that the energies and skill of the professional investor and speculator are mainly occupied otherwise. For most of these persons are, in fact, largely concerned, not with making superior long-term forecasts of the probable yield of an investment over its whole life, but with forecasting changes in the conventional basis of valuation a short time ahead of the general public. They are concerned, not with what an investment is really worth to a man who buys it "for keeps," but with what the market will value it at, under the influence of mass psychology, three months or a year hence.[18]

The stock market in the short run is unpredictable, and it is wise to have a "margin of safety" at all times. While it is necessary to forecast the

---

[18]J. M. Keynes, *The General Theory of Employment, Interest and Money* (New York: Harcourt, Brace, 1936), pp. 154–55.

value of an individual stock and the market in general, we should recognize the possibility that actual market prices can sometimes deviate substantially from the forecasted level. Therefore, we should be realistic enough to have reservations about our own forecast or the forecast of anyone else, expert or not.

Five approaches to valuation were discussed. They are: present value of future income approach, price-earnings approach, cash-flow approach, price/sales approach, and intrinsic value approach. Many analysts use the price-earnings approach in the valuation of common stocks.

In recent years, many researchers have endeavored to pinpoint the factors that seem to determine the P/E level of an individual stock. Four factors seem to be particularly important:

1. Expected growth rate of earnings per share
2. Degree of confidence in the realization of the expected earnings growth rate
3. Level of market interest rate
4. Actual earnings growth rate per share in the last five to seven years

Another useful way to evaluate common stock is by comparing the stock with the industry average or the general market index over a period of years.

Valuation of the "general market" is probably even more important than valuation of individual stocks, because it provides a feeling as to whether the "general market" at the time is relatively high, low, or about right. The methods of valuing the general market are basically the same as the valuation of individual stocks.

QUESTIONS AND PROBLEMS

1. An investor is considering a stock that paid $1.60 in dividends in the last four quarters. The dividend is expected to grow annually at 10 percent for the next five years. The price of the stock is now at $30 and is expected to command a price of $45 in five years. The investor demands a return of 12 percent. What is the present value of the stock? Should the investor buy the stock?

2. A stock paid $1 in dividends in the last twelve months. It is expected that the long-term growth rate of dividends and earnings will be 7 percent. The current yield on a Treasury bill is 6 percent. The investor feels that a 4 percent premium for risk should be added. What is the present value of this stock?

3. An investor has the following estimates for a growth stock:

   a. Initial growth rate of dividend   14%
   b. Terminal growth rate of dividend   5%

      c. Transition period   12 years
      d. Discount rate   11%

The stock pays an annual dividend of $2. What is the present value of this growth stock?

4. What are some of the important factors that seem to determine the P/E level of an individual stock? Why?

5. What are some of the decision rules suggested by Benjamin Graham to individual investors for the purchase of common stocks? Evaluate these rules.

6. Evaluate RCA common stock on the basis of comparison to the industry average or general market index or both.

7. Evaluate the outlook for the general level of stock prices in the coming year, using one of the following approaches:

    a. Present worth approach
    b. Capitalizing average past earnings approach
    c. Price-earnings approach
    d. Multiple regression approach

8. Prepare a table listing the current price-earnings ratios for thirty industry groups. Explain why some industry groups are selling at high P/E whereas a few others are selling at very low P/E.

9. If the value of common stock is dependent on earnings, why is it that common stock of companies without earnings still have a market value?

10. What are the dangers involved in purchasing a high P/E growth stock?

11. Select two promising stocks listed on the New York Stock Exchange at current market prices. Substantiate your judgment with analysis and valuation of each.

12. Evaluate the following six stocks and find out which one is most attractive and which is least attractive based on current market price:

    U.S. Steel common
    Bethlehem Steel common
    Polaroid common
    Eastman Kodak common
    Goodyear Tire common
    Firestone common

APPENDIX: Derivation of the Valuation Formula (Equation 13.3) with Constant Growth Rate of Dividend

Rewrite Equation 13.1 as follows:

$$P_0 = \frac{D_0(1 + g)^1}{(1 + k)^1} + \frac{D_0(1 + g)^2}{(1 + k)^2} + \frac{D_0(1 + g)^3}{(1 + k)^3} + \cdots + \frac{D_0(1 + g)^n}{(1 + k)^n}$$

$$= D_0\left[\frac{(1 + g)}{(1 + k)} + \frac{(1 + g)^2}{(1 + k)^2} + \frac{(1 + g)^3}{(1 + k)^3} + \cdots + \frac{(1 + g)^n}{(1 + k)^n}\right] \quad \text{(A.1)}$$

Multiply both sides of the equation by $(1 + k)/(1 + g)$:

$$\left[\frac{(1 + k)}{(1 + g)}\right]P_0 = D_0\left[1 + \frac{(1 + g)}{(1 + k)} + \frac{(1 + g)^2}{(1 + k)^2} + \cdots \frac{(1 + g)^{n-1}}{(1 + k)^{n-1}}\right] \quad \text{(A.2)}$$

Subtract Equation A.1 from Equation A.2 to obtain:

$$\left[\frac{(1 + k)}{(1 + g)} - 1\right]P_0 = D_0\left[1 - \frac{(1 + g)^n}{(1 + k)^n}\right]$$

$$\left[\frac{(1 + k) - (1 + g)}{(1 + g)}\right]P_0 = D_0\left[1 - \frac{(1 + g)^n}{(1 + k)^n}\right] \quad \text{(A.3)}$$

Assuming k is larger than g, as n approaches infinity, the term in brackets on the right side of Equation A.3 approaches 1, leaving

$$\left[\frac{(1 + k) - (1 + g)}{(1 + g)}\right]P_0 = D_0,$$

which simplifies to Equation A.4:

$$(k - g)P_0 = D_0(1 + g) = D_1.$$

$$P_0 = \frac{D_1}{k - g} \quad \text{(A.4)}$$

REFERENCES

Bauman, W. Scott. *Estimating the Present Value of Common Stocks by the Variable Rate Method*. Ann Arbor, Mich.: University of Michigan, 1963.

———. "Investment Returns & Present Values." *Financial Analysts Journal*, Nov.–Dec. 1969.

Bernhard, Arnold. "Investing in Common Stocks." *The Value Line Investment Survey,* 1975.

Chugh, Lal, and Meader, Joseph. "The Stock Valuation Process: The Analysts' View." *Financial Analysts Journal,* Nov.–Dec. 1984.

Cohen, Jerome B. "Analysis of Common Stock." *Financial Analyst's Handbook.* Homewood, Ill.: Dow Jones-Irwin, 1975.

D'Ambrosio, Charles A. "Truth, Reality and Financial Analysis." *Financial Analysts Journal,* July–Aug. 1982.

Ellis, Charles D. "Ben Graham: Ideas as Mementos." *Financial Analysts Journal,* July–Aug. 1982.

Elton, E. J., and Gruber, M. J. *Security Evaluation and Portfolio Analysis.* Englewood Cliffs, N.J.: Prentice-Hall, 1972.

Financial Analysts Research Foundation. *The Renaissance of Value.* Charlottesville, Virginia, 1964.

Fisher, Kenneth L. "Price-Sales: A New Tool for Measuring Stock Popularity." *American Association of Individual Investors Journal,* June 1984.

Givoly, Dan, and Lakonishok, Josef. "The Quality of Analysts' Forecast of Earnings." *Financial Analysts Journal,* Sept.–Oct. 1984.

Goodman, David A., and Peavy, John W., III. "Industry Relative Price-Earnings Ratios as Indicators of Investment Returns." *Financial Analysts Journal,* July–Aug. 1983.

Gray, William S., III. "Long-Term Outlook for the Stock Market." *Financial Analysts Journal,* July–Aug. 1979.

Graham, B., Dodd, D. L., and Cottle, S. *Security Analysis,* 4th ed. New York: McGraw-Hill, 1962, Part 4.

Griffin, Paul A. "Competitive Information in the Stock Market: An Empirical Study of Earnings, Dividends and Analysts Forecasts." *The Journal of Finance,* May 1976.

Hayes, D., and Bauman, W. *Investments: Analysis & Management,* 3rd ed. New York: Macmillan, 1976, Chapters 16–17.

Huang, Stanley S. C. *Techniques of Investment Analysis.* New York: Intext Educational Publishers, 1972, Chapters 7–8.

————. *Corporate Earning Power and Valuation of Common Stock.* Larchmont, N.Y.: Investors Intelligence, Inc., 1966.

Keran, Michael W. "Expectations, Money, and the Stock Market." *Review,* Federal Reserve Bank of St. Louis, Jan. 1971.

Keynes, J. M. *The General Theory of Employment, Interest, and Money.* New York: Harcourt & Brace, 1936, Chapter 12.

Makridakis, Spyros, Wheelwright, Steven C., and McGee, Victor E. *Forecasting: Methods & Applications.* New York: John Wiley & Sons, 1983.

Malkiel, Burton G. "Equity Yields, Growth and the Structure of Share Prices." *American Economic Review,* Dec. 1963.

Metz, Robert. "Calculating Price of Growth." *New York Times,* April 16, 1981.

Milne, Robert D. "Regression Analysis." *Financial Analyst's Handbook.* Homewood, Ill.: Dow Jones-Irwin, 1975.

Modigliani, Franco, and Cohen, R. A. "Inflation and the Stock Market." *The Financial Analysts Journal,* March–April 1979.

Murray, Roger. "Graham and Dodd: A Durable Discipline." *Financial Analysts Journal,* Sept.–Oct. 1984.

Oppenheimer, Henry R. "A Test of Ben Graham's Stock Selection Criteria." *Financial Analysts Journal*, Sept.–Oct. 1984.

Soldofsky, R. M., and Murphy, J. T. *Growth Yields on Common Stocks, Theory and Tables*. Iowa City, Iowa: State University of Iowa, 1963.

Umstead, David A. "Forecasting Stock Market Prices." *The Journal of Finance*, May 1977.

Wilcox, Jarrod W. "The P/B-ROE Valuation Model." *Financial Analysts Journal*, Jan.–Feb. 1984.

Zacks, Leonard. "EPS Forecasts — Accuracy is not Enough." *Financial Analysts Journal*, March–April 1979.

IV

Analysis of Preferred Stock, Convertible Securities, Options, and Financial Futures

14

The Hybrids: Preferred Stock, Convertible Preferred, and Convertible Bonds

Preferred stock is a hybrid security. Legally, it represents a part of equity or ownership of a firm, but it has only a limited claim on the earnings and properties of the corporation. The general characteristics of preferred stock are:

Preference. Preferred stock has preference over common stocks as to the distribution of dividends and assets in the event of liquidation.

Par Value. Preferred stock usually has a par value, and this value establishes the amount due to the preferred stockholders in the event of liquidation.

Dividend. Preferred stock has a fixed amount of dividend that is usually expressed as a percentage of the par value of the preferred stock.

Cumulative Dividend. Dividends on preferred stocks are usually cumulative. Dividends that are omitted in one year have to be made up in following years before common dividends can be paid.

No Maturity. Preferred stocks do not have maturity dates. They are perpetual securities.

Non-Voting. Preferred stockholders usually do not have voting rights. When preferred stock dividends are not paid for a certain period of time, preferred stockholders are entitled to elect a certain number of directors to the company's board of directors in order to protect their rights and interests.

Call Provision. Some preferred stocks may include a call provision, which states at what time and price the issuer may call the preferred stock for redemption.

Sinking Fund. Some preferred stocks may include a sinking fund provision, which specifies that the issuer will allocate funds annually to purchase in the open market a certain percentage of the preferred stock outstanding.

> *Market Behavior.* The annual dividend income from preferred stock is fixed. High-grade preferred stocks behave in the market place much like high-grade corporate bonds. Their prices are affected mainly by the variations in market interest rates. The prices of speculative, low-grade preferred stocks, on the other hand, depend mainly on the financial and business outlook of the firm.

PREFERRED STOCK

Preferred stock is a part of equity. Usually it has no maturity. Failure to pay dividends on preferred stock will forbid the corporation to pay dividends on common stock. Such an action, while tarnishing the image of the firm, will not force the corporation into any legal problems. Often, when a corporation is doing poorly but is still able to pay dividends on preferred stocks, the board of directors of the corporation may choose instead to omit the dividend on preferred stocks because there is no severe punishment to the corporation if it does so.

Theoretically, because they are riskier, the yield on preferred stock should be more than the yield on corporate bonds of the same rating. Graham, Dodd, and Cottle suggest that dividend-oriented investors should not buy preferred stock unless they can obtain both safety and a yield differential of one percent over that afforded by a bond of similar safety.[1]

Actual Market Yield on Preferred Stock

The actual market yields on the S&P AA utility bonds and high-grade preferred stocks from 1955 to 1984 are shown in Table 14–1. The yield on preferred stock has been lower than the yield on AA utility bonds for each year since 1963. In the ten years 1975–84, the average spread in yield between preferred stock and bonds was a negative 1.19 percent.

The seemingly abnormal spread between the yield on high-grade preferred stocks and the yield on high-grade bonds can be traced to the influence of two tax provisions.

First, interest expenses on bonds are a deductible expense in the computation of net income of the issuing corporation, whereas the dividends on preferred stock are paid from net profits and are not deductible for income tax purposes. This provision provides an incentive to a corporation to issue bonds rather than preferred stock if the capital structure of the corporation permits. As a consequence, in recent years a limited supply of new high-grade preferred stock has been coming to the marketplace.

---

[1]B. Graham, Dodd, D. L., and Cottle, S. *Security Analysis* (New York: McGraw-Hill, 1962), p. 382.

TABLE 14–1   Yield Comparisons: Utility Bonds versus Preferred Stocks, 1955–1984

	Standard & Poor's AA Utility Bonds	Standard & Poor's High-Grade Preferred Stocks	Yield on Preferred Stocks over Utility Bonds
1955	3.14	4.01	0.87
56	3.48	4.25	0.77
57	4.05	4.63	0.58
58	3.90	4.45	0.55
59	4.53	4.69	0.16
60	4.54	4.75	0.21
61	4.52	4.66	0.14
62	4.34	4.50	0.16
63	4.32	4.30	−0.02
64	4.44	4.32	−0.12
65	4.55	4.33	−0.22
66	5.23	4.87	−0.36
67	5.67	5.34	−0.33
68	6.36	5.78	−0.58
69	7.39	6.41	−0.98
70	8.35	7.22	−1.13
71	7.71	6.75	−0.96
72	7.53	6.88	−0.65
73	7.83	7.23	−0.60
74	8.63	8.24	−0.39
75	9.17	8.36	−0.81
76	8.82	7.98	−0.84
77	8.44	7.61	−0.83
78	9.06	8.25	−0.81
79	9.97	9.11	−0.86
80	12.26	10.60	−1.66
81	14.67	12.36	−2.31
82	14.04	12.53	−1.51
83	12.01	11.02	−0.99
84	12.89	11.62	−1.27

Source: Data from Standard & Poor's *Statistical Section.*

Second, as we mentioned in Chapter 2, to avoid double or triple taxation, 85 percent of dividends on common and preferred stock received by corporate investors are tax-exempt. As a result, institutional investors like insurance companies would prefer to buy high-grade preferred stocks rather than bonds. This bids up the price of preferred stock and reduces the yield on preferred stock to a level actually lower than on bonds. Since the risk of holding high-grade preferred stocks is not materially greater than holding high-grade bonds, the legal weakness in the preferred contract does not create any problem to some institutional investors.

Investment Implications for Individual Investors

Because the dividends on preferred stocks are wholly taxable to individual investors, and the yield on preferred stocks is actually lower than on bonds of the same grade, there is no logical reason for individual investors to buy preferred stocks. If they are interested in dependable income, they should buy high-grade corporate bonds or municipal bonds. On the other hand, if they are interested in appreciation as well as income, then they should look into common stocks.

Speculative, low-grade preferred stocks do offer a tempting yield, but here the risk is substantial. Buyers of such securities are speculators rather than investors. In general, investors should be warned that they should not buy preferred stocks for higher yield at a sacrifice of quality.

CONVERTIBLE PREFERRED STOCK

A convertible preferred stock is a preferred stock with the additional feature that the preferred stock can be converted into a specified number of common shares of the issuing company at the option of the holder of the preferred stock. For the analysis of convertible preferred stock, a few terms need to be explained:

Conversion Ratio. This is simply the number of shares of common stock for which the preferred stock can be exchanged. A conversion ratio of five means that the preferred stock can be exchanged for five shares of common stock of the issuing company.

Conversion Price. The conversion price is obtained by dividing the conversion ratio into the par value of the preferred stock, which is usually $100. In the current example, the conversion price is:

$$\text{Conversion price} = \frac{\$100}{5} = \$20$$

Conversion Value. The conversion value is the current market price of the common stock multiplied by the conversion ratio. If the market price of the common stock is now at $15 per share, then the conversion value of the preferred stock is $15 \times 5 = \$75$.

Investment Value. The investment value of the preferred stock is the estimated value of the preferred stock without the conversion feature. In other words, it is the value at which a straight preferred stock of the same rating and dividend would sell in the marketplace. The investment value provides downside protection in the event that the price of common stock of the issuing company should decline and make the conversion feature almost worthless.

Premium over Conversion Value. The premium over conversion value, which is usually expressed as a percent, can be obtained from the following formula:

$$\text{Premium over conversion value (\%)} = \frac{\text{Market price of preferred} - \text{Conversion value}}{\text{Conversion value}}$$

In the current example, if the preferred stock is selling at $90, the premium over conversion value is:

$$\frac{\$90 - 75}{\$75} = 20\%$$

The premium over conversion value indicates the extent to which the common stock must appreciate before the preferred stockholder would begin to have capital gain.

In Figure 14–1 we see the relationships among price of common stock, conversion value, investment value, and market price of convertible preferred stock. When the price of common stock declines, the price of preferred stock usually declines less. On the other hand, when the price of common stock rises, the convertible preferred would also rise, but not as fast. Only after the convertible preferred rises above par value will it rise proportionally with common, because at that time the convertible preferred is simply selling as a multiple number of common shares. In the figure, we assume that the convertible preferred stock would sell for $70 without the conversion feature.

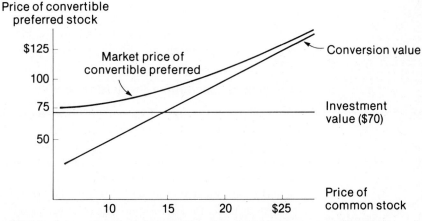

FIGURE 14–1   **Relationships among the Price of Common, Conversion Value, Investment Value, and Market Price of Convertible Preferred**

Advantages of Convertible Preferred Stock

Some of the possible advantages of owning convertible preferred stock, from the standpoint of investors, are

1. The convertible preferred stock as regular preferred stock has preference over common stock in the payment of dividends and the distribution of property in the case of liquidation.
2. If the company's earning power grows, resulting in higher prices for its common stock, the convertible preferred stock representing a certain number of common shares will receive capital gains.
3. The dividend yield on convertible preferred stock is usually higher than the dividend yield on common stock.
4. In times of adverse economic developments and general decline in stock prices, convertible preferred stock usually declines less than common stock because of the relatively higher fixed return of dividends.

Disadvantages of Convertible Preferred Stock

The disadvantages of convertible preferred stock are:

1. The yield on convertible preferred stock is usually less than the yield on straight preferred stock of the same quality or rating.
2. A call provision is usually included in the certificate of convertible preferred stock. The call provision limits the degree of possible appreciation if the company prospers.
3. Because of the lower yield on convertible preferred stock than on straight preferred stock, the adverse impact from rising interest rates in the future, if they occur, can be much greater than on straight preferred stock.
4. Sometimes the conversion feature is added by the issuing company to help distribute a preferred stock of relatively low quality.

Analysis of Convertible Preferred Stock

The analysis of convertible preferred stock consists of four steps. The first step is to evaluate the convertible preferred stock as if it were a straight preferred stock. The analysis of a straight preferred stock, as in the analysis of a corporate bond, requires the investigation and evaluation of the economic significance of the company and the industry in which it operates, the quality of the management of the firm, financial resources of the firm, and the provisions in the preferred contract. The purpose of the analysis is to find out whether the corporation can meet its obligations on the preferred stock under all conceivable economic circumstances, including severe recessions.

The second step is to investigate how much yield the buyers of convertible preferred stock have to give up for the conversion privilege. Related to this is the assessment of the extent of the price decline that may occur if market interest rates rise in the future.

The third step is to determine how much an investor will likely gain from the conversion privilege if the company prospers.

The final step is to weigh prospective gain against prospective loss and decide whether the convertible preferred stock is an attractive buy compared to other investment opportunities.

CONVERTIBLE BONDS

Convertible bonds, like convertible preferred stocks, are hybrid securities. They are bonds and at the same time common stocks. The conversion ratio indicates the number of shares of common stocks into which the bond can be converted.

The advantages of convertible bonds are:

1. The convertible bond is debt of the issuing corporation. It has a fixed claim on the earnings and assets of the corporation ahead of common and preferred stocks.
2. The yield on convertible bond is usually much higher than the dividend yield on the underlying common stock.
3. If the issuing company grows in earning power, resulting in higher prices of common stock, the convertible bond can participate in the upward price movements of the underlying common stock.
4. In times of adverse economic developments and decline in stock prices, the convertible bond usually declines less than the underlying common stocks because of the relatively higher interest income than dividend on common stock.

However, these advantages are counterbalanced by several disadvantages:

1. The yield on convertible bonds is usually less than the yield on nonconvertible bonds of the same corporation or of the same rating.
2. There is usually a call provision, which limits the possibility of capital gain.
3. As a senior security, the price of a convertible bond can be adversely affected if the market interest rate rises.
4. The fall in price of the underlying common stock can make the conversion feature less attractive, and, therefore, can cause the price of convertible bonds to decline.

Analysis of Convertible Bonds

The analysis of convertible bonds is similar to the analysis of convertible preferred stock and involves several steps:

1. Evaluate the convertible bond as if it were a nonconvertible bond to determine its investment grade or quality.
2. Determine the yield difference between nonconvertible bonds and convertible bonds of the same quality. The difference in yield is the yield sacrifice in exchange for the conversion feature.
3. Determine the premium over conversion value, which indicates to what extent the common stock must appreciate before the convertible bond will begin to have capital appreciation.
4. Assess the possibility of a rise in interest rates and the extent of a possible decline in the price of the convertible bond.
5. Evaluate the common stock and the possibility and extent of a rise in its price.
6. Weigh both the favorable and unfavorable factors to make a final assessment of the attractiveness of convertible bonds.

Sample Analysis of Eastman Kodak Convertible Bond

We select the Eastman Kodak convertible bond as an example to illustrate the method of analyzing a convertible bond. The pertinent information on the Eastman Kodak convertible bond and common stock in August, 1985, is listed as follows[2]:

Description: $8\frac{1}{4}$ percent convertible subordinate debentures, maturing in 2007:

Total amount outstanding	$275 million
Call price	107.43 ($1,074.3)
Conversion ratio: Each bond convertible to 14.67 shares of common stock (Conversion price = $1000/14.67 = $68.17)	
Price of convertible bond on 8/21/85	$93\frac{1}{2}$ ($935)
Current yield	82.50/935 = 8.82%
Yield to maturity	9.20%

Current information on Eastman Kodak common stock:

Price of common stock on 8/21/85	$44.25
Price range, last 12 months	$52 − $41\frac{1}{4}
Dividend, last 4 quarters	$2.40
Dividend yield	2.40/44.25 = 5.42%
Earnings per share estimated for 1985	$3.40
Estimated price-earnings ratio	44.25/3.40 = 13

[2] Source of data: *Value Line Investment Survey* and *New York Times*.

Quality of the Convertible Bond

The first step in the analysis of a convertible bond is to evaluate the quality of the convertible bond as if it were a straight bond. Eastman Kodak is the world's largest producer of photographic products. It is also a leading producer of synthetic textile fibers, plastics, and chemicals.

Some of the important business and financial statistics of the company for the period 1980–85 are taken from the *Value Line Investment Survey* and presented in Table 14–2.

The growth rate of sales per share over the period 1980–85 was about 3.8 percent per year. Earnings per share had a moderate decline during the same period. However, even in its worst year, 1983, the company made almost enough profits to maintain its regular dividend requirements for common stock.

The company used very little leverage until 1984. The ratio of long-term debt to net worth is expected to increase in the future to 18.6 percent by *Value Line*, but that is still very low compared with other companies.

The overall picture indicates that Eastman Kodak is a strong company and has a well-established industry position. Its capital structure is very conservative. The convertible bond is of high quality; this is confirmed by the AA rating given it by Moody's Investors Service.

Yield Sacrifice and Possibility of Price Decline

The second step in the analysis of a convertible bond is to find out the amount of yield sacrificed due to the conversion privilege and, in addition, the extent of a possible price decline if interest rates increase. See Table 14–3 for the relevant data and some computations.

The yield sacrifice is 3.18 percent, a 26.5 percent reduction from the yield on a nonconvertible bond of the same quality. The yield sacrifice, though substantial, is reasonable in terms of normal experience. The investment value of the convertible bond is the value at which the bond would provide a yield equivalent to that offered by a nonconvertible bond, which is 12 percent in this case. The investment value indicates the level of protection if the common stock does not look good and the conversion feature becomes almost worthless.

TABLE 14–2   Business and Financial Statistics of Eastman Kodak Corp., 1980–1985

	1980	1981	1982	1983	1984	1985 Est.
Sales per share	40.21	42.41	43.56	40.95	45.42	48.15
Earnings per share	$ 4.77	5.11	4.75	2.27	3.81	3.40
Total net profits (in $ million)	$1153.6	1239.0	1162.0	565.0	923.0	780.0
Long-term debt (in $ million)	$ 207.9	208.0	489.0	630.0	612.0	1360.0
Net worth (in $ million)	$6027.8	6770.0	7541.0	7520.0	7137.0	7325.0
Long-term debt to net worth	3.4%	3.1%	6.5%	8.4%	8.6%	18.6%

Source: Data from *Value Line Investment Survey,* 1985.

TABLE 14–3   Analysis of Yield Sacrifice and Possibility of Price Decline of the Eastman Kodak Convertible Bond

Current yield on convertible bond 82.50/935	8.82%
Current yield on nonconvertible bond of the same quality	12.0%
Yield sacrifice on the convertible bond	3.18%
Yield sacrifice in percent 3.18/12	26.5%
Current market price of convertible bond	$935
Investment value of convertible bond 82.50/.12	$687.50
Investment value as percent of market price 687.50/935	73.5%

Source: Data from *Moody's Bond Survey,* 1985.

Since the convertible bond is partly a fixed-return security, it will be affected by future movement in interest rates. The prospect of rising interest rates usually does not favor the prices of both the convertible bond and the common stock into which it can be converted. Since a rise in interest rates affects the yield on the convertible bond and may also push down the price of common stock, it is most likely that the extent of a price decline of the convertible bond will be greater than the percentage increase in market interest rates. Hence, the prospect of the trend of interest rates is a critical question that must be examined carefully by the potential buyer of a convertible bond.

Possibility of Capital Gain

The third step in the analysis of a convertible bond is to appraise the possibility and extent of a capital gain due to the conversion feature. Some relevant data and computations are shown in Table 14–4.

TABLE 14–4   Analysis of the Possibility of Capital Gain of an Eastman Kodak Convertible Bond

Conversion ratio: Each share of convertible bond is convertible to 14.67 shares of common stock	
Market price of convertible bond	$935
Market price of Eastman Kodak's common stock	$ 44.25
Conversion value: $44.25 × 14.67	$649.15
Premium over conversion value $\dfrac{\$935 - 649.15}{\$649.15} =$	44%
Yield on convertible bond 82.5/935	8.82%
Yield on Eastman Kodak common stock 2.40/44.25	5.42%
Earnings per share of common stock estimated for 1985	$3.40
Estimated price-earnings ratio for 1985 44.25/3.40	$ 13

Average annual price-earnings ratio of common stock in last five years:

	1980	1981	1982	1983	1984	
Average P/E	8.1	9.4	11	22.1	12.3	
Relative P/E	1.08	1.14	1.21	1.87	1.13	
Price range of Eastman Kodak common stock, last twelve months						$52–41¼

Source: Data from *Value Line Investment Survey,* 1985 and *Moody's Bond Survey,* 1985.

The premium over conversion value was 44 percent. This means that the common stock has to appreciate more than 44 percent before the convertible bond can begin to have capital gains on the common stock to which it can be converted. The premium of 44 percent is much more than the normal range of 20 to 30 percent.

The current yield on the convertible bond is 8.82 percent, which exceeds the yield of common (5.42 percent) by more than 60 percent.

Eastman Kodak is expected to earn $3.40 per share in 1985, which is lower than the $3.81 earned in 1984. However, *Value Line* estimates that the earnings per share will improve substantially to $4.40 in 1986.

The average P/E of the stock during the years 1980–1984, excluding 1983, was 10.2, and the relative P/E (relative to all dividend-paying stocks under *Value Line* review) during the same four years was 1.14. Currently (August, 1985), the stock is selling at a P/E of 13 and the relative P/E is $13/11.8 = 1.1$. The stock is, therefore, selling at higher P/E now than its average P/E in the four prior years, but the stock is not selling at higher P/E relative to the market.

Should the stock earn as much as $4.40 per share in 1986 as estimated by *Value Line,* and if the current P/E of 13 remains in 1986, the stock will sell for $13 \times \$4.40 = \$57.20$. But these are two big *ifs,* and we are skeptical of both assumptions. On the other hand, if the stock earns $4 and the P/E will be 12 in 1986, the stock will sell for $12 \times \$4 = \$48$, which is about $8\frac{1}{2}$ percent higher than the current market price at $44.25 per share.

Conclusion of Analysis

The analysis of the Eastman Kodak convertible bond has been completed. Now we need to pull together both the favorable and unfavorable factors and make a final assessment as to the attractiveness of the convertible bond.

The convertible bond is of investment grade. The current yield of 8.82 percent can be considered quite satisfactory, although there is a yield sacrifice of 3.18 percent compared with a nonconvertible bond of the same grade. The premium over conversion value is, however, too high at 44 percent. Eastman Kodak common is selling currently at a P/E of 13, compared to an average of 10.2 in the years, 1980–84 (excluding 1983, an abnormal year). The stock is selling at a relative P/E of 1.1, about the same in the years 1980–84 (excluding 1983). As the stock improves its earning picture in 1986, as expected by *Value Line,* there is a likelihood that the price of the stock will also gradually improve.

Weighing all the evidence, it seems that the favorable factors about the stock are almost counterbalanced by the unfavorable factors. If the investor is a genuine long-term investor, the Eastman Kodak convertible bond can be purchased. On the other hand, if the investor is looking for quick capital gains, he or she should avoid this convertible bond and look elsewhere.

PERFORMANCE OF CONVERTIBLE SECURITIES

In Table 14–5 we see the performance of convertible bonds and preferred stocks compared to nonconvertible securities during the period 1960–75.[3] The annual rate of return is defined as (1) the dividends or interest received during the year, plus (2) the change in the market price of the security during the year, both divided by the market price at the beginning of the year.

Note in the second half of Table 14–5 the risk-return measurements of different classes of securities for four subperiods during the period 1960–73. Risk was measured by standard deviation of annual returns. On the basis of the table, the following observations can be noted:

1. From 1960 to 1975, the average annual return on convertible bonds of BBB rating was 0.052, which was slightly better than the yield of 0.034 for nonconvertible bonds of the same rating. However, the risk as measured by standard deviation was also greater for convertible bonds than for nonconvertible bonds.

2. From 1960 to 1975, the average annual return on convertible preferred stock of BBB rating was about the same as the return for medium-grade nonconvertible preferred stock. However, the risk as measured by standard deviation was much greater for convertible preferred than for nonconvertible preferred.

3. In the more recent period 1970–75, the nonconvertible bond of BBB rating performed better than the convertible bond of the same rating. The medium-grade nonconvertible preferred stock also performed better than the convertible stock in BBB rating. However, the reverse was true in the previous period 1965–69.

4. In recession years 1960, 1970, and 1973, nonconvertible bonds and preferred stocks performed better than convertible bonds and preferred stocks. However, in the recession year of 1974, the performance was comparable between convertible and nonconvertible securities.

5. For the different classes of convertible bonds and preferred stocks, the risk measured by standard deviation increased as quality of the issue declined. This demonstrates the extent to which the increase in risk is a function of quality assessment.

The overall record seems to indicate that the average performance of convertible securities was about the same as nonconvertible bonds and pre-

[3]R. M. Solodofsky, Stevenson, R. A., and Phillips, S. M. "Convertible Securities: New Issues, Conversions, and Performance Record," in *Investment Environment, Analysis, and Alternatives,* edited by R. A. Stevenson and S. M. Phillips (St. Paul, Minn.: West Publishing Co., 1977).

TABLE 14–5 Performance of Convertible Securities by Quality Class, and S&P 500, 1960 to 1975

Part I - Annual Yields

	Corporate Bonds				Preferred Stock						
	BBB Non-conv.	Convertible			Medium Grade Non-conv.	A	Convertible			S&P 500
		BBB	BB	B			BBB	BB	B	
1960	+.070	+.021	-.007	-.070	+.057	-----	-.043	-.019	-.075	-.003
1961	+.056	+.140	+.213	+.097	+.080	-----	+.075	+.121	+.272	+.293
1962	+.065	-.029	-.103	-.214	+.072	-----	+.009	-.022	-.071	-.093
1963	+.066	+.058	+.069	+.091	+.110	-----	+.080	+.052	+.047	+.216
1964	+.053	+.134	+.088	+.103	+.122	-----	+.095	+.140	-.033	+.162
1965	+.017	+.272	+.212	+.220	+.024	-----	+.091	+.208	+.308	+.123
1966	-.075	-.088	-.094	-.109	-.078	-----	-.053	-.048	-.120	-.079
1967	-.051	+.157	+.152	+.378	-.025	-----	+.277	+.293	+.442	+.204
1968	+.046	+.130	+.091	+.104	+.054	-----	+.239	+.163	+.089	+.149
1969	-.093	-.123	-.280	-.311	-.095	-----	-.235	-.198	-.366	-.113
1970	+.107	+.072	+.005	-.081	+.147	+.060	+.050	-.001	-.043	+.026
1971	+.170	+.071	+.252	+.234	+.125	+.228	+.122	+.141	+.063	+.132
1972	+.144	+.069	-.009	+.083	+.058	+.022	+.081	+.115	+.102	+.213
1973	-.029	-.131	-.126	-.125	-.035	-.173	-.235	-.225	-.123	-.162
1974	-.093	-.092	-.089	-.223	-.217	-.213	-.228	-.132	-.026	-.267
1975	+.155	+.293	+.239	+.383	+.258	+.402	+.437	+.494	+.226	+.369

Part II - Risk-Return Measurements

	BBB Non-conv.	BBB	BB	B	Medium Grade Non-conv.	A	BBB	BB	B	S&P 500
1960-64	+.062 (.006)	+.063 (.065)	+.047 (.105)	-.007 (.126)	+.088 (.024)	----- -----	+.042 (.052)	+.052 (.068)	+.020 (.130)	+.106 (.143)
1965-69	-.033 (.054)	+.059 (.152)	-.001 (.181)	+.026 (.245)	-.026 (.057)	----- -----	+.046 (.190)	+.068 (.181)	+.028 (.294)	+.049 (.128)
1970-75	+.071 (.100)	+.038 (.138)	+.035 (.149)	+.024 (.212)	+.044 (.151)	+.032 (.215)	+.013 (.230)	+.042 (.232)	+.027 (.113)	+.029 (.218)
1960-75	+.034 (.083)	+.052 (.125)	+.027 (.149)	+.015 (.203)	+.035 (.109)	----- -----	+.032 (.179)	(+.053) (.179)	(+.025) (.192)	+.059 (.173)

Note: The numbers in parenthesis represent one standard deviation of the average returns. The returns for the three subperiods and 16-year period are geometric returns.

ferred stocks. However, the variation in returns from year to year seemed to be greater for convertible securities than for nonconvertible securities. The empirical evidence dampens to some extent the enthusiasm shown by some who favor the use of convertible securities as investment vehicles on theoretical grounds.

QUESTIONS AND PROBLEMS

1. What are some of the general characteristics found in preferred stocks?
2. Do individual investors find preferred stocks attractive as a vehicle of investment?
3. Explain some advantages and disadvantages of convertible preferred stock.
4. How do you determine the premiums of a convertible security?
5. What are some of the analytic procedures for the analysis of convertible preferred stock?
6. What are some of the advantages and disadvantages of owning convertible bonds?
7. Select one convertible bond from *Moody's Bond Record* and analyze its investment attractiveness on the basis of current market price.
8. Under what circumstances will convertible securities, in general, likely decline in price?
9. What is the significance of the call price of a convertible security (a) from the issuer's viewpoint, and (b) from the investor's viewpoint?
10. Under what conditions is a convertible security deemed attractive?
11. Select an attractive convertible preferred stock or bond on the basis of current price and substantiate your recommendation with analysis.

REFERENCES

Arnold Bernhard Co. *More Profits and Less Risks: Convertible Securities & Warrants*. New York: Arnold Bernhard Co., 1970.

Baumol, W., Malkiel, B., and Quandt, R. "The Valuation of Convertible Securities." *Quarterly Journal of Economics*, Feb. 1966.

Brennan, M. J., and Schwartz, E. S. "Convertible Bonds: Valuation and Optimal Strategies for Call and Conversion." *Journal of Finance*, Dec. 1977.

———. "Analyzing Convertible Bonds." *Journal of Financial and Quantitative Analysis*, Nov. 1980.

Darst, David M. *The Complete Bond Book*. New York: McGraw-Hill, 1975, Chapter 10.

Hayes, D., and Bauman, W. *Investments: Analysis & Management*. New York: Macmillan, 1976, Chapter 3.

Jennings, Edward H. "An Estimate of Convertible Bond Premiums." *Journal of Financial & Quantitative Analysis*, Jan. 1974.

Liebowitz, Martin L. "Analysis of Convertible Bonds." *Financial Analyst's Handbook, Vol. 1*. Homewood, Ill.: Dow Jones-Irwin, 1975.

Noddings, Thomas C. *The Dow Jones-Irwin Guide to Convertible Securities*. Homewood, Ill.: Dow Jones-Irwin, 1973.

———. *Advanced Investment Strategies*. Homewood, Ill.: Dow Jones-Irwin, 1978.

Solodofsky, Robert M. "Yield-Risk Performance of Convertible Securities." *Financial Analysts Journal*, March–April 1971.

Solodofsky, R., Stevenson, R., and Phillips, S. "Convertible Securities: New Issues, Conversions, and Performance Record." *Investment Environment, Analysis, and Alternatives, A Book of Readings*, edited by Richard A. Stevenson and Susan M. Phillips. St. Paul, Minn.: West Publishing, 1977.

Walter, James E., and Que, Augustin V. "The Valuation of Convertible Bonds." *Journal of Finance*, June 1973.

Weil, Roman, Segall, Joel, and Green, David. "Premiums on Convertible Bonds." *Security Evaluation and Portfolio Analysis*, edited by E. J. Elton and M. J. Gruber. Englewood Cliffs, N.J.: Prentice-Hall, 1972.

15

Options and Warrants

OPTIONS

Options are contracts giving the holder the right to buy or sell a stated number of shares of a given security at a fixed price within a specified period of time. There are two basic types of options: calls and puts.

A call option is a contract giving the holder the right to purchase (call) 100 shares of a given security at a specified price (called the *exercise price* or *striking price*) within a specific period of time. The holder (buyer) of the call option pays a price called a *premium*.

A put option, on the other hand, is an option to sell. The holder has the right to sell to the writer (seller) of the option 100 shares of a given security at a specified price within a specific period of time. The holder or buyer of a put option pays a premium to the seller or writer of the option.

Some believe that options are very speculative and that investors should stay away from them. On the other hand, there are those who believe that the options market is the place to make quick and big money. Neither statement is true. Options, like stocks and bonds, are investment vehicles. One may make conservative use of the vehicle or one may speculate with them. Actually, if an investor has some basic understanding of the options market and options strategies, he or she can improve the chances of success in investment by using both options and stocks at the same time. In Wall Street there is a famous proverb: "To err is human, to hedge is divine." To hedge means to take counterbalancing action to protect possible losses. Options are the most flexible investment one can use to hedge a commitment.

THE OPTIONS MARKET

Over-the-Counter Market

Prior to the introduction of the Chicago Board Options Exchange, transactions in put and call options in the United States were all carried out in the over-the-counter market. About two dozen dealers and brokers were active in the market, and they were members of the Put and Call Dealers Association. These dealers and brokers usually served as middlemen between would-be buyers and sellers of options. They rarely took the position as the maker of options themselves.

Each call or put contract was individually negotiated between the buyer and the seller as to exercise price, maturity date, and amount of premium. There was no standardization either in exercise price or on dates of maturity. One call contract could be slightly different from another, even though the underlying stock was the same. Consequently, the resale of an option was both expensive (the difference between buying and selling price was substantial) and time consuming. Many times the maker (writer) and holder of options would have to sit out the duration of the contract, even though their option contracts were in bearer form and transferable.

Chicago Board Options Exchange (CBOE)

The creation of the Chicago Board Options Exchange (CBOE) in April of 1973 changed the whole picture of the options market and trading in the United States. The innovations introduced by the CBOE made trading in options as easy as trading in stocks. Investors and speculators responded with great enthusiasm. Now options are traded not only on the CBOE but also on the American Exchange, the Philadelphia Exchange, the Midwest Exchange, and the Pacific Exchange. Options traded on exchanges now account for more than 90 percent of the total volume.

The innovations introduced by the CBOE are the following:

1. *Standardization of maturity dates.* Under the present practice of exchanges, the expiration months are in three-month cycles. Some options expire in January, April, July, and October, while others expire in February, May, August, and November.
2. *Standardization of exercise price (or striking price).* The exercise price is the price per share at which the holder of the option may purchase the underlying stock upon exercise. Standardization of exercise price is accomplished in the following manner. When trading is introduced in a new expiration month, the exercise price is fixed at a dollar per share figure approximating the market price of the underlying stock. For example, if the market price of XYZ stock is 21 when trading is initiated in XYZ October options, the exercise price would ordinarily be set at 20; if the market price of the underlying stock were 48, the exercise price would ordinarily be set at 50; and if the market price were 107, the exercise price would ordinarily be set at 110. For stocks with prices below $200, the interval between exercise prices is usually $5 (for some stocks the interval can be $2.50). For stocks with prices over $200, the interval between exercise prices is $10.

3. *Range of striking prices.* New options are introduced from time to time after substantial price movements on underlying stocks. When significant price movements take place in an underlying stock, additional options with exercise prices reflecting such price movements may be opened for trading. For example, if stock option was first introduced at a striking price of $50, and the stock rises to $67, a new option will probably be offered at a striking price of $70.

4. *Central marketplace.* CBOE provides a central marketplace for continuous trading in call and put options, both new and old, issued by the Chicago Board.

5. *Adjustments to exercise price.* Unlike options traded in the over-the-counter market, no adjustment is made by the CBOE to reflect the declaration or payment of *ordinary cash dividends* as defined in the rules of the exchange. However, in the case of other distributions (stock dividend, stock split, or recapitalization), either the exercise price of options with respect to such stock is reduced by the value per share of the distributed property, or such options are equitably adjusted to include the equivalent property which a holder of the underlying stock would be entitled to receive.

6. *Assignment of responsibility.* The Options Clearing Corporation is the primary issuer and obliger on every option issued on the CBOE. Ordinarily, whenever a Chicago Board Option is issued to a buyer, there must exist a writer (seller) of this option. However, the holder of an option does not look to any particular writer (seller) for performance; instead, the clearing corporation bears full responsibility for honoring all the options issued on the CBOE.

7. *Certificateless trading.* Ordinarily no option certificates are issued by the Clearing Corporation to evidence the issuance of Chicago Board Options. Rather, the clearing corporation maintains a daily record of options issued in each account of its clearing members, and each clearing member is required to maintain a continuous record of his respective customers' position in Chicago Board Options. The ownership of Chicago Board Options is evidenced by the confirmations and periodic statements that customers receive from their brokers.

CALL OPTIONS

Buying Calls

As mentioned above, a call option is a contract giving the holder the right to purchase 100 shares of a given security at a specified price (the exercise price or striking price) within a specified period of time. The holder (buyer) of the call option pays a price called a premium. Currently call options are offered for three maturities: three months, six months, and nine months.

The *New York Times* on August 24, 1985, reported that call options on GM stock were traded on the Chicago Board Options Exchange (CBOE) on the previous day as follows:

Strike price of call options	Maturity			GM stock closing price
	Sept.	Dec.	March	
65	$2\frac{3}{4}$	$4\frac{3}{8}$	5	$66\frac{7}{8}$
70	$\frac{9}{16}$	$1\frac{13}{16}$	$2\frac{3}{4}$	$66\frac{7}{8}$
75	$\frac{1}{16}$	$\frac{3}{4}$	$1\frac{5}{16}$	$66\frac{7}{8}$
80	$\frac{1}{16}$	$\frac{3}{16}$	s	$66\frac{7}{8}$

(*s* means no option is offered.)

GM stock closed on the previous day at $66\frac{7}{8}$ per share. The maturity months for call options on GM stock were September, 1985, December, 1985, and March, 1986. The third Friday of the maturity month is fixed as the maturity date. Therefore, the maturity dates for the above call options will be the third Friday of September, 1985, December, 1985, and March, 1986, respectively.

There are four strike prices (also called exercise price or contract price) for GM call options. They are $65, $70, $75, and $80. The buyer can select any one of them. The higher the strike price, the lower the premium one has to pay. For example, for the December, 1985, maturity, the premium for strike price at $80 was only $$\frac{3}{16}$ per share, whereas for the strike price at $65, the premium was $$4\frac{3}{8}$ per share.

There are three maturities. The buyer can select any of them. The longer the maturity, the higher the premium the buyer has to pay. For example, at strike price of $70 for the September maturity the premium was $$\frac{9}{16}$ per share, whereas for a maturity in March, 1986, the premium was $$2\frac{3}{4}$ per share.

One option contract represents 100 shares of underlying stock. Assuming that Investor A bought one unit (100 shares) of the $70 March, 1986, call option at a premium of $$2\frac{3}{4}$ per share, the total price paid would be $2\frac{3}{4} \times 100 = 275 plus commission. This would entitle Investor A to buy 100 shares of GM stock at $70 each any time before maturity in March, 1986.

The buyer of call options must be bullish on the price of the underlying stock. In this case, Investor A must anticipate a rise in the price of GM stock before the end of next March. After purchasing the call option, the buyer has three choices:

1. Sell the option on the CBOE before the expiration of the option.
2. Exercise the option before expiration, which means the investor will buy the shares at the exercise price.

3. Let the option lapse on the date of expiration, which means the investor will lose the premium paid.

Let us now discuss some of the objectives or strategies and associated risks in buying call options:

1. *Buying a call for speculation with maximum leverage.* If Investor A in our example is optimistic about GM stock, the stock can be bought directly. Assuming that Investor A has about $7000, he will be able to buy 100 shares of GM at $66\frac{7}{8}$ each. But if Investor A is a speculator and interested in maximum leverage, he can buy 25 call options to purchase 2500 shares on GM with an exercise price at $70 and maturity in March, 1986.

    If Investor A is right, and the price of GM stock rises to $75 before the end of next March, he can exercise his call option at $70 and sell the stock in the market. Ignoring commissions, Investor A would realize a gross profit of ($75 − $70 − $2\frac{3}{4}$) × 2500 = $5,625. The investor could also sell his call options in the market and get a comparable amount of profit without exercising the call option.

    On the other hand, should he buy the stocks directly, he would receive a profit of ($75 − $66\frac{7}{8}$) × 100 = $812.50. The amount of profit from purchasing the call option is nearly seven times the profit from direct purchase of the stock.

    However, one should note that the high leverage in Investor A's case was bought with high risk. Should the price of GM stock decline to $69 before the end of next March, the purchaser of stock would have a small paper profit. On the other hand, had he purchased the $70 March call option, he would have lost all the money he paid for the options.

2. *Buy a call to protect a short sale.* Investor B is pessimistic about a stock or the whole market. He sold short 100 shares of ABC stock at $50 each. However, he realizes that the potential risk of selling short is very great. If unexpected good news develops for the stock or the stock market in general, or for both, the stock may rise to $75 or even $100. If that happens, he could lose $2,500 to $5,000 on this stock. Therefore, in order to limit the risk from selling short, he simultaneously bought a call option on ABC stock with a $50 exercise price and a six-month duration. The option price, say, amounted to $400 for 100 shares. Now he is in a secured position. If his judgment is correct, and the stock later falls to $30 or $35, he can buy the stock to cover his short position and secure a profit. Should the market turn against him and the stock rise to $75 or even $100, he can exercise his call option to acquire the stock to cover his short sale. In effect, his maximum loss is limited to the cost of the option premium plus commissions.

3. *Sell stock at profit and buy a call for continued interest*
Investor C bought 100 shares of ABC stock some months back at
$30 each. Now the stock is $45. She is now wary about the outlook
of the stock market though she thinks the stock can rise further. In
order to protect the possibility of market downturn, she sells the
stock to realize her profits. At the same time, she purchases a
100-share nine-month call option on this stock and pays a premium
for, say, $350. In this case, she pays about one-fourth of her real-
ized profit ($350/$1,500) to maintain her position in the stock, and
at the same time protects herself against the risk of losing her paper
profit in the event of a downturn.

4. *Buy a call instead of a volatile glamour stock in a new commitment.*
Often individuals buy stocks in vogue without much investigation
because at the time brokers are pushing the stock, and friends are
reported to have made money on the stock. However, the end
result turns out to be more often disastrous rather than profitable
for these individuals. The correct strategy under these circumstances is to buy a call option on the stock, if available, instead of
the stock itself. Should the tip work out well and the stock soar, the
buyer of the call option can either sell the call or exercise the call
to acquire stock and sell it in the market at a good profit. On the
other hand, if the stock declines, the most the individual has lost
is the cost of the calls.

Selling (Writing) Call Options

First, let us define again what is meant by writing (selling) a call option. For
example, Investor B wrote (sold) a March, 1986, $50 call option on GE stock
for $300. This means Investor B will stand ready to sell to the holder of this
option 100 shares of GE stock at $50 each any time before the end of March
1986. The reward to the investor is the receipt of the premium.

There are two ways of selling call options. One way is to sell the call
option against stock in one's portfolio. The other way is to sell the call option
without owning the underlying stock.

1. *Selling (writing) call option against stock in portfolio.* One
profitable strategy many sophisticated investors have been using is
to sell calls on stocks in their portfolios. If prices rise, the stocks will
be called away, but the investor receives premiums on the calls
written. In a sense, he is selling shares at prices higher than
the current market prices when the call is written. He can then use
the sales proceeds to buy other stocks on which he can again write
calls. On the other hand, if prices fall, call options will not
be exercised, and he can pocket the premium as income. By and
large, the writers of call options can expect to receive premiums in

the order of 6 percent to 8 percent of the stock price for six-month calls. On an annual basis, premiums will amount to 12 percent to 15 percent of the stock price. After deducting commissions and including dividends, the owners of a portfolio can expect to receive on the average a net return of about 15 percent with moderate risk.

2. *Selling (writing) call option without owning the stock.* Investor Y is bearish about a stock. She writes one unit call option on this stock at $50 exercise price for six months for a premium of $350. However, she does not own this stock in her portfolio; she writes this call purely for speculation. She is required to deposit cash in her account as margin. If the stock falls as anticipated by Investor Y, the call will not be exercised, and she can pocket the premium as profit. On the other hand, if the stock rises, and the call is exercised, Investor Y has to buy the stock for delivery to the holder of the call option. In the case of sharp increases in the price of the stock, Investor Y can lose a substantial amount of money. Therefore, this strategy should not be used except by experienced traders who are fully aware of the risks involved.

PUT OPTIONS

Buying Put Options

A put option is a contract giving the holder the right of delivery to the maker, within a specified length of time, of a given number of shares of a certain stock at a price fixed by the contract. The put options of GM stock, for example, were traded on the CBOE on August 23, 1985, as follows:

Strike price of put options	Maturity			GM stock closing price
	Sept.	Dec.	March	
65	$\frac{9}{16}$	$1\frac{3}{4}$	$2\frac{5}{8}$	$66\frac{5}{8}$
70	$3\frac{3}{8}$	$4\frac{1}{2}$	$5\frac{5}{8}$	$66\frac{7}{8}$
75	r	$8\frac{1}{4}$	$8\frac{1}{2}$	$66\frac{7}{8}$

(r means the option was not traded.)

The put options on GM stock had three exercise prices — $65, $70, and $75. Each exercise price had three maturity dates. In all, there were nine choices to the buyer and seller of put options on this stock.

Assuming that Investor A bought one unit of a March $70 put option on GM stock that day, the premium he paid would amount to $5\frac{5}{8} \times 100 =$ $562.50, plus the commission to the broker. This would entitle Investor A to sell 100 shares of GM stock at $70 each any time before maturity in March, 1986.

The buyer of put options must believe that the price of the underlying stock will drop.

Below are some of the possible objectives or strategies in buying put options.

1. *Buy put options for speculation with maximum leverage.* Investor B is bearish on GM stock, which is now selling at $66\frac{7}{8}$. Investor B does not own this stock, but he is a speculator who wants to make a big profit on small capital. He bought five units of a December $70 put option of GM stock for a premium of $4\frac{1}{2} \times 500 = \$2,250$, plus commission to the broker. If his judgment is correct, and the price of GM stock falls to $60 before the end of December, he can buy 500 shares of GM stock at this price and deliver them to the maker of the put option at $70 each. Ignoring commission, he makes a gross profit of ($70 − $60) × 500 = $5000 on a capital of $2,250 within a short period of time. Alternately, when the GM stock goes down to $60, the put option must appreciate accordingly in the marketplace. Instead of exercising the put option, Investor A can sell his put in the market to reap a comparable profit.

    On the other hand, if the stock goes up above $70, against his expectation, then the put option is of no use to him and becomes worthless. So, the higher leverage of this speculative strategy is balanced by high risk to the buyer.

2. *Buy a put to protect profit.* Investor C bought 100 shares of ABC stock some months back at $30 a share. Now the stock has risen to $45. She feels the stock has the potential to go up more. However, she is wary about the stock market as a whole. She fears if the market does go down as anticipated now, this may also bring down the price of ABC stock. Yet, she is not willing to sell the stock at $45 at this moment. She is in a dilemma. The best strategy under these circumstances is to buy a put and hold on to this stock. Suppose Investor C did follow this strategy and bought a six-month put on ABC stock at a $45 exercise price for a premium of $300. If the stock falls to $35 within the next six months, she can deliver her ABC stock at $45 and make a gross profit of ($45 − 30) × 100 = $1,500. After deduction of the put premium, she still makes $1,200, without deducting the commissions. On the other hand, if the stock rises to $55, she can sell the shares at this price and realize a gross profit of ($55 − $30) × 100 = $2,500. After subtracting the premium she gets $2,200, ignoring the commissions.

3. *Buy a put to limit risk in the purchase of a volatile stock.* Investor A gets some high recommendations from both his broker and friends on a volatile glamour stock. They say that this stock has high prospects. Investor A, after some study on his own, is convinced that he should acquire some shares of this stock at the current market price of $30. However, he knows this stock has had

a fast rise in the past several months and could be subject to a precipitous decline if people begin taking profits or some unexpected adverse news should develop. So Investor A wants to limit his risks on the downside.

The best strategy Investor A can follow under these circumstances is to buy the stock and at the same time purchase a put, if available, at about the current market price. If the stock rises, everything will be fine. On the other hand, should the stock decline against his expectation, he can sell the stock to the maker of the put option. His loss will be limited to the amount he paid.

Selling (Writing) Put Options

Let us define again what is meant by writing a put. Assume that Investor E wrote (sold) a December, 1985, $70 put on GM for $4\frac{1}{2} \times 100 = \$450$; this means that she will stand ready to buy 100 shares of GM stock at $70 from the holder of this put option any time before the maturity date in December, 1985. The reward to Investor E is the receipt of the put premium. Some of the objectives or strategies of writing put options are:

1. *Writing a put for speculation.* Investor E is bullish on GM stock at the current market price of $66\frac{7}{8}$. She writes a December, 1985, $70 put for $4\frac{1}{2} \times 100 = \$450$. If she is right, the price of GM stock will rise above $70, and the put premium will be her profit. On the other hand, if the stock finishes at a price lower than $70 before the end of December, 1985, the put will be exercised and Investor E will have to buy the stock at $70 from the holder of this put option.

2. *Writing a put to buy stocks.* Investor F is interested in GE stock at the current market price of $60. However, he prefers to buy the stock at a lower price. The appropriate strategy under these circumstances is to write a put on GE at the current market price. If the stock rises and the put is not exercised, the premium is profit. If the stock, on the other hand, declines and the put is exercised, he will get the stock at the exercise price. But the net price he will pay is lower by the amount of the premium he previously received in writing the put option.

3. *Writing puts to increase investment return.* Mr. G is a conservative investor who is only interested in a good, steady return on his portfolio. His objective can be accomplished through selling puts on a few selected quality stocks that he would be willing to buy and own at current market prices. If these stocks rise, the premium from selling puts is income. If these stocks fall, he gets the shares at prices lower than the current market price because of the premiums received. He can then sell calls on the stocks put to him until they are called away. Each operation earns him a premium.

He can continue these operations (selling either puts or calls) and the average annual net return he gets will likely exceed 15 percent, including dividends. The risk involved is relatively moderate.

COMBINATIONS OF OPTIONS

Puts and calls are sometimes combined and traded as a unit. Some of these strategies are described below.

Straddle

A *straddle* is a combination of a put and a call on the same security and with identical exercise price and expiration date. Either option is exercisable or salable separately. This means the holder of a straddle has the right to buy from and/or sell to the maker a certain number of shares of a given stock at a specified price within a fixed period of time.

The buyer of a straddle is usually a person who believes that the underlying stock is very volatile. It can go up or down significantly, but the buyer does not know which way the stock will likely go. The seller of a straddle can be a speculator who does not own the stock and is betting that the price of the stock will likely fluctuate within a narrow range. For example, the market price of a stock is $50 and the exercise price of the straddle is also set at $50, and the put and call premiums are $5 each for a duration of nine months; the seller of a straddle hopes that the price of the stock will not change much from the exercise price during the option period. In this example, if the stock ends before expiration within a range of $40 to $60, the seller of the straddle will have a profit, ignoring commissions.

The seller of a straddle can also be a person who owns the underlying stock. If this person is willing to buy more shares of this stock at a reduced price or to sell the shares at a higher price, he can sell a straddle. In the previous example ($50 stock price and also exercise price, $5 each for put and call), if the stock falls below $50 before expiration, the put will be exercised, and he buys the stock at a net price of $40 ($50 exercise price minus $10 premium received). On the other hand, if the stock rises to above $50 before expiration, the call will be exercised and he gets a net price of $60 ($50 exercise price plus $10 premium).

Strip

A *strip* is a combination of two puts and a call. It consists of three separate options, all written at the same time, expiring at the same time, and all exercisable at the same price. The purchaser of a strip, in other words, has the right to sell 200 shares and/or buy 100 shares of a certain stock at the exercise price within a specific period of time. He must be by and large bearish on the underlying stock, but also want to have a call as insurance for unexpected outcome.

Strap

A *strap* is the reverse of a strip. It consists of two calls and one put. The holder of a strap may sell 100 shares and/or buy 200 shares of a given stock at the same exercise price within a specific period of time.

The purchaser of a strap must be by and large bullish on the underlying stock, but also wants to have a put as insurance in case of an unexpected decline of the stock. The drawback of both strip and strap is the fact that the premiums charged are usually quite expensive relative to the price of the underlying stock.

HEDGING STRATEGIES

Options provide a good investment vehicle for employing hedging strategies, which are very useful to both institutional and individual investors. By *hedging* we mean buying one option long while simultaneously selling another short, both in the same stock. For example, on August 27, 1985, call options on Merrill Lynch common stock were traded on the American Stock Exchange as follows:

Call options and exercise price	Maturity			Closing price of common stock
	Sept.	Oct.	Jan.	
$25	r	7	r	$32
30	$2\frac{1}{5}$	$2\frac{3}{4}$	$3\frac{3}{4}$	32
35	$\frac{3}{16}$	$\frac{5}{8}$	$1\frac{9}{16}$	32
40	$\frac{1}{16}$	$\frac{3}{16}$	$\frac{1}{2}$	32

(r means the option was not traded.)

In hedging, a trader may buy a call on Merrill Lynch at $30 and at the same time sell a call at $35, or vice versa, both for the same maturity. This is known as "money-spread" hedging. Or, one can buy a call on Merrill Lynch at $30 with a January maturity and at the same time sell short a call at $35 with an October maturity. This is known as "time-spread" hedging.

The purpose of hedging is twofold:

1. To limit losses if the future price of the stock in question moves against original expectation.
2. To provide an adequate profit to the hedger if the future price trend of the stock is in line with the original expectation. The following example will clarify these points.

Bullish "Money-Spread" Hedging Strategy

If one is bullish on Merrill Lynch, the correct hedging is to buy the call option with a low exercise price and sell short the call option with a higher exercise price, both of the same maturity.

For example, to implement the strategy, the hedger buys a January $30 call option on Merrill Lynch for $3\frac{3}{4}$ and sells a January $35 call option for $1\frac{9}{16}$. The net cost to the transaction, ignoring commissions, are;

Buy Jan. $30	Cost	$3\frac{3}{4}$ each	100 shares:	$375.00
Sell Jan. $35	Receive	$1\frac{9}{16}$ each	100 shares:	156.25
			Net investment:	$218.75

If Merrill Lynch finishes at $37 at the end of January, 1986, both call options will be exercised. Ignoring commissions, the result will be:

Exercise of Jan. $35 call, receive	$35 \times 100 = $3,500
Exercise of Jan. $30 call, cost	$30 \times 100 = 3,000
Difference	$ 500
Less net investment	218.75
Profit	$ 281.25

On the other hand, if Merrill Lynch finishes below $30 at the end of January, 1986, both call options will not be exercised and, therefore, will be worthless. The hedger will lose the net investment of $218.75. What would the consequence be if the investor did not hedge? If he were bullish and bought the January $30 call option, he would lose $3\frac{3}{4} \times 100 = $375.

From this example, we see that a hedging strategy can limit losses and also provide a reasonable profit if the future price of the stock moves as expected. Of course, hedging will also limit the extent of gain. Many professional traders believe that a hedging strategy in the long run works better than a one-way strategy of either buying calls or selling calls.

Bearish "Money-Spread" Hedging Strategy

The bearish hedging strategy is the reverse of the bullish hedging strategy. That is, the hedger should buy the call option with a higher exercise price and at the same time sell the call option with a lower exercise price, both of the same maturity.

In the example above of Merrill Lynch, the bearish hedger should, for instance, buy an October $35 call option and sell the October $30 call option. The hedger will receive the difference between the premiums of the two options ($2\frac{3}{4}$ − $\frac{5}{8}$) × 100 = \$212.50. If the stock falls below \$30 at the end of October, both call options will not be exercised, and the \$212.50 would be profit to the hedger, ignoring commissions.

What happens if the stock finishes at \$37 at the end of October? Will the hedger lose money? If so, how much? We leave this to the reader to figure out.

"Time-Spread" Hedging Strategy

"Time-spread" hedging strategy means buying one option and simultaneously selling another option on the same stock, both of the same exercise price, but of different maturity. If an investor is bullish on a stock for the near term but bearish long-term, or vice versa, he can employ the "time-spread" hedging strategy.

Near-Term Bearish, Long-Term Bullish Strategy

Again using Merrill Lynch as an example, if an investor is bearish near-term but bullish long-term on Merrill Lynch, he can sell the October \$30 call option and simultaneously buy the January \$30 call.

If Merrill Lynch finishes below \$30 at the end of October, the October call option will not be exercised, and the premium $2\frac{3}{4}$ × 100 = \$275 is profit. In the following months, if the stock bounces back, the January call option will appreciate in the marketplace. He can sell the January call option and realize profits.

On the other hand, if Merrill Lynch finishes higher than \$30 at the end of October and the October call option is exercised, the hedger can exercise the January call immediately, or simply ask the broker to use the January call to offset the October call. In this case, he will lose ($3\frac{3}{4}$ − $2\frac{3}{4}$) × 100 = \$100. Alternatively, if he wants to hold on to the January call, he would have to buy the stock at the market price and deliver the shares to the holder of the October call option at an exercise price of \$30 per share.

Near-Term Bullish, Long-Term Bearish Strategy

If an investor is near-term bullish but long-term bearish on Merrill Lynch stock, he should buy, for instance, a September or October \$30 call and at the same time sell the January \$30 call.

The calculation of profit or loss is the same as above, with one difference: The call option sold is of longer duration than the call option the hedger purchases. The long option is, therefore, not deemed adequate to cover the short option, and the hedger is required to deposit some additional funds to cover the margin requirements.

Ratio Hedging Strategies

The hedging strategy does not have to be on a one-to-one basis, that is, buying one call and selling another call. In fact, many professional traders believe that ratio hedging is better, that is, buying one call and selling two or three other calls, or vice versa.

One ratio hedging option strategy sophisticated traders often employ is to write (sell) two calls on each 100 shares of stocks owned. For example, an investor bought 100 shares of a stock at $50 each, and immediately sold two calls at a $50 exercise price for a duration of six months. The premium for the call was $3\frac{1}{2}$ per share.

The profit and loss picture of this operation at various stock prices, ignoring commissions, is shown in Figure 15–1.

If the stock finishes at $50 before the expiration of the call option, the two calls will not be exercised and the hedger will receive a profit of ($3.50 × 200) = $700. If the stock finishes at $53, the two calls will be exercised and the hedger has to buy an additional 100 shares of the stock at $53 and deliver them at $50. She will lose $300 on this new purchase. However, from selling two calls she received a premium of $700. So, she still comes out with a profit of $400.

If the stock finishes at $48, the two calls will not be exercised, and the $700 premiums would be profit. However, she has a paper loss of $200 on the stock. The net profit in this case would be $500.

The figure shows that the hedger will make money if the stock finishes within a range of $43 to $57, ignoring commissions. Since in normal markets, most stocks will not appreciate or decline more than 10 percent in a period of six months, the chances of making a profit for the ratio hedger are quite good. This strategy is particularly interesting when the underlying stock is not moving in either direction.

Classification of Option Strategies in Terms of Degree of Risk

The various uses or strategies of options and their risks have been examined. It is useful to group them together in terms of degree of risk:

Low-Risk Strategies

1. Write call options on stocks in one's portfolio.
2. Write put options on stocks one is willing to purchase now at current market price.
3. Use part of dividend and interest income from a portfolio to buy call or put options.

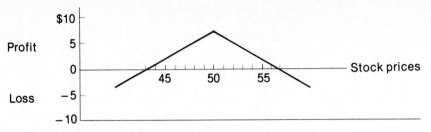

FIGURE 15–1 Profit and Loss Chart of Ratio Hedging Strategy

Moderate-Risk Strategies

1. Hedging — Buy a call option and sell short another call option of the same stock.
2. Ratio hedging — Write (sell) two calls for each 100 shares of stock owned.
3. Sell a straddle (call and put combined).
4. Purchase the stock and sell a straddle on the stock.

High-Risk Strategies

1. Purchase a call.
2. Purchase a put.
3. Sell a call without owning the underlying stock.
4. Sell a put for speculation.
5. Purchase a straddle.

OPTIMUM OPTION STRATEGY WITH DIFFERENT EXPECTATIONS

We now turn to examine the question of which option strategy one should adopt with different expectations. Before we discuss the appropriate strategies, let us assume that an ABC stock is selling at $50, and both the call and put premiums at exercise price $50 for a six-month duration are $3 each per share.

Very Bullish on the Stock

If an investor is very bullish on the stock, the appropriate strategy is to buy calls on the stock. If he is wrong, the most he will lose is $3 per share plus commissions. However, if he is right, the stock can rise to $60 or beyond. In that case, he will make $10 or more per share.

Very Bearish on the Stock

If the investor is very bearish on the stock, the appropriate strategy is to buy puts on the stock. If he is wrong, he will lose, at most, the premium of the put. On the other hand, if he is right and the stock declines to $40 or lower, he can make $10 or more per share.

Moderately Bullish on the Stock

If the investor is moderately bullish on the stock, he should sell puts. If he is right, the put will not be exercised, and the premium received would be his profit. If the investor, instead, buys calls, the stock may rise a few points, which may be just sufficient to cover the cost of the premium of the call he bought. Besides the strategy of selling puts, the investor can also employ a bullish "money-spread" hedging strategy if he is only moderately bullish on the underlying stock.

Moderately Bearish on the Stock

If the investor is moderately bearish on the stock, the appropriate strategy is to sell calls. If he is right, the call will not be exercised, and the premium received will be his profit. On the other hand, should he buy puts, the stock may decline a few points, giving him just enough profit to cover the cost of buying puts. Aside from the strategy of selling calls, the investor, if only moderately bearish on the stock, can also employ a bearish "money-spread" hedging strategy.

Neutral on the Stock

If the investor feels that the stock will not change much either way from the current market price in a six-month period, the proper strategy to use is to sell a straddle (a call and a put). In the current example of ABC stock, the investor can receive a premium of $6 per share. If the stock finishes before the end of the six-month option period within a range of $44 to $56, the investor will receive a profit, ignoring commissions.

Another strategy to use is to employ a ratio hedging strategy. Using the current example, the investor buys 100 shares of the stock at $50 each and sells two calls at $50 for a premium of $3 per share for a duration of six months. If the stock price finishes at $50, the calls will not be exercised, and the premium $3 × 200 = $600 is profit. If the stock finishes at $56, the investor has to buy 100 shares in the market at $56 and deliver them for $50 each together with his own 100 shares. The investor loses $6 per share on the new purchase, but this is just offset by the premium he previously received. Therefore, he breaks even at $56. On the downside, he is protected up to $44 because his cost was $50 per share and he received $600 in premiums, and, therefore, his net cost per share was $44.

OPTIONS ON MARKET INDEXES

Aside from options on individual stocks, options on market indexes are now available. Among the major market indexes are:

1. S&P 100 Index on CBOE
2. Major Market Index on AMEX
3. Market Value Index on AMEX
4. NYSE Composite Index on NYSE

The S&P 100 Index, which includes 100 major companies from the S&P 400 Industrial Index, attracts the most volume of transactions in options on market indexes. The options of the S&P 100 index were traded on CBOE on November 21, 1984 as shown in Table 15–1.

One difference between the options on the market indexes and the options on individual stocks is that there is no delivery of stocks if one exercises a call or put option. Instead, the transaction is settled in cash on the basis of the market price of the index. Consequently, the purchaser of the option will usually either sell the option later or let the option expire on the date of maturity.

Option Strategies with Market Indexes

The option strategies with market indexes are basically the same as option strategies on individual stocks.

TABLE 15–1   S&P 100 Call and Put Options

S&P 100 Call Option and Strike Price	Maturity			Closing Price
	Dec.	Jan.	Feb.	
155	$9\frac{1}{2}$	$10\frac{1}{2}$	$11\frac{3}{4}$	162.73
160	$5\frac{1}{2}$	$7\frac{3}{8}$	$8\frac{1}{2}$	162.73
165	$2\frac{7}{16}$	$4\frac{1}{4}$	$5\frac{1}{4}$	162.73
170	$\frac{13}{16}$	$2\frac{1}{8}$	$3\frac{1}{8}$	162.73
175	$\frac{1}{4}$	$\frac{15}{16}$	$1\frac{3}{4}$	162.73
Put Options				
155	$\frac{1}{4}$	$\frac{3}{4}$	$1\frac{1}{4}$	162.73
160	$1\frac{1}{8}$	$1\frac{7}{8}$	$2\frac{3}{4}$	162.73
165	$3\frac{1}{8}$	$3\frac{7}{8}$	$4\frac{3}{4}$	162.73
170	$7\frac{3}{8}$	$7\frac{1}{4}$	8	162.73
175	$11\frac{5}{8}$	12	$13\frac{1}{4}$	162.73

Bullish strategies. If one is bullish on the trend of stock prices in general, one can implement a variety of bullish strategies, as discussed above. For instance, one can:

1. Buy a call at an exercise price either below or above the current price of market index (162.73).
2. Establish a bullish spread—for example,
   Buy a February $160 call for $8\frac{1}{2}$ each
   Sell a February $170 for $3\frac{1}{8}$ each
3. Establish a ratio bullish spread—for example,
   Buy two February $160 calls for $\quad$ $8\frac{1}{2} \times 200 = \$1,700$
   Sell three February $170 calls for $\quad$ $3\frac{1}{8} \times 300 = 937.50$

$$\text{Net investment } \$762.50$$

Bearish strategies. If the investor is bearish on the overall market, she can implement one of the following strategies:

1. Buy a put, say, February $160 for $2\frac{3}{4} \times 100 = \$275$
2. Establish a bearish spread—for example,
   Buy a February $165 call for $5\frac{1}{4}$ each
   Sell a February $160 call for $8\frac{1}{2}$ each
   or, using the put option instead as follows:
   Buy a February $165 put for $4\frac{3}{4}$ each
   Sell a February $160 put for $2\frac{3}{4}$ each
3. Establish a ratio bearish spread—for example,
   Buy one February $165 put for $4\frac{3}{4}$ each
   Sell two February $155 puts for $1\frac{1}{4}$ each

FACTORS AFFECTING OPTION PREMIUMS

The premium of an option on the Option Exchanges is determined by bids and asks of buyers and makers (sellers) of options. The major factors that determine the bids and asks of buyers and sellers of options (both call and put options) are these:

1. *The duration of the option contract.* The longer the length of the option contract, the higher the premium. The reason is this: The longer the duration of the contract, the longer the period during which the price of the underlying stock may appreciate in the case of a call or may decline in the case of a put.

2. *The relationship between exercise price and stock price.* If the stock price is higher than the exercise price in the case of a call, the option is already worth something, and, therefore, commands a higher premium. By the same token, if the stock price is less than the exercise price, the option premium is lower.

   The reverse applies to a put option. That means, if the exercise price is lower than the stock price, the premium would be less.

3. *The volatility of the stock.* Generally, more volatile stock has more speculative potential and, therefore, commands a higher premium.

4. *Dividend yield of the stock.* Stock with a higher dividend yield is generally more stable and less volatile than low-yield stock. The premium on high-yield stock is usually lower than on low-yield stock.

   Points 3 and 4 both relate to the factor of volatility. In other words, when the volatility of a stock is high, the potential reward is high, the price for that potential (payment of the premium for an option) should also be high, and vice versa.

5. *Current risk-free interest rate (such as yield on ninety-day Treasury bills).* This factor is not as important as the above four factors, and members in the financial community disagree as to the extent to which interest rates actually affect option prices. However, the interest rate remains a factor in most mathematical models for pricing options (see the Black-Scholes model discussed below).

   The reason why interest rate affects the premium of options is quite involved; that is also the reason why there has been disagreement in the financial community as to the possible impact of interest rate on option premiums. To cite one example, Professors Elton and Gruber suggest why interest rate affects call premium in these words:

   Finally, the higher the riskless rate of interest, the greater the value of the calls. This follows logically from the fact that the higher the riskless rate the lower the present value of the amount that must be paid to exercise the call.[1]

DETERMINING THE VALUE OF OPTIONS

As in the case of stocks, investors in general would like to know or determine the value of a given option. A number of theorists have developed mathematical formulas for that purpose. The most well-known formula for the

---

[1] Edwin J. Elton and Martin J. Gruber, *Modern Portfolio Theory and Investment Analysis* (New York: John Wiley & Sons, 1981), p. 463.

determination of the fair value of an option was developed by Black and Scholes.[2] Their equation is as follows:

$$P_o = P_s N(d_1) - \frac{E}{e^{rt}} N(d_2)$$

$$d_1 = \frac{\ln(P_s/E) + (r + .5\sigma^2)t}{\sigma\sqrt{t}}$$

$$d_2 = \frac{\ln(P_s/E) + (r - .5\sigma^2)t}{\sigma\sqrt{t}}$$

where:

P_o = the current value of the option

P_s = the current price of the stock

E = the exercise price of the option

e = 2.71828

t = the time remaining before expiration (in years)

r = the market interest rate on Treasury bills

σ = the standard deviation of the annual rate of return on the stock

$\ln(P_s/E)$ = the natural logarithm of (P_s/E)

$N(d)$ = cumulative normal density function

Their equation was based on a number of assumptions. The key assumptions are:

1. The stock pays no dividend.
2. There are no transaction costs or taxes.
3. Borrowing or lending is possible at a stable rate of interest.
4. The stock price follows a random walk, and the distribution of possible stock prices at the end of option period is log-normal.
5. There are no penalties for short selling.

Application of the Formula

The application of the formula requires the following inputs: current stock price (P_s), exercise price (E), the market interest rate (r), the time to maturity (t), and the standard deviation of annual returns on the stock (σ).

[2] Fisher Black and Myron Scholes, "The Pricing of Options and Corporate Liabilities." *The Journal of Political Economy*, May–June 1973.

For example, the variables for a given option are these:[3]

$P_s = \$36$

$E = \$40$

$r = .05$ (the rate of interest on 90-day Treasury bill)

$t = .25$ year (90 days)

$\sigma = .50$ (the standard deviation of annual returns on the stock is 50%)

Then, by substituting the variables in the equations, we get:

$$d_1 = \frac{\ln(36/40) + [.05 + .5(.50)^2].25}{.50\sqrt{.25}} = -.25$$

$$d_2 = \frac{\ln(36/40) + [.05 - .5(.50)^2].25}{.50\sqrt{.25}} = -.50$$

Using the accompanying Table 15–2 of values of $N(d)$, we can find the corresponding values of $N(d_1)$ and $N(d_2)$ as:

$N(d_1) = N(-.25) = .4013$

$N(d_2) = N(-.50) = .3085$

Therefore, the value of the option is:

$$P_o = (36 \times .4013) - \left[\frac{40}{e^{(.05 \times .25)}} \times .3085\right] = \$2.26$$

Using Nomograms

The calculations for the preceding example, requiring the use of logarithm square root, and statistical table, are quite involved and time-consuming. Because of this, investors could be inhibited from using the equations for providing indications of fair values of options currently available in the market. To help investors, Elroy Dimson has developed nomograms on the basis of the Black-Scholes equation for the calculation of the fair value of options.[4]

The use of nomograms is quite simple. The investor needs to know only four items: (1) the maturity of the option, (2) the share price expressed as a

[3] The current example and the table of values of $N(d)$ is taken from *Investments* by William F. Sharpe, pp. 375–76, Prentice-Hall, 1978.

[4] Elroy Dimson, "Instant Option Valuation." *Financial Analysts Journal*, May–June 1977; "Option Valuation Nomograms." *Financial Analysts Journal*, Nov.–Dec. 1977.

TABLE 15–2   Values of N(d) for Selected Values of d

d	N(d)	d	N(d)	d	N(d)
		−1.00	.1587	1.00	.8413
−2.95	.0016	−.95	.1711	1.05	.8531
−2.90	.0019	−.90	.1841	1.10	.8643
−2.85	.0022	−.85	.1977	1.15	.8749
−2.80	.0026	−.80	.2119	1.20	.8849
−2.75	.0030	−.75	.2266	1.25	.8944
−2.70	.0035	−.70	.2420	1.30	.9032
−2.65	.0040	−.65	.2578	1.35	.9115
−2.60	.0047	−.60	.2743	1.40	.9192
−2.55	.0054	−.55	.2912	1.45	.9265
−2.50	.0062	−.50	.3085	1.50	.9332
−2.45	.0071	−.45	.3264	1.55	.9394
−2.40	.0082	−.40	.3446	1.60	.9452
−2.35	.0094	−.35	.3632	1.65	.9505
−2.30	.0107	−.30	.3821	1.70	.9554
−2.25	.0122	−.25	.4013	1.75	.9599
−2.20	.0139	−.20	.4207	1.80	.9641
−2.15	.0158	−.15	.4404	1.85	.9678
−2.10	.0179	−.10	.4602	1.90	.9713
−2.05	.0202	−.05	.4801	1.95	.9744
−2.00	.0228	.00	.5000	2.00	.9773
−1.95	.0256	.05	.5199	2.05	.9798
−1.90	.0287	.10	.5398	2.10	.9821
−1.85	.0322	.15	.5596	2.15	.9842
−1.80	.0359	.20	.5793	2.20	.9861
−1.75	.0401	.25	.5987	2.25	.9878
−1.70	.0446	.30	.6179	2.30	.9893
−1.65	.0495	.35	.6368	2.35	.9906
−1.60	.0548	.40	.6554	2.40	.9918
−1.55	.0606	.45	.6736	2.45	.9929
−1.50	.0668	.50	.6915	2.50	.9938
−1.45	.0735	.55	.7088	2.55	.9946
−1.40	.0808	.60	.7257	2.60	.9953
−1.35	.0885	.65	.7422	2.65	.9960
−1.30	.0968	.70	.7580	2.70	.9965
−1.25	.1057	.75	.7734	2.75	.9970
−1.20	.1151	.80	.7881	2.80	.9974
−1.15	.1251	.85	.8023	2.85	.9978
−1.10	.1357	.90	.8159	2.90	.9931
−1.05	.1469	.95	.8289	2.95	.9984

percentage of the exercise price, (3) market interest rate, and (4) the volatility of the share (the standard deviation of the annual rate of return on the stock). Figure 15–2 is Dimson's nomogram, which can be used to value a call option. There are four steps in the use of a nomogram:

Step 1. Draw a vertical line through the maturity.

Step 2. Draw a horizontal line from the point of intersection with the interest rate, through the lower right-hand quadrant of the nomogram.

Step 3. Draw a vertical line from the point of intersection with the share price as a percentage of the exercise price, through the upper right-hand quadrant.

Step 4. Draw a horizontal line from the point of intersection with the standard deviation, through the upper right-hand quadrant.

The result is the intersecting point of the two lines in the upper right-hand quadrant of the nomogram. The intersecting point indicates the option value as a percent of stock price.

The rectangular box in Figure 15–2 illustrates the valuation of an option with the following characteristics:

Exercise price	$40
Current price of common stock	$52
Annual interest rate	10%
Maturity	8 months
Annual standard deviation of rates of return on the stock	60%

The intersecting point in the upper right-hand quadrant was at 34 percent. That means the option value is 34% × $52 = $17.68.

The Black-Scholes equation and the nomogram based on it assume that the stock is paying no cash dividend. If a stock does pay a dividend, an adjustment is necessary. The adjustment involves subtracting from the share price the present value of dividends payable to maturity, discounted at the market interest rate. For example, if a $1.50 dividend is payable within the next eight months, and the market interest rate is 10 percent, the present value of the dividend is roughly $1.40. The investor would then adjust the share price of $52 in the example to $50.60.

Value of Options versus an Estimate of Movement of Stock Price

Success in buying or selling options depends on two factors:

1. Correct prediction of the movement of the price of the underlying stock in the option period.
2. Correct assessment of the value of options available in the market. Other things being equal, the sophisticated investor prefers to buy underpriced options and to sell overpriced options.

The important question is: How should investors weigh the two factors in investment decisions on options? Should they treat the two factors as

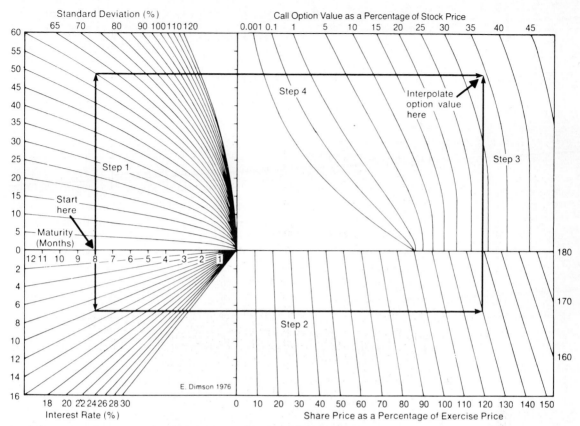

FIGURE 15–2   Dimson's Nomogram for Valuing a Call Option

equally important, or consider one factor as more important than the other? Unfortunately there is no unanimous answer to this question, even among experts.

One inclination would be to weigh the first factor more importantly than the second, even if one buys a group of underpriced call options. If the movement of the underlying stock price of most options in their option periods is predicted incorrectly, one would still lose money. On the other hand, if one buys only underpriced options and sells only overpriced options, without any prediction of the movements of their underlying stocks, the law of large numbers will ensure profits to the investor if he has many transactions among many different stocks and over many time periods. This may be true in the long run provided that the investor is willing to forgo the prediction of movement of stock prices and concentrate only on the criterion of whether a given option is overpriced or underpriced.

The final decision of the relative importance of the two factors rests, of course, with the philosophy or "taste" of the decision maker. The purpose of the discussion here is simply to raise the relevant issues for the consideration of the reader.

THE ROLE OF OPTIONS IN AN INVESTMENT PROGRAM

Having examined the nature, various strategies, and risks of options, we now consider their proper role in an investment program.

1. The options market is a part of the securities markets. Whoever is interested in owning and selling securities either for speculation or investment should acquire a working knowledge of the options market. At one time or another, options could play a useful role in one's investment decision making or investment program.

2. The funds employed for operation in the options market generally should represent a small fraction of one's investment funds. The general rule is that no more than 25 percent of one's funds should be used in this sector of the securities markets. Moreover, one should observe the rule of diversification. Instead of concentrating on one stock, spreading over several issues is generally preferred.

3. Buying options purely for speculation is generally not recommended. According to statistics, less than 40 percent of options are being exercised. That means that the odds are in favor of those who write options rather than those who purchase them.

4. Buying options as a device for limiting risk is generally favored over pure speculation.

5. Writing options against a portfolio of stocks or a pool of liquid funds for the purpose of obtaining an increase in investment return is a relatively dependable strategy. It is very worthwhile for investors to look into if they usually maintain a portfolio of stocks and if their aim is only for a reasonable rate of profit.

6. Buying stocks or options is in some ways like playing poker. If you always stay in the game, you have the fun of always having cards to look at but rarely profits. On the other hand, if you come in only infrequently — only when the probability is clearly in your favor — you may miss the fun of the action, but financially it could be very rewarding.

Federal Tax Regulations on Options Contracts[5]

With respect to the holder of a call option, the Internal Revenue Service has ruled as follows:

1. The cost of the option is a nondeductible capital expenditure.

[5]Source: *Prospects of the Options Clearing Corporation*. Chicago, 1985.

2. If the option is sold prior to exercise, any gain or loss realized by the holder constitutes capital gain or loss.
3. If the option is allowed to expire unexercised, the expiration is treated as a sale or exchange of the option on the expiration date. The resulting loss is a capital loss.
4. If the option is exercised, its cost is treated as an addition to the basis of the stock purchased (in the case of a call), or as a reduction in the amount realized on the sale of the underlying stock (in the case of a put). Gain or loss on such sale is capital gain or loss.

With respect to the writer of an option, the Internal Revenue Service has ruled as follows:

1. The premium received for writing the option is not included in income at the time of receipt, but is carried in a deferred account until the writer's obligation expires in time, until the writer sells the underlying stock pursuant to the exercise of a call or purchases the underlying stock pursuant to the exercise of a put, or until the writer engages in a closing transaction.
2. If the option is exercised, the premium received is treated as part of the proceeds of the sale of the underlying stock (in the case of a call), or as a reduction in the cost of the underlying stock (in the case of a put).

WARRANTS

A warrant is a long-term option to purchase a specified number of shares of common stock of a given corporation at a stated price (exercise price). Warrants are issued by corporations and usually attached to a new issue of bonds or preferred stocks. The purpose of issuing warrants is to make the bonds or preferred stock more salable or at a lower interest rate or dividend rate or both.

Theoretical Value

The theoretical value (V) of a warrant can be obtained from the following formula:

$$V = N(P_M - E)$$

where:

N = the number of shares of common stock that can be purchased with a warrant

E = the exercise price of the warrant

P_M = the market price of a share of common stock

For example, the ABC Corporation has some warrants outstanding. Each warrant is entitled to buy half a share of common stock at the exercise price of $10 each share. The warrant has a life of five years and the market price of the stock is $15. The theoretical value in this case is:

$$V = N(P_M - E) = .5(\$15 - \$10) = \$2.50$$

It is more common, however, to find that the exercise price of a warrant is higher than the market price of the stock. For instance, suppose GAF Corporation issues new shares of preferred stock with warrants attached; each warrant entitles the shareholder to buy 1.5 shares of common stock at a price of $40 per share, and the warrant has a life of five years. If GAF stock is now selling at $30 in the marketplace, the theoretical value of the GAF warrant is:

$$V = N(P_M - E) = 1.5(\$30 - \$40) = -\$15$$

According to the calculation, the theoretical value is −$15. Since a negative theoretical value is meaningless, we treat the theoretical value of the warrant as zero.

Premium of Warrant

The theoretical value of the GAF warrant was just calculated as zero or worthless, but in the marketplace the warrant could be selling at, say, around $4. How can this be explained? Or, why should anybody be willing to pay $4 for a warrant that, for the moment, is useless?

The answer lies in potential capital gain and high leverage. If the stock is expected to rise to $45 in three years, the warrant would be worth 1.5($45 − $40) = $7.50 at that time. On the other hand, if the stock is expected to double within five years, then the future worth of the warrant would be 1.5($60 − $40) = $30, which is more than seven times the market price of the warrant at $4.

The excess of the price of the warrant over its theoretical value is called a premium. The premium of the GAF warrant is $4 − 0 = $4.

The premium of a warrant is usually calculated as a percentage to indicate at what point the warrant would begin to show a capital gain. The formula is:

$$\text{Premium } (\%) = \frac{WP/N + E}{P_M} - 1$$

where:

WP = market price of warrant

N = number of shares of common each warrant can buy

E = exercise price of the warrant

P_M = market price of the stock

The premium of the GAF warrant in percentage terms is:

$$\text{Premium } (\%) = \frac{\$4/1.5 + 40}{30} - 1 = \frac{42.67}{30} - 1 = 42.2\%$$

The premium of the GAF warrant amounted to 42.2%. In other words, the common has to appreciate 42.2% before the theoretical value of the GAF warrant will begin to exceed the price of the warrant ($4).

Factors Determining the Attractiveness of a Warrant

The attractiveness of a warrant depends on a number of factors:

1. The prospect of the underlying stock must be good. In other words, there is a good possibility that the price of the stock will appreciate in future years.
2. The warrant must have a relatively long life (at least three years).
3. The premium of the warrant must be relatively low, preferably less than 20 percent.
4. There must be provisions in the warrant to protect warrant holders from dilution in the case of stock dividends, stock splits, mergers, combinations, and all recapitalizations.
5. The warrant must be actively traded, preferably on organized exchanges.
6. The dividend payout ratio of the stock is not excessive so that it will not adversely affect the potential growth of earnings per share.
7. The warrant is not subject to call.

SUMMARY

Call options give the holder the right to buy a security at a given price within a specified period of time. Put options, on the other hand, give the holder the right to sell a security at a given price before the expiration of the option. Call and put options can be purchased or sold as a means to implement either defensive or aggressive strategies.

Hedging means buying one option and, at the same time, selling another option, both in the same stock. The purpose of hedging is to limit loss, if the future price of the stock moves against expectations; and to provide an adequate profit, if the future price of the stock moves in line with expectations.

In terms of degree of risk, option strategies may be classified into several categories:

Low-Risk Strategies

1. Write call options on stocks in one's portfolio.
2. Write put options on stocks one is willing to purchase now at the current market price.
3. Use part of dividend and interest income from a portfolio to buy call or put options.

Moderate-Risk Strategies

1. Hedging—buy a call option and sell another call option of the same stock.
2. Ratio hedging—write two calls on each 100 shares of stock owned.
3. Sell a straddle (call and put combined).
4. Purchase the stock and sell a straddle on the stock.

High-Risk Strategies

1. Purchase a call.
2. Purchase a put.
3. Sell a call without owning the underlying stock.
4. Sell a put for speculation.
5. Purchase a straddle.

A warrant is a long-term option that gives the holder the right to purchase a specified number of shares of common stock from the issuing corporation at a stated price.

The essential difference between a call option and a warrant on the same stock is maturity. The longest call option on organized exchanges is nine months, whereas the maturity for a warrant is usually three to fifteen years and occasionally even for an indefinite period.

Since most warrants are long-term, the market price of a warrant usually exceeds its theoretical value. The premium in most cases varies from 10 percent to 50 percent.

The attractiveness of a warrant depends primarily on two factors: (1) the long-term outlook of the stock and (2) the extent of the warrant's premium over its theoretical value.

When a stock has both call options and long-term warrants outstanding, the choice between buying calls or warrants rests on other factors besides whether the investor is interested in the long term or short term. In such cases, the investor should examine both the call option and the warrant carefully before making a decision. Sometimes one can substitute for the other or one may be a better vehicle than the other.

QUESTIONS AND PROBLEMS

1. What innovations did the Chicago Board Options Exchange introduce in the trading of options?
2. What are the advantages and disadvantages of buying calls on a stock instead of purchasing the stock itself?
3. What is meant by writing call options?
4. Explain a few objectives or strategies in buying put options.
5. What is a straddle? How can it be properly utilized?
6. Explain the nature of hedging strategies in options.
7. What is meant by ratio hedging? Discuss the advantages of this strategy.
8. Name a few low-risk option strategies.
9. Name a few high-risk option strategies.
10. If one is very bearish on a stock, what option strategy is most appropriate? Why?
11. On a given day, ABC stock closed at $46. The calls on the stock were traded as follows:

Exercise Price	Maturity		
	3 Months	6 Months	9 Months
$45	$3\frac{1}{2}$	5	$6\frac{1}{2}$
$50	$1\frac{1}{2}$	3	4

Questions: a. Establish a bullish "money-spread" hedging strategy.
b. Establish a "time-spread" hedging strategy.
c. Explain the purpose of the "time-spread" strategy just established under (b).
12. Using the information given in Question 11,
a. Establish a ratio-hedging strategy.
b. Explain the purpose of the strategy.

13. On a given day, a YW stock closed at $52. The calls and puts on the stock were traded as follows:

Exercise Price	Maturity		
	3 Months	*6 Months*	*9 Months*
45 (Call)	$7\frac{1}{2}$	$8\frac{1}{4}$	$8\frac{3}{4}$
45 (Put)	$\frac{1}{2}$	$1\frac{1}{4}$	$1\frac{3}{4}$
50 (Call)	$3\frac{1}{2}$	$4\frac{1}{2}$	$5\frac{1}{2}$
50 (Put)	$1\frac{1}{4}$	$2\frac{1}{4}$	3

The investor is neither bullish nor bearish. He feels that the stock will fluctuate in a narrow range within the next six to nine months. What option strategy should he employ? Establish an example and explain.

14. Using the information given in Question 13, if a given investor is moderately bullish on the stock, what option strategy should he employ? Give an example and explain.

15. Using the information given in Question 13, give an example of ratio writing and explain the purpose.

16. ABC Corporation has some warrants outstanding. Each warrant is entitled to buy 1.4 shares of common stock at $40 each. The warrant has a maturity of ten years. The market price of common is $28, and the market price of warrant is $5 each.

   a. Calculate the theoretical value of the warrant.

   b. Explain the discrepancy between the theoretical value and market price of the warrant.

REFERENCES

Ansbacher, Max G. *The New Options Market,* rev. ed. New York: Walker, 1979.

Black, F., and Scholes, M. "The Valuation of Option Contracts and a Test of Market Efficiency." *Journal of Finance,* May 1972.

———. "The Pricing of Options and Corporate Liabilities." *The Journal of Political Economy,* May–June 1973.

Brennan, M. J., and Schwartz, E. S. "The Valuation of American Put Options." *Journal of Finance,* May 1977.

Clasing, H. K., Jr. *The Dow Jones-Irwin Guide to Put and Call Options,* rev. ed. Homewood, Ill.: Dow Jones-Irwin, 1978.

Cleeton, Claud E. *Strategies For the Options Trader.* New York: John Wiley & Sons, 1979.

Cox, John C., and Rubinstein, Mark. *Options Markets.* Englewood Cliffs, N.J.: Prentice-Hall, Inc., 1985.

Culp, Michael. "A Catalog of Option Strategies." *The Outlook,* Nov. 15, 1976.

Cunnion, J. D. *How to Get Maximum Leverage from Puts and Calls*. Larchmont, N.Y.: Business Reports, Inc., 1966.

Dimson, Elroy. "Instant Option Valuation." *Financial Analysts Journal*, May–June 1977.

——. "Option Valuation Nomograms." *Financial Analysts Journal*, Nov.–Dec. 1977.

Filer, Herbert. *Understanding Put and Call Options*. New York: Popular Library, 1966.

Fisher, Stanley. "Call Option Pricing When the Exercise Price is Uncertain, and the Valuation of Index Bonds." *Journal of Finance*, March 1978.

Gastineau, G. L. *The Stock Options Manual*, 2nd ed. New York: McGraw-Hill, 1979.

Hettenhouse, G. W., and Puglisi, D. J. "Investor Experience with Options." *Financial Analysts Journal*, July–Aug. 1975.

Malkiel, B. G., and Quandt, R. E. *Strategies and Rational Decisions in the Securities Option Market*. Cambridge, Mass.: M.I.T. Press, 1969.

Merton, R. C. "Theory of Rational Option Pricing." *Bell Journal of Economics and Management Science*, Spring 1973.

——. "The Impact of Option Pricing of Specification Error in the Underlying Stock Price Returns." *Journal of Finance*, May 1976.

Murray, R. F. "Options as an Investment Tool." *Forbes*, Oct. 1, 1975.

Nodding, T. C., and Zagove, E. *CBOE Call Options: Your Daily Guide to Portfolio Strategy*. Homewood, Ill.: Dow Jones-Irwin, 1975.

——. *Advanced Investment Strategies*. Homewood, Ill.: Dow Jones-Irwin, 1978.

Prendergast, S. L. *Uncommon Profits Through Stock Purchase Warrants*. Homewood, Ill.: Dow Jones-Irwin, 1973.

Prospectus of the Options Clearing Corporation, current issue.

Reback, Robert. "Risk and Return in Option Trading." *Financial Analysts Journal*, July–Aug. 1975.

Scholes, Myron. "Taxes and the Pricing of Options." *Journal of Finance*, May 1976.

16

Financial and Other Futures

Futures markets are the markets in which contracts for future delivery are traded. In other words, one individual agrees to buy and another individual agrees to sell the item in the contract at a stated price with delivery and payment to be made at a specified future date. The items in futures contracts may be financial instruments (such as Treasury bills or GNMA certificates), foreign currency, agricultural commodities, metals, and many other things. In addition, some futures contracts deal with items that are not actually bought and sold, such as stock index futures and futures on economic measures like the consumer price index.

During the last decade, futures markets have grown rapidly, with particular growth in financial futures. There are several reasons for this growth. First, volatile interest rates have created a need for methods of reducing interest rate risk, and interest rate futures serve this purpose. Second, with the growth of international trade and fluctuations in exchange rates, foreign exchange futures have become an important method of reducing exchange rate risk. Third, futures contracts on stock indexes and options on those futures have provided additional opportunities for both investors and speculators. Moreover, as they have become better understood by participants in financial markets, futures have been used to a greater extent.

HISTORY OF FUTURES MARKETS IN THE UNITED STATES[1]

The need for a futures market was apparent to commodity traders by the mid-1800s. During the early fall large numbers of farmers brought their harvested grain to Chicago. Given the quantity of grain dumped on the market, there was a substantial drop in grain prices. Later in the year shortages developed that caused prices to reach high levels. Because of the wide movement in prices, there was considerable uncertainty both for farmers who were selling the grain and the processors who purchased the grain.

[1]Much of this historical information comes from M. Drabenstott and A. McDonley, "Futures Markets: A Primer for Financial Institutions." *Economic Review*, Federal Reserve Bank of Kansas City, November 1984.

Futures markets were, therefore, developed as a mechanism that enabled buyers and sellers to reduce the risk of fluctuating grain prices. In 1848, the Chicago Board of Trade was organized for the purpose of buying and selling grain. Purchases and sales could be for both immediate cash delivery or for delivery at some future time. Contracts made for future delivery enabled the participants to avoid the price uncertainty of the cash, or "spot", market.

Buyers and sellers who used commodity futures to protect themselves against price risk became known as hedgers. Another group that became interested in futures markets were speculators. They purchased or sold contracts without the intention of owning or selling grain. Their objective was to buy and sell contracts for the purpose of making quick profits. In pursuing their objectives they provided liquidity to the markets. In other words, with additional buyers and sellers of contracts in the market, hedging transactions were easier to implement.

The Scope of Contracts Traded

The Chicago Board of Trade was a successful operation, and its growth stimulated the establishment of futures exchanges in other cities. As the number of exchanges increased, so too did the number of commodities traded. Over time the prices of a growing variety of items could be hedged with futures contracts.

The introduction of financial futures is a relatively new development that started in the 1970s. In 1972, the Chicago Mercantile Exchange initiated trading in futures of foreign currencies. Between 1975 and 1979, a variety of interest rate futures appeared. In the early 1980s, trading began on stock index futures and on options on futures.

In 1985, there were seven major categories of futures traded on exchanges in the Unites States: grains and oilseeds, livestock and meats, food and fiber, wood, metals and petroleum, financial, and economic indexes.

LISTINGS OF FUTURES PRICES

A sample of listings of Futures Prices appears in Table 16–1. We will examine in detail several listings that are of interest to investors.

Gold Listings

Gold futures prices are shown under the Metals and Petroleum group in Table 16–1. The top line reads:

Gold (CMX) — 100 troy oz.; $ per troy oz.

TABLE 16–1   Futures Prices

Monday, August 19, 1985.

Open Interest Reflects Previous Trading Day.

Columns for each section: Open, High, Low, Settle, Change, Lifetime High, Lifetime Low, Open Interest

— GRAINS AND OILSEEDS —

CORN (CBT) 5,000 bu.; cents per bu.

	Open	High	Low	Settle	Change	Lifetime High	Lifetime Low	Open Interest
Sept	231½	231¾	230½	231¼	− ¾	321½	225¼	24,137
Dec	224¼	224¾	223	223¾	− 1½	295	221	58,396
Mar86	232¼	232¾	231¼	232	− 1¼	297	230	26,701
May	237	237¾	236	236½	− ¾	291¼	234¾	10,646
July	237	238¼	236½	237	− ½	286	233¾	4,664
Sept	227	229	226¾	226½	− ½	270	225	1,147
Dec	224¾	225	223	223	− 2	228¾	220½	1,991

Est vol 22,000; vol Fri 25,696; open int 127,682, +2342.

CORN (MCE) 1,000 bu.; cents per bu.

Sept	231½	232¾	230½	231¼	− ¾	315½	225⅞	1,234
Dec	224¼	224¾	223¼	223¾	− 1½	289¾	221	16,150
Mar86	232	232¼	231¼	232	− 1½	295½	230	462
May	236½	236½	236½	236½	− ¾	291	226	114
Sept	228	228	228	228	− 1½	244¾	225	16

Est vol 900; vol Fri 859; open int 18,182, +19.

OATS (CBT) 5,000 bu.; cents per bu.

Sept	120¾	120¾	119¾	119¼	− ¾	179	116½	1,063
Dec	129¾	129¾	128	128¼	− 2	172½	124	1,890
Mar86	132	132	129¾	129¾	− 2¾	167¾	126½	337
May	130	130	129¾	129¾	− 2½	163	127½	236

Est vol 300; vol Fri 556; open int 3,740, −9.

SOYBEANS (CBT) 5,000 bu.; cents per bu.

Aug	520½	522½	518¾	519	− 2¾	756	516	2,834
Sept	510	510	505¼	506	− 4	657	504½	2,887
Nov	512	512½	509	509	− 4½	668	509	35,745
Jan86	520	522	518	518	− 4	679	518	6,648
Mar	529	532	528	528½	− 3¾	657	535½	4,642
May	537	540	535½	536½	− 4	657	535½	1,731
July	540	544½	539½	540¼	− 2½	658	539½	2,084
Aug	537½	537½	537½	537½	− 1	609	537	314
Nov	533	535	530½	530½	− 3¾	587	528	293

Est vol 23,000; vol Fri 27,567; open int 64,620, −1353.

SOYBEANS (MCE) 1,000 bu.; cents per bu.

Aug	520	522½	519	519	− 2¾	684	513½	188
Sept	508	509	505½	506	− 4½	668	505½	686
Nov	512	512½	508½	509	− 4½	671	508½	8,591
Jan86	520	521¼	517½	518	− 4½	674	517½	848
Mar	529	530	527¼	528½	− 3¾	647	527¼	741
May	538	539¾	536	536½	− 4	657	536	117
July	541	541½	540	540¾	− 2½	656	535½	125

Est vol 2,717; vol Fri 2,417; open int 11,364, +103.

SOYBEAN MEAL (CBT) 100 tons; $ per ton.

Aug	122.80	123.50	122.40	122.40	− 1.30	180.00	117.70	352
Sept	123.70	124.10	123.00	123.10	− 1.30	179.50	120.60	9,711
Oct	125.30	125.60	124.50	124.60	− 1.30	166.00	121.00	8,370
Dec	128.80	128.80	127.60	127.70	− 1.50	184.00	126.30	14,828
Jan86	130.00	130.00	129.20	129.30	− 1.60	163.00	127.80	2,868
Mar	132.00	133.00	131.80	131.80	− 1.70	166.00	130.00	1,461
May	135.50	135.50	134.00	134.00	− 1.10	162.50	132.50	1,080
July	137.50	137.50	137.00	137.00	− 1.00	163.00	134.00	2,135
Aug				136.50	− 2.00			137

Est vol 2,000; vol Fri 8,350; open int 40,924, −150.

SOYBEAN OIL (CBT) 60,000 lbs.; cents per lb.

Aug	22.45	22.45	22.22	22.25	− .32	31.95	22.22	1,098
Sept	22.42	22.48	22.21	22.23	− .31	31.10	22.21	14,410
Oct	22.38	22.40	22.18	22.21	− .29	30.37	22.18	8,798
Dec	22.38	22.43	22.20	22.21	− .27	29.55	22.20	17,808
Jan86	22.45	22.55	22.31	22.31	− .29	29.07	22.31	3,514
Mar	22.75	22.85	22.51	22.53	− .27	28.60	22.51	3,154
May	22.90	23.10	22.75	22.75	− .20	28.60	22.75	2,199
July	22.95	23.05	22.90	22.90	− .15	25.25	22.90	1,334
Aug	23.00	23.00	22.93	22.93	− .07	25.15	22.93	610
Sept	22.90	23.00	22.86	22.86	− .05	24.05	22.86	244

Est vol 17,000; vol Fri 18,159; open int 54,541, +870.

WHEAT (CBT) 5,000 bu.; cents per bu.

Sept	292	292	287½	287¾	− 5¾	374	284½	11,298
Dec	305	305½	302	302	− 4¾	364	292½	18,110
Mar86	309¼	309¾	307½	307¾	− 3¾	354¾	293½	5,597
May	299½	301¼	299	299	− 4¼	350	284	1,607
July	278	279	276½	276¾	− 3¼	310	265	3,086

Est vol 10,365; open int 39,761, +55.

WHEAT (KC) 5,000 bu.; cents per bu.

Sept	301½	302	299	299¼	− 3¼	363¼	284½	9,725
Dec	309½	309¾	306	306	− 3¼	352	291	15,561
Mar86	309½	309½	306	306½	− 3½	349	308½	1,588
May	295¼	296½	295½	295½	− 2½	325	281	364
July	275	275½	274	275	− 2	301	263½	378

Est vol 2,780; vol Fri 4,113; open int 27,172, −565.

WHEAT (MPLS) 5,000 bu.; cents per bu.

Sept	319¾	320½	319½	319½	− 3	367¼	309¾	3,467
Dec	329	329½	325½	325½	− 4½	372¼	314½	2,555
Mar86	329	332	327½	327½	− 3¼	383¼	315	493
May	323	323	322	322	− 2	326	314¼	173

Est vol 1,791; vol Fri 2,000; open int 6,715, −71.

— LIVESTOCK & MEAT —

CATTLE—FEEDER (CME) 44,000 lbs.; cents per lb.

Aug	65.50	65.60	64.40	65.00	− .45	73.70	58.30	388
Sept	63.85	63.85	62.85	63.05	− .95	73.00	57.45	1,064
Oct	62.40	62.50	61.65	61.95	− .87	72.32	57.17	3,533
Nov	64.00	64.10	63.15	63.35	− .92	73.20	58.30	1,535
Jan86	65.60	65.60	64.55	64.90	− .75	70.80	60.60	441
Mar	65.70	65.70	64.65	65.05	− .75	70.55	61.10	299
Apr	65.70	65.70	64.65	65.05	− .75	69.05	61.15	199

Est vol 1,783; vol Fri 5,565; open int 7,743, +17.

CATTLE—LIVE (CME) 40,000 lbs.; cents per lb.

Aug	54.85	55.00	54.50	54.77	− .17	67.67	50.72	1,091
Oct	56.40	56.55	55.70	56.22	− .47	65.90	53.63	22,298
Dec	58.05	58.20	57.47	57.87	− .35	67.85	55.15	12,613
Feb86	58.55	58.70	57.90	58.27	− .55	66.40	56.00	4,333
Apr	59.60	59.80	59.10	59.25	− .55	67.07	57.30	1,650
June	60.60	60.75	60.40	60.40	− .35	66.60	58.10	543

Est vol 14,572; vol Fri 11,228; open int 42,540, −142.

HOGS (CME) 30,000 lbs.; cents per lb.

Aug	44.45	44.45	43.35	43.87	− .82	54.37	41.92	776
Oct	37.65	37.65	36.45	36.47	− 1.47	51.75	36.45	9,114
Dec	39.90	39.95	38.80	38.92	− 1.37	49.85	38.80	5,411
Feb86	41.60	41.60	40.40	40.42	− 1.47	50.47	40.35	2,367
Apr	38.40	38.65	37.30	37.67	− 1.10	48.00	37.30	696
June	41.60	41.60	40.40	40.77	− .75	49.05	40.40	555
July	41.75	41.90	40.40	41.30	− .82	49.05	40.40	301

Est vol 5,541; vol Fri 5,565; open int 19,267, +122.

PORK BELLIES (CME) 38,000 lbs.; cents per lb.

Aug	49.20	49.20	46.65	46.65	− 2.00	80.90	46.05	460
Feb86	58.50	58.85	56.52	56.72	− 1.95	76.00	56.72	5,332
Mar	58.55	58.55	56.50	56.62	− 1.82	75.50	56.50	369
May	59.85	59.85	58.30	58.30	− 2.00	75.00	58.30	183
July	59.10	60.25	58.25	58.25	− 1.85	76.10	58.25	100

Est vol 4,788; vol Fri 4,445; open int 6,381, −147.

— FOOD & FIBER —

COCOA (CSCE) 10 metric tons; $ per ton.

Sept	2,090	2,095	2,086	2,086	− 10	2,415	1,963	1,502
Dec	2,168	2,175	2,146	2,166	− 1	2,337	1,945	10,087
Mar86	2,212	2,218	2,202	2,208	− 1	2,220	1,955	5,294
May	2,226	2,231	2,226	2,233	− 2	2,241	1,960	940
July				2,256	+ 1	2,255	1,960	651
Sept				2,291	+ 6	2,210	2,055	1,060

Est vol 2,717; vol Fri 3,303; open int 19,602, −257.

COFFEE (CSCE)—37,500 lbs.; cents per lb.

Sept	136.30	136.70	135.70	136.05	+ .19	150.20	127.00	3,176
Dec	139.30	139.70	138.70	139.55	+ .85	150.40	129.25	5,186
Mar86	140.25	140.50	139.80	140.00	+ .90	149.75	129.00	2,393
May	140.49	140.90	140.00	140.86	+ .91	148.75	131.00	411
July				141.13	+ .38	148.00	135.50	110

Est vol 2,270; vol Fri 1,937; open int 11,301, −61.

COTTON (CTN)—50,000 lbs.; cents per lb.

Oct	58.09	58.22	57.65	58.10	+ .20	77.50	57.65	2,666
Dec	58.55	58.75	58.15	58.56	+ .16	73.00	58.15	9,989
Mar86	59.85	59.90	59.55	59.60	− .20	71.50	59.13	2,746
May	60.10	60.10	59.90	59.99	− .06	70.00	59.30	1,322
July	59.65	59.75	59.60	59.78	+ .03	70.05	59.10	1,216
Oct				54.85	+ .18	65.50	54.40	431
Dec	53.70	54.00	53.75	53.95	+ .25	59.25	53.15	1,685

Est vol 1,800; vol Fri 2,572; open int 20,055, +326.

ORANGE JUICE (CTN)—15,000 lbs.; cents per lb.

Sept	135.50	135.90	133.50	134.75	− .05	182.00	130.55	2,187
Nov	131.50	131.75	130.05	131.25	+ .45	181.00	127.40	1,512
Jan86	128.90	129.00	127.75	128.95	+ .95	180.00	123.50	727
Mar	127.50	127.50	127.00	127.50	+ .45	177.50	123.00	450

Est vol 400; vol Fri 356; open int 4,934, +98.

SUGAR—DOMESTIC (CSCE)—112,000 lbs.; cents per lb.

Nov	20.50	20.51	20.40	20.41	− .09	22.15	20.42	2,313
Jan86	20.85	20.85	20.85	20.84	− .09	22.00	20.85	311
Mar	21.12	21.12	21.05	21.07	− .05	22.00	21.05	2,392
May	21.25	21.25	21.21	21.20	− .07	21.90	21.21	1,402
July	21.20	21.20	21.19	21.19	− .10	21.60	21.15	381
Sept	21.20	21.20	21.20	21.00	− .07	21.40	21.00	668

Est vol 902; vol Fri 109; open int 7,471, +36.

— METALS & PETROLEUM —

COPPER (CMX)—25,000 lbs.; cents per lb.

Aug	60.75	60.75	60.75	59.90	− 1.55	60.80	58.70	8
Sept	61.30	61.30	59.65	59.99	− 1.60	82.10	57.50	33,428
Oct	62.50	62.50	60.90	61.15	− 1.65	84.25	58.50	26,767
Mar86	63.45	63.45	62.00	62.10	− 1.65	80.00	59.60	8,748
Dec	62.80	62.80	62.65	62.65	− 1.65	74.00	61.10	3,264
May	64.50	64.50	63.25	63.50	− 1.65	72.55	61.30	4,195
Sept	64.25	64.25	63.70	63.60	− 1.65	70.90	62.45	2,534
Dec	65.80	65.80	65.80	64.65	− 1.65	72.50	63.70	346

Est vol 12,200; vol Fri 6,154; open int 79,479, −77.

GOLD (CMX)—100 troy oz.; $ per troy oz.

Aug	341.00	342.20	337.50	338.10	+	.20	485.00	291.00	1,360
Sept	344.00	345.80	339.60	341.40	+	.20	493.00	297.00	18,617
Oct	348.00	350.20	344.20	345.80	+	.20	489.50	301.50	48,785
Feb86	352.00	354.70	349.40	350.30	+	.20	485.50	306.00	10,568
Apr	357.50	359.00	354.50	354.80	+	.20	496.80	314.70	12,314
June	362.50	362.50	360.80	359.80	+	.20	433.50	320.50	10,098
Aug	368.00	369.50	362.50	365.00	+	.20	427.50	331.00	9,805
Oct	373.00	373.00	371.00	370.40	+	.20	395.70	335.00	7,538
Dec	379.50	379.50	375.50	376.40	+	.20	388.20	339.00	7,496
Feb87	383.50	383.50	381.60	381.60	+	.20	393.00	352.50	3,574

Est vol 30,000; vol Fri 39,124; open int 135,750, +6002.

PLATINUM (NYM)—50 troy oz.; $ per troy oz.

Aug	335.00	335.00	335.00	338.30	+ 8.90	335.00	275.00	1
Oct	341.00	347.00	330.00	338.20	+ 8.90	393.00	249.00	8,087
Jan86	351.00	351.00	333.00	342.10	+ 9.50	373.00	257.50	4,149
Apr	357.00	357.00	336.00	345.80	+10.20	357.00	264.50	1,565
July	363.00	363.00	345.00	350.30	+10.30	363.00	273.00	518
Oct	363.00	363.00	350.00	355.60	+10.30	360.00	303.50	177

Est vol 9,278; vol Fri 8,278; open int 14,497, +1,779.

SILVER (CBT)—1,000 troy oz.; cents per troy oz.

Aug	695.0	640.0	628.0	628.0	− 13.0	1135.0	570.0	22
Oct	650.0	650.0	632.0	633.5	− 14.0	1137.0	580.0	2,890
Dec	659.0	660.0	642.0	643.0	− 14.0	940.5	590.0	4,458
Feb86	673.0	673.0	650.0	653.0	− 14.0	876.0	640.5	1,535
Apr	685.0	685.0	663.0	663.0	− 14.0	813.5	615.0	860
June	695.0	695.0	675.0	674.0	− 14.0	765.0	625.0	1,910
Aug	700.0	700.0	687.0	687.0	− 14.0	765.0	645.0	525

Est vol 6,000; vol Fri 8,289; open int 23,587, +906.

NY GASOLINE, leaded reg. (NYM) 42,000 gal.; $ per gal.

Sept	.7520	.7565	.7510	.7515	− .0027	.7760	.7040	3,916
Oct	.7335	.7365	.7290	.7325	− .0009	.7675	.6855	3,758
Nov	.7180	.7180	.7140	.7140	− .0065	.7810	.6640	1,243
Dec	.7100	.7100	.7070	.7090	− .0058	.7810	.6640	1,032
Jan86	.7015	.7015	.7015	.7015	− .0055	.7715	.6500	865
Feb	.6925	.6925	.6925	.6925	− .0073	.7600	.6600	1,048
Mar	.7025	.7025	.7025	.7025	− .0083	.7465	.6833	117

Est vol 1,381; vol Fri 1,566; open int 12,580, +34.

HEATING OIL NO. 2 (NYM) 42,000 gal.; $ per gal.

Sept	.7375	.7405	.7315	.7330	− .0077	.7610	.6690	8,253
Oct	.7470	.7495	.7420	.7435	− .0076	.7765	.6752	8,253
Nov	.7555	.7560	.7445	.7472	− .0083	.7590	.6833	4,130
Dec	.7620	.7625	.7550	.7552	− .0084	.7825	.6915	4,130
Jan86	.7600	.7600	.7500	.7517	− .0082	.7800	.6000	1,770
Feb	.7515	.7540	.7500	.7517	− .0071	.7595	.7000	1,078

Est vol 4,170; vol Fri 4,024; open int 25,598, −415.

— FINANCIAL —

BRITISH POUND (IMM)—25,000 pounds; $ per pound

Sept	1.3960	1.4010	1.3920	1.3965	+ .0005	1.4275	1.0190	30,217
Dec	1.3865	1.3925	1.3800	1.3870		1.4190	1.0185	11,270
Mar86	1.3840	1.3840	1.3790	1.3810	− .0005	1.4160	1.0650	992

Est vol 9,487; vol Fri 8,576; open int 42,527, +206.

CANADIAN DOLLAR (IMM)—100,000 dlrs.; $ per Can $

Sept	.7373	.7378	.7362	.7372	− .0012	.7585	.7025	6,910
Dec	.7365	.7365	.7347	.7355	− .0013	.7568	.7006	882
Mar86				.7339	− .0015	.7504	.6981	271
June	.7341	.7341	.7324	.7324	− .0016	.7360	.7070	116

Est vol 760; vol Fri 1,011; open int 8,179, −295.

JAPANESE YEN (IMM) 12.5 million yen; $ per yen (.00)

Sept	.4231	.4233	.4225	.4230	+ .0002	.4268	.3870	30,784
Dec	.4252	.4252	.4246	.4250	+ .0002	.4483	.3905	3,202

Est vol 7,363; vol Fri 6,972; open int 34,062, −9.

SWISS FRANC (IMM)—125,000 francs; $ per franc

Sept	.4438	.4450	.4425	.4446	+ .0010	.4830	.3480	31,552
Dec	.4478	.4489	.4461	.4483	+ .0008	.4494	.3525	4,561
Mar86	.4510	.4525	.4510	.4526	+ .0011	.4545	.3790	194

Est vol 17,677; vol Fri 16,700; open int 36,307, +525.

W. GERMAN MARK (IMM)—125,000 marks; $ per mark

Sept	.3630	.3636	.3621	.3634	− .0002	.3847	.2925	50,923
Dec	.3666	.3668	.3651	.3667	− .0002	.3680	.2971	8,043
Mar86	.3702	.3702	.3693	.3702	− .0002	.3712	.3040	901

Est vol 19,571; vol Fri 19,198; open int 59,871, +1,557.

EURODOLLAR (IMM)—$1 million; pts. of 100%

	Open	High	Low	Settle	Chg	Yield Settle	Yield Chg	Open Interest
Sept	91.92	91.96	91.89	91.94	+ .03	8.06	− .03	54,749
Dec	91.52	91.60	91.50	91.59	+ .07	8.41	− .07	45,453
Mr86	91.09	91.20	91.09	91.19	+ .08	8.81	− .08	14,272
June	90.80	90.82	90.77	90.81	+ .09	9.19	− .09	7,069
Sept	90.38	90.46	90.38	90.47	+ .10	9.53	− .10	4,052
Dec	90.06	90.12	90.06	90.15	+ .11	9.85	− .11	3,099
Mr87	89.78	89.81	89.77	89.84	+ .12	10.16	− .12	1,624
June	89.50	89.54	89.49	89.55	+ .12	10.45	− .12	1,728

Est vol 27,208; vol Fri 37,093; open int 132,046, +4,792.

GNMA 8% (CBT)—$100,000 prncpl.; pts. 32nds of 100%

Sept	76-14	76-14	76-04	76-10	+ 11	11.819	− .069	724
Dec	75-21	75-21	75-21	75-17	+ 10	11.975	− .063	2,318
Mr86				74-27	+ 11	12.114	− .070	490
June				74-08	+ 11	12.235	− .077	521
Sept	73-16	73-16	73-16	73-20	+ 8	12.364	− .052	99

Est vol 249; open int 4,152, +55.

TREASURY BONDS (CBT)—$100,000; pts. 32nds of 100%

Sept	76-19	76-26	76-19	77-03	+ 11	10.822	− .052	140 965
Dec	76-17	76-24	76-17	76-00	+ 11	10.989	− .054	50,761
Mr86	74-16	75-02	74-16	75-00	+ 11	11.146	− .055	14,237
June	73-19	74-03	73-19	74-02	+ 11	11.296	− .056	7,178
Sept	72-26	73-06	72-24	73-06	+ 11	11.439	− .057	11,586
Dec	72-09	72-12	72-07	72-12	+ 11	11.574	− .058	3,476
Mr87	71-20	71-20	71-20	71-20	+ 11	11.701	− .059	1,374
June				70-30	+ 11	11.819	− .060	1,335
Sept				70-07	70-10	70-07	70-10	+ 11	11.928	− .061	1,365

Est vol 165,000; vol Fri 189,109; open int 232,305, +1048.

TREASURY NOTES (CBT)—$100,000; pts. 32nds of 100%

Sept	86-08	86-25	86-08	86-21	+ 8	10.156	− .044	40,366
Dec	85-12	85-23	85-12	85-20	+ 8	10.340	− .046	21,387
Mr86	84-16	84-25	84-16	84-23	+ 9	10.505	− .052	3,058
June	84-00	84-00	84-00	84-08	+ 8	10.661	− .046	307
Sept	83-05	83-07	83-03	83-04	+ 7	10.801	− .041	471

Est vol 10,000; vol Fri 11,210; open int 65,622, −2313.

TREASURY BILLS (IMM)—$1 mil.; pts. of 100%

	Open	High	Low	Settle	Chg	Discount Settle	Discount Chg	Open Interest
Sept	92.90	92.98	92.90	92.97	+ .04	7.03	− .04	19,959
Dec	92.58	92.67	92.56	92.66	+ .05	7.34	− .05	13,682
June	92.25	92.32	92.25	92.32	+ .07	7.68	− .07	1,211
Sept	91.93	91.97	91.93	91.97	+ .07	8.03	− .07	1,211
Dec	91.62	91.64	91.62	91.67	+ .08	8.33	− .08	501
Mar	91.32	91.39	91.32	91.39	+ .07	8.61	− .08	219

Est vol 5,520; vol Fri 9,545; open int 38,194, +486.

BANK CDs (IMM)—$1 million; pts. of 100%

Sept	92.29	92.29	92.22	92.27	+ .03			1,410
Dec	91.88	91.92	91.87	91.92	+ .06	8.08	− .06	689
Mr86				91.52	+ .08	8.48	− .08	174
June				91.14	+ .09	8.86	− .09	152
Sept				91.30	− .10	9.20	− .10	168

Est vol 139; vol Fri 139; open int 2,681, −42.

S&P 500 FUTURES INDEX (CME) 500 Times Index

Sept	186.85	187.80	186.70	187.40	+ .65	190.90	156.837	35,837
Dec	189.30	190.25	189.30	189.90	+ .60	200.85	175.40	5,312
Mar86	192.10	193.00	192.10	192.70	+ .60	203.75	188.80	240

Est vol 43,373; vol Fri 44,640; open int 62,406, −347.

S&P 500 STOCK INDEX (Prelim.)

186.46	186.82	186.14	186.38	+ .26

MAJOR MARKET INDEX (CBT) $100 Times Index

Sept	257⅝	259⅝	256¾	257¼	+ 1	276¾	250¼	3,568
Dec	260⅜	260⅝	259¼	260¼	+ 1¾	270¾	253⅝	80

Est vol 3,000; vol Fri 8,713; open int 11,732, +1653.

MAJOR MARKET INDEX (Prelim.)

255.71	256.65	255.66	255.94	+ 17

NYSE COMPOSITE FUTURES (NYFE) 500 Times Index

Dec	108.25	108.80	108.15	108.60	+ .40	115.35	91.35	7,311
Mar86	109.80	110.45	109.80	110.20	+ .35	117.20	101.20	1,994
June	111.60	112.00	111.60	111.80	+ .35	118.75	109.50	348

Est vol 7,880; vol Fri 6,456; open int 9,704, +140.

NYSE COMPOSITE STOCK INDEX

108.16	108.26	107.86	108.10	+ .19

KC VALUE LINE FUTURES (KC) 500 Times Index

Sept	198.80	199.75	198.70	199.05	+ .05	213.50	185.75	9,571
Dec	202.75	203.30	202.35	202.60	+ .10	217.05	200.00	1,718

Est vol 3,600; vol Fri 3,318; open int 11,291, −654.

KC VALUE LINE COMPOSITE STOCK INDEX

197.78	197.91	197.58	197.71	+ .01

CMX refers to the Commodity Exchange in New York, which is where the gold contracts shown in the Table are traded. At the bottom of the middle column in Table 16–1 one can read the initials of the many exchanges where futures contracts are bought and sold. In fact, because many exchanges may have the same commodities, there is not enough space to show every listing from every exchange. The 100 troy ounces refers to the number of ounces of gold covered by each contract, and $ per ounce means the numerical units in the listings are dollars per ounce of gold.

The first column in the gold listings shows the month of delivery for each of the gold futures contracts. We will examine the August, 1986, contract.

	Open	High	Low	Settle	Change	Lifetime Low	High	Open Interest
August 1986	368.00	369.50	362.50	365.00	+.20	427.50	331.00	9,805

The opening price was $368 per ounce, the high for the day was $369.50, and the low was $362.50. The settlement price, $365, is an estimate of the closing price. The reason why it is described as an estimate is because there are often many transactions at the end of the trading day at somewhat different prices. The Change column, +.20, shows the settlement price per ounce increased by 20¢ from the previous day. Lifetime High and Low shows that for the entire period that the August, 1986 contract has been in existence, the highest price was $427.50, and the lowest price was $331.00.

The last column, Open Interest, shows that the number of contracts currently outstanding on this group of futures is 9,805. It is an indicator of the extent to which participants in the futures market are using this contract. Total Open Interest for all gold futures at the CMX are reported at the bottom of Table 16–1 and amount to 135,750, an increase of 6,002 from the previous day. Volume numbers show estimated sales for Monday, August 19, 1985, at 30,000, while sales for the previous Friday were 59,124. Some individuals may confuse volume with open interest, and a detailed explanation is provided in Appendix A at the end of this chapter.

Prices of futures contracts represent prices at which the participants agree to implement the contracts on the specified future dates. In addition, prices of futures contracts represent the consensus view of the market as to the probable spot or cash prices that will prevail on those future dates. If one glances down the Settlement column, one observes that the prices of gold futures rise with delivery months that are later in the future. This is due to two factors. First, there is the expectation of inflation, which would cause gold to sell at higher prices as we move farther into the future. Second, futures prices also reflect carrying costs of those who hold a commodity and sell it for future delivery.

Listings of Financial Futures

In Table 16–1 the foreign currency futures at the top of the right column and the stock index futures at the bottom of the column have the same basic format as the gold listings. However, other financial futures appear differently. For example, consider the futures prices of GNMAs, Treasury bonds, and Treasury notes. They are quoted in 32nds of 1 percent, just as the listings shown for those securities in Chapter 7. Thus, an entry such as 74–08 refers to $74\frac{8}{32}$ percent or 0.7425 times par value. The change column shows the movement in settlement price from the previous day in terms of 32nds of 1 percent. A +8 would mean that the contract value increased by $\frac{8}{32} \times 1\% \times \$100,000 = \$250$.

To the right of the change column, the yield to maturity for the security is shown based on the price, coupon, and years to maturity of the instrument in the contract. This column is followed by the change in yield to maturity from the previous day. Since investors are concerned with interest rate movements, the yield column provides important information. One can also observe from Table 16–1 that on the day of the listings the market anticipated that interest rates would rise in future periods. For example, Treasury bond interest rates were expected to rise from 10.822 percent in September, 1985, to 11.439 percent in September, 1986, and to 11.928 percent in September, 1987.

Just as bond prices move in the opposite direction of interest rate movements, so too do prices of interest rate futures. Thus, if the rates implied in the contracts are rising, the prices of those contracts are falling.

PARTICIPANTS IN FUTURES TRADING

Buyers and Sellers of Contracts

Those who trade in futures markets can either purchase or sell contracts. The buyer of a contract is said to take a *long position*. These individuals will make a profit if they can later sell the contract at a higher price, just as do investors who hold long positions in stocks. In the case of interest rate futures, those with long positions are looking for declining interest rates to cause prices to rise.

Participants who sell futures contracts are said to be taking *short positions*. They are promising to deliver the item in the contract at a specified price on a future date. If the price of that futures falls, they can make a reverse trade and repurchase the contract at a lower price. In this sense, a short position in the futures market is similar to a short position in the stock market.

Buyers and sellers of futures contracts usually do not make or take delivery of the item in the contract. In some cases, such as foreign currency, delivery is possible, but even here it is generally infrequent. In cases such as stock index futures, an actual instrument does not exist in the market. Generally, those who hold positions will at some point make a reverse trade to offset the initial position. Thus, if they go long on a particular futures, they would later go short on that same futures. The opposite procedure would occur for those who originally went short. A profit or loss would be made depending on the change in contract price. A major reason why delivery is rare on financial instruments that do exist in the market is because futures markets are mainly used for hedging or speculation, and delivery is not necessary in either case.

Hedgers and Speculators

As stated earlier, hedgers participate in the futures market in order to reduce risk attributable to price fluctuations in the cash or spot market. (See Table 16–2 for a sample listing of cash market prices.) Short hedgers own the commodities or financial instruments that correspond to the futures contract that they sell. In this way, they can protect themselves against price declines. Long hedgers purchase futures contracts on commodities or financial instruments that they intend to buy at some future time. Using futures, they can obtain protection against price increases.

Speculators take action for entirely different motives. They accept the risks hedgers try to avoid in order to make a profit. Speculators attempt to forecast prices. If those prices exceed prices in the futures markets, they take long positions. If speculators anticipate lower prices than the futures markets, they take short positions. Speculators comprise the largest number of traders on futures markets and, consequently, they are a very important ingredient in maintaining market efficiency.

Clearinghouse of the Exchange

As soon as a transaction is completed between the buyer and seller of a futures contract at the price agreed upon, the clearinghouse of the futures exchange steps in. The clearinghouse is made up of members of the exchange, and it guarantees that both buyers and sellers will honor their contracts. In effect, after the buyer and seller agree on the transaction, they separately become obligated to the clearinghouse, which, in turn, has an obligation to those individuals.

Brokers of Futures Contracts

To trade on futures markets, one must have an account with a broker who performs this service. Some large stock brokerage firms, but not all of them, do handle futures trading. There are also firms that advertise on the futures page of The *Wall Street Journal* and other publications that cover futures prices.

TABLE 16–2

CASH PRICES
Tuesday August 20, 1985.
(Quotations as of 4 p.m. Eastern time)

GRAINS AND FEEDS

	Tues.	Mon.	Yr. Ago
Alfalfa Pellets, dehy. Neb., ton	62.0-64.0	62.0-64.0	87.00
Barley, top-quality Mpls., bu	2.05-2.15	2.10-2.15	2.47½
Bran, (Wheat middling) KC ton ...	49.00	51.00	87.00
Brewer's Grains, Milw. ton	55.00	55.00	80.00
Corn, No. 2 yel. Cent-Ill. bu	bp2.53	2.51	3.14½
Corn Gluten Feed, Chgo., ton	74.00	74.00	80.00
Cottnsd Meal, Clksdle,Miss. ton ..	97.50	97.50	160.00
Flaxseed, Mpls., bu	b6.15	6.35	6.85
Hominy Feed, Ill., ton	75.00	75.00	93.00
Linseed Meal, Mpls., ton	78.00	78.00	115.00
Meat-Bonemeal 50%-pro, Ill. ton ..	140.00	137.50	165.00
Oats, No. 2 milling, Mpls., bu	1.23	1.22	1.75½
Rice, No. 2 milled fob Ark. cwt	17.5-18.0	17.5-18.0	18.50
Rye, No. 2 Mpls., bu	2.22	2.30	2.10
Sorghum, (Milo) No. 2 Gulf cwt ...	3.84	4.07	4.86
Soybean Meal, Decatur, Ill. ton ...	119.50	120.00	147.00
Soybeans, No. 1 yel Cent.-Ill. bu ..	bp5.05½	5.04½	6.17
Sunflwr Sd No. 1 Duluth/Supr cwt	b9.50	9.50	11.75
Wheat, Spring 14%-pro Mpls. bu ..	r3.50¾	3.53½	4.03½
Wheat, amber durum, Mpls. bu ...	3.72-4.30	3.70-4.20	4.65
Wheat, No. 2 sft red, St.Lou. bu ..	h2.77	2.84	3.42½
Wheat, No. 2 hard KC, bu	3.02¼	3.06¾	3.79¾

FOODS

Beef, 700-900 lbs. Mid-U.S.,lb.fob ..	.81	.81	.96
Beef, boxed, gross, Mid-US cwt ...	f92.58	92.64	98.45
Broilers, Dressed "A" NY lb	x.5436	.5340	.5400
Butter, AA, Chgo., lb.	1.39¾	1.39¾	1.50
Cocoa, Ivory Coast, smetric ton ..	g2,557	2,541	2,410
Coffee, Brazilian, NY lb.	n1.33	1.33	1.45
Eggs, Lge white, Chgo doz.	.66-.69	.66-.69	.65
Flour, hard winter KC cwt	8.70	8.75	9.50
Hams, 17-20 lbs. Mid-US lb fob	.62	.65	.84
Hogs, Iowa-S.Minn. avg. cwt	43.50	44.50	51.50
Hogs, Omaha avg cwt	e42.60	43.75	51.70
Orange Juice, frz con, NY lb.	1.37	z	z
Pepper, black, NY lb.	a1.77	1.77	1.05
Pork Bellies, 12-14 lbs Mid-US lb ..	.50	.53	.60
Pork Loins, 14-17 lbs. Mid-US lb ...	.95	.97	1.02
Potatoes, rnd wht, 50 lb., fob	y1.50	1.50-.62½	4.00
Steers, Omaha choice avg cwt	52.38	52.62	64.40
Steers, Tex.-Okla. ch avg cwt	e54.25	54.75	64.00
Steers, Feeder, Okl City, av cwt ...	66.00	66.00	65.50
Sugar, beet, ref. Chgo-Wst lb fob ..	.3150	.3150	.3150
Sugar, cane, raw NY lb. del.	z	z	.2170
Sugar, cane, raw world, lb. fob ...	.0410	.0411	.0377
Sugar, cane, ref NY lb. fob	.3260	.3260	.3260

FATS AND OILS

Coconut Oil, crd, N. Orleans lb. ...	xxn.24½	.25	.65
Coconut Oil, crd, N. Orleans lb. cif	yyn.19	.18¾	.36½
Corn Oil, crd wet mill, Chgo. lb. ...	.22	.21¾	.25½
Corn Oil, crd dry mill, Chgo. lb. ...	n.23	.23	.28
Cottonseed Oil, crd Miss Vly lb. ...	.22	.22	.32
Grease, choice white, Chgo lb.	a.13½	.13½	z
Lard, Chgo lb.	.18	.18½	.28¾
Linseed Oil, raw Mpls lb.	.34	.34	.32
Palm Oil, ref. bl. deod. N.Orl. lb. ..	n.24½	.24½	.28
Peanut Oil, crd, Southeast lb.	n.38	.38	.54
Soybean Oil, crd, Decatur, lb.	.2360	.2325	.2783
Tallow, bleachable, Chgo lb.	a.14	.14	.20
Tallow, bleachable, Mo. River lb. ..	a.13	.13	.19
Tallow, edible, Chgo lb.	.18	.18½	.26½

FIBERS AND TEXTILES

Burlap, 10 oz. 40-in. NY yd	n.2820	.2820	.3385
Cotton 1 1/16 in str lw-md Mphs lb	.5665	.5635	.6300
Print Cloth, cotton, 48-in NY yd ...	s.60	.60	.76
Print Cloth, pol/cot 48-in NY yd ...	1.48	.49	.54
Satin Acetate, NY yd	.72	.72	.67
Sheetings, 60x60 48-in. NY yd	.72	.72	.81
Wool, fine staple terr. Boston lb ..	2.03	2.03	2.42

METALS

Aluminum ingot lb	p.815	.815	.815
Cobalt cathodes 99.9% NY lb.	jp11.70	11.70	11.70
Copper cathodes lb	p.66c	.66-.66½	.63½
Copper Scrap, No 2 wire NY lb ...	k.44½	.44½	.48
Lead, lb.	p.19	.19-.26	.30
Mercury 76 lb. flask NY	317.00	317.00	305.00
Nickel plating grade lb	p3.29	3.29	3.29
Steel Scrap 1 hvy mlt Chgo ton ...	80.00	82.00	87.00
Tin Metals Week composite.lb.	6.2677	6.3046	6.2380
Zinc High grade lb	p.41	.41	.45

MISCELLANEOUS

Hides, hvy native strs lb fob	.55½	.55½	.70
Newspapers, old No. 1 Chgo ton ...	25.0-30.0	25.0-30.0	47.50
Rubber, smoked sheets, NY lb.	n.41¾	.42	.46¼

PRECIOUS METALS

Gold, troy oz			
Engelhard indust bullion	.334.55	341.30	346.40
Engelhard fabric prods	351.28	358.37	363.72
Handy & Harman base price	334.40	341.15	346.00
London fixing AM 335.50 PM ...	334.15	340.90	346.00
Krugerrand, whol	a339.50	342.00	358.00
Platinum, troy ounce (Contract) .	475.00	475.00	475.00
Platinum, troy ounce (Free Mkt.)	331.50	336.00	n.a.
Silver, troy ounce			
Engelhard indust bullion	6.275	6.375	7.500
Engelhard fabric prods	6.714	6.821	8.025
Handy & Harman base price	6.265	6.340	7.495
London Fixing (in pounds)			
Spot (U.S. equiv. $6.260)	4.4715	4.5620	5.6990
3 months	4.5945	4.6860	5.8455
6 months	4.7075	4.8020	5.9895
1 year	4.9450	5.0420	6.3285
Coins, whol $1,000 face val	a5.180	5.210	6.655

MARGIN AND VARIATION IN EQUITY

Buyers and sellers of futures are required to deposit a certain minimum sum of money, known as the *initial margin requirement*, with their brokerage firm. The required amount is essentially a deposit designed to guarantee that buyers and sellers will fulfill their obligations as specified in the futures contract. The initial margin required is often in the range of 5 percent to 10 percent of the value of the contract. The exact dollar amount will depend on the degree of fluctuation of the contract's value, and it can change over time as risk associated with the particular futures changes.

The initial deposit in a futures account constitutes the trader's equity at that time. After a futures contract is bought or sold, fluctuations in price will change the value of the contract. For example, assume the price of a gold futures contract is $440 per ounce with the contract for 100 ounces. A speculator buys one contract, and the initial contract value is therefore $440 × 100 = $44,000. Assume further that the initial margin is $4,000 (approximately 9 percent of the contract value). Given that the required $4,000 is in the account, the speculator's equity at that time is $4,000.

What if the market moves up as the speculator had anticipated, and the price of the gold futures rises to $450? The value of the contract is now $45,000, and the speculator has a profit of $1,000 ($45,000 − $44,000). The equity in the speculator's account is now $4,000 (initial deposit) plus $1,000 (profit on futures contract), or $5,000.

In general, the equity (E) in an account is calculated as:

$$E = \text{Cash} + \text{Profits on current positions}$$

$$- \text{Losses on current positions} \qquad (16.1)$$

Cash refers to both cash payments as well as liquid assets such as money market fund deposits or Treasury bills, which some brokers will accept for margin requirements. Profits minus losses refers to the possibility that a trader has several different futures contracts outstanding, some of which have profits and some which have losses. The term "current position" refers to the fact that the contracts are still "open" and have not been reversed or "offset."

If our speculator had been wrong about gold, and if the price had dropped to $425, the value of the contract would have fallen to $42,500, a loss of $1,500 from the original value. The equity would have dropped substantially to $4,000 − $1,500 = $2,500. Just as stockbrokers have maintenance margin requirements, so too do futures brokers. These requirements are usually 75 percent to 80 percent of the initial margin requirement. Both initial and maintenance margin are usually stated in terms of dollars, and the exact amounts are available from the broker. In the example above, current equity is 2500/4000 = 62.5% of initial margin, and the speculator probably received a margin call. If additional cash is not deposited soon enough, the speculator's position may be reversed, or "closed," by the broker.

Futures trading is sometimes described as a zero-sum game. What a long position gains a short position loses and vice versa. In the gold futures example above, the short position also had an initial margin requirement of $4,000 when the contract price was $440. If the contract price rose to $450, the short position lost the $1,000 that the long position gained, and the short position equity would be reduced by $1,000 to $3,000. If the contract price drops to $425, the short position gains the $1,500 lost by the long position, and the short position equity rises to $5,500.

PURCHASE OF PRECIOUS METALS VERSUS PRECIOUS METALS FUTURES CONTRACTS

Assume a speculator has $4,000 to invest and believes the price of gold will rise substantially. Assume the cash or spot price today is $400 per ounce (t = 0 below) with futures prices of $420 for delivery in six months and $440 for delivery in one year. In other words, the market expects gold to be 5 percent higher after six months and 10 percent higher after a year. The speculator, however, expects gold to rise to $500 by year-end, and he or she is considering whether to buy gold or a gold futures contract. (Methods used to forecast by speculators are described in Appendix B.) Purchase of a futures contract is feasible, for the initial margin requirement by the futures broker is assumed to be $4,000.

<pre>
   t = 0   t = 6 months   t = 1 year
   ●─────────────────●──────────────────●
   $400 $420 $440
</pre>

If the metal is purchased at $400 per ounce, 10 ounces can be obtained. If after six months the price of gold rises to $450, the speculator has a profit of 50/400 = 12.5% for a six-month holding period.

Assume next that the one-year contract has been purchased at $440. If the spot price at the end of six months is $450, the futures contract price should also be higher given the normal pattern of futures prices that we saw in Table 16–1. The futures contract has six months remaining to delivery date, and the price would be approximately $472.50 if the market still expected a 5 percent rise six months into the future. See Table 16–3 for a summary.

Using the assumption of $472.50 as the contract price, the value of the futures is now $472 × 100 = $47,250, a gain of $3,250 over the initial contract value of $44,000 ($440 × 100). In this case, the speculator has the following return on the $4,000 of invested equity:

TABLE 16–3 Purchase of Gold versus Purchase of Gold Futures

$t = 0$ Initial Investment = $4,000	
Buy 10 oz. of gold	Buy futures contract at $440 Contract value = $44,000

Case 1	$t = 6$ Months; Price Rises to $450
Value of 10 oz. of gold at $450 per ounce = $4,500, a gain of $500 Return = $\dfrac{500}{4,000}$ = 12.5%	Value of futures contract at $472.50 = $47,250 Profit = $47,250 − $44,000 = $3,250 Return = $\dfrac{3,250}{4,000}$ = 81.25%

Case 2	$t = 6$ Months; Price Falls to $360
Value of 10 oz. of gold at $360 per ounce = $3,600, a loss of $400 Return = $\dfrac{-400}{4,000}$ = −10%	Value of futures contract at $378 = $37,800 Loss = $44,000 − $37,800 = $6,200 Return = $\dfrac{-6,200}{4,000}$ = −155%

$$3250/4000 = 81.25\%$$

The example shows that the futures market enables gains on equity to be magnified by leverage, just as we saw in margin trading on stocks (Chapter 3). At the same time, however, losses are magnified, as we shall see below.

Suppose the spot price of gold dropped unexpectedly to $360 at the end of six months. If 10 ounces of gold had been purchased, the loss would be $-40/400 = -10\%$. If the one gold futures contract had been purchased, the contract would have six months remaining, and assuming the futures price was still 5 percent higher for such a contract, the price would be $360 × 1.05 = 378$. The contract value would drop to $37,800, a decline of $6,200 from the initial $44,000 value. The return to the speculator is $-6200/4000 = -155\%$. Again, see Table 16–3 for a summary.

It should be noted that for such a loss to occur, the speculator must have added sufficient equity to the account to comply with maintenance margin requirements. Many speculators would close or offset their position before the losses became so large. However, in some cases, rapid price changes may not permit the speculator to close the position when desired, and there have been occasions where speculators have lost more than their initial equity investment. In short, it is apparent that the purchase of precious metals is less risky than using equity funds to speculate in the futures market.

TYPES OF ORDERS

The types of orders in the futures market are the same as in the purchase and sale of securities:

Market order. It instructs the broker to execute the order immediately at the best prevailing price.

Limit order. The order is placed at a price higher than market price in the case of a sale order, and lower than market price in the case of a buy order.

Stop order. Stop orders are contingency orders. They are of two kinds: stop sell order and stop buy order. A stop sell order is always placed at a price lower than the market price. When the market falls to the assigned price, the stop sell order becomes a market order. For example, assume a trader bought an S&P 500 stock index future at 214. To limit possible losses, a stop sell order may be placed at 212. If the market price falls to 212, the broker will sell the contract. The trader will get a price of 212 or less depending on market conditions. The stop sell order was placed to provide a floor to the loss. The stop buy order, on the other hand, is always placed at a price higher than the market price. A short-seller uses this type of order to limit potential losses.

Time limit of orders. The trader can specify the time limit of the order. Most orders are day orders, that is, they expire at the close of the day if they are not executed by that time. Market orders usually belong in this category. On limit orders and stop orders, the trader can specify the time limit — a day, a week, or an indefinite period until the order is canceled.

Price Fluctuation Limit

The individual futures exchanges establish maximum daily permissible price changes for most futures contracts. The purpose of the daily limit is to prevent a major price change from being carried too far by its own momentum. In this way, drastic daily price fluctuations are avoided. Trading in a futures contract usually ceases when the market "equilibrium" price moves beyond the price limit. There is some debate over the merits of such limits, and some contracts, such as stock index futures, have no daily price limit.

Regulation of Trading

All trading in futures markets is regulated by the individual exchanges and by the Commodity Futures Trading Commission (CFTC). Individual exchanges establish rules of fair business practices and periodically check the books and records of their members for violations of the rules established. The CFTC enforces all provisions of the Commodity Futures Trading Commission Act, passed by Congress in 1974. The CFTC, patterned on the SEC, is an independent federal commission. It possesses broad and flexible regulatory powers over the market practices and the conduct of individual exchanges and their members in the futures market.

DIFFERENCES BETWEEN OPTIONS AND FUTURES

We discussed the options market in securities in Chapter 15. Since options also cover a future period, there may be some confusion between futures and options. The fundamental difference between the purchase of an option and a futures contract is that an option represents a right to buy or sell a given security (or index of security prices) at a certain price, whereas the purchase of a futures contract is a real contract to buy a given commodity (or group of securities), at a certain price with actual settlement in a future month.

Now let us compare the selling of an uncovered call option and the selling of a futures contract without owning the item in the contract. Both transactions require a deposit of margin, but the amount of margin required in the selling of a call option is much greater, in terms of percentage, than the selling of a futures contract. The possible losses in both types of selling are not limited to the initial margin put up, unless the positions are offset or closed rapidly enough.

It should be noted that options and futures are not mutually exclusive entities. Options on futures do exist, and we will discuss how they work in a later section.

HEDGING WITH FUTURES

To protect themselves against risk in cash markets, hedgers take a futures position that is opposite to the transaction planned for the cash market. In implementing a hedge, the instruments in the cash and futures market should be the same or nearly the same in terms of price movements. In addition, the value of the cash and futures markets positions should be equal.

A Long Hedge with Stock Index Futures

Assume that it is now January, and a wealthy individual expects to have $100,000 to invest in April. The funds will be placed in a mutual fund that holds a portfolio identical to the S&P 500. The investor expects the stock market to be strong and expects the S&P 500 to rise from 200 in January to 215 by April. Assume that the earliest S&P futures contract available that matures after the $100,000 will be received is the June futures. Assume further that traders in futures markets are less optimistic than the investor, and the June futures price is 205. What happens if the investor decides to hedge and purchases a June contract? Details are shown in Table 16–4.

The next step is to consider the situation in April. The S&P 500 is assumed to rise to 210, which is higher than the futures market anticipated but less than the investor's expectations. At this point, we assume that expectations in the futures market in April are quite optimistic, and the June S&P 500 futures is still five points above the spot price and stands at 215.

In this scenario the investor was unable to invest $100,000 into the S&P 500 fund in January. As a result, she could not benefit from the ten-point rise in the index that would have provided a 5%, or $5,000, gain. However, through the long position in the futures market, a ten-point gain that provided $5,000 (10 points × $500 per point) was obtained. Thus, the hedge was quite successful. In fact, this case is an example of a "perfect hedge," for the $5,000 forgone gain in the mutual fund, or cash market, was exactly offset by the $5,000 gain in the futures market.

Basis

Perfect hedges are rare because of the existence of basis risk. *Basis* is the difference between the existing price in the futures market and the price in the cash market. In our example, the basis in January was $205 - 200 = 5$, and in April it was $215 - 210 = 5$. Because the basis was the same in both time periods, the ten-point gain in the cash market carried over as a ten-point gain in the futures contract.

Basis tends to be fairly stable, and when it changes it is often predictable. There are several reasons why basis behaves in this manner. First, the

TABLE 16–4   A Long Hedge Using Stock Index Futures

Cash Market	*Futures Market*
January	
S&P 500 Index = 200	Purchase a June S&P 500 contract at 205[a]
April	
S&P 500 Fund at 210	Sell June S&P 500 contract at 215
Percentage Increase in index between January and April = 10/200 = 5%	Profit on futures: 10 × $500 = $5,000
Missed capital gain on fund: 5% of $100,000 = $5,000	

[a]The number of contracts used for this particular hedge is 1. The value of one contract is 500 × $205 = $102,500, which comes closest to exactly covering the $100,000 of funds the investor wanted to allocate for stock in January. In later sections, further details are provided on the number of contracts needed in hedges.

same economic forces that affect the cash market will also affect the futures market. Higher corporate profits in future periods should raise both the spot and futures S&P 500 indexes. A second factor influencing basis is the convergence of the delivery date with the current date in the cash market. As we get close to the delivery date, the futures contract price would not be much different from the cash price of an identical item, and the basis will become smaller and smaller.

In the example shown in Table 16–4, chances are that the basis would have been smaller in April than in January. A more realistic futures price, given the 210 spot price, may be 212. If this were the case, the June contract would have brought a profit of $(212 - 205) \times \$500 = \$3,500$. The investor obtained a substantial gain, but we no longer have a perfect hedge.

While the basis is usually predictable, basis risk does exist. Changes in the economic and financial environment can have different impacts on the cash and futures markets. This is particularly true in cases where the item in the futures market and the item being hedged in the cash market are not identical. This is discussed further later in this chapter.

Locking in a Price

In some cases a hedger may be able to use the futures market to lock in a price for future delivery. Assume that it is August, and an importer of Canadian goods, who is located in Seattle, Washington, must make a payment of $200,000 in Canadian dollars to a Canadian supplier in December. Assume further that the cash price in August is 77¢ U.S. for a Canadian dollar, and the December futures price is 75¢ U.S. for the Canadian dollar.

The importer has doubts that the Canadian dollar will drop as low as 75¢ and wants to lock in that price. He or she buys two December futures contracts, each for $100,000. As the delivery date approaches, the cash and futures prices converge. Assume the cash price and futures price at that time are both 76¢ (basis = 0). The importer does not want to take delivery of the Canadian dollars at the futures market (which is in Chicago) and closes the position by selling two futures at 76¢. The transactions are summarized in Table 16–5.

The importer will pay 76¢ U.S. for Canadian dollars on the cash market, but with the 1¢ profit from the futures market, the net cost is 75¢.

TABLE 16–5   A Long Hedge with Foreign Currency Futures

1. In August, purchase two December Canadian dollar futures (each covering $100,000 Canadian at 75¢ U.S. per Canadian dollar.
2. In December, sell two December Canadian dollar futures at 76¢ U.S. per Canadian dollar.
3. Profit = 1¢ U.S. per Canadian dollar.
4. Buy $200,000 Canadian in the local cash market at 76¢ U.S.
5. Net cost in U.S. currency: 76¢ less 1¢ profit in futures market = 75¢.

This strategy works because the futures position is offset just before delivery date, and the basis is zero.

If the importer had been wrong, and the Canadian dollar dropped to 73¢ U.S. in December, there would have been a 2¢ loss in the futures market. The total cost of the Canadian dollars would then be the 73¢ cash price plus 2¢ loss in the futures market. Thus, in our example, the importer would get the Canadian dollars at the price specified in the contract whether or not the December spot price equals 75¢.

Cross-Hedges

Very often, people who deal in commodities or financial assets do not hold items identical to those traded in futures markets. For example, in Table 16–1 there is only one bond in that listing, a Treasury bond, which happens to have an 8 percent coupon and a twenty-year maturity. However, because different long-term interest rates tend to move parallel to each other, Treasury bond futures can be used to hedge a wide range of long-term securities.

The use of the 8 percent coupon Treasury bond futures to hedge securities, such as other Treasury bonds or corporate bonds, is an example of a *cross-hedge*. In general, a cross-hedge involves using a futures contract to hedge a cash market instrument or commodity that is similar but not identical to the item in the futures contract. The usefulness of a cross-hedge is contingent on how well the price of the item in the futures contract correlates with the price of the item in the cash market. There is greater basis risk in cross-hedges than when identical instruments are involved. For example, changes in interest rate risk premiums will affect the basis between Treasury bond futures and cash prices of corporate bonds.

A Short Cross-Hedge Using Interest Rate Futures

Assume it is now September and a wealthy investor owns a portfolio of 300 Baa-rated bonds. The bonds mature in twenty-five years; they have a coupon of 13 percent; the yield to maturity is 12 percent, and the price of each bond is $1,078.40. The investor has a capital gain on the bonds and is concerned about the possibility of rising interest rates and falling bond prices. However, she does not want to sell until February of the following year because of taxes and other considerations. A March Treasury bond (T-bond) future is trading at that time for 75–00 (75 percent of par) and has a yield of 11.146 percent. The investor decides to hedge the corporate bonds using Treasury bond futures.

The current market value of the investor's bonds is $300 \times \$1,078.40 = \$323,520$. The value of one T-bond future is $75\% \times \$100,000 = \$75,000$. The number of futures needed to cover the cash position is 323,502/

TABLE 16–6   A Short Hedge Using Treasury Bond Futures

Cash Market	Futures Market
September	
Value of bond portfolio: $1,078.40 × 300 = $323,520	Sell four T-bond futures at 75–00
February	
Value of bond portfolio: $1,000 × 300 = $300,000	Purchase four T-bond futures at 70–08
Loss: $323,520 − $300,000 = $23,520	Gain: 4 × (75% of $100,000 − 70 8/32% of $100,000) = $300,000 − $281,000 = $19,000
Net loss = $23,520 − $19,000 = $4,520	

75,000 = 4.3. Since fractional contracts are not available, we assume the investor decides to sell four T-bond contracts.[2] See Table 16–6.

Assume that between September and February interest rates do in fact rise, and the new yield to maturity on the corporate bonds rises to 13 percent, while the rate on March T-bond futures rises to 11.939 percent. The price of the corporate bonds drop to $1,000, while the T-bond futures are now selling for 70–08. As shown in Table 16–6, most of the $23,520 loss on the portfolio is made up by a $19,000 gain in the futures market. It is not a perfect hedge because the four contracts do not completely cover the portfolio, and the spread between T-bond rates and Baa corporate bond interest rates had increased. The latter factor is one of the causes of basis risk. Had the investor anticipated the greater spread in interest rates in September, she might have decided to sell five T-bond futures instead of four. If so, the gain in the futures market would have been $23,750, which is $230 more than the loss on the portfolio. This transaction may also be viewed as hedging with 4.3 contracts and speculating with 0.7 contracts.

PROGRAMMED TRADING

Programmed trading represents a use of financial futures by institutional investors and some wealthy individual investors. These trades frequently involve a purchase (sale) of a group of stocks together with a simultaneous sale (purchase) of stock index futures. Such transactions may be viewed as a form of arbitrage. Financial instruments are being purchased in one market and

[2]Some exchanges, like the Mid-America Commodity Exchange, have smaller contract sizes and could provide more complete coverage.

simultaneously being sold in another market to increase profits. (See Chapter 24 for discussion of arbitrage in the context of international exchange rates.) Programmed trading may also include strategies involving stock options and indexes on options.

A simplified example will illustrate the incentive underlying programmed trading. Assume that the S&P 500 index stands at 250 and S&P 500 futures contracts, which expire in three months, also stand at 250. Assume also that an institutional investor holds a $1 million portfolio of stocks, which moves in close conformity with that index. The investor may sell the stocks and buy eight S&P 500 futures contracts with a value of $8 \times 500 \times 250 =$ $1 million. Assume the proceeds of the sale of the stocks are invested in three-month interest-bearing securities, which pay an annual rate of 8 percent compared to, say, a 4 percent annual dividend yield on the stock. (Some of the interest-bearing securities would satisfy futures margin requirements.) At the end of the three-month period, the investor will sell the futures and use matured interest-bearing securities to repurchase stock previously owned.

If the S&P 500 index at the time of expiration is 260 (an increase of 4 percent over the original 250), the return is 4 percent on the futures plus 2 percent for holding the interest-bearing securities for three months, which totals 6 percent (less transactions costs). At that time the investor would take the profit by selling the futures at 260 and use the profits plus proceeds from the matured interest-bearing securities to repurchase the stock portfolio at 260. Investors who did not implement the programmed trade and instead held the S&P 500 portfolio during this period would receive only a 5 percent return consisting of a 4 percent capital gain plus a 1 percent dividend yield for three months.

Next, let us consider what would have happened if the market had dropped. Assume the market fell to 240, a decline of 4 percent. The return on the programmed trade and interest-bearing securities would be −4 percent + 2 percent = −2 percent. This compares to −4 percent + 1 percent = −3 percent for the strategy of holding the S&P 500 portfolio. Regardless of market movements, the programmed trading strategy in our example provided a higher return.

It should be noted that sales of stock and purchases of futures, described at the beginning of our example, would cause futures prices to rise above spot prices until there was no further gain to such trades. On other occasions, the futures index may be high in relation to the spot index, and investors may be motivated to purchase stock and sell futures. In doing so, stock prices would rise relative to futures, and the spread would narrow to a normal alignment where there would be no further profits by making such trades. It should also be noted that the success of programmed trades is contingent on proper timing in the futures and stock markets. If, for example, at the time of expiration the transactions do not occur simultaneously in each market, things may not work out as described. The purchase in one market may be at a higher price than the sale in the other market, reducing or eliminating any gains to the strategy. Furthermore, the size of the transaction must be large enough and spreads in the markets must be appropriate to justify the costs of the transactions.

Programmed trading has drawn considerable attention because on a number of occasions it has generated substantial purchase or sales of stocks which resulted in sharp changes in stock prices. In particular, special attention has been given to periods when stock options, options on stock indexes, and stock index futures contracts all expire on the same day. On those days the effects of programmed trades on stock prices have tended to be greater, and regulators have been considering ways to reduce price fluctuations caused by programmed trading. However, although programmed trading has increased volatility on particular days, it does not appear to have longer term effects on stock prices.

FUTURES OPTIONS

Futures options permit the buyer to purchase or sell a futures contract at a specified price for a limited period of time. They are like stock options except that the put or call applies to a futures contract. An example of a few listings is shown in Table 16–7.

TABLE 16–7 Sample Listing of Options on Futures

T-BONDS (CBT) $ 100,000; points and 64ths of 100%

Strike	Calls – Last			Puts – Last		
Price	Sep-C	Dec-C	Mar-C	Sep-P	Dec-P	Mar-P
74	3-49	3-17	3-15	0-01	0-49	1-50
76	1-46	2-03	2-18	0-02	1-30	2-49
78	0-17	1-08	1-33	0-35	2-33	3-52
80	0-01	0-36	0-62	2-18	3-57	5-13
82	0-01	0-18	0-38	4-18	5-37	6-50

Est. vol. 75,000, Tues.; vol. 31,010 calls, 22,689 puts
Open interest Tues.;218,428 calls, 226,908 puts

T-NOTES (CBT) $ 100,000; points and 64ths of 100%

Strike	Calls – Last			Puts – Last		
Price	Sep-C	Dec-C	Mar-C	Sep-P	Dec-P	Mar-P
82	5-10	4-20	....	0-01	0-18	....
84	3-10	2-48	....	0-01	0-42	....
86	1-12	1-35	....	0-03	1-28	....
88	0-03	0-49	....	0-60	....	....
90	0-01	....	....	....	....	....
92	....	....	....	....	....	....

Est. vol. 400, Tues.; vol. 95 calls, 56 puts
Open interest Tues.;4,921 calls, 5,447 puts

NYSE COMPOSITE INDEX (NYFE) $500 times premium

Strike	Calls – Settle			Puts – Settle		
Price	Sep-C	Dec-C	Mar-C	Sep-P	Dec-P	Mar-P
106	3.95	6.20	....	.15	.80	....
108	2.35	4.75	6.50	.55	1.25	1.60
110	1.15	3.45	5.30	1.25	2.00	2.15
112	.50	2.45	4.15	2.55	2.95	2.95
114	.15	1.65	3.10	4.25	4.10	3.90
116	.05	1.10	2.35	6.10	5.50	5.10

Est. vol. 428, Tues vol. 493 calls, 378 puts
Open interest Tues;7,453 calls, 4,081 puts

Source: The Wall Street Journal, August 22, 1985. Reprinted by permission of *The Wall Street Journal,* © 1985. World rights reserved.

The month columns show expiration dates of calls and puts. For example, based on the listings, one could purchase an option (call) to buy a December Treasury bond futures at a price of 78 by paying a premium of $1\frac{8}{64}$ percent of $100,000, or $1,125. The right to sell that contract (put) could be purchased for $2\frac{33}{64}$ percent of $100,000, or $2,515.63.

It may seem that options on futures are complicated instruments without much purpose. However, they can be useful to both hedgers and speculators. In business transactions, many firms have bought options to do things such as buy land or purchase machinery. Some futures prices and spot prices are closely correlated, and an option on a futures contract may be a good substitute for an option to purchase the actual item. Options on financial futures may be useful for hedging just as futures are used for this purpose. If an option is purchased, possible losses are limited by the premium paid. Speculators may also use these options, just as they make use of stock options. However, as in the case of stock options, there is considerable risk that much or all of the premium will be lost.

SPREAD STRATEGIES

The purpose of a spread strategy is to reap gains from *anticipated* changes in *relative* prices of a commodity between different maturities or between related commodities of the same maturity. The spread strategies are of three types:

1. *Intracommodity spread.* The speculator buys a futures contract of one maturity and sells another futures contract of a different maturity. Both contracts are for the same commodity or financial instrument. The investor is speculating on the *relative* change in the prices of two different maturities. For example, assume in January of year t = 0, the June gold futures of year t = 0 closes at $406.60 per ounce and the August gold futures of year t = 1 closes at $460 per ounce. If an investor felt that the spread (difference) between the prices of the two maturities will narrow in the next few months, he or she could sell the August t = 1 futures and buy at the same time the June t = 0 futures. In this case, the investor is speculating that the August futures will rise more slowly than the June futures if there is a rise in the future price of gold, or that the August futures will decline faster than June futures if there is a fall in the future price of gold.

   Assuming that the investor was right in the expectation, and the price difference between the two maturities decreases to $30, then he or she can buy back the August contract and sell the June contract. The investor will reap a profit amounting to ($460 − $406.60) − $30 = $23.40 per ounce, ignoring commissions.

As another example, assume that on October $t = 0$ the May $t = 1$ soybean meal futures was selling at $197 per ton, and the October $t = 1$ soybean meal futures was selling at $202.90 per ton. If the speculator feels that the difference between the two maturities ($5.90) was too narrow, and that the May futures would likely gain on the October futures in the next few months, he or she can establish a spread by buying a contract on the May futures and selling a contract on the October futures. If this expectation is correct, the investor can later realize the gain by unwinding the spread — selling the May and buying back the October future.

2. *Intercommodity spread.* Many agricultural commodities are related because of common usage or origin — for example, wheat and corn, hogs and pork bellies, oats and corn, soybeans and soybean meal and oil, and Idaho and Maine potatoes. From studies of past prices of these related products over a number of years, some patterns, seasonal and otherwise, can be observed. If the speculator finds the differentials in the futures prices of these related commodities either too small or too large, profitable spread strategies can be instituted.

   For example, wheat is normally harvested in July and August and corn is harvested in October. A popular intercommodity spread among traders is long December wheat and short December corn instituted in July and closed sometime in November. The strategy may work because wheat is relatively cheap during harvest season in July and corn may be relatively expensive at the time. By November, corn prices may be depressed because of the recent harvest, and wheat prices could be higher than a few months before. Of course, when a trading strategy becomes too popular, it loses its effectiveness because the market may have discounted it.

3. *Intermarket spread.* Many commodities are traded in more than one market. Wheat is traded on the Chicago Board of Trade and the Minneapolis Grain Exchange. Although the type of wheat traded in each exchange is different, they are interchangeable for many purposes. If a speculator has found that the price differentials among these wheat futures are out of line with one another, considering the differences in characteristics and location, he or she can institute a spread between markets by buying futures contracts of the lower-priced wheat and at the same time selling the futures contracts of the higher-priced grain. When the price differentials later return to normalcy as expected, he can unwind the spread by reversing the transaction.

Advantages of the Spread Strategy

The spread strategy has its advantages over a net long or short strategy in the commodities market. First, since the spreader takes both a long and short position in a commodity, the change in price of a commodity in either direction will create a gain on one position and a loss on another position. Most of the gain or loss will offset each other. Therefore, the risk is much less than in the case of a net long or short position. The gain or loss of the spreader depends on whether the price differentials of two maturities or two related commodities widen or narrow as expected. Second, since the risk assumed by the spreader is less, brokers also require less margin in a spread position than on a net long or short position. Third, the spread strategy is particularly suitable for beginners when they are in the process of learning how to trade in the commodities market. It requires less margin and exposes the trader to less risk.

Common Mistakes in the Use of Spread Strategies

There are a few common mistakes that inexperienced, new traders often make in the commodities market.

First, since the margin is low, the spreader may take on a large position in relation to available equity capital. He or she ends up taking more risk and paying more in commissions than would otherwise be incurred in a net long or short position.

Second, the speculator does not originally intend to take a spread position but is called on to deposit more margin on a losing net position (short or long). Instead of closing out the position, the speculator converts the position into a spread in order to avoid putting up more margin (spreads require less margin). This kind of bailing out from a bad speculative position frequently works against the spreader in terms of more commissions and possibly more losses.

Third, the spreader does not execute the long and short positions at the same time. Instead, he or she takes one position (long or short) first, and waits for a better chance to execute the other position. Often the market works against the spreader's expectations and forces him or her to (1) take a net position, which was not planned or (2) convert the net position into a less favorable spread. In addition, the opportunity to pay less commissions is lost when both long and short positions are not executed at the same time.

RULES THAT EXPERIENCED TRADERS OBSERVE[3]

Trading in the futures market is a high-risk venture. To trade successfully requires a great deal of experience, sophistication, and discipline — as well

---

[3]Stanley W. Angrist, *Sensible Speculating in Commodities* (New York: Simon and Schuster, 1972), Chapter 14; Benton E. Gup, *The Basics of Investing* (New York: John Wiley

as luck—on the part of the trader. Many experienced traders follow certain time-tested rules. Some of these rules and a few guidelines for speculation include the following:

1. The funds used for speculation in the futures market should be genuine risk capital.
2. The risk capital should be large enough to withstand a series of initial losses.
3. Successful speculation requires a highly disciplined personality. A trader must have the discipline to recognize a mistake when it is made and take the loss.
4. Futures trading is basically a game of skill in predicting prices and managing capital in a risk situation. The trader must develop forecasting skills, continually review new information coming to the market, and gauge the market reactions.
5. The trader should have a plan: price objective, maximum capital to be committed in a trade, and the limit of loss.
6. The trader must diversify his or her positions.
7. The trader should limit trades to a few commodities or financial futures he or she knows best.
8. The trader should not overtrade in relation to available risk funds.
9. The trader should generally employ stop-loss orders.
10. The trader should use both fundamental analysis and technical analysis in forecasting futures prices.

SUMMARY

During the last decade, futures markets have grown rapidly with particular growth in financial futures. There are several reasons for this growth. First, volatile interest rates have created a need for methods of reducing interest rate risk, and interest rate futures serve this purpose. Second, with the growth of international trade and fluctuations in exchange rates, foreign exchange futures have become an important method of reducing exchange rate risk. Futures contracts on stock indexes and options on those futures have provided additional opportunities for both investors and speculators.

The buyer of a futures contract is said to take a long position and obtains a profit if the contract price rises. The seller of a contract takes a short position and obtains a profit from declining futures prices. Hedgers participate in futures markets in order to reduce risk attributable to price fluc-

& Sons, 1979), pp. 428–29; Thomas A. Hieronymus, *Economics of Futures Trading* (New York: Commodity Research Bureau, 1971), p. 253.

tuation in the cash or spot market. Short hedgers own the commodities or financial instruments that correspond to the futures contract that they sell. In this way they can protect themselves against price declines. Long hedgers purchase futures contracts on commodities or financial instruments they intend to buy at some future time. Using futures, they can obtain protection against price increases.

Speculators take action for entirely different motives. They accept the risks that hedgers try to avoid in order to make a profit. Speculators attempt to forecast prices which will exist in the future. If those prices exceed prices in the futures markets, they take long positions. If speculators anticipate lower prices than the futures markets, they take short positions. Speculators comprise the largest number of traders on futures markets, and consequently, they are a very important ingredient in maintaining market efficiency.

Buyers and sellers of futures contracts must comply with margin requirements. These represent required deposits which serve to guarantee that the obligations specified in the contracts will be fulfilled. The equity in the account of the buyer or seller is equal to cash in the account plus profits on current positions minus losses on current positions.

Futures options permit the buyer to purchase or sell a futures contract at a specified price for a limited period of time. They are like stock options except the put or call applies to a futures contract. Some futures prices and spot prices are closely correlated, and an option on a futures contract may be a good substitute for an option to purchase the actual item. Options on financial futures may serve a useful purpose for hedging just as futures are used for this purpose.

QUESTIONS AND PROBLEMS

1. What is the economic function of the futures market?
2. Using the *Wall Street Journal* or other comprehensive source, list the different items for which futures contracts exist.
3. Who are the major participants in commodities and financial futures markets?
4. Why is the trading in the futures market considered very risky?
5. Compare the purchase of a call option in the securities market with the purchase of a futures contract in the futures market.
6. Compare the purchase of a stock on margin with the purchase of a futures contract in the futures market.
7. Can the exchange-imposed price limits protect futures traders from losses in the futures market?
8. What is meant by hedging? Give an example.
9. What is a spreading strategy? What is its purpose? Give an example.

10. Examine current quotations on interest rate futures and explain what is the implicit market forecast of future interest rates. Do you agree with the market forecast?
11. What are some of the rules that experienced traders usually observe in the futures market? Why do they make sense?
12. Assume a speculator has a short position on a gold futures contract of 100 ounces. The futures price of the contract is $500, and initial margin is 10 percent of contract value. If the investor's equity equals initial margin, calculate the investor's rate of return if
    a. The futures price of gold rises by 10 percent.
    b. The futures price of gold falls by 12 percent.
13. What is a cross-hedge?
14. What is the difference between long hedgers and short hedgers?
15. How might business enterprises use options on futures?
16. The closing prices and yields on Treasury bills on the IMM on April 30, t = 0, were as follows:

Maturity	Price	Yield (%)
June t = 0	89.90	10.10
Sept.	90.49	9.51
Dec.	90.76	9.24
March t = 1	90.85	9.15
June	90.79	9.21
Sept.	90.72	9.28
Dec.	90.76	9.24
March t = 2	90.71	9.29

a. Investor C is a speculator. She feels that the yield on Treasury bills will be much lower than what is forecasted by the above market prices. What kind of strategy should she employ?
b. Investor H is a speculator. He feels the spread between the different maturities between March t = 1 and March t = 2 is too narrow. He would like to employ a spread strategy. What should he do? Why?

17. In March an investor with $220,000 is considering two investment strategies for a six-month period:
    a. Place the money in a mutual fund whose price moves according to the S&P 500 index. The annual dividend yield is 5 percent of the March price index, which stands at 220 for both the fund and the S&P 500 index.
    b. Purchase $220,000 of Treasury bills and buy two September S&P 500 futures contract. The Treasury bills have an annual yield of 8 percent and assume that two Treasury bills can serve as margin in the futures account. Also assume that the investor will receive the interest on those two Treasury bills together with the interest on the other bills.

If the September S&P 500 futures index stands at 222 in March when the strategy is being planned, calculate which strategy will maximize the investor's wealth in September if

a. The S&P 500 index drops to 210 in September.

b. The S&P 500 index rises to 230 in September.

APPENDIX A: Volume and Open Interest

The two terms, *volume* and *open interest*, sometimes create confusion. An example may indicate more clearly the differences between the two terms. Suppose in the morning of a given day, Investor A bought ten contracts and Investor B sold ten contracts of February, 1989, gold. The completion of the transaction by Investors A and B will increase both the volume of trading and open interest by ten contracts. Since each transaction involves both a purchase and a sale, the volume of trading is counted only once either by sales or by purchases.

In the afternoon of the same day, Investor A sells his newly purchased contracts to a new trader, Investor C. After the completion of the transaction, the volume of trading for the day is increased to twenty contracts. The open interest, however, remains at ten contracts, because there was only a transfer of ownership between Investors A and C.

If Investor A, on the other hand, sells the newly purchased contract to Investor B, who is now covering his earlier sale, the volume of trading would be increased to twenty contracts, but the open interest will be zero, because both Investors A and B are no longer obligated to anyone for contracts outstanding and yet unfulfilled.

In other words, a resale of an existing contract can affect the open interest figure differently, depending on who the new buyer is. If the new buyer is covering earlier sales, the open interest will be reduced. On the other hand, if the buyer is a new trader taking a position, the open interest will not be affected. The increase of open interest, on the other hand, can only be caused by the initiation of new contracts between traders.

APPENDIX B: Price Forecasting

The degree of success in speculation in the futures market depends mostly on how accurately the speculator can forecast the direction and the extent of future price movements of the commodities concerned. Speculators generally employ two different ways of making a forecast: the fundamental approach and the technical approach.

FUNDAMENTAL APPROACH

The speculator who follows the fundamental approach usually examines all the important factors that he or she believes will influence the future price movement of the commodity. Some factors that will certainly be studied are:

1. The current estimates of supply and demand of the commodity by the government and by private advisory services.

2. The role of government in the commodity, including loan rates and acreage control.
3. Seasonal price pattern of the commodity.
4. Inflationary expectations in the economy.
5. The current price of the commodity relative to prices in previous years and relative to the prices of competing commodities.

Many speculators prefer the fundamental approach in making price forecasts because they want to know why prices are moving higher or lower, and they are more interested in long-term price swings than the day-to-day fluctuations. In addition, they get the satisfaction of analyzing a situation piece by piece and then drawing conclusions from the analysis.

TECHNICAL APPROACH

The technical approach followed in the futures market is basically the same as followed in the securities market. The following explains some of the basic ingredients of this approach. (See Chapter 17 for a discussion of technical analysis.)

Assumption. The speculators in the commodity markets who follow the technical approach share the same belief as their counterparts in the securities markets that prices of commodities move in trends and trends can be recognized and taken advantage of.

Charts. Charts are technicians' tools. Both bar charts and point-and-figure charts are used. The bar chart has the advantage that it can demonstrate seasonal patterns of the commodity, if any, and also volume of transactions. The point-and-figure chart, on the other hand, has the advantage of displaying patterns of price fluctuations and "break-outs" more visibly.

Moving averages. Moving averages of commodity prices for different periods—five or ten days, five or ten weeks— are calculated by traders to recognize the current short-term and longer-term trends. Some traders also calculate rates of change in commodity prices the same way as shown in Chapter 17 on technical analysis. The purposes of calculating moving averages are twofold: (1) to find the direction of the trend and (2) to find the speed or momentum of the current trend. Most traders subscribe to several technical services in order to avoid the drudgery of performing calculations and plotting graphs.

Volume and open interest. Most technicians also follow closely the trend of volume of transactions and open interest. This is a correct approach, because prices, volume of transactions, and open interest represent the three types of raw data available on which one can perform some analysis. Experienced technicians compare the trends found in prices, volume of transactions, and open interest in order to have a better perspective on the strength and possible development of the current trend believed in existence. For most agricultural commodities, there is a seasonal pattern in open interest. For purposes of comparison with price and volume of transaction, the seasonally adjusted trend in open interest should be used.

Many traders believe that the general relationships among volume of transactions, open interest, and price are the following:

1. If prices are up and the transaction volume and open interest are also up, the market is believed to be strong.
2. If prices are up and the transaction volume and open interest are down, the up market is believed to be weak.
3. If prices are down and transaction volume and open interest are up, the down market will likely continue.
4. If prices are down and transaction volume and open interest are also down, the technical position of the market is believed strong and the market may soon turn around.

These relationships among transaction volume, open interest, and price changes are the *beliefs* shared by many traders, but they are not empirically tested. The fourth statement is particulary troublesome, because it is difficult to reconcile with observations and findings.[4] Since the relationships among transaction volume, open interest, and prices are important to a trader following the technical approach, logically the trader should do some empirical study to find out what relationships, if any, really do exist among transaction volume, open interest, and price changes in different types of markets.

> *Support and resistance.* The concepts of support and resistance areas are deemed of much importance by technicians. The support area is the area from which the stock or commodity previously rose and where much volume was transacted. The resistance area is the area of previous highs where much volume was transacted and from which the stock or commodity began its decline. These concepts were formulated by technicians on the basis of their observations of behavioral patterns of buyers and sellers in the security market.
>
> *Chart patterns.* Technicians consider certain configurations of price fluctuation bullish, neutral, or bearish. For example, the following are a few patterns with assumed implications:

[4]Stanley S. C. Huang, *Stock Market Timing*. Investigators Intelligence, Inc., 1973.

1. Bullish patterns — Saucers (round bottom), double bottom, ascending triangle
2. Neutral patterns — Flat channel (line formation)
3. Bearish patterns — Head and shoulder, double tops, round top, descending triangle

Trading tactics. Experienced speculators using the technical approach generally observe the following trading rules:

1. Stay with the trend — go along when market is up and vice versa.
2. Employ stop order with every position taken — when one is bullish, place a stop-loss order at a given percent below market price. As the market moves up, the speculator also moves up his stop-loss order. In selling short, the speculator places the stop buy order at a given percent higher than the price at which he sold short. As the market moves down, he also moves his stop buy order downward.

These procedures will force the speculator to liquidate the position at small losses when he is wrong and at the same time allow him to stay in and ride out a profitable position.

REFERENCES

Angrist, Stanley W. *Sensible Speculating in Commodities*. New York: Simon & Schuster, 1972.

Belongia, Michael, and Santoni, G. "Hedging Interest Rate Risk with Financial Futures: Some Basic Principles." *Review,* Federal Reserve Bank of St. Louis, October 1984.

Chicago Board of Trade. *Financial Instruments Markets: Cash Futures Relationships,* 1982.

Dow Jones & Company. *Wall Street Journal, Education Edition,* 1984.

Drabenstott, M., and McDonley, A. "Futures Market: A Primer for Financial Institutions." *Economic Review,* Federal Reserve Bank of Kansas City, November 1984.

Garbade, Kenneth. *Securities Markets*. New York: McGraw-Hill, 1982, Chapters 15–16.

Gendreau, Brian, "New Markets in Foreign Currency Options." *Business Review,* Federal Reserve Bank of Philadelphia, July–August 19894.

Gup, Benton E. *The Basics of Investing*. New York: John Wiley & Sons, 1979, Chapter 18.

Hieronymus, Thomas A. *Economics of Futures Trading*. New York: Commodity Research Bureau, 1971.

Huff, Charles, and Marinacci, Barbara. *Commodity Speculation for Beginners*. New York: McGraw-Hill, 1982.

Loosigian, Alan. *Interest Rate Futures*. Homewood, Ill.: Dow Jones-Irwin, 1980.

Rendleman, Richard J., Jr., and Carabini, C. E. "The Efficiency of the Treasury Bill Futures Market." *The Journal of Finance,* Sept. 1979.

Sharpe, William F. *Investments*. Englewood Cliffs, N.J.: Prentice-Hall, 1985, Chapter 17.

Spruga, Ronald. *A Practical Guide to the Commodities Market*. Englewood Cliffs, N.J.: Prentice-Hall, 1983.

Teweles, R. J., Harlow, C. V., and Stone, H. L. *The Commodity Futures Game, Who Wins? Who Loses? Why?* New York: McGraw-Hill, 1977.

V

Short-term Trading in Securities

17

Technical Analysis

TECHNICAL ANALYSIS VERSUS SECURITY ANALYSIS

In the previous chapters, we discussed securities in terms of their underlying economic and management factors, such as growth of sales, earnings and dividends, quality of management, industry characteristics and problems, prospects for the company, the industry, and for the whole economy. With this approach we hope to estimate long-term security value compared to current market price; this is usually called the *fundamental approach* because it deals with the fundamental economic factors that determine security values in the long run.

In this chapter we discuss an entirely different approach, called the *technical* or *market approach*. The technical approach studies the day-to-day price and volume changes of securities in the market itself. Therefore it is also called market analysis. The goal is to predict short-term price movements of securities as well as of the general market. Since it is important for investors of all types and inclinations to understand thoroughly the differences between the two approaches, we compare them as follows in Table 17–1.

THE DOW THEORY

The Dow theory is the foundation of much modern-day technical market analysis. The theory was formulated by Charles H. Dow and expressed in articles and editorials he wrote for the *Wall Street Journal* around the turn of the century. The theory was later interpreted, expanded, and refined by William P. Hamilton and Robert Rhea. Present-day Dow theory is therefore a synthesis of the thoughts of Dow, Hamilton, and Rhea.[1] We will briefly describe the basic ideas of Dow's theory.

[1]Readers interested in the development and more detailed exposition of the Dow theory are advised to consult William P. Hamilton, *The Stock Market Barometer* (New York: Richard Russell Associates, 1960); Robert Rhea, *The Dow Theory* (Boulder, Colo.: Rhea, Greiner & Co., 1959); and Richard Russell, *The Dow Theory Today* (New York: Richard Russell Associates, 1961).

TABLE 17–1   A Comparison of the Technical Approach and the Fundamental Approach

	Technical Approach (market analysis)	*Fundamental Approach* (security analysis)
Objective	To predict short-term price movements of securities and security markets in general	To gauge long-run values of securities
Object of study	Action of the stock market, particularly price and volume changes of individual issues and the general market	Earnings and dividends record, sales, product mix, profit margins, the quality of management, outlook of profit of the individual companies, industries, and the whole economy
Type of buyer	Mostly short-term traders	Mainly long-term security holders
Strategy and tactics	Follow trading rules such as placing stop-loss orders, cut losses quickly and let profits run; identify and take advantage of current trends in movements of security prices	Buy securities at reasonable prices in terms of both historical record and outlook, ignore short-term price movements after acquisition
Philosophy or conviction	Short-term price movements can be predicted on basis of price-volume study, chart pattern of individual stocks, and other technical market indicators	Long-term security values can be gauged on the basis of study of fundamental factors

Three Movements

The "market," meaning the price of stocks in general, is always to be considered as having three movements, all going on at the same time. The first and the most important one is the primary trend, which is a broad upward or downward movement lasting usually a few years. The upward movement is also known as a *bull market,* and the downward movement as a *bear market.* The second movement represents intermediate reactions to the major trend—namely, important declines in a bull market or advances in a bear market. These interruptions in the major trend usually last several weeks to several months, retracing one-third to two-thirds of the price change in the preceding primary swing. The third movement represents day-to-day changes in security prices. Except as building blocks of the secondary movement, these daily fluctuations are not considered important by Dow theorists.

Determining the Primary Trend

A major upward trend is said to be in existence when successive rallies penetrate preceding high points with ensuing declines terminating above preceding low points. Conversely, a major downward movement is signified by successive rallies failing to reach preceding high points with ensuing declines carrying below preceding low points. In Figure 17–1, signals for bull and bear markets are indicated.

Principles of Confirmation

A major upward movement found in the Dow Jones Industrial Average does not automatically signal that a bull market is in existence. For a bull market to be in existence, a similar upward movement has to be found also in the Dow Jones Transportation Average. Conversely, a bear market is signaled when both averages are found to be in a major downtrend. Should the Dow Jones Transportation Average fail to confirm the major movement of the Dow Jones Industrial Average, the current movement of the DJIA is suspect and the previous trend is considered still intact.

The "Line" Formation

The "line" formation, in Dow theory parlance, represents a sidewise movement of several weeks duration during which the price variations in both the Dow Jones Industrial and Transportation Averages move within a range of approximately 5 percent. The formation indicates that supply and demand are more or less in equilibrium. Simultaneous advances beyond the narrow range signify stronger forces of demand and predict higher prices,

Bull Market Signal

Bear Market Signal

Dow Jones
Industrial
average

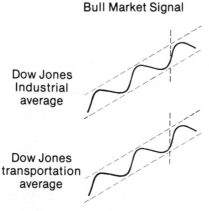

Dow Jones
transportation
average

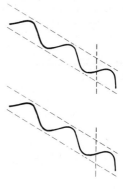

FIGURE 17–1 Market Trend Signals

whereas simultaneous declines below the "line" formation indicate lower prices to follow.

Relationship Between Volume and Price Movement

The Dow theory as originally formulated by Charles H. Dow was based primarily on price movements of two averages. However, Dow believed that volume pointed out the trend of prices. Whereas William P. Hamilton rarely discussed the relationship of volume to price movement, Robert Rhea stated clearly the relationship between the two:

> A market which has been overbought becomes dull on rallies and develops actively on declines; conversely, when a market is oversold, the tendency is to become dull on declines and active on rallies. Bull markets terminate in a period of excessive activity and begin with comparatively light transactions.[2]

Nevertheless, volume in Dow theory serves primarily as supporting evidence that may aid interpretation in practice. Trend signals are still dictated by changes solely in price movements.

Defects of the Dow Theory

Having explained the basic tenets of the Dow theory, we now list several deficiencies of the theory as seen by its critics.

1. The theory is always late in identifying the major trend, because the two averages must be confirmed.
2. The Dow theory is designed to identify the major trend, and therefore, renders little help to intermediate trend traders.
3. The Dow theory is designed to tell the direction of a major trend, but tells nothing about what stocks to buy or sell.
4. The Dow theory is primarily based on the study of price movements; volume data do not receive sufficient attention.

OTHER TECHNICAL THEORIES AND INDICATORS

As we mentioned, the followers of the technical approach, or market analysis, believe that the short-term price movements of the general market and individual stocks are by and large predictable. Their tools include studies on changes in the prices of stocks and stock groups, volume changes, patterns of individual stocks, and a variety of technical market indicators. The technical indicators are most derived from observations of the actions con-

[2]Robert Rhea, *The Dow Theory* (Boulder, Colo.: Rhea, Greiner, 1959), p. 15.

summated in the stock market itself, including the behavior patterns of particular groups of stock buyers. Let us first examine a few widely held technical indicators, the validity of which may be doubtful in view of empirical evidence.

The Short Interest Theory

Short selling in the securities market means selling securities the seller does not own. The short-seller, anticipating a decline in price, sells a given security and borrows it from his brokerage firm for delivery to the buyer. He expects to be able to buy back the security later at a lower price.

One of the technical theories, which has a wide following in Wall Street, is the *short interest theory*. The theory says that a rising volume of short interest or a rising short interest ratio (short interest divided by average daily volume of transactions) is bullish because the short-seller will eventually buy back the stock he sold short. The short interest represents latent demand. The greater the short interest, the more likely it is that the price of the security will go up. By the same token, if the short interest or short interest ratio declines, it signals a bearish trend because the latent demand is diminishing. This theory applies to both individual securities and the stock market as a whole.

Although this theory has been widely held among technicians and investors, many analysts question its validity. They point out three different types of short selling: fundamental shorts, technical shorts, and shorts against the box. Each type is different in terms of intention and the timing of cover and, therefore, their influences would not be the same.

Fundamental shorts are made by investors influenced by fundamental factors like prospective earnings and dividends. They foresee a period of declining prices and they do not plan to buy back within a short period of time. Their influences certainly cannot be considered bullish. Technical shorts are usually made by short-term traders who are more likely to cover their shorts within a short period of time. Shorts against the box are made by people who already own the security but decide to sell short the security now, either for tax advantages from long-term capital gains or to transfer the gains to the next year. It is more likely that they will cover their shorts within the next few months. Since the shorts are of different kinds and there is no way to separate them from the published figures, it is erroneous to interpret their influences as if there were only one kind of short.[3]

Empirical Evidence

Joseph J. Senaca used regression analysis to determine the effect of short interest on stock prices. He related data on stock prices jointly to

---

[3] H. A. Latané, D. L. Tuttle, and C. P. Jones, *Security Analysis and Portfolio Management*, 2nd ed. (New York: The Ronald Press, 1975), pp. 415–17.

dividends and short interest positions for the period January, 1946, to July, 1965. He found that there was no relationship between short selling and stock price.[4] Another study, made by Barton M. Biggs, tested the validity of short interest theory against thirty-three individual stocks over a period of sixteen months. The results indicated no meaningful correlation: sixteen of the thirty-three stocks performed exactly contrary to the theory, fourteen behaved as they should, and no conclusive trend was evident in three others.[5] Randall D. Smith examined the empirical relationship between short interest and stock price on large samples of stocks on both the New York and American Exchanges by means of statistical and simulation techniques. He found that a high short interest did not have an upward price impact on stocks, and the strategy of buying stocks with high short positions did not produce better results than one of buying stocks randomly.[6]

In Figure 17–2 we see the short interest ratio from 1976 to 1985 with the DJIA. From 1970 to 1980, the short interest ratio had a range of 0.75 to 2.0 with a mean of about 1.25. During the five years 1981 to 1985, the short interest ratio had a range from 1.2 to 2.8 with a mean of about 2.0.

During 1976–77, the short interest ratio was rising, but the general market as measured by DJIA was declining. This happened again in 1981–82. However, in the recent period 1983–85, the short interest ratio did rise and fall with somewhat parallel movements in the DJIA. The overall record of the indicator seems mixed in the last ten years.

Odd-Lot Short Sales Ratio

Besides the overall short interest ratio on the NYSE, followers of the technical approach pay special attention to the odd-lot short interest ratio, which is derived by dividing odd-lot short sales by total odd-lot sales. The technical followers believe that the odd-lot short-sellers are usually wrong in timing, especially around the turning points of cycles of security prices. At the market top, they are afraid to sell short, and at the market bottom, they increase short selling sharply. The technical followers, therefore, consider the odd-lot short sales ratio as a good *reverse indicator*.

The Odd-Lot Theory

An odd-lot transaction is a purchase or sale of a lot less than 100 shares. Odd-lot transactions are usually made by small investors. There is a popular theory among followers of technical analysis that the small investor is usually

[4] Joseph J. Senaca, "Short Interests — Bearish or Bullish," *The Journal of Finance,* March 1967.

[5] Barton M. Biggs, "The Short Interest — A False Proverb," *Financial Analysts Journal,* July–Aug. 1966.

[6] Randall D. Smith, "Short Interest and Stock Prices," *Financial Analysts Journal,* Nov.–Dec. 1968.

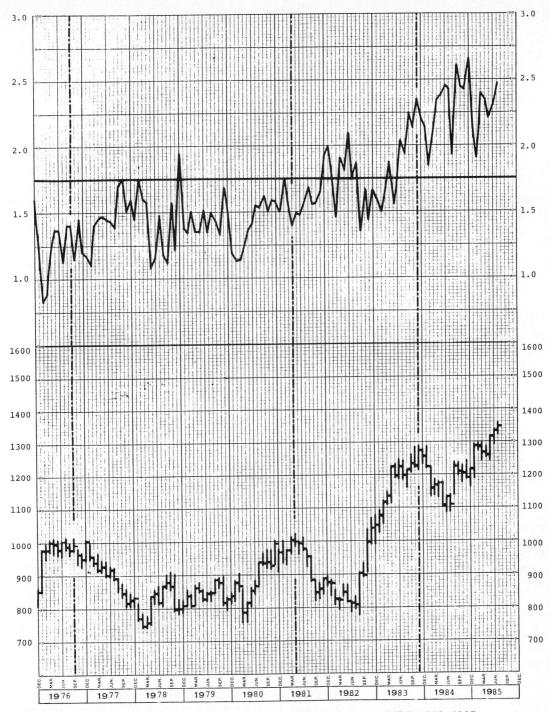

FIGURE 17–2 Ratio of Short Interest to Average Daily Volume—NYSE, 1976–1985

Source: Stone & Mead, Inc., *Long Term Technical Trends*, August 1985.

wrong in timing. The reason is probably that the small investor is less sophisticated in the art of investment and easily influenced by the prevalent wave of optimism or gloom. Market analysts who subscribe to the theory follow the pattern of odd-lot transactions for clues to future price movements.

The odd-lot theory maintains that the odd-lotters have established a consistent pattern of behavior over the cycle of stock prices. In the initial phase of recovery, they view rising stock prices with skepticism and sell, but after a persistent uptrend in prices, they shift to buying and near the top they buy heavily. In the initial phase of price decline, they turn to buying for "bargains," and when the decline persists, they reduce their buying, and near the bottom of the market they turn to heavy selling.

The idea that odd-lot investors are less sophisticated than round-lot investors may have been true at one time. However, both odd-lot and round-lot investors are capable of learning from past mistakes. It is difficult to believe that the buying and selling pattern of odd-lotters would remain consistently poor so that their behavior pattern in the market place can be used as a reverse indicator.

See Figure 17–3 for the odd-lot purchase to sales ratio and the DJIA over the period 1970–79. The figure shows that near each peak of the DJIA, the odd-lotters were selling more than buying, and near each trough of the DJIA their purchases rose more than their sales. The overall timing seems quite good in recent years. This contradicts much of the thesis underlying the odd-lot theory.

New-High and New-Low Indicator

A rising market should normally witness an expanding number of stocks hitting new high prices and a decreasing number of stocks reaching new low prices. Conversely, a declining market is usually accompanied by an increasing number of new lows and decreasing number of new highs.

Many technical analysts believe that when the movement of new-high–new-low data diverges from the movement of market averages, the movement of new-high–new-low data will usually provide clues for future price movement.

Defect of the New-High–New-Low Data

Before examining the evidence, it should be pointed out that the reporting system of new highs and new lows suffers an important defect. That is, the reporting of new highs and new lows is not based on the closing price of the day, but, instead, based on any price occurring that day. In other words, a stock that is reported as having a new high price over the range of prices of the previous fifty-two weeks could actually close lower than the closing price of the previous day. Because of this basic defect, it is doubtful that the new-high–new-low data can serve as a leading indicator of stock prices.

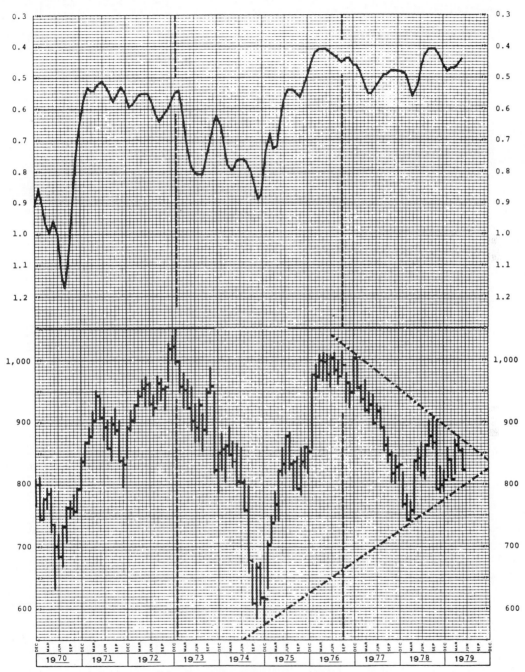

FIGURE 17–3　Odd-lot Purchase to Sales Ratio and DJIA, 1970–79

Source: Stone & Mead, Inc., *Long-Term Technical Trends*, June 1979.

A study was prepared by the author several years ago.[7] Table 17–2, reproduced here, compares the new-high–new-low index (new high as percentage of new-high–new-low combined) with the DJIA for the period September 1968 to March 1969, during which time the stock market peaked out. The peak of the market was established at a DJIA of 985.1 in the week ending December 2, 1968. But the proportion of new highs to the combined total of new highs and new lows was not under the 50 percent neutral line until six weeks later. Therefore, the index was actually a lagging indicator.

Table 17–3 compares the index with the DJIA for a different period, February to September of 1970, during which the market reached its bottom

TABLE 17–2   Dow Jones Industrial Average Compared to the Ratio of New Highs to New Highs and New Lows Combined

Week Ending	New High	New Low	Total	New High as % of Total	3-Week Moving Average	DJIA
9-16-68	178	31	209	85	—	917.2
9-23	235	25	250	94	—	924.4
9-30	250	18	268	93	91	933.8
10-7	290	13	303	96	94	953.0
10-14	222	27	249	89	93	949.6
10-21	263	36	299	88	91	967.5
10-28	251	25	276	91	89	961.3
11-4	181	36	217	83	87	948.4
11-11	154	39	193	80	85	959.0
11-18	295	27	322	92	85	965.9
11-25	331	23	354	94	89	967.1
12-2	368	7	375	98	95	985.1H
12-9	334	20	354	94	95	978.2
12-16	291	36	327	89	94	981.3
12-23	229	61	290	79	87	967.0
12-30	86	64	150	57	75	952.5
1-6-69	68	53	121	56	64	951.9
1-13	25	78	103	25*	46*	925.5
1-20	37	61	98	38	40	935.5
1-27	72	38	110	65	43	938.6
2-3	103	50	153	67	57	946.1
2-10	108	54	162	67	66	947.9
2-17	70	35	105	67	67	952.0
2-24	23	105	128	18	51	916.7
3-3	9	211	220	4	30	905.2
3-10	19	186	205	9	10	911.2
3-17	22	183	205	11	8	904.3
3-24	28	186	214	13	11	920.0
3-31	129	309	438	29	18	935.5

H: High
* First time below 50% level, which is the neutral line.

[7] Stanley S. C. Huang, *Stock Market Timing* (Larchmont, N.Y.: Investors Intelligence, Inc., 1973), pp. 49–51.

TABLE 17–3   Dow Jones Industrial Average Compared to the Ratio of New Highs to New Highs and New Lows Combined

Week Ending	New High	New Low	Total	New High as % of Total	3-Week Moving Average	DJIA
2-16-70	30	249	279	11	—	753.3
2-23	37	195	232	16	—	757.5
3-2	33	94	127	26	18	777.6
3-9	42	59	101	42	28	784.1
3-16	11	95	106	10	26	772.1
3-23	95	300	395	24	25	763.7
3-30	168	188	356	47	27	791.1
4-6	207	129	336	62	44	791.8
4-13	122	245	367	33	47	790.5
4-20	51	515	566	9	35	775.9
4-27	27	703	730	37	26	747.3
5-4	8	956	964	1	16	733.6
5-11	11	845	856	1	13	717.7
5-18	3	1082	1085	0	1	702.2
5-25	6	1237	1243	1	1	662.2L
6-1	8	1322	1330	1	1	700.4
6-8	25	129	154	16	6	695.0
6-15	12	227	239	5	7	684.2
6-22	18	209	227	8	10	720.4
6-29	10	345	355	3	5	687.8
7-6	7	477	484	2	4	689.1
7-13	12	501	573	2	3	700.1
7-20	27	158	185	15	6	735.1
7-27	26	80	106	24	14	730.2
8-3	33	70	103	32	24	734.1
8-10	18	96	114	16	24	725.7
8-17	10	168	178	6	18	710.8
8-24	36	113	149	24	15	745.4
8-31	78	42	120	65*	32	765.8
9-7	66	16	82	80	56*	771.1
9-14	50	7	57	88	78	761.8
9-21	60	19	79	76	81	758.5
9-28	56	15	71	79	81	761.8

L: Low
* First time above 50% level, which is the neutral line.

and recovered. The bottom was established at the DJIA of 662.2 in the week ending May 25, 1970. But the new-high proportion did not move beyond the 50 percent netural line until some thirteen to fourteen weeks later.

The data on new highs and new lows in a more recent period, from April to August of 1979, as shown in the Appendix to this chapter, confirmed our previous finding that the new-high–new-low data cannot be classified as a coincidental, but actually as a lagging indicator of stock prices.

Trends and Moving Average

Followers of the technical approach believe that stock prices tend to move in trends. Besides the Dow theory, they also employ the moving-average method to identify trends. To identify major trends, they usually use a 200-day moving average, or alternately a thirty-week moving average of weekly prices, and to identify intermediate trends they usually use a ten-week moving average. For trading purposes, they also employ a ten-day moving average.

A ten-week moving average of the DJIA can be arrived at by simply summing the closing weekly prices of the DJIA for 10 weeks and dividing the total by 10 to get the first average figure, and then dropping the first week's price and adding on the closing price of another week, and dividing the sum by 10 to get the second average figure, and so on.

See Figure 17–4 for a hypothetical picture of weekly prices of the DJIA with its thirty-week moving average line. The moving average line represents the basic trend of stock prices as represented by the DJIA. The interpretation of the moving average line is governed by two basic principles as follows. A bull market (upward market) is believed to be in existence when (a) the moving average line moves upward, and (b) the actual prices of the DJIA are above the moving average line. Conversely, a bear market (downward market) is believed in existence when (a) the moving average line is moving downward, and (b) the actual prices of the DJIA are below the moving average line. In Figure 17–4, at point A the moving average line is descending, and the actual prices of the DJIA are above the moving average line. Since the moving average line represents the trendline, the trend at point A is still considered downward.

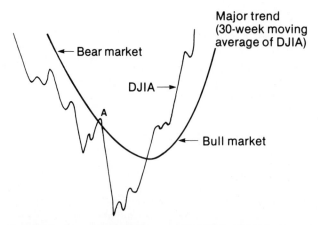

FIGURE 17–4   Hypothetical Chart of Weekly Closing Prices of the DJIA and Its Thirty-week Moving Average

The Advance-Decline Line

The advance-and-decline line measures the cumulative net difference between the number of issues advanced and declined. The starting point can be any time. See Table 17–4 for a computation of the advance-decline line and the DJIA for the period June 17 to August 27, 1985. The basic idea underlying the advance-and-decline line is to find out whether the daily price movement registered in a stock average, such as the DJIA, is reflected in the market as a whole in terms of the number of issues advanced or declined. It is believed that continued price advances in thirty blue-chip stocks in the DJIA cannot be maintained long if these advances are not shared by the majority of issues on the New York Stock Exchange. Conversely, if more issues are going up than down and if the DJIA is also going up, the price advance is considered likely to continue.

Technical analysts also believe that when the cumulative number of advances exceeds declines by 2000 over a ten-day period, the market may be "overbought," meaning that it may be susceptible to some reactions. By the same token, when the cumulative number of declines exceeds advances by 2000 over a ten-day period, the market may soon have a rebound.

Many market analysts believe that comparing the advance-decline line with the DJIA provides a useful indicator of future price movements.

Rate of Change Analysis

If stock prices do move in trends, as followers of the technical approach believe, one way to examine the trend of stock prices and its momentum is to perform a rate of change analysis. In Table 17–5 we present a rate of change analysis for the period from January 2 to May 17, 1985.

The idea behind the rate of change analysis is that change in trend does not occur abruptly, but only gradually. That is, before a rising trend turns downward, it usually slows down at first in its advance, then flattens out, and finally begins to decline. The same sequence of events applies also to the change of a downtrend to an uptrend. Technical analysts believe that by closely following the rates of change in stock averages, they can gauge the direction of the next movement in stock prices.

Price versus Volume Change

Followers of the technical approach generally believe that the relationships between stock prices and volume changes are of vital importance in predicting future movements of stock prices, both of stock averages and individual issues. Their common beliefs with respect to volume changes are these:[8]

---

[8] H. D. Schultz & S. Coslow (eds.), *A Treasury of Wall Street Wisdom*, (Palisades Park, N.J.: Investors Press, 1966), p. 250.

TABLE 17-4 Cumulative Advance-Decline Differential NYSE, versus the DJIA

Date 1985	Advance NYSE Comp.	Decline NYSE Comp.	Difference	Ten-day Cumulative Difference	DJIA
June 17	680	854	−174	—	1298.39
18	1000	614	386	—	1304.77
19	813	793	20	—	1297.38
20	714	823	−109	—	1299.73
21	1034	551	483	—	1324.48
24	725	852	−127	—	1320.56
25	964	615	349	—	1323.03
26	787	730	57	—	1323.81
27	977	590	387	—	1332.21
28	948	619	329	1601	1335.46
July 1	903	684	219	1994	1337.14
2	837	756	81	1689	1334.01
3	793	759	34	1703	1326.39
5	1118	400	718	2530	1334.45
8	658	917	−259	1788	1328.41
9	696	837	−141	1774	1321.91
10	993	584	409	1834	1332.89
11	971	627	344	2121	1337.70
12	873	670	203	1937	1338.60
15	875	691	184	1792	1335.46
16	1211	437	774	2347	1347.89
17	976	683	293	2559	1357.97
18	614	1009	−395	2130	1350.92
19	1059	553	506	1918	1359.54
22	553	1053	−500	1677	1357.54
23	622	983	−361	1457	1351.81
24	669	1006	−337	711	1348.90
25	708	900	−192	175	1353.61
26	763	802	− 39	− 67	1357.08
29	359	1314	−955	−1206	1343.86
30	703	880	−177	−2157	1346.10
31	977	611	366	−2084	1347.45
Aug. 1	1053	557	496	−1193	1355.62
2	685	831	−146	−1845	1353.05
5	458	1156	−698	−2043	1346.89
6	398	1253	−855	−2537	1325.16
7	634	949	−315	−2515	1325.04
8	1096	484	612	−1711	1329.86
9	659	895	−236	−1908	1320.79
12	574	947	−373	−1326	1314.29
13	708	782	− 74	−1223	1315.30
14	883	616	267	−1322	1316.98
15	768	710	58	−1760	1317.76
16	422	1073	−651	−2265	1312.72
19	795	712	83	−1484	1312.50
20	930	587	343	− 286	1323.70
21	989	566	423	452	1329.53
22	575	1004	−429	− 589	1318.10
23	708	758	− 50	− 403	1318.32
26	790	732	58	28	1317.65
27	877	626	251	353	1322.47

TABLE 17–5 Rate of Change Analysis of DJIA, January–May, 1985

Date 1985	DJIA	Rate of Change Against 5 Days Ago	3 Days Moving Average	Date 1985	DJIA	Rate of Change Against 5 Days Ago	3 Days Moving Average
Jan. 2	1198.87	—	—	Mar. 18	1249.67	0.985	0.986
3	1189.82	—	—	19	1271.09	0.999	0.989
4	1184.96	—	—	20	1265.24	1.003	0.996
7	1190.59	—	—	21	1268.22	1.006	1.003
8	1191.70	—	—	22	1267.45	1.016	1.008
9	1202.74	1.003	—	25	1259.94	1.008	1.010
10	1223.50	1.028	—	26	1259.72	0.991	1.005
11	1218.09	1.028	1.020	27	1264.91	1.000	1.000
14	1234.54	1.037	1.031	28	1260.71	0.994	0.995
15	1230.79	1.033	1.033	29	1266.78	0.999	0.998
16	1230.68	1.023	1.031	Apr. 1	1272.75	1.010	1.001
17	1228.69	1.004	1.020	2	1265.68	1.005	1.005
18	1227.36	1.008	1.012	3	1258.06	0.995	1.003
21	1261.37	1.022	1.011	4	1259.05	0.999	1.000
22	1259.50	1.023	1.018	8	1252.98	0.989	0.994
23	1274.73	1.036	1.027	9	1253.86	0.985	0.991
24	1270.43	1.034	1.031	10	1259.94	0.995	0.990
25	1276.06	1.040	1.037	11	1263.69	1.004	0.995
28	1277.83	1.013	1.029	12	1265.68	1.005	1.001
29	1292.62	1.026	1.026	15	1266.78	1.011	1.007
30	1287.88	1.010	1.016	16	1269.55	1.013	1.010
31	1286.77	1.013	1.016	17	1272.31	1.010	1.011
Feb. 1	1277.72	1.001	1.008	18	1265.13	1.001	1.008
4	1290.08	1.010	1.008	19	1266.56	1.001	1.004
5	1285.23	0.994	1.002	22	1266.56	1.000	1.001
6	1280.59	0.994	0.999	23	1278.71	1.007	1.003
7	1290.08	1.003	0.997	24	1278.49	1.005	1.004
8	1289.97	1.010	1.002	25	1284.78	1.016	1.009
11	1276.06	0.989	1.001	26	1275.18	1.007	1.009
12	1276.61	0.993	0.997	29	1259.72	0.995	1.006
13	1297.92	1.014	0.999	30	1258.06	0.984	0.995
14	1287.88	0.998	1.002	May 1	1242.05	0.971	0.983
15	1282.02	0.994	1.002	2	1242.27	0.967	0.974
19	1280.59	1.004	0.999	3	1247.24	0.978	0.972
20	1283.13	1.005	1.001	6	1247.79	0.991	0.979
21	1279.04	0.985	0.998	7	1252.76	0.996	0.988
22	1275.84	0.991	0.994	8	1249.78	1.006	0.998
25	1277.50	0.996	0.991	9	1260.27	1.014	1.005
26	1286.11	1.004	0.997	10	1274.18	1.022	1.014
27	1281.03	0.998	0.999	13	1277.50	1.024	1.020
28	1284.01	1.004	1.002	14	1273.30	1.016	1.021
Mar. 1	1299.36	1.018	1.007	15	1273.52	1.019	1.020
4	1289.53	1.009	1.010	16	1278.05	1.014	1.016
5	1291.85	1.004	1.010	17	1285.34	1.009	1.014
6	1280.37	0.999	1.004				
7	1271.53	0.990	0.998				
8	1269.66	0.977	0.989				
11	1268.55	0.984	0.984				
12	1271.75	0.984	0.982				
13	1261.70	0.985	0.984				
14	1260.05	0.991	0.987				
15	1247.35	0.982	0.986				

1. When volume tends to increase during price declines, it is a bearish indication.
2. When volume tends to increase during advances, it is a bullish indication.
3. When volume tends to decrease during price declines, it is a bullish indication.
4. When volume tends to decrease during price advances, it is a bearish indication.

These beliefs, however, as in the case of their other views, have not been empirically tested.

A careful empirical study of the relationships between changes in market prices and changes in volume was conducted by C. Ying in 1966. The findings were very interesting. They are not in close correspondence with the beliefs of the technicians, especially the third statement that "When volume tends to decrease during price declines, it is a bullish indication." The findings of Dr. Ying were:[9]

1. A small volume is usually accompanied by a fall in price.
2. A large volume is usually accompanied by a rise in price.
3. A large increase in volume is usually accompanied by either a large rise in price or a large fall in price.
4. A large volume is usually followed by a rise in price.
5. If the volume has been decreasing consecutively for a period of five trading days, there will be a tendency for the price to fall over the next four trading days.
6. If the volume has been increasing consecutively for a period of five trading days, there will be a tendency for the price to rise over the next four trading days.

The studies made by the author[10] both on deductive and empirical bases had findings similar to Dr. Ying's. In essence, a bull market (upward market) is characterized by high and rising volume, whereas a bear market (downward market) is characterized by low and declining volume. Volume actually leads price changes both upward and downward.

Mutual Fund Cash Position

In recent years, technical analysts have followed the cash position of mutual funds as an indicator of future trends in security prices. The mutual funds (open-end investment companies) usually keep 4 percent to 6 percent of

---

[9] C. Ying, "Market Prices and Volume of Sales," *Econometrics*, July 1966, pp. 676–85.

[10] Stanley S. C. Huang, *A New Technical Approach to Stock Market Timing* (Larchmont, N.Y.: Investors Intelligence, Inc., 1973), Chapter 9.

their portfolio in cash or cash equivalents (short-term monetary investments like Treasury bills, commercial paper, or certificates of deposit) for purposes of redemption. When the cash position reaches a proportion of 10 percent or higher, it is considered bullish, because the excess cash piled up by these mutual funds will soon pour back into the equity market, thus causing security prices to rise.

See Figure 17–5 for the mutual fund cash ratio and the DJIA during 1976–85. At the market bottom in both 1970 and 1974 (not shown in Figure 17–5), the cash ratio was about 12 percent or higher. The record seems to indicate that when mutual funds as a group increased their cash position, their combined action was an important factor in sending stock prices downward. By the same token, when they reduced their cash position, they created a powerful force that pushed equity prices upward. Historically, when their cash position was between 10 percent and 12 percent, the market seemed to be close to the bottom.

The Theory of Contrary Opinion

Many technicians and stock traders believe in what is known as "contrary opinion theory." The pioneering work on this theory was done by Humphrey Neill in his book, *The Art of Contrary Thinking*, published in 1960.[11] The theory may be summarized as follows:

1. Stock prices in general or of some groups are sometimes pushed to the extreme by mass psychology.
2. Profits in the stock market cannot be made by the majority of participants. Only a small minority in the end will win.
3. When an idea or knowledge is known and widely pursued by the general public, its usefulness is usually over.
4. The best investment strategy is to do the contrary of what the general public has firmly believed in — the future direction of the stock market or stock groups will head upward or downward.

Advantages

The contrary opinion theory does have several advantages. First, the premise that stock prices are sometimes pushed to unwarranted levels by mass psychology is basically true, but it is usually discovered in retrospect. Second, the theory states correctly that any idea when it is widely known and pursued cannot be profitable in most cases. In the stock market, the popular idea at the moment may be already discounted or even overdiscounted by the market. Third, the theory warns spectators and investors to beware of being swept into a popular crowd psychology only to end up holding the bag,

[11] Humphrey Neill, *The Art of Contrary Thinking* (Caldwell, Ohio: The Caxton Printers, 1966); David N. Dreman, *Psychology and the Stock Market* (New York: AMACOM, 1977).

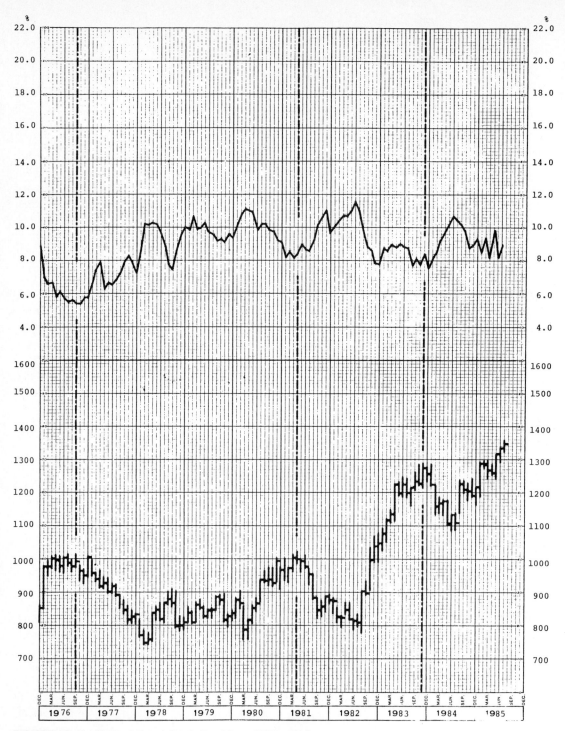

FIGURE 17–5 Mutual Fund Cash Position, 1976–1985

Source: Stone & Mead, Inc., *Long-Term Technical Trends,* August 1985.

so to speak. Fourth, the theory encourages participants in the stock market to be financial loners, thinking for themselves and searching diligently for factors beneath the surface and for the moment completely ignored by the public.

Limitations

There are also several limitations to the theory. First, it is difficult to identify the consensus of the prevailing public view and also the depth of the view. Some technicians take the prevailing sentiment of investment advisory services as the consensus of the market participants. Investors Intelligence, Inc., periodically publishes an Advisory Sentiment Index, indicating the percentage of advisory services that are bullish at the moment. But the record reveals that the advisors have been right on trends just about as often as they have been wrong on turning points.[12] Second, to follow the contrary opinion theory means to adopt at times an investment course just the opposite of what brokers, analysts, and others are recommending. It requires a combination of some personal characteristics and discipline not common to most people. Moreover, in the initial stage even a correct strategy based on contrary opinion may incur some losses rather than gains. This may create enough pressures to dissuade the investor from his original conviction. Third, the extremes of mass psychology happen only infrequently. What should the follower of contrary opinion do in between? Fourth, the theory is not so precise and quantitative as is generally believed. A great deal of judgment is still required on the part of the investor or speculator who follows this approach.

Other Technical Indicators

We have mentioned several of the more popular technical concepts or indicators. In addition, most technical analysts actually follow many other technical indicators. Some of these are listed below.

Call/put ratio
General Motors indicator
Insiders sell/buy ratio
Margin debt in brokerage accounts
Buy/sell differential by members of NYSE
Short selling by members of NYSE
Most active stocks
Speculation index
Short selling by specialists on NYSE

[12] Norman G. Fosback, *Stock Market Logic* (New York: The Institute for Economic Research, 1976), p. 87.

TECHNICAL ANALYSIS OF INDIVIDUAL STOCKS

In deciding which stock to buy and when, technical market analysts usually examine two factors, the outlook for the general market and the chart pattern of the stock. We have examined the first factor in detail and now we turn to the examination of the second factor, chart patterns of individual stocks.

Chart Reading and Analysis

Chartists claim that stock prices move in trends and that price fluctuations usually form characteristic patterns that are useful in signaling the likely course of further movement. Edwards and Magee enunciated their theory of chart reading as follows:

> No one of experience doubts that prices move in trends and trends tend to continue until something happens to change the supply-demand balance. Such changes are usually detectable in the action of the market itself. Certain patterns or formations, levels or areas, appear on the charts which have a meaning, can be interpreted in terms of probable future trend development. They are not infallible, it must be noted, but the odds are definitely in their favor.[13]

Another market analyst, William L. Jiler, also explained the theory of chart reading in his book on the subject:

> The purpose of "chart reading" or "chart analysis" is to determine the probable strength of demand versus pressure of supply at various price levels, and thus to predict the probable direction in which a stock will move, and where it will probably stop.
>
> The clues are provided by the history of a stock's price movements, as recorded on a chart. In the market, history does not repeat itself—often. On the charts, price fluctuations tend, with remarkable consistency, to fall into a number of patterns, each of which signifies a relationship between buying and selling pressures. Some patterns, or "formations," indicate that demand is greater than supply, others suggest that supply is greater than demand, and still others imply that they are likely to remain in balance for some time.[14]

Some Basic Premises in Chart Reading

Trends

The most basic premise or belief of the chartist is that stock prices tend to move in trends. The movement of stock prices is often likened to the

[13] Robert D. Edwards and John Magee, *Technical Analysis of Stock Trends* (Springfield, Mass.: John Magee, 1951), p. 6.

[14] William L. Jiler, "How Charts Can Help You in the Stock Market," *Trendline*, 1962, p. 21.

physical law of inertia or momentum—that is, an object in motion will continue in motion in the same direction until it meets an opposing force. Chartists agree that stock prices in like manner are more likely to continue to move in the same direction (up, down, or sideways) than not, until they meet a change in the supply-demand relationship.

"Volume Goes with Trend"

This is one of the tenets of the Dow theory as discussed earlier. The idea is that in a major upward trend, volume normally increases with price advances and decreases with price declines. In a major downward trend, the reverse will happen. Volume will usually increase as prices decline and dwindle as prices rally. Most chartists subscribe to this thesis and apply it to the price movement of individual stocks. This becomes another basic premise in chart reading.

Support and Resistance Levels

Another basic premise involves the assumed behavior of investors. According to the chartist, the typical pattern of behavior of investors is as follows. When investors make mistakes and find prices declining after a purchase, they usually grit their teeth and hang on, hoping that they will later be able to get out without a loss. When prices actually start to recover, they usually grasp the first chance to get out at the prices they originally paid. This kind of behavior creates the phenomenon that at certain price levels there will be a considerable increase in supply and the price of a stock will find it difficult to go beyond this level, which in the language of the chartist is called the resistance level. Since more investors buy high than buy low and there is usually high volume at former highs, the resistance level for a stock tends to establish at its former highs.

A support level, on the other hand, is the level at which a falling stock may expect a considerable increase in demand. The support level is usually established at the level from which a stock had previously been rising and where the volume of transactions was heavy. At this support level, a variety of investors may come in to buy the stock. They include (1) those who regretted that they did not buy before when the stock was advancing, (2) short-sellers who sold short before and now buy back to take profits, and (3) "value-conscious" investors.

In Figure 17–6 support and resistance levels are shown in pattern F.

Important Chart Patterns

As mentioned earlier, chartists believe that several characteristic formations or chart patterns of stock prices do have predictive value. Their interpretations of these chart formations, however, rely heavily on the three basic premises just discussed.

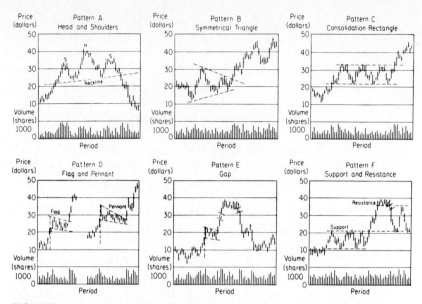

FIGURE 17–6   Typical Graphic Patterns Used in Technical Analysis
Source: Sidney M. Robbins, *Managing Securities* (Boston, Houghton Mifflin Company, 1954), p. 502.

1. Stock prices move in trends.
2. Volume goes with trends.
3. The typical pattern of behavior of investors shows up in establishing support and resistance levels.

A few important chart patterns are selected and described here. They are: head-and-shoulders formation; triangles or coils; rectangles; flags and pennants; gaps; line-and-saucer formation; and V-formation.

Head-and-Shoulders Formation
Chartists consider the head-and-shoulders formation one of the most important and reliable of the major *reversal* patterns. It is a bearish pattern. A typical head-and-shoulders formation as shown in pattern A in Figure 17–6 consists of four basic elements.

1. A strong rally, climaxing a more or less extensive advance, on which trading volume becomes very heavy, followed by a minor decline on which volume runs considerably less than it did during the days of rise and at the top. This is the "left shoulder."
2. Another high volume advance which reaches a higher level than the top of the left shoulder and then another reaction on less volume

which takes prices down to somewhere near the bottom level of the preceding recession, somewhere lower perhaps or somewhere higher but, in any case, below the top of the left shoulder. This is the "head."

3. A third rally, but this time on decidedly less volume than accompanied the formation of either the left shoulder or the head, which fails to reach the height of the head before another decline sets in. This is the "right shoulder."

4. Finally, decline of prices in this third recession down through a line (the "neckline") drawn across the bottoms of the reactions between the left shoulder and head and the head and right shoulder, respectively, and a close below that line by an amount approximately equivalent to 3 percent of the stock's market price. This is the "confirmation" or "breakout."[15]

The inverted head and shoulders look exactly the same in the figure as a normal head and shoulders except that it is upside down. It signals the end of a downward trend rather than the end of an advance.

Triangles or Coils

A triangle or coil represents a pattern of uncertainty. It is difficult to predict which way the price will break out. The triangle can be of four different shapes. They are shown in Figure 17–7 and are called, respectively, symmetrical triangle, ascending triangle, descending triangle, and inverted triangle. William L. Jiler suggested several guidelines on market tactics concerning triangles as follows:

The analysis of triangles should, of course, be tied in with other chart information such as trendlines, support and resistance, and other formations.

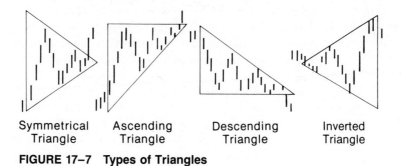

Symmetrical	Ascending	Descending	Inverted
Triangle	Triangle	Triangle	Triangle

FIGURE 17–7   Types of Triangles

---

[15] Edwards and Magee, *Technical Analysis of Stock Trends*, p. 50.

The following guidelines are offered as a checklist in following triangle developments:

1. Odds are favorable that any triangle will eventually result in a continuation of the trend that preceded it.
2. The odds favoring a continuation decrease according to which of the four basic triangles develops, in the following order; ascending, symmetrical, descending, inverted.
3. Purchases should be made at the lowest possible levels within a triangle, or after the subsequent trend has been well defined, because triangles are especially treacherous. They are subject to many false moves, and among the least reliable of all chart formations.[16]

Rectangles

Rectangles represent another chart pattern of uncertainty. Like triangles, a rectangle area pattern may represent either a consolidation or the beginning of a reversal movement. However, more often than not, it represents a consolidation rather than a reversal formation. Pattern C in Figure 17–6 shows a consolidation rectangle.

Flags and Pennants

Pattern D in Figure 17–6 shows formations commonly described as flags and pennants, which often appear after a swift, upward movement of prices. These area patterns usually represent consolidation or continuation patterns. In other words, they typically signify a pause after which the previous price trend will likely resume.

Gaps

A gap represents a price range in which no shares change hands. A gap occurs when the lowest price at which a stock is traded on a given day is higher than the highest price of the preceding day. Technicians recognize several types of gaps, such as breakaway gap, runaway gap, and exhaustion gap. Depending on their location, they may have little significance or may signify the vigor or the start of an important move.

Line-and-Saucer Formation

These formations are easy to recognize and they are reliable. They constitute the dream pattern of the chartist. However, they are rare among popular, actively traded stocks. The line formation represents a narrow range within which price has been moving sideways for a long period of time. It usually represents a long base from which a meaningful upward move will eventually start. Only infrequently does it represent a major top from which

[16] William L. Jiler, "How Charts Can Help You in the Stock Market," p. 120.

a subsequent decline develops. The saucer formation is characterized by a curving upward or downward movement of prices. The curve usually indicates the probable direction of price movement.

V-Formation

Many chartists brush off the existence of V-formations, yet their existence cannot be denied. Not infrequently stocks are found to turn around and move in the other direction without making reversal patterns and without warning. William L. Jiler, contrary to the view of others, not only recognized the V-formation, but considered it as one of the important reversal patterns. However, because it strikes with little warning, he acknowledged that the V-formation is the most difficult to analyze.

Charting

Charts are important tools of the followers of the technical approach. The technicians usually subscribe to several charting services, and, in addition, they do some charting themselves. Charts are of two types: (1) bar charts and (2) point-and-figure charts. Many technicians use both types of charts.

Bar Charts

Figure 17–8 shows a bar chart of the prices of Texaco stock. The bar chart usually shows the daily price range, closing price, and volume of transaction. In this chart, a fifty-day moving average of stock prices and a relative strength line of the stock are also included. The relative strength line showing the strength of the stock compared to the market is derived by dividing the price of the stock by the S&P 500 composite index. An upward slope in the line means that the stock is doing relatively better than the S&P 500.

The bar chart has the advantage of showing price fluctuations in a chronological order and, in addition, the volume of transactions which, as we discussed before, is an important item of information for technical analysis.

Point-and-Figure Charts

Figure 17–9 is a point-and-figure chart for ABC stock. The vertical scale measures the price of the stock. The point-and-figure chart does not have a time dimension, and the horizontal scale is not a time scale. Price is recorded only when the change in price reaches a predetermined magnitude such as $\frac{1}{2}$, 1, or 2 points. What is most commonly used is a one-point scale. That means the price will not be recorded unless it reaches a round figure such as 1, 2, or 3. Fractional change will not be recorded.

When the price of a stock rises, an X is recorded to indicate the price change. When the price of a stock is going down, an O is recorded to indicate the price change. X's and O's never appear in the same column. Each column represents either an upmove or a downmove; it cannot represent both. When there is a change in price in a different direction (rise after previous

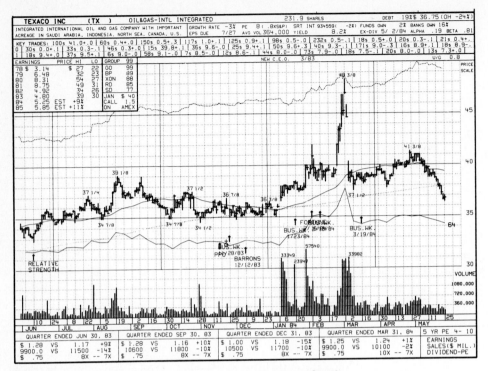

FIGURE 17–8   Daily Graph of Texaco, Inc., Common Stock

Source: Courtesy Daily Graphs, P.O. Box 24933, Los Angeles, CA 90024.

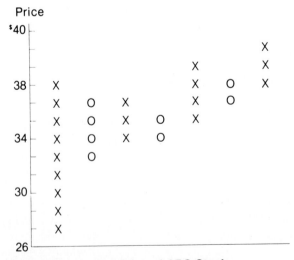

FIGURE 17–9   The Price of ABC Stock

declines, or decline after previous increases), the price is recorded in the next column to the right. The first entry on the chart can be labeled by a square or any other sign.

For purposes of illustration, let us say the daily closing prices of XYZ stock in the last twenty days were as follows:

$$\$30,\ 30\tfrac{1}{4},\ 31,\ 31\tfrac{1}{2},\ 32,\ 32\tfrac{1}{2},\ 33,\ 32\tfrac{3}{4},\ 32\tfrac{1}{2},\ 32,\ 32\tfrac{1}{4},\ 32\tfrac{3}{4},$$
$$33,\ 33\tfrac{1}{2},\ 34,\ 35,\ 36,\ 35,\ 34,\ 33\tfrac{1}{2}$$

In Figure 17–10 see the resulting point-and-figure chart of XYZ stock on the basis of these prices.

Objectives of Point-and-Figure Chart

Through eliminating the time scale and small changes, the point-and-figure chart is designed to compress the recording of price fluctuations of a stock into congested areas so that different chart patterns or formations will emerge clearly. According to technical people, as discussed earlier, some chart patterns are bullish, others are bearish, and still others are basically uncertain. In explaining the basic rationale and the use of point-and-figure charts, a well-known chartist, A. W. Cohen, stated:[17]

> The basic premise of Point and Figure charting and trading is that the Law of Supply and Demand, and nothing else, governs the price of a stock. When Demand exceeds Supply, the price of a stock goes up; when Supply exceeds Demand, the price of a stock goes down. When Supply and Demand are contesting for supremacy, the price of a stock moves sideways.
>
> Every Point and Figure chart constructed in the manner we have described, consists of the following elements: (1) a vertical column of Xs go-

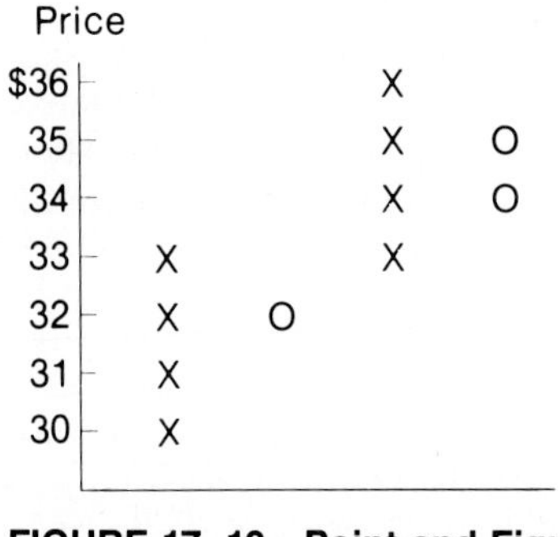

FIGURE 17–10 Point-and-Figure Chart of XYZ Stock

---

[17] A. W. Cohen, *How to Use the Three-Point Reversal of Point & Figure Stock Market Trading* (Larchmont, N.Y.: Chartcraft, Inc., 1982), p. 15.

ing straight up (Demand has overcome Supply); (2) a vertical column of Os going straight down (Supply has overcome Demand); and (3) an interruption in these vertical columns by short alternating columns of Xs and Os (Supply and Demand are contesting for supremacy).

The Point and Figure chart is, therefore, a pictorial record of the contest between the forces of Supply and Demand.

In any chart picture of the price action of a stock, it is the short columns of alternating Xs and Os—the sideways movement—that is of the utmost importance and significance. It is this sideways movement that will give us the clue as to whether a particular stock should be bought or sold. The clue will be given us through the medium of one or more chart patterns. The sideways move—the picture of the contest between the forces of Supply and Demand—always takes on a definite pattern out of which an up or down move will emerge. . . . Once we learn to recognize and interpret these patterns, we know the correct position to take, marketwise, at any particular time.

THE RANDOM-WALK THEORY AND TECHNICAL ANALYSIS

As mentioned above, the most basic premise of the technical approach is the belief that stock prices move in trends. Should this belief be proven untrue or cast in serious doubt, the theoretical foundation of the approach will likewise become vulnerable.

The random-walk theory, which enjoys a large number of advocates among economists and statisticians from academic circles, says just the contrary. It says that where trends seem to be observable, they are merely interpretations, read in after the fact, of a process that really follows a random pattern. The future changes in speculative prices are independent of previous changes. Various statistical analyses of the past behavior of speculative prices have found no positive serial correlation of successive changes in speculative prices. In other words, knowledge of past price changes does not enable a person to predict successfully future price changes.[18]

However, the random walk thesis of speculative prices is by no means universally accepted by statisticians. Some statisticians argue that the statistical tests employed to support the random-walk thesis are either too simple or too inflexible to capture the principles that technical analysts

---

[18] For purpose of reference, some important articles on the controversy over the random-walk theory of speculative prices are P. H. Cootner, "Stock Prices: Random Vs. Systematic Changes," *Industrial Management Review*, Spring 1962; M. G. Kendall, "The Analysis of Economic Time Series—Part I: Prices," *Journal of the Royal Statistical Society*, vol. 96, 1953; H. Houthakker, "Systematic and Random Elements in Short-Term Price-Movements," *American Economic Review*, May 1961; Robert A. Levy, "Random Walk: Reality or Myth," *Financial Analysts Journal*, Nov.–Dec. 1967; M. C. Jensen, "Random Walks: Reality or Myth—Comment," *Financial Analysts Journal*, Nov.–Dec. 1967; H. C. Wallish, "Random Walk and Security Analysts," *Financial Analysts Journal*, March–April 1968; P. A. Rinfret, "Investment Managers are Needed," *Financial Analysts Journal*, March–April 1968.

are supposed to follow. Others counter with their own statistical findings that indicate nonrandomness in the changes of stock prices. For illustration, we cite briefly the methods and findings of two statistical studies.

Findings by Sidney Alexander

Alexander attacked the problem this way: If it is true that stock prices are a random walk, there should be no strategy that will consistently yield profits. On the other hand, if such a strategy is found, then price changes cannot be considered random. He outlined his strategy as follows:[19]

> Suppose we tentatively assume the existence of trends in stock market prices but believe them to be masked by the jiggling of the market. We might filter out all movements smaller than a specified size and examine the remaining movements. The most vivid way to illustrate the operation of the filter is to translate it into a rule of speculative market action. Thus, corresponding to a 5% filter we might have the rule: if the market moves up 5% go long and stay long until it moves down 5% at which time sell and go short until it again moves up 5%. Ignore moves of less than 5%. The more stringent the filter, the fewer losses are made, but also the smaller the gain from any move that exceeds the filter size.

He applied this filter technique to daily closing prices of two indexes, the Dow Jones Industrials from 1897 to 1929 and the Standard & Poor Industrials from 1929 to 1959. He concluded his findings as follows:[20]

> Taken altogether the evidence runs strongly against the hypothesis that from 1928 to 1961 the movement of the Standard & Poor's Industrials is consistent with a random walk with drift. The inconsistency of the data with the hypothesis may be largely linked with the "special events" of 1928–1940, but that is just a plausible conjecture. The formulas tested show substantial profits over the entire period, formulas which would be expected to do only a little better than break even if applied to a random walk with drift equal to the observed drift, since they go short as often as they go long.

Findings by Robert Levy

An important tenet of technical analysis is that relative strength of individual securities tends to persist for a significant period of time. If this tenet is valid, replacing weak issues with currently strong issues should prove to be a successful portfolio strategy. With a view to testing the validity of this tenet of technical analysis, Levy constructed a number of variable ratio models in which the portfolios were composed of both stocks and bonds. The stock portion would be increased if the market has been relatively strong,

[19] Sidney S. Alexander, "Price Movement in Speculative Markets: Trends or Random Walks?" *Industrial Management Review,* May 1961.

[20] Sidney S. Alexander, "Price Movements in Speculative Markets—Trends or Random Walks, Number 2," *Industrial Management Review,* vol. 5, no. 2, Spring 1964, p. 44.

and decreased if the market has been relatively weak. The performances of these portfolios which used this upgrading strategy were found to be much better than a random buy-and-hold policy could produce during the period 1960–65. Based on these findings, Levy argued that "stock prices followed discernible trends and patterns which have predictive significance; and the theory of random walks has been refuted."[21]

Even though statisticians like Alexander and Levy may express dissenting views on the random-walk thesis, the dominant view today still favors the idea of this thesis. Unless and until the technical analysts produce more rigorous evidence to validate their claims that they can predict stock prices from past trends and patterns, their approach remains suspect, at least in academic circles.

SUMMARY

The technical approach studies the day-to-day changes in prices of securities and volumes of transactions. The purpose of the approach is to predict short-term movements of securities and the security market in general.

The basic premise of the technical approach is that security prices move in *trends* and that the trends can be recognized and taken advantage of. The basic premise of the technical approach is contrary to the random-walk theory of security prices.

Many of the concepts embraced by followers of the technical approach can be traced to the Dow theory, which was developed by Charles Dow and later expanded and refined by Hamilton and Rhea. The basic idea is to recognize the *major* trend and to swing with it.

Adherents to the technical approach follow many technical indicators. They believe that these indicators will enable them to predict short-term changes in security prices. However, some of the commonly followed indicators seem of doubtful value in the light of empirical evidence. These indicators include short interest theory, odd-lot theory, and new-high–new-low indicators.

On the other hand, a few other indicators or analytical techniques may be useful in gauging the probability of future movement of stock prices. Such indicators or procedures include the moving-average method, advance-decline line, rate of change analysis, price versus volume changes, mutual fund cash position, and the contrary opinion theory.

Followers of the technical approach use two types of charts, bar charts, and point-and-figure charts. Technicians believe that some characteristic

[21] Robert A. Levy, "Random Walks: Reality or Myth?" *Financial Analysts Journal,* Nov.–Dec. 1967, p. 76.

formations or patterns on charts of stock prices do have predictive value. However, this claim is basically unproved.

The random-walk theory challenges the basic premise of the technical approach that stock prices move in trends. So far, the followers of the technical approach have failed to present convincing evidence that their belief is true. The practitioners of the technical approach seem to be mostly short-term traders.

QUESTIONS AND PROBLEMS

1. What is the rationale of technical or market analysis?
2. Indicate the differences between security analysis and market analysis.
3. What is the essence of the Dow theory? Is there any connection between the Dow theory and modern-day technical analysis?
4. How may the advance-decline line be used by the student of technical analysis?
5. Explain the odd-lot theory.
6. How does a student of the technical approach make use of the moving-average method?
7. What is the theory of chart reading? Explain a few important chart patterns from a technician's point of view.
8. How do you construct a point-and-figure chart? What advantages and disadvantages does a point-and-figure chart possess?
9. What is the random-walk theory? Does it weaken or strengthen the technical market analysis?
10. What do you think of the technical approach?
11. Is it possible for an investor to combine the use of both the technical and fundamental approaches? How?
12. What are some of the important technical indicators of the stock market?
13. Draw a one-point interval, point-and-figure chart on the basis of the following prices: 20, $20\frac{1}{4}$, 21, $20\frac{1}{2}$, 21, $20\frac{3}{4}$, $21\frac{1}{2}$, 22, $20\frac{1}{4}$, 21, 20, 19, $19\frac{1}{2}$, 20, $20\frac{1}{4}$, 21, 22, 23, 24, 25, $24\frac{3}{4}$, 24, $23\frac{1}{2}$, 23, 22, 21, 20.

REFERENCES

Cohen, A. W. *How to Use the Three-Point Reversal Method of Point and Figure Stock Market Trading*. Larchmont, N.Y.: Chartcraft, 1982.

Cohen, J., Zinbarg, E., and Zeikel, A. *Investment Analysis and Portfolio Management*, 4th ed. Homewood, Ill.: R. D. Irwin, 1982, Chapter 8.

Crounch, Robert L. "Market Volume and Price Changes." *Financial Analysts Journal*, July–Aug. 1970.

Drew, Garfield A. *New Methods for Profit in the Stock Market*. Wells, Vt.: Fraser Publishing, 1966.

Edwards, R. D., and Magee, J. *Technical Analysis of Stock Trends*. Springfield, Mass.: John Magee, 1958.

Fosback, Norman G. *Stock Market Logic*. New York: The Institute for Economic Research, 1976.

Gehm, Fred. "Who Is R. N. Elliott and Why Is He Making Waves?" *Financial Analysts Journal*, Jan.–Feb. 1983.

Gordon, William. *The Stock Market Indicators*. Palisades Park, N.J.: Investors' Press, 1968.

Granville, Joseph E. *A Strategy of Daily Stock Market Timing for Maximum Profit*. Englewood Cliffs, N.J.: Prentice-Hall, 1960.

Hamilton, Willilam P. *The Stock Market Barometer*. New York: Richard Russell Associates, 1960.

Huang, Stanley S. C. *Techniques of Investment Analysis*. New York: Intext Educational Publishers, 1972, Chapter 9.

———. *A New Technical Approach to Stock Market Timing*. Larchmont, N.Y.: Investors Intelligence, Inc., 1973.

Jiler, William L. *How Charts Can Help You in the Stock Market*. New York: Trend-line, Standard & Poor Corp., 1962.

Kerrigan, Thomas J. "Behavior of the Short-Interest Ratio." *Financial Analysts Journal*, Nov.–Dec. 1974.

Krow, Harvey A. *Stock Market Behavior*. New York: Random House, 1969.

Levy, Robert A. *The Relative Strength Concept of Common Stock Price Forecasting*. Larchmont, N.Y.: Investors Intelligence, 1968.

———. "Conceptual Foundations of Technical Analysis." *Financial Analysts Journal*, July–Aug. 1966.

Neill, Humphrey. *The Art of Contrary Thinking*. Caldwell, Ohio: Caxton Printers, 1960.

Nelson, S. A. *The ABC of Stock Speculation*. Wells, Vt.: Fraser Publishing, 1964.

Pinches, George E. "The Random Walk and Technical Analysis." *Financial Analysts Journal*, March–April 1970.

Pring, Martin J. *Technical Analysis Explained*. New York: McGraw-Hill, 1980.

Rhea, Robert. *The Dow Theory*. Boulder, Colo.: Rhea, Griener, 1959.

Russell, Richard. *The Dow Theory Today*. New York: Richard Russell Associates, 1961.

Schultz, H. D., and Coslow, S., eds. *A Treasury of Wall Street Wisdom*. Palisades Park, N.J.: Investors' Press, 1966.

Schultz, John W. *The Intelligent Chartist*. New York: WRSM Financial Service Corp., 1962.

Seligman, Daniel. "Playing the Market with Charts." *Fortune*, Feb. 1962.

———. "The Mystique of Point-and-Figure." *Fortune*, March 1962.

Shaw, Alan R. "Technical Analysis." *Financial Analysts' Handbook, Vol. 1*. Homewood, Ill.: Dow Jones-Irwin, 1975.

Stone & Mead, Inc. *Long-Term Technical Trends*, current issue.

Treynor, Jack L., and Ferguson, Robert. "In Defense of Technical Analysis." *The Journal of Finance*, July 1985.

APPENDIX : Number of Stocks Reaching New Annual Highs and Lows Compared to the DJIA, April–August 1979

Date	DJIA	New High	New Low	Date	DJIA	New High	New Low
April 2	855.3	31	30	6	835.5	85	27
3	868.3	65	16	7	837.0	91	18
4	869.8	108	15	8	835.2	49	19
5	877.6	76	12	11	837.6	43	16
6	875.7	85	17	12	845.3	97	11
9	873.7	50	22	13	842.2	72	10
10	H 878.7	75	15	14	842.3	50	12
11	871.7	50	14	15	843.3	62	7
12	870.5	29	10	18	839.4	52	7
16	860.5	24	22	19	839.4	40	15
17	857.9	28	17	20	839.8	49	13
18	860.3	30	16	21	843.6	62	11
19	855.3	43	23	22	849.1	68	14
20	857.0	20*	27	25	844.3	54	12
23	860.1	37	14	26	837.7	55	13
24	866.9	62	22	27	840.5	63	16
25	867.5	64	18	28	843.0	103	11
26	861.0	48	44	29	842.0	97	13
27	856.6	37	51	July 2	834.0	40	20
30	854.9	37	38	3	835.6	35	13
May 1	855.5	38	36	5	835.8	58	8
2	855.5	42	24	6	846.2	110	6
3	857.6	36	32	9	H 853.0	161	8
4	847.5	32	40	10	850.3	104	11
7	833.4	9	81	11	843.9	41	16
8	834.9	1	89	12	836.9	35	12
9	838.6	6	54	13	833.5	21	18
10	828.9	8	59	16	834.9	40	14
11	830.6	8	62	17	828.5	34	25
14	L 825.0	12	67	18	828.6	18*	30
15	825.9	12	76	19	827.3	27	10
16	828.5	10	63	20	828.1	34	12
17	843.0	21	50	23	L 825.5	33#	13
18	841.9	30#	27	24	829.8	38	8
21	842.4	40	32	25	839.5	72	7
22	H 845.4	37	32	26	839.8	73	4
23	837.4	47	21	27	839.8	68	7
24	837.7	37	30	30	838.7	83	8
25	836.3	44	23	31	846.4	106	6
29	832.6	46	28	Aug. 1	850.3	103	5
30	822.2	22*	31	2	848.0	121	2
31	822.3	17	32	3	846.2	70	4
June 1	L 821.2	31#	24	6	848.6	66	6
4	821.9	41	25	7	859.8	127	2
5	831.3	74	22	8	863.1	135	2

Date	DJIA	New High	New Low	Date	DJIA	New High	New Low
9	858.3	72	4	17	883.4	80	3
10	867.0	105	5	20	H 886.5	111	6
13	875.3	172	5	21	886.0	114	4
14	876.7	145	3	22	885.8	106	6
15	885.8	174	4	23	880.4	91	4
16	884.0	159	4	24	880.2	74	6

H: High
L: Low
*: New low exceeds new high
#: New high exceeds new low

From the table, it can be seen that the number of new highs continued to exceed the number of new lows for four to six days after the DJIA had already begun its decline. However, when the DJIA began to turn around from a low, new highs began to exceed new lows almost at the same time in two out of three cases.

VI

Modern Portfolio Theory

18

Efficient Portfolios

In this chapter we will discuss modern theories on how to construct optimum portfolios for investors. Modern portfolio theories differ from traditional views in several important respects. First, modern theories treat different aspects of portfolio construction, such as level of risk, degree of diversification, market influence, interrelationships of securities, and attitudes of the investor toward risk-return tradeoff, in a systematic manner to arrive at an optimum portfolio for a given investor. Second, modern portfolio theories are mostly quantitative. Third, modern portfolio theories also include discussions on the degree of efficiency of the security markets.

The pioneer of modern portfolio theory is Harry M. Markowitz. His portfolio theories are contained in an article, "Portfolio Selection," in the *Journal of Finance* in March of 1952, and also in a monograph, *Portfolio Selection: Efficient Diversification of Investments*, published in 1959.

RETURN AND RISK OF A SECURITY

Before we discuss the return and risk of a portfolio, we should first review the measurement of return and risk of a security. In Chapter 12, we discussed four alternative ways of measuring return and risk of a security:

- Measuring risk in terms of expectation
- Measuring risk in terms of historical record
- Measuring risk on basis of comparison with industry average and the S&P 400 Industrials
- *Value Line* system of measuring risks of a security.

These alternative methods of measuring risks are interrelated and supplementary to each other. Modern portfolio theories discuss risk of securities mostly in terms of expectation. The procedure of measuring risk and return of a security on the basis of expectations was discussed in Chapter 12 and is summarized in the following.

The rate of return on common stocks includes both dividend and price change of a stock. The formula for the calculation of the rate of return on an annual basis is:

$$\text{Annual rate of return} = \frac{D + (P_1 - P_0)}{P_0}$$

where:

D = the dividend for the year
P_0 = the price of the stock at the beginning of the year
P_1 = the price of the stock at the end of the year

Expected Return

Assume that you are now considering the purchase of GM stock. As an intelligent investor, you have to estimate the expected return and risk of the stock. To estimate the expected return and risk of the GM stock, you need to:

1. Estimate and list the realistically obtainable returns from the investment in GM stock.
2. Estimate the likelihood of occurrence of each possible return.

In other words, you have to formulate a probability distribution of possible returns from the investment.

The expected return on GM stock is the most likely return, which is obtained by multiplying each possible return by its probability and then summing them up. In the form of an equation, the expected return can be expressed as:

$$E(r_i) = \sum P_i r_i \qquad\qquad (18.1)$$

where:

$E(r_i)$ = the expected return
r_i = each possible return
P_i = probability of occurrence of each possible return

Expected Risk

The risk of the investment lies in the fact that the actual return to be realized can be quite different from the expected return. The expected risk of the stock depends on the degree of variability of possible returns from the expected return. The best statistical method to measure this variability is the standard deviation. The formula for computing it is:

$$\sigma_i = \sqrt{\sum_{i=1}^{n} P_i[r_i - E(r_i)]^2} \tag{18.2}$$

where:

σ_i = the standard deviation of the expected return
P_i = the probability of occurrence of each possible return
r_i = the possible rate of return
$E(r_i)$ = the expected return.

In Tables 12–1 and 12–2 in Chapter 12, we perform the calculations. The expected return on the GM stock is 6.25 percent and the expected risk as measured by standard deviation is 7.6 percent based on the probability distribution of possible returns of the investor.

EXPECTED RETURN OF A PORTFOLIO

The calculation of expected return of a portfolio is relatively simple. The formula for its calculation is:

$$E_p = \sum_{i=1}^{N} X_i E_i \tag{18.3}$$

where:

E_p = expected return of a portfolio
X_i = proportion of total portfolio invested in security i
E_i = expected return of security i
N = total number of securities in a portfolio.

For example, Investor A has a portfolio of three stocks. He gives us the following information:

Stock	Price per Share	Shares Purchased	Value	Proportion	Expected Return
A	$15	200 sh.	$ 3,000	30%	10%
B	30	100	3,000	30%	15%
C	40	100	4,000	40%	20%
			$10,000	100%	

The expected return of his portfolio is therefore:

$$E_p = \Sigma X_i E_i = .3 \times 10\% + .3 \times 15\% + .4 \times 20\% = 15.5\%$$

In other words, the expected return of a portfolio is the weighted-average return of the portfolio.

EXPECTED RISK OF A PORTFOLIO

Assume that Investor A also provided us with the expected risk of each stock as measured by standard deviation in his portfolio as follows:

Stock	Proportion	Expected Risk (σ)
A	30%	12%
B	30%	20%
C	40%	30%

He wanted us to calculate the expected risk of his portfolio. Can we do it? Unfortunately, the answer is no. You may wonder why we cannot calculate portfolio risk in the same way we calculate the expected return of a portfolio. In other words, why can't we use the weighted-average of the risks of individual securities in the portfolio as the risk of the portfolio? The answer to the question is involved. Briefly, the risk of a portfolio is usually less than the weighted-average of the risk of individual securities in a portfolio. The explanation lies in the fact that the risk of a portfolio, the standard deviation of expected return of a portfolio, depends not only on the risks (standard deviation) of individual securities, but also on the covariation or relationships between the returns of securities in the portfolio.

To clarify this point, we set up three hypothetical portfolios of two stocks each. In Figure 18–1, there are six subcharts. The three charts on the left indicate the returns of individual stocks over time, and the three charts on the right indicate the returns of three portfolios composed of stocks A and B, C and D, and E and F, respectively.

In portfolio I, A and B are both cyclical stocks. They may be in the same industry or related cyclical industries. A and B's returns fluctuated over business cycles in the same direction and magnitude. In statistical terms, the coefficient of correlation between the returns of the two stocks is +1. The variation of the return of the portfolio or the portfolio risk was not reduced.

In portfolio II, the returns of C and D vary inversely, and the coefficient of correlation was −1. The return of the portfolio did not have any variation over time. In other words, the portfolio risk was zero.

In portfolio III, the return on F was random and had no relationship with the return of security E. In other words, the coefficient of correlation

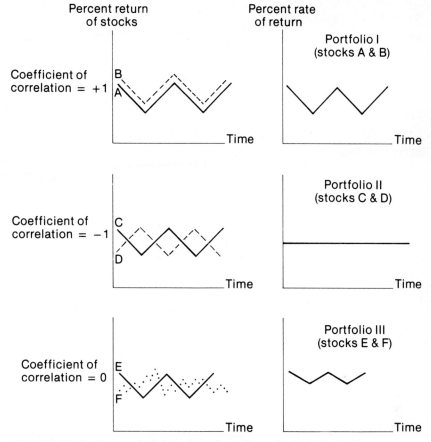

FIGURE 18–1   Rates of Return for Three Hypothetical Portfolios

between the two was zero. The return of portfolio III did fluctuate over time, but at a rate substantially less than that of security E.

Hence Markowitz stated that:[1]

> The standard deviation of a portfolio is determined by:
> (a) the standard deviation of each security,
> (b) the correlation between each pair of securities, and, of course,
> (c) the amount invested in each security.

The formula for the computation of portfolio risk of a two-security portfolio is:

$$p = \sqrt{X_a^2 \sigma_b^2 + X_b^2 \sigma_b^2 + 2X_a X_b \, \mathrm{Cov}_{ab}} \qquad (18.4)$$

[1] Harry M. Markowitz, *Portfolio Selection: Efficient Diversification of Investments* (New York: John Wiley & Sons, Inc., 1959), p. 19.

where:

σ_p = standard deviation of the portfolio's return
X_a = percentage of total portfolio value in security A
X_b = percentage of total portfolio value in security B
σ_a = standard deviation of security A
σ_b = standard deviation of security B
Cov_{ab} = covariance between securities A and B

The covariance between returns of two securities is related to the coefficient of correlation between the two securities in the following manner:

$$\text{Cov}_{ab} = P_{ab}\sigma_a\sigma_b$$

where P_{ab} stands for the coefficient of correlation between securities A and B. The formula for computing portfolio risk of a two-security portfolio can be, therefore, expressed also as:

$$\sigma_p = \sqrt{X_a^2\sigma_a^2 + X_b^2\sigma_b^2 + 2X_aX_b(P_{ab}\sigma_a\sigma_b)} \qquad (18.5)$$

If the portfolio consists of three securities, the formula for portfolio risk would be:

$$\sigma_p = \sqrt{\begin{array}{c} X_a^2\sigma_a^2 + X_b^2\sigma_b^2 + X_c^2\sigma_c^2 + 2X_aX_b(P_{ab}\sigma_a\sigma_b) + \\ 2X_aX_c(P_{ac}\sigma_a\sigma_c) + 2X_bX_c(P_{bc}\sigma_b\sigma_c) \end{array}} \qquad (18.6)$$

For N securities in a portfolio, the formula for portfolio risk is:

$$\sigma_p = \sqrt{\sum_{i=1}^{N} X_i^2\sigma_i^2 + 2\sum_{i=1}^{N-1}\sum_{j=i+1}^{N} X_iX_jP_{ij}\sigma_i\sigma_j} \qquad (18.7)$$

where:

σ_p = standard deviation of the portfolio's returns
σ_i = standard deviation of returns of security i
σ_j = standard deviation of returns of security j
X_i = percentage of total portfolio value in security i
X_j = percentage of total portfolio value in security j
P_{ij} = coefficient of correlation between securities i and j.

Remember when Investor A wanted us to calculate the risk of his portfolio and we said, "Sorry, we cannot." The reason was that we did not know the coefficient of correlation between the returns of each pair of stocks in his portfolio. Assume that Investor A also provides us with these coefficients of correlations plus the information formerly provided as follows:

Stocks in Portfolio	Proportion	Expected Return	Std. Deviation of Each Stock (Risk)	Coefficient Correlation
A	30%	10%	12%	$P_{ab} = .5$
B	30%	15%	20%	$P_{ac} = .7$
C	40%	20%	30%	$P_{bc} = .9$

The expected return of Investor A's portfolio, as calculated before, is:

$$E_p = \Sigma X_i E_i = .3 \times 10\% + .3 \times 15\% + .4 \times 20\% = 15.5\%$$

The risk of Investor A's portfolio can now be calculated as:

$$\sigma_p = \sqrt{\begin{array}{l}(.3)^2(12)^2 + (.3)^2(20)^2 + (.4)^2(30)^2 + 2(.3)(.3)(.5)(12)(20) \\ + 2(.3)(.4)(.7)(12)(30) + 2(.3)(.4)(.9)(20)(30)\end{array}}$$

$$= \sqrt{12.96 + 36 + 144 + 21.6 + 60.48 + 129.6}$$

$$= \sqrt{404.64} = 20.11 \ (\%)$$

From the calculation, we know that the risk of the portfolio as measured by standard deviation of portfolio return is 20.11 percent.

From statistics, we know that the expected return $\pm 1\sigma$ takes up about 68.3 percent of the area under the normal curve. Assuming that the possible return of the portfolio would look like a normal distribution as shown in Figure 18–2, the actual return of Investor A's portfolio will likely fall within a range of −4.61 percent to 35.61 percent (15.5% ± 20.11%) roughly two-thirds of the time.

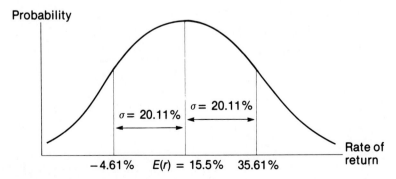

FIGURE 18–2   Possible Rates of Return on Investor A's Portfolio

Coefficient of Correlation

In statistics, the formula for computing the coefficient of correlation between two variables is:

$$P_{ab} = \pm\sqrt{1 - \frac{\Sigma(y_i - y_i')^2}{\Sigma(y_i - \overline{y})^2}} \begin{array}{l} \leftarrow \text{unexplained variability} \\ \leftarrow \text{total variability} \end{array}$$

In Figure 18–3, the dots represent rates of return on stocks A and B for a given period. Line Cy' represents the least-squares regression line. $\overline{y}$ represents the mean of returns of stock A, and $\Sigma(y_i - \overline{y})^2$ measures the total variability in the rates of return of stock A.

 y_i' represents values on the regression line, and $\Sigma(y_i - y_i')^2$ measures the unexplained variability in the rates of return of stock A. The statistic P_{ab}, known as the coefficient of correlation, measures the strength of linear relationship between the two variables A and B. The coefficient of correlation can vary between $+1$ and -1 as shown in Figure 18–4.

Implications for Investors from the Measurement of Portfolio Risk

The implications are quite obvious. If the investor is conservative and interested in low variability of portfolio returns from the expected return (actual realizable return not far from expected return), he or she should:

1. Invest his or her funds in securities with low standard deviations, and also
2. Ensure that the securities chosen for the portfolio have relatively low coefficients of correlation with one another.

 Theoretically, if it is possible, the investor should include some securities with negative coefficients of correlation with other securities in the portfolio.

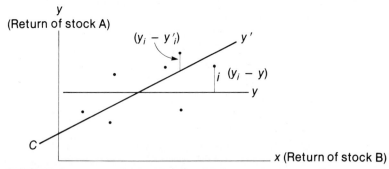

FIGURE 18–3 Correlation Between Rates of Return on Stocks A and B

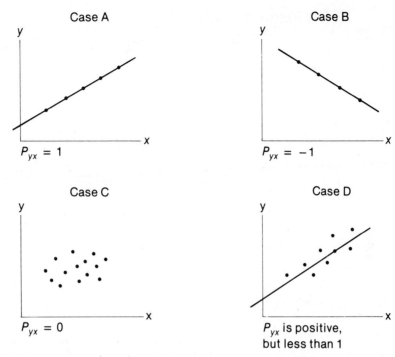

FIGURE 18–4   Coefficients of Correlation in Four Hypothetical Cases

However, in reality, with the exception of gold stocks, most stocks are positively correlated in their returns. The only difference is in the degree of correlation.

EFFICIENT PORTFOLIOS

In previous sections we explained how to calculate the expected return and risk of a portfolio. The risk of a portfolio depends on:

1. Standard deviation of each security in the portfolio,
2. The coefficient of correlation or covariance between each pair of securities in the portfolio, and
3. The percentage of funds invested in each security.

Markowitz argued that most investors are risk-averse. Investors are not willing to take up more risk unless there is an expectation of higher return. By the same token, at a given level of return they seek portfolios that will minimize the risk. He stated that portfolios can be, therefore, classified into two categories: (1) efficient portfolios and (2) inefficient portfolios.

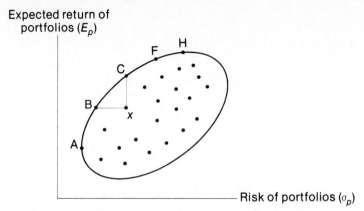

FIGURE 18–5   Expected Return and Risk of Portfolios

    The efficient portfolios are those that provide the highest return at a given level of risk or alternatively minimize the risk for a given level of return.

    In Figure 18–5, the leaflike area represents all possible portfolios of different risk-return combinations. Each dot in the leaflike area represents the return-risk of a portfolio.

    Portfolio X is inferior to portfolio C, because both portfolios X and C are of the same level of risk, and yet portfolio X receives less expected return. Portfolio X is also inferior to portfolio B, because both portfolios X and B receive the same expected return, and yet portfolio X incurs greater risk. Portfolio X is dominated by portfolios B and C, and, therefore, is an inefficient portfolio.

    Portfolios A, B, C, F, and H, on the other hand, are efficient portfolios. They are efficient because they provide the highest return at a given level of risk, or impose the minimum risk at a given level of return. The ABCFH curve at the edge of the leaflike space of investment opportunities is called the *efficient frontier*. Any portfolio to the right of the efficient frontier and within this leaflike investment space is inferior to the portfolios on the efficient frontier and, therefore, is inefficient.

    The investment implication from these discussions of the character-istics of portfolios is obvious: investors should try to get on the efficient frontier and select efficient portfolios as their model for investing their funds.

ATTITUDES OF INVESTORS TOWARD RISK AND RETURN

    Individuals differ in financial ability as well as in attitudes toward the amount of risk they are willing to assume in the quest for higher return. For example, some investors may be only willing to buy stocks like American Telephone

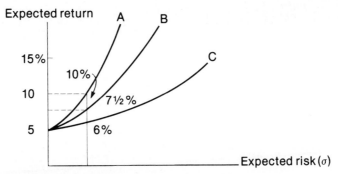

**FIGURE 18–6   Indifference Curves of Risk and Return
for Three Investors**

& Telegraph, while other investors may be totally unattracted to this type of
stock because they like high-risk–high-return stocks.

In Figure 18–6, we use the concept of the indifference curve to denote
the attitudes of three investors toward their risk-return tradeoff.

Each indifference curve measures the tradeoff between return and risk
for the individual investor. Investor A, for example, is indifferent toward any
particular selection of points on his indifference curve. Any point on his
indifference curve represents the same level of satisfaction. That is why the
curve is called the indifference curve.

The relative venturesomeness of each investor is measured by the slope
of his individual indifference curve. As shown in the chart, with zero risk
each investor is content with a 5 percent return. If the risk of the security or
portfolio as measured by standard deviation (σ) is 5 percent, Investor A
demands a return of 10 percent, B demands a return of 7.5 percent, but C
demands only a 6 percent return. In other words, A is basically a conservative investor, C is a speculator, and B is a middle-of-the-road investor.

For each individual, there is a family of indifference curves, representing different levels of satisfaction. As shown in Figure 18–7, three indifference curves are drawn for Investor B. Each indifference curve represents
a given level of satisfaction. I_3 provides higher satisfaction than I_2 which, in
turn, provides higher satisfaction than I_1. In other words, if the individual has
a choice among the indifference curves, he will always want to get on the
higher indifference curve, because he will get higher satisfaction. For example, if risk is zero, Investor B obviously prefers a 9 percent return to one
of 5 percent or 7 percent.

OPTIMUM PORTFOLIO FOR A GIVEN INVESTOR

The previous section showed the locus of the efficient frontier and portfolios
that represent the best available portfolios. The map of indifference curves,
on the other hand, shows the subjective attitudes of an investor toward the

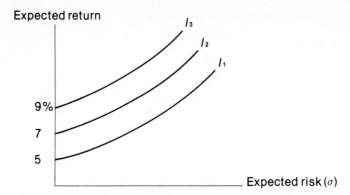

FIGURE 18–7   Family of Indifference Curves for Investor B

tradeoff between expected return and risk. Armed with this information, we can now decide which one of the efficient portfolios is the optimum portfolio for a given investor.

As shown in Figure 18–8, the optimum portfolio for a given investor is the portfolio in which the indifference curve is tangent to the efficient frontier. The optimum portfolio for Investor B is portfolio C. Portfolios B and F lie on I_2, and portfolios A and H lie on I_1. Portfolio C is on I_3, providing the highest level of satisfaction possible to Investor B. I_4 is not reachable by any efficient portfolio.

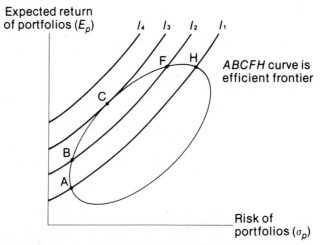

FIGURE 18–8   The Optimum Portfolio for Investor B

DIFFICULTIES IN APPLYING MARKOWITZ'S PORTFOLIO THEORY

Markowitz's portfolio theories represent a beautiful theoretical structure of diverse elements (risk and return of individual securities, risk and return of portfolios, and tradeoff between risk and return) that concludes with the selection of an optimum portfolio for a given investor. It was a theoretical masterpiece. However, the actual application of his theories was much delayed. One main reason is that the application of his theories demands an enormous amount of data inputs and calculations. For example, in dealing with a universe of only 100 securities, the portfolio analysis requires (1) expected returns of each of the 100 securities, (2) the standard deviation of the returns of each of the 100 securities, and (3) $(N^2 - N)/2 = [(100)^2 - 100]/2 = 4950$ coefficients of correlations or covariances. The heavy demand for data inputs applies not only in the initial setup of a portfolio but also in each subsequent revision of the portfolio.

CORRELATION OF RETURN OF SECURITIES TO RETURNS ON MARKET INDEX

Markowitz was aware of the problem of requiring enormous amounts of computation in the application of his theories. He suggested that if we assume that returns of securities are related only through the common market factor, the number of computations can be substantially reduced.[2] W. F. Sharpe took up the suggestion and developed a simplified model.[3]

The simplified model developed by Sharpe was based on the assumption that the returns of various securities are related only through common relationships with some basic underlying factors, and these factors are reflected in the overall market performance. Based on its relationship with returns on the general market index, the return of an individual security can be expressed as:

$$R_i = a_i + \beta_i I + c_i \tag{18.8}$$

where:

R_i = return on security i

a_i = intercept of the regression line of the vertical axis, or "alpha coefficient"

---

[2] Markowitz, *Portfolio Selection: Efficient Diversification of Investments*, p. 100.

[3] W. F. Sharpe, "A Simplified Model for Portfolio Analysis," *Management Science*, Jan. 1963.

I = returns on market index such as the Standard & Poor's 500 Composite

C_i = a random variable with an expected value of zero and standard deviation Q_i

In Figure 18–9 we see the historical relationships between the returns of a hypothetical security and the returns of a market index. Assume that on the basis of these historical data we arrive at a regression equation through the least-squares method:

$$R_i = 2\% + .8I$$

The a_i (called "alpha") is the intercept of the regression line and is 2 percent in this case, which means that when the return on the market index is zero, the return of this stock is 2 percent.

The β_i (called "beta") is the slope of the regression line, which measures the sensitivity of the stock's return to the movements in the returns on market index. In this case, the slope is 0.8, which means that when return of the market index changes by 1 percent, the return of the stock changes by 0.8 percent, excluding the alpha of the stock.

Portfolio Sensitivity or Volatility (beta$_p$)

The beta (β_i) of an individual security measures the sensitivity of its returns to changes in the returns on a broad market index. The portfolio sensitivity or beta depends on two factors: (1) the beta of the individual security in the portfolio and (2) the percentage of funds invested in each security. The formula for portfolio beta is:

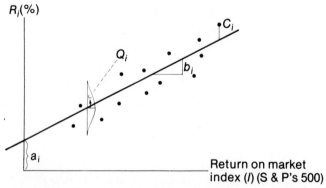

FIGURE 18–9   Correlation Between Hypothetical Rate of Return R_i and Market Index

$$\beta_p = \sum_{i=1}^{N} X_i \beta_i \qquad\qquad (18.9)$$

where:

β_i = beta of individual security in the portfolio
X_i = the percentage of portfolio funds invested in security i
β_p = beta of the portfolio.

The Expected Return of a Portfolio Based on beta Analysis

Based on Sharpe's method, the expected return of a portfolio can be calculated as:

$$E_p = \Sigma X_i(a_i + \beta_p I) = \Sigma X_i a_i + \Sigma X_i \beta_i I$$
$$= \Sigma X_i a_i + \beta_p I \qquad\qquad (18.10)$$

where:

E_p = expected return of the portfolio
X_i = percentage of funds invested in security i
β_i = beta of an individual security
β_p = beta of the portfolio
I = expected return on market index

Assume that Investor A has three securities in his portfolio. He provided us with the following information on his portfolio and estimates on the market index:

Security	X_i Proportions	a_i Intercept	β_i beta	Standard Deviation of Residuals (Q_i)	Expected Return	Standard Deviation
X	30%	2%	1.3	4%		
Y	45%	1%	0.8	2%		
Z	25%	−2%	1.1	2.5%		
Market index (S&P 500)					10%	7%

What is the portfolio beta and expected return of Investor A's portfolio?

The portfolio beta is:

$$\beta_p = \sum X_i \beta_i = .3 \times 1.3 + .45 \times 0.8 + .25 \times 1.1$$

$$= .39 + .36 + .275$$

$$= 1.025$$

The expected return of Investor A's portfolio is:

$$E_p = \sum X_i a_i + \beta_p I = .3 \times 2 + .45 \times 1 + .25 \times (-2) + 1.025\,(10)$$

$$= .6 + .45 - .5 + 10.25 = 11.8(\%)$$

Portfolio Risk Based on beta Analysis

Based on Sharpe's method, the expected risk of a portfolio is calculated by the following formula:

$$\sigma_p = \sqrt{\left[\left(\sum_{i=1}^{N} X_i \beta_i\right)^2 S_I^2\right] + \left[\sum_{i=1}^{N} X_i^2 Q_i^2\right]}$$

$$= \sqrt{[\beta_p^2 S_I^2] + \left[\sum_{i=1}^{N} X_i^2 Q_i^2\right]}$$

where:

σ_p = standard deviation of the expected return of the portfolio
β_p = portfolio beta
S_I^2 = variance of the return of the market index
X_i = percentage of funds invested in security i
Q_i = standard deviation of residuals from values on the regression
   line as shown in Figure 18–9

The first component of this formula, $\beta_p^2 S_I^2$, measures the variation in the return of the portfolio from the general market influence. This portion of the portfolio risk is called systematic or market risk, which cannot be eliminated by diversification of the portfolio.

The second component of the formula, $\sum X_i^2 Q_i^2$, measures the variation in the return of the portfolio, which was originated from the independent variation in returns of individual securities. This portion of portfolio risk is called specific or nonsystematic risk, which can be diversified away. It is expected that in a well-diversified portfolio most of the specific risks of individual securities will cancel out. What is left in the portfolio will be mainly the market or systematic risks of the portfolio.

The risk of Investor A's portfolio can be now calculated as follows:

$$\sigma_p = \sqrt{(1.025)^2 (7)^2 + (.3)^2 (4)^2 + (.45)^2 (2)^2 + (.25)^2 (2.5)^2}$$

$$= \sqrt{(1.050625)(49) + (.09)(16) + (.2025)(4) + (.0625)(6.25)}$$

$$= \sqrt{51.48 + 1.44 + .81 + .39} = \sqrt{54.12}$$

$$= 7.36(\%)$$

In summary, the characteristics of Investor A's portfolio are as follows:

Portfolio sensitivity (β_p)	1.025
Expected return of the portfolio (E_p)	11.8%
Expected risk of the portfolio (σ_p)	7.36%

For comparison, the characteristics of the market index are:

Sensitivity of the market index	1
Expected return of the market index (I)	10%
Expected risk of the market index (S_I)	7%

MODIFIED EFFICIENT FRONTIER WITH POSSIBILITIES OF LENDING AND BORROWING

When Markowitz discussed his efficient frontier, he did not take into consideration the possibility that the investor may invest part of his funds in risk-free assets, such as ninety-day Treasury bills, or use margin to leverage his portfolio. When these possibilities are included, the efficient frontier, Sharpe pointed out, will be different.

In Figure 18–10, OT represents the risk-free interest rate. TB is a line tangent to the efficient frontier. If the investor is ultraconservative, he or she can invest 100 percent of the portfolio in risk-free Treasury bills (in this case, one is lending money to the government). OT will be the expected return and there will be zero risk. On the other hand, if the investor wants to take chances, he or she can invest in the risky portfolio R, giving RX expected return with OX expected risk. If he or she takes a middle-of-the-road approach, investing partly in portfolio R, the expected return and risk will fall between the two types of assets. In other words, TR now replaces ER as the efficient frontier.

Sharpe further argued that if investors can be assumed to borrow at funds at risk-free interest rate, RB will replace RF as the efficient frontier. In other words, with the possibilties of lending and borrowing and the

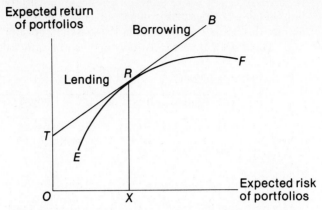

FIGURE 18–10   Efficient Frontier with Lending and Borrowing

assumption of borrowing at a risk-free interest rate, the new efficient frontier will be the line TRB, replacing the EF curve of the original Markowitz model.

Application of the beta Analysis

The advantages of Sharpe's simplified model over Markowitz's original model are clear. For example, in dealing with a universe of 100 securities, Markowitz's model will require, in addition to funds allocation, the following:

> 100 expected returns
>
> 100 standard deviations
>
> 4950 coefficient of correlations or covariances

Sharpe's simplified model, on the other hand, requires, in addition to funds allocations, only the following data inputs:

> 100 intercepts (a_i)
>
> 100 betas (β_i)
>
> 100 standard deviations of residuals
>
> 1 expected return on the market index
>
> 1 expected standard deviation of the returns on the market index

The advantage of Sharpe's simplified model is, therefore, in the vast reduction of data requirements and in the time required for computations for portfolio analysis. In other words, Sharpe introduced a way for the practical application of the Markowitz model for portfolio analysis. The disadvantage of Sharpe's model, on the other hand, is the question of whether too much useful information from the covariances among returns of individual securities was lost in the simplified procedure.

Variation of beta over Time

The first question with regard to the application of beta analysis is whether the beta values of individual securities and portfolios are relatively stable over time. According to most studies, the beta of individual securities does change from period to period. However, the betas of diversified portfolios, due to the operation of the law of large numbers, tend to remain quite stationary over time.

Marshall Blume examined the empirical behavior of the risk measures for portfolios composed of NYSE-listed stocks during the period between 1933 and 1968. He found that the correlation coefficients between betas of the same portfolios of ten securities or more in two adjacent periods were over 90 percent.[4] Besides, there was also a tendency for a portfolio with a high or low beta in one period to have a less extreme beta in the next period. In a later study,[5] he reported beta values for portfolios of 100 securities on both adjusted and unadjusted bases and compared them with betas of subsequent periods, as shown in Table 18–1. The figures again show a close correlation between betas of adjacent periods.

Gerald Levitz examined the market risk as measured by the beta of well-diversified portfolios composed from a universe of 800 stocks of broad institutional interest over the period from January 1963 to January 1972.[6] His findings were similar to Blume's. The adjusted beta[7] of large portfolios in the previous three years predicted quite correctly the beta of these portfolios in the following year.

Historical beta and Future Portfolio Performance

The beta of large portfolios was found to be quite stationary over time. The next question is, can we use the historical beta of a large diversified portfolio to predict its future performance? In other words, can we be sure that, in a market advance, high beta portfolios will perform better than low beta portfolios, or that, in a market decline, low beta portfolios will outperform high beta portfolios?

Levitz found that the returns of diversified portfolios appeared to be correlated with estimated market risk in the way beta theory suggests. However, a closer examination of the evidence indicated that the relationships

[4]Marshall E. Blume, "On the Assessment of Risk," *Journal of Finance*, March 1971.

[5]Marshall E. Blume, "Betas and their Regression Tendencies," *Journal of Finance*, June 1975.

[6]Gerald D. Levitz, "Market Risk and the Management of Institutional Equity Portfolios," *Financial Analysts Journal*, Jan.–Feb. 1974.

[7]Ibid.,p. 56. The adjusted beta was obtained by adjusting the historic beta with the formula: adj. beta = .30 + .75 × hist. beta.

TABLE 18–1   Beta Coefficients for Portfolios of 100 Securities

| | Grouping Period | | | |
Portfolio	Unadjusted for Order Bias	Adjusted for Order Bias	First Subsequent Period	Second Subsequent Period
	7/26-6/33		7/33-6/40	7/40-6/47
1	0.50	.54	0.61	0.73
2	0.85	.86	0.96	0.92
3	1.15	1.14	1.24	1.21
4	1.53	1.49	1.42	1.47
	7/33-6/40		7/40-6/47	7/47-6/54
1	0.38	.43	0.56	0.53
2	0.69	.72	0.77	0.86
3	0.90	.91	0.91	0.96
4	1.13	1.12	1.12	1.11
5	1.35	1.32	1.31	1.29
6	1.68	1.63	1.69	1.40
	7/40-6/47		7/47-6/54	7/54-6/61
1	0.43	.50	0.60	0.73
2	0.61	.65	0.76	0.88
3	0.73	.76	0.88	0.93
4	0.86	.88	0.99	1.04
5	1.00	1.00	1.10	1.12
6	1.21	1.19	1.21	1.14
7	1.61	1.54	1.36	1.20
	7/47-6/54		7/54-6/61	7/61-6/68
1	0.36	.48	0.57	0.72
2	0.61	.68	0.71	0.79
3	0.78	.82	0.88	0.88
4	0.91	.93	0.96	0.92
5	1.01	1.01	1.03	1.04
6	1.13	1.10	1.13	1.02
7	1.26	1.21	1.24	1.08
8	1.47	1.39	1.32	1.15
	7/54-6/61		7/61-6/68	
1	0.37	.53	0.62	
2	0.56	.67	0.68	
3	0.72	.79	0.85	
4	0.86	.89	0.85	
5	0.99	.99	0.95	
6	1.11	1.08	0.98	
7	1.23	1.17	1.07	
8	1.43	1.32	1.25	

between returns and market risk were not consistent throughout the entire range of market risk. Within the range of 0.80 and 1.50 for adjusted beta, there was little relationship between returns and estimated market risk of portfolios.[8]

[8]Ibid., p. 59.

To study the predictive power of conventionally estimated betas, Fouse, Jahnke, and Rosenberg carried out a study comparing the returns of portfolios with historic beta of the previous five years over the period 1956 to 1973.[9] The results are shown in Figure 18–11. The returns of portfolios were plotted in the chart from left to right in increasing order by betas. The average returns for all stocks in the sample for the year are shown by the broken line.

Out of eighteen years, beta performed correctly in eleven years. In two years, 1959 and 1962, "the predictions were neither helpful nor harmful, in the sense that high- and low-beta deciles did about equally well. In 1961, 1964, 1966, 1968, and 1972, the results contradicted the predicted pattern; high-beta deciles did less well when they were expected to do better, and vice versa.[10]

Studies by Levy,[11] and by Black-Jensen Scholes,[12] (whose findings will be cited in the next chapter on capital market theory), also yielded mixed results on the relationships between beta and portfolio returns.

A study by Bowlin and Dukes was designed to analyze the risk-return relationships of stock portfolios for the 1968–1972, 1973–1977, and 1975–1976 subperiods and for the 1968–1977 overall period.[13] They found both a positive and a negative functional relationship between beta values and holding period returns of stock portfolios during the 1968–1977 period and the three subperiods, 1968–1972, 1973–1977, and 1975–1976, as shown in Table 18–2.

They also found that the beta values greater than 1.0 were relatively good predictors of portfolio returns, whereas the beta values of less than 1.0 were poor predictors.

While no one disputes the idea that the investment markets generally provide higher returns for higher risks, the question remains: Which types of risks — systematic risks, specific risks, or inefficiencies in the marketplace — are receiving higher compensations? Arnott used a number of measures to indicate the risks of securities in his study, and he found that securities in the marketplace were priced in accordance to the *concensus perceived risk,* and that there is much discrepancy between the consensus perceived risk and the nondiversifiable risk of securities. Based on his study,

---

[9]W. L. Fouse, W. W. Jahnke, and B. Rosenberg, "Is beta Phlogiston?" *Financial Analysts Journal,* Jan.–Feb. 1974.

[10]Ibid., p. 71.

[11]Robert A. Levy, "beta as a Predictor of Return," *Financial Analysts Journal,* Jan.–Feb. 1974.

[12]Michael C. Jensen (ed.), *Studies in the Theory of Capital Markets* (New York: Praeger Publishers, 1972).

[13]Oswald D. Bowlin and William P. Dukes, "The Dual Nature of beta Responsiveness," *The Journal of Portfolio Management,* Winter 1983.

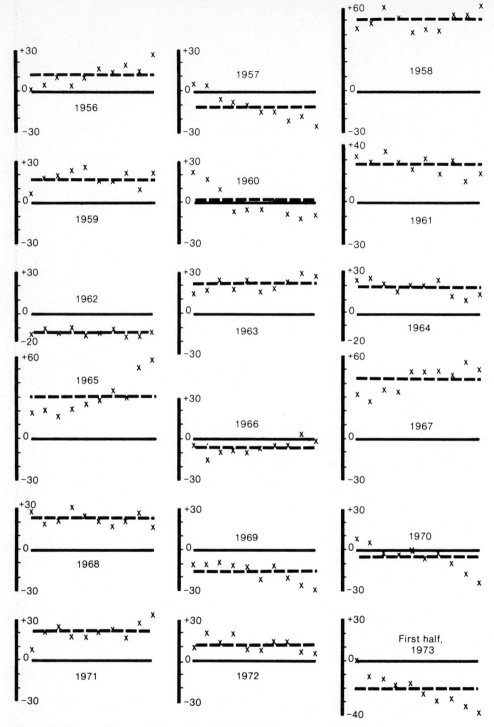

FIGURE 18–11 Annual Returns by beta Deciles

468

TABLE 18–2 Risk-Return Correlations for Thirty-Stock Portfolios

	Portfolio Groups	HPR_p vs. β_p
1968–1972		
Beta > 1	(21)	−.898 (.0005)
Beta < 1	(30)	.109 (.300)
1973–1977		
Beta > 1	(49)	−.739 (.0005)
Beta < 1	(44)	−.005 (.400)
1968–1977		
Beta > 1	(20)	−.884 (.0005)
Beta < 1	(30)	.148 (.200)
1975–1976		
Beta > 1	(55)	.825 (.0005)
Beta < 1	(45)	.091 (.90)

Source: Oswald D. Bowlin and William P. Dukes, "The Dual Nature of beta Responsiveness," *The Journal of Portfolio Management*, Winter 1983.

Arnott said, "We have seen demonstrations that beta has little to do with returns."[14]

Underlying Assumptions of beta Analysis

As mentioned above, beta analysis was predicted on the assumption that the returns of securities are correlated because they are influenced by the common market environment. After the removal of market influence, the covariance of all pairs of securities are assumed to be zero.

Livingston's study was aimed at determining how true this basic assumption was. He reported that his study indicated "approximately 18 percent of total variance was explained by residual industry effects. The mean coefficient of determination of each security's rate of return with S&P Composite Index was 23 percent. Thus, the residual industry effect was $\frac{3}{4}$'s the size of market comovement of the securities."[15] He concluded that Sharpe's single-index model overlooked a significant part of the comovement of securities' rate of return. In other words, the underlying assumption that covariances of pairs of securities, after removal of market influence, were zero was found invalid.

[14]Robert D. Arnott, "What has MPT Wrought: Which Risks Reap Rewards?" *Journal of Portfolio Management*, Fall 1983.

[15]Miles Livingston, "Industry Movements of Common Stocks," *Journal of Finance*, June 1977, p. 873.

Response by Some Institutional Investors to beta Analysis

To obtain some ideas about the way institutional investors are reacting to beta analysis, Karen Sterling sent twenty-nine questionnaires to various banking, investment, and insurance firms in the Philadelphia area asking whether they used beta analysis in constructing their portfolios, and if not, what were their reasons.[16] Of the nineteen replies she received, three firms used beta analysis, one firm is seriously considering using it, and fifteen do not use it.

Two of the firms using beta reported returns higher than what is consistent with the theory. The third firm reported that the returns have been consistent only when two factors were present: R^2 is extremely close to 1 and the number of securities in the portfolio is greater than thirty. None of the three firms had been using this technique for more than three years.

While a few of the firms reporting nonuse of beta analysis gave such reasons as limited funds or the use of other measures of risk, such as the mean absolute deviation from the S&P 500, most of the firms rejected beta analysis on the grounds of instability of the beta and a distrust of a "mechanical" tool. Some comments were as follows:

> Firm 1 — "Evidence seems to be that beta is not reliable in predicting volatility."
>
> Firm 2 — "beta coefficients change too much."
>
> Firm 3 — "We prefer to rely on our own analysis of a situation rather than a mechanical-historical tool."
>
> Firm 4 — "If there is one reason . . . [it is] a general skepticism as to the ability to quantify the concept with precision that is often attempted."
>
> Firm 5 — "If betas were as accurate as they are sometimes claimed to be, then the betas would not need constant revision."
>
> Firm 6 — "Apparently something further needs to be studied, whether it be alpha in itself or some additional error term, we remain to be converted." [This firm has had their portfolio measured for spot beta on several occasions and holds superior performance of a magnitude that could not be explained by beta or the assumption of superior timing.]

Estimating and Predicting Future beta

The future beta of a security will most likely differ from its betas of past periods. The degree of difference depends on whether or not important events take place currently or in the future to affect the characteristics of the company and/or its industry group. For purposes of superior investment decision making — portfolio revision and selection of individual securities — it is important to make use of currently available knowledge about the

---

[16]Karen Sterling, "Risk and Return," a study completed in the Graduate School of Rider College in 1976, unpublished.

developments affecting the company and the industry in the estimate and prediction of the future beta of the security. The historic betas of the security in past periods are useful, but must be properly adjusted in terms of current developments.

Barr Rosenberg and James Guy showed some examples of how to adjust historic betas to arrive at an estimate of a future beta of a stock.[17]

For firm A in Figure 18–12, the historic betas were available for fifteen years, during which there were two pronounced drops: one due to the acquisition of a less risky firm and the other from a recent offering of equity that reduced the debt and the leverage of the firm. The best forecast in this case is indicated by the heavy line extending to the right, and the probable range of future values of betas is indicated by the dotted lines.

The historic betas of firm B had a tendency to drift toward an industry norm, assumed at a level of 1.2 beta. The tendency of the drift toward an industry norm may be caused by management's decision to assume a risk exposure no higher than the industry average, or it may be caused by the disappearance of abnormal transitory factors of the firm. In the absence of other information, the best forecast of a future beta of the firm is indicated by the declining heavy line.

The historic betas of firm C changed sharply due to the changing nature of the firm. The historic betas are no longer relevant. The best forecast should be based on a more timely estimate of the nature of the company. In the absence of further information, the best forecast of future beta is at the current level and indicated by the heavy line.

The historic betas of firm D were quite stable in the past. However, the security is heavily exposed to one kind of economic event—an energy crisis—and the variance of that event is known to be increasing in the future. In this case, the past stable beta will not provide a basis for an estimate of future beta. The best forecast of future beta is indicated by the ascending heavy line.

The historic betas of firm E were quite stable in the past, and there was no known change in the fundamentals of the company and its industry group. The best forecast of a future beta in this case is probably for it to continue at the current stable level. However, the range of fluctuation of future beta values could be greater than in the past on the basis of other information that might become available.

Wells Fargo Approach—Combining beta Analysis with Security Analysis

Wells Fargo Investment Advisors, investment subsidiary of the San Francisco bank, as reported by Paul Blustein in *Forbes*,[18] has designed and

---

[17] Barr Rosenberg and James Guy, "beta and Investment Fundamentals," *Financial Analysts Journal*, May–June and July–Aug. 1976.

[18] Paul Blustein, "What's the Big Fuss about Modern Portfolio Theory?" *Forbes*, June 12, 1978.

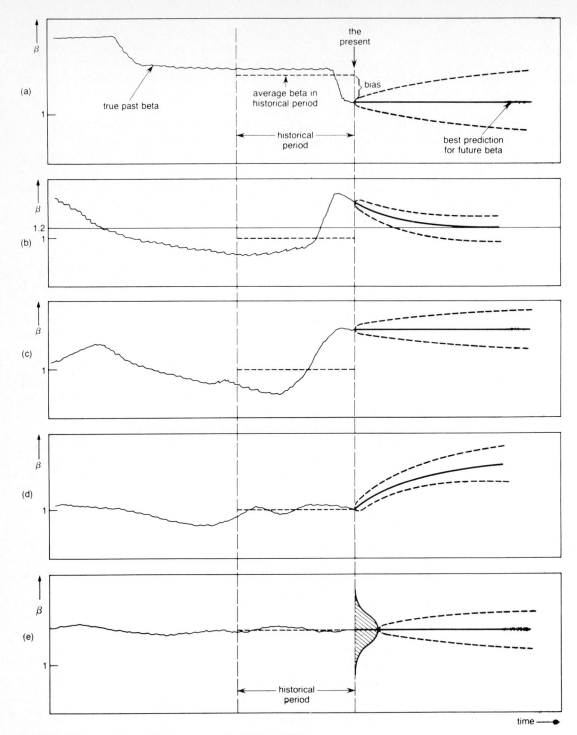

FIGURE 18–12   Using Historic betas in Forecasting

followed an approach that is unique and interesting. The approach combines the beta analysis with security analysis. The program seems to consist of the following procedures:

1. They calculated betas of 370 securities of broad institutional interest. The historic betas were then adjusted on the basis of knowledge of current developments affecting the company and its industrial group for estimate and prediction of future beta of the security. This step is similar to what Barr Rosenberg and James Guy had proposed. Actually, Barr Rosenberg was their consultant until 1976 when he organized his own advisory firm.

2. A team of security analysts was called on to formulate as accurately as possible the estimates of future dividends of the 370 securities. Then, the current market price of the security, treated as the present value of future dividends, and the estimates of future dividends were substituted in the formula.

$$\text{Present value of future dividends} = \frac{D_1}{(1 + r)^1} + \frac{D_2}{(1 + r)^2} + \cdots + \frac{D_\infty}{(1 + r)^\infty}$$

and the equation was solved for r. The r was the implied discount rate of the security or, in other words, the expected return on the current price of the security.

3. They plotted the expected beta and return (r) of each security in a chart, as shown in Figure 18–13, and drew a least-squares regression line through the observations. The regression line is the expected "Security Market Line" for the future period. Securities

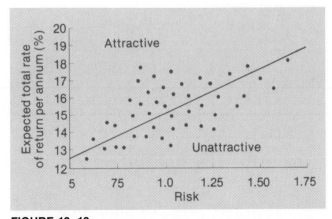

FIGURE 18–13
Source: Forbes, June 12, 1978.

above the regression line were considered attractive, and those below the line unattractive.

4. In Figure 18–14, an estimated AAA bond yield is also drawn for comparison with the expected "Security Market Line." When the security market line is high as in 1974 and 1978, as shown in Figure 18–14, stocks were attractive relative to bonds. When the security market line slopes upward steeply, the more risky securities are attractive relative to safer securities.

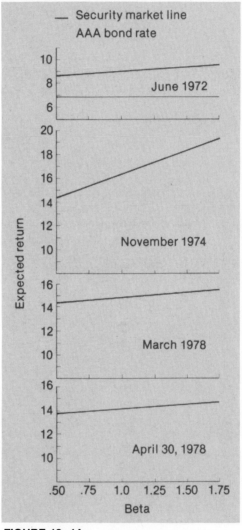

FIGURE 18–14

Source; Forbes, June 12, 1978.

Some Comments on the Wells Fargo Approach

The Wells Fargo approach overcomes the limitations of historic beta by using current information that affects the company and its industry in the estimation of a future beta for each security. It relies on analysts' estimates of future dividends of the security to find what the implied rate of return is on the current price of the security. The estimated risk and return of 370 securities provides a quantitative picture of the external investment environment. The regression line between expected return and risk, together with the estimated AAA bond yield, provides rational bases for the decision of investment policy and the selection of individual securities.

So long as the estimates of future dividends of securities are fairly good and consistent with one another, the end result should be satisfactory, and quite possibly outstanding.

Along the same line of reasoning as Wells Fargo, Frankfurter and Phillips have suggested an approach on how to integrate the application of modern portfolio theory and security analysis.[19]

SUMMARY

The expected return of a portfolio is the weighted-average of the expected returns of individual securities in the portfolio. The expected risk of a portfolio, on the other hand, is determined by three factors:

1. The expected risk of each security in the portfolio.
2. The correlation between each pair of securities in the portfolio.
3. The proportion of each security represented in the portfolio.

The general formula for portfolio risk is:

$$\sigma_p = \sqrt{\sum_{i=1}^{N} X_i^2 \sigma_i^2 + 2 \sum_{i=1}^{N-1} \sum_{j=i+1}^{N} X_i X_j P_{ij} \sigma_i \sigma_j}$$

where X, σ, and P_{ij} represent the proportion of each security, the standard deviation of the returns of each security, and the coefficient of correlation between each pair of securities, respectively.

To reduce portfolio risk, investors should look for securities with low standard deviations and low coefficients of correlation between securities in the portfolio. If possible, the investor should include some securities with negative coefficients of correlation with other securities in the portfolio.

[19] George M. Frankfurter and Herbert E. Phillips, "MPT plus security analysis for better performance," *The Journal of Portfolio Management,* Summer 1982.

Assuming that investors are averse to risk, the efficient portfolios are the portfolios that provide the highest return at a given level of risk, or alternatively the minimum risk at a given level of return.

Individual investors differ in attitudes toward risk and return. The risk-return tradeoff of an investor can be expressed by indifference schedule or curves in a graph.

The efficient portfolios represent the best portfolios available at the time, whereas the map of indifference curves of an investor represents subjective attitudes toward the tradeoff between risk and return.

Represented graphically, the optimum portfolio for a given investor is shown by the portfolio for which the indifference curve is tangent to the efficient frontier (the curve linking up the efficient portfolios).

The theory of efficient portfolios and portfolio diversification was developed by Markowitz. The application of his brilliant theory requires, however, an enormous amount of calculations. If we assume that returns of individual securities are related to one another because of a common market influence, the mathematical calculation required can be substantially reduced. Professor Sharpe developed a simplified model on that assumption, which relates the returns of a security to the returns on a market index. The relationships are expressed by an equation as:

$$R_i = a_i + \beta_i I + c_i$$

where:

R_i = return on security i

a_i = intercept of the regression line

I = returns on market index such as the S&P 500

c_i = a random deviation from the regression line, with an expected value of zero and standard deviation Q_i

The coefficient β — called the "beta" — is the slope of the regression line. The beta measures the sensitivity of the stock's return to the changes in the returns on a market index.

For a given portfolio, using Sharpe's approach we can derive sensitivity of the portfolio (β_p), expected return of the portfolio (E_p), and portfolio risk (σ_p) by the following formulas:

$$\beta_p = \sum_{i=1}^{N} X_i \beta_i$$

$$E_p = \sum X_i a_i + \beta_p I$$

$$\sigma_p = \sqrt{(\beta_p^2 \sigma_I^2) + \sum_{i=1}^{N} X_i^2 Q_i^2}$$

The usefulness of beta as a measure of relative risk or volatility of a security or a portfolio is widely recognized in both the academic and investment communities. However, using beta to predict the returns of an individual stock or a portfolio is a different matter. There is growing doubt on its reliability as a predictor of returns.

QUESTIONS AND PROBLEMS

1. Investor A provided us the following information:

Stocks in Portfolio	Shares Owned	Market Price	Expected Return	Std. Deviation of Returns of Each Stock	Coefficient of Correlation
A	100 sh.	$40	10%	8%	$P_{ab} = .6$
B	200 sh.	30	12%	15%	$P_{ac} = .9$
C	300 sh.	20	20%	25%	$P_{bc} = -.7$

Find (a) expected return of the portfolio and (b) expected risk of the portfolio.

2. What is meant by beta? How do you calculate the beta of a stock? What is the purpose of calculating beta? How does it relate to a portfolio?

3. What is meant by efficient frontier? How do you identify the efficient frontier? According to Markowitz, how do you arrive at an optimum portfolio?

4. An investor has estimated the potentials of a stock as follows:

Possible Return	Probability
−5%	.10
0%	.20
5%	.30
10%	.20
15%	.10
20%	.10

Find (a) expected return, and (b) standard deviation.

5. One investor has three stocks in her portfolio. She invested 20 percent of her funds in stock A, 50 percent in stock B, and 30 percent in stock C. The relationships between the general market and these stocks are as follows:

	Stock A	Stock B	Stock C
Intercept term (a)	2%	−1%	−2%
Slope term (b)	1.1	1.4	2
Residual standard deviation	3%	6%	8%

The expected return for the general market in the next year is estimated to be 10 percent, while the risk is estimated at 7 percent. Find (a) portfolio volatility, (b) portfolio risk, and (c) estimated portfolio return for next year.

6. What are the assumptions underlying beta analysis?
7. What are some of the drawbacks of beta analysis as viewed by critics?
8. How can it be explained that while betas of individual securities do change over time, the beta of a large portfolio seems to be quite stationary over time?
9. Under the assumption that the investor can borrow and lend at the same risk-free interest rate, Professor Sharpe arrived at an efficient frontier different from the efficient frontier in the Markowitz model. Show their differences.
10. The annual rates of return of Company H and the S&P 500 Composite Index in the last ten years were as follows:

Year	Company H	S&P 500
1	−15%	− 8.5%
2	10	4.0
3	12	14
4	20	15
5	−20	−14
6	−15	−26
7	25	37
8	30	24
9	−10	−7.0
10	3	6.5

Find the following;
a. beta (slope of the regression line)
b. Alpha (intercept of the regression line)
c. Residual standard deviation (nonsystematic risk)
d. Coefficient of correlation
e. Coefficient of determination
   (*Note:* Review materials in Appendix A or use a computer program for simple regression analysis.)
11. The annual rates of return of two stocks, X and Y, in the last eight years were:

Year	Stock X	Stock Y
1	10%	15%
2	15%	10%
3	− 5%	−15%
4	−14%	− 5%
5	25%	15%
6	15%	5%
7	5%	10%
8	− 4%	−10%

Find the following:
a. Standard deviation of returns for stock X and Y
b. Covariance between the two stocks
c. Coefficient of correlation between the two stocks
(*Note:* Review Appendix B.)

12. The expected returns, standard deviations, and the correlations between the returns of four securities are as follows:

Security	Expected Return	Std. Deviation	A	B	C	D
			\multicolumn{4}{c}{*Correlations*}
A	.20	.14	1	.5	.8	.4
B	.14	.18		1	−.6	.8
C	.10	.8			1	.5
D	.07	.6				1

a. Determine the expected return and standard deviation of a portfolio composed of 30 percent security A and 70 percent security B.
b. Determine the expected return and standard deviation of a portfolio composed of 40 percent security C and 60 percent security D.
c. Determine the expected return and standard deviation of a portfolio with equal investments in the four securities.
d. If an investor wants to hold two securities in his portfolio and expects a return of 12 percent with minimum risk, what do you advise him to do?

APPENDIX A: Calculation of Alpha, Beta, and Residual Variance: The Palmer Company

X = S&P 500 annual rate of return n = number of observations
Y = Palmer Co. annual rate of return

Year	X	Y	XY	X^2	Y^2
1	.123	.1564	.0192	.0151	.0244
2	−.100	.1161	−.0116	.0100	.0135
3	.237	.5300	.1256	.0561	.2809
4	.108	.2944	.0318	.0116	.0867
5	−.083	.1277	−.0106	.0069	.0163
6	.028	.3103	.0087	.0008	.0963
7	.142	.5355	.0760	.0202	.2867
8	.173	.6008	.1039	.0299	.3610
9	−.130	.2736	−.0356	.0169	.0748
	$\Sigma X = .498$	$\Sigma Y = 2.9448$	$\Sigma XY = .3074$	$\Sigma X^2 = .1676$	$\Sigma Y^2 = 1.2406$
	$\bar{X} = .0553$	$\bar{Y} = .3272$			

Formulas:

Beta (the slope of the line):

$$b = \frac{n\Sigma XY - (\Sigma X)(\Sigma Y)}{n\Sigma X^2 - (\Sigma X)^2} = \frac{(9)(.3074) - (.498)(2.9448)}{(9)(.1676) - (.248)} = \underline{+1.03}$$

Alpha (the intercept of the line):

$$a = \bar{Y} - b\bar{X} = .3272 - [(1.03)(.0553)] = \underline{+.27}$$

Residual variance (unsystematic risk):

$$e^2 = \frac{\Sigma Y^2 - a\Sigma Y - b\Sigma XY}{n} = \frac{(1.2406) - (.27)(2.9448) - (1.0315)(.3074)}{9} = \underline{.0142}$$

Correlation coefficient (an estimate of the extent to which the rate of return on the stock is correlated to the rate of return on the market):

$$r = \frac{n\Sigma XY - (\Sigma X)(\Sigma Y)}{\sqrt{n\Sigma X^2 - (\Sigma X)^2}\sqrt{n\Sigma Y^2 - (\Sigma Y)^2}} = \frac{(9)(.3074) - [(.498)(2.9448)]}{\sqrt{[(9)(.1676)] - (.248)}\sqrt{[(9)(1.2407)] - (8.672)}}$$

$$= +.73$$

Coefficient of determination (the percentage of variation in the stock's rate of return explained by the variation in the market's rate of return). It is the square of the correlation coefficient:

$$r^2 = (.73)^2 = .53$$

Source: Donald E. Fischer and Ronald J. Jordan, *Security Analysis and Portfolio Management,* 2nd ed., (Englewood Cliffs, N.J.: Prentice-Hall, Inc., 1979), p. 517.

APPENDIX B: Calculation of Standard Deviation of Annual Return σ_i, Covariance σ_{ij} and Coefficient of Correlation P_{ij} Between Returns of Two Companies

Year	1 Annual Rate of Return (R) Co. A	2 Annual Rate of Return (R) Co. B	3 $R - \bar{R}$ Co. A	4 $(R - \bar{R})^2$ Co. A	5 $R - \bar{R}$ Co. B	6 $(R - \bar{R})^2$ Co. B	7 (3×5) $(R_A - \bar{R}_A) \times$ $(R_B - \bar{R}_B)$
1	.07	.04	−.01	.0001	−.02	.0004	.0002
2	.05	0	−.03	.0009	−.06	.0036	.0018
3	.10	.05	.02	.0004	−.01	.0001	−.0002
4	.14	.12	.06	.0036	.06	.0036	.0036
5	.08	.10	0	0	.04	.0016	0
6	.08	.07	0	0	.01	.0001	0
7	.12	.10	.04	.0016	.04	.0016	.0016
8	.15	.10	.07	.0049	.04	.0016	.0028
9	.06	0	−.02	.0004	−.06	.0036	.0012
10	−.05	.02	−.13	.0169	−.04	.0016	.0052
	$\bar{R} = .08$	$\bar{R} = .06$		$\Sigma = .0288$		$\Sigma = .0178$	$\Sigma = .0162$

Standard deviation of returns of Co. A:

$$\sigma_A = \sqrt{\frac{\Sigma(R - \bar{R})^2}{N}} = \sqrt{\frac{.0288}{10}} = \sqrt{.00288} = .054$$

Standard deviation of returns of Co. B:

$$\sigma_B = \sqrt{\frac{\Sigma(R - \bar{R})^2}{N}} = \sqrt{\frac{.0178}{10}} = \sqrt{.00178} = .042$$

Covariance between the returns of the two companies:

$$\sigma_{AB} = \Sigma \frac{1}{N} (R_A - \bar{R}_A)(R_B - \bar{R}_B) = \frac{.0162}{10} = .00162$$

Coefficient of correlation between the returns of the two companies:

$$P_{AB} = \frac{\sigma_{AB}}{\sigma_A \sigma_B} = \frac{.00162}{(.054)(.042)} = \frac{.00162}{.002268} = .71$$

481

REFERENCES

Arnott, Robert D. "What has MPT Wrought: Which Risks Reap Rewards?" *The Journal of Portfolio Management*, Fall 1983.

Blume, Marshall E. "On the Assessment of Risk." *Journal of Finance*, March 1971.

———. "betas and Their Regression Tendencies." *Journal of Finance*, June 1975.

Blustein, Paul. "What's the Big Fuss about Modern Portfolio Theory?" *Forbes*, June 12, 1978.

Bowlin, Oswald D., and Dukes, William P. "The Dual Nature of beta Responsiveness." *The Journal of Portfolio Management*, Winter 1983.

Brealey, Richard A. *An Introduction to Risk and Return from Common Stocks*. Cambridge, Mass.: M.I.T. Press, 1969.

Elton, E. J., and Gruber, M. J., eds. *Security Evaluation and Portfolio Analysis*. Englewood Cliffs, N.J.: Prentice-Hall, 1972.

Elton, E. J., Gruber, M. J., and Urich, T. J. "Are betas Best?" *Journal of Finance*, Dec. 1978.

Fabbozzi, F. J., and Francis, J. C. "Stability Tests for Alphas and betas over Bull and Bear Market Conditions." *Journal of Finance*, Sept. 1977.

Francis, J. C., and Stephen, A. *Portfolio Analysis*. Englewood Cliffs, N.J.: Prentice-Hall, 1971.

Frankfurter, George M., and Phillips, Herbert E. "MPT plus Security Analysis for Better Performance," *The Journal of Portfolio Management*, Summer 1982.

Fouse, W. L., Jahnke, W. W., and Rosenberg, B. "Is beta Phlogiston?" *Financial Analysts Journal*, Jan.–Feb. 1974.

Harrington, Diana. "Whose Beta is Best?" *Financial Analysts Journal*, July–Aug. 1983.

Haugen, Robert A. "Common Stock Quality Ratings and Risk." *Financial Analysts Journal*, March–April 1979.

Hawawini, Gabriel. "Why Beta Shifts as the Return Interval Changes." *Financial Analysts Journal*, May–June 1983.

Jensen, Michael C., ed. *Studies in the Theory of Capital Markets*. New York: Praeger Publishers, 1972.

Levitz, Gerald D. "Market Risk and The Management of Institutional Equity-Portfolios." *Financial Analysts Journal*, Jan.–Feb. 1974.

Levy, Haim. "Measuring Risk and Performance Over Alternative Investment Horizons." *Financial Analysts Journal*, March–April 1984.

Levy, Robert A. "Beta as a Predictor of Return." *Financial Analysts Journal*, Jan.–Feb. 1974.

Livingston, Miles, "Industry Movements of Common Stocks." *Journal of Finance*, June 1977.

Lorie, J. H. and Hamilton, M. T. *The Stock Market, Theories and Evidence*. Homewood, Ill.: R. D. Irwin, 1973.

Markowitz, Harry M. *Portfolio Selection: Efficient Diversification of Investments*. New York: John Wiley & Sons, 1959.

Miller, Edward M. "Risk, Uncertainty, and Difference of Opinion." *Journal of Finance*, Sept. 1977.

Rosenberg, Barr, and Guy, James. "Beta and Investment Fundamentals." *Financial Analysts Journal*, May–June 1976.

————. "Beta and Investment Fundamentals—II." *Financial Analysts Journal,* July–Aug. 1976.

Sarnat, Marshall. "Capital Market Imperfections and the Composition of Optimal Portfolio." *Journal of Finance,* Sept. 1974.

Sharpe, William F. "A Simplified Model for Portfolio Analysis." *Management Science,* Jan. 1963.

————. *Portfolio Theory and Capital Markets.* New York: McGraw-Hill, 1970.

————. *Investments.* Englewood Cliffs, N.J.: Prentice-Hall, 1968, Chapters 5, 6, and 11.

19

The Efficient Market Hypothesis and the Capital Market Theory

In the last twenty-five years, many researchers in the academic and financial community have very carefully examined the question of whether the security market is efficient. By efficiency we mean by and large the following:

1. Historical price and volume information is of no value in forecasting price movements.
2. Investors in general are rational and averse to risk. They are alert and able to distinguish between efficient and inefficient securities.
3. News disseminates quickly among investors of all kinds.
4. Security prices adjust quickly to new information.
5. No special group of investors has monopolistic access to important investment information; no special group of investors has special influence on security prices.
6. Security prices are accurate reflections of their "intrinsic value" because they reflect all available information.

Lorie explained what is meant by an efficient security market in these words:[1]

Efficiency in this context means the ability of the capital markets to function so that prices of securities react rapidly to new information. Such efficiency will produce prices that are "appropriate" in terms of current knowledge, and investors will be less likely to make unwise investments. A corollary is that investors will also be less likely to discover great bargains and thereby earn extraordinary high rates of return.

THREE FORMS OF THE EFFICIENT MARKET HYPOTHESIS

The efficient market hypothesis has three forms: the weak form, the semi-strong form, and the strong form.

[1]James H. Lorie, "Public Policy for American Capital Markets," U.S. Department of the Treasury, 1974, p. 3.

Weak Form

This is the oldest statement of the hypothesis. It is also known as the "random-walk" hypothesis. It holds that the security market is by and large efficient. Security prices are determined by the inflow of news, which enters into the market randomly. A knowledge of past prices would not provide information about future prices and would not enable the investor to earn a rate of return higher than a simple buy-and-hold strategy. The weak form of the efficient market hypothesis is a direct challenge to technical market analysis discussed in Chapter 17.

Semistrong Form

The semistrong form of the efficient market hypothesis requires a high level of market efficiency. It holds that all publicly available information, which comes from such sources as newspapers, company releases, brokerage reports, and investment advisory services, is immediately reflected in market prices. The analysis of publicly available information as done in traditional security analysis and discussed in previous chapters of this text will not provide a higher rate of return than a simple procedure of buy-and-hold for a randomly selected portfolio. The semistrong form of the efficient market hypothesis represents clearly a direct challenge to the traditional security analysis based on publicly available data.

Strong Form

The strong form of the efficient market hypothesis holds that the present market prices of securities reflect all the information that can be known about a company, including privileged information that might be available to corporate insiders, specialists on the exchange, and superior analysts from in-depth studies.

EMPIRICAL EVIDENCE FOR THE EFFICIENT MARKET HYPOTHESIS

Weak Form

Over the last twenty-five years, the findings of numerous studies basically support the weak form of the efficient market hypothesis. Let us cite the findings of a few major studies.

Eugene Fama tested the independence of successive price changes by measuring serial correlations for the thirty stocks in the Dow Jones Industrial Index during a five-year period from 1957 to 1962.[2] Table 19–1 shows the results of his correlation studies. In column 1 are the correlation coefficients

---

[2]Eugene F. Fama, "The Behavior of Stock Market Prices," *Journal of Business*, Jan. 1965.

TABLE 19–1   Correlation Coefficients: Daily Price Changes versus Lagged Price Changes for Each Dow Jones Industrial Company

Stock	\multicolumn{10}{c}{Lag in Days}
	1	2	3	4	5	6	7	8	9	10
Allied Chemical	.02	−.04	.01	−.00	.03	.00	−.02	−.03	−.02	−.01
Alcoa	.12	.04	−.01	.02	−.02	.01	.02	.01	−.00	−.03
American Can	−.09	−.02	.03	−.07	−.02	−.01	.02	.03	−.05	−.04
AT&T	−.04	−.10	.00	.03	.01	−.01	.00	.03	−.01	.01
American Tobacco	.11	−.11	−.06	−.07	.01	−.01	.01	.05	.04	.04
Anaconda	.07	−.06	−.05	−.00	.00	−.04	.01	.02	−.01	−.06
Bethlehem Steel	.01	−.07	.01	.02	−.05	−.10	−.01	.00	−.00	−.02
Chrysler	.01	−.07	−.02	−.01	−.02	.01	.04	.06	−.04	.02
DuPont	.01	−.03	.06	.03	−.00	−.05	.02	.01	−.03	.00
Eastman Kodak	.03	.01	−.03	.01	−.02	.01	.01	.01	.01	.00
General Electric	.01	−.04	−.02	.03	−.00	.00	−.01	.01	−.00	.01
General Foods	.06	−.00	.05	.00	−.02	−.05	−.01	−.01	−.02	−.02
General Motors	−.00	−.06	−.04	−.01	−.04	−.01	.02	.01	−.02	.01
Goodyear	−.12	.02	−.04	.04	−.00	−.00	.04	.01	−.02	.01
Int'l. Harvester	−.02	−.03	−.03	.04	−.05	−.02	−.00	.00	−.05	−.02
Int'l. Nickel	.10	−.03	−.02	.02	.03	.06	−.04	−.01	−.02	.03
Int'l. Paper	.05	−.01	−.06	.05	.05	−.00	−.03	−.02	−.00	−.02
Johns Manville	.01	−.04	−.03	−.02	−.03	−.08	.04	.02	−.04	.03
Owens Illinois	−.02	−.08	−.05	.07	.09	−.04	.01	−.04	.07	−.04
Procter & Gamble	.10	−.01	−.01	.01	−.02	.02	.01	−.01	−.02	−.02
Sears	.10	.03	.03	.03	.01	−.05	−.01	−.01	−.01	−.01
Standard Oil (Cal.)	.03	−.03	−.05	−.03	−.05	−.03	−.01	.07	−.05	−.04
Standard Oil (N.J.)	.01	−.12	.02	.01	−.05	−.02	−.02	−.03	−.07	.08
Swift & Co.	−.00	−.02	−.01	.01	.06	.01	−.04	.01	.01	.00
Texaco	.09	−.05	−.02	−.02	−.02	−.01	.03	.03	−.01	.01
Union Carbide	.11	−.01	.04	.05	−.04	−.03	.00	−.01	−.05	−.04
United Aircraft	.01	−.03	−.02	−.05	−.07	−.05	.05	.04	.02	−.02
U.S. Steel	.04	−.07	.01	.01	.01	−.02	.04	.04	−.02	−.04
Westinghouse	−.03	−.02	−.04	−.00	.00	−.05	−.02	.01	−.01	.01
Woolworth	.03	−.02	.02	.01	.01	−.04	−.01	.00	−.09	−.01
Average	.03	−.04	−.01	.01	−.01	−.02	.00	.01	−.02	−.01

Source: From Fama, "Behavior of Stock Market Prices," *Journal of Business,* Vol. 39, No. 1, January 1965. Reprinted by permission of The University of Chicago Press.

between price changes of successive days for each stock in the DJIA. These coefficients are close to zero. The second column shows the correlation coefficients with a lag of two days. The results are similar. The other columns show correlation coefficients with a lag of three to ten days. The results are all close to zero, suggesting that there was only a negligible degree of relationship between successive price changes with a lag of one to ten days.

Correlation coefficients may be dominated by a few unusual or extreme price changes. In that case, an alternative statistical procedure called a "series of runs" is better. This method focuses on the directional signs of successive price changes to see if runs tend to persist.

Fama again used the same data on stocks in the DJIA. Each daily price change was simply classified as $+$, 0, or $-$, regardless of the amount of change. For example, a series of price changes, such as $+\,+\,-\,-\,-\,+\,+\,0\,-\,-$, constitutes five runs. If price changes tend to persist, the average length of runs will be longer and the number of runs will be less than if the series were random.

In Table 19–2, the first column shows the actual number of continuous runs for each Dow Jones stock. The second column shows the number of

TABLE 19–2   Runs of Consecutive Price Changes in Same Direction: Actual versus Expected for Each Dow Jones Industrial Company

Stock	Daily Changes		4-Day Changes		9-Day Changes		16-Day Changes	
	Ac-tual	Ex-pected	Ac-tual	Ex-pected	Ac-tual	Ex-pected	Ac-tual	Ex-pected
Allied Chemical	683	713	160	162	71	71	39	39
Alcoa	601	671	151	154	61	67	41	39
American Can	730	756	169	172	71	73	48	44
AT&T	657	688	165	156	66	70	34	37
American Tobacco	700	747	178	173	69	73	41	41
Anaconda	635	680	166	160	68	66	36	38
Bethlehem Steel	709	720	163	159	80	72	41	42
Chrysler	927	932	223	222	100	97	54	54
DuPont	672	695	160	162	78	72	43	39
Eastman Kodak	678	679	154	160	70	70	43	40
General Electric	918	956	225	225	101	97	51	52
General Foods	799	825	185	191	81	76	43	41
General Motors	832	868	202	205	83	86	44	47
Goodyear	681	672	151	158	60	65	36	36
Int'l. Harvester	720	713	159	164	84	73	40	38
Int'l. Nickel	704	713	163	164	68	71	34	38
Int'l. Paper	762	826	190	194	80	83	51	47
Johns Manville	685	699	173	160	64	69	39	40
Owens Illinois	713	743	171	169	69	73	36	39
Procter & Gamble	826	859	180	191	66	81	40	43
Sears	700	748	167	173	66	71	40	35
Standard Oil (Cal.)	972	979	237	228	97	99	59	54
Standard Oil (N.J.)	688	704	159	159	69	69	29	37
Swift & Co.	878	878	209	197	85	84	50	48
Texaco	600	654	143	155	57	63	29	36
Union Carbide	595	621	142	151	67	67	36	35
United Aircraft	661	699	172	161	77	68	45	40
U.S. Steel	651	662	162	158	65	70	37	41
Westinghouse	829	826	198	193	87	84	41	46
Woolworth	847	868	193	199	78	81	48	48
Averages	735	760	176	176	75	75	42	42

Source: From Fama, "Behavior of Stock Market Prices," *Journal of Business,* Vol. 39, No. 1, January 1965. Reprinted by permission of the University of Chicago Press.

continuous runs that could be expected with a perfectly random distribution. The data indicate a very slight tendency (760 versus 735) for the one-day runs to persist. As the test is extended for successive runs of four, nine, and sixteen days, the persistence disappears, and on the average the overall results conform closely to a random distribution.

We have examined empirical evidence from two types of statistical analyses: coefficient of correlation and series of runs. Both tests have found that the empirical evidence seemed to fit with random distribution. Now we will discuss the empirical evidence of yet another type of test, called the "filter test."

The filter theory states that if security prices move in trends, but not randomly as followers of the technical approach would argue, mechanical trading strategies may be developed that will obtain rates of return higher than a simple buy-and-hold strategy. A trading strategy based on the Dow theory may be applied in the following manner:

> If the daily closing price of a security moves up at least X%, buy the security until its price moves down at least X% from a subsequent high, at which time simultaneously sell and go short. The short position should be maintained until the price rises at least X% above a subsequent low, at which time cover and buy.

The selection of the size of the filter X will influence the number of transactions, commission costs, and the actual performance of the strategy. If a low percentage is chosen for the filter X, the investor will participate in most of the move, but at the disadvantage of having too many transactions at too high commission costs. On the other hand, if a high value is chosen for the filter X, there will be fewer transactions and lower commission costs, but at the disadvantage that the investor may miss most of the move in security prices.

Eugene Fama and Marshall Blume applied the filter test to each stock in the DJIA over the period from 1957 to 1962. Table 19–3 summarizes the results of the study. The first two columns of the table show the returns of a programmed trading strategy at different sizes of filter X. The third column shows the return of a simple buy-and-hold strategy of a random portfolio. The comparison shows that only when the filter was at its smallest did the programmed strategy prove superior to the buy-and-hold strategy. But this was before commissions. After commissions, the programmed trading strategy at different sizes of the filter all produced returns inferior to the simple buy-and-hold strategy.

Tests of the Semistrong and Strong Forms

Fama, Fisher, Jensen, and Roll conducted a study to find out the speed and accuracy with which the market reacted to the announcement of stock splits

TABLE 19–3 Average Annual Rates of Return Per Stock

Value of x	Return with Trading Strategy	Return with Buy-and-Hold Strategy	Total Transactions with Trading Strategy	Return with Trading Strategy, After Commissions
0.5%	11.5%	10.4%	12,514	−103.6%
1.0	5.5	10.3	8.660	−74.9
2.0	0.2	10.3	4,784	−45.2
3.0	−1.7	10.3	2,994	−30.5
4.0	0.1	10.1	2,013	−19.5
5.0	−1.9	10.0	1,484	−16.6
6.0	1.3	9.7	1,071	−9.4
7.0	0.8	9.6	828	−7.4
8.0	1.7	9.6	653	−5.0
9.0	1.9	9.6	539	−3.6
10.0	3.0	9.3	435	−1.4
12.0	5.3	9.4	289	2.3
14.0	3.9	10.3	224	1.4
16.0	4.2	10.3	172	2.3
18.0	3.6	10.0	139	2.0
20.0	4.3	9.8	110	3.0

Source: R. A. Brealey, *An Introduction to Risk and Return from Common Stocks* (Cambridge, Mass.: M.I.T. Press, 1969). From Fama and Blume, "Filter Rules and Stock Market Trading," *Journal of Business*, January 1966, pp. 226–241.

and anticipated dividend increases.[3] Their study covered the stock splits of 940 stocks listed on the NYSE during the period 1927 to 1959. Their analysis centered on each stock's behavior in the period thirty months before and after the split. Figure 19–1 summarizes the results of the study. From the sharp upward trend of market prices prior to the split, it can be inferred that the market was efficient in anticipating the pending split and subsequent dividend increases.

Ball and Brown conducted a test of the stock market's ability to anticipate changes in annual earnings.[4] They selected a sample of 261 large firms. The actual earnings per share of each company were compared with the earnings per share forecasted. The companies were then classified into two groups:

1. Firms with "increased earnings" relative to the forecast.
2. Firms with "decreased earnings" relative to the forecast.

[3]Eugene F. Fama, Lawrence Fisher, Michael C. Jensen, and Richard Roll, "The Adjustment of Stock Prices to New Information," *International Economic Review*, Feb. 1969.

[4]Ray Ball and Philip Brown, "An Empirical Evaluation of Accounting Income, Number 5," *Journal of Accounting Research*, Autumn 1968.

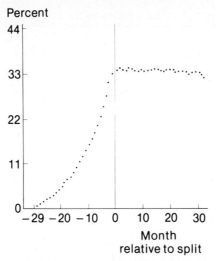

Percent

FIGURE 19–1   Relative Peformance of 940 Stocks over the Period of a Split

Source: Fama, Fisher, Jensen, and Roll, "Adjustment of Stock Prices."

The results of the study are summarized in Figure 19–2. Stock prices of firms with better than expected earnings increased in the twelve months prior to the announcement of annual earnings and plateaued in the following six months. Stock prices of firms with worse than expected earnings declined in the twelve months prior to the announcement of annual earnings and then drifted sideways in the following six months. The study shows that the market was able to anticipate the changes in annual earnings.

Diefenback examined the one-year market performance of stocks previously recommended by the institutional research departments of twenty-four brokerage and advisory firms.[5] The study covered 1209 buy recommendations during the period 1967 to 1969. The performance of each recommendation in the subsequent fifty-two weeks was compared with the Standard & Poor's Industrial Index.

In Table 19–4 we summarize the findings of the study. It was found that about 50 percent of the recommendations did better than the market index, and the other 50 percent did worse than the market index. The mean performance of all the recommendations was −0.3 percent and was only 2.7 percent better than the market index. The findings raised the question of whether the quality of institutional research was any better than the random selection.

[5]Robert E. Diefenback, "How Good Is Institutional Brokerage Research?" *Financial Analysts Journal*, Jan.–Feb. 1972.

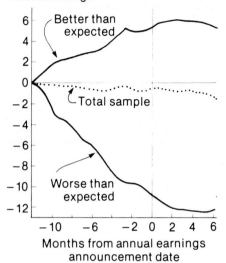

FIGURE 19–2 Stock Market Price Change Attributable to Earnings Announcements

Source: After Ball and Brown, "Empirical Evaluation of Accounting Income."

Friend, Blume, and Crockett analyzed the performance of 136 mutual funds in the period 1960 to 1968.[6] They compared the performance of these funds with hypothetical portfolios randomly selected from stocks listed on the NYSE with betas corresponding closely to each of the funds.

Their results were somewhat mixed. The funds did not match the performance of equally weighted random portfolios. But they did fully match the performance of proportionally weighted random portfolios, and the high-risk funds (high betas) even surpassed the performance of such random portfolios.

EMPIRICAL EVIDENCE AGAINST THE EFFICIENT MARKET HYPOTHESIS

Weak Form

The number of studies whose findings are against the weak form of the efficient market hypothesis are not as many as the studies in support of the efficient market hypothesis. However, we can cite several studies.

---

[6] I. Friend, M. Blume, and J. Crockett, *Mutual Funds and Other Institutional Investors* (New York: McGraw-Hill, 1970).

TABLE 19–4 Fifty-two Week Market Performance of Recommendations of Institutional Research Departments

Broker or Investment Advisor	Number of Buy Recom- mendations	Mean Price Change	Percentage Outperforming S&P's 425 Industrials	Mean Performance Differential from S&P's 425 Industrials
A	12	+24.6%	75%	+25.9%
B	11	+ 6.7	36	+13.8
C	26	+ 1.8	54	+13.7
D	5	− 1.6	60	+11.8
E	12	+ 8.9	50	+11.6
F	288	+10.8	56	+ 9.8
G	49	+ 3.5	51	+ 6.9
H	192	+ 5.8	47	+ 5.9
I	13	+ 0.7	38	+ 5.7
J	91	+ 3.2	48	+ 4.3
K	59	+ 7.2	53	+ 4.0
L	24	− 1.5	50	+ 0.1
M	21	− 8.0	48	− 0.2
N	39	−13.9	46	− 1.6
O	147	−11.1	39	− 4.0
P	67	− 9.6	43	− 4.5
Q	39	−11.4	36	− 4.9
R	33	−10.7	39	− 6.3
S	14	−18.7	21	−11.1
T	23	−21.6	35	−11.7
U	9	−25.5	11	−13.4
V	8	−26.0	0	−19.3
W	9	−29.5	22	−21.3
X	18	−38.8	17	−25.3
Aggregate: All sources .	1,209	− 0.3	47	+ 2.7

Source: From Robert Diefenback, "How Good Is Institutional Brokerage Research?" *Financial Analysts Journal*, Jan.–Feb. 1972.

Julius Shiskin applied the same statistical "series of runs" method as used by Eugene Fama to test whether the changes in security prices are random. For a random series of 120 monthly observations (ten years' data), the average duration of run should be within the range of 1.36 to 1.75 about 95 percent of the time. However, from an examination of the data of 120 months on the S&P 500 stock price index, he found that:[7]

> The average duration of run for stock prices is 2.37, well above the limits for a random series. Since stock prices had a pronounced upward trend from 1948 to 1966, the average duration of run was also computed for the series after the trend was eliminated. It proved to be 2.30, also well above the limits for a random series.

[7]Julius Shiskin, "Systematic Aspects of Stock Price Fluctuations," University of Chicago, *Seminar on the Analysis of Security Prices*, May 1968.

Sidney Alexander applied the filter test to daily closing prices of two indexes, the Dow Jones Industrials from 1897 to 1929 and the Standard & Poor Industrials from 1929 to 1959. In appraising his findings, he concluded:[8]

> Taken altogether the evidence runs strongly against the hypothesis that from 1928 to 1961 the movement of the Standard & Poor's Industrials is consistent with a random walk with drift.

Cheng and Deets tested the independence of successive price changes for the thirty stocks in the DJIA. They compared the portfolio return under the buy-and-hold (B&H) strategy with the portfolio return under a rebalancing (RB) strategy over a thirty-one-year period, 1937 to 1969.

Under the B&H strategy, a fixed portfolio is purchased at the beginning of the period and held until the terminal period. Under the RB strategy, a portfolio is purchased at an initial period and rebalanced at the end of each one-week period. Rebalancing means selling some of those securities that have experienced superior performance and replacing them with securities that have experienced a relatively inferior return. They concluded their study with the following statements:[9]

1. The random-walk theory is not supported by the evidence.
2. The buy-and-hold strategy is overwhelmingly inferior to the rebalancing strategy.
3. There is a tendency for performance to improve as the frequency of rebalancing increases.
4. In summary, the fact that rebalancing yields greater returns than does buy-and-hold indicates security prices are not independent.

Semistrong and Strong Forms

A number of studies provide evidence against the semistrong and strong forms of the efficient market hypothesis. In this section we discuss some of them.

S. Basu compared the performance of low P/E stocks against high P/E stocks over the fifteen-year period, 1956 to 1971.[10] The 750 companies included were ranked according to size of their P/E ratio and were then divided into five P/E groups. Basu found that the low P/E groups performed better than the high P/E groups. These findings raised questions about the efficiency of the market with respect to discounting future returns.

[8]Sidney S. Alexander, "Price Movements in Speculative Markets — Trends or Random Walks, Number 2," *Industrial Management Review,* vol. 5, no. 2, Spring 1964.

[9]Pao L. Cheng and M. King Deets, "Portfolio Returns and the Random-Walk Theory," *Journal of Finance,* March 1971.

[10]S. Basu, "The Investment Performance of Common Stocks in Relation to Their Price Earnings Ratios: A Test of the Efficient Market Hypothesis," *Journal of Finance,* June 1977.

Fisher Black tested the performance of the ranking system of the *Value Line Investment Survey* from 1965 to 1970 to determine if it supported the efficient market hypothesis. *Value Line* ranked each stock under its review from 1 (best) to 5 (poorest) according to its expected performance for the next twelve months. The *Value Line* rankings were based on fundamental analysis of each company, including earnings trend, P/E ratios, and trend in market prices. Having used various statistical techniques to test the historical data from 1965 to 1970, Black concluded that the *Value Line* system of ranking was meaningful. He stated:[11]

> In conclusion, it does appear that there is hope that traditional methods of portfolio management and security analysis can succeed. However, I must continue to maintain that it is a rather small hope. The *Value Line* ranking system is one of only two or three clear examples I have seen that show significant performance over a reasonable period of time.

Henry C. Wallich cited stock price gyration in the 1968 to 1970 period as evidence to question the claim of the efficient market hypothesis that stock prices are efficiently determined in the market. He commented that such extreme gyrations seem to show that these stocks were not correctly valued and that the application of wisdom and good sense could discover this.[12]

Charles Kuehner supported Wallich's contention by citing the gyrations in security prices in the 1971 to 1973 period. Table 19–5 shows the price spread for each stock in the DJIA during 1971–1973.[13] The price spread was calculated by the formula: (Annual High − Low)/Low. If a stock's price ranged from a low of 30 to a high of 40, the price spread would be 33 percent [(40 − 30)/30].

The price spreads in the table range from a minimum of 19 percent (General Motors in 1972) to a maximum of 173 percent (Chrysler in 1973). The average price spread for the thirty stocks was 46 percent in 1971, 38 percent in 1972, and 70 percent in 1973. This raises the question of whether the underlying value of these established securities really did fluctuate as much as shown by the price gyration.

Arbel, Carvell, and Strebel examined market efficiency from a different perspective. Their analysis covered 510 firms over the ten-year period 1971 to 1980. Their results indicate that shares of those firms neglected by institutions outperform significantly the shares of firms widely held by institutions. These firms may offer a premium as a compensation for information defi-

[11]Fisher Black, *Yes, Virginia, There is Hope: Tests of the Value Line Ranking System,* University of Chicago, Center for Research in Security Prices, May 1971.

[12]Henry C. Wallich, "Traditional vs. Performance Stock Valuation," *Commercial & Financial Chronicle,* Feb. 18, 1971.

[13]Charles D. Kuchner, "Legal Implications of Random Walk Hypothesis," New York University Law School Seminar, Feb. 1974.

**TABLE 19–5   Price Spread: Low to High Dow Jones 30
Industrials (1971–1973)**

	1971	1972	1973
Allied Chemical	48%	29%	72%
Alcoa	94	47	68
American Can	55	36	45
AT&T	32	30	21
American Brands	34	24	51
Anaconda	107	40	70
Bethlehem Steel	51	37	45
Chrysler	36	49	173
DuPont	22	28	40
Eastman Kodak	39	61	47
Esmark	57	31	95
Exxon	23	31	23
General Electric	43	25	38
General Foods	42	54	40
General Motors	24	19	89
Goodyear	29	26	155
Int'l. Harvester	47	51	76
Int'l. Nickel	86	25	40
Int'l. Paper	43	27	73
Johns-Manville	26	52	128
Owens Illinois	62	35	59
Procter & Gamble	45	48	35
Sears Roebuck	41	28	58
Standard Oil of Cal.	28	52	37
Texaco	34	34	73
Union Carbide	30	24	77
United Aircraft	84	71	123
U.S. Steel	44	27	43
Westinghouse	16	43	95
Woolworth (F.W.)	57	56	102

Source: Charles D. Kuehner, at New York University Law School Seminar,
"Legal Implications of Random Walk Hypothesis." in February 1974.

ciencies associated with lack of coverage and/or because pricing inefficiencies
exist as a result of the lack of information.[14]

These neglected firms are primarily companies with small capitalization. Being small, they are unsuitable for institutional investors such as
financial institutions, and they attract relatively little research coverage by
security analysts. The authors suggest that there is a "neglected firm effect"
that may provide rewarding opportunities for individuals and institutions.

EVALUATION OF THE EFFICIENT MARKET HYPOTHESIS

Because the efficient market hypothesis has an important bearing on the
investment policy one adopts, we have cited many studies, both for and

[14]Avner Arbel, Steven Carvell, and Paul Strebel, "Giraffes, Institutions, and Neglected
Firms," *Financial Analysts Journal,* May/June 1983.

against the hypothesis. It may be interesting to note the appraisal of the efficient market hypothesis by a few other authorities.

Malkiel has indicated his own views on the validity of the efficient market hypothesis roughly along the following lines.[15] He prefers a middle road, and is cautious because the random-walk theory rests on several fragile assumptions. He is not comfortable with the claim that market prices are the best estimates of their intrinsic value, because there have been many times in the past when stock prices were swept up in waves of frenzy. News, in his view, does not travel instantaneously, as the random-walk suggests, and he doubts that there will ever be a time in the future when all useful inside information is immediately disclosed. Finally, fast transmission of news is one thing, but there is enormous difficulty in translating known information about stocks into estimates of true value.

In a seminar on the efficient capital market and random-walk hypotheses sponsored by the Financial Analysts Research Foundation, Edmund A. Mennis, a senior investment officer of a large bank, commented on the hypothesis of the efficient market as follows:[16]

1. Information is objective in nature, but the *interpretation* by the recipients is not necessarily uniform. The recipient may have different experience, different investment objectives, and a different time horizon than another investor.
2. The efficient market hypothesis holds that, although there are many independent estimates of a stock's value, the correct price will reflect the mean of estimates. He indicates that he cannot agree with the proposition. In his view, the price of a stock is not set by the estimates of all of those who make estimates but rather by the estimates of buyers and sellers.
3. One of the assumptions of the capital asset pricing model is that invesors are risk-averse and, therefore, should seek to diversify away the specific risk of individual securities. His own observation suggests that investors actually seek to expose themselves to risk where they believe the opportunity exists for higher returns.

To summarize Malkiel's views, while he acknowledges that the security market is by and large reasonably efficient, there are always differences of opinion on the meaning of the "news" and its implication for security prices. Moreover, the price of a security is determined by the estimates of buyers and sellers, and not by the mean of estimates of all investors and analysts.

[15]Burton G. Malkiel, *A Random Walk Down Wall Street* (New York: W. W. Norton & Co., Inc., 1981).

[16]Edmund A. Mennis, "Efficient Capital Markets—A Practitioner's View," the *Proceedings of a Seminar on the Efficient Capital Market and Random Walk Hypotheses*, The Financial Analysts Foundation, Charlottesville, Va., 1975.

In a more recent study, Boldt and Arbit examined the accumulated evidence on the efficient market hypothesis.[17] They contend that the hypothesis has more shortcomings than most academics admit, but at the same time, the hypothesis is more valid than most professional investors choose to believe. Boldt and Arbit state that there are times when information on certain events is too complex to be fully understood, and there can be a lag before the stocks involved are efficiently priced. Given the system under which investment professionals have to operate, consensus prices can be biased by "groupthink." These biases can offer rewarding opportunities to investors who perceive and act upon them. At the same time, professional investors err if they completely ignore the efficient market hypothesis. While the market may not be entirely efficient, there are economic incentives for a considerable degree of efficiency.

Our views are very similar to the views of these investment writers just cited. We set them forth as follows:

1. The security market is efficient in the sense that news transmits quickly, there are many knowledgeable buyers and sellers, and there are no special groups that seem to dominate the market.
2. Security prices reflect their underlying value reasonably well perhaps most of the time. However, at the time of peaks and troughs of business cycles, when extreme sentiment prevails toward certain types of stocks or particular sectors of the economy, security prices become so severely depressed or inflated that they hardly represent their underlying normal value.
3. Transmission of news is one thing. The assessment of news in terms of its real meaning on the outlook of individual companies and industries requires expertise and judgment, which varies among investors.
4. The efficient market hypothesis can be considered as a "rough approximation" of the nature of the security market.

CAPITAL MARKET THEORY

Capital market theory is built on the Markowitz portfolio theory. Capital market theory describes how capital assets are priced in the market if all investors are risk-averse diversifiers (as assumed by Markowitz) and if there are conditions of equilibrium in the security market.

Sharpe was mainly responsible for developing the theory.[18] He made the following assumptions:

[17]Bob Boldt and Hal Arbit, "Efficient Markets and the Professional Investor," *Financial Analysts Journal*, July–August, 1984, pp. 22–34.

[18]W. F. Sharpe, "Capital Asset Prices: A Theory of Market Equilibrium under Conditions of Risk," *Journal of Finance*, Sept. 1964; *Portfolio Theory & Capital Markets* (New York: McGraw-Hill, 1970).

1. All investors are Markowitz's efficient diversifiers who delineate and seek to get on the efficient frontier.
2. Any amount of money can be borrowed or lent at the risk-free interest rate.
3. All investors have the same "one period" time horizon.
4. All investors have the same expectations of future returns and risks of individual securities.
5. Securities are infinitely divisible; fractional shares can be purchased.
6. There are no taxes and transaction costs.
7. Security markets are in equilibrium, that is, there are no pressures for changes in security prices and the holdings of all investors.

The assumptions of the theory are obviously arbitrary and not realistic. However, readers should not immediately discard a theory on the basis of seemingly unrealistic assumptions, because some of the assumptions can later be modified or dropped. Moreover, the worth of a theory depends ultimately on its predictive power. The purpose of capital market theory, according to Sharpe,[19] is to predict the relationships among important variables in equilibrium. Two questions are of particular interest:

1. What will the relationship be between expected return and risk for portfolios?
2. What will the relationship be between expected return and risk for securities?

A related question is: What are the appropriate measures of risk for a portfolio and for a security?

The Capital Market Line

As discussed in the previous chapter, when it is possible to lend and borrow at risk-free interest rates, the Markowitz efficient frontier shown in Figure 19–3 is replaced by a straight line, PZ, which starts at OP (the risk-free interest rate) and is tangent to the EF curve. R is the portfolio when the PZ line touches the EF curve.

Under conditions of equilibrium and the other conditions assumed previously, Professor Sharpe argued that the optimal combination of risky securities must include all securities; moreover, the proportion of each security must equal its proportionate value in the market as a whole.

In Figure 19–4, the vertical axis represents expected return of portfolios, and the horizontal axis represents the risk of portfolios as measured by

---

[19]W. F. Sharpe, *Portfolio Theory & Capital Markets* (New York: McGraw-Hill, 1970), p. 78.

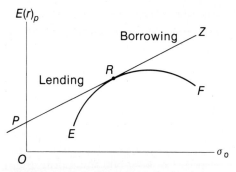

FIGURE 19–3   Efficient Frontier with Lending and Borrowing

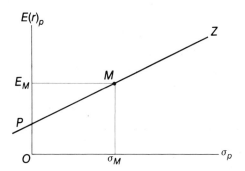

FIGURE 19–4   Capital Market Line

standard deviation of expected return. The portfolio M represents the optimal portfolio or the market portfolio. OP represents the risk-free interest rate. PM represents portfolios of all possible combinations between risk-free assets and the optimal market portfolio M. MZ represents the expected returns and risks of portfolios which are financed partly by borrowing at a risk-free interest rate.

In equilibrium, Sharpe argued, all investors will choose some point along the line PMZ. The PMZ line is called the capital market line. In equilibrium, there will be a linear relationship between risk (measured by standard deviation of expected return) and expected return for *efficient portfolios*. The capital market line can be expressed mathematically by the following equation:

$$E(R)_p = R_f + \frac{E(R)_M - R_f}{\sigma_M} \sigma_p \tag{19.1}$$

where:

$E(R)_p$ = the expected return of an efficient portfolio

$$R_f = \text{risk-free return}$$
$$E(R)_M = \text{the expected return on the market (index)}$$
$$\sigma_p = \text{the standard deviation of return on the efficient portfolio}$$
$$\sigma_M = \text{the standard deviation of return on the market.}$$

The component $(E(R_M) - R_f)/\sigma_M$ is called the *reward-to-variability ratio*. The numerator indicates the reward in excess return for bearing risk. The denominator indicates the risk (uncertainty) borne. For example, if the risk-free interest rate is 5 percent, the market portfolio's return as represented by the Standard & Poor 500 Composite Index is 14 percent and its standard deviation is 18 percent, the reward-to-risk ratio would be:

$$\frac{E(R_M) - R_f}{\sigma_M} = \frac{14\% - 5\%}{18\%} = .5$$

which means the reward in return is .5 percent for each 1 percent of risk assumed.

In empirical work, the actual results over a number of periods are often used to obtain estimates for $E(R_M)$, σ_M, and R_f.

The value of the capital market line, according to Sharpe, lies in the fact that it provides a basis for estimating the future returns of efficient portfolios.

For instance, if we have the following estimates:

$$E(R_M) = 10\% \qquad R_f = 6\%$$
$$\sigma_M = 12\% \qquad \sigma_p = 15\%$$

then the expected return of this portfolio (efficient) will be:

$$E(R_p) = R_f + \frac{E(R_M) - R_f}{\sigma_M}\sigma_p = 6\% + \frac{10\% - 6\%}{12\%} \times 15\%$$
$$= 6\% + 5\% = 11\%$$

In Equation 19.1, the risk of a portfolio is measured by the standard deviation of its rate of return. The relationship implied in the equation does not hold for inefficient portfolios or individual securities. For them, other measures of risk must be used.

The Security Market Line (Also Known as the Capital Asset Pricing Model)

Thus far the analysis has shown that the expected return of efficient portfolios under conditions of equilibrium is a linear function of the portfolio's risk as measured by the standard deviation of its expected return. The next question we consider is: What determines the rate of return of an individual security under conditions of equilibrium?

Sharpe argued that the essence of Markowitz's diversification is to combine securities with either low or negative covariance, or alternatively, securities with low or negative beta. As a result, securities with low or negative beta will be in great demand, causing their prices to rise and their expected returns to be pushed down. On the other hand, securities with high systematic risk (beta) will experience low demand, causing their prices to fall and their expected return to be pushed up. Consequently, under conditions of equilibrium, securities will be priced in the market in such a way that securities with low systematic or market risk will receive low expected return, and securities with high systematic risk will receive relatively high expected return. The relationship is depicted in Figure 19–5 where:

$E(r_i)$ = expected return of securities

OR = risk-free interest rate such as yield on ninety-day Treasury bill

β_i = beta of securities

Under conditions of equilibrium, all securities will tend to locate on the security market line. If security H (Figure 19–5) has a return that is higher for the amount of systematic risk associated with it, then the market will bid up its price until its expected return falls to the equilibrium level at H′. For the same reason, security L, whose return is relatively low compared to its equilibrium level, will be under selling pressure until it falls sufficiently to bring forth a return at equilibrium level L′.

In a nutshell, what Sharpe argues is that under conditions of equilibrium, the expected return of a security does not depend on its total risk,

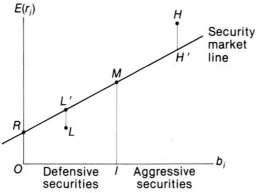

FIGURE 19–5　Security Market Line

but on its systematic risk (beta). The greater the systematic risk a security has, the more is the expected return of the security.

The capital asset pricing model proposed by Sharpe and depicted in Figure 19–5 can be expressed mathematically by the following equation:

$$E(r_i) = R_f + [E(r_M) - R_f]\beta_i \qquad\qquad (19.2)$$

where:

$E(r_i)$ = the expected return of security i

R_f = risk-free interest rate

$E(r_M)$ = the expected return on the market (index)

β_i = beta of security i

The relationship shown in Figure 19–5 and Equation 19.2 holds not only for individual securities, but also for any combination of securities (that is a portfolio)—efficient or inefficient.[20]

Capital Market Line with Some Assumptions Relaxed

The capital market theory discussed above was based on a number of assumptions, some of which are seemingly unrealistic. Now, let us consider the impact on the capital market line if some of the key assumptions were dropped.

Different Lending and Borrowing Rates
In the real world, investors cannot borrow funds at the same rate as the federal government. In margin accounts, they usually pay interest rates of about 2 percent to 3 percent higher than the yield on ninety-day Treasury bills.

In Figure 19–6, if the investor does not borrow, his efficient frontier would be LM, with OL representing the risk-free interest rate. However, if he borrows funds at interest rate OB to leverage his account, his efficient frontier would be MHG. The MH section is not a straight line, but a curve. As a result, the capital market line is now a curve LMHG, if differential lending and borrowing rates are recognized.

Differing Investment Expectations
Investors indeed have different expectations of the future returns and risks of individual securities. That is the basic reason why trading in securities arises.

[20] Ibid., p. 90.

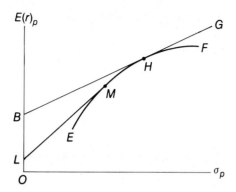

FIGURE 19–6   Efficient Frontier with Different Lending and Borrowing Rates

If we recognize that investors do have different expectations, then the capital market line would be different for different investors. In effect, the capital market line would not be a line, but rather a zone or channel in which the capital market lines of most investors would be situated as shown in Figure 19–7.

If we recognize both different expectations and different lending and borrowing rates, we can visualize a capital market zone, rising at first with higher risk (σ), and later declining due to higher leverage costs. The width of the zone would most likely expand with risk increasing as shown in Figure 19–8.

The other assumptions of capital market theory are not as critical as the two assumptions we have just discussed. Hence, we shall not discuss the impact if we were to relax them.

Empirical Evidence and Capital Market Theory

The usefulness of a theory, as discussed before, ultimately depends on whether it can yield sufficiently accurate predictions. Now let us examine what the theory says in relation to empirical evidence.

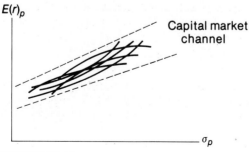

FIGURE 19–7

$E(r)_p$

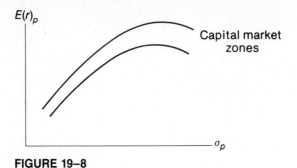

Capital market
zones

σ_p

FIGURE 19–8

The capital market theory has two basic contentions. First, under conditions of equilibrium, the expected return of efficient portfolios will be a linear function of their riskiness as measured by their standard deviation. Second, under conditions of equilibrium, the rate of return on individual assets will be determined by their contribution to the riskiness of portfolios as measured by the beta coefficients of their returns and the returns on the market.

The empirical findings so far are mixed. They seem to confirm some of the implications of the capital market theory, while at the same time reject their other implications. Some of the major findings are summarized in the following:

1. Most studies confirm that the average long-run relationship between risk and return is positive. That is, on the average, investors are compensated in the securities market for bearing systematic risk as measured by the beta of their portfolio. In other words, the higher the portfolio risk (beta), the greater the return they usually receive.

2. The average long-run relationship between return and risk is mostly linear, except for the region of high risk. For example, Shannon Pratt studied the relationship between risk and return of all stocks listed on the NYSE during a thirty-year period from 1929 to 1960. He divided all the stocks into quintiles, designated grades A through E on the basis of the magnitude of the risk factor as measured by the standard deviation of monthly returns during the two preceding periods of three to five years. He stated that:[21]

    In summary, the findings showed that, during the 30 years covered by the study, the average rate of return increased, but at a decelerating rate, with increasing risk, from Grade A to Grade D stocks; with the data for Grade E vs. Grade D inconclusive, based on the arithmetic means, but suggesting a flattening out of the risk-return curve.

[21] Shannon P. Pratt, *Relationship between Risk and Rate of Return for Common Stocks*, Ph.D. dissertation, Indiana University, 1966, p. 135.

The fact that high-risk stocks may not yield more return than low-risk stocks, as found by Pratt and others, not only contradicts a part of the implications of the capital market theory but also is quite puzzling to many students of investments. A common hypothesis is that high-risk stocks resemble lottery tickets. Investors know that their expected value is small or even negative, but they are willing to place the bets (pay higher prices on high-risk stocks than justified by underlying value) because of the lure of the possibility of high winnings.

3. Black, Jensen, and Scholes, in their study of the portfolio returns for various levels of beta during the period 1926 to 1966, found that the capital asset pricing model does not yield an accurate description of the structure of security returns.[22] As shown in Figure 19–9, the actual regression line between returns and systematic risk (beta) for the period 1931 to 1965 had a slope less than predicted by the capital asset pricing model. On the average, the low-risk (low-beta) stocks earned higher returns than the pricing model implies, and high-risk (high-beta) stocks earned lower returns than the theory implies.

4. For the short run of several months or even years, the average long-run relationship between return and risk is much less dependable. As cited in Chapter 18, Fouse, Jahnke, and Rosenberg compiled a study comparing the returns of portfolios with their betas of the previous five years over the period 1956 to 1973. They found that out of eighteen years, the betas performed correctly in eleven years. In two years, 1959 and 1962, the results were mixed. In 1961, 1964, 1966, 1968, and 1972, the results contradicted the predicted pattern; high-beta deciles did less well when they were expected to do better, and vice versa.[23]

One of the implications of the capital market theory is that high-beta stocks in general are expected to do better than the market in bullish years, and worse in bear markets. In a study on the performance of 500 stocks on the NYSE during 1960–1970, Levy compared the performance of each stock to its beta in preceding years. He found that four of the periods support the hypothesis; two periods support an opposite hypothesis; two periods show insignificant performance differences; and one period shows a negatively significant correlation during a flat market.[24]

---

[22] Fisher Black, Michael C. Jensen, and Myron Scholes, "The Capital Asset Pricing Model: Some Empirical Tests," in *Studies in the Theory of Capital Markets*, Michael C. Jensen (ed.), (New York: Praeger Publishers, 1972).

[23] W. L. Fouse, W. W. Jahnke, and B. Rosenberg, "Is beta Phlogiston?" *Financial Analysts Journal*, Jan.–Feb. 1974, p. 71.

[24] Robert A. Levy, "beta Coefficients as Predictors of Return," *Financial Analysts Journal*, Jan.–Feb. 1974.

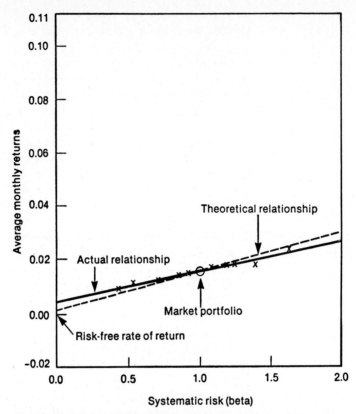

FIGURE 19–9   Average Monthly Returns Versus Systematic Risk (beta) for Ten Different Portfolios and the Market Portfolio, over the Period 1931–1965

Source: Black, Jensen, and Scholes, "The Capital Asset Pricing Model: Some Empirical Tests."

In the same study, Levy compared the performance of ten portfolios with their betas in both advancing and declining markets during 1960–1970. He summarized that

the hypothesis that returns and betas are positively correlated during bull markets, and negatively correlated during bear markets, is confirmed with some reservations. The bear market results are unambiguous. The bull market results, while tending in all three cases to support the hypothesis, are statistically significant in only one.

5. One basic contention of the capital asset pricing theory is that the return of individual securities is determined not by the total risk of the security, but by its contribution to the riskiness of the portfolio. In a portfolio the nonsystematic risk of securities would cancel out,

and only the market risk (betas) of individual securities in the portfolio would be left.

This basic contention was tested by Miller and Scholes,[25] who found that the returns of individual securities were related to both systematic and nonsystematic risks. However, they cautioned that the relationship between return and nonsystematic risk could be partly due to statistical problems rather than to the true nature of capital markets.

Friend, Westerfield, and Granito also looked into the question of whether the returns of individual securities are solely related to their betas. In their study covering a period 1973–1977, they found that the capital asset pricing model did not seem to be able to explain the observed data in their study. The residual standard deviation seems to be at least as important as the beta coefficient in explaining the observed data in their study.[26] This finding corresponds with Miller and Scholes's earlier study and is also in accord with Miles Livingston's findings on industry effects, which were cited in the previous chapter. Together these findings represent a serious challenge to one of the basic propositions of the capital asset pricing model.

6. Since, according to the capital asset pricing theory, returns of individual securities are determined by their market risk (beta), it should follow that investors in general would consider only beta as a measure of risk when they evaluate securities.

Arthur Gooding conducted a study looking into the perceptions of risk by institutional portfolio managers.[27] He found that portfolio managers' average risk perceptions are multidimensional. Company risk, beta, and standard deviation of return, together, describe institutional portfolio managers' risk perceptions extremely well. This finding seems to be inconsistent with the behavior of institutional portfolio managers as assumed in the capital asset pricing model.

Blume and Friend surveyed over 1000 individual stockholders in 1975. When 82 percent of the stockholding families were asked what measures of risk they used in the evaluation of securities, 45 percent stated that they used earnings volatility, 30 percent price volatility, and 17 percent betas.[28] The answers to

[25] Morton H. Miller and Myron Scholes, "Rates of Return in Relation to Risk: A Reexamination of Some Recent Findings," in *Studies in the Theory of Capital Markets*, Michael C. Jensen (ed.), (New York: Praeger Publishers, 1972).

[26] Irwin Friend, Randolph Westerfield and Michael Granito, "New Evidence on the Capital Asset Pricing Model," *The Journal of Finance*, June 1978.

[27] Arthur E. Gooding, "Perceived Risk and Capital Asset Pricing," *The Journal of Finance*, Dec. 1978.

[28] M. Blume and I. Friend, *The Changing Role of the Individual Investor* (New York: John Wiley & Sons, 1978).

other questions in the survey suggested that the majority of investors had little conception of the beta of a security as contributing to the riskiness of a portfolio. This finding seems inconsistent with the theory of capital asset pricing.

7. Another problem in the use of betas is deciding which betas the investor should use. Diana Harrington found that betas provided by different investment services varied greatly for the same stocks.[29] Similar findings were obtained by Gabriel Hawawini, who found that betas calculated using daily returns may differ substantially from betas calculated using monthly returns. These results occurred even if both betas were estimated over the same time period.[30]

ARBITRAGE PRICING THEORY

Because of the problems associated with the Capital Asset Pricing Model, an alternative model has been presented to explain security pricing. This approach, called *Arbitrage Pricing Theory (APT)*, was developed by Stephen Ross.[31] Under APT a security's return can be represented with the following equation:

$$R_i = E_i + a_{i1} V_1 + a_{i2} V_2 + \ldots + a_{in} V_n + u_i \qquad (19.3)$$

where:

R_i = actual rate of return on asset i

E_i = expected rate of return on asset i

a_{ij} = sensitivity of asset i to variable V $(j = 1 \ldots n)$

V_j = a risk factor with a zero mean that affects returns on all securities $(j = 1 \ldots n)$

u_i = unique or particular effects on asset i that can be eliminated through diversification

A major problem with Arbitrage Pricing Theory is that the precise risk factors, the V_js, are not clearly identified in the theoretical framework. Roll and Ross, however, have identified four such factors, which they state are the

[29] Diana Harrington, "Whose Beta Is Best?" *Financial Analysts Journal*, July/August, 1983.

[30] Gabriel Hawawini, "Why Beta Shifts as the Return Interval Changes," *Financial Analysts Journal*, May/June, 1983.

[31] Stephen Ross, "The Arbitrage Theory of Capital Asset Pricing," *Journal of Economic Theory*, December 1976.

primary influences on the stock market.[32] These factors are (1) unanticipated inflation, (2) changes in the expected level of industrial production, (3) unanticipated shifts in risk premiums, and (4) unanticipated movements in the shape of the term structure of interest rates. A number of empirical studies have been performed to test various aspects of APT, and at present there is a continuing debate on the degree of usefulness of the theory.[33]

SUMMARY

Security markets are quite efficient in the sense that news is transmitted quickly, there are many knowledgeable buyers and sellers, and there are no special groups that seem to dominate the market. Security prices reflect their underlying values reasonably well most of the time. However, at times of peaks and troughs of business cycles, extreme sentiment prevails toward certain types of stocks or particular sectors of the economy. At such times, security prices become so severely depressed or inflated that they often may not represent underlying normal value. As a result, the efficient market hypothesis can be considered as a "rough approximation" of the nature of the security market.

Capital market theory was built on Markowitz portfolio theory plus a number of restrictive conditions. The theory provides us with a theoretical framework describing the interrelationships of factors such as the risk-free interest rate, beta of a portfolio, return on the market, and the return of the portfolio under some assumed conditions. Since the real world is substantially different from the assumed conditions, and since the model is concerned with long-run tendencies among the related factors, it is expected that empirical findings would not correspond exactly to what is predicted by the capital asset pricing model. Nonetheless, the theory is useful. It enables investors to derive some approximate estimates of the expected returns of their portfolios if they are sufficiently diversified.

QUESTIONS AND PROBLEMS

1. What is meant by an "efficient securities market"?
2. Describe briefly the three forms of efficient market hypothesis.
3. What is meant by the random-walk hypothesis? Do you agree with it? Why? Why not?

---

[32]See Richard Roll and Stephen Ross, "The Arbitrage Theory Approach to Strategic Portfolio Planning," *Financial Analysts Journal,* May/June 1984.

[33]See P. Dhrymes, I. Friend, and N. Gultekin, "A Critical Reexamination of the Empirical Evidence on the Arbitrage Pricing Theory," *Journal of Finance,* June 1984.

4. What evidence supports the efficient market hypothesis?
5. What kinds of empirical evidence were produced to reject the efficient market hypothesis?
6. How do you characterize the nature of the securities markets? Which of the three forms of efficient market hypothesis do you think is valid? Why?
7. What does the efficient market hypothesis imply with respect to (a) technical market analysis, (b) fundamental analysis, and (c) portfolio policy of investors?
8. What conditions were assumed for the capital market theory?
9. How does the capital market theory measure risks of individual securities and portfolios?
10. Point out the differences between the efficient frontier under capital market theory and under the Markowitz approach.
11. What is meant by the security market line? Explain the rationale behind the security market line.
12. What would the capital market line look like if different investment expectations and different borrowing and lending rates were recognized?
13. Describe a few empirical findings on capital market theory.
14. What is your assessment of the capital market theory?
15. An investor has the following estimates for next year:

Risk-free interest rate	8%
Expected return on market index	12%
beta of his portfolio	1.3

What is the expected return of the portfolio if he applied the equation of the capital market theory? Can the investor be sure of the expected return thus obtained? Why or why not?

REFERENCES

Arbel, Avner, Carvell, Steven, and Strebel, Paul. "Giraffes, Institutions, and Neglected Firms." *Financial Analysts Journal*, May/June 1983.

Basu, S. "The Investing Performance of Common Stocks in Relation to their Price-Earnings Ratios: A Test of the Efficient Market Hypothesis." *Journal of Finance*, June 1977.

Black, F., Jensen, M. C., and Scholes, M. "The Capital Asset Pricing Model: Some Empirical Tests." In *Studies in the Theory of Capital Markets*, Michael C. Jensen, ed. New York: Praeger Publishers, 1972.

Blume, M. E. "On the Assessment of Risk." *Journal of Finance*, March 1971.

Boldt, Bob, and Arbit, Hal. "Efficient Markets and the Professional Investor." *Financial Analysts Journal*, July/August 1984.

Brown, Stewart L. "Earnings Changes, Stock Prices, and Market Efficiency." *Journal of Finance*, March 1978.

Campanella, F. B. *The Measurement of Portfolio Risk Exposure*. Lexington, Mass.: Lexington Books, 1972.

Dhrymes, P., Friend, I., and Gultekin, N. "A Critical Reexamination of the Empirical Evidence on the Arbitrage Pricing Theory." *Journal of Finance*, June 1984.

Friend, I., Westerfield, R., and Granito, M. "New Evidence on the Capital Asset Pricing Model." Papers & Proceedings, *Journal of Finance*, June 1978.

————, Blume, M, and Crockett, J. *Mutual Funds and Other Institutional Investors*. New York: McGraw-Hill, 1970.

Gooding, A. E. "Perceived Risk and Capital Asset Pricing." *Journal of Finance*, Dec. 1978.

Harrington, Diana. "Whose Beta Is Best?" *Financial Analysts Journal*, July/August 1983.

Hawawini, Gabriel. "Why Beta Shifts as the Return Interval Changes." *Financial Analysts Journal*, May/June 1983.

Jensen, Michael C., ed. *Studies in the Theory of Capital Markets*. New York: Praeger Publishers, 1972.

————. *Tests of Capital Market Theory and Implications of the Evidence*. The Financial Analysts Research Foundation, University of Virginia, 1975.

Kuchner, C. D. "Efficient Markets and Random Walk." *Financial Analysts' Handbook*. Homewood, Ill.: Dow Jones-Irwin, 1975.

Levy, R. A. "Beta as a Predictor of Return." *Financial Analysts Journal*, Jan.–Feb. 1974.

Lorie, J. H., Dodd, Peter, and Hamilton, M. T. *The Stock Market: Theories and Evidence*. Homewood, Ill.: R. D. Irwin, 1985.

Malkiel, B. G. *A Random Walk Down Wall Street*. New York: W. W. Norton, 1981.

Modigliani, Franco, and Pogue, G. A. "An Introduction to Risk and Return: Concepts and Evidence." *Financial Analysts Journal*, March–April and May–June 1974.

Pinches, G. E. "The Random Walk Hypothesis and Technical Analysis." *Financial Analysts Journal*, March–April 1970.

Roll, Richard, and Ross, Stephen. "The Arbitrage Theory Approach to Strategic Portfolio Planning." *Financial Analysts Journal*, May/June 1984.

Ross, Stephen. "The Arbitrage Theory of Capital Asset Pricing." *Journal of Economic Theory*, December 1976.

————. "The Current Status of the Capital Asset Pricing Model." *Journal of Finance*, June 1978.

Shanken, Jay. "The Arbitrage Pricing Theory: Is it Testable?" *Journal of Finance*, December 1982.

Sharpe, William F. "Capital Asset Prices: A Theory of Market Equilibrium under Conditions of Risk." *Journal of Finance*, Sept. 1964.

————. *Portfolio Theory & Capital Markets*. New York: McGraw-Hill, 1970.

————. *Investments*. Englewood Cliffs, N.J.: Prentice-Hall, 1985.

20

Evaluation of Portfolio Performance

$\mathbf{T}$o help improve future decision making in investment, investors need to periodically evaluate their own performance and the performance of some institutional investors, such as mutual funds and closed-end investment companies. This is done for purposes of comparison and for investment selection in the future.

The first major effort to specify a system of objective measurements of investment performance was carried out by a group of academicians under the chairmanship of James H. Lorie of the University of Chicago on behalf of the Bank Administration Institute. They worked closely with a group of bankers experienced in investments and in 1968 published their findings and recommendations.[1] Though the report was written for pension funds, its findings are equally applicable to evaluation of all types of portfolios. Accordingly, the major recommendations of their study are summarized as follows:

1. Measurement of performance should be in two dimensions: rate of return and risk.
2. Rates of return should be based on income and on changes in the market value of assets held. To measure the portfolio manager's success in making investment decisions, a time-weighted rate of return should be used. For measuring the overall performance of the portfolio, a dollar-weighted rate of return should be used.[2]
3. Measurement of rates of return and risk should be based on calculations for calendar quarters in order to facilitate interfund comparisons.
4. Although it is not clear what the best method of measuring risk is, the variability of the time-weighted quarterly rate of return method, in general, and the mean-absolute-deviation method, in particular, are recommended until better methods are developed.

[1] James H. Lorie, et al., *Measuring the Investment Performance of Pension Funds for the Purpose of Inter-fund Comparison* (Park Ridge, Ill., Bank Administration Institute, 1968); K. Smith and D. Eiteman, *Essentials of Investing* (Homewood, Ill.: Irwin, 1974), Chapter 21.

[2] Time-weighted and dollar-weighted returns will be explained in following sections of this chapter.

5. For diagnostic purposes, the investment assets of a portfolio should be classified as follows: common stocks and warrants, convertible securities, cash and short-term fixed-income securities, long-term fixed-income securities, assets directed by a trustee and other assets, such as real estate and commodities.

6. The group of portfolios used as the basis for comparisons should be as large as possible.

7. Further research should be conducted, particularly on the concept and measurement of risk.

RATE OF RETURN

The rate of return of a security or portfolio should be based on changes in the market value of securities held plus the value of dividends, interests, and other payments received.

The formula for calculating rate of return is:

$$\text{Rate of return } (R) = \frac{(P_1 - P_0) + I}{P_0}$$

where:

P_1 = value of asset or assets at end of the period

P_0 = value of asset or assets at the beginning of the period

I = income (dividend or interest) received during the period

Suppose that you managed your investment program in securities. You bought $10,000 worth of securities at the beginning of 1987. The value of the portfolio declined to $9,000 a year later, but appreciated to $13,000 two years later. During 1987 you received $500 dividends and during 1988 you received $600 dividends. What was the rate of return in each year and what was the average return during the two years?

	1/1/87	1/1/88	1/1/89
Portfolio worth	$10,000	$9000	$13,000
	$500 (Div.)		$600 (Div.)

The negative rate of return for 1987 was:

$$R = \frac{(\$9000 - \$10,000) + \$500}{\$10,000} = \frac{-\$500}{\$10,000} = -5\%$$

The rate of return for 1988 was:

$$R = \frac{(\$13{,}000 - \$9000) + \$600}{\$9000} = \frac{\$4600}{\$9000} = 51.11\%$$

Two methods are used to calculate the average rate of return. One is the arithmetic average and the other is the geometric average. It is, of course, easier to compute the arithmetic average, but the result is not as accurate as the geometric average, which provides an accurate compound rate of return over the whole period.

For instance, you bought a $100 security two years ago, which appreciated 50 percent to $150 in the first year. But, it declined 50 percent in the second year to $75. What was the average rate of return during the two years?

The arithmetic average gives an answer of 0%:

$$(50\% - 50\%) \div 2 = 0\%$$

Obviously, this is not the correct answer, because the security is worth $75 now compared to an original investment of $100. The correct answer is provided by the geometric average, or time-weighted method:

$$\text{Average rate of return} = \sqrt{\frac{150}{100} \times \frac{75}{150}} - 1 = \sqrt{1.5 \times .5} - 1$$

$$= \sqrt{.75} - 1 = .866 - 1$$

$$= -13.4\%$$

Returning to the example given before, the average rate of return on your portfolio during the two years 1987–1988 was:

$$\begin{aligned}\text{Average rate of} \\ \text{return } 1987\text{--}1988\end{aligned} = \sqrt{\frac{9500}{10{,}000} \times \frac{13{,}600}{9000}} - 1$$

$$= \sqrt{.95 \times 1.511} - 1 = \sqrt{1.43545} - 1$$

$$= 1.198 - 1$$

$$= 19.8\%$$

Time-Weighted versus Dollar-Weighted Rate of Return

Let us assume that you had $50,000 in funds on January 1, 1987, and entrusted them to an investment advisor or bank trust department to invest in securities for you.

	1/1/87	1/1/88	1/1/89
Portfolio's worth, excluding dividends	$50,000	$46,000	$46,200
Dividend received and reinvested		2,500	2,000
Withdrawal		10,000	0
Net worth of portfolio		$38,500	$48,200

As shown in the accompanying table, you withdrew $10,000 on January 1, 1988. Your account received $2,500 in dividends in 1987 and $2,000 in dividends in 1988. The dividend was assumed to be received at each year end and promptly reinvested by your investment advisor. We need to answer two questions:

1. What rate of return did your advisor achieve on the investment?
2. What rate of return did you experience as an investor?

The answer to the two questions should be identical if there were no withdrawal or new deposit of funds. With no withdrawal and no new deposit, the rate of return your advisor has achieved is also your rate of return, excluding management fee. In the current case, the answers to the two questions are not the same.

Let us answer the first question, that is, the performance of your advisor. The method of calculation is the same as in the previous example, and is called the *time-weighted method*.

The performance of the investment advisor was:

$$1987: R = \frac{(\$46,000 - \$50,000) + \$2500}{\$50,000} = \frac{\$-1500}{\$50,000} = -.03 = -3\%$$

$$1988: R = \frac{(\$46,200 - \$38,500) + \$2000}{\$38,500} = \frac{\$9700}{\$38,500} = .252 = 25.2\%$$

The geometric average rate of return for 1987–88 was:

$$\text{Average time-weighted rate of return} = \sqrt{\frac{48,500}{50,000} \times \frac{48,200}{38,500}} - 1$$

$$= \sqrt{.97 \times 1.252} - 1$$

$$= \sqrt{1.21444} - 1$$

$$= .102$$

$$= 10.2\%$$

Dollar-Weighted Return for the Investor

The correct method for calculating the rate of return experienced by the investor is the internal rate of return method, or the *dollar-weighted method*. In this case, your original investment was $50,000, and your benefits included a withdrawal of $10,000 a year later and a portfolio worth $48,200 two years later. So the internal rate of return is calculated as follows:

$$\$50,000 = \frac{\$10,000}{(1 + r)^1} + \frac{\$48,200}{(1 + r)^2}$$

where r stands for the dollar-weighted rate of return or the discount rate at which the future benefits discounted would equal the original investment.

Through trial and error, we found that the r was about 8.7 percent. That was the rate of return you experienced as an investor. The investment advisor, on the other hand, would insist that he achieved an average of 10.2 percent for the two years. You may wonder what could have caused the difference between the two rates, or why you actually experienced a lower rate of return than the rate of return achieved by the advisor.

The reason was, of course, your withdrawal of $10,000 and the bad timing of the withdrawal. The investment advisor achieved a 25.2 percent return in 1988; your withdrawal of $10,000 missed that opportunity. This factor adversely affected the internal rate of return you actually experienced as an investor.

Since the magnitude and timing of withdrawal and new deposits were beyond the control of the investment advisor, his performance should be measured by the time-weighted method, and not the dollar-weighted or the internal rate of return method.

MEASUREMENT OF RISK

The evaluation of the performance of a portfolio must take into account not only the rate of return achieved but also the level of risk the investor was subjected to. It is undesirable or unwise for all investors to subject themselves to the same degree of risk, and therefore not all investors should expect the same rate of return.

The risk of a portfolio can be measured in a number of ways. The Bank Administration Institute study mentioned earlier recommended that the risk of a portfolio be measured by the variability of the quarterly rates of return of the portfolio. They were particularly in favor of using the mean-absolute-deviation method to measure the variability of returns. Sharpe and others held the same view, that portfolio risk should be measured by the variability of its rates of returns. However, they are in favor of using the standard deviation method to measure the variability of returns.

Another way to measure the risk of a portfolio is to use the beta of the portfolio as a measure of risk. The beta of a portfolio can be found by regressing the rates of return of the portfolio on the rates of return on the market index such as the S&P 500 Composite. The slope of the regression line is the beta of the portfolio. The beta of the portfolio measures the systematic risk of the portfolio, and the nonsystematic risks in a well-diversified portfolio are expected mostly to cancel out.

RISK-ADJUSTED RETURN

Since both return and risk are important in the evaluation of a portfolio, we are confronted with the problem of how to combine these two factors into an index for the evaluation of a portfolio.

Sharpe's Approach

Sharpe suggested that an index of performance be calculated in the following manner:[3]

$$\text{Performance Index of Portfolio (P.I.)} = \frac{\overline{R}_p - R_f}{\sigma_p}$$

where:

$\overline{R}_p$ = average rate of return of the portfolio
R_f = riskless rate of interest
σ_p = standard deviation of rates of return of the portfolio

The numerator $(\overline{R}_p - R_f)$ represents excess return (or risk premium) for assuming risk. The denominator (σ_p) measures the degree of risk assumed. The performance index measures excess return per unit of risk. The greater the index, the better is the portfolio's performance.

For example, we will compare the performance of two portfolios with the market portfolio as measured by the S&P 500 Composite. Information about the three portfolios based on records of the past three years is given below.

	$\overline{R}_p$	σ_p	R_f
Portfolio A	14%	18%	5%
Portfolio B	10%	12%	5%
Market portfolio (S&P 500)	12%	10%	5%

[3] William F. Sharpe, "Mutual Fund Performance," *Journal of Business,* Security Prices: A Supplement, Jan. 1966.

The performance indexes for the three portfolios are:

$$\text{P.I. A} = \frac{14\% - 5\%}{18\%} = \frac{9\%}{18\%} = .5$$

$$\text{P.I. B} = \frac{10\% - 5\%}{12\%} = \frac{5\%}{12\%} = .4167$$

$$\text{P.I. Mkt} = \frac{12\% - 5\%}{10\%} = \frac{7\%}{10\%} = .7$$

In terms of rate of return alone, portfolio A was the best. However, on a risk-adjusted return basis, the market index was the best. For each percent of risk assumed, the market index received 0.7 percent excess return, higher than both portfolios A and B.

The comparison of the three portfolios is also shown graphically in Figure 20–1. The performance index of each portfolio is indicated by the slope of the line linking the risk-free interest rate and the point representing the individual portfolio. The market portfolio has the highest slope and, therefore, was the best performer among the three portfolios.

Treynor's Approach

Jack Treynor conceived an index of portfolio performance on the basis of the systematic risk of the portfolio as measured by the beta coefficient of the portfolio. His formula is:[4]

$$\text{Performance Index (P.I.)} = \frac{\overline{R}_p - R_f}{\beta_p}$$

where:

$\overline{R}_p$ = average rate of return of the portfolio
R_f = riskless rate of interest
β_p = beta coefficient of the portfolio

The numerator $(\overline{R}_p - R_f)$ representing excess return is the same as in Sharpe's index. The denominator (β_p) indicates the systematic risk of a portfolio as measured by the beta coefficient between the rates of returns of the portfolio and the market index. In a well-diversified portfolio, the specific risks of individual securities are expected mostly to cancel out, and only the systematic risk is left in the portfolio. Therefore, Treynor suggests that

[4] Jack L. Treynor, "How to Rate Management of Investment Funds," *Harvard Business Review*, Jan.–Feb. 1965.

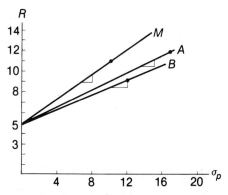

FIGURE 20–1   Return, Risk Premium, and Total Risk of Three Portfolios

the excess return of a portfolio be compared to the systematic risk, rather than the total risk of a portfolio.

Jensen's Approach

Jensen's measure of portfolio performance is based on the capital asset pricing model, which was discussed in Chapter 19.[5] The basic version of the CAPM is expressed by the equation:

$$E(r_p) = R_f + [E(r_M) - R_f]\beta_p \qquad\qquad (20.1)$$

where:

$$E(r_p) = \text{expected return of a portfolio}$$
$$R_f = \text{risk-free interest rate}$$
$$E(r_M) = \text{expected return of a market index}$$
$$\beta_p = \text{beta of a portfolio}$$

This equation expresses *ex ante* relationships. If expectations are realized the equation is empirically valid, and it can be stated in empirical form as:

$$\bar{r}_p = \bar{R}_f + (\bar{R}_M - \bar{R}_F)\beta_p \qquad\qquad (20.2)$$

Jensen's approach to evaluating portfolio performance involves two steps. First, using Equation 20.2, he calculates what the return of a given portfolio should be on the basis of β_p, R_M and R_f. Second, he compares the

---

[5] Michael C. Jensen, "The Performance of Mutual Funds in the Period 1945–1964," *Journal of Finance*, May 1968.

actual realized return of the portfolio with the calculated or predicted return. The greater the excess of realized return over the calculated return, the better the performance of the portfolio.

For example, assume we are comparing the performance of three port-folios and the market index as represented by the S&P 500 Composite. The actual results of portfolios and the market index in the last three years were as follows:

Portfolio	Return of Portfolio r_p	Portfolio beta β	Risk-free Interest Rate R
1	13%	1.2	5%
2	10%	0.8	5%
3	16%	1.5	5%
Market S&P 500	11%	1.0	5%

The return of the three portfolios on the basis of the CAPM should be:

Portfolio 1　　$5\% + (11\% - 5\%) \times 1.2 = 5\% + 7.2\% = 12.2\%$

Portfolio 2　　$5\% + (11\% - 5\%) \times\ \ .8 = 5\% + 4.8\% = \ \ 9.8\%$

Portfolio 3　　$5\% + (11\% - 5\%) \times 1.5 = 5\% + 9\% \ \ \ = 14\%$

The differences between actual realized returns and the calculated return for the three portfolios are:

Portfolio 1　　$13\% - 12.2\% = 0.8\%$

Portfolio 2　　$10\% - \ \ 9.8\% = 0.2\%$

Portfolio 3　　$16\% - 14\% \ \ \ = 2.0\%$

The risk-adjusted performances of the three portfolios based on Jensen's approach indicate that portfolio 3 was the best, portfolio 1 second-best, and portfolio 2 the worst.

Using Treynor's approach, the performance index of each portfolio would be:

Portfolio 1　　$\dfrac{\overline{R} - \overline{R}_f}{\beta_p} = \dfrac{13\% - 5\%}{1.2} = 6.67$

Portfolio 2　　$= \dfrac{10\% - 5\%}{.8} = 6.25$

Portfolio 3　　$= \dfrac{16\% - 5\%}{1.5} = 7.33$

Treynor's approach indicates the same ranking of the three portfolios as Jensen's approach. The two approaches are related, because they both use beta to represent risk of a portfolio.

Comparison of Sharpe and Treynor Indexes

Both performance indexes are risk-adjusted. The difference between the two lies in the fact that Treynor's index relates excess return to the systematic risk of a portfolio, whereas Sharpe's index relates excess return to total risk of a portfolio.

Sharpe ranked the performance of thirty-four mutual funds for the period 1954–1963 by both his own index and the Treynor index. In Figure 20–2 we show the rankings of these thirty-four funds by both indexes. As can be seen from the chart, both methods produced very similar rankings for the funds. The coefficient of rank correlation between the two methods was 97 percent. Therefore, these two indexes, though differing somewhat conceptually, will in practice yield very similar evaluations of the performance of portfolios.[6]

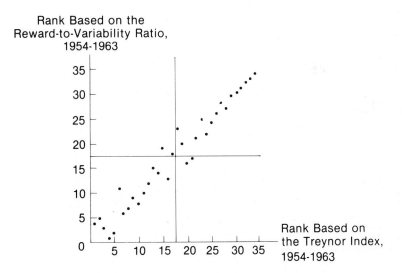

Rank Correlation Coefficient = 0.974

FIGURE 20–2   Ranking of Thirty-Four Mutual Funds by Sharpe's Index versus Treynor's Index

Source: Sharpe, "Mutual Fund Performance."

[6] W. F. Sharpe, "Mutual Fund Performance," *Journal of Business,* Security Prices: A Supplement, Jan. 1966.

EVALUATION OF INVESTMENT PERFORMANCE OF MUTUAL FUNDS

Among the institutional investors—which include mutual funds, closed-end investment companies, pension funds, investment advisors, bank-administered trust funds, life insurance and casualty insurance companies, and endowment funds—the performance data most available for public examination are for mutual funds, because they are legally obligated to reveal fully their operating results.

A number of studies have been conducted on the performance of the mutual funds. One such comprehensive study was prepared by Irwin Friend, Marshall Blume, and Jean Crockett. Their report, "Mutual Funds and Other Institutional Investors, A New Perspective," was published in 1970. The important findings of their study are summarized in the following:

1. The overall annual rates of return on investment of 136 funds covered by the study averaged 10.7 percent for the period from January 1960 through June 1968.

2. For the same period, hypothetical portfolios investing equal amounts in randomly selected stocks on the NYSE would produce an average annual return of 12.4 percent.

3. For the same period, hypothetical portfolios investing weighted amounts (weighted in proportion to the value of stocks outstanding), in randomly selected stocks on the NYSE would produce an average annual return of 9.9 percent.

4. Compared with random portfolios of *the same level of risk,* the higher-risk funds clearly outperformed the weighted random portfolios during 1960–1968. The medium-risk funds also came out somewhat ahead, while the low-risk funds did worse compared to the weighted random portfolios.

5. In the view of the three authors, it is fairer to compare hypothetical portfolios on a weighted basis than on an unweighted basis. They feel that an average of the performances of beta-weighted and unweighted random portfolios would probably be an even better basis for comparison with actual results of the funds.

6. When funds were classified by fund size, sales charges, management expenses, portfolio turnover, and investment objectives, no consistent relationship was found between these factors and investment performance properly adjusted for risk.

7. The evidence also shows that the rate of return for no-load funds (no sales charges) with risk held constant was fully as high as for load funds (with sales charges).

8. The findings, indicating the absence of any consistent relationships between the characteristics of mutual funds and their investment performance, suggest that there may not be any consistent re-

lationship between performance for a given fund in different periods of time.

9. The evidence suggests that the funds seem just as likely to invest in a NYSE stock that proves to be overvalued in the light of its later earnings as in an undervalued issue.

10. The overall evidence is mixed. The funds have been no more efficient in their equity investment policy than the stock market generally. The funds have nonetheless served a useful economic function. First, they have provided small investors with a convenient vehicle for spreading risk at a cost that is generally not too high when compared with the alternatives. Second, they have raised the average return realized by small investors when investment alternatives were mostly fixed-interest-bearing assets, like bonds.

In Table 20–1 we provide a statistical summary for the comparison of investment performance of mutual funds and random portfolios for the period January, 1960, to June, 1968. Several points we noted above were based on this table.

Another study was performed by the Securities and Exchange Commission. Using monthly data from 1965 through 1969, a number of findings emerged.[7] First, no-load funds did about as well as load funds before deduction of the load fund commission. After commission costs, the no-load group had superior performance. Second, performance was about the same for large and small funds. Third, the extent of trading by funds, as measured by turnover, was important and had a negative effect on performance. In short, trading activity tended to lower returns after transactions costs.

Evaluation of Investment Performance by Individual Investors

Many individuals manage their own investment program. The techniques and methods of evaluating investment performance discussed in this chapter apply to institutional investors as well as to individual investors. As individuals we all know that one of the ways to improve ourselves is to review the past, to see where we made mistakes, and where we can improve.

As far as investment is concerned, we should review the past results with respect to the following:

1. *Degree of risk assumed.* Was the portfolio properly diversified, or was it underdiversified or overly diversified? Did the investor use margin? If so, was it too much? Many individuals' accounts were

---

[7]U.S. Securities and Exchange Commission, *Institutional Investors Study Report,* 1971.

TABLE 20–1 Comparison of Investment Performances of Mutual Funds and Random Portfolios (January 1960–June 1968)

Comparison of Investment Performances of Mutual Funds and Random Portfolios (January 1960–June 1968)

Risk class (beta coefficient)	Number in sample		Mean beta coefficient		Mean variance		Mean return			
	Mutual funds	Equally weighted random portfolios[a]	Mutual funds	Equally weighted random portfolios[a]	Mutual funds	Equally weighted random portfolios[a]	Mutual funds	Equally weighted random portfolios[a]	Proportionally weighted random portfolios, variant 1[b,d]	Proportionally weighted random portfolios, variant 2[c,d]
Low risk ($\beta = .5-.7$)	28	17	.614	.642	0.000877	0.000872	0.091	0.128	0.116	0.101
Medium risk ($\beta = .7-.9$)	53	59	.786	.800	0.001543	0.001293	0.106	0.131	0.097	0.084
High risk ($\beta = .9-1.1$)	22	60	.992	.992	0.002304	0.001948	0.135	0.137	0.103	0.092

[a] NYSE stocks only, assuming an equal investment as of beginning of period in each stock included. Number in sample and mean beta coefficients within each of the three risk classes are approximately the same for equally weighted and proportionally weighted random portfolios. Mean variance was not computed for proportionally weighted random portfolios.

[b] Variant 1: NYSE stocks only, assuming probability of investment in each stock proportional to amount outstanding as of beginning of period and equal amount invested in each stock included.

[c] Variant 2: NYSE stocks only, assuming equal probability of security inclusion, and amount invested in included stock proportional to amount outstanding as of beginning of period.

[d] Portfolios selected by either variant 1 or 2 would have the same expected return. The differences in the mean returns between these two variants suggest that there is a wide variability in the returns realized by particular random portfolios.

Source: Friend, Blume and Crockett, *Mutual Funds and Other Institutional Investors: A New Perspective (New York: McGraw-Hill Book Company; 1970).*

wiped out because of margin calls and forced sales of securities in previous recessions.

2. *Selection of individual securities.* Did the investor have the ability to select undervalued issues? This can be determined by comparing the percentage gain of the newly purchased issues with the market performance. If the percentage gain exceeds the market index, it shows that the buyer had made good selections. If one had done this consistently, it shows skill in selecting undervalued issues.

3. *Cyclical and market timing.* Did the investor try to adjust the portfolio into aggressive, neutral, or defensive positions on the basis of anticipating the market swings? If so, was the investor successful? On what basis—technical or fundamental factors—did he formulate his anticipations of market swings? What improvements can be made? Or, would it seem that he should better invest his energies elsewhere?

4. *Risk-adjusted return.* The investor should compute (a) annual rates of return on the portfolio, (b) the level of risk assumed in terms of beta of the portfolio or variability of returns, and (c) the risk-adjusted returns. Then, the investor should compare the risk-adjusted returns with those experienced by:
   a. The market index as measured by the S&P 500 Composite.
   b. The average of stock funds and balanced mutual funds.
   c. A few selected no-load mutual funds.

An evaluation of the portfolio performance by the investor along the lines suggested, if done consistently once every year, should reveal weaknesses and strengths, and provide means to improve overall ability in managing the investment program.

SUMMARY

To evaluate the performance of a portfolio properly, one must take into account the risk of the portfolio as well as its rate of return. The rate of return on an investment depends on the income derived from the portfolio and changes in the market value of the securities held. Risk-adjusted rates of return may be calculated using the approaches suggested by William Sharpe, Jack Treynor, or Michael Jensen.

A number of studies on the performance of mutual funds have been performed. Two of the major studies, that of the SEC and the study by Friend, Blume, and Crockett, indicated that no-load funds did about as well as load funds before deduction of the load fund commission. After commission costs the no-load group had superior performance.

QUESTIONS AND PROBLEMS

1. The Bank Administration Institute study recommends that a time-weighted rate of return should be used for measuring the success of the portfolio manager in making investment decisions. Why?

2. Explain how you calculate a dollar-weighted return. What does it measure?

3. Explain the performance index designed by Sharpe.

4. What was the difference between the Sharpe and Treynor indexes of portfolio performance? Which one do you prefer? Why?

5. Why is ranking mutual funds by their rates of return a poor way to evaluate their performance?

6. Name a few essential findings from the Friend, Blume, and Crockett study of the performance of mutual funds.

7. In the evaluation of investment performance by individual investors, what things should they examine and compute?

8. Do you think individuals should buy mutual funds? If so, which types? Why?

9. On January 1, 1986, an investor invested $10,000 in three stocks. The record of performance in the next three years, 1986–1988, was as follows:

	End of 1986	End of 1987	End of 1988
Worth of portfolio	$11,000	$13,500	$13,000

The investor received dividends of $500 in 1986, $600 in 1987, and $650 in 1988. Dividends were not reinvested.

a. Find the rates of return for 1986, 1987, and 1988 respectively.

b. Find the geometric average rate of return for the period 1986–1988.

10. The performance records of the portfolios of three investors are as follows:

	Investor A	Investor B	Investor C
Rate of return of portfolio	18%	14%	10%
Variability of return	12%	5%	6%
Risk-free interest rate	7%	7%	7%

Find whose performance is best and whose performance is worst on a risk-adjusted basis.

11. The average results of these portfolios and the market index in the last three years were as follows:

Portfolio	Return of Portfolio	beta of Portfolio	Risk-free Interest Rate
A	10%	0.8	6%
B	14%	1.2	6%
C	20%	1.5	6%
Mkt Index S&P 500	12%	1	6%

Find the risk-adjusted performance of the three portfolios on the basis of (a) Treynor's approach and (b) Jensen's approach.

REFERENCES

Cottle, Sidney. "The Future of Pension Management." *Financial Analysts Journal*, May–June 1977.

Dietz, Peter, and Kirschman, Jeannette. "Evaluating Portfolio Performance." In *Managing Investment Portfolios*, ed. J. Maginn and D. Tuttle. Boston: Warren, Gorham, & Lamont, 1983.

Forbes, Annual Mutual Fund Survey.

Friend, I., Blume, M., and Crockett, J. *Mutual Funds and Other Institutional Investors*, New York: McGraw-Hill, 1970.

Jensen, Michael C. "The Performance of Mutual Funds in the Period 1945–1964." *Journal of Finance*, May 1968.

Kon, S. J., and Jen, F. C. "Estimation of Time-Varying Systematic Risk and Performance for Mutual Fund Portfolios: An Application of Switching Regression." *Journal of Finance*, May 1978.

Latane, H. A., Tuttle, D. L., and Jones, C. *Security Analysis and Portfolio Management*. New York: Ronald, 1975, Chapter 22.

Lorie, J. H., Dodd, P., and Hamilton, M. T. *The Stock Market: Theories and Evidence*. Homewood, Ill.: R. D. Irwin, 1985.

Lorie, J. H., et al. *Measuring the Investment Performance of Pension Funds*. Park Ridge, Ill.: Bank Administration Institute, 1968.

Mains, Norman. "Risk, The Pricing of Capital Assets and the Evaluation of Investment Portfolios: Comment." *Journal of Business*, July 1977.

Malkiel, B. G. *A Random Walk Down Wall Street*. New York: W. W. Norton, 1981.

Schlarbaum, G. G., Lewellen, W. G. and Lease, R. C. "The Common Stock Portfolio Performance Records of Individual Investors: 1964–70." *Journal of Finance*, May 1978.

Sharpe, W. F. "Mutual Fund Performance." *Journal of Business*, Security Prices: A Supplement, Jan. 1966.

———. *Investments*. Englewood Cliffs, N.J.: Prentice-Hall, 1985.

Treynor, J. L. "How to Rate Management of Investment Funds." *Harvard Business Review*, Jan.–Feb. 1965.

U.S. Securities and Exchange Commission, *Institutional Investors Study Report*, 1971.

21

Investment Decision Making by Individuals

This chapter deals with investment decision making and portfolio management of individual investors. Individual investors are not homogeneous. They differ in personal and financial circumstances, motivation, the degree of risk they are willing to assume, training, experience, and ability to evaluate potential risks and rewards of individual securities. In the following discussions, we classify investors arbitrarily into five broad categories:

1. Passive investors willing to accept minimum risk
2. Passive investors willing to assume moderate risk
3. Active investors willing to assume moderate risk
4. Active investors willing to assume high risk
5. Speculative investors willing to assume very high risk in the quest for exceptional returns

PERSONAL AND FAMILY FINANCIAL PLANNING

Before setting up an investment program, investors need to formulate an overall financial plan for themselves or their families. The financial plan should include a proper amount of insurance. In the case of a young family with one breadwinner and several dependents, it is imperative that the breadwinner have sufficient insurance to cover any emergency. If the family cannot afford all straight-life insurance, it should supplement with a liberal amount of term insurance. The desirability of owning a home should also be considered in the financial plan. If the family's goal is to own a home, then the first priority should be to accumulate sufficient savings for a down payment.

The financial plan should also include an adequate amount of liquid reserve. In a democratic country where individuals enjoy personal freedom, such as the United States, individuals should be prepared to pay a price for the vagaries of business cycles, business failures of employers, and the consequences of mergers and acquisitions. One should be realistic enough to realize that the loss of a job or a layoff can happen to anybody, at any time, due to a general business downturn, or particular failures of the employer-company, or due to elimination of jobs because of merger. It is general knowledge that looking for a job after a layoff during a business slump is usually not productive in the first six months when the economy is going through its recessionary adjustments. In addition, the compensation from unemployment insurance is generally inadequate for one's needs. Because of these uncertainties, each individual or family should consider setting aside at least sufficient reserve funds for the requirements of one year.

After proper allowances are made for insurance coverage, home ownership, and emergency reserve funds, then one can proceed to consider a proper investment program for the additional funds he or she may have.

FACTORS DETERMINING APPROPRIATE INVESTMENT POLICY

The optimum investment policy for a given individual investor depends on many factors. Some of the more important factors are:

1. *Objectives.* Such as safety of principal, dependable income, preservation of purchasing power, long-term growth and capital gain, short-term capital gain, or some combination of the above objectives.
2. *Degree of risk to be assumed.* Is the investor willing to accept fluctuations in the current return on the securities? Is the investor willing to accept a capital loss? To what extent?
3. *Personal characteristics.* Did the investor receive some form of education or training in investment, including self-study? Did he or she have prior experience in investment? Is the investor willing to devote part of his or her spare time in the study of the security market and in the evaluation of individual securities? Is the investor able to make independent judgments or is he or she more likely to follow the crowd?
4. *Assessment of the investment environment and the different investment approaches.* How efficient does the investor think the security market is? Moderately efficient or highly efficient? How useful does the investor deem the discipline of security analysis? Does he or she think technical analysis is useful? Does he or she think one can do better than the average mutual funds in managing one's own investments?

These four factors are somewhat related. High investment objectives usually go with higher risk exposure. High objectives demand some personal characteristics, such as previous training, experience, devoting time to study, and, most of all, the ability to formulate an independent judgment and having the guts to stick to it. To achieve high objectives, the investor has to understand correctly the investment environment and also skillfully execute the investment approach.

Frequently, investors follow high-risk–high-return investment policies without realizing that they are not qualified or suited for that type of agressive approach. The investor may ill afford the possible losses, may lack the training or experience, or both. The investor may have received some training, and may have had some experience, but he or she may be that type of person who is quite emotional and usually follows the crowd. The crowd, buying securities mostly when they are rising fast and selling them when they are declining rapidly, cannot make a return higher than the market, but rather receives a return, most of the time, well below the market.

THE PASSIVE INVESTOR DESIRING MINIMUM RISK EXPOSURE

For different reasons, many investors choose an investment policy with minimum risk exposure. These investors do not want to handle their own investments, and yet they are not satisfied with the returns that a passbook savings account can offer.

For them, the best strategy may be to allocate most of their funds for the purchase of shares in no-load mutual funds or money market funds. Money market funds invest only in short-term monetary instruments, such as Treasury bills, commerical paper, short-term certificates of deposits issued by banks, and bankers' acceptances. Since all these investments are usually of high grade and mature in a few months, there is very little price risk. These funds provide a return approximating the average yield on short-term monetary instruments. If the investor is in need of funds, he can redeem part of his shares anytime without a charge.

The no-load mutual funds employ no salespeople and impose no sales charge, and that is why they are called no-load mutual funds. The investors who are interested in the purchase of no-load funds (liquid asset and other types) should first select the funds and then buy shares directly from the issuers of these funds.

The passive investor desiring minimum risk exposure, besides allocating most of his or her funds to the purchase of no-load liquid assets funds, can invest remaining funds in one or several no-load balanced funds. The balanced funds may provide a return higher than the liquid assets funds in the long run. The balanced funds the investor selects should be the better-known and larger funds that have had a good track record in both up and down markets in the last ten years. (In Chapter 22, Investing in Mutual Funds, we discuss methods of analysis of mutual funds, funds' selection, and funds switch approach.)

THE PASSIVE INVESTOR ASSUMING MODERATE RISK

For the investor who does not want to handle his or her own investments and is willing to assume moderate risk, the best strategy may be to purchase no-load investment funds. However, since the investor is willing to assume moderate risks, the funds should probably be allocated evenly among three types of no-load funds, namely, liquid asset funds, balanced funds (stocks and bonds), and stock funds.

Should the investor feel that he or she has the ability to recognize when stock prices in general are either too high or too low, he or she should do some switching among the three categories of funds. For example, when the general public is very bullish on the stock market, pushing prices higher and higher, and the investor believes that the market is too high at the moment in terms of underlying economic factors, he or she should reduce commitments in stock funds and balanced funds, and buy more of the no-load liquid asset funds. On the other hand, in time of general pessimism and depressed stock prices, the investor should reduce the commitments in liquid asset funds and balanced funds and buy more of the stock funds.

THE ACTIVE INVESTOR ASSUMING MODERATE RISK

The active investor chooses to manage his or her own investment program. In this case, the investor chooses to assume a *moderate* level of risk, which may have two meanings. First, a moderate level of risk may mean that one is prepared to incur some market risk, but at a maximum loss of principal to the extent of, say, not beyond 30 percent. Second, the assumption of a moderate level of risk may mean that one refrains from risky market strategies in selection, timing, and otherwise. To be logical, the investor in this category should probably observe some guidelines to his or her investment program as follows:

1. A portion of funds should be invested in no-load liquid asset funds as reserve.
2. One should maintain a diversified portfolio of six to ten securities. If the investor has more than ten securities in his or her portfolio, he or she may not be able to follow these securities closely.
3. The selection of securities should be based on long-term economic values.
4. The investor should not try to forecast and take advantage of the short swing of the market.
5. One should not use margin. If one does, the margin amount must be less than 25 percent of the amount of one's own funds.

6. The investor should consider using the option market. However, he or she should employ only defensive strategies such as:
   a. Write call options on stocks in the portfolio.
   b. Write options on stocks he or she is willing to purchase now at current market prices.
   c. Employ hedging strategy.
   d. Use part of the dividend and interest income from the portfolio to buy call and put options on individual securities or a market index.
7. The investor should evaluate the general level of stock prices to assess whether they are too high, too low, or about right based on underlying macro- and microeconomic factors. On the basis of this assessment, he or she adjusts the portfolio in terms of liquidity, risk, and potential. However, this adjustment is gradual and infrequent and differs from in-and-out trading.

THE ACTIVE INVESTOR ASSUMING HIGH RISK

This investor chooses to manage his or her own investment program and is willing to assume high risk in the quest for high rewards. To be consistent with these goals, he or she might observe several guidelines as follows:

1. A portion of the funds should be invested in liquid asset funds as reserve.
2. The investor maintains a diversified portfolio of five to seven securities. Because he or she aims for high gains, he or she needs some diversification, but also requires relative concentration on those securities which will, in his or her view, perform best.
3. The investor will most likely use margin for leverage. However, it is not advisable to use margin amounting to more than 50 percent of one's own funds.
4. This investor will likely use the option market. He or she will probably employ both defensive and agressive option strategies.
5. Because of the desire for high gain, this investor is more likely to try to forecast and take advantage of the short swings of the stock market.
6. This investor may also sell short when bearish for certain securities or for the market in general.

This type of high-risk approach to investment is obviously not suitable for most investors. Those who desire to employ this approach probably should possess the following characteristics:

a. Are highly motivated.

    b.   Are knowledgeable about the security market and have many years of experience in investment.

    c.   Have confidence in their ability in trading and judging security values.

    d.   Can afford to lose a substantial amount of their capital.

    e.   Have time to keep close watch on developments in the security markets.

THE SPECULATIVE INVESTOR

In the final category of investors are high-risk speculators. They may at times use 100 percent margin. At times they may use part of their funds in the futures market. They are most likely in-and-out traders. They are aiming for a return of 50 percent or more in a year and are also prepared to lose a substantial portion of their funds if the market should develop against their expectations. They are speculators or may be, more appropriately, gamblers.

To have any hope of success in the long run, they must be knowledgeable in the security markets, possess many years of experience in speculation, have some innate ability as fast-moving traders, and also have some luck. Those whose occupation is in the security markets, such as account executives, analysts, portfolio managers, investment advisors, and brokerage house partners, may have more chance of success than others in following this approach because they have the expertise, the contacts, and the proximity to the market. However, even though they probably do have an advantage over the general public, it does not mean that they have a high degree of success in following this type of approach. There are not many millionaires among those professionals.

Common sense tells us the general public should not follow this approach. Those who follow this approach must be fully aware that the chance of success in the long run is very slim.

REVIEWING THE EXPERIENCE OF EQUITY AND BOND INVESTMENT IN THE LAST THIRTY-FIVE YEARS

Investors in general always want to have some ideas as to what future investment in stocks and bonds will bring. Before we address this question, we need to review the past experience of equity and bond investment.

In Table 21–1 we see the annual total returns on common stocks, long-term corporate bonds, and U.S. Treasury bills compared to the rate of change in the consumer price index from 1950 to 1984. These figures are based on a study prepared by Ibbotson and Sinquefield.[1]

[1]Roger G. Ibbotson and Rex A. Sinquefield, *Stocks, Bonds, Bills and Inflation, 1926–1982* (Charlottesville, Vir.: Financial Analysis Research Foundation, 1983).

TABLE 21–1 Annual Total Returns in Percent on Common Stocks, Long-Term Corporate Bonds, and U.S. Treasury Bills

	Common Stocks	Long-Term Corporate Bonds	U.S. Treasury Bills	Change in Consumer Price Index (%)
1950	31.71	2.12	1.20	5.79
1	24.02	−2.69	1.49	5.87
2	18.37	3.52	1.66	.88
3	−.99	3.41	1.82	.62
4	52.62	5.39	.86	−.50
1950–54 Average	25.15	2.35	1.41	2.53
1955	31.56	.48	1.57	.37
6	6.56	−6.81	2.46	2.86
7	−10.78	8.71	3.14	3.02
8	43.36	−2.22	1.54	1.76
9	11.95	−.97	2.95	1.50
1955–59 Average	16.53	−.16	2.33	1.90
1960	.47	9.07	2.66	1.48
1	26.89	4.82	2.13	.67
2	−8.73	7.95	2.73	1.22
3	22.80	2.19	3.12	1.65
4	16.48	4.77	3.54	1.19
1960–64 Average	11.58	5.76	2.84	1.24
1965	12.45	−.46	3.93	1.92
6	−10.06	.20	4.76	3.35
7	23.98	−4.95	4.21	3.04
8	11.06	2.57	5.21	4.72
9	−8.50	−8.09	6.58	6.11
1965–69 Average	5.79	−2.15	4.94	3.83
1970	4.01	18.37	6.53	5.49
1	14.31	11.01	4.39	3.36
2	18.98	7.26	3.84	3.41
3	−14.66	1.14	6.93	8.80
4	−26.47	−3.06	8.00	12.20
1970–74 Average	−.77	6.94	5.94	6.65
1975	37.20	14.64	5.80	7.01
6	23.84	18.65	5.08	4.81
7	−7.18	1.71	5.12	6.77
8	6.56	−.07	7.18	9.03
9	18.44	−4.18	10.38	13.31
1975–79 Average	15.77	6.15	6.71	8.19
1980	32.42	−2.62	11.24	12.40
1	−4.91	−0.96	14.71	8.94
2	21.41	43.76	10.53	3.87
3	22.30	6.70	8.60	3.90
4	6.20	16.20	9.60	4.00
1980–84 Average	15.48	12.62	10.94	6.62
Average over seven periods	12.79	4.50	5.02	4.42
Average 1965–1985	9.07	5.89	7.13	6.32
Average 1970–1985	10.16	8.57	7.86	7.15

Sources: 1950–82: Roger G. Ibbotson and Rex A. Sinquefield, *Stocks, Bonds, Bills and Inflation, 1926–1982* (Charlottesville, Vir.: Financial Analysis Research Foundation, 1983.) 1983–84: Estimated by authors.

Common stocks had the best returns during the period 1950–54 and lowest performance during 1970–74. The average of the returns in seven five-year periods amounted to 12.79 percent per year, including both dividend and capital appreciation. The average return during the fifteen years, 1970–85, was 10.16 percent. The average rate of inflation as measured by changes in the consumer price index was 4.42 percent for the seven five-year periods, and was 7.15 percent during the fifteen years, 1970–85. So the average returns on common stocks were ahead of inflation by about 3 percent a year during 1970–84. However, the year-to-year variation in returns on common stocks were substantial.

Long-term corporate bonds performed very poorly in two periods: 1955–59 and 1965–69. The average of the returns in seven five-year periods was 4.50 percent per year, lower than the average return on U.S. Treasury bills (5.02 percent) and about the same as the average inflation rate of 4.42 percent as measured by the consumer price index. The average rate of return on bonds in the fifteen years, 1970–85, was higher at 8.57 percent and also was ahead of inflation, which averaged 7.15 percent a year.

Comparing returns on stocks with bonds, stocks were ahead of bonds in six out of seven five-year periods with the exception of 1970–74. In the five years, 1980–84, the average return on stocks was 15.48 percent compared to 12.62 percent on bonds. However, for individual years there was no consistent relationship in returns between stocks and bonds.

Reviewing the experience in the last twenty years, 1965–84, stocks seemed to be vulnerable to recession plus high inflation and high interest rates, as in 1973 and 1974. However, they were not so vulnerable if there was high inflation and high interest rates without business recession, as shown in the returns on common stocks during the last seven years, 1978–84, of either high inflation or high interest rates or both.

Future Returns on Equity and Bond Investment

The future performance of common stocks depends on a number of key economic variables, such as the rate of growth of real GNP, the rate of growth of earnings and dividends, and trends in inflation and interest rates.

Some major problems in the economy are the federal budget deficit, amounting to about 5 percent of GNP, huge and growing deficits in international trade, high nominal and real interest rates relative to European trade partners and Japan, problems in the farming sector, dislocations in the industrial sector, and a declining savings rate. These problems are interrelated. The root problem rests with the continuing huge federal deficit.

What the future returns on common stocks will be in the next five years or so will depend primarily on how soon progress can be made on the deficit problem. Indicators are that both Congress and the present administration are at least realizing the seriousness of the problem and are trying to do something about it.

In December, 1985, Congress passed an important piece of legislation, the Gramm-Rudman Act, which will bind the government to reduce gradually the deficit and have a balanced budget by 1992. This act, if enforced, will reduce future inflation and interest rates which, in turn, can have a favorable impact on future returns on both equity and bond investments.

QUESTIONS AND PROBLEMS

1. Do you think common stocks in general are fairly priced, too high, or too low at the current level of the DJIA?
2. An investor is seeking your help in establishing an investment portfolio. She has $20,000 to invest and is willing to assume moderate risk. How do you advise her in this case?
3. Another investor has $30,000. He is willing to assume moderate risk. He wants to invest all his funds in a stock portfolio. What do you suggest he should buy and in what proportions?
4. Let us assume that you have a rich uncle. As a graduation gift, he is going to give you $10,000 with only one stipulation, that you will not spend the money, but invest it. How will you invest the money?
5. Someone has said that to be successful in investment is really more difficult than in other lines of business. Do you agree with the statement? Why or why not?
6. What determines the optimum investment policy of a given investor? Discuss.
7. What are some of the common errors individual investors make?
8. At the moment, which is more attractive for investment: bonds, stocks, or Treasury bills? Why?
9. In your view, how efficient is the security market? If you have funds for investment, which of the following approaches would you use: (1) modern portfolio theory, (2) security analysis, or (3) technical analysis? Explain.

REFERENCES

Appleman, Mark J. "How to Shake the Habit of Losing." *Exchange*, May 1974.

Arnott, Robert D., and Copeland, William A. "The Business Cycle and Security Selection." *Financial Analysts Journal*, March–April 1985.

Arnott, Robert D., and Von Germeten, James N. "Systematic Asset Allocation." *Financial Analysts Journal*, Nov.–Dec. 1983.

Blustein, Paul. "What Is the Big Fuss about Modern Portfolio Theory?" *Forbes*, June 12, 1978.

Einhorn, Steven G., and Shangquan, Patricia. "Using the Dividend-Discount Model for Asset Allocation." *Financial Analysts Journal*, May–June 1984.

Ellis, Charles D. "The Loser's Game." *Financial Analysts Journal*, July–August 1975.

Forbes, Annual Mutual Fund Survey, August, current year.

Grauer, Robert R. and Hakansson, Nils H. "Returns on Levered, Actively Managed Long-Run Portfolios of Stocks, Bonds and Bills, 1934–1983." *Financial Analysts Journal*, Sept.–Oct. 1985.

Helms, Gary B. "Toward Bridging the Gap." *Financial Analysts Journal*, Jan.–Feb. 1978.

Ibbotson, R. G., and Sinquefield, R. A. *Stocks, Bonds, Bills and Inflation, 1926–1982*. Charlottesville, Vir.: Financial Analysis Research Foundation, 1983.

Lease, R. C., Lewellen, W. G., and Schlarbaum, G. G. "The Individual Investor: Attributes and Attitudes." *The Journal of Finance*, May 1974.

Modigliani, Franco. "A Message for Reagan and Why the Deficit Must be Slashed." *New York Times*, Nov. 3, 1985.

Moffit, Donald. "Ed Miller's New Paper Shows Why Investors in Securities Win by Playing 'Loser's Game.'" *Wall Street Journal*, Jan. 22, 1979.

Peavy, John W., III, and Goodman, David A. "How Inflation, Risk and Corporate Profitability Affect Common Stock Returns." *Financial Analysts Journal*, Sept.–Oct. 1985.

Rosenberg, Barr. "How Active Should Your Portfolio Be?" *Financial Analysts Journal*, Jan.–Feb. 1979.

Sauvain, Harry C. *Investment Management*, 4th ed. Englewood Cliffs, N.J.: Prentice-Hall, 1973.

Schlarbaum, G. G., Lewellan, W. G., and Lease, R. C. "The Common Stock Portfolio Performance Records of Individual Investors, 1964–70." *The Journal of Finance*, May 1978.

Vartan, Vartanig G. "What Ails Portfolios?" *New York Times*, May 9, 1976.

———. "Crowd Psychology and the Stock Market." *New York Times*, Jan. 30, 1977.

VII

Alternative Investments, International Investing, and the Use of the Personal Computer

22

Investing in Mutual Funds

Investing is a business. To succeed in any business requires effort: learning, supervising, managing, and above all, having good judgment. Investing is no different from any other business except that it is probably even more difficult to succeed in, as we discussed in Chapter 21.

Most of us work outside the investment business. Daily pressure on the job leaves us little time to devote to another business. Therefore, for most individuals the most sensible approach in our view is *indirect* rather than *direct* investing. By indirect investing we mean investing in mutual funds, particularly no-load mutual funds.

There are two types of investment companies; the *closed-end* investment company and the *open-end* investment company. The closed-end investment company is like other business corporations. The amount of common equity is fixed. Their common stocks are traded daily in the market. Investors who are interested in them can instruct their brokers to buy them in the market.

The open-end investment company is commonly known as a mutual fund. It is called open-end because the amount of common equity of the company is not fixed. Each day the investment company computes the net asset value per share of stock. The fund offers to buy or sell these shares at the computed net asset value per share. So, the total amount of common equity changes every day.

There are two types of open-end investment companies. *Load funds* employ salespeople to sell their shares. New buyers of shares are usually charged a sales charge of 7 percent to 8 percent, which is deducted from the initial investment. No-load funds do not employ salespeople. Usually, they have advertisements in newspapers like the *Wall Street Journal* and in magazines like *Forbes* and *Barron's*. Investors can buy their shares through the mail. They have no sales charge. Both load and no-load funds charge a management fee from .5 percent to 1.5 percent per year of the net asset value of the company to defray the costs of managing the portfolio.

According to available studies, the load funds as a group over the years have not performed any better than the no-load funds as a group. Therefore, we prefer no-load funds to load funds, which impose a sales charge. Some funds, like the Fidelity Magellan Fund, which has had an outstanding past record but charges a low load (3 percent compared to normal load of 6 percent to 8 percent), can also be considered.

THE ADVANTAGES OF INVESTING IN MUTUAL FUNDS

Investing in mutual funds offers several advantages to the individual investor.

1. *Professional management*. Mutual funds employ professional advisors and researchers to counsel the management of funds in respect to specific issues to be purchased or sold, the time of these transactions, and the proportions of various types of assets to be held in the portfolio at different times. The managers of funds are usually professionals themselves. Both the advisors and the managers monitor the investment markets on a full-time basis.

2. *Diversification*. Individuals usually have a limited amount of funds. By themselves, they cannot hold a properly diversified portfolio. Buying securities on an odd-lot basis (usually less than 100 shares) would incur an odd-lot fee and proportionally higher commissions. Investing in mutual funds provides individuals with wide diversification because mutual funds usually own more than 100 securities of different industries in the portfolio. According to modern portfolio theories and empirical evidence, diversification cuts down risk but not expected return. Therefore, buying mutual funds by individuals represents gaining an important, cost-free advantage. Furthermore, since funds often require low minimum investments, typically $1,000 or less, investors with small amounts of money can assemble a portfolio that includes a variety of different types of funds, so that a single mistake will not spell financial disaster.

3. *Saving time in managing one's portfolio*. One of the requirements of successful direct investing is that the investor devote quite a bit of time to monitoring the markets, keeping abreast of current economic and financial developments, and watching for opportunities to buy or sell, or change the portfolio mix. Investing in mutual funds requires only careful selection of individual funds in the beginning, and from then on the daily management of the investor's funds is shifted to the shoulders of the fund management and advisors.

4. *Other benefits*. No-load mutual funds provide other benefits, such as:
   a. Opportunity to redeem shares at net asset value (announced every day) without paying any commission.
   b. Automatic reinvestment of dividend and capital gain distributions.

    c. Privilages to switch to other types of funds in the family of funds administered by the same management at little or no cost.

    d. Systematic withdrawal plan.

SELECTING NO-LOAD MUTUAL FUNDS

As mentioned above, investing in no-load mutual funds requires careful selection in the *beginning*, and from then on the investor is practically free from the responsibility of managing the funds. We cannot overemphasize the importance of properly selecting the no-load mutual funds. The logical steps in the selection of the funds are these:

1. Know your objectives and select funds with the same objectives.
2. Examine the issues in the portfolio of the funds. They are listed in the prospectus.
3. Measure the rate of return achieved by the fund over a long enough period—five to ten years.
4. Measure the risk level of the fund.
5. Compute an index of return per unit of risk for the fund and compare it to other similar funds.

Know Your Objectives and Match Them with Selected Funds

First, you need to ask yourself: What are my objectives? Do you seek (1) safety and income, or (2) maximum capital appreciation, or (3) long-term growth and future income, or (4) some combination of the three objectives?

Then ask what types of companies you prefer included in the portfolio of the funds—blue chips, large growth companies, small and emerging growth companies, quality medium-sized companies, resource companies, or foreign companies? In addition, do you prefer mutual funds investing all in stocks, all in bonds, or partly in stocks and partly in bonds; or specialized funds such as gold funds, option funds, energy funds, international funds, tax-exempt funds, and so on?

Once you have established clearly your investment objectives and preferences, you can proceed to select either one fund or a group of funds to accomplish your objectives. Investors, if they can afford it, should invest in more than one no-load mutual fund.

The objectives of each fund are clearly stated in its prospectus and annual reports, which the investor can obtain by telephoning and requesting them. The potential investor needs to examine carefully the stated objectives of the fund and the ways they propose to accomplish their objectives. Moreover, the potential investor should take a look at the issues in the portfolio to see whether they fit his or her taste.

Measure the Performance of the Fund

After matching the objectives of the investor with that of the funds, the next step in the selection of no-load mutual funds is to measure the performance of the fund. Table 22–1 is a financial statement of the Fidelity Magellan Fund covering 1974 to 1983.

The performance of the fund for a given year can be computed by the following formula:

$$\text{Rate of return} = \frac{NAV_1 + D + G}{NAV_0} - 1$$

where:

NAV_1 = net asset value per share at the end of the year
NAV_0 = net asset value per share at the beginning of the year
D = dividend distribution
G = capital gain distribution

TABLE 22–1   Magellan Fund, 1974–1983

PER-SHARE DATA
Selected data for a share outstanding throughout each year
(adjusted for a 3 for 1 split paid December 19, 1980)
(See Report of Independent Certified Public Accountants on page 32):

	Years Ended March 31,									
	1983	1982	1981	1980	1979	1978	1977	1976	1975	1974
Investment income	$ .44	$ .61	$ .80	$ .66	$ .36	$ .30	$ .20	$ .18	$ .18	$ .12
Expenses	.11	.23	.30	.22	.18	.13	.09	.08	.08	.09
Investment income—net	.33	.38	.50	.44	.18	.17	.11	.10	.10	.03
Dividends from investment income—net	(.33)	(.58)	(.39)	(.17)	(.16)	(.12)	(.08)	(.09)	(.02)	—
Realized and unrealized gain (loss) on investments—net	15.80	(.02)	14.46	2.17	3.99	1.43	.71	1.88	(.59)	(2.40)
Distributions from net realized gain from security transactions and other capital sources	(1.23)	(9.92)	(.13)	—	—	—	—	—	(.01)*	(1.39)
Net increase (decrease) in net asset value	14.57	(10.14)	14.44	2.44	4.01	1.48	.74	1.89	(.52)	(3.76)
Net asset value:										
Beginning of year	19.68	29.82	15.38	12.94	8.93	7.45	6.71	4.82	5.34	9.10
End of year	$34.25	$19.68	$29.82	$15.38	$12.94	$8.93	$7.45	$6.71	$4.82	$5.34
Ratio of expenses to average net assets	.85%	1.34%	1.23%	1.40%	1.52%	1.60%	1.49%	1.30%	1.68%	1.25%
Ratio of net investment income to average net assets	2.56%	2.39%	2.08%	2.77%	1.49%	2.03%	1.98%	1.68%	2.10%	.45%
Portfolio turnover rate	120%	194%	277%	338%	249%	238%	205%	169%	90%	179%
Shares outstanding at end of year (000 omitted)	23,403	5,896	1,971	2,096	2,358	2,598	2,868	948	1,013	1,138

*Paid from principal

In order to maintain the historical base for the shares of the Fund actually outstanding through June 19, 1981, (the date of the merger with Salem Fund, Inc. described in Note 6 to the financial statements) the information shown in the table above, is presented on the basis of the results of operations of the Fund prior to the merger with Salem Fund, Inc. In management's judgment, the separate Per-Share Data for the Salem Fund, Inc. is not necessary for making an informed investment decision in that such data would provide no meaningful information concerning the operations of Fidelity Magellan Fund, Inc.

Source: Magellan Fund Annual Report, 1984.

For example, the rate of return of the Fidelity Magellan Fund for 1982 was:

$$\text{Rate of return (82)} = \frac{19.68 + .58 + 9.92}{29.82} - 1 = .012 \text{ or } 1.2\%$$

The Fidelity Magellan Fund did not do well in 1982. However, in 1983, it performed exceedingly well. The rate of return for 1983 was:

$$\text{Rate of return (83)} = \frac{34.25 + .33 + 1.23}{19.68} - 1 = .8196 \text{ or } 81.96\%$$

Measure Risk Level of the Fund

The third step in the analysis of a fund is very important — measuring the risk level that the fund has incurred. Good performance in some years followed by bad performance in other years would not do the investor any good. In investment as in competitive sport, what counts is consistency rather than occasional brilliant performance.

So, how do we measure risk of a fund? We measure it by consistency. If you leave money in a bank for a fixed duration, you know what the return will be. There will be no fluctuation, so there is no risk. Risk stems from the fact that you do not know what the rate of return will be. The more variable the past returns of a fund have been, the more likely that the future returns will also be quite variable.

The formula for the computation of risk is suggested as follows:

$$\text{Risk measurement} = \frac{\Sigma // (rr - ARR)}{\text{Number of years}}$$

where:

rr = rate of return of the fund for a given year
ARR = average annual rate of return of the fund
$//$ = the absolute difference between the rate of return of a given year and the average annual rate of return for the whole period
Σ = summation sign

The numerator represents the sum of variations of return from the mean of the period. The whole equation indicates the average annual variation of returns of the fund from the mean of the period. It shows the degree of fluctuation, and, therefore, the risk level of the fund.

In Table 22–2, we use the data of the Fidelity Magellan Fund for illustration.

The first column of Table 22–2 shows the rate of return of the fund for each year. The second column shows the mean annual return for the period 1974–83. The third column shows the deviation of rate of return of each year from the mean return of the period. This column shows the degree of variability of each year's return. The average annual variation measures the risk level of the fund. In the case of the Fidelity Magellan Fund, the risk level was 30.45 percent, which was quite high.

Relating Rate of Return to Risk Level

Finally, we need to relate the rate of return of the fund to the risk level incurred. A relative performance index can be obtained through the use of the following formula:

$$\text{Relative performance index} = \frac{\text{Average annual return}}{\text{Average annual variation}}$$

For example, the relative performance index of the Fidelity Magellan Fund for the period 1974–83 was:

$$\text{Relative performance index} = \frac{28.69\%}{30.45\%} = .94$$

TABLE 22–2 Rate of Return, Mean Return, and Variation of Return from Mean, Fidelity Magellan Fund, 1974–1983

Years	Rate of Return % (1)	Mean Return % (2)	Absolute Difference Between Rate of Return and Mean Return (%) (3) = (1) − (2)
1974	−26.04	28.69	54.73
75	− 9.18	28.69	37.87
76	41.08	28.69	12.39
77	12.22	28.69	16.47
78	21.48	28.69	7.21
79	46.70	28.69	18.01
80	20.17	28.69	8.52
81	97.27	28.69	68.58
82	1.20	28.69	27.49
83	81.96	28.69	53.27
Average annual return, 1974–83 28.69%			
Average annual variation (risk level)			30.45%

This means the fund achieved a .94 percent return for every percentage of risk assumed. The relative performance index, which compares return with risk for the same fund, can also be used for comparison of performance among funds of the same type or of different types. The higher the relative performance index, the better the fund. Therefore, the investor should first decide which type of fund he or she likes to invest in, and then proceed to calculate the relative performance index to determine which fund is best on the basis of risk-adjusted performance in the past.

Risk Measurement by beta of the Portfolio

In modern investment theory, the risk of a security or portfolio is divided into two categories:

1. Market risk or systematic risk
2. Non-market risk or specific risk

The market risk of a security or portfolio relates to overall factors in the economy like trends in general business, corporate profits, inflation, interest rates, and so on. The non-market risk, on the other hand, relates to success or failure of the company and/or its industry.

The market risk of a security can be measured by relating the rates of return on the security to the rate of return on an index such as the Standard & Poor 500. By using regression analysis, we can obtain a beta for the security. If beta is 1.0, that means that the volatility of the returns of the security is the same as that of the overall market index. If beta is more than 1.0, the security is more volatile than the market, whereas if it is less than 1.0, the security is less volatile than the market.

Modern investment theory further indicates that in a large, well-diversified portfolio, most of the non-market risks of individual securities cancel out and what is left is the market risk, indicated by the beta of the portfolio. The beta of the portfolio is simply the weighted average of the beta of individual securities in the portfolio.

If beta is used to measure the risk of the portfolio of a fund, the relative performance index of the fund can be obtained by the following formula:

$$\text{Relative performance index} = \frac{\text{Average annual return}}{\text{beta of the portfolio}}$$

Some studies have revealed that either measure of risk, beta, or variability of returns provides similar numbers on relative performance index. Hence, the investor can use either method to measure the risk of the portfolio of a fund.

STUDIES ON PERFORMANCE OF MUTUAL FUNDS

Shawky studied the performance of 255 mutual funds for the period January, 1973, to December, 1977. This group of funds included sixty-one funds for maximum captial gains, eighty-four for growth, sixty-four balanced funds, and forty-six funds for income. He found that the beta estimates of these four groups of funds were consistent with their declared investment objectives, which means the higher the investment goals the higher were the beta estimates of the funds. The returns on the funds as a whole were found to be about the same as the equally-weighted NYSE returns.[1]

Kon studied the record of performance of thirty-seven mutual funds for the period January, 1960, to June, 1976. The distribution of funds by objectives included four funds for maximum capital gain, ten funds for growth, eleven for growth/income, nine balanced funds, and three funds for income. He reported that

> the empirical results indicate that at the individual fund level there is evidence of significant superior timing ability and performance. However, the multivariate tests were not inconsistent with the efficient markets hypothesis. That is, fund managers as a group have no special information regarding the information of expectation on the returns of the market portfolio.[2]

Chang and Lewellen studied the record of performance of sixty-seven mutual funds for the period January, 1971, to December, 1979. The value-weighted stock index of the Center for Research in Security Prices of the University of Chicago was employed as a representation of the market portfolio of equities. Based on their findings, they concluded that few fund managers appear to have displayed much market-timing skill. Thus the general conclusion of prior studies by other scholars that mutual funds have been unable collectively to outperform a passive investment strategy still seems valid.[3]

SOURCES OF INFORMATION ON MUTUAL FUNDS

Forbes

Forbes rates the mutual funds industry each year on the basis of these variables:

[1] Hany A. Shawky, "An Update on Mutual Funds: Better Grades," *The Journal of Portfolio Management*, Winter 1982.

[2] Stanley J. Kon, "The Market-Timing Performance of Mutual Fund Managers," *The Journal of Business*, July 1983.

[3] Eric C. Chang and Wilber G. Lewellen, "Market Timing and Mutual Fund Investment Performance," *The Journal of Business*, Jan. 1984.

1. Consistency of performance in both up and down markets
2. Average annual total return in the last ten years
3. Rate of return in the last twelve months.

Forbes ranks funds relative to one another. To get a high rating, a fund must perform consistently well in all three up or down markets. In up markets, the top 12.5 percent of all funds get an A+; the next 12.5 percent an A; the next 25 percent, a B; the next 25 percent, a C; and the bottom quartile, a D. In down markets, ratings range from A to F, with a similar distribution.

For purposes of comparison, *Forbes* also provides statistics on average annual return in the last ten years and the rate of return in the last twelve months by all stock funds, and the S & P 500 Stock Index.

Because *Forbes'* ratings are based on consistency of performance and show a separate rating for both up and down markets, their ratings are quite meaningful. We urge our readers to use their ratings for reference in their selection of funds.

A sample page from the 1985 ratings is shown in Table 22–3. At the top of the table one can observe average annual return for the 1976–85 period. The average return for the S & P 500 was 12.5 percent, and the average return for stock funds reviewed by Forbes was 15.2 percent. The return for the most recent twelve months was 30.9 percent for the S & P 500, of which 4.2 percent was income dividends. The *Forbes* composite fund index showed a total return of 22.9 percent, of which 2.7 percent was income from dividends.

The Forbes annual evaluation of mutual funds contains a wealth of information. It provides the performance record and *Forbes* ratings of over 1000 individual funds clasified into load and no-load stock funds, closed-end stock funds, stock funds investing abroad, load and no-load balanced funds, closed-end balanced funds, load and no-load bonds and preferred stock funds, exchange funds, dual-purpose funds, international funds, new funds, money market funds, and municipal bond funds.

Other Surveys of Mutual Funds

In addition to the information from *Forbes,* one can obtain useful information from other sources that review mutual funds. One is the *Individual Investor's Guide to No-Load Mutual Funds*.[4] A sample page is presented in Table 22–4.

The analysis covers performance data of the Mutual Shares Fund for six years from 1978 to 1983. Items in the analysis are briefly explained as follows:

Net investment income	Includes dividend and interest income on a per-share basis.

---

[4] Published by the American Association of Individual Investors, Chicago, Ill.

TABLE 22–3   1985 Fund Ratings

1985 Fund Ratings

Stock funds

Performance in UP —markets—	in DOWN	Fund/distributor	Average annual total return 1976-85	Latest 12 months total return	Latest 12 months return from income dividends	Total assets 6/30/85 (millions)	Total assets % change '85 vs '84	Maximum sales charge	Annual expenses per $100
		Standard & Poor's 500 stock average	12.5%	30.9%	4.2%				
		FORBES stock fund composite	15.2%	22.3%	2.7%				
D	C	Corp Leaders Tr Fund Certificates Ser B/Lexington	12.6%	24.9%	4.8%	$60	21%	†	$0.11
C	D	Country Capital Growth Fund/Country Capital	11.2	30.1	2.2	65	25	7.50%	1.00
C	D	de Vegh Mutual Fund/Alliance	10.3	24.3	2.1	55	7	none	1.13‡
		Dean Witter Developing Growth Secs/Dean Witter	—*	10.9	2.2	175	−2	5.00b	1.83‡
		Dean Witter Dividend Growth Secs/Dean Witter	—*	31.6	3.5	221	339	5.00b	1.24‡
•C	•D	Dean Witter Industry-Valued Secs/Dean Witter	—*	25.6	2.8	41	11	5.00b	1.16‡
		Dean Witter Natural Resource Dev/Dean Witter	—*	6.4	3.2	23	−20	5.00b	1.28‡
		Dean Witter Option Income Trust/Dean Witter	—*	—*	—*	442	—	5.00b	1.88‡
		Dean Witter World Wide Invest/Dean Witter	—*	13.4	2.4	100	−2	5.00b	1.58‡
D	A	Decatur Income Fund/Delaware	15.9	32.6	5.3	774	35	8.50	0.66
C	B	Delaware Fund/Delaware	15.7	36.7	3.6	348	33	8.50	0.78
B	B	Delta Trend Fund/Delaware	16.8	18.8	1.3	87	22	8.50	1.30
		Depositors Fund of Boston/†	11.1	24.1	2.5	53	12	NA	0.79
		Diversification Fund/†	12.4	28.1	2.5	59	11	NA	0.77
		Dividend/Growth-Dividend Series/AIM Mgmt		29.8	3.4	5	35	none	2.00‡
C	C	Dodge & Cox Stock Fund/Dodge & Cox	14.5	30.2	3.8	33	27	none	0.69
C	B	Drexel Burnham Fund/Drexel Burnham	13.9	29.6	4.5	85	22	3.50	1.20
		Drexel Series-Option Income/Drexel Burnham	—*	—*	—*	19	—	5.00b	2.50‡
C	B	Dreyfus Fund/Dreyfus	14.8	28.7	3.8	2,168	29	8.50	0.76
A	C	Dreyfus Growth Opportunity Fund/Dreyfus	16.0	9.1	2.1	417	12	none	1.02
B	B	Dreyfus Leverage Fund/Dreyfus	16.7	33.2	3.0	465	37	8.50	0.99
B	C	Dreyfus Third Century Fund/Dreyfus	16.8	31.0	2.7	177	50	none	1.01
D	C	Eagle Growth Shares/Universal	12.3	16.3	2.1	5	2	8.50	1.38
D	C	Eaton & Howard Stock Fund/Eaton Vance	11.5	35.7	4.4	82	33	7.25	0.89
C	B	Eaton Vance Growth Fund/Eaton Vance	16.3	26.8	1.7	71	23	8.50	0.93
B	B	Eaton Vance Special Equities Fund/Eaton Vance	17.0	18.8	0.3	47	13	7.25	1.04
		Eaton Vance Tax-Managed Trust/Eaton Vance	—*	42.3	none	570	3	8.50	0.91
		Emerging Medical Technology Fund/closed end	—*	—*	—*	9	—	NA	1.85
B	C	Energy Fund/Neuberger	14.1	20.6	4.4	382	10	none	0.88
•B	•D	Engex/closed end	—*	−1.1	none	13	−39	NA	0.94
		Equity Strategies Fund/closed end	—*	12.5	none	7	14	NA	1.66
		EuroPacific Growth Fund/American Funds	—*	12.6	1.0	36	187	8.50	1.80‡
A+	B	Evergreen Fund/Lieber	26.4	29.6	1.5	323	50	none	1.10
•C	•A	Evergreen Total Return Fund/Lieber	—*	38.0	7.2	124	151	none	1.31
		Exchange Fund of Boston/†	13.9	30.2	2.3	55	17	NA	0.82
A	B	Explorer Fund/Vanguard	20.7	6.9	1.2	348	47	†	1.00
A	F	Fairfield Fund/National Secs	13.4	27.1	0.4	52	15	8.50	1.17
		Fairmont Fund/Sachs	—*	35.9	1.0	38	122	none	1.77‡
D	C	Farm Bureau Growth Fund/PFS Management	11.3	22.9	2.9	45	6	none	0.53‡

Total return is for 9/30/76 to 6/30/85. Funds are added to this guide when they exceed $5 million in net assets and deleted when they drop below $2 million. Stock and balanced funds are rated only if in operation since 11/30/80.   *Fund not in operation for full period.   •Fund rated for two periods only; maximum allowable grade A.   †Fund not currently selling new shares.   ‡Fund has 12b-1 plan pending or in force (see story, p. 82)   b: Includes back-end load.   NA: Not applicable or not available.

Table of distributors, showing addresses and phone numbers, begins on p. 150.

Source: ©Forbes, September 16, 1985.

TABLE 22–4 Mutual Shares

(Years Ending 12/31)	Recent Price $52.16	Dividend Yield 3.7%				
	1978	1979	1980	1981	1982	1983
Net Investment Income ($)	.86	1.14	1.84	1.78	2.00	1.40
Dividends from Net Investment Income ($)	.80	1.05	1.93	1.67	2.12	1.37
Net Gains (Losses) on Investments ($)	4.58	12.54	5.92	1.86	3.15	13.51
Distributions from Net Realized Capital Gains ($)	2.35	3.75	4.77	3.63	2.68	4.63
Net Asset Value End of Year ($)	31.95	40.83	41.89	40.23	40.58	49.49
Ratio of Expenses to Net Assets (%)	1.00	.86	.80	.75	.78	.83
Portfolio Turnover Rate (%)	56	75	73	88	78	70
Number of Shares Year End (000 omitted)	1,465	2,188	2,578	3,145	3,789	4,872
Total Assets: End of Year (Millions $)	46.8	89.3	108.0	126.5	153.8	241.1
Annual Rate of Return on Investment (%)	18.1	42.8	19.0	8.7	12.8	36.7

Five-year Appreciation	188.7%	Degree of Diversification	B	Beta	.63	Bull	B	Bear	B

Investment objectives and policy:	Seeks either short- or long-term capital growth. It invests in securities of companies involved in prospective mergers, consolidations, liquidations and reorganizations so long as the value of such invesments does not exceed 50% of total assets.
Year first offered:	1949
Minimum investment:	Initial $1,000 Subsequent None
Approved for sale in:	All states except IA, LA, MS, TX
Investor services:	IRA, Keo, Auto, Withdr
Telephone exchange privilege:	None
Number of stocks held:	159 (12/31/83/)
Portfolio:	(12/31/83) Common stocks 70%, Corporate bonds 9%, Commercial paper 4%, Bonds in reorganization 9%, Preferred stocks 8%. Largest stock holdings: Natural resources 12%, Financial companies 12%.
Dividends paid:	Income June, Dec Capital gains June, Dec

Source: Gerald W. Perritt and L. Kay Shannon, *The Individual Investor's Guide to No-Load Mutual Funds* (Chicago, Ill.: American Association of Individual Investors, 1984), p. 126.

Dividends from net investment income:	Dividend distributions to shareholders of the funds.
Net gains (losses) in investments:	Per share realized and unrealized capital gains.
Distributions from net realized capital gains:	Capital gains distributions to shareholders of the fund.
Net asset value:	Net asset value per share or the share price.
Ratio of expenses to net assets (%):	The sum of administrative expenses and investment advisor fees as a percent of the average net asset value of the fund.
Portfolio turnover rate (%):	The lesser of purchases or sales for the fiscal year divided by monthly average value of securities owned by the fund. One hundred percent means a complete asset turnover.
Annual rate of return:	Same as our previous definition: $(NAV_1 + D + G/NAV_0) - 1$
Five-year appreciation:	Including dividends and capital gains distributions, which are assumed to have been reinvested.
Degree of diversification:	Ranging from A to E, A being a highly diversified and E being a highly concentrated portfolio.
Beta:	Measures the volatility of the returns of the fund relative to the market returns.
Bull:	Reflects performance of the fund in an up market (7/82–11/83), with rankings from A to E.
Bear:	Reflects performance of the fund in a down market (11/80–7/82), with rankings from A to E.

This type of analysis is useful to individual investors in their selection of no-load mutual funds.

Money Magazine

Every six months, *Money Magazine* ranks all mutual funds having assets over $10 million. They publish their rankings in the May and November issues. In the May, 1984, issue, they ranked 458 funds, which were classified into eight categories:

Maximum-capital gain funds

Long-term growth funds
Growth and income fund
Income funds
Gold and precious metals funds
Balanced funds
Corporate bond funds
Municipal bonds funds

For each fund, they provide the following information:

Percent gain or loss in the last twelve months
Percent gain or loss in the last five years
Percent gain or loss in the last ten years
A risk rating from 1 to 5 (1 being the least volatile, 5 being the most
    volatile)
Percentage sales charges (no-load, low-load, or high-load)
Privilege of switching to other funds within the family at no cost
Telephone number of the fund

From the rankings, the investor can prepare a preliminary list of ten to fifteen interesting candidates for investing in no-load or low-load funds. Once the list is completed, the investor can call for prospectuses from these funds. From there, the investor can examine the objectives of the fund, the ways they propose to achieve these objectives, types of issues in the portfolio, variability of past returns, the makeup of current management and investment advisors, and so on.

Money Magazine, therefore, is a very useful source of information on no-load and low-load mutual funds; it should not be overlooked by the investor.

Other Sources of Information

To obtain information on particular no-load mutual funds, the investors should consult the following:

1. *Investment Companies* (yearly and monthly supplements), published by Wiesenberger Services, Inc.
2. *Mutual Funds Almanac* (Yearly and quarterly supplements), published by Hirsch Organization, Inc.
3. Directory and free publications by the No-Load Mutual Fund Association (475 Park Avenue South, New York, N.Y. 10016).
4. *Risk-Adjusted Mutual Fund Performance Review*, published quarterly by Computer Directions Advisors, Inc.
5. *Handbook for No-Load Fund Investors* (annual) (Box 283, Hastings-on-Hudson, N.Y. 10706).

A List of Better-Performing No-Load Stock Funds

In Table 22–5 we selected eighteen better-performing no-load stock funds for the reference of our readers. The funds are selected from *Forbes'* 1984 Mutual Fund Survey (August 27, 1984). They have had to qualify by two standards:

1. In up markets, the fund should have a *Forbes* rating of B or above, and
2. In down markets, the fund should have a *Forbes* rating of C or above.

TABLE 22–5   A Selected List of Better-Performing No-Load Stock Funds

Forbes Performance Rating			*Percent Gain (or Loss) to April 1, 1984*			
Up Markets	*Down Markets*	*Name of Fund*	*5 yrs.*	*10 yrs.*	*Risk Rating*	*Telephone Switch*
B	B	Acorn (312–621–0630)	120.7	435.0	3	yes
A+	C	The Evergreen Fund (914–698–5711)	164.9	830.4	4	yes
A	C	Explorer Fund (800–523–7025)	187.0	355.1	4	no
B	C	Financial Industrial Fund (800–525–9831)	99.1	235.7	3	yes
B	C	Guardian Mutual Fund (800–367–0770)	134.6	328.8	3	yes
B	B	Janus Fund (800–225–2618)	225.5	438.6	3	yes
B	C	Mathers Fund (312–236–8215)	111.4	374.2	4	no
B	A	Mutual Shares (212–908–4047)	173.9	735.7	3	no
B	B	Nicholas Fund (414–272–6133)	183.1	491.7	3	no
A	A	Pennsylvania Mutual Fund (800–221–4268)	165.9	694.8	3	no
B	C	Plitrend Fund (800–231–0808)	93.8	325.7	4	yes
A	C	SAFECO Growth Fund (800–426–6730)	106.6	400.5	3	yes
B	C	Scudder Development Fund (800–225–2470)	128.1	376.7	3	yes
B	C	Stratton Growth Fund (215–542–8025)	99.7	279.1	4	yes
A+	C	20th Century Select Investors (816–531–5575)	234.1	773.3	3	no
A	C	United Services Gold Shares (800–531–5777)	500.3	143.7	5	yes
A	C	The *Value Line* Special Situations (800–223–0818)	149.0	401.6	3	yes
B	A	Windsor Fund (800–523–7025)	158.3	451.5	3	yes

Source: Data from "Mutual Funds 1984," *Forbes*, Aug. 27, 1984; "Special Report on Mutual Funds," *Money Magazine*, May 1984.

The other figures in the table are taken from *Money Magazine*, May, 1984. As mentioned above, *Money Magazine* has a risk-rating system from 1 to 5, with 1 being the least volatile and 5 the most volatile.

In terms of performance in the last five years, aside from the United Services Gold Fund whose performance was caused by the sharp rise in gold price in the last few years, the 20th Century Selected Investors performed best, scoring a gain of 234.1 percent, and the Janus Fund was second, with a gain of 225.5 percent. In terms of performance in the last ten years, the Evergreen Fund was best, scoring a gain of 830.4 percent, and the 20th Century Fund was second, with a gain of 773.3 percent.

Table 22–5 may be useful as a preliminary screening step. Readers can proceed to obtain prospectuses from these funds and then examine their objectives, types of issues in the portfolio, the makeup of current management and advisors, and so on.

SUMMARY

Investing in mutual funds, particularly no-load funds, provides several important advantages to investors. The advantages include professional management, diversification, saving time in managing one's own portfolio.

Since there are hundreds of no-load funds in the marketplace, the investor needs to carefully select the right funds. The logical steps in the selection of funds are these:

1. Know one's objectives and select funds with the same objectives.
2. Examine issues in the portfolio of the funds.
3. Measure the rate of return achieved by the fund over a long enough period—five to ten years.
4. Measure the risk level of the fund.
5. Compute the index of return per unit of risk for the fund and compare it to similar funds.

Several studies indicate that most mutual funds have produced returns in the past comparable to returns on the market index. Yet, there were very few funds that did consistently outperform the market index.

QUESTIONS AND PROBLEMS

1. What is the difference between load fund and no-load fund?
2. How do you measure the risk of a fund?

3. In selecting a mutual fund, which factor is more important: the historical rate of return of the fund, or the consistency of return of the fund? Why?

4. If your objective is to outperform the market index, do you think you can achieve it by investing in mutual funds? Why?

5. If a fund has had good performance in the past few years, do you think that the fund will continue to do well in the next few years? Why or why not?

6. Name a few good sources of information on mutual funds.

7. Can you analyze the results of funds in terms of (a) selection ability and (b) timing ability? How?

8. From materials in the library on mutual funds, select three funds each for the following objectives:
   a. Maximum capital gains
   b. Growth
   c. Income

REFERENCES

Chang, Eric C., and Lewellen, Wilber G. "Market Timing and Mutual Fund Investment Performance." *The Journal of Business*, Jan. 1984.

Kon, Stanley J. "The Market-Timing Performance of Mutual Fund Managers." *The Journal of Business*, July 1983.

Forbes. Annual Review of Mutual Funds.

Money Magazine. Current issue on mutual funds.

Perritt, Gerald W., and Shannon, L. Kay. *The Individual Investors' Guide to No-Load Mutual Funds*. Chicago: American Association of Individual Investors, latest annual edition.

Shawky, Hany A. "An Update on Mutual Funds: Better Grades." *The Journal of Portfolio Management*, Winter 1982.

Wiesenberger Investment Company Service. Latest annual edition.

23

Home Ownership as an Investment and Real Estate Investment Trusts

HOME OWNERSHIP VERSUS RENTING

For most people, the purchase of a home is their largest single investment. In the analysis that follows, we develop a detailed example in which we examine some of the financial aspects of purchasing a home. We consider the problem from the point of view of a homeowner-investor who can either use personal savings to make a down payment on a home, or rent and invest those savings into securities. We then calculate the increase in the investor's wealth from the purchase decision and compare it to the additional accumulated wealth if a decision to rent had instead been made. The objective is to illustrate the type of information needed by the potential home buyer and to show how to process that information in order to determine whether home ownership is preferable to renting.

Dwelling Units Defined

In using the terms *home* or *house* we are referring to either a condominium, a townhouse, or a single-family detached house. The dwelling to be rented will be described as an apartment, but it could also be a house. In comparing the costs of a house and apartment, it will be assumed that the investor receives the same nonmonetary benefits from renting or purchasing the units under consideration. If this were not true, some adjustments would be necessary. For example, the investor may desire the amount of space in a four-bedroom house. This means that a two-bedroom apartment would not be an equally suitable alternative. In cases where the investor is reluctantly willing to live in less favorable accommodations, an estimate of how much he or she would be willing to pay for the lost benefits of the house would have to be estimated. That amount would then be added to the cost of renting.

Fixed-Rate and Variable-Rate Mortgages

Home buyers today may select from a wide range of financing plans. Prior to the 1980s, mortgages generally contained fixed interest rates for terms ranging from fifteen to thirty years. The advantage of a fixed-rate mortgage is that the monthly payment of the borrower for principal and interest is fixed for the term of the mortgage. If interest rates should subsequently rise, the borrower's payment would not be affected. On the other hand, if interest rates drop, the borrower could repay the mortgage loan, sometimes with a prepayment penalty, and refinance at a lower rate. Thus the fixed-rate mortgage offers a combination of safety and flexibility.

In the early 1980s, variable- or adjustable-rate mortgages, ARMs, became very popular. Under these plans, the mortgage is still paid over fifteen to thirty years, but the interest rate periodically changes. Depending on the type of ARM, the interest rate may be adjusted semiannually, annually, or every few years. Whether the rate moves up or down depends on the movements of designated market interest rates. Many ARMs are limited to a maximum increase each year, such as 2 percent, and many also have a cap or ceiling interest rate, which would be the maximum rate the lender can charge at any point over the entire term of the mortgage. Whenever the interest rate is adjusted, the mortgage payments change. Therefore, much of the risk of changes in interest rates is transferred to the borrower. If one obtains an ARM at the wrong time, the monthly payments may rise substantially.

The advantage of ARMs is that the interest rate is normally lower than on a fixed-rate mortgage during the first year. The differences between interest rates on ARMs and on fixed-rate mortgages vary among different financial institutions — the spread could be between 1 and 4 percentage points. Some individuals who cannot afford to buy with a high fixed-rate mortgage may be able to purchase a home with an ARM. The borrower should carefully weigh the benefits against the risks in deciding which type of loan best meets his or her needs.

Points

When a mortgage loan is obtained, the borrower frequently must pay a certain number of *points*. This payment may also be called a *loan origination fee*. For example, assume a household borrows $60,000 to buy a $75,000 home with the balance of $15,000 coming from personal savings. The particular financial institution making the mortgage loan requires 3 points. This means that the household must pay the lender 3 percent of the $60,000 mortgage, or $1,800, in order to get the loan. Part of $1,800 may be paid prior to taking possession of the house (the time of closing or settlement), and the balance will be paid at the closing. The payment of points is similar to making a loan under the discount method. The net effect is that the lender is not providing $60,000 in the example above, but rather $60,000 − $1,800 = $58,200. Interest on the loan, however, is based on the full $60,000. This means that the interest rate usually quoted by the lender understates the true cost to the borrower.

The Home to Be Purchased

As stated at the beginning of this chapter, the importance of the following analysis is to provide the reader with a framework to analyze whether home ownership or renting is more preferable to an investor. In the example, numbers are specified for the price of a hypothetical house, costs of owning and maintaining the house, and the rent on a hypothetical apartment. Because of very wide differences across the country and because of price changes which are constantly occurring, the numbers we will use may not be applicable to many readers. In such cases, the reader may want to make separate calculations using estimates which apply to his or her area and situation. In any case, in going through our analysis the reader should be focusing on the type of information he or she will need and what types of computations will be required to make a decision. At the close of our example we discuss how our results might have changed if we had made different assumptions and had chosen different numbers.

We will continue with the example above and assume that an investor has an opportunity to buy a home for $75,000.[1] He plans to make a down payment of $15,000 and obtain a thirty-year mortgage of $60,000. The terms of the mortgage are a fixed-interest rate of 12 percent and 3 points. This means the investor must also have $1,800 for the loan origination fee in addition to the $15,000 down payment.

There are also many other costs associated with the purchase and the closing. A loan application fee may amount to $300. A survey of the property and a title search are necessary, and title insurance must be obtained. The investor will require the services of a competent lawyer to protect his interests and make sure everything is done properly. Other fees and charges, in addition to the above, are also normally incurred. We estimate that total transactions costs, including points, are $3,000. It is assumed that the $15,000 down payment plus the $3,000 transactions cost are financed from personal savings. This means that the initial investment requires a total of $18,000 of equity from the investor.

Apartment and Housing Expenses

If the investor does not purchase a home we assume he rents a one-bedroom apartment. We will also establish a three-year planning horizon. The investor expects to remain in the present location for three years and wants to determine whether the apartment or a home purchase is financially superior for that period. They estimate the average rent for the three years to be $525 per month, which includes heat, maintenance, and water.

Similarly, if a home is purchased, the holding period is estimated as three years, after which the investor expects to sell the dwelling and move elsewhere. We have selected three years to limit the amount of calculation.

[1] In 1985, the median price of an existing single-family house was approximately $75,000, and down payments in the 10 percent to 30 percent range were very common.

In calculating the monthly costs of owning a home, we start with the mortgage payment. Since the stated interest rate is 12 percent per year, the lender will take this to be one percent per month.[2] The equation to calculate the payment is the following:

$$\$60,000 = PV = M \times (\text{Present value of \$1 per period at 1\% for } 360 \text{ periods})$$

where:

PV = present value of mortgage payments
M = monthly (annuity) payment

In other words, the present value of the monthly payments is equal to the amount borrowed, $60,000. From an expanded version of Table 8A–3 we can look up the present value of $1 per period at 1 percent per period. Since that value is 97.218, we calculate the monthly payment to be $60,000/ 97.218 = $617.

Other estimated annual expenses are shown in Table 23–1. Property taxes are $1,600, and the sum of heating, maintenance, insurance, and utilities is $1,500. While the apartment dweller will also have an expense for utilities and possibly renter's insurance, the cost to the homeowner will be greater. The components comprising the $1,500 represent the excess of the homeowner's expense over the renter's comparable expense. It should be noted that the estimated expenses in Table 23–1 are subject to great variation

TABLE 23–1   Outlays at Time of Purchase

Down Payment	$15,000
Points	1,800
Other Transactions Costs	1,200
Total Outlay	$18,000

Annual Costs

	House	Apartment
Mortgage	$ 7,400	Rent $6,300
Taxes	1,600	
Heating	550	
Maintenance	550	
Insurance	250	
Water and Other Utilities	150	
Total	$10,500	

[2] This implies the effective annual rate is greater than 12 percent per year because of monthly compounding.

depending on the location of the house, its physical condition, and the discretion of the homeowner in controlling some of the costs.

In order to simplify the calculations to follow, we assume that all payments are made once per year, in the middle of the year, instead of on a monthly basis. Given that we are working with so many estimates, any error generated by this procedure will be relatively unimportant. Thus, the annual mortgage payment will be taken as $7,400 (approximately 12 × $617), compared to an annual rental expense of $6,300.

Tax Benefits of Home Ownership

As can be observed from Table 23–1, the before-tax annual costs of home ownership are much larger than the apartment's rent. However, after considering the tax deductions from the house, the difference between the annual costs is substantially reduced.

Our next step, therefore, is to calculate the tax benefits that reduce the burden on the homeowner under 1986 tax law. The computations of deductions and tax savings are shown in Table 23–2. In the upper panel, mortgage payments are divided into the components representing interest and payment of principal. Of the two components, only the payment for interest is a deductible expense.

In the lower panel, total deductions and the annual tax savings are shown. Under 1986 tax laws, the value of the points can be immediately

TABLE 23–2   Expenses, Deductions, and Tax Savings in Owning the House

Year	Mortgage Balance Beginning of Year	Breakdown of Mortgage Payments Annual Mortgage Payment	Interest[a]	Principle
1	$60,000	$7,400	$7,200	$200
2	59,800	7,400	7,180	220
3	59,580	7,400	7,150	250

Year	Points	Interest[b]	Tax Savings Property Tax	Total Deductions	Tax Savings[b,c]
1	$1,800	$7,200	$1,600	$10,600	$3,530
2	0	7,180	1,600	8,780	2,930
3	0	7,150	1,600	8,750	2,920

[a] Calculated as 12 percent of the mortgage balance at the beginning of the year and rounded to the nearest $10. The interest numbers shown are slightly overestimated because the mortgage payments are made monthly and not annually. The average mortgage balance during the first year is less than $60,000 but more than the $59,800 balance at the beginning of the second year. The true interest payment is approximately 12 percent of the average mortgage balance during the year.
[b] Rounded to the nearest $10.
[c] Household in thirty-three and one-third percent tax bracket (see footnote in text).

deducted. Although the expense was incurred during the closing at the start of year 1, the $1,800, for simplicity, is included with the year 1 deductions which are entered at mid-year. In addition to interest expense, property taxes are also deductible.

To compute the tax savings for the investor, we must know his or her tax bracket. A thirty three and one third percent tax rate is assumed, and we also assume the household previously itemized deductions.[3] Under these conditions the full tax savings would be realized. If a standard deduction had previously been used because it was larger than total itemized deductions, then some of the deductions from the house would not have reduced taxes. The investor would gain only to the extent that his or her total deductions increase beyond the standard deduction.

Additional Wealth Through Rental Savings

In Table 23–3 after-tax home ownership costs are compared to renter costs. While the tax savings have significantly reduced the expense of owning a house, it is still cheaper to rent the apartment. We assume the renter will invest his or her annual savings from not buying a house. In addition, the total initial outlay of $18,000, which included down payment and closing costs, is saved by renting. These sums are assumed to be invested in an interest-bearing account that pays 9 percent. In Figure 23–1 we show a time line that illustrates when the deposits are made.

Given the renter's tax rate, the after-tax yield on the securities is 6 percent. The balance in the renter's account at the end of year 3, FV, is calculated as follows:

$$FV = 18,000(1.06)^3 + 670(1.06)^{2.5} + 1,270(1.06)^{1.5} + 1,280(1.06)^{.5}$$

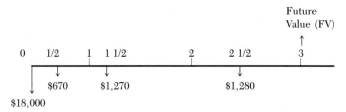

Figure 23–1 Funds Available to Renter for Investment

---

[3] As previously noted in Chapter 1, it is possible that an investor's overall marginal income tax rate will be higher than 28 percent in 1988 and beyond. This could occur because of the added effect of state and local income taxes and because of a scheduled federal surtax which would be applicable in certain income ranges.

TABLE 23–3 After-Tax Annual Costs

	Home Ownership			Apartment	
Year	Before-Tax Expenses (Table 23–1)	Tax Savings (Table 23–2)	After-Tax Expenses	Rent	Renter's Saving
1	$10,500	$3,530	$6,970	$6,300	$ 670
2	10,500	2,930	7,570	6,300	1,270
3	10,500	2,920	7,580	6,300	1,280

and rounding to the nearest $10,

$$= 21,440 + 780 + 1,390 + 1,320$$
$$= 24,930$$

Accumulation of Wealth Through Home Ownership

The computation of gains from home ownership has more details than the computation of wealth generated through rental savings. One must estimate the increase in home prices, transactions costs, and capital gains taxes (if any) upon the sale of the house. Estimates of some of these variables are shown in Table 23–4.

We have assumed that the house appreciates at a rate of 6 percent per year, resulting in a selling price of $89,330 at end of year 3. In computing

TABLE 23–4 Returns on Home Ownership — Three Years

Annual price increase	6%
Selling price	$89,330
Transactions costs	5,800
Proceeds before mortgage repayment	83,530
Mortgage outstanding	59,330
Proceeds before taxes	24,200
Maximum Capital Gains Tax	
Proceeds before mortgage repayment	$83,530
Purchase price of home	$75,000
Transactions costs at purchase not previously deducted (Table 23–1)	$ 1,200
Basis of capital gain	76,200
Capital gain	7,330
Capital gains tax (33⅓%)[1]	2,440
Net proceeds after taxes (proceeds before taxes less capital gains tax)	21,760

[1] It is very possible that the overall capital gains tax rate on the home sale will be lower than 33⅓ percent even if the overall marginal tax rate on ordinary income were 33⅓ percent. A number of states that tax interest and capital gains on securities may not tax the capital gain due to someone selling their home.

transactions costs we have assumed a broker has been used who charges a 6 percent fee, or $5,360. The remaining $440 in transactions costs consist of attorney fees plus some small incidental fees.

The main factor affecting the transactions costs is whether a real estate broker is utilized. Most people use brokers to sell their homes for several reasons. First, brokers provide useful information and advice. Second, their marketing network enables them to reach a large group of potential buyers. Third, they can screen many buyers so that people most likely to be interested in the property will visit. At the same time, the broker's fee of approximately 6 percent of the selling price is paid by the seller. Therefore, in deciding whether to use a broker, the selling household must weigh the considerable benefits against the considerable costs.

After payment of the transactions costs there is a balance of $83,530. A major portion of this sum will repay the outstanding mortgage. From Table 23–2 the mortgage balance was $59,580 at the beginning of year 3. After the third mortgage payment, which includes a $250 repayment of principal, the balance is $59,330. Repayment of the latter amount leaves the seller with $24,200.

The amount of tax that the seller must pay is subject to a number of criteria. If another house is purchased within a certain time interval, and if the price is greater than the $83,530 proceeds before mortgage repayment, it may be possible that taxes can be avoided at that time. If the owner of the home is over fifty-five years old, it may be possible to avoid a capital gains tax even if no new home is purchased. The seller should consult a competent accountant or tax attorney on these tax provisions. Thus, it is possible that the $24,200 of proceeds may not be taxed when the home is sold.

An estimate of a potential tax that could be incurred in our example if no avoidance were possible, is computed in the lower panel of Table 23-4. One starts with the selling price minus transactions costs, which we have labeled as proceeds before mortage repayment. Next one calculates the "basis" for computing the capital gain. It includes the purchase price plus transactions costs relating to the purchase which were not previously deducted. The cost of making improvements on the house can also be added to the basis. While we have not listed improvements, it is possible that some of the maintenance expenditures would fall into this category. As stated earlier, a professional accountant would be familiar with the latest tax laws.

Assessment of the Results

In our example, the investor had somewhat more wealth at the end of the three-year period if he or she had rented ($24,930) than if a home had been purchased (between $21,760 and $24,200). However, the results could easily have been different under alternative assumptions. The following changes in variables would increase the incentives for home ownership and could have made it more profitable than renting in our example.

1. Home prices rise more rapidly than assumed.[4]
2. The house was sold at the price shown without using a real estate broker, and the investor avoided the commission.
3. The home is owned more than three years before selling. This would lower the ratio of transactions costs to price increase of the house. For example, if the house had been sold immediately after its purchase, there would have been little, if any, increase in price. At the same time, there would have been a large brokerage fee, significant legal expenses, and other fees. The more time that passes, the greater the increase in the price of the house to cover those expenses.
4. The rent on the apartment is higher than we specified.
5. The investor moves into a higher tax bracket. This would increase the tax savings from deductions and reduce the after-tax return from renting and investing in interest-bearing securities.
6. Reductions in the annual costs of home ownership, shown in Table 23–1.

At the same time, if factors were to move in the opposite direction as those just described, home ownership would become less attractive. In addition, possible future changes in the tax laws, such as the elimination or reduction of allowable property tax deductions, would increase the costs of home ownership. Thus there are many factors to consider in deciding whether to buy a home. However, through the analytical framework shown in this chapter, the investor can simulate the outcome of a home purchase under a variety of different assumptions.

REAL ESTATE INVESTMENT TRUSTS

Another type of real estate investment involves indirect ownership in real estate by purchasing shares of real estate investment trusts (REITS) in the securities exchanges. REITs are closed-end investment companies that invest in mortgages and investment real estate. They are required to return most of their earnings to their shareholders in the form of dividends and capital gains.

REITs can be classified into three types:

1. Mortgage trusts make short-term and intermediate term loans to builders, and long-term mortgage loans to large real estate buyers.
2. Equity trusts own property outright and seek their profits from rental income and capital gains.

---

[4] In 1985 and 1986 home prices rose much more rapidly than 6% per year in many areas.

3. Hybrid trusts are a mixture of the above two types; they invest in real estate directly and also own real estate mortgages in their portfolios.

The 1973–75 recession severely depressed investment real estate, and REITs performed poorly. Many mortgage trusts went bankrupt. Many markets were overbuilt, and the recession brought a slackening in rental demand and higher construction costs. Many REITs were simply poorly managed. Equity trusts were also hurt, but not as badly. Consequently, the individual investor is probably better off by investing in Equity trusts and Hybrids than investing in a Mortgage trust.

Selection of an investment like a REIT is similar to analyzing other investments. It involves a determination of the various risks and deciding which ones the investor can afford to take. Evaluating alternative REITs involves examining their prospectuses for information about past performance, management experience, the capital structure (degree of leverage used), trust objectives, and composition of their assets. For example, does the trust own properties that are well-located, well-leased, and have proven cash flows? Obviously, some general knowledge of real estate market trends and economic and financial trends is an advantage.

SUMMARY

Prospective home buyers have a number of considerations in deciding whether to purchase a home or rent an apartment. A home purchase and sale involve substantial transactions costs, and the buyer is likely to encounter much higher monthly costs than would be associated with an apartment. Because of these factors, a minimum amount of price appreciation is necessary before the investment on a home provides a better return than renting. The home, however, offers substantial tax advantages, the prospect of capital appreciation, and a number of nonmonetary benefits.

Aside from direct ownership of real estate such as through ownership, investors can acquire indirect ownership in real estate through the purchase of shares in real estate investment trusts (REITs). Most REITs are organized as close-end investment companies designed to invest in diversified portfolios of real estate and mortgage investments. They distribute over 90 percent of their current income to their shareholders in the form of dividends and capital gains.

QUESTIONS AND PROBLEMS

1. What is the difference between an adjustable-rate mortgage and a fixed-rate mortgage? What are the rates for your area?

2. What are points?
3. What federal tax deductions do homeowners receive that are not available to renters?
4. Why might renting be more desirable than home ownership if the individual will only hold the house for a relatively short period of time?
5. Given you know the purchase and sales price for a home, what factors or deductions can reduce the capital gains tax?
6. What are the main features of the three types of real estate investment trusts?
7. What are the risks in investing in REITS?

REFERENCES

Allen, Robert G. *Creating Wealth*. New York: Simon & Schuster, 1983.

Case, Fred E. "The Attraction of Home Ownership." *Journal of the American Real Estate and Urban Economics Association*, Spring 1979.

Hall, Craig. *Craig Hall's Book of Real Estate Investing*. New York: Holt, Rinehart & Winston, 1982.

Mader, Chris. *The Dow Jones-Irwin Guide to Real Estate Investing*. Homewood, Ill.: Dow Jones-Irwin, 1983.

Stevenson, Richard, and Jennings, Edward. *Fundamentals of Investments*. St. Paul, Minn.: West, 1984.

24

Other Investment Opportunities: Foreign Investments and Precious Metals

INTERNATIONAL INVESTING

Modern portfolio theory emphasizes the idea that a well-diversified portfolio reduces risk but not expected return. A well-diversified portfolio requires low covariance among the securities within it. In 1970, nearly 70 percent of the total value of the aggregate world equity market was in the United States. By 1986, just under 50 percent was in the United States. In other words, investors are choosing to put more of their funds overseas. One reason for this was the fall in the value of the dollar against major foreign currencies in 1985 and 1986. More fundamentally, there have been a number of countries outside the U.S. that have had faster economic growth, higher productivity, and higher personal savings rates. These developments have contributed to superior growth in companies located in those countries. Finally, of course, there is the objective of diversification. In effect, if one invests in only U.S. firms, one is limiting oneself to about half the available investments in the world.

The effect of risk reduction through national and international diversification is shown by Solnick's study, as illustrated in Figure 24–1.[1] The horizontal axis shows the number of stocks in the portfolio, and the vertical axis shows the risk of the portfolio as a percentage of the average risk of an individual stock. The number 30 means the risk of the portfolio is 30 percent of the risk of an average stock.

Two curves are shown in the chart, one for a portfolio of U.S. stocks and the other for a portfolio of internationally diversified securities. Looking at the chart, if the portfolio consists of thirty-five stocks, the portfolio of U.S. stocks has a risk of about 30 percent, whereas the portfolio of internationally diversified securities contains risk of only about 17 percent.

[1]B. H. Solnick, "Why Not Diversify Internationally Rather Than Domestically?" *Financial Analysts Journal,* July–Aug. 1974.

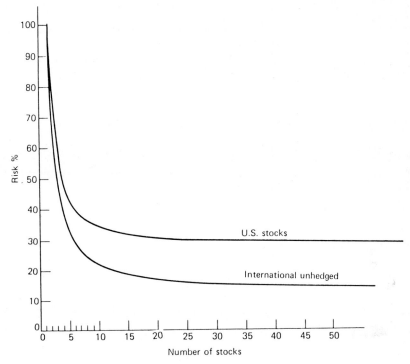

FIGURE 24–1   Risk Reduction Through National and International Diversification

Source: B. H. Solnik, "Why Not Diversify Internationally Rather Than Domestically?" *Financial Analysts Journal,* July–Aug. 1974. Reprinted by permission of the publisher.

Correlation of Returns in the Equity Market Among Countries

Reduction of risk of internationally diversified portfolios can also be viewed from the correlation of returns among countries. Table 24–1 shows cross-correlations of returns of world equities for the period 1960–80.[2] The correlations among securities from different countries are much lower than the correlations among securities from the same country. This suggests that portfolios that include securities from several countries should have much less risk than the portfolios composed of securities from a single country.

The table also shows that U.S. equities had low correlations with countries like Austria, Denmark, France, Germany, Italy, Norway, Spain, and

[2]R. G. Ibbotson, R. C. Carr, and A. W. Robinison, "International Equity and Bond Returns," *Financial Analysts Journal,* July–Aug. 1982.

TABLE 24–1   World Equities: Cross-Correlations of Annual U.S.-Dollar-Adjusted Total Returns, 1960–1980

Series	Austria	Belgium	Denmark	France	Germany	Italy	Nether-lands	Norway
Austria	−1.000							
Belgium	0.308	1.000						
Denmark	0.224	0.387	1.000					
France	0.155	0.559	0.259	1.000				
Germany	0.258	0.303	0.058	0.273	1.000			
Italy	0.180	−0.104	0.156	0.398	−0.004	1.000		
Netherlands	−0.012	0.567	0.342	0.484	0.537	0.031	1.000	
Norway	0.343	0.359	−0.100	0.188	−0.212	0.119	0.010	1.000
Spain	0.260	0.208	0.413	0.326	−0.075	0.338	−0.102	0.171
Sweden	−0.038	0.311	0.281	0.277	0.285	0.131	0.429	−0.100
Switzerland	0.454	0.465	0.134	0.444	0.700	0.129	0.658	−0.021
United Kingdom	−0.349	0.284	0.152	0.432	0.258	0.104	0.675	−0.136
Europe Total	−0.039	0.493	0.266	0.643	0.505	0.289	0.783	−0.039
Hong Kong	0.127	0.447	0.743	0.387	0.131	0.324	0.729	0.046
Japan	0.216	0.331	0.831	0.361	0.302	0.307	0.284	−0.257
Singapore	0.260	0.510	0.921	0.404	0.311	0.353	0.614	−0.157
Asia Total	0.211	0.337	0.845	0.365	0.281	0.314	0.308	−0.228
Australia	−0.241	0.281	0.213	0.504	0.321	0.420	0.766	0.089
Canada	0.239	0.623	0.341	0.441	−0.037	0.269	0.554	0.469
Other Total	0.029	0.544	0.329	0.528	0.157	0.363	0.743	0.358
Non-U.S. Total Equities	0.062	0.559	0.557	0.646	0.470	0.390	0.774	−0.114
U.S. Total Equities	−0.076	0.389	0.243	0.214	0.210	0.208	0.730	0.009
World Total Equities	−0.042	0.483	0.358	0.384	0.322	0.281	0.804	−0.045

Series	Spain	Sweden	Switzer-land	United Kingdom	Europe Total	Hong Kong	Japan	Singa-pore
Spain	1.000							
Sweden	0.313	1.000						
Switzerland	0.127	0.233	1.000					
United Kingdom	−0.039	0.301	0.454	1.000				
Europe Total	0.178	0.471	0.712	0.882	1.000			
Hong Kong	0.418	0.376	0.563	0.487	0.598	1.000		
Japan	0.337	0.340	0.240	0.171	0.374	0.707	1.000	
Singapore	0.585	0.439	0.584	0.338	0.547	0.898	0.927	1.000
Asia Total	0.338	0.337	0.244	0.198	0.391	0.759	0.997	0.952
Australia	0.090	0.282	0.432	0.674	0.731	0.667	0.184	0.512
Canada	0.260	0.312	0.350	0.360	0.505	0.791	0.231	0.598
Other Total	0.195	0.340	0.432	0.550	0.676	0.800	0.247	0.609
Non-U.S. Total Equities	0.242	0.522	0.643	0.716	0.905	0.785	0.688	0.826
U.S. Total Equities	−0.115	0.398	0.454	0.617	0.627	0.814	0.216	0.579
World Total Equities	−0.015	0.470	0.557	0.703	0.774	0.848	0.385	0.700

(continued)

TABLE 24–1, continued

Series	Asia Total	Aus-tralia	Canada	Other Total	Non-U.S. Total Equities	U.S. Total Equities	World Total Equities
Asia Total	1.000						
Australia	0.224	1.000					
Canada	0.280	0.577	1.000				
Other Total	0.296	0.863	0.907	1.000			
Non-U.S. Total Equities	0.704	0.704	0.586	0.717	1.000		
U.S. Total Equities	0.260	0.699	0.710	0.787	0.667	1.000	
World Total Equities	0.422	0.753	0.716	0.818	0.831	0.967	1.000

Source: R. G. Ibbotson, R. C. Carr, and A. W. Robinson, "International Equity and Bond Returns," *Financial Analysts Journal*, July–Aug. 1982. Reprinted by permission of the publisher.

Japan. On the other hand, the correlations among U.S. equities and equities in such countries as the United Kingdom, Canada, Australia, and Singapore were higher.

Equity Returns Among Countries

We know the portfolios of internationally diversified securities can cut down risk, but how about returns?

Before we address this question, let us first look at the market returns of equities in different countries in recent years. The study by Errunza shows the return and risk of various countries for the period 1976–80 as follows in Table 24–2.[3]

The study shows that the returns for most foreign markets were higher than in the U.S., including on a risk-adjusted basis (returns divided by standard deviation shows returns per unit of risk).

In respect to returns of internationally diversified portfolios, Errunza provided the following estimates, as shown in Table 24–3.

If the U.S. investor owned a portfolio of internationally diversified securities of thirteen countries (U.S. and twelve emerging markets) and the portfolio were equally weighted, the annual return would be 30.3 percent, compared to 8 percent on portfolios of all U.S. equities. At the same time, the standard deviation would also be lower for the internationally diversified portfolio.

However, if the internationally diversified portfolio were weighted by market capitalization, then the gain in annual return would have been much smaller: 9.8 percent for the internationally diversified portfolio and 8 percent for portfolios of all U.S. securities.

[3]Vihang R. Errunza, "Emerging Markets: A New Opportunity for Improving Global Portfolio Performance," *Financial Analysts Journal*, Sept.–Oct. 1983. Reprinted by permission of the publisher.

TABLE 24–2   Return and Risk—U.S. $ Terms (1976–1980)

	Annualized Market Return* (%)	Monthly Standard Deviation (%)
Emerging Markets		
Argentina	97.3	23.1
Brazil	4.8	9.5
Chile	122.6	13.3
Greece	3.2	3.3
Hong Kong	41.4	8.9
Jordan	40.4	8.5
Korea	30.3	9.6
Mexico	47.0	9.7
Singapore	29.8	7.1
Spain	−18.6	6.8
Thailand	21.5	9.0
Zimbabwe	30.4	9.4
Developed Markets		
Australia	20.0	6.9
Austria	5.5	3.6
Belgium	0.9	5.0
Canada	17.0	6.4
Denmark	1.7	4.0
France	10.3	7.8
Germany	5.2	4.8
Italy	13.8	8.0
Japan	19.7	4.7
Netherlands	11.3	4.6
Norway	16.6	8.6
Sweden	1.7	5.6
Switzerland	11.0	4.8
U.K.	18.8	7.0
U.S.	8.0	4.2

*Returns are not adjusted for withholding or any other taxes.
Returns are annualized by compounding mean monthly returns.

On the other hand, if the investor is a global investor owning a world portfolio composed of securities from twenty-seven countries (see Table 24–3) on an equally weighted basis, then the average annual return would be 19.6 percent for the period 1976–80 and the standard deviation would be 3.05 percent, compared to an 8 percent annual return and a 4.15 percent standard deviation for the portfolio of all U.S. securities during the same period.

In summary, Errunza shows that the returns of internationally diversified portfolios can be substantially higher than portfolios of all domestic securities, while the standard deviation of the internationally diversified portfolios is also lower.

TABLE 24–3   Gains from Diversification (1976–1980) in U.S. $

Portfolio	Number of Countries in Portfolio	Equally Weighted Portfolios		Market-Cap.-Weighted Portfolios	
		Annual Return[a] (%)	Monthly Stand. Dev. (%)	Annual Return[a] (%)	Monthly Stand. Dev. (%)
U.S. Investor					
U.S.	1	8.0	4.15	8.0	4.15
U.S. & 12 Emerging Markets	13	30.3	3.29	9.8	3.92
Global Investor					
DCs	15	10.6	3.68	11.5	3.51
DCs, Mexico Korea, Hong Kong, Singapore, Spain[b]	20	13.6	3.72	12.1	3.51
DCs & 12 Emerging Markets (World Portfolio)	27	19.6	3.05	12.5	3.46

[a] Returns are annualized by compounding mean monthly returns.
[b] Mexico, Korea, Hong Kong, Singapore and Spain are the available EMs.

Problems in International Investing

International investing does pose some additional problems for the investor. These additional problems include the following.

Exchange Risk

Buying a foreign security involves converting domestic currency to foreign currency at the time of purchase and the reverse at the time of sale. If one buys a French stock, one's eventual gain or loss will depend on two factors: 1) the performance of the stock and 2) the exchange rate between the French franc and U.S. dollar at the time of sale. If the stock appreciates 20 percent in the local market at the time of sale and the franc declines in value by 20 percent against the U.S. dollar, the net result is no gain or loss (ignoring buying and selling commissions). Therefore, the U.S. investor in foreign securities has one additional variable to consider, the future exchange rate between the foreign currency and the U.S. dollar.

Availability of Information

The second problem in international investing relates to the availability and adequacy of information on a company, its industry, and the foreign economy. In general, there is less information available on a foreign company and its industry than what is available on a U.S. company and its industry. Besides, there are differences in accounting standards and practices. For instance, many foreign countries do not require consolidated statements.

Other Problems

An obvious problem in international investing is the political environment under which foreign corporations function. This varies substantially from country to country. In general, there is more uncertainty in terms of government regulation than with the U.S. counterpart.

Another problem is the difficulty of settling trades because time periods for transactions vary from country to country. Commission costs for foreign security trades are usually higher. The net quoted price can include a transfer tax, the commission of the local broker in a foreign country, and any fees of the U.S. broker.

Limiting Risks in International Investing

To limit the risks in international investing, it is advisable for investors to limit their consideration of candidates for purchase to widely traded international companies.

There are about 600 foreign companies whose equities are traded on the New York Stock Exchange, American Stock Exchange, and the over-the-counter markets in the U.S. For these companies, trading is done through an instrument called an American Depositary Receipt (ADR). ADRs are certificates issued by U.S. banks to represent receipts of foreign stocks. The ADRs are always registered in the name of the owner and they can be easily bought and sold.

Since most of these international companies are big companies and command a lot of interest by both institutional and individual investors, they are usually followed by analysts in big brokerage firms and investment advisory firms such as Standard & Poor and *Value Line*. Individual investors, therefore, should have no difficulty in obtaining timely information on these companies as well as the opinions of analysts concerning them. This will help investors in evaluating the attractiveness of each company.

International Mutual Funds

The most popular way for Americans to invest overseas is through mutual funds. At the end of 1985, there were nineteen global funds that had at least 25 percent of their portfolios overseas, and twenty-five international funds, which had nearly all their assets in securities outside the United States.

One can choose from no-load, low-load, or load international funds. These mutual funds have full-time professionals following different foreign markets, selecting attractive stocks or bonds, and changing the mix of their portfolios as circumstances require.

Investors in these funds get wide diversification among foreign securities and at the same time, it is much easier for investors to evaluate and buy these funds than individual foreign securities. We include below in Table 24–4 a list of selected international mutual funds by the *Fact Magazine,* a *Value Line* publication.

Arbitrage

Arbitrage is an important process in both international and domestic financial markets. It is basically the process in which someone purchases something in one or more financial markets at a low price and immediately resells it in one or more other markets at a higher price, earning a profit after any transactions costs. When arbitrage occurs, the prices in the markets will soon move into "proper alignment," and the arbitrage will then cease.

For example, consider the following situation that relates to foreign currency markets. Assume that in the New York foreign exchange market $1 can be exchanged for 201 Japanese yen or for 10 French francs. Assume further that in Paris, 1 franc can be converted into 20 yen. As we will see, market prices are out of line, and arbitragers can take advantage of this situation.

Assume a foreign currency trader at a bank in New York has $10 million, which is enough to purchase 2.01 billion yen in the New York market. At the same time, the trader sells 2.01 billion yen for 100.5 million francs (1 franc = 20 yen) in Paris, and also sells 100.5 million francs in New York for $10.05 million ($1 = 10 francs). The trader has an instant profit of $50,000. Other arbitragers will try to do the same thing, or our New York trader may try to implement a larger transaction than we specified above. In any case, such transactions will bid up the cost of the yen and the number of yen per dollar will drop below 201. In addition, the exchange rate between yen and francs will adjust until there are no longer profits to be made by buying these currencies in one market and selling them in other markets. At that time, exchange rates will be in line with each other.

PRECIOUS METALS

Investors who are concerned about high or rising rates of inflation often maintain some investments in precious metals. There are several methods in which such investments can be made. These methods include taking possession of the metal, precious metal certificates, shares in mining stocks, and futures markets. Each of these ways of investing is discussed below.

Methods of Taking Possession of Precious Metals

There are two principal forms in which precious metals are held for investment purposes. Generally, the metals can be obtained as bullion (bars),

TABLE 24–4 Selected International Mutual Funds

U.S.A. Based Funds

Dean Witter World Wide Investment Trust	Keystone International Fund	Putnam International Equities Fund
One World Trade Center	99 High Street	One Post Office Square
New York, NY 10048	Boston, MA 02110	Boston, MA 02109
212-938-4554	800-225-1587, 617-338-3250	617-292-1000
Minimum investment: $1,000 initial,	Minimum investment: $250 initial,	Minimum investment: $500 initial,
$100 subsequent	$25 subsequent	$50 subsequent
Sales charge: none	Sales charge: none	Sales charge: 8.5 percent
Redemption charge: 5 percent first year	Redemption charge: 4 percent first year declining	
decreases to zero after six years	to zero in the fifth year	
		Scudder International Fund, Inc.
Fidelity Overseas Fund	Merrill Lynch International Holdings, Inc.	Scudder Fund Distributors
82 Devonshire	633 Third Avenue	175 Federal Street
Boston, MA 02109	New York, NY 10017	Boston, MA 02110
800-544-6666	212-692-2939	800-225-2470
Minimum investment: $2,500 initial,	Minimum investment: $1,000 initial,	Minimum investment: $1,000 initial,
$250 subsequent	$50 subsequent	none subsequent
Sales charge: 3 percent	Sales charge: 8.5 percent	No-load fund
Redemption fees: none		
	New Perspective Fund, Inc.	Shearson Global Opportunities Fund
Financial Group Portfolios, Inc.	333 South Hope Street	Shearson Lehman/American Express
Pacific Basin Portfolio	Los Angeles, CA 90071	14 Wall Street
P.O. Box 2040	213-486-9200	New York, NY 10005
Denver, CO 80201	Minimum investment: $250 initial,	212-577-5822
800-525-9831, 303-779-1233	$50 subsequent	Minimum investment: $2,000 initial,
		$200 subsequent

Minimum investment: $1,000 initial, $100 subsequent
No-load fund

First Investors International Securities Fund
120 Wall Street
New York, NY 10005
212-825-7900
Minimum investment: $200 initial, $50 subsequent
Sales charge: 8.5 percent

G.T. Pacific Fund, Inc.
601 Montgomery Street, Suite 1400
San Francisco, CA 94111
415-392-6181, 800-824-1580
Minimum investment, $500 initial, $100 subsequent
No-load fund

Kemper International Fund, Inc.
Kemper Financial Services
120 South La Salle Street
Chicago, IL 60603
312-781-1121
Minimum investment: $1,000 initial, $100 subsequent
Sales charge: 8.5 percent

Sales charge: 8.5 percent

Paine Webber ATLAS Fund, Inc.
140 Broadway
New York, NY 10005
800-544-9300
Minimum investment: $1,000 initial, $100 subsequent
Sales charge: 8.5 percent

T. Rowe Price International Fund, Inc.
100 East Pratt Street
Baltimore, MD 21202
800-638-5660, 301-547-2308
Minimum investment: $1,000 initial, $100 subsequent
No-load fund

Prudential-Bache Global Fund, Inc.
2 Heritage Drive
North Quincy, MA 02171
800-225-1852, 617-328-5000
Minimum investment, $1,000 initial, $100 subsequent
Sales charge: none
Redemption fee: 5 percent first year declining to zero in the sixth year

Sales charge: 5 percent

Templeton Funds, Inc.
(Templeton World, Global I and Global II Funds)
405 Central Avenue
P.O. Box 3942
St. Petersburg, FL 33731
800-237-0738
Minimum investment: $500 initial, $25 subsequent
Sales charge: 8.5 percent

Transatlantic Fund, Inc.
c/o Kleinwort Benson International Investment Ltd.
100 Wall Street
New York, NY 10005
212-747-0440
Minimum investment: $5,000 initial, $1,000 subsequent
No-load fund

Source: Fact Magazine, Feb.–March, 1985.

and in the case of gold and silver, they may be purchased in the form of coins. Whichever method is used, the investor must carefully check out the integrity of the supplier. During the early 1980s a number of individuals lost substantial sums by purchasing from dishonest firms.

There are several disadvantages associated with holding precious metals. There may be storage and insurance costs. If the investor holds the metal with no insurance, he or she bears the risk of losses due to theft, fire, or other causes. Another negative feature of holding the metal is the lost interest and dividends that could have been earned from holding investments in securities.

The advantage of holding the metal as bullion or coins rather than in forms such as jewelry is the lower transaction costs. Ordinarily, the spread between a jeweler's buying and selling price is much higher than the price spread of dealers in bullion. Coins with no numismatic or rare coin value also tend to have low spreads, but if there is numismatic value in a coin, the spread between the buying and selling prices could be large. Regardless of how investors purchase precious metals, they should first find out how much they can receive if they should immediately attempt to sell their holdings. If a wide spread between buying and selling prices exists, investors may want to acquire a position in the metal in some other manner.

Precious Metal Certificates

Some firms, including mutual funds, offer investors certificates on precious metals. In such cases, the firm holds the metal as bullion for the investor. In addition to commissions and a spread between bid and asked prices, there are usually storage fees. Again, the investor should be sure of the firm's integrity before buying precious metal certificates.

Shares in Mining Stocks

Shares in mining stocks tend to fluctuate with the metal. The correlation is not perfect, however, for several reasons. First, the firm may be mining more than one metal. A silver mining firm may also be extracting other metals or substances. Second, the management and efficiency of the firm can also affect share price. Third, some firms have facilities overseas and can be affected by foreign political problems. In the mid-1980s, shares in South African gold mining firms dropped due to political unrest in that country. Fourth, mining shares may pay dividends that tend to reduce, to some extent, fluctuation in share prices. An investor who is contemplating the purchase of mining company shares should analyze the historical relationship between previous fluctuations in the metal's price and the return on the firm's shares.

Futures Markets in Precious Metals

Futures markets may be used by investors who expect the prices of precious metals to rise to higher levels than those that prevail on futures exchanges. The use of futures markets by individuals who anticipate an increase in prices was discussed in Chapter 16, where we provided an example that compared a strategy of purchasing precious metals to one involving the purchase of commodity futures. In our example, we illustrated how both risk and potential returns are magnified through the use of futures.

SUMMARY

International investments provide the investor with additional diversification beyond that available in domestic securities markets. In addition, returns on foreign securities markets have often been higher than on U.S. securities markets. There are, however, problems associated with international investing. These problems include exchange rate risk, less information on foreign companies, and political risk.

Arbitrage is basically the process in which someone purchases something in one or more markets at a low price and immediately resells it in one or more other markets at a higher price, earning a profit after any transactions costs. When arbitrage occurs, the prices in the markets will soon move into "proper alignment," and the arbitrage will then cease.

Investors who are concerned about high or rising rates of inflation often maintain some investments in precious metals. There are several methods in which these investments can be made, including taking possession of the metal, precious metal certificates, shares in mining stocks, and futures markets.

QUESTIONS AND PROBLEMS

1. What are the benefits of international investing?
2. What are some of the problems associated with international investing?
3. What are American Depository Receipts?
4. How can U.S. investors make international investments?
5. What is arbitrage? Give an example outside of foreign currency markets.
6. How can someone invest in precious metals?
7. What are some of the problems associated with investing in precious metals?

REFERENCES

Adler, Michael. "Global Fixed-Income Portfolio Management." *Financial Analysts Journal*, Sept.–Oct. 1983.

Berss, Marcia. "Just How Alluring Are Foreign Stocks Now?" *Forbes*, July 29, 1985.

Errunza, Vihang R. "Emerging Markets: A New Opportunity for Improving Global Portfolio Performance." *Financial Analysts Journal*, Sept.–Oct. 1983.

Fact Magazine. Feb.–March 1985, Section on International Investing.

Forbes. Section on International Business, July 29, 1985.

Farrell, James L., Jr. *Guide to Portfolio Management*. New York: McGraw-Hill, 1983, Chapter 9.

Forsyth, Randall W. "Investing Abroad: How to Buy Foreign Stocks and Bonds." *Barron's*, Sept. 2, 1985.

Ibbotson, R. G., Carr, R. C., and Robinson, A. W. "International Equity and Bond Returns." *Financial Analysts Journal*, July–Aug. 1982.

Mattews, G. Paul. "International Investing: The Far East." *AAII Journal*, May 1984.

Reilly, Frank K. *Investment Analysis and Portfolio Management*. Hinsdale, Ill.: The Dryden Press, 1985, Chapter 21.

Stevenson, Richard, and Jennings, Edward. *Fundamentals of Investments*. St. Paul, Minn.: West, 1984, Chapter 21.

25

The Investor and the Personal Computer

Good investment decisions, like good decisions in other areas, come from the following ingredients:

1. Gathering *relevant* information
2. *Analyzing* the information gathered
3. Forming *good judgment* on the basis of the analysis performed
4. Taking *action*
5. *Completing* the action at the *right time or price*

These ingredients of good investment decisions do not necessarily require the use of computers. Since the introduction of computers more than twenty years ago most investment institutions have been using them, but the use of computers has not guaranteed them investment success. Some institutions have done well, others have not. Some institutions have done well in some periods, but poorly in other periods. What counts is not the use of computers, but whether management possesses by and large the above-mentioned ingredients of good investment decision making.

HOW COMPUTERS CAN HELP INVESTORS

The personal computer, such as an IBM PC or Apple II, like the big computers of years ago, possesses tremendous memory capacity and high-speed processing ability. The personal computer can help the investor gather information from a data base, and process and analyze the information according to certain instructions. The instructions can be an investor's own method, or program, or they may be ready-made investment program software.

The benefits of using a personal computer, therefore, fall into three categories. First, a computer can save the investor hours of work gathering information and making computations. Second, it broadens the universe of securities with which the investor can deal. Third, it provides the results of analysis almost instantaneously.

Therefore, should the investor use a personal computer? The answer is definitely yes, if one can afford the initial investment, if one makes investment decisions frequently, and if the investor uses the computer with an understanding of its limitations in the area of investment analysis and management.

COMPUTER SOFTWARE

Most investment software falls into four broad categories:

1. Portfolio management
2. Technical analysis
3. Fundamental analysis
4. Financial planning

Software for portfolio management enables an investor to track the record and evaluate the performance of individual securites and an entire portfolio.

Software for technical analysis enables the trader to manipulate market price and volume data, compute different moving averages, and display on the screen movements of individual stocks together with their moving averages so that the trader can pick up buy or sell signals immediately.

Software for fundamental analysis enables the investor to screen a large universe of stocks on the basis of selected characteristics. The investor can then do further research on the stocks that have met these characteristics.

Software for financial planning enables the investor to formulate plans for various financial needs, such as insurance programs, liquid fund accumulation, contingency funds, retirement needs, tax shelters, and estate planning.

Computer Applications with Technical Analysis

Technical analysis, or market analysis, is aimed at trading. We have examined it in detail in Chapter 17. Most professional traders use technical analysis to make trading decisions in securities, commodities, and the foreign exchange markets. However, technical analysis, in our view, offers limited advantages to the general public for trading purposes, as we have explained in Chapters 1 and 17, for these reasons:

1. The investors hold jobs away from the market. These investors cannot take advantage of fast-changing developments in the market.

2. Most investors do not have enough knowledge of technical market analysis. Moreover, they cannot afford to subscribe to the many different technical advisory and chart services

3. The average investors do not follow strictly the trading rules as do the technical analysis professionals.

4. Most investors do not have enough financial resources to implement the principles of diversification, nor do they have sufficient financial reserves necessary to offset the enormous risks involved.

The Nonprofessional Trader Using Technical Analysis with Computer Assistance

Suppose our nonprofessional trader, who holds a regular full-time job not related to the security market, invests $4000 to $6000 in a computer hardware, software, and modem (for communication with data bases and with other computers). Does our amateur trader improve the chances of success in trading using technical analysis software?

Our amateur trader, in his or her spare time after work, would use the computer to review the day's developments in the marketplace. First, one would probably get a summary of news, and then on to price and volume changes in major market indexes, advances and declines, up volume and down volume, and other market indicators. Next, the investor would take a look at the most active issues, those issues with a large percentage change in volume, and those issues advancing or declining most during the day. Finally, one would look at those stocks that one has been following. On the screen would appear price and volume charts of these stocks with moving averages superimposed over them.

After having completed that, the investor would probably come up with some opinion about the market trend and individual securities. Once the investor makes a decision, orders can be sent to the brokerage firm via the modem to buy or sell specific securities at limit prices. All this could not have been done before without a personal computer and its software: it certainly has enabled the investor to follow market developments more closely, and in all likelihood will improve the chances of success in trading. However, if there had been other important trading opportunities while the investor was not at the computer, he or she could not have taken advantage of them. The securities markets are known for their volatility, and important changes can happen any time. Being away from the market during the day can be a very important drawback to our average trader. Nonetheless, the availability of a personal computer and its software does help the amateur trader using technical analysis make some trading decisions much more easily.

Now suppose we go a step further — our amateur trader is one who can watch developments in security markets on the computer screen part of the time during trading hours. Now, of course, he or she has the additional advantage of being able to follow market developments. This investor is not as disadvantaged as far as concerns knowing what is going on in the security markets and using technical data to make decisions.

In conclusion, the availability of a personal computer and its software does make it easier for the general-public investor to do some trading using technical analysis. It also improves to some extent the chances of success.

Computer Applications with Fundamental Analysis

Before the introduction of the personal computer, one of the problems investors encountered was that fundamental analysis was time-consuming. Moreover, the number of securities that one could deal with was quite limited. Now, with the availability of a personal computer and its software, the investor using fundamental analysis can deal with a universe of hundreds of stocks. For instance, the Value/Screen software by *Value Line* brings data and ratios on 1650 stocks to the screen and enables one to review and locate stocks meeting the criteria set up by the investor.

In investment, as in general shopping, good values on some securities become visible after one has compared many of them. Comparative valuation of many securities using advanced statistical techniques known as multiple regression and correlation analysis is now feasible on a personal computer. (See Chapter 13.) In addition, there are many software programs developed for specific purposes, such as determining the value of option premiums, devising option strategies, analysis of futures markets, generating macro-economic forecasts, bond analysis, real estate analysis, and so on. There are also programs designed to help investors to develop their own analytical tools. The use of these programs can save an enormous amount of time the investor would otherwise spend if a personal computer and its software were unavailable.

In short, with the availability of a personal computer and the many investment software products on the market, the investor can now develop in-depth securities analysis and research which was possible years ago only in universities and large investment institutions. In other words, the availability of a personal computer and software to investors using fundamental analysis has narrowed the advantage investment institutions have enjoyed over individuals.

However, investors using a personal computer with fundamental analysis should be warned that simple methods such as screening stocks by P/E ratios, past earnings growth rate, and so forth, unless backed up by further careful analysis, would be unlikely to yield much benefit. The investment business is highly competitive and academicians have told us for a long time that the securities markets are quite efficient, meaning that security prices are, by and large, fair representations of the value of the stock on the basis of current available information. Consequently, better-than-average profits would have to come from research not of average quality, but of high quality.

Several recent articles by successful investment managers relate how they have used computers to select securities and portfolios, and how individual investors, they feel, should use their personal computers for fundamental investment analysis. The views expressed are sound and interesting. The articles are listed below:

Albert Nicholas, "A Bottom-Up Approach to Stock Market Timing," *Journal of American Association of Individual Investors*, July 1984.

Thomas M. Nourse, "Screening Screens: Selections for a Sequential Approach," *Journal of American Association of Individual Investors*, Oct. 1984.

Dean LeBaron, "Contrary, Value-Oriented Approach Focuses on Strategy," *Journal of American Association of Individual Investors*, Sept. 1984.

SOURCES OF INFORMATION

Books

A particularly useful book, updated annually, is *The Individual Investor's Microcomputer Resource Guide,* edited by Norm Nicholson, and published by the American Association of Individual Investors. The book covers developments in microcomputer technology, and describes investment software products, including prices and addresses of the vendors.

Other very useful books include:

Albert I. A. Bookbinder. *Computer Assisted-Investment Handbook.* Programmed Press, 1983 (2301 Bayle's Ave., Elmont, N.Y. 10003).

Riley and Montgomery. *Guide to Computer Assisted-Investment Analysis.* McGraw-Hill, 1982.

Donald Woodwell, *Automating Your Financial Portfolio,* Dow Jones-Irwin, 1983.

Magazines

There are many magazines on the market. Two good ones are: *Wall Street Computer Review,* from Dealer's Digest, Inc., 150 Broadway, New York, N.Y. 10038, and *Computer Investing,* from the American Association of Individual Investors, 612 No. Michigan Avenue, Chicago, Ill. 60611.

Recommended Software

Which software is best is practically impossible to determine. First of all, there are new products constantly coming on the market and one cannot keep up with them. Thus it is useful to read a magazine, such as *Computer Investing*, which reviews most of the products. *Money Magazine* published an article that listed the following products as their favorites (Jordan E. Goodman and June Bruedy, "Computers: 25 Top Personal Finance Programs," *Money Magazine*, November 1984, pp. 230-46). It can serve as a suitable starting point for the interested investor.

For Fundamental Analysis

- Stockpak II. Standard & Poor Corporation; program and one year of diskettes containing data on 1500 companies.
- Dow Jones Market Microscope. Dow Jones & Co.; the program can 1) tap the Dow Jones News/Retrieval, a data book, and 2) rank companies according to your criteria.
- Value/Screen. *Value Line*, Inc.; includes program and one year of monthly data disks.

For Technical Analysis

- Brandon Stock System. Brandon Information Management.
- Market Analyzer. Dow Jones & Company.
- The Technical Investor. Savant Corporation.
- Market Analyst. Andidata Incorporated.
- Winning on Wall Street. Summa Software Corporation.

Recently, we came across a very informative article in *Forbes* on use of personal computer, investment software, and data bases. The article, "The Electronic Edge," was written by Janet Bamford and appeared in *Forbes* on May 6, 1985.

SUMMARY

The availability and use of a personal computer provides several important benefits to the individual investor who understands what the computer can and cannot do in the area of investment management. One is the saving of enormous amounts of time and effort in gathering information and making calculations. Second, a computer broadens the universe of securities the investor can effectively research. Third, it provides the results of analysis almost instantaneously.

However, good investment decisions require more than the availability of a personal computer and ready-made investment software. Good investment decisions require:

1. Gathering *relevant* information.
2. *Properly analyzing* the information gathered.
3. Forming *good judgment* on the basis of the analysis performed.
4. Taking *action*.
5. *Completing* the action at *the right time or price*.

What counts in the final anaylsis is the *quality* of judgment. But, a computer can help in the endeavor for investment success.

Glossary

Accrued Interest.   Interest that has accrued on a bond since the most recent interest payment. For many types of bonds the buyer must pay the sum of market price plus any accrued interest.

Active Investors.   Investors who formulate and manage their own investment program. Active investors adjust their portfolios as their needs and opportunities change.

Adjustable Rate Mortgage (ARM).   A mortgage loan in which the interest rate is periodically adjusted by the lender, depending on the movements of other, designated interest rates, such as the prime rate.

ADR.   See *American Depository Receipts*.

American Depository Receipts (ADR).   Certificates issued by U.S. banks that represent ownership of shares in specified foreign firms.

Annuity.   A series of equal payments made at regular intervals.

Arbitrage.   The purchase of financial assets in one or more markets at a low price coupled with the immediate resale of those financial assets in one or more other markets at a higher price.

Arbitrage Pricing Theory.   A theory in which a security's return is specified to depend on the expected return on that security plus several risk factors.

ARM.   See *Adjustable Rate Mortgage*.

Asked Price.   The price the investor must pay the dealer on an over-the-counter market transaction.

Bankers' Acceptances.   Drafts that originate in the financing of foreign trade and are guaranteed by a commercial bank for payment on specified dates.

Basis.   The difference between the existing price in the futures market and the price in the cash market.

Basis Point.   A measure of interest rate change. A basis point is 1/100 of 1 percentage point.

Bear Market.   An extended period of time during which security prices are generally declining in a market.

Best Efforts.   Instances when investment bankers are not underwriting a group of securities but are merely using their best efforts to sell those securities.

Beta (β).   A measure of risk that indicates the sensitivity of a security or a portfolio to a specified market index.

Bid Price.   The price the investor receives in selling to a dealer on an over-the-counter market transaction.

Black-Scholes Formula.   An equation used to determine the fair market value of a call option.

Block Trading.   Single trades involving 10,000 or more shares.

Bond.   Long-term promissory note in which principal, and interest payments in the case of coupon bonds, are due at specified dates.

Book Value Per Share.   The value of common shareholder equity from the balance sheet divided by the number of common shares outstanding.

Broker.   Someone who implements or arranges a transaction for a buyer or a seller and receives a commission for this service.

Bull Market.   An extended period of time during which security prices are generally increasing.

Business Risk.   The unpredictability in a firm's profits due to variation in revenues and operating expenses.

Call Option.   An option that gives the owner the right to buy a specified number of shares of stock at a stated price for a given period of time.

Call Price.   The price a bond issuer must pay for each bond if the bonds are redeemed prior to maturity.

Call Provisions.   Provisions in a bond indenture that state the conditions under which a bond issuer may redeem the bonds prior to maturity.

Capital Asset Pricing Model (CAPM).   The theory that relates the required return on a security or portfolio to a risk-free rate, the beta of the security or portfolio, and the difference between the expected return on the market and the risk-free rate.

Capital Gain.   The profit realized when assets are sold for more than the purchase cost.

Capital Loss.   The loss when securities or certain real assets are sold for less than the purchase cost.

Cash Price.   The price for immediate delivery of a commodity.

Certificates of Deposit (CD).   Certificates that represent deposits in commercial banks. Negotiable certificates of deposit have large denominations and mature within one year.

Chartist.   A technical analyst who uses charts showing recent patterns of price movements in an attempt to forecast future price movements of securities.

Churning.   The situation where an investor makes many purchases and sales at the suggestion or direction of a broker who is primarily concerned with generating commissions and has little if any concern about the investor's return.

Closed-End Fund.   A fund of an investment company in which the number of shares issued by the fund to the public is fixed.

Coincidental Indicators.   Economic and financial indicators that tend to show peaks and troughs when the economy as a whole shows peaks and troughs.

Commercial Paper.   Short-term, unsecured promissory notes issued usually by large, well-known firms.

Common Stock.   Securities held by residual owners of a corporation and represent their share of ownership.

Contrarian. An investor who tends to place funds in groups of stocks associated with generally negative opinion and are currently out of favor with most investors.

Conversion Price. The par value of a convertible security divided by the conversion ratio.

Conversion Ratio. The number of shares of common stock that the owner of a convertible security can receive if conversion occurs.

Conversion Value. Conversion ratio times current price per share of the stock underlying a convertible security. The market value of the shares that could be obtained through conversion.

Convertible Securities. Corporate bonds or preferred stock that can be converted into a specified number of shares of stock.

Coupon Bonds. Bonds that pay interest periodically and pay the par value at maturity.

Coupon Rate. The annual interest payment on a bond divided by the par value of the bond.

Coupon Reinvestment Risk. Risk associated with reinvesting future interest payments on bonds at uncertain future interest rates.

Cross-Hedge. A hedge in which the item being hedged and the item in the futures contract used for hedging are not identical but share a number of similarities.

Cumulative Dividends. Dividends on most issues of preferred stock in which dividends omitted in one year must be paid before common dividends can be paid.

Current Yield. The ratio of the annual interest payment on a bond divided by the current price of the bond.

Day Order. An order to buy or sell securities that expires if it is not executed by the end of the trading day specified by the investor.

Dealer. A participant in financial markets who either buys or sells certain groups of securities. Dealers buy and sell out of their own account and earn profits on the spread between their buying (bid) and selling (asked) prices.

Debenture. An unsecured corporate bond backed only by the creditworthiness of the firm.

Default. The situation in which an issuer of an interest-bearing asset does not make an interest payment or payment of principal as scheduled.

Delivery Date. The date on which the item in a futures contract is to be delivered and payment is due.

Diffusion Index. A statistical series indicating the percentage of items in a group of series that is rising at a given time.

Discount Broker. A broker who charges low commission rates and supplies little or no researched information on securities.

Diversification. The purchase of a variety of different securities to reduce investment risk.

Dividends. Payments made to shareholders by the corporation.

Dividend Yield. The ratio of the annual dividend to the current market price of the stock.

Dow Jones Industrial Average (DJIA).   An index of stock market prices based on the stock prices of thirty well-established industrial firms.

Dow Theory.   The foundation of modern-day technical analysis. The theory is concerned with market trends and whether a bull market or bear market is currently underway.

Duration.   A weighted average of when payments are scheduled to be made on a bond. Duration provides information on the sensitivity of the bond's price to interest rate changes.

Earnings Per Share.   Net income due common shareholders divided by the number of common shares outstanding.

Efficiency Frontier.   The set of all portfolios that simultaneously maximize expected returns for each given level of risk and minimize risk for each given level of expected return.

Efficient Markets.   Markets characterized by many buyers and sellers, good information flows, and prices that reflect the latest information.

Efficient Portfolio.   A portfolio that has minimum risk for its level of expected return and maximum expected return for its level of risk.

Equity Margin.   Equity in the investor's brokerage account divided by the market value of securities subject to margin requirements.

Eurodollars.   Short-term interest-bearing deposits that are held in banks outside of the United States.

Exchange Risk.   Price risk associated with international investments due to fluctuations in currency exchange rates.

Exercise Price.   The price paid by the owner of a call if the call is exercised, or the price at which the owner of a put sells if the put is exercised.

Expectation Theory.   A theory on the term structure of interest rates in which long-term rates are stated to equal some average of a current interest rate and interest rates expected to exist in future periods.

Expiration Date.   The last day on which a particular put or call option can be exercised.

Federal Agency Securities.   Securities issued by different agencies in some way affiliated with the federal government.

Federal Funds Rate.   The interest rate on federal funds, which are overnight loans of excess reserves made by one commercial bank to another.

Financial Futures.   Contracts in which financial assets or price indexes of financial assets are bought and sold for future delivery.

Financial Risk.   Risk associated with the use of borrowed funds.

Fisher Equation.   The relationship in which the market interest rate is stated to equal a real interest rate plus the expected rate of inflation.

Fixed-Rate Mortgage.   A mortgage in which the interest rate is fixed by the lender over the life of the loan.

Floor Traders.   Members of a stock exchange, such as the New York Stock Exchange, who trade for their own account while on the exchange floor. They do not act for the public or for other members.

Full-Service Broker. A broker who provides research and other services for his clients and whose commissions reflect the cost of providing these services.

Fundamental Analysis. Analysis of external and internal factors relevant to a firm to assess the true worth or intrinsic value of the company's stock.

Futures Contract. A contract in which something is bought or sold for future delivery with the delivery price of the item determined when the contract is made.

Futures Option. Puts or calls on listed futures contracts.

General Obligation Bonds. Tax-exempt state and local bonds that are backed by the full taxation power of the issuer.

GNMA Securities. "Pass-through" securities issued by the Government National Mortgage Association (GNMA). Holders receive income derived from payments of principal, and interest on pools of mortgages. The GNMA guarantees that investors will receive their payments as scheduled.

Hedger. Someone who buys or sells instruments on financial markets, such as options or futures contracts, in order to reduce risks associated with other transactions.

Immunization. The process of "locking in" a target future value when making an investment. The locked-in value would not change with subsequent fluctuations in market interest rates.

Indenture. A contract associated with a bond issue that specifies the provisions of the bond.

Individual Retirement Account (IRA). An account in which deposits are often tax-deductible, and interest and dividends are tax-deferred. Amounts withdrawn out of the IRA account before a specified date are subject to penalties and taxation.

Industry Life Cycle Theory. A theory that discusses how industries evolve from the initial rapidly growing stages to later mature, slower growing stages.

Inflation Risk. Risk associated with the uncertainty of real returns on investments due to fluctuations in the rate of inflation.

Initial Margin. The margin requirement that applies on the date the securities were purchased. Initial margin is set by the Federal Reserve Board.

Insider Trading. Purchases or sales of shares by important corporate officers, members of the board of directors, or major stockholders.

Institutional Investors. Organizations such as mutual funds and other investment companies, pension funds, insurance companies, and so on, which manage sizable portfolios.

Interest Rate Futures. Futures contracts on fixed-income securities.

Interest-Rate Risk. Risk of fluctuation in security prices caused by unanticipated movements in interest rates.

International Fund. A mutual fund or other investment company that holds a portfolio of foreign securities.

Investment. The purchase of assets at one point in time with the expectation of future returns.

Investment Bankers.   Firms that specialize in the marketing of new securities.

Investment Companies.   Firms that pool the money of many individual investors and purchase a diversified portfolio of securities.

Investment Value.   The value of a convertible security as straight debt, excluding the conversion features.

IRA.   See *Individual Retirement Account*.

Junk Bonds.   Bonds rated BB or lower by Standard and Poor or Ba or lower by Moody's Investors Service. They represent speculative bonds.

Lagging Indicators.   Economic or financial indicators that reach peaks or troughs after the economy as a whole does so.

Leading Indicators.   Economic or financial indicators which reach peaks or troughs prior to the economy as a whole.

Leverage.   The use of borrowed funds in an investment strategy.

Limit Order.   An order to buy securities if the price is at or below a specified level or to sell securities if the price is at or above a specified level.

Liquidity.   The ability to convert an asset into cash quickly and with no loss in value of principal.

Liquidity Premium Theory.   A theory on term structure of interest rates. It holds that the long-term interest rate is related to short-term rates as stated in the expectations theory except that a premium for price risk should be added.

Load Funds.   Mutual funds in which there is a sales charge to purchase shares, and so purchase price exceeds the net asset value which normally is the selling price.

Long Hedge.   The strategy where someone purchases futures contracts on commodities or financial instruments that they intend to buy at some future time.

Long Position.   Someone who purchases securities or futures contracts and will profit on that transaction if the price rises is said to be holding a long position.

M1.   The basic measure of money supply, consisting of currency, demand deposits, and other checkable deposits.

M2.   A measure of money supply that equals M1 plus savings, small-denomination time deposits, and money market funds.

Maintenance Margin.   Established by brokers and exchanges, indicating the minimum equity margin the investor has to have in his or her account.

Margin.   Partial payment by an investor for his purchase of a security or his equity in the transaction.

Margin Call.   The demand from a broker to the investor for the deposit of additional funds into the latter's account to cover loans made by the broker.

Margin Requirement.   Amount established by the Federal Reserve Board in regulations concerning the percentage of a security purchase that must be paid for in cash, and the amount that can be lent the investor by the broker.

Marked to the Market.   In the futures market, gains and losses are calculated daily, that is, marked to the market.

Market Index. A measure of the general level of security prices, like the S & P 500 or the DJIA.

Market Order. An order to buy or sell securities at the market price prevailing at the time.

Market Risk. The general rise or decline in security prices, whose risk cannot be avoided through diversification.

Merger. The joining of two companies to form a new one.

Monetary Policy. The Federal Reserve Board's policy regulating monetary conditions of the U.S.

Money Market. The market for short-term securities with maturities of one year or less.

Mortgage bond. A bond secured by real assets.

Municipal bond. A debt obligation issued by a state or local government.

Mutual fund. An open-end investment company that invests in a portfolio of securities for investors and also redeems their shares at the net asset value of the shares.

NASD. National Association of Securities Dealers in the over-the-counter market.

NASDAQ. The National Association of Securities Dealers Automated Quotations, an automated price quotation system of the NASD for the over-the-counter market.

Negotiated Market. A market based on a net of security dealers like the OTC.

Net Asset Value. The per-share value of an investment company, based on current market prices of its portfolio.

No-load Fund. A mutual fund that imposes no sales charge.

Odd Lot. Less than 100 shares of a given security.

Open-end Investment Company. Also known as a mutual fund; capitalization of the investment company constantly changes due to new sales and redemptions.

Open Interest. The number of uncovered future contracts outstanding.

Open Market Operation. The purchase or sale of government securities by the Federal Reserve to affect the reserves of the banking system.

Option. A financial contract that gives the holder the right to buy or sell securities at a fixed price within a given period of time.

Option Premium. The price that a buyer of a call or put option must pay for the option.

Over-the-Counter Market. A communications network allowing for trading in securities not traded on organized exchanges.

Par Value. The value assigned to a security when it is issued.

Payout Ratio. The ratio of dividends to earnings.

P/E Ratio. The ratio of stock price to historical earnings, current earnings, or estimated future earnings.

Preferred Stock. A security issued by corporations that has a fixed dividend payment that will be paid before common-stock holders are paid.

Premium.   In the options market, the price of an option.

Premium Bond.   A bond with a market price above the par value of the bond.

Primary EPS.   The earnings per share on the common stock after accounting for the conversion of common stock equivalents.

Primary Market.   The market for new issues of securities.

Private Placement.   The sale of an issue of securities directly to institutional investors.

Point-and-Figure Chart.   A type of chart without time dimension, usually used by a technical analyst.

Portfolio.   A group of financial assets owned by an investor or an institution.

Program Trading.   Hedge operations in stocks, stock options, options on stock indexes, and in stock futures market. Computer programs are often used to indicate opportunities for initiating hedge operations.

Proxy.   The authorization given to an agent to vote for the shareholder.

Public Offering.   The issuance of a new security offered for sale to the general public.

Purchasing-Power Risk.   Risk arising from changes in the rate of inflation.

Put Option.   An option to sell securities at a fixed price within a given period of time.

Random-Walk Theory.   A theory that states security prices fluctuate randomly due to news constantly arriving in the marketplace.

Real Return.   A return after allowance for inflation.

Registered Bond.   A bond registered on the books of the issuing corporation.

REIT.   A real estate investment trust, a type of investment company specializing in real estate investments for tax benefits.

Retained Earnings.   Earnings retained in the business for reinvestment.

Return on Assets.   The ratio of total earnings to total assets of the firm.

Return on Equity.   The ratio of earnings per share to book value per share.

Revenue Bond.   A municipal bond supported by the revenue of a project financed by the issuance of the municipal bond.

Risk Aversion.   The unwillingness to accept risk without adequate return.

Risk-free Assets.   This usually refers to short-term securities issued by the U.S. government.

Risk-Free Rate.   The yield on short-term securities issued by the U.S. government.

Risk-Return Trade-off.   Increasing return generally goes with increasing risk.

Round lot.   The standard unit of trading on an exchange, usually 100 shares.

S & P 500.   Standard and Poor's market index which includes 500 common stocks.

SEC.   Securities and Exchange Commission.

Secondary Market.   Market for trading in existing securities.

Security Market Line.   A line expressing the equilibrium relationship between expected return and systematic risk.

Short Sale.   The sale of a borrowed security in the hope that the price of the security will fall.

Sinking Fund.   A fund established for the orderly retirement of an issue of bond.

Specialist.   A member of an organized exchange responsible for the maintenance of an orderly market in the stock assigned to him.

Spread.   The difference between bids and asks of a security offered by the dealer.

Standard Deviation.   A statistical measure of the dispersion or variablity of the return of a security.

Stock Dividend.   The issuance of dividend in the form of additional shares of common stock.

Stock Index Futures.   Futures contracts on stock indexes like the S & P 500, the NYSE Index, and the *Value Line* Index.

Stock Split.   The issuance of more shares (greater than 25 percent) for existing shareholders.

Stop Order.   An order to buy or sell a security when its price reaches a certain level.

Striking Price.   The contract price for an option.

Systematic Risk.   The risk of a security associated with the overall market fluctuation in security prices.

Tax-Exempt Bonds.   Bonds issued by state and municipal governments and agencies, the interest on which is exempt from federal income taxes.

Technical Analysis.   Study of market conditions by reference to price and volume changes.

Technical Analyst.   An analyst who follows the technical approach in studying and charting the price and volume changes in securities and market indexes.

Term Structure of Interest Rates.   This refers to the relationship between yields and time to maturities of securities.

Third Market.   An OTC market for trading in exchange-listed securities.

Total Risk.   The unsystematic risk plus systematic risk of a security or a portfolio.

Treasury Bill.   Short-term security issued by the U.S. government.

Treasury Bond.   A longer-term bond issued by the U.S. government.

Treasury Note.   A U.S. security with a maturity of one to ten years.

Underwriting.   The purchase of an issue of a security of a corporation by investment bankers, who then resell it to the public.

Undiversified Risk.   Also known as systematic risk, which cannot be eliminated through diversification.

Unlisted Security.   A security not listed on one of the exchanges.

Unsystematic Risk.   Also known as specific risk, the risk attributable to factors unique to the security and its industry.

Utility.   The level or amount of satisfaction to a consumer or investor.

Value.   Estimated worth of a security.

Value Line **Index.**   A stock market index published by the *Value Line Investment Survey,* based on the performance of about 1700 stocks; each stock is given the same weight.

Variance.   A measure of variability or risk equal to the square of the standard deviation.

Volatility.   Fluctuations in the price or return of a security or a portfolio.

Warrant.   A long-term option giving the holder the right to purchase a specified number of shares within a certain period of time at a specified price.

Writing an Option.   Selling an option.

Yield.   The dividend or interest income as a prcent of the price of the security.

Yield Curve.   A graphic presentation of the relationship between maturity and yield for securities of the same risk class.

Yield to Maturity.   The yield of a bond if the holder keeps the bond until maturity.

Zero-Coupon Bonds   Bonds that pay no coupon interest and are issued at discount from their face value. They pay full par value at maturity.

Index

A

Accounting principles, 212–213
Accrued interest, 130
Active investors, 531–533
Adjustable-rate mortgage, 557–558
ADR. *See* American Depository
    Receipts
Altman model, 233–236
American Depository Receipts, 574
American Stock Exchange, 28–29
Annuity, 182–183
Arbitrage, 393–395, 575
Arbitrage Pricing Theory, 508–509
ARM. *See* Adjustable-rate mortgage
Asked price, 42
Auction market, 41

B

Bankers' acceptances, 15, 128
Basis, 390
Basis point, 107*n*, 142
Bearer bonds, 134
Best efforts, 28
Beta, 21–22, 500–502, 505–508
    beta and future portfolio
        performance, 465–469
    estimating future betas, 471–475
    use by institutional investors,
        470–471
Bid price, 42
Block trading, 43
Bonds, 12–14, 130–144, 148–174
    analysis of corporate bonds, 12–13,
        130–131, 137–141
    call provisions, 13, 141
    duration, 157–161
    immunization, 162–163
    indenture, 140–141
    investment strategies, 173–174
    markets and quotes, 130–134
    municipal bonds, 14, 141–145
    ratings, 134–137, 171–172
    term structure, 164–169
    Treasury securities, 13, 131–132
    valuation, 148–150
    yield curve, 164–169
    zero-coupon bonds, 131, 150,
        183–185
Brokers, 42–43
Business risk, 20

C

Call options, 348–352
Call provisions of bonds, 13, 141
Capital Asset Pricing Model, 500–502
Capital gains, 7
Capital market line, 498–500
Capital market theory, 497–508
    empirical evidence, 503–508
Cash market, 379
Central market, 45
Certificate of Deposit (CD), 15, 127
Churning, 6
Closed-end investment companies, 18
Closing costs, 558–559
Coincidental indicators, 83, 86
Commercial paper, 15, 128
Commodity Futures Trading
    Commission, 388
Common stock, 15–16, 294–321
    dividend valuation, 294–302
    Graham approach, 311–313
    market valuation, 314–321
    price-earnings ratio, 302–310
Computerized information sources,
    62–63

Computers, 581–585. *See also* Personal
  computer
Convertible securities, 16, 334–341
  advantages and disadvantages, 336,
    338
  convertible bonds, 337–341
  convertible preferred stock, 334–337
  performance, 342–343
Coupon bonds, 12
Coupon rate, 12, 130
Coupon reinvestment risk, 163
Cross hedges, 392
Cumulative dividends, 16
Current yield, 130–131

D

Dealers, 42
Debenture, 12
Default, 136
Delivery date, 381
Discount broker, 43
Diversification, 21, 568–571
Dividends, 16, 294–302
Dow Jones Industrial Average. *See*
  Indexes of securities prices
Dow theory, 411–412
Duration, 157–161

E

Earnings quality, 219–221
Economic function of investment, 9–10
Economic indicators, 83–85
Efficient frontier, 498–499
Efficient market hypothesis, 484–497
  empirical evidence, 485–495
  evaluation, 495–497
  random-walk hypothesis, 485, 493,
    496
  semistrong form, 485, 488–491,
    493–495
  strong form, 485, 488–491, 493–495
  weak form, 485–488, 491–493
Efficient portfolio, 455–456
Equity margin, 35
Errors of individual investors, 9
Eurodollars, 15, 128
Exchange rate risk, 573
Expectations theory, 166–167

F

Federal agency securities, 13–14,
  132–134
Federal funds rate, 111
Federal Reserve, 35, 109–112
  discount rate, 112
  margin requirements, 35
  monetary policy, 109–112
Filter test, 488, 493
Financial futures
  foreign currency futures, 391–392
  hedging, 389–393
  interest rate futures, 382, 392–393
  listings, 382
  programmed trading, 393–395
  stock index futures, 389–391,
    393–395
Financial risk, 20
Financial statement analysis, 210–235
  balance sheet, 210–211
  common-size statement analysis,
    224–227
  deficiencies of statements, 213–218
  income statement, 211–212
  ratio analysis, 227–232
Fisher equation, 112
Fixed-rate mortgage, 557–558
Floor broker, 30
Forecasting, 82–96, 113–120
  business conditions, 83–95
  diffusion indexes, 85, 87
  econometric models, 92–93
  futures markets, 94–95, 403–406
  indicators, 83–85, 117–120
  interest rates, 113–120
  monetarist approach, 93–94
  national income and product
    accounts, 89–92
  organizations, 95–99
  surveys, 87, 89
Forward interest rate, 166
Full-service broker, 42–43
Future returns on stocks and bonds,
  535–536
Future value tables, 178–179
Future values with compound interest,
  177
Futures, 378–399. *See also* Financial
  futures

brokers of futures contracts, 383
categories of items traded, 379
clearinghouse of exchange, 383
forecasting prices, 403–406
hedging, 379, 383, 389–393
history of markets, 378–379
listings, 379–382
locking in a price, 391
margin, 385–386
orders, 388
price fluctuation limit, 388
regulation, 388–389
speculators, 379, 383
spread strategies, 396–398
Futures options, 395–396

G

General obligation bonds, 141, 143–144
GNMA securities, 13–14, 134
Government agency securities. *See*
    Federal agency securities
Government National Mortgage
    Association. *See* GNMA
    securities
Groupthink, 497
Growth analysis
    determination of earnings per share,
        241–244
    estimating EPS growth, 244–259
    importance of earnings growth,
        239–240

H

Hedging on futures markets, 379, 383,
    389–393
Historical performance of securities,
    22–24
Home ownership, 557–565
    closing costs, 558–559
    expenses, 559–561
    mortgages, 557–558
    real estate brokers, 563
    tax benefits, 561–562

I

Immunization, 162–163
Indenture, 13, 140–141

Indexes of securities prices, 63–77
    Dow Jones Industrial Average,
        63–66, 73, 76
    NYSE index, 67
    Standard & Poor indexes, 67–70, 76
    Value Line averages, 70, 73, 77
Individual investors, 528–536
    active investor, 531–533
    errors, 9
    financial planning, 528–529
    passive investor, 530–531
    speculator, 533
Individual Retirement Accounts,
    144–145
Industry analysis
    classification of industries, 189–192
    competition, 195
    costs and profitability, 195–196
    importance, 189
    input-output analysis, 197–199
    outlook for sales and profits, 196–197
    sources of information, 199–206
    stages of industry development,
        191–193
    technology and research, 196
Inflation and interest rates, 112–113
Inflation risk, 19–20
Information sources
    advisory services, 55–59
    brokerage houses, 60–61
    computer-based data, 62–63
    corporate reports, 58–60
    magazines, 54
    newspapers, 54
    trade publications, 62
    U.S. government, 61
Initial margin, 35
Institutional investors, 43–44
Interest rate futures, 382, 392–393
Interest rate risk, 20, 155–163
Interest rates, 107–121, 171–172
    forecasting rates, 113–120
    historical data, 108–110, 172
    inflation and interest rates, 112–113
    monetary policy, 109–112
International investing, 568–575
    diversification, 568–571
    returns, 571–572
    risk, 573–574
International mutual funds, 574–575

Inventory valuation, 213–215
Investment advice and costs, 6
Investment advisory services, 55–61
Investment bankers, 27
Investment companies, 17
Investment management
  active investors, 531–533
  passive investors, 530–531
  speculators, 533
Investment objectives, 3–5
IRA. *See* Individual Retirement
      Accounts

J

Jensen performance measure, 519–521
Junk bonds, 136

L

Lagging indicators, 83, 86
Leading indicators, 83, 85–86
Leverage, 37
Limit order, 33
Liquidity, 4, 123
Liquidity premium theory, 167–168
Load funds, 18
Long hedge, 383
Long position, 40, 382

M

Maintenance margin, 35
Manipulating income, 218–219
Margin call, 35
Margin on futures, 385–386
Margin requirements, 35
Margin trading on stocks, 35–41
Market indexes. *See* Indexes of
      securities prices
Market order, 33
Market portfolio, 498–499
Market risk, 20
Monetarists, 93–94
Monetary policy, 109–112
Money market accounts, 18, 123–124
Money market funds, 18, 123–124
Money market instruments, 14–15,
      123–130
Money rates, 129

Money supply, 111–112
Mortgage bonds, 12
Mortgage securities, 13–14, 128
Mortgages, 557–558
Municipal securities, 14, 128, 141–145
  general obligation bonds, 141,
      143–144
  revenue bonds, 141, 144
  yields, 153–155
Mutual funds, 18, 542–555, 574–575
  advantages, 542–543
  measuring the performance of the
      fund, 544–545
  measuring the risk level of the fund,
      545–547
  performance of mutual funds, 491,
      548
  selecting no-load funds, 543–547
  sources of information on funds,
      548–555

N

NASD, 42
NASDAQ, 42
National market system, 45
Neglected firms, 494–495
Negotiated markets, 41
Net asset value, 18
New York Stock Exchange. *See* Stock
      exchanges
No-load fund, 18

O

Odd lot, 34
Open-end investment company, 18
Open interest, 381
Open market operations, 111
Optimum portfolio, 457–458
Options
  buying calls, 348–351
  buying puts, 352–354
  Chicago Board Options Exchange,
      347–348
  classification of options strategy in
      terms of degree of risk, 359–360
  combinations of options, 355–356
  compared with futures, 389

factors affecting options premiums, 363–364

federal tax regulations on options contracts, 370–371

optimum option strategy with different expectations, 360–362

role of options in investment program, 370

selling calls, 351–352

selling puts, 354–355

strategies of hedging, 356–359

strategies with market indexes, 362–363

value of option versus movement of stock price, 368–370

value of options, 364–368

Orders, 33–35

Over-the-counter market, 41–42, 130

P

Par value, 12

Perfect hedge, 390

Personal computer

benefits of using computer, 581–582

computer applications with fundamental analysis, 584–585

computer applications with technical analysis, 582–584

computer software, 582

sources of information, 585–586

Portfolio performance, 512–525, 533–535

bond investment, 533–535

equity investment, 533–535

individual investors, 523–524

mutual fund performance, 522–523

performance measures, 517–521

Portfolio risk, 450–455

Portfolio theory

Markowitz, 447–458

Sharpe, 459–463

Precious metals, 575–579

Preferred stocks

comparison with bonds in yields and risks, 333

general characteristics, 331–332

investment implications for individual investors, 332–334

Present value analysis, 177–185

Present value tables, 180–181, 183–184

Price-earning ratio, 493

Primary markets, 27

Profits and stock prices, 96, 100–102

Programmed trading, 393–395

Proxy battle, 16

Put option, 17

R

Random walk hypothesis, 485, 493, 496

Rate of return, 18–19, 513–516

dollar-weighted method, 516

time-weighted method, 515

Ratings of bonds, 134–137, 171–172

Ratio analysis of financial statements, 227–232

Real estate brokers, 563

Real estate investment trusts (REITs), 565–566

Real investment, 3

Real return, 112–113

Regional exchanges. *See* Stock exchanges

Registered bonds, 134

Regulation

futures markets, 388–389

securities markets, 46–49

Repurchase agreements, 15, 128

Reward to risk ratio, 500

Risk analysis

components of risk, 19–21

international investing, 573–574

measuring risk, 21–22, 516–521

risk of owning common stocks, 263–264

risk measurement in terms of expectations, 267–274

risk measurement in terms of historical record

based on comparison with market averages, 283–287

based on financial ratios, 281–282

risk of individual security vs. portfolio risk, 288–289

Value Line system, 287–288

variation in EPS, 278–281

variation in price of stock, 275–276

Risk analysis, *continued*
   variation in rate of return of stock,
     277–278
   variation in rate of return on net
     worth, 278
Round lot, 34

S

Savings bonds, 132
Secondary markets, 28–30, 41–46
Securities analysis, 5
Securities and Exchange Commission
   (SEC), 42, 46–48
Security market line, 500–502
Segmented market theory, 168
Settlement price, 381
Share ownership, 43–45
Sharpe performance index, 517–518,
   521
Short hedge, 383
Short sales, 34, 39–41
Sinking fund, 140
Small (neglected) firms, 494–495
Specialist, 30–32
Speculation versus investment, 7–8
Speculators on futures markets, 379,
   383
Spot interest rate, 166
Spot market, 379, 383
Spread strategies on futures, 396–398
   intercommodity spread, 397
   intermarket spread, 397
   intracommodity spread, 396–397
Standard deviation, 21
Standard & Poor's indexes. *See* Indexes
   of securities prices
State and local government securities.
   See Municipal securities
Stock exchanges
   American Stock Exchange, 28–29
   New York Stock Exchange, 28–33
   regional exchanges, 28–29
Stock index futures, 389–391
Stock splits, 488–489
Stop order, 33
Surveys, 87, 89
Systematic risk, 19

T

Taxable and tax-exempt yields, 153–155
Tax Reform Act of 1986, 215–217
Taxes, 7, 153–155
Tax-exempt securities. *See* Municipal
   securities
Technical market analysis
   advance-decline line, 423
   bar charts, 435–436
   basic premises of chart reading,
     430–431
   chart patterns, 431–435
   Dow theory, 411–414
   market analysis vs. security analysis,
     411
   mutual fund cash position, 426–427
   new-high and new-low indicator,
     418–421
   odd-lot short sales ratio, 416–418
   point-and-figure charts, 435–438
   price vs. volume change, 423–426
   random walk theory and technical
     analysis, 438–440
   rate of change analysis, 423–425
   short-interest theory, 415–416
   theory of chart reading and analysis,
     430–431
   theory of contrary opinion, 427–429
   trends and moving averages, 422
Term structure of interest rates,
   164–169
Third market, 44–45
Time limit order, 33
Time value of money, 177–185
Treasury bills, 13–14, 124–127
Treasury bonds, 13, 131–132
Treasury notes, 13, 131–132
Treynor performance index, 518–519,
   521

U

Uncertainty of return of common stocks
   factors contributing to uncertainty,
     263–264
   how to deal with uncertainty,
     264–267

the Markowitz approach, 267–274
views on how best to deal with
    uncertainty, 274–275
Underwriting, 27
Unsystematic risk, 20
Up-tick, 34
U.S. Savings Bonds, 132

V

Valuation of common stocks
    analysts' view, 321
    based on cash flow, 309–310
    based on comparison with industry
        average or general market index,
        307–309
    Graham's "intrinsic value" approach,
        311–313
    price/dividend table, 300
    price-earnings approach, 302–307
    price/sales per share, 310–311
    theory of present worth, 294–298
Valuation of the "general market"
    capitalizing average past earnings,
        315–318
    multiple regression and correlation
        analysis, 316, 319–321

present worth approach, 314–315
Value Line index. *See* Indexes of
    securities prices
Variable rate mortgage, 557–558
Volume and open interest, 403

W

Warrants
    factors determining the attractiveness
        of a warrant, 373
    premium of a warrant, 372–373
    theoretical value, 371–372
Wells Fargo approach, 465–468

Y

Yield curve, 164–169
Yield spreads, 169–173
Yield to call, 151–153
Yield to maturity, 150–153

Z

Zero-coupon bonds, 131, 150, 183–185
Zero-sum game, 386
Z score, 233–236